SEVEN CENTURIES OF ENGLISH VERSE

Cyrus F. Rea II, Editor

©2017 by Tomogo Lakes Press, LLC.
100 Broadway, Suite 560
San Antonio, Texas 78205
All rights reserved.

No part of this publication may be reproduced, stored in a retrieval system, or transmitted in any form or by any means (including electronic, mechanical, photocopying, recording, or otherwise) without prior written permission from the publisher.

ISBN-13: 978-0-9986656-6-5
ISBN-10: 0-9986656-6-5

Dedicated to Brenda Canales,
the ideal woman whom all the poets had in mind,

and

Ivanna Valentina Rea,
who insisted "Twinkle Twinkle, Little Star" be included.

Seven Centuries of English Verse

Introduction

Can a string of a few carefully chosen words encapsulate eternal truths? Rarely. But, within these pages, you'll find examples of Poets who accomplished just that. The selections were written from the late Fourteenth to early Twentieth Century by authors ranging from kings to vagabonds. All are united by a common thread—this magical ability to capture a glimpse of the eternal with a gossamer web of words.

Poets have their Muses to assist in their work. An anthologist, on the other hand, has no Muse... instead, he has to settle for two nasty little Imps. The first Imp torments the anthologist by forcing him to choose what goes in and what gets cut. The second one bedevils with second-guessing regarding the work's arrangement. In regard to the first, I have endeavored to select pieces that transcend the time in which they were written. With a few notable exceptions, each poem is capable of appreciation without too much knowledge of any particular historical setting or event. In addition, while most of the poets herein hail from the British Isles, the reader will find a smattering from virtually every corner of the English-speaking world. (Indeed, sufficient American poets have been included to necessitate sprinkling a few Stars on the cover's Union Jack design.)

In regard to the second Imp, he insisted the selections be organized by theme. With much trepidation, I have ignored his advice. Instead, the poems are roughly grouped together according to the poet's date of birth (when known), and within these groups, the poems have been arranged to minimize awkward page breaks. This somewhat chronological arrangement will permit the reader to notice what has stayed the same and what has changed as poetry (and the English language) evolved over time.

While the earliest poems in this collection retain the original inflections and spellings, an effort has been made to modernize some archaic elements in the later poems. In regard to formatting, as there is not always a consensus on a particular poem's line indentations (or even number of stanzas) I have endeavored to present the poems as they appear in the majority of other anthologies.

Finally, with a few exceptions, no poems from the past seventy years have been included. As a practical matter, copyright laws preclude the easy inclusion of more recent works. But, more importantly, I noticed something upon reviewing dozens of anthologies from centuries past: usually, the most recent poems in each collection weren't all that great. This fact tempered my temptation to include selections from the latter-half of the twentieth century. Poems, I suppose, must age a little before one can determine their greatness. Consequently, I'll leave it to the future editor of *Eight Centuries of English Verse* to decide whether these modern masters make the cut.

Cyrus F. Rea II
2017

The Poems

Seven Centuries of English Verse

Praise of Women   1

No thyng ys to man so dere
As wommanys love in gode manere.
A gode womman is mannys blys,
There her love right and stedfast ys.
There ys no solas under hevene
Of alle that a man may nevene
That shulde a man so moche glew
As a gode womman that loveth true.
Ne derer is none in Goddis hurde
Than a chaste womman with lovely worde.
                ROBERT MANNYNG OF BRUNNE (1269–1340)

nevene: *name*; glew: *gladden*; hurde: *flock*

This World's Joy   2

Wynter wakeneth al my care,
Nou this leves waxeth bare;
Ofte I sike ant mourne sare
  When hit cometh in my thoht
  Of this worldes joie, hou hit goth al to noht.

Nou hit is, and nou hit nys,
Al so hit ner nere, ywys;
That moni mon seith, soth hit ys:
  Al goth bote Godes wille:
  Alle we shule deye, thah us like ylle.

Al that gren me graueth grene,
Nou hit faleweth albydene:
Jesu, help that hit be sene
  Ant shild us from helle!
  For y not whider y shal, ne hou longe her duelle.
                ANONYMOUS (c. 1300)

this leves: *these leaves*; sike: *sigh*; nys: *is not*;
al so hit ner nere: *as though it had never been*; soth: *sooth*;
bote: *but, except*; thah: *though*; faleweth: *fadeth*; albydene: *altogether*;
y not whider: *I know not whither*; her duelle: *here dwell*

Freedom   3

A! Fredome is a noble thing!
Fredome mays man to haiff liking;
Fredome all solace to man giffis,
He levys at ese that frely levys!
A noble hart may haiff nane ese,
Na ellys nocht that may him plese,
Gyff fredome fail; for fre liking
Is yarnyt our all othir thing.
Na he that ay has levyt fre
May nocht knaw weill the propyrte,
The angyr, na the wretchyt dome
That is couplyt to foule thyrldome.

　　　　　　Bot gyff he had assayit it,
　　　　　　Than all perquer he suld it wyt;
　　　　　　And suld think fredome mar to prise
　　　　　　Than all the gold in warld that is.
　　　　　　Thus contrar thingis evirmar
　　　　　　Discoweryngis off the tothir ar.
　　　　　　　　　　　　JOHN BARBOUR (1320?–1395)

liking: *liberty*; na ellys nocht: *nor aught else*; yarnyt: *yearned for*; perquer: *thoroughly, by heart*

4　　　　　THE LOVE UNFEIGNED
　　　　O yonge fresshe folkes, he or she,
　　　　In which that love up groweth with your age,
　　　　Repeyreth hoom from worldly vanitee,
　　　　And of your herte up-casteth the visage
　　　　To thilke god that after his image
　　　　Yow made, and thinketh al nis but a fayre
　　　　This world, that passeth sone as floures fayre.

　　　　And loveth him, the which that right for love
　　　　Upon a cros, our soules for to beye,
　　　　First starf, and roos, and sit in hevene a-bove;
　　　　For he nil falsen no wight, dar I seye,
　　　　That wol his herte al hoolly on him leye.
　　　　And sin he best to love is, and most meke,
　　　　What nedeth feyned loves for to seke?
　　　　　　　　　　　GEOFFREY CHAUCER (1340?–1400)

repeyreth: *repair ye*; starf: *died*

5　　　　　　　BALADE
　　　　Hyd, Absolon, thy gilte tresses clere;
　　　　Ester, ley thou thy meknesse al a-doun;
　　　　Hyd, Jonathas, al thy frendly manere;
　　　　Penalopee, and Marcia Catoun,
　　　　Mak of your wyfhod no comparisoun;
　　　　Hyde ye your beautes, Isoude and Eleyne;
　　　　My lady cometh, that al this may disteyne.

　　　　Thy faire body, lat hit nat appere,
　　　　Lavyne; and thou, Lucresse of Rome toun,
　　　　And Polixene, that boghten love so dere,
　　　　And Cleopatre, with al thy passioun,
　　　　Hyde ye your trouthe of love and your renoun;
　　　　And thou, Tisbe, that hast of love swich peyne;
　　　　My lady cometh, that al this may disteyne.

　　　　Herro, Dido, Laudomia, alle y-fere,
　　　　And Phyllis, hanging for thy Demophoun,
　　　　And Canace, espyed by thy chere,
　　　　Ysiphile, betraysed with Jasoun,
　　　　Maketh of your trouthe neyther boost ne soun;
　　　　Nor Ypermistre or Adriane, ye tweyne;
　　　　My lady cometh, that al this may disteyne.
　　　　　　　　　　　GEOFFREY CHAUCER (1340?–1400)

disteyne: *bedim*; y-fere: *together*

MERCILES BEAUTE
A TRUPLE ROUNDEL
1. CAPTIVITY

Your eyen two wol slee me sodenly,
I may the beaute of hem not sustene,
So woundeth hit through-out my herte kene.

And but your word wol helen hastily
My hertes wounde, whyl that hit is grene,
  Your eyen two wol slee me sodenly,
  I may the beautè of hem not sustene.

Upon my trouthe I sey yow feithfully,
That ye ben of my lyf and deeth the quene;
For with my deeth the trouthe shal be sene.
  Your eyen two wol slee me sodenly,
  I may the beautè of hem not sustene,
  So woundeth hit through-out my herte kene.

2. REJECTION

So hath your beautè fro your herte chaced
Pitee, that me ne availeth not to pleyne;
For Daunger halt your mercy in his cheyne.

Giltles my deeth thus han ye me purchaced;
I sey yow sooth, me nedeth not to feyne;
  So hath your beautè fro your herte chaced
  Pitee, that me ne availeth not to pleyne.

Allas! that nature hath in yow compassed
So greet beautè, that no man may atteyne
To mercy, though he sterve for the peyne.
  So hath your beautè fro your herte chaced
  Pitee, that me ne availeth not to pleyne;
  For Daunger halt your mercy in his cheyne.

3. ESCAPE

Sin I fro Love escaped am so fat,
I never thenk to ben in his prison lene;
Sin I am free, I counte him not a bene.

He may answere, and seye this or that;
I do no fors, I speke right as I mene.
  Sin I fro Love escaped am so fat,
  I never thenk to ben in his prison lene.

Love hath my name y-strike out of his sclat,
And he is strike out of my bokes clene
For ever-mo; ther is non other mene.
  Sin I fro Love escaped am so fat,
  I never thenk to ben in his prison lene;
  Sin I am free, I counte him not a bene.

GEOFFREY CHAUCER (1340?–1400)

halt: *holdeth*; sclat: *slate*

OF A ROSE, A LOVELY ROSE

Lestenyt, lordynges, both elde and yinge,
How this rose began to sprynge;
Swych a rose to myn lykynge
    In al this word ne knowe I non.

The Aungil came fro hevene tour,
To grete Marye with gret honour,
And seyde sche xuld bere the flour
    That xulde breke the fyndes bond.

The flour sprong in heye Bedlem,
That is bothe bryht and schen:
The rose is Mary hevene qwyn,
    Out of here bosum the blosme sprong.

The ferste braunche is ful of myht,
That sprang on Cyrstemesse nyht,
The sterre schon over Bedlem bryht
    That is bothe brod and long.

The secunde braunche sprong to helle,
The fendys power doun to felle:
Therein myht non sowle dwelle;
    Blyssid be the time the rose sprong!

The thredde braunche is good and swote,
It sprang to hevene crop and rote,
Therein to dwellyn and ben our bote;
    Every day it schewit in prystes hond.

Prey we to here with gret honour,
Che that bar the blyssid flowr,
Che be our helpe and our socour
    And schyd us fro the fyndes bond.

                                ANONYMOUS (c. 1350)

lestenyt: *listen*; word: *world*; xuld: *should*; schen: *beautiful*;
hevene qwyn: *heaven's queen*; bote: *salvation*

LAMENT FOR CHAUCER

Allas! my worthi maister honorable,
This landes verray tresor and richesse!
Deth by thy deth hath harme irreparable
Unto us doon: hir vengeable duresse
Despoiled hath this land of the swetnesse
Of rethorik; for unto Tullius
Was never man so lyk amonges us.

Also who was hier in philosophie
To Aristotle in our tonge but thou?
The steppes of Virgile in poesie
Thou folwedist eeke, men wot wel ynow.
Thou combre-worlde that the my maister slow—
Wolde I slayn were!—Deth, was to hastyf
To renne on thee and reve the thi lyf...

She myghte han taried hir vengeance a while
Til that sum man had egal to the be;
Nay, lat be that! sche knew wel that this yle
May never man forth brynge lyk to the,
And hir office needes do mot she:
God bad hir so, I truste as for the beste;
O maister, maister, God thi soule reste!
                    THOMAS HOCCLEVE (1369?–1450?)

hier: heir; *combre-worlde: encumberer of earth*; *slow: slew*

VOX ULTIMA CRUCIS   9
Tarye no lenger; toward thyn heritage
Hast on thy weye, and be of ryght good chere.
Go eche day onward on thy pylgrymage;
Thynke howe short tyme thou hast abyden here.
Thy place is bygged above the sterres clere,
Noon erthly palys wrought in so statly wyse.
Come on, my frend, my brother most entere!
For the I offered my blood in sacryfice.
                    JOHN LYDGATE (1370?–1450?)

bygged: built; *palys: palace*

SPRING SONG OF THE BIRDS   10
Worschippe ye that loveris bene this May,
For of your blisse the Kalendis are begonne,
And sing with us, Away, Winter, away!
  Cum, Somer, cum, the suete sesoùn and sonne!
  Awake for schame! that have your hevynnis wonne,
    And amorously lift up your hedis all,
    Thank Lufe that list you to his merci call!
                    KING JAMES I OF SCOTLAND (1394–1437)

suete: sweet; *Lufe: Love*

MAY IN THE GREEN-WOOD   11
In somer when the shawes be sheyne,
  And leves be large and long,
Hit is full merry in feyre foreste
  To here the foulys song.

To se the dere draw to the dale
  And leve the hilles hee,
And shadow him in the leves grene
  Under the green-wode tree.

Hit befell on Whitsontide
  Early in a May mornyng,
The Sonne up faire can shyne,
  And the briddis mery can syng.

"This is a mery mornyng," said Litulle Johne,
  "Be Hym that dyed on tre;
A more mery man than I am one
  Lyves not in Christianteè.

> "Pluk up thi hert, my dere mayster,"
>   Litulle Johne can say,
> "And thynk hit is a fulle fayre tyme
>   In a mornynge of May."
>
> ANONYMOUS (15th Cent.)

sheyne: *bright*

12   CAROL

> I sing of a maiden
>   That is makeles;
> King of all kings
>   To her son she ches.
>
> He came al so still
>   There his mother was,
> As dew in April
>   That falleth on the grass.
>
> He came al so still
>   To his mother's bour,
> As dew in April
>   That falleth on the flour.
>
> He came al so still
>   There his mother lay,
> As dew in April
>   That falleth on the spray.
>
> Mother and maiden
>   Was never none but she;
> Well may such a lady
>   Goddes mother be.
>
> ANONYMOUS (15th Cent.)

makeles: *matchless*; ches: *chose*

13   QUIA AMORE LANGUEO

> In a valley of this restles mind
> I sought in mountain and in mead,
> Trusting a true love for to find.
> Upon an hill then took I heed;
> A voice I heard (and near I yede)
> In great dolour complaining tho:
> See, dear soul, how my sides bleed
>   *Quia amore langueo.*
>
> Upon this hill I found a tree,
> Under a tree a man sitting;
> From head to foot wounded was he;
> His hearte blood I saw bleeding:
> A seemly man to be a king,
> A gracious face to look unto.
> I askèd why he had paining;
>   [He said,] *Quia amore langueo.*

I am true love that false was never;
My sister, man's soul, I loved her thus.
Because we would in no wise dissever
I left my kingdom glorious.
I purveyed her a palace full precious;
She fled, I followed, I loved her so
That I suffered this pain piteous
   Quia amore langueo.

My fair love and my spouse bright!
I saved her from beating, and she hath me bet;
I clothed her in grace and heavenly light;
This bloody shirt she hath on me set;
For longing of love yet would I not let;
Sweete strokes are these: lo!
I have loved her ever as I her het
   Quia amore langueo.

I crowned her with bliss and she me with thorn;
I led her to chamber and she me to die;
I brought her to worship and she me to scorn;
I did her reverence and she me villany.
To love that loveth is no maistry;
Her hate made never my love her foe:
Ask me then no question why—
   Quia amore langueo.

Look unto mine handes, man!
These gloves were given me when I her sought;
They be not white, but red and wan;
Embroidered with blood my spouse them brought.
They will not off; I loose hem nought;
I woo her with hem wherever she go.
These hands for her so friendly fought
   Quia amore langueo.

Marvel not, man, though I sit still.
See, love hath shod me wonder strait:
Buckled my feet, as was her will,
With sharpe nails (well thou may'st wait!)
In my love was never desait;
All my membres I have opened her to;
My body I made her herte's bait
   Quia amore langueo.

In my side I have made her nest;
Look in, how weet a wound is here!
This is her chamber, here shall she rest,
That she and I may sleep in fere.
Here may she wash, if any filth were;
Here is seat for all her woe;
Come when she will, she shall have cheer
   Quia amore langueo.

I will abide till she be ready,
I will her sue if she say nay;
If she be retchless I will be greedy,
If she be dangerous I will her pray;
If she weep, then bide I ne may:
Mine arms ben spread to clip her me to.
Cry once, I come: now, soul, assay
   Quia amore langueo.

Fair love, let us go play:
Apples ben ripe in my gardayne.
I shall thee clothe in a new array,
Thy meat shall be milk, honey and wine.
Fair love, let us go dine:
Thy sustenance is in my crippe, lo!
Tarry thou not, my fair spouse mine,
   Quia amore langueo.

If thou be foul, I shall thee make clean;
If thou be sick, I shall thee heal;
If thou mourn ought, I shall thee mene;
Why wilt thou not, fair love, with me deal?
Foundest thou ever love so leal?
What wilt thou, soul, that I shall do?
I may not unkindly thee appeal
   Quia amore langueo.

What shall I do now with my spouse
But abide her of my gentleness,
Till that she look out of her house
Of fleshly affection? love mine she is;
Her bed is made, her bolster is bliss,
Her chamber is chosen; is there none mo.
Look out on me at the window of kindeness
   Quia amore langueo.

My love is in her chamber: hold your peace!
Make ye no noise, but let her sleep.
My babe I would not were in disease,
I may not hear my dear child weep.
With my pap I shall her keep;
Ne marvel ye not though I tend her to:
This wound in my side had ne'er be so deep
   But *Quia amore langueo.*

Long thou for love never so high,
My love is more than thine may be.
Thou weepest, thou gladdest, I sit thee by:
Yet wouldst thou once, love, look unto me!
Should I always feede thee
With children meat? Nay, love, not so!
I will prove thy love with adversitè
   Quia amore langueo.

Wax not weary, mine own wife!
What mede is aye to live in comfort?
In tribulation I reign more rife
Ofter times than in disport.
In weal and in woe I am aye to support:
Mine own wife, go not me fro!
Thy mede is marked, when thou art mort:
  Quia amore langueo.

ANONYMOUS (15th Cent. (?))

yede: *went*; het: *promised*; bait: *resting-place*; weet: *wet*;
in fere: *together*; crippe: *scrip*; mene: *care for*

THE NUT-BROWN MAID   14

He.
  Be it right or wrong, these men among
    On women do complain;
  Affirming this, how that it is
    A labour spent in vain
  To love them wele; for never a dele
    They love a man again:
  For let a man do what he can
    Their favour to attain,
  Yet if a new to them pursue,
    Their first true lover than
  Laboureth for naught; for from her thought
    He is a banished man.

She.
  I say not nay, but that all day
    It is both written and said
  That woman's faith is, as who saith,
    All utterly decayd:
  But nevertheless, right good witnèss
    In this case might be laid
  That they love true and continùe:
    Record the Nut-brown Maid,
  Which, when her love came her to prove,
    To her to make his moan,
  Would not depart; for in her heart
    She loved but him alone.

He.
  Then between us let us discuss
    What was all the manere
  Between them two: we will also
    Tell all the pain in fere
  That she was in. Now I begin,
    So that ye me answere:
  Wherefore all ye that present be,
    I pray you, give an ear.
  I am the Knight. I come by night,
    As secret as I can,
  Saying, Alas! thus standeth the case,
    I am a banished man.

She.	*And I your will for to fulfil*
	   In this will not refuse;
	Trusting to show, in wordes few,
	   That men have an ill use—
	To their own shame—women to blame,
	   And causeless them accuse.
	Therefore to you I answer now,
	   All women to excuse—
	Mine own heart dear, with you what cheer?
	   I pray you, tell anone;
	For, in my mind, of all mankind
	   I love but you alone.

He.	It standeth so: a deed is do
	   Whereof great harm shall grow:
	My destiny is for to die
	   A shameful death, I trow;
	Or else to flee. The t' one must be.
	   None other way I know
	But to withdraw as an outlaw,
	   And take me to my bow.
	Wherefore adieu, mine own heart true!
	   None other rede I can:
	For I must to the green-wood go,
	   Alone, a banished man.

She.	O Lord, what is this worldis bliss,
	   That changeth as the moon!
	My summer's day in lusty May
	   Is darked before the noon.
	I hear you say, farewell: Nay, nay,
	   We dèpart not so soon.
	Why say ye so? whither will ye go?
	   Alas! what have ye done?
	All my welfàre to sorrow and care
	   Should change, if ye were gone:
	For, in my mind, of all mankind
	   I love but you alone.

He.	I can believe it shall you grieve,
	   And somewhat you distrain;
	But afterward, your paines hard
	   Within a day or twain
	Shall soon aslake; and ye shall take
	   Comfort to you again.
	Why should ye ought? for, to make thought,
	   Your labour were in vain.
	And thus I do; and pray you to,
	   As hartely as I can:
	For I must to the green-wood go,
	   Alone, a banished man.

She.	Now, sith that ye have showed to me
	The secret of your mind,
	I shall be plain to you again,
	Like as ye shall me find.
	Sith it is so that ye will go,
	I will not live behind.
	Shall never be said the Nut-brown Maid
	Was to her love unkind.
	Make you ready, for so am I,
	Although it were anone:
	For, in my mind, of all mankind
	I love but you alone.
He.	Yet I you rede to take good heed
	What men will think and say:
	Of young, of old, it shall be told
	That ye be gone away
	Your wanton will for to fulfil,
	In green-wood you to play;
	And that ye might for your delight
	No longer make delay
	Rather than ye should thus for me
	Be called an ill woman
	Yet would I to the green-wood go,
	Alone, a banished man.
She.	Though it be sung of old and young
	That I should be to blame,
	Theirs be the charge that speak so large
	In hurting of my name:
	For I will prove that faithful love
	It is devoid of shame;
	In your distress and heaviness
	To part with you the same:
	And sure all tho that do not so
	True lovers are they none:
	For in my mind, of all mankind
	I love but you alone.
He.	I counsel you, Remember how
	It is no maiden's law
	Nothing to doubt, but to run out
	To wood with an outlaw.
	For ye must there in your hand bear
	A bow ready to draw;
	And as a thief thus must you live
	Ever in dread and awe;
	Whereby to you great harm might grow:
	Yet had I liever than
	That I had to the green-wood go,
	Alone, a banished man.

She.	I think not nay but as ye say;
	  It is no maiden's lore;
	But love may make me for your sake,
	  As I have said before,
	To come on foot, to hunt and shoot,
	  To get us meat and store;
	For so that I your company
	  May have, I ask no more.
	From which to part it maketh my heart
	  As cold as any stone;
	For, in my mind, of all mankind
	  I love but you alone.

He.	For an outlaw this is the law,
	  That men him take and bind:
	Without pitie, hangèd to be,
	  And waver with the wind.
	If I had need (as God forbede!)
	  What socours could ye find?
	Forsooth I trow, you and your bow
	  For fear would draw behind.
	And no mervail; for little avail
	  Were in your counsel than:
	Wherefore I'll to the green-wood go,
	  Alone, a banished man.

She.	Right well know ye that women be
	  But feeble for to fight;
	No womanhede it is, indeed,
	  To be bold as a knight:
	Yet in such fear if that ye were
	  With enemies day and night,
	I would withstand, with bow in hand,
	  To grieve them as I might,
	And you to save; as women have
	  From death men many one:
	For, in my mind, of all mankind
	  I love but you alone.

He.	Yet take good hede; for ever I drede
	  That ye could not sustain
	The thorny ways, the deep valleys,
	  The snow, the frost, the rain,
	The cold, the heat; for dry or wete,
	  We must lodge on the plain;
	And, us above, no other roof
	  But a brake bush or twain:
	Which soon should grieve you, I believe;
	  And ye would gladly than
	That I had to the green-wood go,
	  Alone, a banished man.

She.   Sith I have here been partynere
            With you of joy and bliss,
        I must alsò part of your woe
            Endure, as reason is:
        Yet I am sure of one pleasùre,
            And shortly it is this—
        That where ye be, me seemeth, parde,
            I could not fare amiss.
        Without more speech I you beseech
            That we were shortly gone;
        For, in my mind, of all mankind
            I love but you alone.

He.   If ye go thyder, ye must consider,
            When ye have lust to dine,
        There shall no meat be for to gete,
            Nether bere, ale, ne wine,
        Ne shetès clean, to lie between,
            Made of thread and twine;
        None other house, but leaves and boughs,
            To cover your head and mine.
        Lo, mine heart sweet, this ill diete
            Should make you pale and wan:
        Wherefore I'll to the green-wood go,
            Alone, a banished man.

She.   Among the wild deer such an archère,
            As men say that ye be,
        Ne may not fail of good vitayle
            Where is so great plentè
        And water clear of the rivere
            Shall be full sweet to me;
        With which in hele I shall right wele
            Endure, as ye shall see;
        And, or we go, a bed or two
            I can provide anone;
        For, in my mind, of all mankind
            I love but you alone.

He.   Lo yet, before, ye must do more,
            If ye will go with me:
        As, cut your hair up by your ear,
            Your kirtle by the knee;
        With bow in hand for to withstand
            Your enemies, if need be:
        And this same night, before daylight,
            To woodward will I flee.
        If that ye will all this fulfil,
            Do it shortly as ye can:
        Else will I to the green-wood go,
            Alone, a banished man.

She.   I shall as now do more for you
         Than 'longeth to womanhede;
     To short my hair, a bow to bear,
         To shoot in time of need.
     O my sweet mother! before all other
         For you I have most drede!
     But now, adieu! I must ensue
         Where fortune doth me lead.
     All this make ye: Now let us flee;
         The day cometh fast upon:
     For, in my mind, of all mankind
         I love but you alone.

He.   Nay, nay, not so; ye shall not go,
         And I shall tell you why—
     Your appetite is to be light
         Of love, I well espy:
     For, right as ye have said to me,
         In likewise hardily
     Ye would answere whosoever it were,
         In way of companỳ:
     It is said of old, Soon hot, soon cold;
         And so is a womàn:
     Wherefore I to the wood will go,
         Alone, a banished man.

She.   If ye take heed, it is no need
         Such words to say to me;
     For oft ye prayed, and long assayed,
         Or I loved you, pardè:
     And though that I of ancestry
         A baron's daughter be,
     Yet have you proved how I you loved,
         A squire of low degree;
     And ever shall, whatso befall
         To die therefore anone;
     For, in my mind, of all mankind
         I love but you alone.

He.   A baron's child to be beguiled,
         It were a cursèd deed!
     To be felaw with an outlaw—
         Almighty God forbede!
     Yet better were the poor squyere
         Alone to forest yede
     Than ye shall say another day
         That by my cursed rede
     Ye were betrayed. Wherefore, good maid,
         The best rede that I can,
     Is, that I to the green-wood go,
         Alone, a banished man.

She.   Whatever befall, I never shall
    Of this thing be upbraid:
But if ye go, and leave me so,
    Then have ye me betrayed.
Remember you wele, how that ye dele;
    For if ye, as ye said,
Be so unkind to leave behind
    Your love, the Nut-brown Maid,
Trust me truly that I shall die
    Soon after ye be gone:
For, in my mind, of all mankind
    I love but you alone.

He.   If that ye went, ye should repent;
    For in the forest now
I have purveyed me of a maid
    Whom I love more than you:
Another more fair than ever ye were
    I dare it well avow;
And of you both each should be wroth
    With other, as I trow:
It were mine ease to live in peace;
    So will I, if I can:
Wherefore I to the wood will go,
    Alone, a banished man.

She.   Though in the wood I understood
    Ye had a paramour,
All this may nought remove my thought,
    But that I will be your':
And she shall find me soft and kind
    And courteis every hour;
Glad to fulfil all that she will
    Command me, to my power:
For had ye, lo, an hundred mo,
    Yet would I be that one:
For, in my mind, of all mankind
    I love but you alone.

He.   Mine own dear love, I see the prove
    That ye be kind and true;
Of maid, of wife, in all my life,
    The best that ever I knew.
Be merry and glad; be no more sad;
    The case is changèd new;
For it were ruth that for your truth
    Ye should have cause to rue.
Be not dismayed, whatsoever I said
    To you when I began:
I will not to the green-wood go;
    I am no banished man.

She. These tidings be more glad to me
  Than to be made a queen,
If I were sure they should endure;
  But it is often seen
When men will break promise they speak
  The wordis on the splene.
Ye shape some wile me to beguile,
  And steal from me, I ween:
Then were the case worse than it was,
  And I more wo-begone:
For, in my mind, of all mankind
  I love but you alone.

He. Ye shall not nede further to drede:
  I will not disparàge
You (God defend), sith you descend
  Of so great a linàge.
Now understand: to Westmoreland,
  Which is my heritage,
I will you bring; and with a ring,
  By way of marriàge
I will you take, and lady make,
  As shortly as I can:
Thus have you won an Earles son,
  And not a banished man.

Here may ye see that women be
 In love meek, kind, and stable;
Let never man reprove them than,
 Or call them variable;
But rather pray God that we may
 To them be comfortable;
Which sometime proveth such as He loveth,
 If they be charitable.
For sith men would that women should
 Be meek to them each one;
Much more ought they to God obey,
 And serve but Him alone.

ANONYMOUS (15th Cent.)

never a dele: *never a bit*; than: *then*; in fere: *in company together*;
rede I can: *counsel I know*; part with: *share with*; tho: *those*;
hele: *health*; yede: *went*; on the splene: *that is, in haste*

15   TO A LADY

Sweet rois of vertew and of gentilness,
Delytsum lily of everie lustynes,
 Richest in bontie and in bewtie clear,
 And everie vertew that is wenit dear,
Except onlie that ye are mercyless

Into your garth this day I did persew;
There saw I flowris that fresche were of hew;
 Baith quhyte and reid most lusty were to seyne,
 And halesome herbis upon stalkis greene;
Yet leaf nor flowr find could I nane of rew.

I doubt that Merche, with his cauld blastis keyne,
Has slain this gentil herb, that I of mene;
   Quhois piteous death dois to my heart sic paine
   That I would make to plant his root againe,—
So confortand his levis unto me bene.
                               WILLIAM DUNBAR (1465–1520?)

rois: *rose*; wenit: *weened, esteemed*; garth: *garden-close*;
to seyne: *to see*; that I of mene: *that I complain of, mourn for*

IN HONOUR OF THE CITY OF LONDON   16

London, thou art of townes *A per se.*
  Soveraign of cities, seemliest in sight,
Of high renoun, riches and royaltie;
  Of lordis, barons, and many a goodly knyght;
  Of most delectable lusty ladies bright;
Of famous prelatis, in habitis clericall;
  Of merchauntis full of substaunce and of myght:
London, thou art the flour of Cities all.

Gladdith anon, thou lusty Troynovaunt,
  Citie that some tyme cleped was New Troy;
In all the erth, imperiall as thou stant,
  Pryncesse of townes, of pleasure and of joy,
  A richer restith under no Christen roy;
For manly power, with craftis naturall,
  Fourmeth none fairer sith the flode of Noy:
London, thou art the flour of Cities all.

Gemme of all joy, jasper of jocunditie,
  Most myghty carbuncle of vertue and valour;
Strong Troy in vigour and in strenuytie;
  Of royall cities rose and geraflour;
  Empress of townes, exalt in honour;
In beawtie beryng the crone imperiall;
  Swete paradise precelling in pleasure;
London, thou art the flour of Cities all.

Above all ryvers thy Ryver hath renowne,
  Whose beryall stremys, pleasaunt and preclare,
Under thy lusty wallys renneth down,
  Where many a swan doth swymme with wyngis fair;
  Where many a barge doth saile and row with are;
Where many a ship doth rest with top-royall.
  O, towne of townes! patrone and not compare,
London, thou art the flour of Cities all.

Upon thy lusty Brigge of pylers white
  Been merchauntis full royall to behold;
Upon thy stretis goeth many a semely knyght
  In velvet gownes and in cheynes of gold.
  By Julyus Cesar thy Tour founded of old
May be the hous of Mars victoryall,
  Whose artillary with tonge may not be told:
London, thou art the flour of Cities all.

Strong be thy wallis that about thee standis;
  Wise be the people that within thee dwellis;
Fresh is thy ryver with his lusty strandis;
  Blith be thy chirches, wele sownyng be thy bellis;
  Rich be thy merchauntis in substaunce that excellis;
Fair be their wives, right lovesom, white and small;
  Clere be thy virgyns, lusty under kellis:
London, thou art the flour of Cities all.

Thy famous Maire, by pryncely governaunce,
  With sword of justice thee ruleth prudently.
No Lord of Parys, Venyce, or Floraunce
  In dignitye or honour goeth to hym nigh.
  He is exampler, loode-ster, and guye;
Principall patrone and rose orygynalle,
  Above all Maires as maister most worthy:
London, thou art the flour of Cities all.
                                WILLIAM DUNBAR (1465–1520?)

gladdith: *rejoice*; Troynovaunt: *New Troy*; fourmeth: *appeareth*;
geraflour: *gillyflower*; are: *oar*; small: *slender*;
kellis: *hoods, head-dresses*; guye: *guide*

17   ON THE NATIVITY OF CHRIST
        Rorate coeli desuper!
          Hevins, distil your balmy schouris!
        For now is risen the bricht day-ster,
          Fro the rose Mary, flour of flouris:
          The cleir Sone, quhom no cloud devouris,
        Surmounting Phebus in the Est,
          Is cumin of his hevinly touris:
            Et nobis Puer natus est.

        Archangellis, angellis, and dompnationis,
          Tronis, potestatis, and marteiris seir,
        And all ye hevinly operationis,
          Ster, planeit, firmament, and spheir,
          Fire, erd, air, and water cleir,
        To Him gife loving, most and lest,
          That come in to so meik maneir;
            Et nobis Puer natus est.

        Synnaris be glad, and penance do,
          And thank your Maker hairtfully;
        For he that ye micht nocht come to
          To you is cumin full humbly
          Your soulis with his blood to buy
        And loose you of the fiendis arrest—
          And only of his own mercỳ;
            Pro nobis Puer natus est.

        All clergy do to him inclyne,
          And bow unto that bairn benyng,
        And do your observance divyne
          To him that is of kingis King:

Encense his altar, read and sing
In holy kirk, with mind degest,
  Him honouring attour all thing
    Qui nobis Puer natus est.

Celestial foulis in the air,
  Sing with your nottis upon hicht,
In firthis and in forrestis fair
  Be myrthful now at all your mycht;
  For passit is your dully nicht,
Aurora has the cloudis perst,
  The Sone is risen with glaidsum licht,
    Et nobis Puer natus est.

Now spring up flouris fra the rute,
  Revert you upward naturaly,
In honour of the blissit frute
  That raiss up fro the rose Mary;
  Lay out your levis lustily,
Fro deid take life now at the lest
  In wirschip of that Prince worthy
    Qui nobis Puer natus est.

Sing, hevin imperial, most of hicht!
  Regions of air mak armony!
All fish in flud and fowl of flicht
  Be mirthful and mak melody!
  All *Gloria in excelsis* cry!
Heaven, erd, se, man, bird, and best,—
  He that is crownit abone the sky
    Pro nobis Puer natus est!
                      WILLIAM DUNBAR (1465–1520?)

schouris: *showers*; cumin: *come, entered*; seir: *various*; erd: *earth*; lest: *least*; synnaris: *sinners*; benyng: *benign*; attour: *over, above*; perst: *pierced*; raiss: *rose*; best: *beast*

LAMENT FOR THE MAKERS 18

I that in heill was and gladnèss
Am trublit now with great sickness
And feblit with infirmitie:—
  Timor Mortis conturbat me.

Our plesance here is all vain glory,
This fals world is but transitory,
The flesh is bruckle, the Feynd is slee:—
  Timor Mortis conturbat me.

The state of man does change and vary,
Now sound, now sick, now blyth, now sary,
Now dansand mirry, now like to die:—
  Timor Mortis conturbat me.

No state in Erd here standis sicker;
As with the wynd wavis the wicker
So wannis this world's vanitie:—
  Timor Mortis conturbat me.

Unto the Death gois all Estatis,
Princis, Prelatis, and Potestatis,
Baith rich and poor of all degree:—
  Timor Mortis conturbat me.

He takis the knichtis in to the field
Enarmit under helm and scheild;
Victor he is at all mellie:—
  Timor Mortis conturbat me.

That strong unmerciful tyrand
Takis, on the motheris breast sowkand,
The babe full of benignitie:—
  Timor Mortis conturbat me.

He takis the campion in the stour,
The captain closit in the tour,
The lady in bour full of bewtie:—
  Timor Mortis conturbat me.

He spairis no lord for his piscence,
Na clerk for his intelligence;
His awful straik may no man flee:—
  Timor Mortis conturbat me.

Art-magicianis and astrologgis,
Rethoris, logicianis, and theologgis,
Them helpis no conclusionis slee:—
  Timor Mortis conturbat me.

In medecine the most practicianis,
Leechis, surrigianis, and physicianis,
Themself from Death may not supplee:—
  Timor Mortis conturbat me.

I see that makaris amang the lave
Playis here their padyanis, syne gois to grave;
Sparit is nocht their facultie:—
  Timor Mortis conturbat me.

He has done petuously devour
The noble Chaucer, of makaris flour,
The Monk of Bury, and Gower, all three:—
  Timor Mortis conturbat me.

The good Sir Hew of Eglintoun,
Ettrick, Heriot, and Wintoun,
He has tane out of this cuntrie:—
  Timor Mortis conturbat me.

That scorpion fell has done infeck
Maister John Clerk, and James Afflek,
Fra ballat-making and tragedie:—
  Timor Mortis conturbat me.

Holland and Barbour he has berevit;
Alas! that he not with us levit
Sir Mungo Lockart of the Lee:—
Timor Mortis conturbat me.

Clerk of Tranent eke he has tane,
That made the anteris of Gawaine;
Sir Gilbert Hay endit has he:—
Timor Mortis conturbat me.

He has Blind Harry and Sandy Traill
Slain with his schour of mortal hail,
Quhilk Patrick Johnstoun might nought flee:—
Timor Mortis conturbat me.

He has reft Merseir his endite,
That did in luve so lively write,
So short, so quick, of sentence hie:—
Timor Mortis conturbat me.

He has tane Rowll of Aberdene,
And gentill Rowll of Corstorphine;
Two better fallowis did no man see:—
Timor Mortis conturbat me.

In Dunfermline he has tane Broun
With Maister Robert Henrysoun;
Sir John the Ross enbrast has he:—
Timor Mortis conturbat me.

And he has now tane, last of a,
Good gentil Stobo and Quintin Shaw,
Of quhom all wichtis hes pitie:—
Timor Mortis conturbat me.

Good Maister Walter Kennedy
In point of Death lies verily;
Great ruth it were that so suld be:—
Timor Mortis conturbat me.

Sen he has all my brether tane,
He will naught let me live alane;
Of force I man his next prey be:—
Timor Mortis conturbat me.

Since for the Death remeid is none,
Best is that we for Death dispone,
After our death that live may we:—
  Timor Mortis conturbat me.

WILLIAM DUNBAR (1465–1520?)

heill: *health*; bruckle: *brittle, feeble*; slee: *sly*; dansand: *dancing*; sicker: *sure*; wicker: *willow*; wannis: *wanes*; mellie: *mellay*; sowkand: *sucking*; campion: *champion*; stour: *fight*; piscence: *puissance*; straik: *stroke*; supplee: *save*; makaris: *poets*; the lave: *the leave, the rest*; padyanis: *pageants*; anteris: *adventures*; schour: *shower*; endite: *inditing*; fallowis: *fellows*; wichtis: *wights, persons*; man: *must*; dispone: *make disposition*

19   To Mistress Margery Wentworth

With margerain gentle,
  The flower of goodlihead,
Embroidered the mantle
  Is of your maidenhead.
Plainly I cannot glose;
  Ye be, as I divine,
The pretty primèrose,
  The goodly columbine.

Benign, courteous, and meek,
  With wordes well devised;
In you, who list to seek,
  Be virtues well comprised.
With margerain gentle,
  The flower of goodlihead,
Embroidered the mantle
  Is of your maidenhead.

JOHN SKELTON (1460?–1529)

margerain: *marjoram*

20   To Mistress Margaret Hussey

Merry Margaret
  As midsummer flower,
  Gentle as falcon
  Or hawk of the tower:
With solace and gladness,
Much mirth and no madness,
All good and no badness;
    So joyously,
    So maidenly,
    So womanly
  Her demeaning
  In every thing,
  Far, far passing
  That I can indite,
  Or suffice to write
Of Merry Margaret
  As midsummer flower,
  Gentle as falcon
  Or hawk of the tower.
As patient and still

And as full of good will
As fair Isaphill,
Coliander,
Sweet pomander,
Good Cassander;
Steadfast of thought,
Well made, well wrought,
Far may be sought,
Ere that ye can find
So courteous, so kind
As merry Margaret,
  This midsummer flower,
  Gentle as falcon
Or hawk of the tower.
                  JOHN SKELTON (1460?–1529)

Isaphill: *Hypsipyle*; coliander: *coriander seed, an aromatic*; pomander: *a ball of perfume*; Cassander: *Cassandra*

CONTENTMENT   21

My mind to me a kingdom is;
  Such perfect joy therein I find
As far excels all earthly bliss
  That God or Nature hath assigned;
Though much I want that most would have,
Yet still my mind forbids to crave.

Content I live; this is my stay,—
  I seek no more than may suffice.
I press to bear no haughty sway;
  Look, what I lack my mind supplies.
Lo, thus I triumph like a king,
Content with that my mind doth bring.

I laugh not at another's loss,
  I grudge not at another's gain;
No worldly wave my mind can toss;
  I brook that is another's bane.
I fear no foe, nor fawn on friend;
I loathe not life, nor dread mine end.

My wealth is health and perfect ease;
  My conscience clear my chief defense;
I never seek by bribes to please
  Nor by desert to give offense.
Thus do I live, thus will I die;
Would all did so as well as I!
                  EDWARD DYER (1545–1607)

AS YE CAME FROM THE HOLY LAND   22

As ye came from the holy land
  Of Walsinghame,
Met you not with my true love
  By the way as you came?

How should I know your true love,
  That have met many a one
As I came from the holy land,
  That have come, that have gone?

She is neither white nor brown,
  But as the heavens fair;
There is none hath her form divine
  In the earth or the air.

Such a one did I meet, good sir,
  Such an angelic face,
Who like a nymph, like a queen, did appear
  In her gait, in her grace.

She hath left me here alone
  All alone, as unknown,
Who sometime did me lead with herself,
  And me loved as her own.

What's the cause that she leaves you alone
  And a new way doth take,
That sometime did love you as her own,
  And her joy did you make?

I have loved her all my youth,
  But now am old, as you see:
Love likes not the falling fruit,
  Nor the withered tree.

Know that Love is a careless child,
  And forgets promise past:
He is blind, he is deaf when he list,
  And in faith never fast.

His desire is a dureless content,
  And a trustless joy;
He is won with a world of despair,
  And is lost with a toy.

Of womenkind such indeed is the love,
  Or the word love abused,
Under which many childish desires
  And conceits are excused.

But true love is a durable fire,
  In the mind ever burning,
Never sick, never dead, never cold,
  From itself never turning.

Anonymous (16th Cent.)

The Lover in Winter Plaineth for the Spring

O Western wind, when wilt thou blow
  That the small rain down can rain?
Christ, that my love were in my arms
  And I in my bed again!

ANONYMOUS (16th Cent. (?))

Balow

Balow my babe, lie still and sleep!
It grieves me sore to see thee weep.
Wouldst thou be quiet I'se be glad,
Thy mourning makes my sorrow sad:
Balow my boy, thy mother's joy,
Thy father breeds me great annoy—
  Balow, la-low!

When he began to court my love,
And with his sugred words me move,
His faynings false and flattering cheer
To me that time did not appear:
But now I see most cruellye
He cares ne for my babe nor me—
  Balow, la-low!

Lie still, my darling, sleep awhile,
And when thou wak'st thoo'le sweetly smile:
But smile not as thy father did,
To cozen maids: nay, God forbid!
But yet I fear thou wilt go near
Thy father's heart and face to bear—
  Balow, la-low!

I cannot choose but ever will
Be loving to thy father still;
Where'er he go, where'er he ride,
My love with him doth still abide;
In weal or woe, where'er he go,
My heart shall ne'er depart him fro—
  Balow, la-low!

But do not, do not, pretty mine,
To faynings false thy heart incline!
Be loyal to thy lover true,
And never change her for a new:
If good or fair, of her have care
For women's banning's wondrous sare—
  Balow, la-low!

Bairn, by thy face I will beware;
Like Sirens' words, I'll come not near;
My babe and I together will live;
He'll comfort me when cares do grieve.
My babe and I right soft will lie,
And ne'er respect man's crueltye—
    Balow, la-low!

Farewell, farewell, the falsest youth
That ever kist a woman's mouth!
I wish all maids be warn'd by me
Never to trust man's curtesye;
For if we do but chance to bow,
They'll use us then they care not how—
    Balow, la-low!

ANONYMOUS (16th Cent.)

25   THE OLD CLOAK

This winter's weather it waxeth cold,
  And frost it freezeth on every hill,
And Boreas blows his blast so bold
  That all our cattle are like to spill.
Bell, my wife, she loves no strife;
  She said unto me quietlye,
Rise up, and save cow Crumbock's life!
  Man, put thine old cloak about thee!

He.   O Bell my wife, why dost thou flyte?
  Thou kens my cloak is very thin:
It is so bare and over worn,
  A crickè thereon cannot renn.
Then I'll no longer borrow nor lend;
  For once I'll new apparell'd be;
To-morrow I'll to town and spend;
  For I'll have a new cloak about me.

She.   Cow Crumbock is a very good cow:
  She has been always true to the pail;
She has helped us to butter and cheese, I trow,
  And other things she will not fail.
I would be loth to see her pine.
  Good husband, counsel take of me:
It is not for us to go so fine—
  Man, take thine old cloak about thee!

He.   My cloak it was a very good cloak,
  It hath been always true to the wear;
But now it is not worth a groat:
  I have had it four and forty year'.
Sometime it was of cloth in grain:
  'Tis now but a sigh clout, as you may see:
It will neither hold out wind nor rain;
  And I'll have a new cloak about me.

She.	It is four and forty years ago
	  Sine the one of us the other did ken;
	And we have had, betwixt us two,
	  Of children either nine or ten:
	We have brought them up to women and men:
	  In the fear of God I trow they be.
	And why wilt thou thyself misken?
	  Man, take thine old cloak about thee!

He.	O Bell my wife, why dost thou flyte?
	  Now is now, and then was then:
	Seek now all the world throughout,
	  Thou kens not clowns from gentlemen:
	They are clad in black, green, yellow and blue,
	  So far above their own degree.
	Once in my life I'll take a view;
	  For I'll have a new cloak about me.

She.	King Stephen was a worthy peer;
	  His breeches cost him but a crown;
	He held them sixpence all too dear,
	  Therefore he called the tailor "lown."
	He was a king and wore the crown,
	  And thou'se but of a low degree:
	It's pride that puts this country down:
	  Man, take thy old cloak about thee!

He.	Bell my wife, she loves not strife,
	  Yet she will lead me, if she can;
	And to maintain an easy life
	  I oft must yield, though I'm good-man.
	It's not for a man with a woman to threap,
	  Unless he first give o'er the plea:
	As we began, so will we keep,
	  And I'll take my old cloak about me.

ANONYMOUS (16th Cent. (?))

flyte: *scold*; cloth in grain: *scarlet cloth*; sigh clout: *a rag for straining*; threap: *argue*

THE TRUE KNIGHT

For knighthood is not in the feats of warre,
As for to fight in quarrel right or wrong,
But in a cause which truth can not defarre:
  He ought himself for to make sure and strong,
    Justice to keep mixt with mercy among:
      And no quarrell a knight ought to take
      But for a truth, or for the common's sake.

STEPHEN HAWES (1502?–1523)

defarre: *undo*

27   AN EPITAPH
O mortal folk, you may behold and see
How I lie here, sometime a mighty knight;
The end of joy and all prosperitee
  Is death at last, thorough his course and might:
  After the day there cometh the dark night,
    For though the daye be never so long,
    At last the bells ringeth to evensong.
          STEPHEN HAWES (1502?–1523)

28   FORGET NOT YET
THE LOVER BESEECHETH HIS MISTRESS NOT TO FORGET
    HIS STEADFAST FAITH AND TRUE INTENT
  Forget not yet the tried intent
  Of such a truth as I have meant;
  My great travail so gladly spent,
    Forget not yet!

  Forget not yet when first began
  The weary life ye know, since whan
  The suit, the service, none tell can;
    Forget not yet!

  Forget not yet the great assays,
  The cruel wrong, the scornful ways,
  The painful patience in delays,
    Forget not yet!

  Forget not! O, forget not this!—
  How long ago hath been, and is,
  The mind that never meant amiss—
    Forget not yet!

  Forget not then thine own approved,
  The which so long hath thee so loved,
  Whose steadfast faith yet never moved:
    Forget not this!
          SIR THOMAS WYATT (1503–1542)

29   THE APPEAL
AN EARNEST SUIT TO HIS UNKIND MISTRESS,
    NOT TO FORSAKE HIM
  And wilt thou leave me thus?
  Say nay, say nay, for shame!
  —To save thee from the blame
  Of all my grief and grame.
  And wilt thou leave me thus?
    Say nay! say nay!

  And wilt thou leave me thus,
  That hath loved thee so long
  In wealth and woe among:
  And is thy heart so strong
  As for to leave me thus?
    Say nay! say nay!

And wilt thou leave me thus,
That hath given thee my heart
Never for to depart
Neither for pain nor smart:
And wilt thou leave me thus?
   Say nay! say nay!

And wilt thou leave me thus,
And have no more pitye
Of him that loveth thee?
Alas, thy cruelty!
And wilt thou leave me thus?
   Say nay! say nay!
Sir Thomas Wyatt (1503–1542)

grame: *sorrow*

A Revocation   30

What should I say?
  —Since Faith is dead,
And Truth away
  From you is fled?
  Should I be led
    With doubleness?
  Nay! nay! mistress.

I promised you,
  And you promised me,
To be as true
  As I would be.
  But since I see
    Your double heart,
  Farewell my part!

Thought for to take
  'Tis not my mind;
But to forsake
  One so unkind;
  And as I find
    So will I trust.
  Farewell, unjust!

Can ye say nay
  But that you said
That I alway
  Should be obeyed?
  And—thus betrayed
    Or that I wist!
  Farewell, unkist!
Sir Thomas Wyatt (1503–1542)

31   Vixi Puellis Nuper Idoneus...

They flee from me that sometime did me seek,
  With naked foot stalking within my chamber:
Once have I seen them gentle, tame, and meek,
  That now are wild, and do not once remember
  That sometime they have put themselves in danger
To take bread at my hand; and now they range,
Busily seeking in continual change.

Thanked be fortune, it hath been otherwise
  Twenty times better; but once especial—
In thin array: after a pleasant guise,
  When her loose gown did from her shoulders fall,
  And she me caught in her arms long and small,
And therewithal so sweetly did me kiss,
And softly said, *"Dear heart, how like you this?"*

It was no dream; for I lay broad awaking:
  But all is turn'd now, through my gentleness,
Into a bitter fashion of forsaking;
  And I have leave to go of her goodness;
  And she also to use new-fangleness.
But since that I unkindly so am served,
"How like you this?"—what hath she now deservèd?

                          Sir Thomas Wyatt (1503–1542)

32   To His Lute

My lute, awake! perform the last
Labour that thou and I shall waste,
  And end that I have now begun;
For when this song is said and past,
  My lute, be still, for I have done.

As to be heard where ear is none,
As lead to grave in marble stone,
  My song may pierce her heart as soon:
Should we then sing, or sigh, or moan?
  No, no, my lute! for I have done.

The rocks do not so cruelly
Repulse the waves continually,
  As she my suit and affectiòn;
So that I am past remedy:
  Whereby my lute and I have done.

Proud of the spoil that thou hast got
Of simple hearts thorough Love's shot,
  By whom, unkind, thou hast them won;
Think not he hath his bow forgot,
  Although my lute and I have done.

Vengeance shall fall on thy disdain,
That makest but game of earnest pain:
  Trow not alone under the sun
Unquit to cause thy lover's plain,
  Although my lute and I have done.

May chance thee lie wither'd and old
The winter nights that are so cold,
  Plaining in vain unto the moon:
Thy wishes then dare not be told:
  Care then who list! for I have done.

And then may chance thee to repent
The time that thou has lost and spent
  To cause thy lover's sigh and swoon:
Then shalt thou know beauty but lent,
  And wish and want as I have done.

Now cease, my lute! this is the last
Labour that thou and I shall waste,
  And ended is that we begun:
Now is this song both sung and past—
  My lute, be still, for I have done.

                            SIR THOMAS WYATT (1503–1542)

DESCRIPTION OF SPRING
WHEREIN EACH THING RENEWS, SAVE ONLY THE LOVER

The soote season, that bud and bloom forth brings,
With green hath clad the hill and eke the vale:
The nightingale with feathers new she sings;
The turtle to her make hath told her tale.
Summer is come, for every spray now springs:
The hart hath hung his old head on the pale;
The buck in brake his winter coat he flings;
The fishes flete with new repaired scale.
The adder all her slough away she slings;
The swift swallow pursueth the flies smale;
The busy bee her honey now she mings;
Winter is worn that was the flowers' bale.

  And thus I see among these pleasant things
  Each care decays, and yet my sorrow springs.
                    HENRY HOWARD, EARL OF SURREY (1516–1547)

make: *mate*; mings: *mingles, mixes*

COMPLAINT OF THE ABSENCE OF HER LOVER BEING UPON THE SEA

  O happy dames! that may embrace
    The fruit of your delight,
  Help to bewail the woful case
    And eke the heavy plight
  Of me, that wonted to rejoice
  The fortune of my pleasant choice:
  Good ladies, help to fill my mourning voice.

In ship, freight with rememberance
   Of thoughts and pleasures past,
He sails that hath in governance
   My life while it will last:
With scalding sighs, for lack of gale,
Furthering his hope, that is his sail,
Toward me, the swete port of his avail.

Alas! how oft in dreams I see
   Those eyes that were my food;
Which sometime so delighted me,
   That yet they do me good:
Wherewith I wake with his return
Whose absent flame did make me burn:
But when I find the lack, Lord! how I mourn!

When other lovers in arms across
   Rejoice their chief delight,
Drowned in tears, to mourn my loss
   I stand the bitter night
In my window where I may see
Before the winds how the clouds flee:
Lo! what a mariner love hath made me!

And in green waves when the salt flood
   Doth rise by rage of wind,
A thousand fancies in that mood
   Assail my restless mind.
Alas! now drencheth my sweet foe,
That with the spoil of my heart did go,
And left me; but alas! why did he so?

And when the seas wax calm again
   To chase fro me annoy,
My doubtful hope doth cause me plain;
   So dread cuts off my joy.
Thus is my wealth mingled with woe
And of each thought a doubt doth grow;
—Now he comes! Will he come? Alas! no, no.
        HENRY HOWARD, EARL OF SURREY (1516–1547)

drencheth: *ie is drenched or drowned*

THE MEANS TO ATTAIN HAPPY LIFE
Martial, the things that do attain
   The happy life be these, I find:—
The richesse left, not got with pain;
   The fruitful ground, the quiet mind;

The equal friend; no grudge, no strife;
   No charge of rule, nor governance;
Without disease, the healthful life;
   The household of continuance;

The mean diet, no delicate fare;
   True wisdom join'd with simpleness;
The night discharged of all care,
    Where wine the wit may not oppress.

The faithful wife, without debate;
   Such sleeps as may beguile the night:
Contented with thine own estate
    Ne wish for death, ne fear his might.
        HENRY HOWARD, EARL OF SURREY (1516–1547)

A TRUE LOVE

What sweet relief the showers to thirsty plants we see,
What dear delight the blooms to bees, my true love is to me!
As fresh and lusty Ver foul Winter doth exceed—
As morning bright, with scarlet sky, doth pass the evening's weed—
As mellow pears above the crabs esteemed be—
So doth my love surmount them all, whom yet I hap to see!
The oak shall olives bear, the lamb the lion fray,
The owl shall match the nightingale in tuning of her lay,
Or I my love let slip out of mine entire heart,
So deep reposed in my breast is she for her desart!
For many blessed gifts, O happy, happy land!
Where Mars and Pallas strive to make their glory most to stand!
Yet, land, more is thy bliss that, in this cruel age,
A Venus' imp thou hast brought forth, so steadfast and so sage.
Among the Muses Nine a tenth if Jove would make,
And to the Graces Three a fourth, her would Apollo take.
Let some for honour hunt, and hoard the massy gold:
With her so I may live and die, my weal cannot be told.
        NICHOLAS GRIMALD (1519–1562)

   fray: *affright*

A BEQUEST OF HIS HEART

Hence, heart, with her that must depart,
   And hald thee with thy soverane!
For I had liever want ane heart,
   Nor have the heart that dois me pain.
   Therefore, go, with thy love remain,
And let me leif thus unmolest;
   And see that thou come not again,
But bide with her thou luvis best.

Sen she that I have servit lang
   Is to depart so suddenly,
Address thee now, for thou sall gang
   And bear thy lady company.
   Fra she be gone, heartless am I,
For quhy? thou art with her possest.
   Therefore, my heart, go hence in high,
And bide with her thou luvis best.

    Though this belappit body here
       Be bound to servitude and thrall,
    My faithful heart is free entier
       And mind to serve my lady at all.
       Would God that I were perigall
    Under that redolent rose to rest!
       Yet at the least, my heart, thou sall
    Abide with her thou luvis best.

    Sen in your garth the lily quhyte
       May not remain amang the laif,
    Adieu the flower of whole delite!
       Adieu the succour that may me saif!
       Adieu the fragrant balme suaif,
    And lamp of ladies lustiest!
       My faithful heart she shall it haif
    To bide with her it luvis best.

    Deploir, ye ladies cleir of hue,
       Her absence, sen she must depart!
    And, specially, ye luveris true
       That wounded bene with Luvis dart.
       For some of you sall want ane heart
    As well as I; therefore at last
       Do go with mine, with mind inwart,
    And bide with her thou luvis best!
                          ALEXANDER SCOTT (1520?–1582?)

hald: *keep*; sen: *since*; belappit: *downtrodden*;
perigall: *made equal to, privileged*; garth: *garden-close*; laif: *rest*;
with mind inwart: *with inner mind, ie in spirit*

A RONDEL OF LOVE

    Lo, quhat it is to love
      Learn ye that list to prove,
  By me, I say, that no ways may
      The ground of grief remove,
But still decay both nicht and day:
    Lo, quhat it is to love!

    Love is ane fervent fire
      Kindlit without desire,
Short pleasure, long displeasure,
      Repentance is the hire;
Ane pure tressour without measour;
    Love is ane fervent fire.

    To love and to be wise,
      To rage with good advice;
Now thus, now than, so gois the game,
      Incertain is the dice;
There is no man, I say, that can
    Both love and to be wise.

Flee always from the snare,
Learn at me to beware;
It is ane pain, and double trane
Of endless woe and care;
For to refrain that danger plain,
Flee always from the snare.

ALEXANDER SCOTT (1520?–1582?)

AMANTIUM IRAE

In going to my naked bed as one that would have slept,
I heard a wife sing to her child, that long before had wept;
She sighed sore and sang full sweet, to bring the babe to rest,
That would not cease but cried still, in sucking at her breast.
She was full weary of her watch, and grieved with her child,
She rocked it and rated it, till that on her it smiled.
Then did she say, Now have I found this proverb true to prove,
The falling out of faithful friends renewing is of love.

Then took I paper, pen, and ink, this proverb for to write,
In register for to remain of such a worthy wight:
As she proceeded thus in song unto her little brat,
Much matter utter'd she of weight, in place whereas she sat:
And provèd plain there was no beast, nor creature bearing life,
Could well be known to live in love without discord and strife:
Then kissèd she her little babe, and sware by God above,
The falling out of faithful friends renewing is of love.

She said that neither king nor prince nor lord could live aright,
Until their puissance they did prove, their manhood and their might.
When manhood shall be matched so that fear can take no place,
Then weary works make warriors each other to embrace,
And left their force that failèd them, which did consume the rout,
That might before have lived their time, their strength and nature out:
Then did she sing as one that thought no man could her reprove,
The falling out of faithful friends renewing is of love.

She said she saw no fish nor fowl, nor beast within her haunt,
That met a stranger in their kind, but could give it a taunt:
Since flesh might not endure, but rest must wrath succeed,
And force the fight to fall to play in pasture where they feed,
So noble nature can well end the work she hath begun,
And bridle well that will not cease her tragedy in some:
Thus in song she oft rehearsed, as did her well behove,
The falling out of faithful friends renewing is of love.

I marvel much pardy (quoth she) for to behold the rout,
To see man, woman, boy and beast, to toss the world about:
Some kneel, some crouch, some beck, some check,
    and some can smoothly smile,

And some embrace others in arm, and there think many a wile,
Some stand aloof at cap and knee, some humble and some stout,
Yet are they never friends in deed until they once fall out:
Thus ended she her song and said, before she did remove,
The falling out of faithful friends renewing is of love.
				RICHARD EDWARDES (1523–1566)

40			A LOVER'S LULLABY
　　Sing lullaby, as women do,
　　　　Wherewith they bring their babes to rest;
　　And lullaby can I sing too,
　　　　As womanly as can the best.
　　With lullaby they still the child;
　　And if I be not much beguiled,
　　Full many a wanton babe have I,
　　Which must be still'd with lullaby.

　　First lullaby my youthful years,
　　　　It is now time to go to bed:
　　For crooked age and hoary hairs
　　　　Have won the haven within my head.
　　With lullaby, then, youth be still;
　　With lullaby content thy will;
　　Since courage quails and comes behind,
　　Go sleep, and so beguile thy mind!

　　Next lullaby my gazing eyes,
　　　　Which wonted were to glance apace;
　　For every glass may now suffice
　　　　To show the furrows in thy face.
　　With lullaby then wink awhile;
　　With lullaby your looks beguile;
　　Let no fair face, nor beauty bright,
　　Entice you eft with vain delight.

　　And lullaby my wanton will;
　　　　Let reason's rule now reign thy thought;
　　Since all too late I find by skill
　　　　How dear I have thy fancies bought;
　　With lullaby now take thine ease,
　　With lullaby thy doubts appease;
　　For trust to this, if thou be still,
　　My body shall obey thy will.

　　Thus lullaby my youth, mine eyes,
　　　　My will, my ware, and all that was:
　　I can no more delays devise;
　　　　But welcome pain, let pleasure pass.
　　With lullaby now take your leave;
　　With lullaby your dreams deceive;
　　And when you rise with waking eye,
　　Remember then this lullaby.
				GEORGE GASCOIGNE (1525?–1577)

Jolly Good Ale and Old   41

I cannot eat but little meat,
  My stomach is not good;
But sure I think that I can drink
  With him that wears a hood.
Though I go bare, take ye no care,
  I nothing am a-cold;
I stuff my skin so full within
  Of jolly good ale and old.
    Back and side go bare, go bare;
    Both foot and hand go cold;
    But, belly, God send thee good ale enough,
    Whether it be new or old.

I love no roast but a nut-brown toast,
  And a crab laid in the fire;
A little bread shall do me stead;
  Much bread I not desire.
No frost nor snow, no wind, I trow,
  Can hurt me if I wold;
I am so wrapp'd and thoroughly lapp'd
  Of jolly good ale and old.
    Back and side go bare, go bare, &c.

And Tib, my wife, that as her life
  Loveth well good ale to seek,
Full oft drinks she till ye may see
  The tears run down her cheek:
Then doth she trowl to me the bowl
  Even as a maltworm should,
And saith, "Sweetheart, I took my part
  Of this jolly good ale and old."
    Back and side go bare, go bare, &c.

Now let them drink till they nod and wink,
  Even as good fellows should do;
They shall not miss to have the bliss
  Good ale doth bring men to;
And all poor souls that have scour'd bowls
  Or have them lustily troll'd,
God save the lives of them and their wives,
  Whether they be young or old.
    Back and side go bare, go bare;
    Both foot and hand go cold;
    But, belly, God send thee good ale enough,
    Whether it be new or old.
                  WILLIAM STEVENSON (1530?–1575)

When Flora had O'erfret the Firth   42

Quhen Flora had o'erfret the firth
  In May of every moneth queen;
Quhen merle and mavis singis with mirth
  Sweet melling in the shawis sheen;

       Quhen all luvaris rejoicit bene
       And most desirous of their prey,
         I heard a lusty luvar mene
       —"I luve, but I dare nocht assay!"

"Strong are the pains I daily prove,
   But yet with patience I sustene,
I am so fetterit with the luve
   Only of my lady sheen,
   Quhilk for her beauty micht be queen,
Nature so craftily alway
   Has done depaint that sweet serene:
—Quhom I luve I dare nocht assay.

"She is so bricht of hyd and hue,
   I luve but her alone, I ween;
Is none her luve that may eschew,
   That blinkis of that dulce amene;
   So comely cleir are her twa een
That she mae luvaris dois affray
   Than ever of Greece did fair Helene:
—Quhom I luve I dare nocht assay!"
                         ANONYMOUS (16th Cent. (Scottish))

o'erfret: *adorned*; shawis: *woods*; sheen: *beautiful*; mene: *mourn*;
hyd: *skin*; blinkis: *gets a glimpse*;
dulce amene: *gentle and pleasant one*; mae: *more*

LUSTY MAY

O lusty May, with Flora queen!
The balmy dropis from Phœbus sheen
   Preluciand beams before the day:
By that Diana growis green
   Through gladness of this lusty May.

Then Esperus, that is so bricht,
Til woful hairtis castis his light,
   With bankis that bloomis on every brae;
And schouris are shed forth of their sicht
   Through gladness of this lusty May.

Birdis on bewis of every birth,
Rejoicing notis makand their mirth
   Richt plesantly upon the spray,
With flourishingis o'er field and firth
   Through gladness of this lusty May.

All luvaris that are in care
To their ladies they do repair
   In fresh morningis before the day,
And are in mirth ay mair and mair
   Through gladness of this lusty May.
                         ANONYMOUS (16th Cent. (Scottish))

sheen: *bright*; til: *into*; schouris: *showers*; bewis: *boughs*; birth: *kind*

My Heart is High Above 44

My heart is high above, my body is full of bliss,
For I am set in luve as well as I would wiss
I luve my lady pure and she luvis me again,
I am her serviture, she is my soverane;
She is my very heart, I am her howp and heill,
She is my joy invart, I am her luvar leal;
I am her bond and thrall, she is at my command;
I am perpetual her man, both foot and hand;
The thing that may her please my body sall fulfil;
Quhatever her disease, it does my body ill.
My bird, my bonny ane, my tender babe venust,
My luve, my life alane, my liking and my lust!
We interchange our hairtis in others armis soft,
Spriteless we twa depairtis, usand our luvis oft.
We mourn when licht day dawis, we plain the nicht is short,
We curse the cock that crawis, that hinderis our disport.
I glowffin up aghast, quhen I her miss on nicht,
And in my oxter fast I find the bowster richt;
Then languor on me lies like Morpheus the mair,
Quhilk causes me uprise and to my sweet repair.
And then is all the sorrow forth of remembrance
That ever I had a-forrow in luvis observance.
Thus never I do rest, so lusty a life I lead,
Quhen that I list to test the well of womanheid.
Luvaris in pain, I pray God send you sic remeid
As I have nicht and day, you to defend from deid!
Therefore be ever true unto your ladies free,
And they will on you rue as mine has done on me.
       ANONYMOUS (16th Cent. (Scottish))

*wiss: wish; heill: health; invart: inward; venust: delightful;
glowffin: blink on awaking; oxter: armpit; a-forrow: aforetime*

Hey Nonny No! 45

 Hey nonny no!
 Men are fools that wish to die!
 Is't not fine to dance and sing
 When the bells of death do ring?
 Is't not fine to swim in wine,
 And turn upon the toe,
 And sing hey nonny no!
 When the winds blow and the seas flow?
 Hey nonny no!

MISCELLANIES & SONGS BY UNNAMED OR UNCERTAIN AUTHORS (16th Cent.)
           from Christ Church MS.

Preparations 46

Yet if His Majesty, our sovereign lord,
Should of his own accord
Friendly himself invite,
And say "I'll be your guest to-morrow night,"
How should we stir ourselves, call and command
All hands to work! "Let no man idle stand!

"Set me fine Spanish tables in the hall;
  See they be fitted all;
  Let there be room to eat
And order taken that there want no meat.
  See every sconce and candlestick made bright,
  That without tapers they may give a light.

"Look to the presence: are the carpets spread,
  The dazie o'er the head,
  The cushions in the chairs,
And all the candles lighted on the stairs?
  Perfume the chambers, and in any case
  Let each man give attendance in his place!"

Thus, if a king were coming, would we do;
  And 'twere good reason too;
  For 'tis a duteous thing
To show all honour to an earthly king,
  And after all our travail and our cost,
  So he be pleased, to think no labour lost.

But at the coming of the King of Heaven
  All's set at six and seven;
  We wallow in our sin,
Christ cannot find a chamber in the inn.
  We entertain Him always like a stranger,
  And, as at first, still lodge Him in the manger.

MISCELLANIES & SONGS BY UNNAMED OR UNCERTAIN AUTHORS (16th Cent.)
from Christ Church MS.

47   PHILLIDA AND CORIDON
    In the merry month of May,
    In a morn by break of day,
    Forth I walk'd by the wood-side
    When as May was in his pride:
    There I spièd all alone
    Phillida and Coridon.
    Much ado there was, God wot!
    He would love and she would not.
    She said, Never man was true;
    He said, None was false to you.
    He said, He had loved her long;
    She said, Love should have no wrong.
    Coridon would kiss her then;
    She said, Maids must kiss no men
    Till they did for good and all;
    Then she made the shepherd call
    All the heavens to witness truth
    Never loved a truer youth.
    Thus with many a pretty oath,
    Yea and nay, and faith and troth,

Such as silly shepherds use
When they will not Love abuse,
Love, which had been long deluded,
Was with kisses sweet concluded;
And Phillida, with garlands gay,
Was made the Lady of the May.

NICHOLAS BRETON (1542–1626)

A CRADLE SONG 48

Come little babe, come silly soul,
Thy father's shame, thy mother's grief,
Born as I doubt to all our dole,
And to thyself unhappy chief:
    Sing lullaby, and lap it warm,
    Poor soul that thinks no creature harm.

Thou little think'st and less dost know
The cause of this thy mother's moan;
Thou want'st the wit to wail her woe,
And I myself am all alone:
    Why dost thou weep? why dost thou wail?
    And know'st not yet what thou dost ail.

Come, little wretch—ah, silly heart!
Mine only joy, what can I more?
If there be any wrong thy smart,
That may the destinies implore:
    'Twas I, I say, against my will,
    I wail the time, but be thou still.

And dost thou smile? O, thy sweet face!
Would God Himself He might thee see!—
No doubt thou wouldst soon purchase grace,
I know right well, for thee and me:
    But come to mother, babe, and play,
    For father false is fled away.

Sweet boy, if it by fortune chance
Thy father home again to send,
If death do strike me with his lance,
Yet mayst thou me to him commend:
    If any ask thy mother's name,
    Tell how by love she purchased blame.

Then will his gentle heart soon yield:
I know him of a noble mind:
Although a lion in the field,
A lamb in town thou shalt him find:
    Ask blessing, babe, be not afraid,
    His sugar'd words hath me betray'd.

Then mayst thou joy and be right glad;
Although in woe I seem to moan,
Thy father is no rascal lad,
A noble youth of blood and bone:
    His glancing looks, if he once smile,
    Right honest women may beguile.

Come, little boy, and rock asleep;
Sing lullaby and be thou still;
I, that can do naught else but weep,
Will sit by thee and wail my fill:
    God bless my babe, and lullaby
    From this thy father's quality.
                  NICHOLAS BRETON (1542–1626)
           from The Arbor of Amorous Devices, 1593–1594

THE LYE

[In Raleigh's day, "to give the lye" meant to call someone a liar. – Ed.]

Goe, soule, the bodie's guest,
  Upon a thanklesse arrant;
Feare not to touche the best—
  The truth shall be thy warrant!
    Goe, since I needs must dye,
    And give the world the lye.

Goe tell the court it glowes
  And shines like rotten wood;
Goe tell the church it showes
  What's good, and doth no good;
    If church and court reply,
    Then give them both the lye.

Tell potentates they live
  Acting by others' actions—
Not loved unlesse they give,
  Not strong but by their factions;
    If potentates reply,
    Give potentates the lye.

Tell men of high condition,
  That rule affairs of state,
Their purpose is ambition,
  Their practice only hate;
    And if they once reply,
    Then give them all the lye.

Tell zeale it lacks devotion;
  Tell love it is but lust;
Tell time it is but motion;
  Tell flesh it is but dust;
    And wish them not reply,
    For thou must give the lye.

Tell wit how much it wrangles
  In tickle points of nicenesse;
Tell wisdome she entangles
  Herselfe in over-wisenesse;
    And if they do reply,
    Straight give them both the lye.

Tell physicke of her boldnesse;
  Tell skill it is pretension;
Tell charity of coldnesse;
  Tell law it is contention;
    And as they yield reply,
    So give them still the lye.

Tell fortune of her blindnesse;
  Tell nature of decay;
Tell friendship of unkindnesse;
  Tell justice of delay;
    And if they dare reply,
    Then give them all the lye.

Tell arts they have no soundnesse,
  But vary by esteeming;
Tell schooles they want profoundnesse,
  And stand too much on seeming;
    If arts and schooles reply,
    Give arts and schooles the lye.

So, when thou hast, as I
  Commanded thee, done blabbing—
Although to give the lye
  Deserves no less than stabbing—
    Yet stab at thee who will,
    No stab the soule can kill.
                        Sir Walter Raleigh (1552–1618)

POLONIUS' ADVICE

See thou character. Give thy thoughts no tongue,
Nor any unproportion'd thought his act.
Be thou familiar, but by no means vulgar:
The friends thou hast, and their adoption tried,
Grapple them to thy soul with hoops of steel;
But do not dull thy palm with entertainment
Of each new-hatch'd, unfledg'd comrade. Beware
Of entrance to a quarrel; but, being in,
Bear't that th' opposed may beware of thee.
Give every man thine ear, but few thy voice:
Take each man's censure, but reserve thy judgment.
Costly thy habit as thy purse can buy
But not expressed in fancy; rich, not gaudy:
For the apparel oft proclaims the man.
Neither a borrower nor a lender be;
For loan oft loses both itself and friend,

And borrowing dulls the edge of husbandry.
This above all: to thine own self be true;
And it must follow, as the night the day,
Thou canst not then be false to any man.
> WILLIAM SHAKESPEARE (1564–1616)
from "Hamlet"

51   A FRAGMENT FROM
           MARK ANTONY'S SPEECH

This was the noblest Roman of them all:
All the conspirators, save only he,
Did that they did in envy of great Cæsar;
He only, in a general honest thought
And common good to all, made one of them.
His life was gentle; and the elements
So mix'd in him, that Nature might stand up,
And say to all the world, "This was a man!"
> WILLIAM SHAKESPEARE (1564–1616)
from "Julius Cæsar"

52   IN YOUTH IS PLEASURE

In a harbour grene aslepe whereas I lay,
The byrdes sang swete in the middes of the day,
I dreamèd fast of mirth and play:
    In youth is pleasure, in youth is pleasure.

Methought I walked still to and fro,
And from her company I could not go—
But when I waked it was not so:
    In youth is pleasure, in youth is pleasure.

Therefore my hart is surely pyght
Of her alone to have a sight
Which is my joy and hartes delight:
    In youth is pleasure, in youth is pleasure.
> ROBERT WEVER (flourit c. 1550)

53   TO HER SEA-FARING LOVER

Shall I thus ever long, and be no whit the neare?
And shall I still complain to thee, the which me will not hear?
  Alas! say nay! say nay! and be no more so dumb,
But open thou thy manly mouth and say that thou wilt come:
  Whereby my heart may think, although I see not thee,
That thou wilt come—thy word so sware—if thou a live man be.
  The roaring hugy waves they threaten my poor ghost,
And toss thee up and down the seas in danger to be lost.
  Shall they not make me fear that they have swallowed thee?
—But as thou art most sure alive, so wilt thou come to me.
  Whereby I shall go see thy ship ride on the strand,
And think and say *Lo where he comes* and *Sure here will he land:*
  And then I shall lift up to thee my little hand,
And thou shalt think thine heart in ease, in health to see me stand.
  And if thou come indeed (as Christ thee send to do!)
Those arms which miss thee now shall then embrace [and hold] thee too:

Each vein to every joint the lively blood shall spread
Which now for want of thy glad sight doth show full pale and dead.
  But if thou slip thy troth, and do not come at all,
As minutes in the clock do strike so call for death I shall:
  To please both thy false heart and rid myself from woe,
That rather had to die in troth than live forsaken so!
        MISCELLANIES & SONGS BY UNNAMED OR UNCERTAIN AUTHORS (1557)
                                        from Tottel's Miscellany

    neare: *nearer*

THE FAITHLESS SHEPHERDESS   54

While that the sun with his beams hot
  Scorchèd the fruits in vale and mountain,
Philon the shepherd, late forgot,
  Sitting beside a crystal fountain
    In shadow of a green oak tree,
    Upon his pipe this song play'd he:
Adieu, Love, adieu, Love, untrue Love!
Untrue Love, untrue Love, adieu, Love!
Your mind is light, soon lost for new love.

So long as I was in your sight
  I was your heart, your soul, your treasure;
And evermore you sobb'd and sigh'd
  Burning in flames beyond all measure:
    —Three days endured your love to me,
    And it was lost in other three!
Adieu, Love, adieu, Love, untrue Love!
Untrue Love, untrue Love, adieu, Love!
Your mind is light, soon lost for new love.

Another shepherd you did see,
  To whom your heart was soon enchained;
Full soon your love was leapt from me,
  Full soon my place he had obtained.
    Soon came a third your love to win,
    And we were out and he was in.
Adieu, Love, adieu, Love, untrue Love!
Untrue Love, untrue Love, adieu, Love!
Your mind is light, soon lost for new love.

Sure you have made me passing glad
  That you your mind so soon removèd,
Before that I the leisure had
  To choose you for my best belovèd:
    For all my love was pass'd and done
    Two days before it was begun.
Adieu, Love, adieu, Love, untrue Love!
Untrue Love, untrue Love, adieu, Love!
Your mind is light, soon lost for new love.
        MISCELLANIES & SONGS BY UNNAMED OR UNCERTAIN AUTHORS (1589)
                              from William Byrd's *Songs of Sundry Natures*

55   CRABBED AGE AND YOUTH
Crabbèd Age and Youth
Cannot live together:
Youth is full of pleasance,
Age is full of care;
Youth like summer morn,
Age like winter weather;
Youth like summer brave,
Age like winter bare.
Youth is full of sport,
Age's breath is short;
Youth is nimble, Age is lame;
Youth is hot and bold,
Age is weak and cold;
Youth is wild, and Age is tame.
Age, I do abhor thee;
Youth, I do adore thee;
O, my Love, my Love is young!
Age, I do defy thee:
O, sweet shepherd, hie thee!
For methinks thou stay'st too long.
MISCELLANIES & SONGS BY UNNAMED OR UNCERTAIN AUTHORS (1599)
from The Passionate Pilgrim

56   THE SILENT LOVER
i.
Passions are liken'd best to floods and streams:
The shallow murmur, but the deep are dumb;
So, when affection yields discourse, it seems
 The bottom is but shallow whence they come.
They that are rich in words, in words discover
That they are poor in that which makes a lover.

ii.
Wrong not, sweet empress of my heart,
 The merit of true passion,
With thinking that he feels no smart,
 That sues for no compassion.

Silence in love bewrays more woe
 Than words, though ne'er so witty:
A beggar that is dumb, you know,
 May challenge double pity.

Then wrong not, dearest to my heart,
 My true, though secret passion;
He smarteth most that hides his smart,
 And sues for no compassion.
SIR WALTER RALEIGH (1552–1618)

His Pilgrimage 57

Give me my scallop-shell of quiet,
  My staff of faith to walk upon,
My scrip of joy, immortal diet,
  My bottle of salvation,
My gown of glory, hope's true gage;
And thus I'll take my pilgrimage.

Blood must be my body's balmer;
  No other balm will there be given:
Whilst my soul, like quiet palmer,
  Travelleth towards the land of heaven;
Over the silver mountains,
Where spring the nectar fountains;
    There will I kiss
    The bowl of bliss;
And drink mine everlasting fill
Upon every milken hill.
My soul will be a-dry before;
But, after, it will thirst no more.

                  SIR WALTER RALEIGH (1552–1618)

The Conclusion 58

Even such is Time, that takes in trust
Our youth, our joys, our all we have,
And pays us but with earth and dust;
  Who in the dark and silent grave,
When we have wander'd all our ways,
Shuts up the story of our days;
But from this earth, this grave, this dust,
My God shall raise me up, I trust.

                  SIR WALTER RALEIGH (1552–1618)

Whilst it is Prime 59

Fresh Spring, the herald of loves mighty king,
In whose cote-armour richly are displayd
All sorts of flowers, the which on earth do spring,
In goodly colours gloriously arrayd—
Goe to my love, where she is carelesse layd,
Yet in her winters bowre not well awake;
Tell her the joyous time wil not be staid,
Unlesse she doe him by the forelock take;
Bid her therefore her selfe soone ready make,
To wayt on Love amongst his lovely crew;
Where every one, that misseth then her make,
Shall be by him amearst with penance dew.
  Make hast, therefore, sweet love, whilest it is prime;
  For none can call againe the passed time.

                  EDMUND SPENSER (1552–1599)

make: *mate*

60
A Ditty In praise of Eliza, Queen of the Shepherds

See where she sits upon the grassie greene,
    (O seemely sight!)
Yclad in Scarlot, like a mayden Queene,
    And ermines white:
Upon her head a Cremosin coronet
With Damaske roses and Daffadillies set:
    Bay leaves betweene,
    And primroses greene,
Embellish the sweete Violet.

Tell me, have ye seene her angelick face
    Like Phœbe fayre?
Her heavenly haveour, her princely grace,
    Can you well compare?
The Redde rose medled with the White yfere,
In either cheeke depeincten lively chere:
    Her modest eye,
    Her Majestie,
Where have you seene the like but there?

I see Calliope speede her to the place,
    Where my Goddesse shines;
And after her the other Muses trace
    With their Violines.
Bene they not Bay braunches which they do beare,
All for Elisa in her hand to weare?
    So sweetely they play,
    And sing all the way,
That it a heaven is to heare.

Lo, how finely the Graces can it foote
    To the Instrument:
They dauncen deffly, and singen soote,
    In their meriment.
Wants not a fourth Grace to make the daunce even?
Let that rowme to my Lady be yeven.
    She shal be a Grace,
    To fyll the fourth place,
And reigne with the rest in heaven.

Bring hether the Pincke and purple Cullambine,
    With Gelliflowres;
Bring Coronations, and Sops-in-wine
    Worne of Paramoures:
Strowe me the ground with Daffadowndillies,
And Cowslips, and Kingcups, and lovèd Lillies:
    The pretie Pawnce,
    And the Chevisaunce,
Shall match with the fayre flowre Delice.

Now ryse up, Elisa, deckèd as thou art
    In royall aray;
And now ye daintie Damsells may depart
    Eche one her way.
I feare I have troubled your troupes to longe:
Let dame Elisa thanke you for her song:
    And if you come hether
    When Damsines I gether,
I will part them all you among.
EDMUND SPENSER (1552–1599)

medled: *mixed*; yfere: *together*; soote: *sweet*; coronations: *carnations*; sops-in-wine: *striped pinks*; pawnce: *pansy*; chevisaunce: *wallflower*; flowre delice: *iris*

FROM "DAPHNAIDA"
AN ELEGY

She fell away in her first ages spring,
Whil'st yet her leafe was greene, and fresh her rinde,
And whil'st her braunch faire blossomes foorth did bring,
She fell away against all course of kinde.
For age to dye is right, but youth is wrong;
She fel away like fruit blowne downe with winde.
Weepe, Shepheard! weepe, to make my undersong.

Yet fell she not as one enforst to dye,
Ne dyde with dread and grudging discontent,
But as one toyld with travaile downe doth lye,
So lay she downe, as if to sleepe she went,
And closde her eyes with carelesse quietnesse;
The whiles soft death away her spirit hent,
And soule assoyld from sinfull fleshlinesse.

How happie was I when I saw her leade
The Shepheards daughters dauncing in a rownd!
How trimly would she trace and softly tread
The tender grasse, with rosie garland crownd!
And when she list advance her heavenly voyce,
Both Nymphes and Muses nigh she made astownd,
And flocks and shepheards caused to rejoyce.

But now, ye Shepheard lasses! who shall lead
Your wandring troupes, or sing your virelayes?
Or who shall dight your bowres, sith she is dead
That was the Lady of your holy-dayes?
Let now your blisse be turned into bale,
And into plaints convert your joyous playes,
And with the same fill every hill and dale.

For I will walke this wandring pilgrimage,
Throughout the world from one to other end,
And in affliction wast my better age:
My bread shall be the anguish of my mind,
My drink the teares which fro mine eyed do raine,
My bed the ground that hardest I may finde;
So will I wilfully increase my paine.

Ne sleepe (the harbenger of wearie wights)
Shall ever lodge upon mine ey-lids more;
Ne shall with rest refresh my fainting sprights,
Nor failing force to former strength restore:
But I will wake and sorrow all the night
With Philumene, my fortune to deplore;
With Philumene, the partner of my plight.

And ever as I see the starres to fall,
And under ground to goe to give them light
Which dwell in darknes, I to minde will call
How my fair Starre (that shinde on me so bright)
Fell sodainly and faded under ground;
Since whose departure, day is turnd to night,
And night without a Venus starre is found.

And she, my love that was, my Saint that is,
When she beholds from her celestiall throne
(In which shee joyeth in eternall blis)
My bitter penance, will my case bemone,
And pitie me that living thus doo die;
For heavenly spirits have compassion
On mortall men, and rue their miserie.

So when I have with sorowe satisfide
Th' importune fates, which vengeance on me seeke,
And th' heavens with long languor pacifide,
She, for pure pitie of my sufferance meeke,
Will send for me; for which I daylie long:
And will till then my painful penance eeke.
Weep, Shepheard! weep, to make my undersong!
                                        EDMUND SPENSER (1552–1599)

62   EASTER

Most glorious Lord of Lyfe! that, on this day,
Didst make Thy triumph over death and sin;
And, having harrowd hell, didst bring away
Captivity thence captive, us to win:
This joyous day, deare Lord, with joy begin;
And grant that we, for whom thou diddest dye,
Being with Thy deare blood clene washt from sin,
May live for ever in felicity!

And that Thy love we weighing worthily,
May likewise love Thee for the same againe;
And for Thy sake, that all lyke deare didst buy,
With love may one another entertayne!
  So let us love, deare Love, lyke as we ought,
  —Love is the lesson which the Lord us taught.
                                        EDMUND SPENSER (1552–1599)

Cards and Kisses 63

Cupid and my Campaspe play'd
At cards for kisses—Cupid paid:
He stakes his quiver, bow, and arrows,
His mother's doves, and team of sparrows;
Loses them too; then down he throws
The coral of his lips, the rose
Growing on 's cheek (but none knows how);
With these, the crystal of his brow,
And then the dimple of his chin:
All these did my Campaspe win.
At last he set her both his eyes—
She won, and Cupid blind did rise.
  O Love! has she done this for thee?
  What shall, alas! become of me?
JOHN LYLY (1553–1606)

Spring's Welcome 64

What bird so sings, yet so does wail?
O 'tis the ravish'd nightingale.
Jug, jug, jug, jug, tereu! she cries,
And still her woes at midnight rise.
Brave prick-song! Who is't now we hear?
None but the lark so shrill and clear;
Now at heaven's gate she claps her wings,
The morn not waking till she sings.
Hark, hark, with what a pretty throat
Poor robin redbreast tunes his note!
Hark how the jolly cuckoos sing
Cuckoo! to welcome in the spring!
Cuckoo! to welcome in the spring!
JOHN LYLY (1553–1606)

Beauty Bathing 65

Beauty sat bathing by a spring,
  Where fairest shades did hide her;
The winds blew calm, the birds did sing,
  The cool streams ran beside her.
My wanton thoughts enticed mine eye
  To see what was forbidden:
But better memory said Fie;
  So vain desire was chidden—
    Hey nonny nonny O!
    Hey nonny nonny!

Into a slumber then I fell,
  And fond imagination
Seemed to see, but could not tell,
  Her feature or her fashion:
But ev'n as babes in dreams do smile,
  And sometimes fall a-weeping,
So I awaked as wise that while
  As when I fell a-sleeping.
ANTHONY MUNDAY (1553–1633)

66 THE BARGAIN

My true love hath my heart, and I have his,
  By just exchange one for another given:
I hold his dear, and mine he cannot miss,
  There never was a better bargain driven:
    My true love hath my heart, and I have his.

His heart in me keeps him and me in one,
  My heart in him his thoughts and senses guides:
He loves my heart, for once it was his own,
  I cherish his because in me it bides:
    My true love hath my heart, and I have his.

SIR PHILIP SIDNEY (1554–1586)

67 SONG

Who hath his fancy pleased
  With fruits of happy sight,
Let here his eyes be raised
  On Nature's sweetest light;
A light which doth dissever
  And yet unite the eyes,
A light which, dying never,
  Is cause the looker dies.

She never dies, but lasteth
  In life of lover's heart;
He ever dies that wasteth
  In love his chiefest part:
Thus is her life still guarded
  In never-dying faith;
Thus is his death rewarded,
  Since she lives in his death.

Look then, and die! The pleasure
  Doth answer well the pain:
Small loss of mortal treasure,
  Who may immortal gain!
Immortal be her graces,
  Immortal is her mind;
They, fit for heavenly places—
  This, heaven in it doth bind.

But eyes these beauties see not,
  Nor sense that grace descries;
Yet eyes deprivèd be not
  From sight of her fair eyes—
Which, as of inward glory
  They are the outward seal,
So may they live still sorry,
  Which die not in that weal.

> But who hath fancies pleased
>   With fruits of happy sight,
> Let here his eyes be raisèd
>   On Nature's sweetest light!
>
> SIR PHILIP SIDNEY (1554–1586)

VOICES AT THE WINDOW   68

Who is it that, this dark night,
  Underneath my window plaineth?
It is one who from thy sight
  Being, ah, exiled, disdaineth
Every other vulgar light.

Why, alas, and are you he?
  Be not yet those fancies changeèd?
Dear, when you find change in me,
  Though from me you be estranged,
Let my change to ruin be.

Well, in absence this will die:
  Leave to see, and leave to wonder.
Absence sure will help, if I
  Can learn how myself to sunder
From what in my heart doth lie.

But time will these thoughts remove;
  Time doth work what no man knoweth.
Time doth as the subject prove:
  With time still the affection groweth
In the faithful turtle-dove.

What if you new beauties see?
  Will not they stir new affection?
I will think they pictures be
  (Image-like, of saints' perfection)
Poorly counterfeiting thee.

But your reason's purest light
  Bids you leave such minds to nourish.
Dear, do reason no such spite!
  Never doth thy beauty flourish
More than in my reason's sight.

SIR PHILIP SIDNEY (1554–1586)

leave: *cease*

PHILOMELA   69

The Nightingale, as soon as April bringeth
  Unto her rested sense a perfect waking,
While late-bare Earth, proud of new clothing, springeth,
  Sings out her woes, a thorn her song-book making;
    And mournfully bewailing,
    Her throat in tunes expresseth
    What grief her breast oppresseth,
For Tereus' force on her chaste will prevailing.

> *O Philomela fair, O take some gladness*
> *That here is juster cause of plaintful sadness!*
> *Thine earth now springs, mine fadeth;*
> *Thy thorn without, my thorn my heart invadeth.*

Alas! she hath no other cause of anguish
  But Tereus' love, on her by strong hand wroken;
Wherein she suffering, all her spirits languish,
  Full womanlike complains her will was broken
      But I, who, daily craving,
      Cannot have to content me,
      Have more cause to lament me,
Since wanting is more woe than too much having.

> *O Philomela fair, O take some gladness*
> *That here is juster cause of plaintful sadness!*
> *Thine earth now springs, mine fadeth;*
> *Thy thorn without, my thorn my heart invadeth.*

Sir Philip Sidney (1554–1586)

70   The Highway

Highway, since you my chief Parnassus be,
And that my Muse, to some ears not unsweet,
Tempers her words to trampling horses' feet
More oft than to a chamber-melody,—
Now blessèd you bear onward blessèd me
To her, where I my heart, safe-left, shall meet;
My Muse and I must you of duty greet
With thanks and wishes, wishing thankfully;
Be you still fair, honour'd by public heed;
By no encroachment wrong'd, nor time forgot;
Nor blamed for blood, nor shamed for sinful deed;
And that you know I envy you no lot
  Of highest wish, I wish you so much bliss,
  Hundreds of years you Stella's feet may kiss!

Sir Philip Sidney (1554–1586)

71   This Lady's Cruelty

With how sad steps, O moon, thou climb'st the skies!
How silently, and with how wan a face!
What! may it be that even in heavenly place
That busy archer his sharp arrows tries?
Sure, if that long-with-love-acquainted eyes
Can judge of love, thou feel'st a lover's case:
I read it in thy looks; thy languish'd grace
To me, that feel the like, thy state descries.
Then, even of fellowship, O Moon, tell me,
Is constant love deem'd there but want of wit?
Are beauties there as proud as here they be?
Do they above love to be loved, and yet
  Those lovers scorn whom that love doth possess?
  Do they call "virtue" there—ungratefulness?

Sir Philip Sidney (1554–1586)

Sleep   72

Come, Sleep; O Sleep! the certain knot of peace,
The baiting-place of wit, the balm of woe,
The poor man's wealth, the prisoner's release,
Th' indifferent judge between the high and low;
With shield of proof shield me from out the prease
Of those fierce darts Despair at me doth throw:
O make in me those civil wars to cease;
I will good tribute pay, if thou do so.
Take thou of me smooth pillows, sweetest bed,
A chamber deaf to noise and blind of light,
A rosy garland and a weary head;
And if these things, as being thine by right,
  Move not thy heavy grace, thou shalt in me,
  Livelier than elsewhere, Stella's image see.
                       Sir Philip Sidney (1554–1586)

prease: *press*

Splendidis Longum Valedico Nugis   73

Leave me, O Love, which reachest but to dust,
And thou, my mind, aspire to higher things!
Grow rich in that which never taketh rust:
Whatever fades, but fading pleasure brings.
Draw in thy beams, and humble all thy might
To that sweet yoke where lasting freedoms be;
Which breaks the clouds and opens forth the light
That doth both shine and give us sight to see.
O take fast hold! let that light be thy guide
In this small course which birth draws out to death,
And think how evil becometh him to slide
Who seeketh Heaven, and comes of heavenly breath.
  Then farewell, world! thy uttermost I see:
  Eternal Love, maintain thy life in me!
                       Sir Philip Sidney (1554–1586)

Splendidis Longum...: *A long farewell to shining trifles.*

Myra   74

I, with whose colours Myra dress'd her head,
  I, that ware posies of her own hand-making,
I, that mine own name in the chimneys read
  By Myra finely wrought ere I was waking:
Must I look on, in hope time coming may
With change bring back my turn again to play?

I, that on Sunday at the church-stile found
  A garland sweet with true-love-knots in flowers,
Which I to wear about mine arms was bound
  That each of us might know that all was ours:
Must I lead now an idle life in wishes,
And follow Cupid for his loaves and fishes?

I, that did wear the ring her mother left,
  I, for whose love she gloried to be blamed,
I, with whose eyes her eyes committed theft,
I, who did make her blush when I was named:
Must I lose ring, flowers, blush, theft, and go naked,
Watching with sighs till dead love be awakèd?

Was it for this that I might Myra see
  Washing the water with her beauty's white?
Yet would she never write her love to me.
  Thinks wit of change when thoughts are in delight?
Mad girls may safely love as they may leave;
No man can *print* a kiss: lines may deceive.
                    FULKE GREVILLE, LORD BROOKE (1554–1628)

chimneys: cheminées, *chimney-screens of tapestry work*;
deceive: *betray*

75   ROSALIND'S MADRIGAL
      Love in my bosom like a bee
            Doth suck his sweet:
      Now with his wings he plays with me,
            Now with his feet.
      Within mine eyes he makes his nest,
      His bed amidst my tender breast;
      My kisses are his daily feast,
      And yet he robs me of my rest:
            Ah! wanton, will ye?

      And if I sleep, the percheth he
            With pretty flight,
      And makes his pillow of my knee
            The livelong night.
      Strike I my lute, he tunes the string;
      He music plays if so I sing;
      He lends me every lovely thing,
      Yet cruel he my heart doth sting:
            Whist, wanton, still ye!

      Else I with roses every day
            Will whip you hence,
      And bind you, when you long to play,
            For your offence.
      I'll shut mine eyes to keep you in;
      I'll make you fast it for your sin;
      I'll count your power not worth a pin.
      —Alas! what hereby shall I win
            If he gainsay me?

      What if I beat the wanton boy
            With many a rod?
      He will repay me with annoy,
            Because a god.

Then sit thou safely on my knee;
Then let thy bower my bosom be;
Lurk in mine eyes, I like of thee;
O Cupid, so thou pity me,
    Spare not, but play thee!
THOMAS LODGE (1556?–1625)

PHILLIS 1   76
My Phillis hath the morning sun
  At first to look upon her;
And Phillis hath morn-waking birds
  Her risings still to honour.
My Phillis hath prime-feather'd flowers,
  That smile when she treads on them;
And Phillis hath a gallant flock,
  That leaps since she doth own them.
But Phillis hath too hard a heart,
  Alas that she should have it!
It yields no mercy to desert,
  Nor grace to those that crave it.
THOMAS LODGE (1556?–1625)

PHILLIS 2   77
Love guards the roses of thy lips
  And flies about them like a bee;
If I approach he forward skips,
  And if I kiss he stingeth me.

Love in thine eyes doth build his bower,
  And sleeps within their pretty shine;
And if I look the boy will lower,
  And from their orbs shoot shafts divine.

Love works thy heart within his fire,
  And in my tears doth firm the same;
And if I tempt it will retire,
  And of my plaints doth make a game.

Love, let me cull her choicest flowers;
  And pity me, and calm her eye;
Make soft her heart, dissolve her lowers
  Then will I praise thy deity.

But if thou do not, Love, I'll truly serve her
In spite of thee, and by firm faith deserve her.
THOMAS LODGE (1556?–1625)

ROSALINE   78
Like to the clear in highest sphere
  Where all imperial glory shines,
Of selfsame colour is her hair
  Whether unfolded or in twines:

    Heigh ho, fair Rosaline!
Her eyes are sapphires set in snow,
  Resembling heaven by every wink;
The gods do fear whenas they glow,
  And I do tremble when I think
    Heigh ho, would she were mine!

Her cheeks are like the blushing cloud
  That beautifies Aurora's face,
Or like the silver crimson shroud
  That Phœbus' smiling looks doth grace.
    Heigh ho, fair Rosaline!
Her lips are like two budded roses
  Whom ranks of lilies neighbour nigh,
Within whose bounds she balm encloses
  Apt to entice a deity:
    Heigh ho, would she were mine!

Her neck like to a stately tower
  Where Love himself imprison'd lies,
To watch for glances every hour
  From her divine and sacred eyes:
    Heigh ho, fair Rosaline!
Her paps are centres of delight,
  Her breasts are orbs of heavenly frame,
Where Nature moulds the dew of light
  To feed perfection with the same:
    Heigh ho, would she were mine!

With orient pearl, with ruby red,
  With marble white, with sapphire blue,
Her body every way is fed,
  Yet soft to touch and sweet in view:
    Heigh ho, fair Rosaline!
Nature herself her shape admires;
  The gods are wounded in her sight;
And Love forsakes his heavenly fires
  And at her eyes his brand doth light:
    Heigh ho, would she were mine!

Then muse not, Nymphs, though I bemoan
  The absence of fair Rosaline,
Since for a fair there's fairer none,
  Nor for her virtues so divine:
    Heigh ho, fair Rosaline!
Heigh ho, my heart! would God that she were mine!
         THOMAS LODGE (1556?–1625)

79   FAIR AND FAIR

Œnone. Fair and fair, and twice so fair,
    As fair as any may be;
    The fairest shepherd on our green,

	A love for any lady.
Paris.	Fair and fair, and twice so fair,
	As fair as any may be;
	Thy love is fair for thee alone
	And for no other lady.
Œnone.	My love is fair, my love is gay,
	As fresh as bin the flowers in May
	And of my love my roundelay,
	My merry, merry, merry roundelay,
	Concludes with Cupid's curse,—
	"They that do change old love for new
	Pray gods they change for worse!"
Ambo Simul.	They that do change old love for new,
	Pray gods they change for worse!
Œnone.	Fair and fair, etc.
Paris.	Fair and fair, etc.
	Thy love is fair, etc.
Œnone.	My love can pipe, my love can sing,
	My love can many a pretty thing,
	And of his lovely praises ring
	My merry, merry, merry roundelays
	Amen to Cupid's curse,—
	"They that do change," etc.
Paris.	They that do change, etc.
Ambo.	Fair and fair, etc.

GEORGE PEELE (1558?–1597)

A FAREWELL TO ARMS   80
(TO QUEEN ELIZABETH)

His golden locks Time hath to silver turn'd;
  O Time too swift, O swiftness never ceasing!
His youth 'gainst time and age hath ever spurn'd,
  But spurn'd in vain; youth waneth by increasing:
Beauty, strength, youth, are flowers but fading seen;
Duty, faith, love, are roots, and ever green.

His helmet now shall make a hive for bees;
  And, lovers' sonnets turn'd to holy psalms,
A man-at-arms must now serve on his knees,
  And feed on prayers, which are Age his alms:
But though from court to cottage he depart,
His Saint is sure of his unspotted heart.

And when he saddest sits in homely cell,
  He'll teach his swains this carol for a song,—
"Blest be the hearts that wish my sovereign well,
  Curst be the souls that think her any wrong."
Goddess, allow this aged man his right
To be your beadsman now that was your knight.

GEORGE PEELE (1558?–1597)

81   SAMELA

    Like to Diana in her summer weed,
       Girt with a crimson robe of brightest dye,
          Goes fair Samela.
    Whiter than be the flocks that straggling feed
       When wash'd by Arethusa faint they lie,
          Is fair Samela.
    As fair Aurora in her morning grey,
       Deck'd with the ruddy glister of her love
          Is fair Samela;
    Like lovely Thetis on a calmed day
       Whenas her brightness Neptune's fancy move,
          Shines fair Samela.

    Her tresses gold, her eyes like glassy streams,
       Her teeth are pearl, the breasts are ivory
          Of fair Samela;
    Her cheeks like rose and lily yield forth gleams;
       Her brows bright arches framed of ebony.
          Thus fair Samela
    Passeth fair Venus in her bravest hue,
       And Juno in the show of majesty
          (For she's Samela!),
    Pallas in wit,—all three, if you well view,
       For beauty, wit, and matchless dignity,
          Yield to Samela.
                    ROBERT GREENE (1560–1592)

82   FAWNIA

    Ah! were she pitiful as she is fair,
    Or but as mild as she is seeming so,
    Then were my hopes greater than my despair,
    Then all the world were heaven, nothing woe.
    Ah! were her heart relenting as her hand,
    That seems to melt even with the mildest touch,
    Then knew I where to seat me in a land
    Under wide heavens, but yet there is not such.
    So as she shows she seems the budding rose,
    Yet sweeter far than is an earthly flower;
    Sovran of beauty, like the spray she grows;
    Compass'd she is with thorns and canker'd flower.
       Yet were she willing to be pluck'd and worn,
       She would be gather'd, though she grew on thorn.

    Ah! when she sings, all music else be still,
    For none must be compared to her note;
    Ne'er breathed such glee from Philomela's bill,
    Nor from the morning-singer's swelling throat.

Ah! when she riseth from her blissful bed
She comforts all the world as doth the sun,
And at her sight the night's foul vapour's fled;
When she is set the gladsome day is done.
  O glorious sun, imagine me the west,
  Shine in my arms, and set thou in my breast!
ROBERT GREENE (1560–1592)

SEPHESTIA'S LULLABY   83

Weep not, my wanton, smile upon my knee;
When thou art old there's grief enough for thee.
  Mother's wag, pretty boy,
  Father's sorrow, father's joy;
  When thy father first did see
  Such a boy by him and me,
  He was glad, I was woe;
  Fortune changed made him so,
  When he left his pretty boy,
  Last his sorrow, first his joy.
Weep not, my wanton, smile upon my knee;
When thou art old there's grief enough for thee.
  Streaming tears that never stint,
  Like pearl-drops from a flint,
  Fell by course from his eyes,
  That one another's place supplies;
  Thus he grieved in every part,
  Tears of blood fell from his heart,
  When he left his pretty boy,
  Father's sorrow, father's joy.
Weep not, my wanton, smile upon my knee;
When thou art old there's grief enough for thee.
  The wanton smiled, father wept,
  Mother cried, baby leapt;
  More he crow'd, more we cried,
  Nature could not sorrow hide:
  He must go, he must kiss
  Child and mother, baby bliss,
  For he left his pretty boy,
  Father's sorrow, father's joy.
Weep not, my wanton, smile upon my knee,
When thou art old there's grief enough for thee.
ROBERT GREENE (1560–1592)

BRIDAL SONG   84

O come, soft rest of cares! come, Night!
  Come, naked Virtue's only tire,
  The reapèd harvest of the light
  Bound up in sheaves of sacred fire.
    Love calls to war:
      Sighs his alarms,
      Lips his swords are,
      The field his arms.

> Come, Night, and lay thy velvet hand
>   On glorious Day's outfacing face;
> And all thy crownèd flames command
>   For torches to our nuptial grace.
>   Love calls to war:
>   Sighs his alarms,
>   Lips his swords are,
>   The field his arms.
>
> GEORGE CHAPMAN (1560–1634)

85

TIMES GO BY TURNS

> The loppèd tree in time may grow again,
> Most naked plants renew both fruit and flower;
> The sorest wight may find release of pain,
> The driest soil suck in some moist'ning shower;
> Times go by turns and chances change by course,
> From foul to fair, from better hap to worse.
>
> The sea of Fortune doth not ever flow,
> She draws her favours to the lowest ebb;
> Her tides hath equal times to come and go,
> Her loom doth weave the fine and coarsest web;
> No joy so great but runneth to an end,
> No hap so hard but may in fine amend.
>
> Not always fall of leaf nor ever spring,
> No endless night yet not eternal day;
> The saddest birds a season find to sing,
> The roughest storm a calm may soon allay:
> Thus with succeeding turns God tempereth all,
> That man may hope to rise, yet fear to fall.
>
> A chance may win that by mischance was lost;
> The net that holds no great, takes little fish;
> In some things all, in all things none are crost,
> Few all they need, but none have all they wish;
> Unmeddled joys here to no man befall:
> Who least, hath some; who most, hath never all.
>
> ROBERT SOUTHWELL (1561–1595)

unmeddled: *unmixed*

86

THE BURNING BABE

> As I in hoary winter's night
>   Stood shivering in the snow,
> Surprised I was with sudden heat
>   Which made my heart to glow;
> And lifting up a fearful eye
>   To view what fire was near,
> A pretty babe all burning bright
>   Did in the air appear;
> Who, scorchèd with excessive heat,
>   Such floods of tears did shed,
> As though His floods should quench His flames,
>   Which with His tears were bred:

"Alas!" quoth He, "but newly born
   In fiery heats I fry,
Yet none approach to warm their hearts
   Or feel my fire but I!"

"My faultless breast the furnace is;
   The fuel, wounding thorns;
Love is the fire, and sighs the smoke;
   The ashes, shames and scorns;
The fuel Justice layeth on,
   And Mercy blows the coals,
The metal in this furnace wrought
   Are men's defiled souls:
For which, as now on fire I am
   To work them to their good,
So will I melt into a bath,
   To wash them in my blood."
With this He vanish'd out of sight
   And swiftly shrunk away,
And straight I callèd unto mind
   That it was Christmas Day.
                ROBERT SOUTHWELL (1561–1595)

ON THE DEATH OF SIR PHILIP SIDNEY   87

Give pardon, blessèd soul, to my bold cries,
If they, importune, interrupt thy song,
Which now with joyful notes thou sing'st among
The angel-quiristers of th' heavenly skies.
Give pardon eke, sweet soul, to my slow eyes,
That since I saw thee now it is so long,
And yet the tears that unto thee belong
To thee as yet they did not sacrifice.
I did not know that thou wert dead before;
I did not feel the grief I did sustain;
The greater stroke astonisheth the more;
Astonishment takes from us sense of pain;
  I stood amazed when others' tears begun,
  And now begin to weep when they have done.
                HENRY CONSTABLE (1562?–1613?)

LOVE IS A SICKNESS   88

Love is a sickness full of woes,
   All remedies refusing;
A plant that with most cutting grows,
   Most barren with best using.
      Why so?

More we enjoy it, more it dies;
If not enjoy'd, it sighing cries—
      Heigh ho!

Love is a torment of the mind,
   A tempest everlasting;
And Jove hath made it of a kind
   Not well, nor full nor fasting.
      Why so?

More we enjoy it, more it dies;
If not enjoy'd, it sighing cries—
      Heigh ho!

SAMUEL DANIEL (1562–1619)

89   ULYSSES AND THE SIREN

Siren.   Come, worthy Greek! Ulysses, come,
    Possess these shores with me:
  The winds and seas are troublesome,
    And here we may be free.
  Here may we sit and view their toil
    That travail in the deep,
  And joy the day in mirth the while,
    And spend the night in sleep.

Ulysses.   Fair Nymph, if fame or honour were
    To be attain'd with ease,
  Then would I come and rest me there,
    And leave such toils as these.
  But here it dwells, and here must I
    With danger seek it forth:
  To spend the time luxuriously
    Becomes not men of worth.

Siren.   Ulysses, O be not deceived
    With that unreal name;
  This honour is a thing conceived,
    And rests on others' fame:
  Begotten only to molest
    Our peace, and to beguile
  The best thing of our life—our rest,
    And give us up to toil.

Ulysses.   Delicious Nymph, suppose there were
    No honour nor report,
  Yet manliness would scorn to wear
    The time in idle sport:
  For toil doth give a better touch
    To make us feel our joy,
  And ease finds tediousness as much
    As labour yields annoy.

Siren.   Then pleasure likewise seems the shore
    Whereto tends all your toil,
  Which you forgo to make it more,

	And perish oft the while.
	Who may disport them diversely
	Find never tedious day,
	And ease may have variety
	As well as action may.

Ulysses. But natures of the noblest frame
    These toils and dangers please;
And they take comfort in the same
    As much as you in ease;
And with the thought of actions past
    Are recreated still:
When Pleasure leaves a touch at last
    To show that it was ill.

Siren. That doth *Opinion* only cause
    That's out of *Custom* bred,
Which makes us many other laws
    Than ever *Nature* did.
No widows wail for our delights,
    Our sports are without blood;
The world we see by warlike wights
    Receives more hurt than good.

Ulysses. But yet the state of things require
    These motions of unrest:
And these great Spirits of high desire
    Seem born to turn them best:
To purge the mischiefs that increase
    And all good order mar:
For oft we see a wicked peace
    To be well changed for war.

Siren. Well, well, Ulysses, then I see
    I shall not have thee here:
And therefore I will come to thee,
    And take my fortune there.
I must be won, that cannot win,
    Yet lost were I not won;
For beauty hath created been
    T' undo, or be undone.

Samuel Daniel (1562–1619)

Beauty, Time, and Love
Sonnets.
I

Fair is my Love and cruel as she's fair;
Her brow-shades frown, although her eyes are sunny.
Her smiles are lightning, though her pride despair,
And her disdains are gall, her favours honey:
A modest maid, deck'd with a blush of honour,
Whose feet do tread green paths of youth and love;

The wonder of all eyes that look upon her,
Sacred on earth, design'd a Saint above.
Chastity and Beauty, which were deadly foes,
Live reconcilèd friends within her brow;
And had she Pity to conjoin with those,
Then who had heard the plaints I utter now?
  For had she not been fair, and thus unkind,
  My Muse had slept, and none had known my mind.

II

My spotless love hovers with purest wings,
About the temple of the proudest frame,
Where blaze those lights, fairest of earthly things,
Which clear our clouded world with brightest flame.
My ambitious thoughts, confinèd in her face,
Affect no honour but what she can give;
My hopes do rest in limits of her grace;
I weigh no comfort unless she relieve.
For she, that can my heart imparadise,
Holds in her fairest hand what dearest is;
My Fortune's wheel's the circle of her eyes,
Whose rolling grace deign once a turn of bliss.
  All my life's sweet consists in her alone;
  So much I love the most Unloving one.

III

And yet I cannot reprehend the flight
Or blame th' attempt presuming so to soar;
The mounting venture for a high delight
Did make the honour of the fall the more.
For who gets wealth, that puts not from the shore?
Danger hath honour, great designs their fame;
Glory doth follow, courage goes before;
And though th' event oft answers not the same—
Suffice that high attempts have never shame.
The mean observer, whom base safety keeps,
Lives without honour, dies without a name,
And in eternal darkness ever sleeps.—
  And therefore, *Delia*, 'tis to me no blot
  To have attempted, tho' attain'd thee not.

IV

When men shall find thy flow'r, thy glory, pass,
And thou with careful brow, sitting alone,
Receivèd hast this message from thy glass,
That tells the truth and says that *All is gone;*
Fresh shalt thou see in me the wounds thou mad'st,
Though spent thy flame, in me the heat remaining:
I that have loved thee thus before thou fad'st—
My faith shall wax, when thou art in thy waning.
The world shall find this miracle in me,
That fire can burn when all the matter's spent:

Then what my faith hath been thyself shalt see,
And that thou wast unkind thou may'st repent.—
  Thou may'st repent that thou hast scorn'd my tears,
  When Winter snows upon thy sable hairs.

V

Beauty, sweet Love, is like the morning dew,
Whose short refresh upon the tender green
Cheers for a time, but till the sun doth show,
And straight 'tis gone as it had never been.
Soon doth it fade that makes the fairest flourish,
Short is the glory of the blushing rose;
The hue which thou so carefully dost nourish,
Yet which at length thou must be forced to lose.
When thou, surcharged with burthen of thy years,
Shalt bend thy wrinkles homeward to the earth;
And that, in Beauty's Lease expired, appears
The Date of Age, the Calends of our Death—
  But ah, no more!—this must not be foretold,
  For women grieve to think they must be old.

VI

I must not grieve my Love, whose eyes would read
Lines of delight, whereon her youth might smile;
Flowers have time before they come to seed,
And she is young, and now must sport the while.
And sport, Sweet Maid, in season of these years,
And learn to gather flowers before they wither;
And where the sweetest blossom first appears,
Let Love and Youth conduct thy pleasures thither.
Lighten forth smiles to clear the clouded air,
And calm the tempest which my sighs do raise;
Pity and smiles do best become the fair;
Pity and smiles must only yield thee praise.
  Make me to say when all my griefs are gone,
  Happy the heart that sighed for such a one!

VII

Let others sing of Knights and Paladines
In aged accents and untimely words,
Paint shadows in imaginary lines,
Which well the reach of their high wit records:
But I must sing of thee, and those fair eyes
Authentic shall my verse in time to come;
When yet th' unborn shall say, *Lo, where she lies!*
Whose beauty made him speak, that else was dumb!
These are the arcs, the trophies I erect,
That fortify thy name against old age;
And these thy sacred virtues must protect
Against the Dark, and Time's consuming rage.
  Though th' error of my youth in them appear,
  Suffice, they show I lived, and loved thee dear.

SAMUEL DANIEL (1562–1619)

91
SONET

Fra bank to bank, fra wood to wood I rin,
  Ourhailit with my feeble fantasie;
  Like til a leaf that fallis from a tree,
Or til a reed ourblawin with the win.

Twa gods guides me: the ane of tham is blin,
  Yea and a bairn brocht up in vanitie;
  The next a wife ingenrit of the sea,
And lichter nor a dauphin with her fin.

Unhappy is the man for evermair
  That tills the sand and sawis in the air;
  But twice unhappier is he, I lairn,
That feidis in his hairt a mad desire,
And follows on a woman throw the fire,
  Led by a blind and teachit by a bairn.
MARK ALEXANDER BOYD (1563–1601)

92
UBIQUE

Were I as base as is the lowly plain,
And you, my Love, as high as heaven above,
Yet should the thoughts of me, your humble swain,
Ascend to heaven in honour of my Love.

Were I as high as heaven above the plain,
And you, my Love, as humble and as low
As are the deepest bottoms of the main,
Wheresoe'er you were, with you my love should go.

Were you the earth, dear Love, and I the skies,
My love should shine on you like to the Sun,
And look upon you with ten thousand eyes,
Till heaven wax'd blind, and till the world were done.

  Wheresoe'er I am,—below, or else above you—
  Wheresoe'er you are, my heart shall truly love you.
JOSHUA SYLVESTER (1563–1618)

93
TO HIS COY LOVE

I pray thee, leave, love me no more,
  Call home the heart you gave me!
I but in vain that saint adore
  That can but will not save me.
These poor half-kisses kill me quite—
  Was ever man thus servèd?
Amidst an ocean of delight
  For pleasure to be starvèd?

Show me no more those snowy breasts
  With azure riverets branched,
Where, whilst mine eye with plenty feasts,
  Yet is my thirst not stanched;

O Tantalus, thy pains ne'er tell!
  By me thou art prevented:
'Tis nothing to be plagued in Hell,
  But thus in Heaven tormented.

Clip me no more in those dear arms,
  Nor thy life's comfort call me,
O these are but too powerful charms,
  And do but more enthral me!
But see how patient I am grown
  In all this coil about thee:
Come, nice thing, let my heart alone,
  I cannot live without thee!
MICHAEL DRAYTON (1563–1631)

THE PARTING   94

Since there's no help, come let us kiss and part—
Nay, I have done, you get no more of me;
And I am glad, yea, glad with all my heart,
That thus so cleanly I myself can free.
Shake hands for ever, cancel all our vows,
And when we meet at any time again,
Be it not seen in either of our brows
That we one jot of former love retain.
Now at the last gasp of Love's latest breath,
When, his pulse failing, Passion speechless lies,
When Faith is kneeling by his bed of death,
And Innocence is closing up his eyes,
  —Now if thou wouldst, when all have given him over,
  From death to life thou might'st him yet recover.
MICHAEL DRAYTON (1563–1631)

SIRENA   95

Near to the silver *Trent*
  SIRENA dwelleth;
She to whom Nature lent
  All that excelleth;
By which the Muses late
  And the neat Graces
Have for their greater state
  Taken their places;
Twisting an anadem
  Wherewith to crown her,
As it belong'd to them
  Most to renown her.
    On thy bank,
    In a rank,
    Let thy swans sing her,
    And with their music
    Along let them bring her.

Tagus and *Pactolus*
  Are to thee debtor,
Nor for their gold to us
  Are they the better:
Henceforth of all the rest
  Be thou the River
Which, as the daintiest,
  Puts them down ever.
For as my precious one
  O'er thee doth travel,
She to pearl paragon
  Turneth thy gravel.
      On thy bank...

Our mournful Philomel,
  That rarest tuner,
Henceforth in Aperil
  Shall wake the sooner,
And to her shall complain
  From the thick cover,
Redoubling every strain
  Over and over:
For when my Love too long
  Her chamber keepeth,
As though it suffer'd wrong,
  The Morning weepeth.
      On thy bank...

Oft have I seen the Sun,
  To do her honour,
Fix himself at his noon
  To look upon her;
And hath gilt every grove,
  Every hill near her,
With his flames from above
  Striving to cheer her:
And when she from his sight
  Hath herself turnèd,
He, as it had been night,
  In clouds hath mournèd.
      On thy bank...

The verdant meads are seen,
  When she doth view them,
In fresh and gallant green
  Straight to renew them;
And every little grass
  Broad itself spreadeth,
Proud that this bonny lass
  Upon it treadeth:

Nor flower is so sweet
  In this large cincture,
But it upon her feet
  Leaveth some tincture.
    On thy bank...

The fishes in the flood,
  When she doth angle,
For the hook strive a-good
  Them to entangle;
And leaping on the land,
  From the clear water,
Their scales upon the sand
  Lavishly scatter;
Therewith to pave the mould
  Whereon she passes,
So herself to behold
  As in her glasses.
    On thy bank...

When she looks out by night,
  The stars stand gazing,
Like comets to our sight
  Fearfully blazing;
As wond'ring at her eyes
  With their much brightness,
Which so amaze the skies,
  Dimming their lightness.
The raging tempests are calm
  When she speaketh,
Such most delightsome balm
  From her lips breaketh.
    On thy bank...

In all our *Brittany*
  There's not a fairer,
Nor can you fit any
  Should you compare her.
Angels her eyelids keep,
  All hearts surprising;
Which look whilst she doth sleep
  Like the sun's rising:
She alone of her kind
  Knoweth true measure,
And her unmatchèd mind
  Is heaven's treasure.
    On thy bank...

Fair *Dove* and *Darwen* clear,
  Boast ye your beauties,
To *Trent* your mistress here
  Yet pay your duties:

My Love was higher born
  Tow'rds the full fountains,
Yet she doth moorland scorn
  And the *Peak* mountains;
Nor would she none should dream
  Where she abideth,
Humble as is the stream
  Which by her slideth.
      On thy bank...

Yet my pour rustic Muse
  Nothing can move her,
Nor the means I can use,
  Though her true lover:
Many a long winter's night
  Have I waked for her,
Yet this my piteous plight
  Nothing can stir her.
All thy sands, silver *Trent*,
  Down to the *Humber*,
The sighs that I have spent
  Never can number.
    On thy bank,
    In a rank,
    Let thy swans sing her,
    And with their music
    Along let them bring her.

MICHAEL DRAYTON (1563–1631)

AGINCOURT

Fair stood the wind for France
When we our sails advance,
Nor now to prove our chance
  Longer will tarry;
But putting to the main,
At Caux, the mouth of Seine,
With all his martial train
  Landed King Harry.

And taking many a fort,
Furnish'd in warlike sort,
Marcheth tow'rds Agincourt
  In happy hour;
Skirmishing day by day
With those that stopp'd his way,
Where the French gen'ral lay
  With all his power.

Which, in his height of pride,
King Henry to deride,
His ransom to provide
  Unto him sending;

Which he neglects the while
As from a nation vile,
Yet with an angry smile
    Their fall portending.

And turning to his men,
Quoth our brave Henry then,
"Though they to one be ten
    Be not amazèd:
Yet have we well begun;
Battles so bravely won
Have ever to the sun
    By fame been raisèd.

"And for myself (quoth he)
This my full rest shall be:
England ne'er mourn for me
    Nor more esteem me:
Victor I will remain
Or on this earth lie slain,
Never shall she sustain
    Loss to redeem me.

"Poitiers and Cressy tell,
When most their pride did swell,
Under our swords they fell:
    No less our skill is
Than when our grandsire great,
Claiming the regal seat,
By many a warlike feat
    Lopp'd the French lilies."

The Duke of York so dread
The eager vaward led;
With the main Henry sped
    Among his henchmen.
Excester had the rear,
A braver man not there;
O Lord, how hot they were
    On the false Frenchmen!

They now to fight are gone,
Armour on armour shone,
Drum now to drum did groan,
    To hear was wonder;
That with the cries they make
The very earth did shake:
Trumpet to trumpet spake,
    Thunder to thunder.

Well it thine age became,
O noble Erpingham,
Which didst the signal aim
    To our hid forces!

When from a meadow by,
Like a storm suddenly
The English archery
    Stuck the French horses.

With Spanish yew so strong,
Arrows a cloth-yard long
That like to serpents stung,
    Piercing the weather;
None from his fellow starts,
But playing manly parts,
And like true English hearts
    Stuck close together.

When down their bows they threw,
And forth their bilbos drew,
And on the French they flew,
    Not one was tardy;
Arms were from shoulders sent,
Scalps to the teeth were rent,
Down the French peasants went—
    Our men were hardy.

This while our noble king,
His broadsword brandishing,
Down the French host did ding
    As to o'erwhelm it;
And many a deep wound lent,
His arms with blood besprent,
And many a cruel dent
    Bruised his helmet.

Gloster, that duke so good,
Next of the royal blood,
For famous England stood
    With his brave brother;
Clarence, in steel so bright,
Though but a maiden knight,
Yet in that furious fight
    Scarce such another.

Warwick in blood did wade,
Oxford the foe invade,
And cruel slaughter made
    Still as they ran up;
Suffolk his axe did ply,
Beaumont and Willoughby
Bare them right doughtily,
    Ferrers and Fanhope.

Upon Saint Crispin's Day
Fought was this noble fray,
Which fame did not delay
    To England to carry.

O when shall English men
With such acts fill a pen?
Or England breed again
   Such a King Harry?

MICHAEL DRAYTON (1563–1631)

bilbos: *swords, from Bilboa*

TO THE VIRGINIAN VOYAGE

You brave heroic minds
  Worthy your country's name,
    That honour still pursue;
    Go and subdue!
Whilst loitering hinds
  Lurk here at home with shame.

Britons, you stay too long:
  Quickly aboard bestow you,
    And with a merry gale
    Swell your stretch'd sail
With vows as strong
  As the winds that blow you.

Your course securely steer,
  West and by south forth keep!
    Rocks, lee-shores, nor shoals
    When Eolus scowls
You need not fear;
  So absolute the deep.

And cheerfully at sea
  Success you still entice
    To get the pearl and gold,
    And ours to hold
Virginia,
  Earth's only paradise.

Where nature hath in store
  Fowl, venison, and fish,
    And the fruitfull'st soil
    Without your toil
Three harvests more,
  All greater than your wish.

And the ambitious vine
  Crowns with his purple mass
    The cedar reaching high
    To kiss the sky,
The cypress, pine,
  And useful sassafras.

> To whom the Golden Age
>   Still nature's laws doth give,
>   No other cares attend,
>   But them to defend
>   From winter's rage,
>   That long there doth not live.
>
> When as the luscious smell
>   Of that delicious land
>   Above the seas that flows
>   The clear wind throws,
>   Your hearts to swell
>   Approaching the dear strand;
>
> In kenning of the shore
>   (Thanks to God first given)
>   O you the happiest men,
>   Be frolic then!
>   Let cannons roar,
>   Frighting the wide heaven.
>
> And in regions far,
>   Such heroes bring ye forth
>   As those from whom we came;
>   And plant our name
>   Under that star
>   Not known unto our North.
>
> And as there plenty grows
>   Of laurel everywhere—
>   Apollo's sacred tree—
>   You it may see
>   A poet's brows
>   To crown, that may sing there.
>
> Thy *Voyages* attend,
>   Industrious Hakluyt,
>   Whose reading shall inflame
>   Men to seek fame,
>   And much commend
>   To after times thy wit.
>
> MICHAEL DRAYTON (1563–1631)

98 THE PASSIONATE SHEPHERD TO HIS LOVE

> Come live with me and be my Love,
> And we will all the pleasures prove
> That hills and valleys, dales and fields,
> Or woods or steepy mountain yields.
>
> And we will sit upon the rocks,
> And see the shepherds feed their flocks
> By shallow rivers, to whose falls
> Melodious birds sing madrigals.

And I will make thee beds of roses
And a thousand fragrant posies;
A cap of flowers, and a kirtle
Embroider'd all with leaves of myrtle.

A gown made of the finest wool
Which from our pretty lambs we pull;
Fair-lined slippers for the cold,
With buckles of the purest gold.

A belt of straw and ivy-buds
With coral clasps and amber studs:
And if these pleasures may thee move,
Come live with me and be my Love.

The shepherd swains shall dance and sing
For thy delight each May morning:
If these delights thy mind may move,
Then live with me and be my Love.
CHRISTOPHER MARLOWE (1564–1593)

HER REPLY

If all the world and love were young,
And truth in every shepherd's tongue,
These pretty pleasures might me move
To live with thee and be thy Love.

But Time drives flocks from field to fold;
When rivers rage and rocks grow cold;
And Philomel becometh dumb;
The rest complains of cares to come.

The flowers do fade, and wanton fields
To wayward Winter reckoning yields:
A honey tongue, a heart of gall,
Is fancy's spring, but sorrow's fall.

Thy gowns, thy shoes, thy beds of roses,
Thy cap, thy kirtle, and thy posies,
Soon break, soon wither—soon forgotten,
In folly ripe, in reason rotten.

Thy belt of straw and ivy-buds,
Thy coral clasps and amber studs,—
All these in me no means can move
To come to thee and be thy Love.

But could youth last, and love still breed,
Had joys no date, nor age no need,
Then these delights my mind might move
To live with thee and be thy Love.
SIR WALTER RALEIGH (1564–1593)

100   SILVIA
Who is Silvia? What is she?
    That all our swains commend her?
Holy, fair, and wise is she;
    The heaven such grace did lend her,
That she might admirèd be.

Is she kind as she is fair?
    For beauty lives with kindness:
Love doth to her eyes repair,
    To help him of his blindness;
And, being help'd, inhabits there.

Then to Silvia let us sing,
    That Silvia is excelling;
She excels each mortal thing
    Upon the dull earth dwelling:
To her let us garlands bring.
                    WILLIAM SHAKESPEARE (1564–1616)

101   THE BLOSSOM
On a day—alack the day!—
Love, whose month is ever May,
Spied a blossom passing fair
Playing in the wanton air:
Through the velvet leaves the wind
All unseen 'gan passage find;
That the lover, sick to death,
Wish'd himself the heaven's breath.
Air, quoth he, thy cheeks may blow;
Air, would I might triumph so!
But, alack, my hand is sworn
Ne'er to pluck thee from thy thorn:
Vow, alack, for youth unmeet;
Youth so apt to pluck a sweet!
Do not call it sin in me
That I am forsworn for thee;
Thou for whom e'en Jove would swear
Juno but an Ethiop were;
And deny himself for Jove,
Turning mortal for thy love.
                    WILLIAM SHAKESPEARE (1564–1616)

102   WHEN DAISIES PIED AND VIOLETS BLUE
When daisies pied and violets blue,
    And lady-smocks all silver-white,
And cuckoo-buds of yellow hue
    Do paint the meadows with delight,
The cuckoo then, on every tree,
Mocks married men; for thus sings he,
            Cuckoo!
Cuckoo, cuckoo!—O word of fear,
Unpleasing to a married ear!

When shepherds pipe on oaten straws,
  And merry larks are ploughmen's clocks,
When turtles tread, and rooks, and daws,
  And maidens bleach their summer smocks
The cuckoo then, on every tree,
Mocks married men; for thus sings he,
        Cuckoo!
Cuckoo, cuckoo!—O word of fear,
Unpleasing to a married ear!
WILLIAM SHAKESPEARE (1564–1616)
from "Love's Labor's Lost"

WHEN ICICLES HANG BY THE WALL   103
When icicles hang by the wall,
  And Dick the shepherd blows his nail,
And Tom bears logs into the hall,
  And milk comes frozen home in pail,
When blood is nipp'd, and ways be foul,
Then nightly sings the staring owl,
        To-whit!
To-who!—a merry note,
While greasy Joan doth keel the pot.

When all aloud the wind doe blow,
  And coughing drowns the parson's saw,
And birds sit brooding in the snow,
  And Marian's nose looks red and raw,
When roasted crabs hiss in the bowl,
Then nightly sings the staring owl,
        To-whit!
To-who!—a merry note,
While greasy Joan doth keel the pot.
WILLIAM SHAKESPEARE (1564–1616)
from "Love's Labor's Lost"

keel: *skim*

OVER HILL, OVER DALE   104
Over hill, over dale,
  Thorough bush, thorough brier,
Over park, over pale,
  Thorough flood, thorough fire,
  I do wander everywhere,
  Swifter than the moonè's sphere;
  And I serve the fairy queen,
  To dew her orbs upon the green:
  The cowslips tall her pensioners be;
  In their gold coats spots you see;
  Those be rubies, fairy favours,
  In those freckles live their savours:
I must go seek some dew-drops here,
And hang a pearl in every cowslip's ear.
WILLIAM SHAKESPEARE (1564–1616)
from "Midsummer Night's Dream"

105   SPOTTED SNAKES WITH DOUBLE TONGUE
                You spotted snakes with double tongue,
                   Thorny hedgehogs, be not seen;
              Newts and blind-worms, do no wrong;
                   Come not near our fairy queen.

                      Philomel, with melody,
                      Sing in our sweet lullaby;
                Lulla, lulla, lullaby; lulla, lulla, lullaby!
                        Never harm,
                        Nor spell nor charm,
                   Come our lovely lady nigh;
                   So, good night, with lullaby.

            Weaving spiders, come not here;
                Hence, you long-legg'd spinners, hence!
            Beetles black, approach not near;
                Worm nor snail, do no offence.

                      Philomel, with melody,
                      Sing in our sweet lullaby;
                Lulla, lulla, lullaby; lulla, lulla, lullaby!
                        Never harm,
                        Nor spell nor charm,
                   Come our lovely lady nigh;
                   So, good night, with lullaby.
                              WILLIAM SHAKESPEARE (1564–1616)
                                    from "A Midsummer Night's Dream"

106   WHERE THE BEE SUCKS
        Where the bee sucks, there suck I:
        In a cowslip's bell I lie;
        There I couch when owls do cry.
        On the bat's back I do fly
        After summer merrily:
          Merrily, merrily, shall I live now,
          Under the blossom that hangs on the bough.
                              WILLIAM SHAKESPEARE (1564–1616)
                                    from "The Tempest"

107   TELL ME WHERE IS FANCY BRED
              Tell me where is Fancy bred,
              Or in the heart or in the head?
              How begot, how nourished?
                  Reply, reply.
              It is engender'd in the eyes,
              With gazing fed; and Fancy dies
              In the cradle where it lies.
                  Let us all ring Fancy's knell:
                  I'll begin it,—Ding, dong, bell.

All.   Ding, dong, bell.
                              WILLIAM SHAKESPEARE (1564–1616)
                                  from "The Merchant of Venice"

Dirge 108

Come away, come away, death,
  And in sad cypres let me be laid;
Fly away, fly away, breath;
  I am slain by a fair cruel maid.
My shroud of white, stuck all with yew,
    O prepare it!
My part of death, no one so true
    Did share it.

Not a flower, not a flower sweet,
  On my black coffin let there be strown;
Not a friend, not a friend greet
  My poor corse, where my bones shall be thrown:
A thousand thousand sighs to save,
    Lay me, O, where
Sad true lover never find my grave
    To weep there!

WILLIAM SHAKESPEARE (1564–1616)
from "Twelfth Night"

cypres: *crape*

It was a Lover and his Lass 109

It was a lover and his lass,
  With a hey, and a ho, and a hey nonino,
That o'er the green corn-field did pass,
  In the spring time, the only pretty ring time,
When birds do sing, hey ding a ding, ding;
Sweet lovers love the spring.

Between the acres of the rye,
  With a hey, and a ho, and a hey nonino,
These pretty country folks would lie,
  In the spring time, the only pretty ring time,
When birds do sing, hey ding a ding, ding;
Sweet lovers love the spring.

This carol they began that hour,
  With a hey, and a ho, and a hey nonino,
How that life was but a flower
  In the spring time, the only pretty ring time,
When birds do sing, hey ding a ding, ding;
Sweet lovers love the spring.

And, therefore, take the present time
  With a hey, and a ho, and a hey nonino,
For love is crownèd with the prime
In the spring time, the only pretty ring time,
When birds do sing, hey ding a ding, ding;
Sweet lovers love the spring.

WILLIAM SHAKESPEARE (1564–1616)
from "As You Like It"

110 AUBADE

Hark! hark! the lark at heaven's gate sings,
 And Phœbus 'gins arise,
His steeds to water at those springs
 On chaliced flowers that lies;
And winking Mary-buds begin
 To ope their golden eyes:
With everything that pretty bin,
 My lady sweet, arise!
  Arise, arise!

WILLIAM SHAKESPEARE (1564–1616)
from "Cymbeline"

111 BRIDAL SONG

[Some suggest this may have been written by John Fletcher. – Ed.]

Roses, their sharp spines being gone,
Not royal in their smells alone,
 But in their hue;
Maiden pinks, of odour faint,
Daisies smell-less, yet most quaint,
 And sweet thyme true;

Primrose, firstborn child of Ver;
Merry springtime's harbinger,
 With her bells dim;
Oxlips in their cradles growing,
Marigolds on death-beds blowing,
 Larks'-heels trim;

All dear Nature's children sweet
Lie 'fore bride and bridegroom's feet,
 Blessing their sense!
Not an angel of the air,
Bird melodious or bird fair,
 Be absent hence!

The crow, the slanderous cuckoo, nor
The boding raven, nor chough hoar,
 Nor chattering pye,
May on our bride-house perch or sing,
Or with them any discord bring,
 But from it fly!

WILLIAM SHAKESPEARE (1564–1616)

DIRGE OF THE THREE QUEENS   *112*

[Some suggest this may have been written by John Fletcher. – Ed.]

>Urns and odours bring away!
> Vapours, sighs, darken the day!
>Our dole more deadly looks than dying;
> Balms and gums and heavy cheers,
> Sacred vials fill'd with tears,
>And clamours through the wild air flying!
>
>Come, all sad and solemn shows,
>That are quick-eyed Pleasure's foes!
>We convènt naught else but woes.
>   WILLIAM SHAKESPEARE (1564–1616)

dole: *lamentation*; convent: *summon*

ORPHEUS   *113*

>Orpheus with his lute made trees
>And the mountain tops that freeze
> Bow themselves when he did sing:
>To his music plants and flowers
>Ever sprung; as sun and showers
> There had made a lasting spring.
>
>Every thing that heard him play,
>Even the billows of the sea,
> Hung their heads and then lay by.
>In sweet music is such art,
> Killing care and grief of heart
> Fall asleep, or hearing, die.
>   WILLIAM SHAKESPEARE (1564–1616)
>   *from "Henry VIII"*

SONNET, NO. 18   *114*

>Shall I compare thee to a Summer's day?
>Thou art more lovely and more temperate:
>Rough winds do shake the darling buds of May,
>And Summer's lease hath all too short a date:
>Sometime too hot the eye of heaven shines,
>And often is his gold complexion dimm'd;
>And every fair from fair sometime declines,
>By chance or nature's changing course untrimm'd:
>But thy eternal Summer shall not fade
>Nor lose possession of that fair thou owest;
>Nor shall Death brag thou wanderest in his shade,
>When in eternal lines to time thou growest:
> So long as men can breathe, or eyes can see,
> So long lives this, and this gives life to thee.
>   WILLIAM SHAKESPEARE (1564–1616)

115
Sonnet, No. 30

When to the Sessions of sweet silent thought
I summon up remembrance of things past,
I sigh the lack of many a thing I sought,
And with old woes new wail my dear time's waste:
Then can I drown an eye, unused to flow,
For precious friends hid in death's dateless night,
And weep afresh love's long-since-cancell'd woe,
And moan th' expense of many a vanish'd sight:
Then can I grieve at grievances foregone,
And heavily from woe to woe tell o'er
The sad account of fore-bemoaned moan,
Which I new pay as if not paid before.
  But if the while I think on thee, dear friend,
  All losses are restored and sorrows end.
William Shakespeare (1564–1616)

116
Sonnet, No. 31

Thy bosom is endeared with all hearts
Which I, by lacking, have supposed dead:
And there reigns Love, and all Love's loving parts,
And all those friends which I thought buried.
How many a holy and obsequious tear
Hath dear religious love stol'n from mine eye,
As interest of the dead!—which now appear
But things removed that hidden in thee lie.
Thou art the grave where buried love doth live,
Hung with the trophies of my lovers gone,
Who all their parts of me to thee did give:
—That due of many now is thine alone:
  Their images I loved I view in thee,
  And thou, all they, hast all the all of me.
William Shakespeare (1564–1616)

117
Sonnet, No. 53

What is your substance, whereof are you made,
That millions of strange shadows on you tend?
Since every one hath, every one, one shade,
And you, but one, can every shadow lend.
Describe Adonis, and the counterfeit
Is poorly imitated after you;
On Helen's cheek all art of beauty set,
And you in Grecian tires are painted new:
Speak of the spring and foison of the year,
The one doth shadow of your beauty show,
The other as your bounty doth appear;
And you in every blessed shape we know.
  In all external grace you have some part,
  But you like none, none you, for constant heart.
William Shakespeare (1564–1616)

foison: *plenty*

Sonnet, No. 57

118

Being your slave, what should I do but tend
Upon the hours and times of your desire?
I have no precious time at all to spend,
Nor services to do, till you require.
Nor dare I chide the world-without-end hour
Whilst I, my sovereign, watch the clock for you,
Nor think the bitterness of absence sour
When you have bid your servant once adieu;
Nor dare I question with my jealous thought
Where you may be, or your affairs suppose,
But, like a sad slave, stay and think of nought
Save, where you are how happy you make those!
  So true a fool is love, that in your Will,
  Though you do any thing, he thinks no ill.

WILLIAM SHAKESPEARE (1564–1616)

Sonnet, No. 94

119

They that have power to hurt and will do none,
That do not do the thing they most do show,
Who, moving others, are themselves as stone,
Unmoved, cold, and to temptation slow—
They rightly do inherit heaven's graces,
And husband nature's riches from expense;
They are the Lords and owners of their faces,
Others, but stewards of their excellence.
The summer's flower is to the summer sweet,
Though to itself it only live and die,
But if that flower with base infection meet,
The basest weed outbraves his dignity:
  For sweetest things turn sourest by their deeds;
  Lilies that fester smell far worse than weeds.

WILLIAM SHAKESPEARE (1564–1616)

Sonnet, No. 97

120

How like a Winter hath my absence been
From thee, the pleasure of the fleeting year!
What freezings have I felt, what dark days seen,
What old December's bareness everywhere!
And yet this time removed was summer's time;
The teeming Autumn, big with rich increase,
Bearing the wanton burden of the prime
Like widow'd wombs after their Lord's decease:
Yet this abundant issue seem'd to me
But hope of orphans and unfather'd fruit;
For Summer and his pleasures wait on thee,
And, thou away, the very birds are mute:
  Or if they sing, 'tis with so dull a cheer
  That leaves look pale, dreading the Winter's near.

WILLIAM SHAKESPEARE (1564–1616)

121
Sonnet, No. 102
My love is strengthen'd, though more weak in seeming;
I love not less, though less the show appear:
That love is merchandised whose rich esteeming
The owner's tongue doth publish everywhere.
Our love was new, and then but in the spring,
When I was wont to greet it with my lays;
As Philomel in summer's front doth sing
And stops her pipe in growth of riper days:
Not that the summer is less pleasant now
Than when her mournful hymns did hush the night,
But that wild music burthens every bough,
And sweets grown common lose their dear delight.
  Therefore, like her, I sometime hold my tongue,
  Because I would not dull you with my song.
WILLIAM SHAKESPEARE (1564–1616)

122
Sonnet, No. 104
To me, fair friend, you never can be old;
For as you were when first your eye I eyed,
Such seems your beauty still. Three Winters cold
Have from the forests shook three Summers' pride;
Three beauteous springs to yellow Autumn turn'd
In process of the seasons have I seen,
Three April perfumes in three hot Junes burn'd,
Since first I saw you fresh, which yet are green.
Ah! yet doth beauty, like a dial-hand,
Steal from his figure, and no pace perceived;
So your sweet hue, which methinks still doth stand,
Hath motion, and mine eye may be deceived:
  For fear of which, hear this, thou age unbred:
  Ere you were born was beauty's summer dead.
WILLIAM SHAKESPEARE (1564–1616)

123
Sonnet, No. 106
When in the chronicle of wasted time
I see descriptions of the fairest wights,
And beauty making beautiful old rime
In praise of Ladies dead and lovely Knights;
Then, in the blazon of sweet beauty's best,
Of hand, of foot, of lip, of eye, of brow,
I see their antique pen would have exprest
Even such a beauty as you master now.
So all their praises are but prophecies
Of this our time, all you prefiguring;
And for they look'd but with divining eyes,
They had not skill enough your worth to sing:
  For we, which now behold these present days,
  Have eyes to wonder, but lack tongues to praise.
WILLIAM SHAKESPEARE (1564–1616)

Seven Centuries of English Verse

SONNET, No. 116   124

Let me not to the marriage of true minds
Admit impediments. Love is not love
Which alters when it alteration finds,
Or bends with the remover to remove:
O, no! it is an ever-fixèd mark,
That looks on tempests and is never shaken;
It is the star to every wand'ring bark,
Whose worth's unknown, although his height be taken.
Love's not Time's fool, though rosy lips and cheeks
Within his bending sickle's compass come;
Love alters not with his brief hours and weeks,
But bears it out even to the edge of doom:—
  If this be error and upon me proved,
  I never writ, nor no man ever loved.

WILLIAM SHAKESPEARE (1564–1616)

SONNET, No. 129   125

Th' expense of Spirit in a waste of shame
Is lust in action; and till action, lust
Is perjured, murderous, bloody, full of blame,
Savage, extreme, rude, cruel, not to trust;
Enjoy'd no sooner but despisèd straight;
Past reason hunted; and, no sooner had,
Past reason hated, as a swallow'd bait
On purpose laid to make the taker mad:
Mad in pursuit, and in possession so;
Had, having, and in quest to have, extreme;
A bliss in proof, and proved, a very woe;
Before, a joy proposed; behind, a dream.
  All this the world well knows; yet none knows well
  To shun the heaven that leads men to this hell.

WILLIAM SHAKESPEARE (1564–1616)

SONNET, No. 146   126

[Line 2 in the original Quatro begins with the words "My sinful earth." This is taken to be a printer's error since it repeats the end of the previous line. Nobody knows how WS originally began the line. – Ed.]

Poor soul, the centre of my sinful earth—
[... ... ...] these rebel powers array—
Why dost thou pine within and suffer dearth,
Painting thy outward walls so costly gay?
Why so large cost, having so short a lease,
Dost thou upon thy fading mansion spend?
Shall worms, inheritors of this excess,
Eat up thy charge? Is this thy body's end?

Then, soul, live thou upon thy servant's loss,
And let that pine to aggravate thy store;
Buy terms divine in selling hours of dross;
Within be fed, without be rich no more:
  So shalt thou feed on Death, that feeds on men;
  And Death once dead, there's no more dying then.
WILLIAM SHAKESPEARE (1564–1616)

127   **LULLABY**

Upon my lap my sovereign sits
And sucks upon my breast;
Meantime his love maintains my life
And gives my sense her rest.
    Sing lullaby, my little boy,
    Sing lullaby, mine only joy!

When thou hast taken thy repast,
Repose, my babe, on me;
So may thy mother and thy nurse
Thy cradle also be.
    Sing lullaby, my little boy,
    Sing lullaby, mine only joy!

I grieve that duty doth not work
All that my wishing would;
Because I would not be to thee
But in the best I should.
    Sing lullaby, my little boy,
    Sing lullaby, mine only joy!

Yet as I am, and as I may,
I must and will be thine,
Though all too little for thyself
Vouchsafing to be mine.
    Sing lullaby, my little boy,
    Sing lullaby, mine only joy!
RICHARD ROWLANDS (1565–1630?)

128   **SPRING**

Spring, the sweet Spring, is the year's pleasant king;
Then blooms each thing, then maids dance in a ring,
Cold doth not sting, the pretty birds do sing—
  Cuckoo, jug-jug, pu-we, to-witta-woo!

The palm and may make country houses gay,
Lambs frisk and play, the shepherds pipe all day,
And we hear aye birds tune this merry lay—
  Cuckoo, jug-jug, pu-we, to-witta-woo!

The fields breathe sweet, the daisies kiss our feet,
Young lovers meet, old wives a-sunning sit,
In every street these tunes our ears do greet—
  Cuckoo, jug-jug, pu-we, to-witta-woo!
    Spring, the sweet Spring!
THOMAS NASHE (1567–1601)

IN TIME OF PESTILENCE
1593

Adieu, farewell earth's bliss!
This world uncertain is:
Fond are life's lustful joys,
Death proves them all but toys.
None from his darts can fly;
I am sick, I must die—
    Lord, have mercy on us!

Rich men, trust not in wealth,
Gold cannot buy you health;
Physic himself must fade;
All things to end are made;
The plague full swift goes by;
I am sick, I must die—
    Lord, have mercy on us!

Beauty is but a flower
Which wrinkles will devour;
Brightness falls from the air;
Queens have died young and fair;
Dust hath closed Helen's eye;
I am sick, I must die—
    Lord, have mercy on us!

Strength stoops unto the grave,
Worms feed on Hector brave;
Swords may not fight with fate;
Earth still holds ope her gate;
Come, come! the bells do cry;
I am sick, I must die—
    Lord, have mercy on us!

Wit with his wantonness
Tasteth death's bitterness;
Hell's executioner
Hath no ears for to hear
What vain art can reply;
I am sick, I must die—
    Lord, have mercy on us!

Haste therefore each degree
To welcome destiny;
Heaven is our heritage,
Earth but a player's stage.
Mount we unto the sky;
I am sick, I must die—
    Lord, have mercy on us!

THOMAS NASHE (1567–1601)

130   CHERRY-RIPE

There is a garden in her face
  Where roses and white lilies blow;
A heavenly paradise is that place,
  Wherein all pleasant fruits do flow:
    There cherries grow which none may buy
    Till "Cherry-ripe" themselves do cry.

Those cherries fairly do enclose
  Of orient pearl a double row,
Which when her lovely laughter shows,
  They look like rose-buds fill'd with snow;
    Yet them nor peer nor prince can buy
    Till "Cherry-ripe" themselves do cry.

Her eyes like angels watch them still;
  Her brows like bended bows do stand,
Threat'ning with piercing frowns to kill
  All that attempt with eye or hand
    Those sacred cherries to come nigh,
    Till "Cherry-ripe" themselves do cry.
                        THOMAS CAMPION (1567?–1619)

131   LAURA

Rose-cheek'd *Laura*, come;
Sing thou smoothly with thy beauty's
Silent music, either other
    Sweetly gracing.

Lovely forms do flow
From concent divinely framed:
Heaven is music, and thy beauty's
    Birth is heavenly.

These dull notes we sing
Discords need for helps to grace them;
Only beauty purely loving
    Knows no discord;

But still moves delight,
Like clear springs renew'd by flowing,
Ever perfect, ever in them-
    selves eternal.
                        THOMAS CAMPION (1567?–1619)

132   DEVOTION

Follow thy fair sun, unhappy shadow!
  Though thou be black as night,
  And she made all of light,
Yet follow thy fair sun, unhappy shadow!

Follow her, whose light thy light depriveth!
  Though here thou liv'st disgraced,
  And she in heaven is placed,
Yet follow her whose light the world reviveth!

Follow those pure beams, whose beauty burneth!
  That so have scorchèd thee
  As thou still black must be,
Till her kind beams thy black so brightness turneth.

Follow her, while yet her glory shineth!
  There comes a luckless night
  That will dim all her light;
And this the black unhappy shade divineth.

Follow still, since so thy fates ordained!
  The sun must have his shade,
  Till both at once do fade,—
The sun still proud, the shadow still disdained.
THOMAS CAMPION (1567?–1619)

FOLLOW YOUR SAINT   133

Follow your saint, follow with accents sweet!
Haste you, sad notes, fall at her flying feet!
There, wrapt in cloud of sorrow, pity move,
And tell the ravisher of my soul I perish for her love:
But if she scorns my never-ceasing pain,
Then burst with sighing in her sight, and ne'er return again!

All that I sung still to her praise did tend;
Still she was first, still she my songs did end;
Yet she my love and music both doth fly,
The music that her echo is and beauty's sympathy:
Then let my notes pursue her scornful flight!
It shall suffice that they were breathed and died for her delight.
THOMAS CAMPION (1567?–1619)

VOBISCUM EST IOPE   134

When thou must home to shades of underground,
And there arrived, a new admirèd guest,
The beauteous spirits do engirt thee round,
White Iope, blithe Helen, and the rest,
To hear the stories of thy finish'd love
From that smooth tongue whose music hell can move;

Then wilt thou speak of banqueting delights,
Of masques and revels which sweet youth did make,
Of tourneys and great challenges of knights,
And all these triumphs for thy beauty's sake:
When thou hast told these honours done to thee,
Then tell, O tell, how thou didst murder me!
THOMAS CAMPION (1567?–1619)

A HYMN IN PRAISE OF NEPTUNE   135

  Of Neptune's empire let us sing,
  At whose command the waves obey;
  To whom the rivers tribute pay,
  Down the high mountains sliding:

To whom the scaly nation yields
Homage for the crystal fields
    Wherein they dwell:
And every sea-dog pays a gem
Yearly out of his wat'ry cell
To deck great Neptune's diadem.

The Tritons dancing in a ring
Before his palace gates do make
The water with their echoes quake,
Like the great thunder sounding:
The sea-nymphs chant their accents shrill,
And the sirens, taught to kill
    With their sweet voice,
Make ev'ry echoing rock reply
Unto their gentle murmuring noise
The praise of Neptune's empery.
                    THOMAS CAMPION (1567?–1619)

136   WINTER NIGHTS
Now winter nights enlarge
    The number of their hours,
And clouds their storms discharge
    Upon the airy towers.
Let now the chimneys blaze
    And cups o'erflow with wine;
Let well-tuned words amaze
    With harmony divine.
Now yellow waxen lights
    Shall wait on honey love,
While youthful revels, masques, and courtly sights
    Sleep's leaden spells remove.

This time doth well dispense
    With lovers' long discourse;
Much speech hath some defence,
    Though beauty no remorse.
All do not all things well;
    Some measures comely tread,
Some knotted riddles tell,
    Some poems smoothly read.
The summer hath his joys,
    And winter his delights;
Though love and all his pleasures are but toys,
    They shorten tedious nights.
                    THOMAS CAMPION (1567?–1619)

137   INTEGER VITAE
The man of life upright,
    Whose guiltless heart is free
From all dishonest deeds,
    Or thought of vanity;

The man whose silent days
  In harmless joys are spent,
Whom hopes cannot delude,
  Nor sorrow discontent;

That man needs neither towers
  Nor armour for defence,
Nor secret vaults to fly
  From thunder's violence:

He only can behold
  With unaffrighted eyes
The horrors of the deep
  And terrors of the skies.

Thus, scorning all the cares
  That fate or fortune brings,
He makes the heaven his book,
  His wisdom heavenly things;

Good thoughts his only friends,
  His wealth a well-spent age,
The earth his sober inn
  And quiet pilgrimage.

THOMAS CAMPION (1567?–1619)

O COME QUICKLY! 138

Never weather-beaten sail more willing bent to shore,
Never tirèd pilgrim's limbs affected slumber more,
Than my wearied sprite now longs to fly out of my troubled breast:
O come quickly, sweetest Lord, and take my soul to rest!

Ever blooming are the joys of heaven's high Paradise,
Cold age deafs not there our ears nor vapour dims our eyes:
Glory there the sun outshines; whose beams the Blessèd only see:
O come quickly, glorious Lord, and raise my sprite to Thee!

THOMAS CAMPION (1567?–1619)

ELIZABETH OF BOHEMIA 139

You meaner beauties of the night,
  That poorly satisfy our eyes
More by your number than your light,
  You common people of the skies;
  What are you when the moon shall rise?

You curious chanters of the wood,
  That warble forth Dame Nature's lays,
Thinking your passions understood
  By your weak accents; what's your praise
  When Philomel her voice shall raise?

You violets that first appear,
  By your pure purple mantles known
Like the proud virgins of the year,
  As if the spring were all your own;
  What are you when the rose is blown?

So, when my mistress shall be seen
  In form and beauty of her mind,
By virtue first, then choice, a Queen,
  Tell me, if she were not design'd
  Th' eclipse and glory of her kind.
Sir Henry Wotton (1568–1639)

140   THE CHARACTER OF A HAPPY LIFE

How happy is he born and taught
That serveth not another's will;
Whose armour is his honest thought,
And simple truth his utmost skill!

Whose passions not his masters are;
Whose soul is still prepared for death,
Untied unto the world by care
Of public fame or private breath;

Who envies none that chance doth raise,
Nor vice; who never understood
How deepest wounds are given by praise;
Nor rules of state, but rules of good;

Who hath his life from rumours freed;
Whose conscience is his strong retreat;
Whose state can neither flatterers feed,
Nor ruin make oppressors great;

Who God doth late and early pray
More of His grace than gifts to lend;
And entertains the harmless day
With a religious book or friend;

—This man is freed from servile bands
Of hope to rise or fear to fall:
Lord of himself, though not of lands,
And having nothing, yet hath all.
Sir Henry Wotton (1568–1639)

141   UPON THE DEATH OF SIR ALBERT MORTON'S WIFE

He first deceased; she for a little tried
To live without him, liked it not, and died.
Sir Henry Wotton (1568–1639)

142   MAN

I know my soul hath power to know all things,
Yet she is blind and ignorant in all:
I know I'm one of Nature's little kings,
Yet to the least and vilest things am thrall.

I know my life's a pain and but a span;
I know my sense is mock'd in everything;
And, to conclude, I know myself a Man—
Which is a proud and yet a wretched thing.
Sir John Davies (1569–1626)

To His Forsaken Mistress 143

I do confess thou'rt smooth and fair,
  And I might have gone near to love thee,
Had I not found the slightest prayer
  That lips could move, had power to move thee;
But I can let thee now alone
As worthy to be loved by none.

I do confess thou'rt sweet; yet find
  Thee such an unthrift of thy sweets,
Thy favours are but like the wind
  That kisseth everything it meets:
And since thou canst with more than one,
Thou'rt worthy to be kiss'd by none.

The morning rose that untouch'd stands
  Arm'd with her briers, how sweet she smells!
But pluck'd and strain'd through ruder hands,
  Her sweets no longer with her dwells:
But scent and beauty both are gone,
And leaves fall from her, one by one.

Such fate ere long will thee betide
  When thou hast handled been awhile,
With sere flowers to be thrown aside;
  And I shall sigh, while some will smile,
To see thy love to every one
Hath brought thee to be loved by none.

                    Sir Robert Ayton (1570–1638)

To an Inconstant One 144

I loved thee once; I'll love no more—
  Thine be the grief as is the blame;
Thou art not what thou wast before,
  What reason I should be the same?
    He that can love unloved again,
      Hath better store of love than brain:
God send me love my debts to pay,
While unthrifts fool their love away!

Nothing could have my love o'erthrown
  If thou hadst still continued mine;
Yea, if thou hadst remain'd thy own,
  I might perchance have yet been thine.
    But thou thy freedom didst recall
      That it thou might elsewhere enthral:
And then how could I but disdain
A captive's captive to remain?

When new desires had conquer'd thee
  And changed the object of thy will,
It had been lethargy in me,
  Not constancy, to love thee still.

Yea, it had been a sin to go
  And prostitute affection so:
Since we are taught no prayers to say
To such as must to others pray.

Yet do thou glory in thy choice—
  Thy choice of his good fortune boast;
I'll neither grieve nor yet rejoice
  To see him gain what I have lost:
    The height of my disdain shall be
    To laugh at him, to blush for thee;
To love thee still, but go no more
A-begging at a beggar's door.
                    SIR ROBERT AYTON (1570–1638)

145   HYMN TO DIANA

Queen and huntress, chaste and fair,
  Now the sun is laid to sleep,
Seated in thy silver chair,
  State in wonted manner keep:
    Hesperus entreats thy light,
    Goddess excellently bright.

Earth, let not thy envious shade
  Dare itself to interpose;
Cynthia's shining orb was made
  Heaven to clear when day did close:
    Bless us then with wishèd sight,
    Goddess excellently bright.

Lay thy bow of pearl apart,
  And thy crystal-shining quiver;
Give unto the flying hart
  Space to breathe, how short soever:
    Thou that mak'st a day of night—
    Goddess excellently bright.
                    BEN JONSON (1573–1637)

146   TO CELIA

Drink to me only with thine eyes,
  And I will pledge with mine;
Or leave a kiss but in the cup
  And I'll not look for wine.
The thirst that from the soul doth rise
  Doth ask a drink divine;
But might I of Jove's nectar sup,
  I would not change for thine.

I sent thee late a rosy wreath,
  Not so much honouring thee
As giving it a hope that there
  It could not wither'd be;

But thou thereon didst only breathe,
   And sent'st it back to me;
Since when it grows, and smells, I swear,
   Not of itself but thee!
BEN JONSON (1573–1637)

SIMPLEX MUNDITIIS   147

Still to be neat, still to be drest,
As you were going to a feast;
Still to be powder'd, still perfumed:
Lady, it is to be presumed,
Though art's hid causes are not found,
All is not sweet, all is not sound.

Give me a look, give me a face
That makes simplicity a grace;
Robes loosely flowing, hair as free:
Such sweet neglect more taketh me
Than all th' adulteries of art;
They strike mine eyes, but not my heart.
BEN JONSON (1573–1637)

THE SHADOW   148

Follow a shadow, it still flies you;
   Seem to fly it, it will pursue:
So court a mistress, she denies you;
   Let her alone, she will court you.
     Say, are not women truly, then,
     Styled but the shadows of us men?

At morn and even, shades are longest;
   At noon they are or short or none:
So men at weakest, they are strongest,
   But grant us perfect, they're not known.
     Say, are not women truly, then,
     Styled but the shadows of us men?
BEN JONSON (1573–1637)

THE TRIUMPH   149

See the Chariot at hand here of Love,
   Wherein my Lady rideth!
Each that draws is a swan or a dove,
   And well the car Love guideth.
As she goes, all hearts do duty
     Unto her beauty;
And enamour'd do wish, so they might
     But enjoy such a sight,
That they still were to run by her side,
Through swords, through seas, whither she would ride.

Do but look on her eyes, they do light
   All that Love's world compriseth!
Do but look on her hair, it is bright
   As Love's star when it riseth!

Do but mark, her forehead's smoother
    Than words that soothe her;
And from her arch'd brows such a grace
    Sheds itself through the face,
As alone there triumphs to the life
All the gain, all the good, of the elements' strife.

Have you seen but a bright lily grow
  Before rude hands have touch'd it?
Have you mark'd but the fall of the snow
  Before the soil hath smutch'd it?
Have you felt the wool of beaver,
    Or swan's down ever?
Or have smelt o' the bud o' the brier,
    Or the nard in the fire?
Or have tasted the bag of the bee?
O so white, O so soft, O so sweet is she!

BEN JONSON (1573–1637)

150   An Elegy

Though beauty be the mark of praise,
  And yours of whom I sing be such
  As not the world can praise too much,
Yet 'tis your Virtue now I raise.

A virtue, like allay so gone
  Throughout your form as, though that move
  And draw and conquer all men's love,
This subjects you to love of one.

Wherein you triumph yet—because
  'Tis of your flesh, and that you use
  The noblest freedom, not to choose
Against or faith or honour's laws.

But who should less expect from you?
  In whom alone Love lives again:
  By whom he is restored to men,
And kept and bred and brought up true.

His falling temples you have rear'd,
  The wither'd garlands ta'en away;
  His altars kept from that decay
That envy wish'd, and nature fear'd:

And on them burn so chaste a flame,
  With so much loyalty's expense,
  As Love to acquit such excellence
Is gone himself into your name.

And you are he—the deity
  To whom all lovers are design'd
  That would their better objects find;
Among which faithful troop am I—

Who as an off'ring at your shrine
   Have sung this hymn, and here entreat
   One spark of your diviner heat
To light upon a love of mine.

Which if it kindle not, but scant
   Appear, and that to shortest view;
   Yet give me leave to adore in you
What I in her am grieved to want!

BEN JONSON (1573–1637)

allay: *alloy*

151. A FAREWELL TO THE WORLD

False world, good night! since thou hast brought
   That hour upon my morn of age;
Henceforth I quit thee from my thought,
   My part is ended on thy stage.

Yes, threaten, do. Alas! I fear
   As little as I hope from thee:
I know thou canst not show nor bear
   More hatred than thou hast to me.

My tender, first, and simple years
   Thou didst abuse and then betray;
Since stir'd'st up jealousies and fears,
   When all the causes were away.

Then in a soil hast planted me
   Where breathe the basest of thy fools;
Where envious arts professed be,
   And pride and ignorance the schools;

Where nothing is examined, weigh'd,
   But as 'tis rumour'd, so believed;
Where every freedom is betray'd,
   And every goodness tax'd or grieved.

But what we're born for, we must bear:
   Our frail condition it is such
That what to all may happen here,
   If't chance to me, I must not grutch.

Else I my state should much mistake
   To harbour a divided thought
From all my kind—that, for my sake,
   There should a miracle be wrought.

No, I do know that I was born
   To age, misfortune, sickness, grief:
But I will bear these with that scorn
   As shall not need thy false relief.

Nor for my peace will I go far,
  As wanderers do, that still do roam;
But make my strengths, such as they are,
  Here in my bosom, and at home.

BEN JONSON (1573–1637)

152 THE NOBLE BALM

High-spirited friend,
I send nor balms nor cor'sives to your wound:
    Your fate hath found
A gentler and more agile hand to tend
The cure of that which is but corporal;
And doubtful days, which were named critical,
    Have made their fairest flight
    And now are out of sight.
Yet doth some wholesome physic for the mind
    Wrapp'd in this paper lie,
Which in the taking if you misapply,
    You are unkind.

    Your covetous hand,
Happy in that fair honour it hath gain'd,
    Must now be rein'd.
True valour doth her own renown command
In one full action; nor have you now more
To do, than be a husband of that store.
    Think but how dear you bought
    This fame which you have caught:
Such thoughts will make you more in love with truth.
    'Tis wisdom, and that high,
For men to use their fortune reverently,
    Even in youth.

BEN JONSON (1573–1637)

153 ON ELIZABETH L. H.
AN EPITAPH

Wouldst thou hear what Man can say
In a little? Reader, stay.
Underneath this stone doth lie
As much Beauty as could die:
Which in life did harbour give
To more Virtue than doth live.
If at all she had a fault,
Leave it buried in this vault.
One name was *Elizabeth*,
The other, let it sleep with death:
Fitter, where it died, to tell
Than that it lived at all. Farewell.

BEN JONSON (1573–1637)

On Salathiel Pavy,   154
a child of Queen Elizabeth's Chapel
An Epitaph

  Weep with me, all you that read
    This little story;
  And know, for whom a tear you shed
    Death's self is sorry.
  'Twas a child that so did thrive
    In grace and feature,
  As Heaven and Nature seem'd to strive
    Which own'd the creature.
  Years he number'd scarce thirteen
    When Fates turn'd cruel,
  Yet three fill'd zodiacs had he been
    The stage's jewel;
  And did act (what now we moan)
    Old men so duly,
  As sooth the Parcæ thought him one,
    He play'd so truly.
  So, by error, to his fate
    They all consented;
  But, viewing him since, alas, too late!
    They have repented;
  And have sought, to give new birth,
    In baths to steep him;
  But, being so much too good for earth,
    Heaven vows to keep him.

                            BEN JONSON (1573–1637)

A Part of an Ode   155
to the Immortal Memory and Friendship of
That Noble Pair, Sir Lucius Cary and Sir H. Morison

  It is not growing like a tree
    In bulk, doth make man better be;
  Or standing long an oak, three hundred year,
  To fall a log at last, dry, bald, and sere:
      A lily of a day
        Is fairer far in May,
    Although it fall and die that night;
    It was the plant and flower of light.
  In small proportions we just beauties see;
  And in short measures, life may perfect be.

    Call, noble *Lucius*, then for wine,
    And let thy looks with gladness shine:
  Accept this garland, plant it on thy head,
  And think—nay, know—thy *Morison's* not dead.
      He leap'd the present age,
      Possest with holy rage
    To see that bright eternal Day
    Of which we Priests and Poets say
  Such truths as we expect for happy men;
  And there he lives with memory—and *Ben*

    Jonson: who sung this of him, ere he went
        Himself to rest,
Or tast a part of that full joy he meant
        To have exprest
     In this bright Asterism
     Where it were friendship's schism—
Were not his *Lucius* long with us to tarry—
        To separate these twy
     Lights, the Dioscuri,
And keep the one half from his *Harry*.
But fate doth so alternate the design,
Whilst that in Heav'n, this light on earth must shine.

     And shine as you exalted are!
     Two names of friendship, but one star:
Of hearts the union: and those not by chance
Made, or indenture, or leased out to advance
        The profits for a time.
        No pleasures vain did chime
     Of rimes or riots at your feasts,
     Orgies of drink or feign'd protests;
But simple love of greatness and of good,
That knits brave minds and manners more than blood.

     This made you first to know the *Why*
     You liked, then after, to apply
That liking, and approach so one the t'other
Till either grew a portion of the other:
        Each stylèd by his end
        The copy of his friend.
     You lived to be the great surnames
     And titles by which all made claims
Unto the Virtue—nothing perfect done
But as a *CARY* or a *MORISON*.

And such the force the fair example had
        As they that saw
The good, and durst not practise it, were glad
        That such a law
     Was left yet to mankind,
     Where they might read and find
FRIENDSHIP indeed was written, not in words,
        And with the heart, not pen,
        Of two so early men,
Whose lines her rules were and records:
Who, ere the first down bloomed on the chin,
Had sow'd these fruits, and got the harvest in.
                  BEN JONSON (1573–1637)

Daybreak 156

Stay, O sweet and do not rise!
The light that shines comes from thine eyes;
The day breaks not: it is my heart,
  Because that you and I must part.
    Stay! or else my joys will die
    And perish in their infancy.

JOHN DONNE (1573–1631)

Song 157

Go and catch a falling star,
  Get with child a mandrake root,
Tell me where all past years are,
  Or who cleft the Devil's foot;
Teach me to hear mermaids singing,
Or to keep off envy's stinging,
    And find
    What wind
Serves to advance an honest mind.

If thou be'st born to strange sights,
  Things invisible to see,
Ride ten thousand days and nights
  Till Age snow white hairs on thee;
Thou, when thou return'st, wilt tell me
All strange wonders that befell thee,
    And swear
    No where
Lives a woman true and fair.

If thou find'st one, let me know;
  Such a pilgrimage were sweet.
Yet do not; I would not go,
  Though at next door we might meet.
Though she were true when you met her,
And last till you write your letter,
    Yet she
    Will be
False, ere I come, to two or three.

JOHN DONNE (1573–1631)

Time and Absence 158

Absence, hear thou my protestation
  Against thy strength,
  Distance and length:
Do what thou canst for alteration,
  For hearts of truest mettle
  Absence doth join and Time doth settle.

Who loves a mistress of such quality,
  His mind hath found
  Affection's ground
Beyond time, place, and all mortality.
  To hearts that cannot vary
  Absence is present, Time doth tarry.

My senses want their outward motion
    Which now within
    Reason doth win,
Redoubled by her secret notion:
    Like rich men that take pleasure
    In hiding more than handling treasure.

By Absence this good means I gain,
    That I can catch her
    Where none can watch her,
In some close corner of my brain:
    There I embrace and kiss her,
    And so enjoy her and none miss her.
                          JOHN DONNE (1573–1631)

159   THE ECSTASY

Where, like a pillow on a bed,
    A pregnant bank swell'd up, to rest
The violet's reclining head,
    Sat we two, one another's best.

Our hands were firmly cèmented
    By a fast balm which thence did spring;
Our eye-beams twisted, and did thread
    Our eyes upon one double string.

So to engraft our hands, as yet
    Was all the means to make us one;
And pictures in our eyes to get
    Was all our propagation.

As 'twixt two equal armies Fate
    Suspends uncertain victory,
Our souls—which to advance their state
    Were gone out—hung 'twixt her and me.

And whilst our souls negotiate there,
    We like sepulchral statues lay;
All day the same our postures were,
    And we said nothing, all the day.
                          JOHN DONNE (1573–1631)

160   THE DREAM

Dear love, for nothing less than thee
Would I have broke this happy dream;
    It was a theme
For reason, much too strong for fantasy.
Therefore thou waked'st me wisely; yet
My dream thou brok'st not, but continued'st it.
Thou art so true that thoughts of thee suffice
To make dreams truths and fables histories;
Enter these arms, for since thou thought'st it best
Not to dream all my dream, let's act the rest.

As lightning, or a taper's light,
Thine eyes, and not thy noise, waked me;
    Yet I thought thee—
For thou lov'st truth—an angel, at first sight;
But when I saw thou saw'st my heart,
And knew'st my thoughts beyond an angel's art,
When thou knew'st what I dreamt, when thou knew'st when
Excess of joy would wake me, and cam'st then,
I must confess it could not choose but be
Profane to think thee anything but thee.

Coming and staying show'd thee thee,
But rising makes me doubt that now
    Thou art not thou.
That Love is weak where Fear's as strong as he;
'Tis not all spirit pure and brave
If mixture it of Fear, Shame, Honour have.
Perchance as torches, which must ready be,
Men light and put out, so thou deal'st with me.
Thou cam'st to kindle, go'st to come: then I
Will dream that hope again, but else would die.

JOHN DONNE (1573–1631)

THE FUNERAL   161

Whoever comes to shroud me, do not harm
    Nor question much
That subtle wreath of hair about mine arm;
The mystery, the sign you must not touch,
    For 'tis my outward soul,
Viceroy to that which, unto heav'n being gone,
    Will leave this to control
And keep these limbs, her provinces, from dissolution.

For if the sinewy thread my brain lets fall
    Through every part
Can tie those parts, and make me one of all;
Those hairs, which upward grew, and strength and art
    Have from a better brain,
Can better do 't: except she meant that I
    By this should know my pain,
As prisoners then are manacled, when they're condemn'd to die.

Whate'er she meant by 't, bury it with me,
    For since I am
Love's martyr, it might breed idolatry
If into other hands these reliques came.
    As 'twas humility
T' afford to it all that a soul can do,
    So 'tis some bravery
That, since you would have none of me, I bury some of you.

JOHN DONNE (1573–1631)

162   A HYMN TO GOD THE FATHER
Wilt Thou forgive that sin where I begun,
  Which was my sin, though it were done before?
Wilt Thou forgive that sin through which I run,
  And do run still, though still I do deplore?
    When Thou hast done, Thou hast not done;
      For I have more.

Wilt Thou forgive that sin which I have won
  Others to sin, and made my sins their door?
Wilt Thou forgive that sin which I did shun
  A year or two, but wallow'd in a score?
    When Thou hast done, Thou hast not done;
      For I have more.

I have a sin of fear, that when I've spun
  My last thread, I shall perish on the shore;
But swear by Thyself that at my death Thy Son
  Shall shine as He shines now and heretofore:
    And having done that, Thou hast done;
      I fear no more.
                              JOHN DONNE (1573–1631)

163   DEATH
Death, be not proud, though some have called thee
Mighty and dreadful, for thou art not so:
For those whom thou think'st thou dost overthrow
Die not, poor Death; nor yet canst thou kill me.
From Rest and Sleep, which but thy picture be,
Much pleasure, then from thee much more must flow;
And soonest our best men with thee do go—
Rest of their bones and souls' delivery!
Thou'rt slave to fate, chance, kings, and desperate men,
And dost with poison, war, and sickness dwell;
And poppy or charms can make us sleep as well
And better than thy stroke. Why swell'st thou then?
  One short sleep past, we wake eternally,
  And Death shall be no more: Death, thou shalt die!
                              JOHN DONNE (1573–1631)

164   PHILOMEL
        As it fell upon a day
        In the merry month of May,
        Sitting in a pleasant shade
        Which a grove of myrtles made,
        Beasts did leap and birds did sing,
        Trees did grow and plants did spring;
        Everything did banish moan
        Save the Nightingale alone:
        She, poor bird, as all forlorn
        Lean'd her breast up-till a thorn,
        And there sung the dolefull'st ditty,
        That to hear it was great pity.

Fie, fie, fie! now would she cry;
Tereu, Tereu! by and by;
That to hear her so complain
Scarce I could from tears refrain;
For her griefs so lively shown
Made me think upon mine own.
Ah! thought I, thou mourn'st in vain,
None takes pity on thy pain:
Senseless trees they cannot hear thee,
Ruthless beasts they will not cheer thee:
King Pandion he is dead,
All thy friends are lapp'd in lead;
All thy fellow birds do sing
Careless of thy sorrowing:
Even so, poor bird, like thee,
None alive will pity me.

RICHARD BARNEFIELD (1574–1627)

SWEET CONTENT 165

Art thou poor, yet hast thou golden slumbers?
  O sweet content!
Art thou rich, yet is thy mind perplexèd?
  O punishment!
Dost thou laugh to see how fools are vexèd
To add to golden numbers golden numbers?
  O sweet content! O sweet, O sweet content!
Work apace, apace, apace, apace;
Honest labour bears a lovely face;
Then hey nonny nonny—hey nonny nonny!

Canst drink the waters of the crispèd spring?
  O sweet content!
Swim'st thou in wealth, yet sink'st in thine own tears?
  O punishment!
Then he that patiently want's burden bears,
No burden bears, but is a king, a king!
  O sweet content! O sweet, O sweet content!
Work apace, apace, apace, apace;
Honest labour bears a lovely face;
Then hey nonny nonny—hey nonny nonny!

THOMAS DEKKER (1575–1641)

MATIN SONG 166

Pack, clouds, away! and welcome, day!
 With night we banish sorrow.
Sweet air, blow soft; mount, lark, aloft
 To give my Love good-morrow!
Wings from the wind to please her mind,
 Notes from the lark I'll borrow:
Bird, prune thy wing! nightingale, sing!
 To give my Love good-morrow!
  To give my Love good-morrow
  Notes from them all I'll borrow.

110

    Wake from thy nest, robin red-breast!
      Sing, birds, in every furrow!
    And from each bill let music shrill
      Give my fair Love good-morrow!
    Blackbird and thrush in every bush,
      Stare, linnet, and cocksparrow,
    You pretty elves, among yourselves
      Sing my fair Love good-morrow!
        To give my Love good-morrow!
        Sing, birds, in every furrow!
                      THOMAS HEYWOOD (1575?–1650)

stare: *starling*

167   THE MESSAGE
    Ye little birds that sit and sing
      Amidst the shady valleys,
    And see how Phillis sweetly walks
      Within her garden-alleys;
    Go, pretty birds, about her bower;
    Sing, pretty birds, she may not lower;
    Ah me! methinks I see her frown!
      Ye pretty wantons, warble.

    Go tell her through your chirping bills,
      As you by me are bidden,
    To her is only known my love,
      Which from the world is hidden.
    Go, pretty birds, and tell her so,
    See that your notes strain not too low,
    For still methinks I see her frown;
      Ye pretty wantons, warble.

    Go tune your voices' harmony
      And sing, I am her lover;
    Strain loud and sweet, that every note
      With sweet content may move her:
    And she that hath the sweetest voice,
    Tell her I will not change my choice:
    —Yet still methinks I see her frown!
      Ye pretty wantons, warble.

    O fly! make haste! see, see, she falls
      Into a pretty slumber!
    Sing round about her rosy bed
      That waking she may wonder:
    Say to her, 'tis her lover true
    That sendeth love to you, to you!
    And when you hear her kind reply,
      Return with pleasant warblings.
                      THOMAS HEYWOOD (1575?–1650)

Sleep   *168*

Come, Sleep, and with thy sweet deceiving
  Lock me in delight awhile;
  Let some pleasing dreams beguile
  All my fancies; that from thence
  I may feel an influence
All my powers of care bereaving!

Though but a shadow, but a sliding,
  Let me know some little joy!
  We that suffer long annoy
  Are contented with a thought
  Through an idle fancy wrought:
O let my joys have some abiding!
                           JOHN FLETCHER (1579–1625)

Bridal Song   *169*

Cynthia, to thy power and thee
  We obey.
Joy to this great company!
  And no day
Come to steal this night away
  Till the rites of love are ended,
And the lusty bridegroom say,
  Welcome, light, of all befriended!

Pace out, you watery powers below;
  Let your feet,
Like the galleys when they row,
  Even beat;
Let your unknown measures, set
  To the still winds, tell to all
That gods are come, immortal, great,
  To honour this great nuptial!
                           JOHN FLETCHER (1579–1625)

Aspatia's Song   *170*

Lay a garland on my herse
  Of the dismal yew;
Maidens, willow branches bear;
  Say, I died true.

My love was false, but I was firm
  From my hour of birth.
Upon my buried body lie
  Lightly, gentle earth!
                           JOHN FLETCHER (1579–1625)

Hymn to Pan   *171*

Sing his praises that doth keep
  Our flocks from harm.
Pan, the father of our sheep;
  And arm in arm
Tread we softly in a round,
Whilst the hollow neighbouring ground
Fills the music with her sound.

>   Pan, O great god Pan, to thee
>   Thus do we sing!
>   Thou who keep'st us chaste and free
>   As the young spring:
>   Ever be thy honour spoke
>   From that place the morn is broke
>   To that place day doth unyoke!
>
>   JOHN FLETCHER (1579–1625)

172   AWAY, DELIGHTS

> Away, delights! go seek some other dwelling,
>   For I must die.
> Farewell, false love! thy tongue is ever telling
>   Lie after lie.
> For ever let me rest now from thy smarts;
>   Alas, for pity go
>   And fire their hearts
> That have been hard to thee! Mine was not so.
>
> Never again deluding love shall know me,
>   For I will die;
> And all those griefs that think to overgrow me
>   Shall be as I:
> For ever will I sleep, while poor maids cry—
>   "Alas, for pity stay,
>   And let us die
> With thee! Men cannot mock us in the clay."
>
>   JOHN FLETCHER (1579–1625)

173   LOVE'S EMBLEMS

> Now the lusty spring is seen;
>   Golden yellow, gaudy blue,
>   Daintily invite the view:
> Everywhere on every green
> Roses blushing as they blow,
>   And enticing men to pull,
> Lilies whiter than the snow,
>   Woodbines of sweet honey full:
>   All love's emblems, and all cry,
>   "Ladies, if not pluck'd, we die."
>
> Yet the lusty spring hath stay'd;
>   Blushing red and purest white
>   Daintily to love invite
> Every woman, every maid:
> Cherries kissing as they grow,
>   And inviting men to taste,
> Apples even ripe below,
>   Winding gently to the waist:
>   All love's emblems, and all cry,
>   "Ladies, if not pluck'd, we die."
>
>   JOHN FLETCHER (1579–1625)

Hear, ye Ladies 174

Hear, ye ladies that despise
  What the mighty Love has done;
Fear examples and be wise:
  Fair Callisto was a nun;
Leda, sailing on the stream
  To deceive the hopes of man,
Love accounting but a dream,
  Doted on a silver swan;
    Danaë, in a brazen tower,
    Where no love was, loved a shower.

Hear, ye ladies that are coy,
  What the mighty Love can do;
Fear the fierceness of the boy:
  The chaste Moon he makes to woo;
Vesta, kindling holy fires,
  Circled round about with spies,
Never dreaming loose desires,
  Doting at the altar dies;
    Ilion, in a short hour, higher
    He can build, and once more fire.

John Fletcher (1579–1625)

God Lyaeus 175

God Lyaeus, ever young,
Ever honour'd, ever sung,
Stain'd with blood of lusty grapes,
In a thousand lusty shapes
Dance upon the mazer's brim,
In the crimson liquor swim;
From thy plenteous hand divine
Let a river run with wine:
  God of youth, let this day here
  Enter neither care nor fear.

John Fletcher (1579–1625)

mazer: *a bowl of maple-wood*

Beauty Clear and Fair 176

Beauty clear and fair,
  Where the air
Rather like a perfume dwells;
  Where the violet and the rose
  Their blue veins and blush disclose,
And come to honour nothing else:

  Where to live near
  And planted there
Is to live, and still live new;
  Where to gain a favour is
  More than light, perpetual bliss—
Make me live by serving you!

Dear, again back recall
   To this light,
A stranger to himself and all!
   Both the wonder and the story
   Shall be yours, and eke the glory;
I am your servant, and your thrall.
JOHN FLETCHER (1579–1625)

177   MELANCHOLY

Hence, all you vain delights,
   As short as are the nights
   Wherein you spend your folly!
There's naught in this life sweet,
If men were wise to see't,
   But only melancholy—
   O sweetest melancholy!
Welcome, folded arms and fixèd eyes,
A sight that piercing mortifies,
A look that's fasten'd to the ground,
A tongue chain'd up without a sound!

Fountain-heads and pathless groves,
Places which pale passion loves!
Moonlight walks, when all the fowls
Are warmly housed, save bats and owls!
   A midnight bell, a parting groan—
   These are the sounds we feed upon:
Then stretch our bones in a still gloomy valley,
Nothing's so dainty sweet as lovely melancholy.
JOHN FLETCHER (1579–1625)

178   WEEP NO MORE

Weep no more, nor sigh, nor groan,
Sorrow calls no time that's gone:
Violets pluck'd, the sweetest rain
Makes not fresh nor grow again.
Trim thy locks, look cheerfully;
Fate's hid ends eyes cannot see.
Joys as wingèd dreams fly fast,
Why should sadness longer last?
Grief is but a wound to woe;
Gentlest fair, mourn, mourn no moe.
JOHN FLETCHER (1579–1625)

179   AURORA

O happy Tithon! if thou know'st thy hap,
   And valuest thy wealth, as I my want,
   Then need'st thou not—which ah! I grieve to grant—
Repine at Jove, lull'd in his leman's lap:
   That golden shower in which he did repose—
      One dewy drop it stains
      Which thy Aurora rains
      Upon the rural plains,
When from thy bed she passionately goes.

Then, waken'd with the music of the merles,
  She not remembers Memnon when she mourns:
That faithful flame which in her bosom burns
From crystal conduits throws those liquid pearls:
  Sad from thy sight so soon to be removed,
    She so her grief delates.
    —O favour'd by the fates
    Above the happiest states,
  Who art of one so worthy well-beloved!
WILLIAM ALEXANDER, EARL OF STIRLING (1580?–1640)

A LITANY   180

  Drop, drop, slow tears,
    And bathe those beauteous feet
  Which brought from Heaven
    The news and Prince of Peace:
  Cease not, wet eyes,
    His mercy to entreat;
  To cry for vengeance
    Sin doth never cease.
  In your deep floods
    Drown all my faults and fears;
  Nor let His eye
    See sin, but through my tears.
PHINEAS FLETCHER (1580–1650)

OF HIS DEAR SON, GERVASE   181

Dear Lord, receive my son, whose winning love
To me was like a friendship, far above
The course of nature or his tender age;
Whose looks could all my bitter griefs assuage:
Let his pure soul, ordain'd seven years to be
In that frail body which was part of me,
Remain my pledge in Heaven, as sent to show
How to this port at every step I go.
SIR JOHN BEAUMONT (1583–1627)

INVOCATION   182

  Phœbus, arise!
  And paint the sable skies
With azure, white, and red;
Rouse Memnon's mother from her Tithon's bed,
That she thy càreer may with roses spread;
The nightingales thy coming each-where sing;
Make an eternal spring!
Give life to this dark world which lieth dead;
Spread forth thy golden hair
In larger locks than thou wast wont before,
And emperor-like decore
With diadem of pearl thy temples fair:
Chase hence the ugly night
Which serves but to make dear thy glorious light.
This is that happy morn,
That day, long wished day

Of all my life so dark
(If cruel stars have not my ruin sworn
And fates not hope betray),
Which, only white, deserves
A diamond for ever should it mark:
This is the morn should bring into this grove
My Love, to hear and recompense my love.
Fair King, who all preserves,
But show thy blushing beams,
And thou two sweeter eyes
Shalt see than those which by Penèus' streams
Did once thy heart surprise:
Nay, suns, which shine as clear
As thou when two thou did to Rome appear.
Now, Flora, deck thyself in fairest guise:
If that ye, winds, would hear
A voice surpassing far Amphion's lyre,
Your stormy chiding stay;
Let zephyr only breathe
And with her tresses play,
Kissing sometimes these purple ports of death.

The winds all silent are;
And Phœbus in his chair
Ensaffroning sea and air
Makes vanish every star:
Night like a drunkard reels
Beyond the hills to shun his flaming wheels:
The fields with flowers are deck'd in every hue,
The clouds bespangle with bright gold their blue:
Here is the pleasant place—
And everything, save Her, who all should grace.
      WILLIAM DRUMMOND, OF HAWTHORNDEN (1585–1649)

183   MADRIGAL

    Like the Idalian queen,
    Her hair about her eyne,
With neck and breast's ripe apples to be seen,
    At first glance of the morn
In Cyprus' gardens gathering those fair flow'rs
    Which of her blood were born,
I saw, but fainting saw, my paramours.
The Graces naked danced about the place,
    The winds and trees amazed
    With silence on her gazed,
The flowers did smile, like those upon her face;
And as their aspen stalks those fingers band,
    That she might read my case,
A hyacinth I wish'd me in her hand.
      WILLIAM DRUMMOND, OF HAWTHORNDEN (1585–1649)

band: *bound*

Spring Bereaved 1 — 184

    That zephyr every year
    So soon was heard to sigh in forests here,
It was for her: that wrapp'd in gowns of green
    Meads were so early seen,
That in the saddest months oft sung the merles,
It was for her; for her trees dropp'd forth pearls.
    That proud and stately courts
Did envy those our shades and calm resorts,
It was for her; and she is gone, O woe!
    Woods cut again do grow,
Bud doth the rose and daisy, winter done;
But we, once dead, no more do see the sun.
        WILLIAM DRUMMOND, OF HAWTHORNDEN (1585–1649)

Spring Bereaved 2 — 185

Sweet Spring, thou turn'st with all thy goodly train,
Thy head with flames, thy mantle bright with flow'rs:
The zephyrs curl the green locks of the plain,
The clouds for joy in pearls weep down their show'rs.
Thou turn'st, sweet youth, but ah! my pleasant hours
And happy days with thee come not again;
The sad memorials only of my pain
Do with thee turn, which turn my sweets in sours.
Thou art the same which still thou wast before,
Delicious, wanton, amiable, fair;
But she, whose breath embalm'd thy wholesome air,
Is gone—nor gold nor gems her can restore.
  Neglected virtue, seasons go and come,
  While thine forgot lie closèd in a tomb.
        WILLIAM DRUMMOND, OF HAWTHORNDEN (1585–1649)

Spring Bereaved 3 — 186

Alexis, here she stay'd; among these pines,
Sweet hermitress, she did alone repair;
Here did she spread the treasure of her hair,
More rich than that brought from the Colchian mines.
She set her by these muskèd eglantines,
—The happy place the print seems yet to bear:
Her voice did sweeten here thy sugar'd lines,
To which winds, trees, beasts, birds, did lend their ear.
Me here she first perceived, and here a morn
Of bright carnations did o'erspread her face;
Here did she sigh, here first my hopes were born,
And I first got a pledge of promised grace:
  But ah! what served it to be happy so?
  Sith passed pleasures double but new woe?
        WILLIAM DRUMMOND, OF HAWTHORNDEN (1585–1649)

Her Passing — 187

    The beauty and the life
    Of life's and beauty's fairest paragon
—O tears! O grief!—hung at a feeble thread
To which pale Atropos had set her knife;

The soul with many a groan
  Had left each outward part,
And now did take his last leave of the heart:
Naught else did want, save death, ev'n to be dead;
When the afflicted band about her bed,
Seeing so fair him come in lips, cheeks, eyes,
Cried, "*Ah! and can Death enter Paradise?*"
        WILLIAM DRUMMOND, OF HAWTHORNDEN (1585–1649)

188   INEXORABLE
  My thoughts hold mortal strife;
  I do detest my life,
  And with lamenting cries
  Peace to my soul to bring
Oft call that prince which here doth monarchise:
  —But he, grim-grinning King,
Who caitiffs scorns, and doth the blest surprise,
Late having deck'd with beauty's rose his tomb,
Disdains to crop a weed, and will not come.
        WILLIAM DRUMMOND, OF HAWTHORNDEN (1585–1649)

189   CHANGE SHOULD BREED CHANGE
  New doth the sun appear,
  The mountains' snows decay,
Crown'd with frail flowers forth comes the baby year.
  My soul, time posts away;
  And thou yet in that frost
  Which flower and fruit hath lost,
As if all here immortal were, dost stay.
  For shame! thy powers awake,
Look to that Heaven which never night makes black,
And there at that immortal sun's bright rays,
Deck thee with flowers which fear not rage of days!
        WILLIAM DRUMMOND, OF HAWTHORNDEN (1585–1649)

190   SAINT JOHN BAPTIST
The last and greatest Herald of Heaven's King,
Girt with rough skins, hies to the deserts wild,
Among that savage brood the woods forth bring,
Which he than man more harmless found and mild.
His food was locusts, and what young doth spring
With honey that from virgin hives distill'd;
Parch'd body, hollow eyes, some uncouth thing
Made him appear, long since from earth exiled.
There burst he forth: "All ye, whose hopes rely
On God, with me amidst these deserts mourn;
Repent, repent, and from old errors turn!"
—Who listen'd to his voice, obey'd his cry?
  Only the echoes, which he made relent,
  Rung from their marble caves "Repent! Repent!"
        WILLIAM DRUMMOND, OF HAWTHORNDEN (1585–1649)

WOOING SONG 191

Love is the blossom where there blows
Every thing that lives or grows:
Love doth make the Heav'ns to move,
And the Sun doth burn in love:
Love the strong and weak doth yoke,
And makes the ivy climb the oak,
Under whose shadows lions wild,
Soften'd by love, grow tame and mild:
Love no med'cine can appease,
He burns the fishes in the seas:
Not all the skill his wounds can stench,
Not all the sea his fire can quench.
Love did make the bloody spear
Once a leavy coat to wear,
While in his leaves there shrouded lay
Sweet birds, for love that sing and play
And of all love's joyful flame
I the bud and blossom am.
 Only bend thy knee to me,
 Thy wooing shall thy winning be!

See, see the flowers that below
Now as fresh as morning blow;
And of all the virgin rose
That as bright Aurora shows;
How they all unleaved die,
Losing their virginity!
Like unto a summer shade,
But now born, and now they fade.
Every thing doth pass away;
There is danger in delay:
Come, come, gather then the rose,
Gather it, or it you lose!
All the sand of Tagus' shore
Into my bosom casts his ore:
All the valleys' swimming corn
To my house is yearly borne:
Every grape of every vine
Is gladly bruised to make me wine:
While ten thousand kings, as proud,
To carry up my train have bow'd,
And a world of ladies send me
In my chambers to attend me:
All the stars in Heav'n that shine,
And ten thousand more, are mine:
 Only bend thy knee to me,
 Thy wooing shall thy winning be!

GILES FLETCHER (1585?–1623)

192   ON THE TOMBS IN WESTMINSTER ABBEY

Mortality, behold and fear!
What a change of flesh is here!
Think how many royal bones
Sleep within this heap of stones:
Here they lie had realms and lands,
Who now want strength to stir their hands:
Where from their pulpits seal'd with dust
They preach, "In greatness is no trust."
Here's an acre sown indeed
With the richest, royall'st seed
That the earth did e'er suck in
Since the first man died for sin:
Here the bones of birth have cried—
"Though gods they were, as men they died."
Here are sands, ignoble things,
Dropt from the ruin'd sides of kings;
Here's a world of pomp and state,
Buried in dust, once dead by fate.

                              FRANCIS BEAUMONT (1586–1616)

193   DAWN

Fly hence, shadows, that do keep
Watchful sorrows charm'd in sleep!
Tho' the eyes be overtaken,
Yet the heart doth ever waken
Thoughts chain'd up in busy snares
Of continual woes and cares:
Love and griefs are so exprest
As they rather sigh than rest.
  Fly hence, shadows, that do keep
  Watchful sorrows charm'd in sleep!

                                     JOHN FORD (1586–1639)

194   THE LOVER'S RESOLUTION

Shall I, wasting in despair,
Die because a woman's fair?
Or make pale my cheeks with care
'Cause another's rosy are?
Be she fairer than the day,
Or the flow'ry meads in May,
  If she think not well of me,
  What care I how fair she be?

Shall my silly heart be pined
'Cause I see a woman kind?
Or a well disposèd nature
Joinèd with a lovely feature?
Be she meeker, kinder, than
Turtle-dove or pelican,
  If she be not so to me,
  What care I how kind she be?

Shall a woman's virtues move
Me to perish for her love?
Or her well-deservings known
Make me quite forget my own?
Be she with that goodness blest
Which may merit name of Best,
  If she be not such to me,
  What care I how good she be?

'Cause her fortune seems too high,
Shall I play the fool and die?
She that bears a noble mind,
If not outward helps she find,
Thinks what with them he would do
That without them dares her woo;
  And unless that mind I see,
  What care I how great she be?

Great, or good, or kind, or fair,
I will ne'er the more despair;
If she love me, this believe,
I will die ere she shall grieve;
If she slight me when I woo,
I can scorn and let her go;
  For if she be not for me,
  What care I for whom she be?

GEORGE WITHER (1588–1667)

A WIDOW'S HYMN

How near me came the hand of Death,
  When at my side he struck my dear,
And took away the precious breath
  Which quicken'd my belovèd peer!
    How helpless am I thereby made!
    By day how grieved, by night how sad!
And now my life's delight is gone,
—Alas! how am I left alone!

The voice which I did more esteem
  Than music in her sweetest key,
Those eyes which unto me did seem
  More comfortable than the day;
    Those now by me, as they have been,
    Shall never more be heard or seen;
But what I once enjoy'd in them
Shall seem hereafter as a dream.

Lord! keep me faithful to the trust
  Which my dear spouse reposed in me:
To him now dead preserve me just
  In all that should performed be!

> For though our being man and wife
> Extendeth only to this life,
> Yet neither life nor death should end
> The being of a faithful friend.
>
> GEORGE WITHER (1588–1667)

peer: *companion*

196 A WELCOME

Welcome, welcome! do I sing,
Far more welcome than the spring;
He that parteth from you never
Shall enjoy a spring for ever.

He that to the voice is near
  Breaking from your iv'ry pale,
Need not walk abroad to hear
  The delightful nightingale.
    Welcome, welcome, then...

He that looks still on your eyes,
  Though the winter have begun
To benumb our arteries,
  Shall not want the summer's sun.
    Welcome, welcome, then...

He that still may see your cheeks,
  Where all rareness still reposes,
Is a fool if e'er he seeks
  Other lilies, other roses.
    Welcome, welcome, then...

He to whom your soft lip yields,
  And perceives your breath in kissing,
All the odours of the fields
  Never, never shall be missing.
    Welcome, welcome, then...

He that question would anew
  What fair Eden was of old,
Let him rightly study you,
  And a brief of that behold.
    Welcome, welcome, then...

WILLIAM BROWNE, OF TAVISTOCK (1588–1643)

197 THE SIRENS' SONG

Steer, hither steer your winged pines,
  All beaten mariners!
Here lie Love's undiscover'd mines,
  A prey to passengers—
Perfumes far sweeter than the best
Which make the Phœnix' urn and nest.
  Fear not your ships,
Nor any to oppose you save our lips;
  But come on shore,
Where no joy dies till Love hath gotten more.

For swelling waves our panting breasts,
    Where never storms arise,
Exchange, and be awhile our guests:
    For stars gaze on our eyes.
The compass Love shall hourly sing,
And as he goes about the ring,
    We will not miss
To tell each point he nameth with a kiss.
    —Then come on shore,
Where no joy dies till Love hath gotten more.
WILLIAM BROWNE, OF TAVISTOCK (1588–1643)

THE ROSE   198

A rose, as fair as ever saw the North,
Grew in a little garden all alone;
A sweeter flower did Nature ne'er put forth,
Nor fairer garden yet was never known:
The maidens danced about it morn and noon,
And learneèd bards of it their ditties made;
The nimble fairies by the pale-faced moon
Water'd the root and kiss'd her pretty shade.
But well-a-day!—the gardener careless grew;
The maids and fairies both were kept away,
And in a drought the caterpillars threw
Themselves upon the bud and every spray.
  God shield the stock! If heaven send no supplies,
  The fairest blossom of the garden dies.
WILLIAM BROWNE, OF TAVISTOCK (1588–1643)

SONG   199

  For her gait, if she be walking;
  Be she sitting, I desire her
  For her state's sake; and admire her
  For her wit if she be talking;
    Gait and state and wit approve her,
    For which all and each I love her.

  Be she sullen, I commend her
  For a modest. Be she merry,
  For a kind one her prefer I.
  Briefly, everything doth lend her
    So much grace, and so approve her,
    That for everything I love her.
WILLIAM BROWNE, OF TAVISTOCK (1588–1643)

MEMORY   200

So shuts the marigold her leaves
  At the departure of the sun;
So from the honeysuckle sheaves
  The bee goes when the day is done;
So sits the turtle when she is but one,
And so all woe, as I since she is gone.

To some few birds kind Nature hath
  Made all the summer as one day:
Which once enjoy'd, cold winter's wrath
  As night they sleeping pass away.
Those happy creatures are, that know not yet
The pain to be deprived or to forget.

I oft have heard men say there be
  Some that with confidence profess
The helpful Art of Memory:
  But could they teach Forgetfulness,
I'd learn; and try what further art could do
To make me love her and forget her too.
              WILLIAM BROWNE, OF TAVISTOCK (1588–1643)

201 An Epitaph
In Obitum M.S. X° Maij, 1614

May! Be thou never graced with birds that sing,
  Nor Flora's pride!
In thee all flowers and roses spring,
  Mine only died.
              WILLIAM BROWNE, OF TAVISTOCK (1588–1643)

202 On the Countess Dowager of Pembroke
An Epitaph

Underneath this sable herse
Lies the subject of all verse:
Sidney's sister, Pembroke's mother:
Death, ere thou hast slain another
Fair and learn'd and good as she,
Time shall throw a dart at thee.
              WILLIAM BROWNE, OF TAVISTOCK (1588–1643)

Robert Herrick
1591-1674

203   To the Virgins, to make much of Time

Gather ye rosebuds while ye may,
  Old Time is still a-flying:
And this same flower that smiles to-day
  To-morrow will be dying.

The glorious lamp of heaven, the sun,
  The higher he's a-getting,
The sooner will his race be run,
  And nearer he's to setting.

That age is best which is the first,
  When youth and blood are warmer;
But being spent, the worse, and worst
  Times still succeed the former.

Then be not coy, but use your time,
  And while ye may, go marry:
For having lost but once your prime,
  You may for ever tarry.
                              Robert Herrick (1591–1674)

204   To the Western Wind

Sweet western wind, whose luck it is,
  Made rival with the air,
To give Perenna's lip a kiss,
  And fan her wanton hair:

Bring me but one, I'll promise thee,
  Instead of common showers,
Thy wings shall be embalm'd by me,
  And all beset with flowers.
                              Robert Herrick (1591–1674)

205   To Electra

I dare not ask a kiss,
  I dare not beg a smile,
Lest having that, or this,
  I might grow proud the while.

No, no, the utmost share
  Of my desire shall be
Only to kiss that air
  That lately kissèd thee.
                              Robert Herrick (1591–1674)

206   To Violets

Welcome, maids of honour!
    You do bring
    In the spring,
And wait upon her.

She has virgins many,
    Fresh and fair;
    Yet you are
More sweet than any.

You're the maiden posies,
   And so graced
   To be placed
'Fore damask roses.

Yet, though thus respected,
   By-and-by
   Ye do lie,
Poor girls, neglected.
ROBERT HERRICK (1591–1674)

207. To Daffodils

Fair daffodils, we weep to see
  You haste away so soon;
As yet the early-rising sun
  Has not attain'd his noon.
    Stay, stay
   Until the hasting day
    Has run
   But to the evensong;
And, having pray'd together, we
  Will go with you along.

We have short time to stay, as you,
  We have as short a spring;
As quick a growth to meet decay,
  As you, or anything.
    We die
   As your hours do, and dry
    Away
   Like to the summer's rain;
Or as the pearls of morning's dew,
  Ne'er to be found again.
ROBERT HERRICK (1591–1674)

208. To Blossoms

Fair pledges of a fruitful tree,
  Why do ye fall so fast?
  Your date is not so past
But you may stay yet here awhile
  To blush and gently smile,
    And go at last.

What! were ye born to be
  An hour or half's delight,
  And so to bid good night?
'Twas pity Nature brought you forth
  Merely to show your worth
    And lose you quite.

But you are lovely leaves, where we
　May read how soon things have
　　Their end, though ne'er so brave:
And after they have shown their pride
　Like you awhile, they glide
　　Into the grave.
　　　　　　　　　　　　ROBERT HERRICK (1591–1674)

209　　　　　　　THE PRIMROSE
Ask me why I send you here
This sweet Infanta of the year?
Ask me why I send to you
This primrose, thus bepearl'd with dew?
I will whisper to your ears:—
The sweets of love are mix'd with tears.

Ask me why this flower does show
So yellow-green, and sickly too?
Ask me why the stalk is weak
And bending (yet it doth not break)?
I will answer:—These discover
What fainting hopes are in a lover.
　　　　　　　　　　　　ROBERT HERRICK (1591–1674)

210　　　THE FUNERAL RITES OF THE ROSE
The Rose was sick and smiling died;
And, being to be sanctified,
About the bed there sighing stood
The sweet and flowery sisterhood:
Some hung the head, while some did bring,
To wash her, water from the spring;
Some laid her forth, while others wept,
But all a solemn fast there kept:
The holy sisters, some among,
The sacred dirge and trental sung.
But ah! what sweet smelt everywhere,
As Heaven had spent all perfumes there.
At last, when prayers for the dead
And rites were all accomplished,
They, weeping, spread a lawny loom,
And closed her up as in a tomb.
　　　　　　　　　　　　ROBERT HERRICK (1591–1674)

　trental: *services for the dead, of thirty masses*

211　　　　　　　CHERRY-RIPE
Cherry-Ripe, ripe, ripe, I cry,
Full and fair ones; come and buy.
If so be you ask me where
They do grow, I answer: There
Where my Julia's lips do smile;
There's the land, or cherry-isle,
Whose plantations fully show
All the year where cherries grow.
　　　　　　　　　　　　ROBERT HERRICK (1591–1674)

A Meditation for his Mistress 212

You are a tulip seen to-day,
But, dearest, of so short a stay
That where you grew scarce man can say.

You are a lovely July-flower,
Yet one rude wind or ruffling shower
Will force you hence, and in an hour.

You are a sparkling rose i' th' bud,
Yet lost ere that chaste flesh and blood
Can show where you or grew or stood.

You are a full-spread, fair-set vine,
And can with tendrils love entwine,
Yet dried ere you distil your wine.

You are like balm enclosèd well
In amber or some crystal shell,
Yet lost ere you transfuse your smell.

You are a dainty violet,
Yet wither'd ere you can be set
Within the virgin's coronet.

You are the queen all flowers among;
But die you must, fair maid, ere long,
As he, the maker of this song.

ROBERT HERRICK (1591–1674)

Delight in Disorder 213

A sweet disorder in the dress
Kindles in clothes a wantonness:
A lawn about the shoulders thrown
Into a fine distraction:
An erring lace, which here and there
Enthrals the crimson stomacher:
A cuff neglectful, and thereby
Ribbands to flow confusedly:
A winning wave, deserving note,
In the tempestuous petticoat:
A careless shoe-string, in whose tie
I see a wild civility:
Do more bewitch me than when art
Is too precise in every part.

ROBERT HERRICK (1591–1674)

Upon Julia's Clothes 214

Whenas in silks my Julia goes,
Then, then, methinks, how sweetly flows
The liquefaction of her clothes!

Next, when I cast mine eyes and see
That brave vibration each way free,
—O how that glittering taketh me!

ROBERT HERRICK (1591–1674)

215   The Bracelet: To Julia

Why I tie about thy wrist,
Julia, this silken twist;
For what other reason is 't
But to show thee how, in part,
Thou my pretty captive art?
But thy bond-slave is my heart:
'Tis but silk that bindeth thee,
Knap the thread and thou art free;
But 'tis otherwise with me:
—I am bound and fast bound, so
That from thee I cannot go;
If I could, I would not so.

                       Robert Herrick (1591–1674)

216   To Daisies, not to Shut So Soon

Shut not so soon; the dull-eyed night
  Has not as yet begun
To make a seizure on the light,
  Or to seal up the sun.

No marigolds yet closèd are,
  No shadows great appear;
Nor doth the early shepherd's star
  Shine like a spangle here.

Stay but till my Julia close
  Her life-begetting eye,
And let the whole world then dispose
  Itself to live or die.

                       Robert Herrick (1591–1674)

217   The Night-piece: To Julia

Her eyes the glow-worm lend thee,
The shooting stars attend thee;
  And the elves also,
  Whose little eyes glow
Like the sparks of fire, befriend thee.

No Will-o'-the-wisp mislight thee,
Nor snake or slow-worm bite thee;
  But on, on thy way
  Not making a stay,
Since ghost there's none to affright thee.

Let not the dark thee cumber:
What though the moon does slumber?
  The stars of the night
  Will lend thee their light
Like tapers clear without number.

Then, Julia, let me woo thee,
Thus, thus to come unto me;
   And when I shall meet
   Thy silv'ry feet,
My soul I'll pour into thee.

ROBERT HERRICK (1591–1674)

To Music, to Becalm his Fever   218
Charm me asleep, and melt me so
  With thy delicious numbers,
That, being ravish'd, hence I go
  Away in easy slumbers.
    Ease my sick head,
    And make my bed,
Thou power that canst sever
    From me this ill,
    And quickly still,
   Though thou not kill
    My fever.

Thou sweetly canst convert the same
  From a consuming fire
Into a gentle licking flame,
  And make it thus expire.
    Then make me weep
    My pains asleep;
And give me such reposes
    That I, poor I,
    May think thereby
   I live and die
    'Mongst roses.

Fall on me like the silent dew,
  Or like those maiden showers
Which, by the peep of day, do strew
  A baptim o'er the flowers.
    Melt, melt my pains
    With thy soft strains;
That, having ease me given,
    With full delight
    I leave this light,
   And take my flight
    For Heaven.

ROBERT HERRICK (1591–1674)

To Dianeme   219
Sweet, be not proud of those two eyes
Which starlike sparkle in their skies;
Nor be you proud that you can see
All hearts your captives, yours yet free;

Be you not proud of that rich hair
Which wantons with the love-sick air;
Whenas that ruby which you wear,
Sunk from the tip of your soft ear,
Will last to be a precious stone
When all your world of beauty's gone.

ROBERT HERRICK (1591–1674)

220   TO ŒNONE

What conscience, say, is it in thee,
  When I a heart had one,
To take away that heart from me,
  And to retain thy own?

For shame or pity now incline
  To play a loving part;
Either to send me kindly thine,
  Or give me back my heart.

Covet not both; but if thou dost
  Resolve to part with neither,
Why, yet to show that thou art just,
  Take me and mine together!

ROBERT HERRICK (1591–1674)

221   TO ANTHEA, WHO MAY COMMAND HIM ANYTHING

Bid me to live, and I will live
  Thy Protestant to be;
Or bid me love, and I will give
  A loving heart to thee.

A heart as soft, a heart as kind,
  A heart as sound and free
As in the whole world thou canst find,
  That heart I'll give to thee.

Bid that heart stay, and it will stay
  To honour thy decree:
Or bid it languish quite away,
  And't shall do so for thee.

Bid me to weep, and I will weep
  While I have eyes to see:
And, having none, yet will I keep
  A heart to weep for thee.

Bid me despair, and I'll despair
  Under that cypress-tree:
Or bid me die, and I will dare
  E'en death to die for thee.

Thou art my life, my love my heart,
  The very eyes of me:
And hast command of every part
  To live and die for thee.

ROBERT HERRICK (1591–1674)

To the Willow-tree 222

Thou art to all lost love the best,
  The only true plant found,
Wherewith young men and maids distrest,
  And left of love, are crown'd.

When once the lover's rose is dead,
  Or laid aside forlorn:
Then willow-garlands 'bout the head
  Bedew'd with tears are worn.

When with neglect, the lovers' bane,
  Poor maids rewarded be
For their love lost, their only gain
  Is but a wreath from thee.

And underneath thy cooling shade,
  When weary of the light,
The love-spent youth and love-sick maid
  Come to weep out the night.

Robert Herrick (1591–1674)

The Mad Maid's Song 223

Good-morrow to the day so fair,
  Good-morning, sir, to you;
Good-morrow to mine own torn hair
  Bedabbled with the dew.

Good-morning to this primrose too,
  Good-morrow to each maid
That will with flowers the tomb bestrew
  Wherein my love is laid.

Ah! woe is me, woe, woe is me!
  Alack and well-a-day!
For pity, sir, find out that bee
  Which bore my love away.

I'll seek him in your bonnet brave,
  I'll seek him in your eyes;
Nay, now I think they've made his grave
  I' th' bed of strawberries.

I'll seek him there; I know ere this
  The cold, cold earth doth shake him;
But I will go, or send a kiss
  By you, sir, to awake him.

Pray hurt him not; though he be dead,
  He knows well who do love him,
And who with green turfs rear his head,
  And who do rudely move him.

He's soft and tender (pray take heed);
  With bands of cowslips bind him,
And bring him home—but 'tis decreed
  That I shall never find him!
                                    ROBERT HERRICK (1591–1674)

224   COMFORT TO A YOUTH THAT HAD LOST HIS LOVE

What needs complaints,
When she a place
Has with the race
    Of saints?

In endless mirth
She thinks not on
What's said or done
    In Earth.

She sees no tears,
Or any tone
Of thy deep groan
    She hears:

Nor does she mind
Or think on't now
That ever thou
    Wast kind;

But changed above,
She likes not there,
As she did here,
    Thy love.

Forbear therefore,
And lull asleep
Thy woes, and weep
    No more.
                                    ROBERT HERRICK (1591–1674)

225   TO MEADOWS

Ye have been fresh and green,
  Ye have been fill'd with flowers,
And ye the walks have been
  Where maids have spent their hours.

You have beheld how they
  With wicker arks did come
To kiss and bear away
  The richer cowslips home.

You've heard them sweetly sing,
  And seen them in a round:
Each virgin like a spring,
  With honeysuckles crown'd.

But now we see none here
  Whose silv'ry feet did tread
And with dishevell'd hair
  Adorn'd this smoother mead.

Like unthrifts, having spent
  Your stock and needy grown,
You're left here to lament
  Your poor estates, alone.

ROBERT HERRICK (1591–1674)

A Child's Grace 226

Here a little child I stand
Heaving up my either hand;
Cold as paddocks though they be,
Here I lift them up to Thee,
For a benison to fall
On our meat and on us all. Amen.

ROBERT HERRICK (1591–1674)

paddocks: *frogs*

An Epitaph upon a Child that Died 227

Here she lies, a pretty bud,
Lately made of flesh and blood:
Who as soon fell fast asleep
As her little eyes did peep.
Give her strewings, but not stir
The earth that lightly covers her.

ROBERT HERRICK (1591–1674)

His Winding-sheet 228

Come thou, who are the wine and wit
  Of all I've writ:
The grace, the glory, and the best
  Piece of the rest.
Thou art of what I did intend
  The all and end;
And what was made, was made to meet
  Thee, thee, my sheet.
Come then and be to my chaste side
  Both bed and bride:
We two, as reliques left, will have
  Once rest, one grave:
And hugging close, we will not fear
  Lust entering here:
Where all desires are dead and cold
  As is the mould;
And all affections are forgot,
  Or trouble not.
Here, here, the slaves and prisoners be
  From shackles free:
And weeping widows long oppress'd
  Do here find rest.
The wrongèd client ends his laws
  Here, and his cause.

Here those long suits of Chancery lie
    Quiet, or die:
And all Star-Chamber bills do cease
    Or hold their peace.
Here needs no Court for our Request
    Where all are best,
All wise, all equal, and all just
    Alike i' th' dust.
Nor need we here to fear the frown
    Of court or crown:
Where fortune bears no sway o'er things,
    There all are kings.
In this securer place we'll keep
    As lull'd asleep;
Or for a little time we'll lie
    As robes laid by;
To be another day re-worn,
    Turn'd, but not torn:
Or like old testaments engross'd,
    Lock'd up, not lost.
And for a while lie here conceal'd,
    To be reveal'd
Next at the great Platonick year,
    And then meet here.
                         ROBERT HERRICK (1591–1674)

Platonick year: *when the revolutions of sun, moon, and planets start anew.*

229   LITANY TO THE HOLY SPIRIT
In the hour of my distress,
When temptations me oppress,
And when I my sins confess,
    Sweet Spirit, comfort me!

When I lie within my bed,
Sick in heart and sick in head,
And with doubts discomforted,
    Sweet Spirit, comfort me!

When the house doth sigh and weep,
And the world is drown'd in sleep,
Yet mine eyes the watch do keep,
    Sweet Spirit, comfort me!

When the passing bell doth toll,
And the Furies in a shoal
Come to fright a parting soul,
    Sweet Spirit, comfort me!

When the tapers now burn blue,
And the comforters are few,
And that number more than true,
    Sweet Spirit, comfort me!

When the priest his last hath pray'd,
And I nod to what is said,
'Cause my speech is now decay'd,
    Sweet Spirit, comfort me!

When, God knows, I'm toss'd about
Either with despair or doubt;
Yet before the glass be out,
    Sweet Spirit, comfort me!

When the tempter me pursu'th
With the sins of all my youth,
And half damns me with untruth,
    Sweet Spirit, comfort me!

When the flames and hellish cries
Fright mine ears and fright mine eyes,
And all terrors me surprise,
    Sweet Spirit, comfort me!

When the Judgment is reveal'd,
And that open'd which was seal'd,
When to Thee I have appeal'd,
    Sweet Spirit, comfort me!
ROBERT HERRICK (1591–1674)

A DIVINE RAPTURE   230

E'en like two little bank-dividing brooks,
  That wash the pebbles with their wanton streams,
And having ranged and search'd a thousand nooks,
  Meet both at length in silver-breasted Thames,
    Where in a greater current they conjoin:
So I my Best-belovèd's am; so He is mine.

E'en so we met; and after long pursuit,
  E'en so we joined; we both became entire;
No need for either to renew a suit,
  For I was flax, and He was flames of fire:
    Our firm-united souls did more than twine;
So I my Best-belovèd's am; so He is mine.

If all those glittering Monarchs, that command
  The servile quarters of this earthly ball,
Should tender in exchange their shares of land,
  I would not change my fortunes for them all:
    Their wealth is but a counter to my coin:
The world's but theirs; but my Belovèd's mine.
FRANCIS QUARLES (1592–1644)

RESPICE FINEM   231
AN EPIGRAM

My soul, sit thou a patient looker-on;
Judge not the play before the play is done:
Her plot hath many changes; every day
Speaks a new scene; the last act crowns the play.
FRANCIS QUARLES (1592–1644)

232   A Contemplation upon Flowers

Brave flowers—that I could gallant it like you,
    And be as little vain!
You come abroad, and make a harmless show,
    And to your beds of earth again.
You are not proud: you know your birth:
For your embroider'd garments are from earth.

You do obey your months and times, but I
    Would have it ever Spring:
My fate would know no Winter, never die,
    Nor think of such a thing.
O that I could my bed of earth but view
And smile, and look as cheerfully as you!

O teach me to see Death and not to fear,
    But rather to take truce!
How often have I seen you at a bier,
    And there look fresh and spruce!
You fragrant flowers! then teach me, that my breath
Like yours may sweeten and perfume my death.
        Henry King, Bishop of Chichester (1592–1669)

233   A Renunciation

We, that did nothing study but the way
To love each other, with which thoughts the day
Rose with delight to us and with them set,
Must learn the hateful art, how to forget.
We, that did nothing wish that Heaven could give
Beyond ourselves, nor did desire to live
Beyond that wish, all these now cancel must,
As if not writ in faith, but words and dust.
Yet witness those clear vows which lovers make,
Witness the chaste desires that never brake
Into unruly heats; witness that breast
Which in thy bosom anchor'd his whole rest—
'Tis no default in us: I dare acquite
Thy maiden faith, thy purpose fair and white
As thy pure self. Cross planets did envy
Us to each other, and Heaven did untie
Faster than vows could bind. Oh, that the stars,
When lovers meet, should stand opposed in wars!

Since then some higher Destinies command,
Let us not strive, nor labour to withstand
What is past help. The longest date of grief
Can never yield a hope of our relief:
Fold back our arms; take home our fruitless loves,
That must new fortunes try, like turtle-doves
Dislodgèd from their haunts. We must in tears
Unwind a love knit up in many years.

In this last kiss I here surrender thee
Back to thyself.—So, thou again art free:
Thou in another, sad as that, resend
The truest heart that lover e'er did lend.
Now turn from each: so fare our sever'd hearts
As the divorced soul from her body parts.
                    HENRY KING, BISHOP OF CHICHESTER (1592–1669)

EXEQUY ON HIS WIFE   234
Accept, thou shrine of my dead saint,
Instead of dirges this complaint;
And for sweet flowers to crown thy herse
Receive a strew of weeping verse
From thy grieved friend, whom thou might'st see
Quite melted into tears for thee.
  Dear loss! since thy untimely fate,
My task hath been to meditate
On thee, on thee! Thou art the book,
The library whereon I look,
Tho' almost blind. For thee, loved clay,
I languish out, not live, the day....
Thou hast benighted me; thy set
This eve of blackness did beget,
Who wast my day (tho' overcast
Before thou hadst thy noontide past):
And I remember must in tears
Thou scarce hadst seen so many years
As day tells hours. By thy clear sun
My love and fortune first did run;
But thou wilt never more appear
Folded within my hemisphere,
Since both thy light and motion,
Like a fled star, is fall'n and gone,
And 'twixt me and my soul's dear wish
The earth now interposed is....
  I could allow thee for a time
To darken me and my sad clime;
Were it a month, a year, or ten,
I would thy exile live till then,
And all that space my mirth adjourn—
So thou wouldst promise to return,
And putting off thy ashy shroud
At length disperse this sorrow's cloud.
  But woe is me! the longest date
Too narrow is to calculate
These empty hopes: never shall I
Be so much blest as to descry
A glimpse of thee, till that day come
Which shall the earth to cinders doom,
And a fierce fever must calcine
The body of this world—like thine,
My little world! That fit of fire
Once off, our bodies shall aspire

To our souls' bliss: then we shall rise
And view ourselves with clearer eyes
In that calm region where no night
Can hide us from each other's sight.
   Meantime thou hast her, earth: much good
May my harm do thee! Since it stood
With Heaven's will I might not call
Her longer mine, I give thee all
My short-lived right and interest
In her whom living I loved best.
Be kind to her, and prithee look
Thou write into thy Doomsday book
Each parcel of this rarity
Which in thy casket shrined doth lie,
As thou wilt answer Him that lent—
Not gave—thee my dear monument.
So close the ground, and 'bout her shade
Black curtains draw: my bride is laid.
   Sleep on, my Love, in thy cold bed
Never to be disquieted!
My last good-night! Thou wilt not wake
Till I thy fate shall overtake:
Till age, or grief, or sickness must
Marry my body to that dust
It so much loves; and fill the room
My heart keeps empty in thy tomb.
Stay for me there: I will not fail
To meet thee in that hollow vale.
And think not much of my delay:
I am already on the way,
And follow thee with all the speed
Desire can make, or sorrows breed.
Each minute is a short degree
And every hour a step towards thee....
   'Tis true—with shame and grief I yield—
Thou, like the van, first took'st the field;
And gotten hast the victory
In thus adventuring to die
Before me, whose more years might crave
A just precedence in the grave.
But hark! my pulse, like a soft drum,
Beats my approach, tells thee I come;
And slow howe'er my marches be
I shall at last sit down by thee.
   The thought of this bids me go on
And wait my dissolution
With hope and comfort. Dear—forgive
The crime—I am content to live
Divided, with but half a heart,
Till we shall meet and never part.

                HENRY KING, BISHOP OF CHICHESTER (1592–1669)

Virtue 235

Sweet day, so cool, so calm, so bright!
The bridal of the earth and sky—
The dew shall weep thy fall to-night;
    For thou must die.

Sweet rose, whose hue angry and brave
Bids the rash gazer wipe his eye,
Thy root is ever in its grave,
    And thou must die.

Sweet spring, full of sweet days and roses,
A box where sweets compacted lie,
My music shows ye have your closes,
    And all must die.

Only a sweet and virtuous soul,
Like season'd timber, never gives;
But though the whole world turn to coal,
    Then chiefly lives.

GEORGE HERBERT (1593–1632)

Easter 236

I got me flowers to straw Thy way,
    I got me boughs off many a tree;
But Thou wast up by break of day,
    And brought'st Thy sweets along with Thee.

Yet though my flowers be lost, they say
    A heart can never come too late;
Teach it to sing Thy praise this day,
    And then this day my life shall date.

GEORGE HERBERT (1593–1632)

Discipline 237

Throw away Thy rod,
Throw away Thy wrath;
    O my God,
Take the gentle path!

For my heart's desire
Unto Thine is bent:
    I aspire
To a full consent.

Not a word or look
I affect to own,
    But by book,
And Thy Book alone.

Though I fail, I weep;
Though I halt in pace,
    Yet I creep
To the throne of grace.

> Then let wrath remove;
> Love will do the deed;
> > For with love
> Stony hearts will bleed.
>
> Love is swift of foot;
> Love's a man of war,
> > And can shoot,
> And can hit from far.
>
> Who can 'scape his bow?
> That which wrought on Thee,
> > Brought Thee low,
> Needs must work on me.
>
> Throw away Thy rod;
> Though man frailties hath,
> > Thou art God:
> Throw away Thy wrath!
>
> GEORGE HERBERT (1593–1632)

238   A DIALOGUE

Man.
> Sweetest Saviour, if my soul
> > Were but worth the having,
> Quickly should I then control
> > Any thought of waving.
> But when all my care and pains
> Cannot give the name of gains
> To Thy wretch so full of stains,
> What delight or hope remains?

Saviour.
> What, child, is the balance thine,
> > Thine the poise and measure?
> If I say, "Thou shalt be Mine,"
> > Finger not My treasure.
> What the gains in having thee
> Do amount to, only He
> Who for man was sold can see;
> That transferr'd th' accounts to Me.

Man.
> But as I can see no merit
> > Leading to this favour,
> So the way to fit me for it
> > Is beyond my savour.
> As the reason, then, is Thine,
> So the way is none of mine;
> I disclaim the whole design;
> Sin disclaims and I resign.

Saviour.
> That is all: if that I could
> > Get without repining;
> And My clay, My creature, would

　　　　　　Follow My resigning;
　　　　　That as I did freely part
　　　　　With My glory and desert,
　　　　　Left all joys to feel all smart—

Man.　　　Ah, no more! Thou break'st my heart!
　　　　　　　　　　　　GEORGE HERBERT (1593–1632)

savour: *savoir, knowing*

THE PULLEY　　　　　　　　　　　239
　　When God at first made Man,
　　　Having a glass of blessings standing by—
　Let us (said He) pour on him all we can;
　Let the world's riches, which dispersèd lie,
　　　Contract into a span.

　　So strength first made a way,
　Then beauty flow'd, then wisdom, honour, pleasure:
　When almost all was out, God made a stay,
　Perceiving that, alone of all His treasure,
　　　Rest in the bottom lay.

　　For if I should (said He)
　Bestow this jewel also on My creature,
　He would adore My gifts instead of Me,
　And rest in Nature, not the God of Nature:
　　　So both should losers be.

　　Yet let him keep the rest,
　But keep them with repining restlessness;
　Let him be rich and weary, that at least,
　If goodness lead him not, yet weariness
　　　May toss him to My breast.
　　　　　　　　　　　GEORGE HERBERT (1593–1632)

LOVE　　　　　　　　　　　　240
Love bade me welcome; yet my soul drew back,
　　Guilty of dust and sin.
But quick-eyed Love, observing me grow slack
　　From my first entrance in,
Drew nearer to me, sweetly questioning
　　If I lack'd anything.

"A guest," I answer'd, "worthy to be here:"
　　Love said, "You shall be he."
"I, the unkind, ungrateful? Ah, my dear,
　　I cannot look on Thee."
Love took my hand and smiling did reply,
　　"Who made the eyes but I?"

"Truth, Lord; but I have marr'd them: let my shame
    Go where it doth deserve."
"And know you not," says Love, "Who bore the blame?"
    "My dear, then I will serve."
"You must sit down," says Love, "and taste my meat."
    So I did sit and eat.

GEORGE HERBERT (1593–1632)

241   A Hymn

O fly, my Soul! What hangs upon
    Thy drooping wings,
    And weighs them down
With love of gaudy mortal things?

The Sun is now i' the east: each shade
    As he doth rise
    Is shorter made,
That earth may lessen to our eyes.

O be not careless then and play
    Until the Star of Peace
Hide all his beams in dark recess!
Poor pilgrims needs must lose their way,
When all the shadows do increase.

JAMES SHIRLEY (1596–1666)

242   Death the Leveller

The glories of our blood and state
  Are shadows, not substantial things;
There is no armour against Fate;
  Death lays his icy hand on kings:
    Sceptre and Crown
    Must tumble down,
  And in the dust be equal made
With the poor crookèd scythe and spade.

Some men with swords may reap the field,
  And plant fresh laurels where they kill:
But their strong nerves at last must yield;
  They tame but one another still:
    Early or late
    They stoop to fate,
And must give up their murmuring breath
When they, pale captives, creep to death.

The garlands wither on your brow,
  Then boast no more your mighty deeds!
Upon Death's purple altar now
  See where the victor-victim bleeds.
    Your heads must come
    To the cold tomb:
Only the actions of the just
Smell sweet and blossom in their dust.

JAMES SHIRLEY (1596–1666)

Song 243

Ask me no more where Jove bestows,
When June is past, the fading rose;
For in your beauty's orient deep
These flowers, as in their causes, sleep.

Ask me no more whither do stray
The golden atoms of the day;
For in pure love heaven did prepare
Those powders to enrich your hair.

Ask me no more whither doth haste
The nightingale when May is past;
For in your sweet dividing throat
She winters and keeps warm her note.

Ask me no more where those stars 'light
That downwards fall in dead of night;
For in your eyes they sit, and there
Fixed become as in their sphere.

Ask me no more if east or west
The Phœnix builds her spicy nest;
For unto you at last she flies,
And in your fragrant bosom dies.

THOMAS CAREW (1595?–1639?)

Persuasions to Joy: a Song 244

If the quick spirits in your eye
Now languish and anon must die;
If every sweet and every grace
Must fly from that forsaken face;
    Then, Celia, let us reap our joys
    Ere Time such goodly fruit destroys.

Or if that golden fleece must grow
For ever free from aged snow;
If those bright suns must know no shade,
Nor your fresh beauties ever fade;
    Then fear not, Celia, to bestow
    What, still being gather'd, still must grow.

Thus either Time his sickle brings
In vain, or else in vain his wings.

THOMAS CAREW (1595?–1639?)

To His Inconstant Mistress 245

When thou, poor Excommunicate
  From all the joys of Love, shalt see
The full reward and glorious fate
  Which my strong faith shall purchase me,
  Then curse thine own inconstancy!

A fairer hand than thine shall cure
  That heart which thy false oaths did wound;
And to my soul a soul more pure
  Than thine shall by Love's hand be bound,
  And both with equal glory crown'd.

Then shalt thou weep, entreat, complain
  To Love, as I did once to thee;
When all thy tears shall be as vain
  As mine were then: for thou shalt be
  Damn'd for thy false apostasy.
                                THOMAS CAREW (1595?–1639?)

246   THE UNFADING BEAUTY
He that loves a rosy cheek,
  Or a coral lip admires,
Or from star-like eyes doth seek
  Fuel to maintain his fires:
As old Time makes these decay,
So his flames must waste away.

But a smooth and steadfast mind,
  Gentle thoughts and calm desires,
Hearts with equal love combined,
  Kindle never-dying fires.
Where these are not, I despise
Lovely cheeks or lips or eyes.
                                THOMAS CAREW (1595?–1639?)

247   INGRATEFUL BEAUTY THREATENED
Know, Celia, since thou art so proud,
  'Twas I that gave thee thy renown.
Thou hadst in the forgotten crowd
  Of common beauties lived unknown,
  Had not my verse extoll'd thy name,
  And with it imp'd the wings of Fame.

That killing power is none of thine;
  I gave it to thy voice and eyes;
Thy sweets, thy graces, all are mine;
  Thou art my star, shin'st in my skies;
  Then dart not from thy borrow'd sphere
  Lightning on him that fix'd thee there.

Tempt me with such affrights no more,
  Lest what I made I uncreate;
Let fools thy mystic form adore,
  I know thee in thy mortal state.
  Wise poets, that wrapt Truth in tales,
  Knew her themselves through all her veils.
                                THOMAS CAREW (1595?–1639?)

imp'd: *grafted with new feathers*

ON THE LADY MARY VILLIERS 248
AN EPITAPH

The Lady Mary Villiers lies
Under this stone; with weeping eyes
The parents that first gave her birth,
And their sad friends, laid her in earth.
If any of them, Reader, were
Known unto thee, shed a tear;
Or if thyself possess a gem
As dear to thee, as this to them,
Though a stranger to this place,
Bewail in theirs thine own hard case:
  For thou perhaps at thy return
  May'st find thy Darling in an urn.

THOMAS CAREW (1595?–1639?)

AN EPITAPH 249

This little vault, this narrow room,
Of Love and Beauty is the tomb;
The dawning beam, that 'gan to clear
Our clouded sky, lies darken'd here,
For ever set to us: by Death
Sent to enflame the World Beneath.
'Twas but a bud, yet did contain
More sweetness than shall spring again;
A budding Star, that might have grown
Into a Sun when it had blown.
This hopeful Beauty did create
New life in Love's declining state;
But now his empire ends, and we
From fire and wounding darts are free;
  His brand, his bow, let no man fear:
  The flames, the arrows, all lie here.

THOMAS CAREW (1595?–1639?)

DIAPHENIA 250

Diaphenia like the daffadowndilly,
  White as the sun, fair as the lily,
Heigh ho, how do I love thee!
  I do love thee as my lambs
  Are belovèd of their dams;
How blest were I if thou would'st prove me.

Diaphenia like the spreading roses,
  That in thy sweets all sweets encloses,
Fair sweet, how do I love thee!
  I do love thee as each flower
  Loves the sun's life-giving power;
For dead, thy breath to life might move me.

Diaphenia like to all things blessèd
When all thy praises are expressèd,
Dear joy, how do I love thee!
  As the birds do love the spring,
  Or the bees their careful king:
Then in requite, sweet virgin, love me!
HENRY CONSTABLE (1562–1613)

251   TO AURORA
O if thou knew'st how thou thyself does harm,
And dost prejudge thy bliss, and spoil thy rest;
Then thou would'st melt the ice out of thy breast
And thy relenting heart would kindly warm.

O if thy pride did not our joys controul,
What world of loving wonders should'st thou see!
For if I saw thee once transform'd in me,
Then in thy bosom I would pour my soul;

Then all my thoughts should in thy visage shine,
And if that aught mischanced thou should'st not moan
Nor bear the burthen of thy griefs alone;
No, I would have my share in what were thine:

And whilst we thus should make our sorrows one,
This happy harmony would make them none.
WILLIAM ALEXANDER, EARL OF STIRLING (1567–1640)

252   CARE-CHARMER SLEEP
Care-charmer Sleep, son of the sable Night,
Brother to Death, in silent darkness born,
Relieve my anguish, and restore the light;
With dark forgetting of my care return.

And let the day be time enough to mourn
The shipwreck of my ill adventured youth:
Let waking eyes suffice to wail their scorn,
Without the torment of the night's untruth.

Cease, dreams, the images of day-desires,
To model forth the passions of the morrow;
Never let rising Sun approve you liars
To add more grief to aggravate my sorrow:

Still let me sleep, embracing clouds in vain,
And never wake to feel the day's disdain.
SAMUEL DANIEL (1562–1619)

253   A RENUNCIATION
If women could be fair, and yet not fond,
Or that their love were firm, not fickle still,
I would not marvel that they make men bond
By service long to purchase their good will;
But when I see how frail those creatures are,
I muse that men forget themselves so far.

To mark the choice they make, and how they change,
How oft from Phœbus they do flee to Pan;
Unsettled still, like haggards wild they range,
These gentle birds that fly from man to man;
Who would not scorn and shake them from the fist,
And let them fly, fair fools, which way they list?

Yet for disport we fawn and flatter both,
To pass the time when nothing else can please,
And train them to our lure with subtle oath,
Till, weary of their wiles, ourselves we ease;
And then we say when we their fancy try,
To play with fools, O what a fool was I!
EDWARD VERE, EARL OF OXFORD (1550–1604)

THIS LIFE WHICH SEEMS SO FAIR   254
This Life, which seems so fair,
Is like a bubble blown up in the air
By sporting children's breath,
Who chase it everywhere
And strive who can most motion it bequeath.
And though it sometimes seem of its own might
Like to an eye of gold to be fix'd there,
And firm to hover in that empty height,
That only is because it is so light.
—But in that pomp it doth not long appear;
For when 'tis most admirèd, in a thought,
Because it erst was nought, it turns to nought.
WILLIAM DRUMMOND, OF HAWTHORNDEN (1585–1649)

LIFE   255
The World's a bubble, and the Life of Man
  Less than a span:
In his conception wretched, from the womb
  So to the tomb;
Curst from his cradle, and brought up to years
  With cares and fears.
Who then to frail mortality shall trust,
But limns on water, or but writes in dust.

Yet whilst with sorrow here we live opprest,
  What life is best?
Courts are but only superficial schools
  To dandle fools:
The rural parts are turn'd into a den
  Of savage men:
And where's a city from foul vice so free,
But may be term'd the worst of all the three?

Domestic cares afflict the husband's bed,
  Or pains his head:
Those that live single, take it for a curse,
  Or do things worse:

Some would have children: those that have them, moan
  Or wish them gone:
What is it, then, to have, or have no wife,
But single thraldom, or a double strife?

Our own affections still at home to please
  Is a disease:
To cross the seas to any foreign soil,
  Peril and toil:
Wars with their noise affright us; when they cease,
  We are worse in peace;—
What then remains, but that we still should cry
For being born, or, being born, to die
FRANCIS BACON (1561–1626)

256   THE LESSONS OF NATURE

Of this fair volume which we World do name
If we the sheets and leaves could turn with care,
Of Him who it corrects, and did it frame,
We clear might read the art and wisdom rare:

Find out His power which wildest powers doth tame,
His providence extending everywhere,
His justice which proud rebels doth not spare,
In every page, no period of the same.

But silly we, like foolish children, rest
Well pleased with colour'd vellum, leaves of gold,
Fair dangling ribbands, leaving what is best,
On the great Writer's sense ne'er taking hold;

Or if by chance we stay our minds on aught,
It is some picture on the margin wrought.
WILLIAM DRUMMOND, OF HAWTHORNDEN (1585–1649)

257   DOTH THEN THE WORLD GO THUS?

Doth then the world go thus, doth all thus move?
Is this the justice which on Earth we find?
Is this that firm decree which all doth bind?
Are these your influences, Powers above?

Those souls which vice's moody mists most blind,
Blind Fortune, blindly, most their friend doth prove;
And they who thee, poor idle Virtue! love,
Ply like a feather toss'd by storm and wind.

Ah! if a Providence doth sway this all,
Why should best minds groan under most distress?
Or why should pride humility make thrall,
And injuries the innocent oppress?

Heavens! hinder, stop this fate; or grant a time
When good may have, as well as bad, their prime!
WILLIAM DRUMMOND, OF HAWTHORNDEN (1585–1649)

The Last Conquerer 258

Victorious men of earth, no more
  Proclaim how wide your empires are;
Though you bind-in every shore
  And your triumphs reach as far
    As night and day,
  Yet you, proud monarchs, must obey
And mingle with forgotten ashes, when
Death calls ye to the crowd of common men.

Devouring Famine, Plague, and War,
  Each able to undo mankind,
Death's servile emissaries are;
  Nor to these alone confined,
    He hath at will
  More quaint and subtle ways to kill;
A smile or kiss, as he will use the art,
Shall have the cunning skill to break a heart.

James Shirley (1596–1666)

Love in Thy Youth 259

Love in thy youth, fair maid; be wise
  Old Time will make thee colder,
And though each morning new arise
  Yet we each day grow older.
Thou as heaven art fair and young,
  Thine eyes like twin stars shining:
But ere another day be sprung,
  All these will be declining;
Then winter comes with all his fears,
  And all thy sweets shall borrow;
Too late then wilt thou shower thy tears,
  And I too late shall sorrow.

Walter Porter (1595?–1659)

Content 260

Sweet are the thoughts that savor of content;
  The quiet mind is richer than a crown;
Sweet are the nights in careless slumber spent,—
  The poor estate scorns Fortune's angry frown:
Such sweet content, such minds, such sleep, such bliss,
Beggars enjoy, when princes oft do miss.

The homely house that harbors quiet rest,
  The cottage that affords no pride or care,
The mean, that 'grees with country music best,
  The sweet consort of mirth's and music's fare.
Obscurèd life sets down a type of bliss;
A mind content both crown and kingdom is.

Robert Greene (1560–1592)

261   ONE DAY I WROTE HER NAME UPON THE STRAND

[It's is worth comparing this verse to "Her Name" by Walter Savage Landor written approximately 250 years later. – Ed.]

> One day I wrote her name upon the strand,
> But came the waves and washèd it away:
> Again I wrote it with a second hand,
> But came the tide and made my pains his prey.
> Vain man (said she) that dost in vain assay
> A mortal thing so to immortalise;
> For I myself shall like to this decay,
> And eke my name be wipèd out likewise.
> Not so (quod I); let baser things devise
> To die in dust, but you shall live by fame;
> My verse your virtues rare shall eternise,
> And in the heavens write your glorious name:
>   Where, when as Death shall all the world subdue,
>   Our love shall live, and later life renew.
>
>   EDMUND SPENSER (1552–1599)

262   ON PARADISE LOST

[It should comfort modern readers, turning to "Paradise Lost" for the first time, that Milton's own friend and colleague had doubtful expectations of the piece. As Marvell discovered — as will all who make it even five pages into Milton's masterpiece — "Paradise Lost" is, without question, the greatest poem ever written. – Ed.]

> When I beheld the poet blind, yet bold,
> In slender book his vast design unfold,
> Messiah crowned, God's reconciled decree,
> Rebelling angels, the forbidden tree,
> Heaven, hell, earth, chaos, all; the argument
> Held me awhile misdoubting his intent,
> That he would ruin (for I saw him strong)
> The sacred truths to fable and old song,
> (So Samson groped the temple's posts in spite)
> The world o'erwhelming to revenge his sight.
>   Yet as I read, soon growing less severe,
> I liked his project the success did fear;
> Through that wide field how he his way should find,
> O'er which lame faith leads understanding blind;
> Lest he perplexed the things he would explain,
> And what was easy he should render vain.
>   Or if a work so infinite he spanned,
> Jealous I was that some less skilful hand
> (Such as disquiet always what is well,
> And by ill imitating would excel)
> Might hence presume the whole creation's day
> To change in scenes, and show it in a play.
>   Pardon me, mighty poet, nor despise
> My causeless, yet not impious, surmise.

But I am now convinced, and none will dare
Within thy labours to pretend a share.
Thou hast not missed one thought that could be fit,
And all that was improper dost omit;
So that no room is here for writers left,
But to detect their ignorance or theft.
   That majesty which through thy work doth reign
Draws the devout, deterring the profane;
And things divine thou treat'st of in such state
As them preserves, and thee, inviolate.
At once delight and horror on us seize,
Thou sing'st with so much gravity and ease,
And above human flight dost soar aloft,
With plume so strong, so equal, and so soft:
The bird named from that paradise you sing
So never flags, but always keeps on wing.
Where couldst thou words of such a compass find?
Whence furnish such a vast expanse of mind?
Just Heaven thee, like Tiresias, to requite,
Rewards with prophecy thy loss of sight.
   Well mightst thou scorn thy readers to allure
With tinkling rhyme, of thy own sense secure,
While the Town-Bayes writes all the while and spells,
And like a pack-horse tires without his bells.
Their fancies like our bushy points appear:
The poets tag them, we for fashion wear.
I too, transported by the mode, offend,
And while I meant to praise thee, mis-commend;
Thy verse created like thy theme sublime,
In number, weight, and measure, needs not rhyme.
                          ANDREW MARVELL (1621–1678)

A Pedlar   263

Fine knacks for ladies! cheap, choice, brave, and new,
  Good pennyworths—but money cannot move:
I keep a fair but for the Fair to view—
  A beggar may be liberal of love.
Though all my wares be trash, the heart is true,
      The heart is true.

Great gifts are guiles and look for gifts again;
  My trifles come as treasures from my mind:
It is a precious jewel to be plain;
  Sometimes in shell the orient'st pearls we find:—
Of others take a sheaf, of me a grain!
      Of me a grain!
    MISCELLANIES & SONGS BY UNNAMED OR UNCERTAIN AUTHORS (1600)
        from John Dowland's Second Book of Songs or Airs

The Now Jerusalem   264

  Hierusalem, my happy home,
    When shall I come to thee?
  When shall my sorrows have an end,
    Thy joys when shall I see?

O happy harbour of the Saints!
  O sweet and pleasant soil!
In thee no sorrow may be found,
  No grief, no care, no toil.

There lust and lucre cannot dwell,
  There envy bears no sway;
There is no hunger, heat, nor cold,
  But pleasure every way.

Thy walls are made of precious stones,
  Thy bulwarks diamonds square;
Thy gates are of right orient pearl,
  Exceeding rich and rare.

Thy turrets and thy pinnacles
  With carbuncles do shine;
Thy very streets are paved with gold,
  Surpassing clear and fine.

Ah, my sweet home, Hierusalem,
  Would God I were in thee!
Would God my woes were at an end,
  Thy joys that I might see!

Thy gardens and thy gallant walks
  Continually are green;
There grows such sweet and pleasant flowers
  As nowhere else are seen.

Quite through the streets, with silver sound,
  The flood of Life doth flow;
Upon whose banks on every side
  The wood of Life doth grow.

There trees for evermore bear fruit,
  And evermore do spring;
There evermore the angels sit,
  And evermore do sing.

Our Lady sings *Magnificat*
  With tones surpassing sweet;
And all the virgins bear their part,
  Sitting about her feet.

Hierusalem, my happy home,
  Would God I were in thee!
Would God my woes were at an end,
  Thy joys that I might see!

MISCELLANIES & SONGS BY UNNAMED OR UNCERTAIN AUTHORS (1601)
from Song of Mary the Mother of Christ

ICARUS   265

Love wing'd my Hopes and taught me how to fly
Far from base earth, but not to mount too high:
    For true pleasure
    Lives in measure,
    Which if men forsake,
Blinded they into folly run and grief for pleasure take.

But my vain Hopes, proud of their new-taught flight,
Enamour'd sought to woo the sun's fair light,
    Whose rich brightness
    Moved their lightness
    To aspire so high
That all scorch'd and consumed with fire now drown'd in woe they lie.

And none but Love their woeful hap did rue,
For Love did know that their desires were true;
    Though fate frowned,
    And now drowned
    They in sorrow dwell,
It was the purest light of heav'n for whose fair love they fell.

MISCELLANIES & SONGS BY UNNAMED OR UNCERTAIN AUTHORS (1601)
from Robert Jones's Second Book of Songs and Airs

MADRIGAL   266

My Love in her attire doth show her wit,
  It doth so well become her;
For every season she hath dressings fit,
  For Winter, Spring, and Summer.
    No beauty she doth miss
      When all her robes are on:
    But Beauty's self she is
      When all her robes are gone.

MISCELLANIES & SONGS BY UNNAMED OR UNCERTAIN AUTHORS (1602)
from Davison's Poetical Rhapsody

HOW CAN THE HEART FORGET HER?   267

At her fair hands how have I grace entreated
With prayers oft repeated!
Yet still my love is thwarted:
Heart, let her go, for she'll not be converted—
    Say, shall she go?
      O no, no, no, no, no!
She is most fair, though she be marble-hearted.

How often have my sighs declared my anguish,
Wherein I daily languish!
Yet still she doth procure it:
Heart, let her go, for I can not endure it—
    Say, shall she go?
      O no, no, no, no, no!
She gave the wound, and she alone must cure it.

But shall I still a true affection owe her,
Which prayers, sighs, tears do show her,
And shall she still disdain me?
Heart, let her go, if they no grace can gain me—
    Say, shall she go?
    O no, no, no, no, no!
She made me hers, and hers she will retain me.

But if the love that hath and still doth burn me
No love at length return me,
Out of my thoughts I'll set her:
Heart, let her go, O heart I pray thee, let her!
    Say, shall she go?
    O no, no, no, no, no!
Fix'd in the heart, how can the heart forget her?

MISCELLANIES & SONGS BY UNNAMED OR UNCERTAIN AUTHORS (1602)
from Davison's Poetical Rhapsody

268   TEARS

Weep you no more, sad fountains;
  What need you flow so fast?
Look how the snowy mountains
  Heaven's sun doth gently waste!
But my Sun's heavenly eyes
    View not your weeping,
    That now lies sleeping
Softly, now softly lies
    Sleeping.

Sleep is a reconciling,
  A rest that peace begets;
Doth not the sun rise smiling
  When fair at even he sets?
Rest you then, rest, sad eyes!
    Melt not in weeping,
    While she lies sleeping
Softly, now softly lies
    Sleeping.

MISCELLANIES & SONGS BY UNNAMED OR UNCERTAIN AUTHORS (1603)
from John Dowland's Third and Last Book of Songs or Airs

269   MY LADY'S TEARS

  I saw my Lady weep,
And Sorrow proud to be advanced so
In those fair eyes where all perfections keep.
  Her face was full of woe;
But such a woe (believe me) as wins more hearts
Than Mirth can do with her enticing parts.

  Sorrow was there made fair,
And Passion wise; Tears a delightful thing;
Silence beyond all speech, a wisdom rare:
  She made her sighs to sing,
And all things with so sweet a sadness move
As made my heart at once both grieve and love.

  O fairer than aught else
The world can show, leave off in time to grieve!
Enough, enough: your joyful look excels:
  Tears kill the heart, believe.
O strive not to be excellent in woe,
Which only breeds your beauty's overthrow.
MISCELLANIES & SONGS BY UNNAMED OR UNCERTAIN AUTHORS (1603)
  from John Dowland's Third and Last Book of Songs or Airs

SISTER, AWAKE!   270
Sister, awake! close not your eyes!
  The day her light discloses,
And the bright morning doth arise
  Out of her bed of roses.

See the clear sun, the world's bright eye,
  In at our window peeping:
Lo, how he blusheth to espy
  Us idle wenches sleeping!

Therefore awake! make haste, I say,
  And let us, without staying,
All in our gowns of green so gay
  Into the Park a-maying!
MISCELLANIES & SONGS BY UNNAMED OR UNCERTAIN AUTHORS (1604)
  from Thomas Bateson's First Set of English Madrigals

DEVOTION   271
Fain would I change that note
To which fond Love hath charm'd me
Long, long to sing by rote,
Fancying that that harm'd me:
Yet when this thought doth come,
"Love is the perfect sum
  Of all delight,"
I have no other choice
Either for pen or voice
  To sing or write.

O Love! they wrong thee much
That say thy sweet is bitter,
When thy rich fruit is such
As nothing can be sweeter.
Fair house of joy and bliss,
Where truest pleasure is,
  I do adore thee:
I know thee what thou art,
I serve thee with my heart,
  And fall before thee.
MISCELLANIES & SONGS BY UNNAMED OR UNCERTAIN AUTHORS (1605)
  from Captain Tobias Hume's The First Part of Airs, etc.

272   SINCE FIRST I SAW YOUR FACE
Since first I saw your face I resolved to honour and renown ye;
If now I be disdainèd I wish my heart had never known ye.
What? I that loved and you that liked, shall we begin to wrangle?
No, no, no, my heart is fast, and cannot disentangle.

If I admire or praise you too much, that fault you may forgive me;
Or if my hands had stray'd but a touch, then justly might you leave me.
I ask'd you leave, you bade me love; is't now a time to chide me?
No, no, no, I'll love you still what fortune e'er betide me.

The Sun, whose beams most glorious are, rejecteth no beholder,
And your sweet beauty past compare made my poor eyes the bolder:
Where beauty moves and wit delights and signs of kindness bind me,
There, O there! where'er I go I'll leave my heart behind me!
    MISCELLANIES & SONGS BY UNNAMED OR UNCERTAIN AUTHORS (1607)
                from Thomas Ford's Music of Sundry Kinds

273   THERE IS A LADY SWEET AND KIND
There is a Lady sweet and kind,
Was never face so pleased my mind;
I did but see her passing by,
And yet I love her till I die.

Her gesture, motion, and her smiles,
Her wit, her voice my heart beguiles,
Beguiles my heart, I know not why,
And yet I love her till I die.

Cupid is wingèd and doth range,
Her country so my love doth change:
But change she earth, or change she sky,
Yet will I love her till I die.
    MISCELLANIES & SONGS BY UNNAMED OR UNCERTAIN AUTHORS (1607)
                from Thomas Ford's Music of Sundry Kinds

274   LOVE NOT ME FOR COMELY GRACE
Love not me for comely grace,
For my pleasing eye or face,
Nor for any outward part,
No, nor for a constant heart:
    For these may fail or turn to ill,
    So thou and I shall sever:
Keep, therefore, a true woman's eye,
And love me still but know not why—
    So hast thou the same reason still
    To doat upon me ever!
    MISCELLANIES & SONGS BY UNNAMED OR UNCERTAIN AUTHORS (1609)
                from John Wilbye's Second Set of Madrigals

The Wakening 275
On a time the amorous Silvy
Said to her shepherd, "Sweet, how do ye?
Kiss me this once and then God be with ye,
    My sweetest dear!
Kiss me this once and then God be with ye,
For now the morning draweth near."

With that, her fairest bosom showing,
Op'ning her lips, rich perfumes blowing,
She said, "Now kiss me and be going,
    My sweetest dear!
Kiss me this once and then be going,
For now the morning draweth near."

With that the shepherd waked from sleeping,
And spying where the day was peeping,
He said, "Now take my soul in keeping,
    My sweetest dear!
Kiss me and take my soul in keeping,
Since I must go, now day is near."

MISCELLANIES & SONGS BY UNNAMED OR UNCERTAIN AUTHORS (1622)
from John Attye's First Book of Airs

A Dirge 276
Call for the robin-redbreast and the wren,
Since o'er shady groves they hover,
And with leaves and flowers do cover
The friendless bodies of unburied men.
Call unto his funeral dole
The ant, the field-mouse, and the mole,
To rear him hillocks that shall keep him warm,
And (when gay tombs are robb'd) sustain no harm;
But keep the wolf far thence, that's foe to men,
For with his nails he'll dig them up again.
    JOHN WEBSTER (*flor.* 1630)

dole: *lamentation*

The Shrouding of 277
The Duchess of Malfi
Hark! Now everything is still,
The screech-owl and the whistler shrill,
Call upon our dame aloud,
And bid her quickly don her shroud!

Much you had of land and rent;
Your length in clay's now competent:
A long war disturb'd your mind;
Here your perfect peace is sign'd.

Of what is't fools make such vain keeping?
Sin their conception, their birth weeping,
Their life a general mist of error,
Their death a hideous storm of terror.
Strew your hair with powders sweet,
Don clean linen, bathe your feet,

And—the foul fiend more to check—
A crucifix let bless your neck:
'Tis now full tide 'tween night and day;
End your groan and come away.
JOHN WEBSTER (*flor.* 1630)

278   VANITAS VANITATUM

All the flowers of the spring
Meet to perfume our burying;
These have but their growing prime,
And man does flourish but his time:
Survey our progress from our birth—
We are set, we grow, we turn to earth.
Courts adieu, and all delights,
All bewitching appetites!
Sweetest breath and clearest eye
Like perfumes go out and die;
And consequently this is done
As shadows wait upon the sun.
Vain the ambition of kings
Who seek by trophies and dead things
To leave a living name behind,
And weave but nets to catch the wind.
JOHN WEBSTER (*floruit* c. 1630)

279   TIME

Time is the feather'd thing,
    And, whilst I praise
The sparklings of thy looks and call them rays,
    Takes wing,
Leaving behind him as he flies
An unperceivèd dimness in thine eyes.
  His minutes, whilst they're told,
    Do make us old;
And every sand of his fleet glass,
Increasing age as it doth pass,
Insensibly sows wrinkles there
Where flowers and roses do appear.
  Whilst we do speak, our fire
  Doth into ice expire,
    Flames turn to frost;
    And ere we can
Know how our crow turns swan,
  Or how a silver snow
Springs there where jet did grow,
Our fading spring is in dull winter lost.

  Since then the Night hath hurl'd
   Darkness, Love's shade,
  Over its enemy the Day, and made
    The world
  Just such a blind and shapeless thing
As 'twas before light did from darkness spring,
  Let us employ its treasure
  And make shade pleasure:
Let's number out the hours by blisses,
And count the minutes by our kisses;
  Let the heavens new motions feel
  And by our embraces wheel;
  And whilst we try the way
  By which Love doth convey
   Soul unto soul,
   And mingling so
  Makes them such raptures know
  As makes them entranced lie
   In mutual ecstasy,
Let the harmonious spheres in music roll!
JASPER MAYNE (1604–1672)

To Roses in the Bosom of Castara   280

Ye blushing virgins happy are
 In the chaste nunnery of her breasts—
For he'd profane so chaste a fair,
 Whoe'er should call them Cupid's nests.

Transplanted thus how bright ye grow!
 How rich a perfume do ye yield!
In some close garden cowslips so
 Are sweeter than i' th' open field.

In those white cloisters live secure
 From the rude blasts of wanton breath!—
Each hour more innocent and pure,
 Till you shall wither into death.

Then that which living gave you room,
 Your glorious sepulchre shall be.
There wants no marble for a tomb
 Whose breast hath marble been to me.
WILLIAM HABINGTON (1605–1654)

Nox Nocti Indicat Scientiam   281

When I survey the bright
 Celestial sphere;
So rich with jewels hung, that Night
 Doth like an Ethiop bride appear:

My soul her wings doth spread
 And heavenward flies,
Th' Almighty's mysteries to read
 In the large volumes of the skies.

    For the bright firmament
        Shoots forth no flame
So silent, but is eloquent
  In speaking the Creator's name.

    No unregarded star
        Contracts its light
Into so small a character,
  Removed far from our human sight,

    But if we steadfast look
        We shall discern
In it, as in some holy book,
  How man may heavenly knowledge learn.

    It tells the conqueror
        That far-stretch'd power,
Which his proud dangers traffic for,
  Is but the triumph of an hour:

    That from the farthest North,
        Some nation may,
Yet undiscover'd, issue forth,
  And o'er his new-got conquest sway:

    Some nation yet shut in
        With hills of ice
May be let out to scourge his sin,
  Till they shall equal him in vice.

    And then they likewise shall
        Their ruin have;
For as yourselves your empires fall,
  And every kingdom hath a grave.

    Thus those celestial fires,
        Though seeming mute,
The fallacy of our desires
  And all the pride of life confute:—

    For they have watch'd since first
        The World had birth:
And found sin in itself accurst,
  And nothing permanent on Earth.
                WILLIAM HABINGTON (1605–1654)

282   A DEVOUT LOVER

I have a mistress, for perfections rare
In every eye, but in my thoughts most fair.
Like tapers on the altar shine her eyes;
Her breath is the perfume of sacrifice;

And wheresoe'er my fancy would begin,
Still her perfection lets religion in.
We sit and talk, and kiss away the hours
As chastely as the morning dews kiss flowers:
I touch her, like my beads, with devout care,
And come unto my courtship as my prayer.

THOMAS RANDOLPH (1605–1635)

AUBADE 283

The lark now leaves his wat'ry nest,
   And climbing shakes his dewy wings.
He takes this window for the East,
   And to implore your light he sings—
Awake, awake! the morn will never rise
Till she can dress her beauty at your eyes.

The merchant bows unto the seaman's star,
   The ploughman from the sun his season takes,
But still the lover wonders what they are
   Who look for day before his mistress wakes.
Awake, awake! break thro' your veils of lawn!
Then draw your curtains, and begin the dawn!

SIR WILLIAM DAVENANT (1606–1668)

TO A MISTRESS DYING 284

Lover.   Your beauty, ripe and calm and fresh
      As eastern summers are,
   Must now, forsaking time and flesh,
      Add light to some small star.

Philosopher.   Whilst she yet lives, were stars decay'd,
      Their light by hers relief might find;
   But Death will lead her to a shade
      Where Love is cold and Beauty blind.

Lover.   Lovers, whose priests all poets are,
      Think every mistress, when she dies,
   Is changed at least into a star:
      And who dares doubt the poets wise?

Philosopher.   But ask not bodies doom'd to die
      To what abode they go;
   Since Knowledge is but Sorrow's spy,
      It is not safe to know.

SIR WILLIAM DAVENANT (1606–1668)

PRAISE AND PRAYER 285

Praise is devotion fit for mighty minds,
   The diff'ring world's agreeing sacrifice;
Where Heaven divided faiths united finds:
   But Prayer in various discord upward flies.

For Prayer the ocean is where diversely
   Men steer their course, each to a sev'ral coast;
Where all our interests so discordant be
   That half beg winds by which the rest are lost.

By Penitence when we ourselves forsake,
'Tis but in wise design on piteous Heaven;
In Praise we nobly give what God may take,
And are, without a beggar's blush, forgiven.

SIR WILLIAM DAVENANT (1606–1668)

286   ON A GIRDLE

[On the day I met my wife-to-be — that is, the day I discovered "love at first sight" is not merely something poets write — I stumbled upon this poem. And, I knew exactly how the long-departed Waller must have felt. – Ed.]

That which her slender waist confined
Shall now my joyful temples bind;
No monarch but would give his crown
His arms might do what this has done.

It was my Heaven's extremest sphere,
The pale which held that lovely deer:
My joy, my grief, my hope, my love,
Did all within this circle move.

A narrow compass! and yet there
Dwelt all that's good, and all that's fair!
Give me but what this ribband bound,
Take all the rest the sun goes round!

EDMUND WALLER (1606–1687)

287   GO, LOVELY ROSE

Go, lovely Rose—
Tell her that wastes her time and me,
   That now she knows,
When I resemble her to thee,
How sweet and fair she seems to be.

   Tell her that's young,
And shuns to have her graces spied,
   That hadst thou sprung
In deserts where no men abide,
Thou must have uncommended died.

   Small is the worth
Of beauty from the light retired:
   Bid her come forth,
Suffer herself to be desired,
And not blush so to be admired.

   Then die—that she
The common fate of all things rare
   May read in thee;
How small a part of time they share
That are so wondrous sweet and fair!

EDMUND WALLER (1606–1687)

Old Age

The seas are quiet when the winds give o'er;
So calm are we when passions are no more.
For then we know how vain it was to boast
Of fleeting things, so certain to be lost.
Clouds of affection from our younger eyes
Conceal that emptiness which age descries.

The soul's dark cottage, batter'd and decay'd,
Lets in new light through chinks that Time hath made:
Stronger by weakness, wiser men become
As they draw near to their eternal home.
Leaving the old, both worlds at once they view
That stand upon the threshold of the new.

EDMUND WALLER (1606–1687)

Hymn on the Morning of Christ's Nativity   289

It was the Winter wilde,
While the Heav'n-born-childe,
  All meanly wrapt in the rude manger lies;
Nature in aw to him
Had doff't her gawdy trim,
  With her great Master so to sympathize:
It was no season then for her
To wanton with the Sun her lusty Paramour.

Only with speeches fair
She woo's the gentle Air
  To hide her guilty front with innocent Snow,
And on her naked shame,
Pollute with sinfull blame,
  The Saintly Vail of Maiden white to throw,
Confounded, that her Makers eyes
Should look so neer upon her foul deformities.

But he her fears to cease,
Sent down the meek-eyd Peace,
  She crown'd with Olive green, came softly sliding
Down through the turning sphear
His ready Harbinger,
  With Turtle wing the amorous clouds dividing,
And waving wide her mirtle wand,
She strikes a universall Peace through Sea and Land.

No War, or Battails sound
Was heard the World around,
  The idle spear and shield were high up hung;
The hookèd Chariot stood
Unstain'd with hostile blood,
  The Trumpet spake not to the armed throng,
And Kings sate still with awfull eye,
As if they surely knew their sovran Lord was by.

But peacefull was the night
Wherin the Prince of light
  His raign of peace upon the earth began:
The Windes with wonder whist,
Smoothly the waters kist,
  Whispering new joyes to the milde Ocean,
Who now hath quite forgot to rave,
While Birds of Calm sit brooding on the charmeed wave.

The Stars with deep amaze
Stand fixt in stedfast gaze,
  Bending one way their pretious influence,
And will not take their flight,

For all the morning light,
  Or Lucifer that often warn'd them thence;
But in their glimmering Orbs did glow,
Untill their Lord himself bespake, and bid them go.

And though the shady gloom
Had given day her room,
  The Sun himself with-held his wonted speed,
And hid his head for shame,
As his inferiour flame,
  The new enlightn'd world no more should need;
He saw a greater Sun appear
Then his bright Throne, or burning Axletree could bear.

The Shepherds on the Lawn,
Or ere the point of dawn,
  Sate simply chatting in a rustick row;
Full little thought they than,
That the mighty Pan
  Was kindly com to live with them below;
Perhaps their loves, or els their sheep,
Was all that did their silly thoughts so busie keep.

When such musick sweet
Their hearts and ears did greet,
  As never was by mortall finger strook,
Divinely-warbled voice
Answering the stringed noise,
  As all their souls in blisfull rapture took
The Air such pleasure loth to lose,
With thousand echo's still prolongs each heav'nly close.

Nature that heard such sound
Beneath the hollow round
  Of Cynthia's seat, the Airy region thrilling,
Now was almost won
To think her part was don,
  And that her raign had here its last fulfilling;
She knew such harmony alone
Could hold all Heav'n and Earth in happier union.

At last surrounds their sight
A Globe of circular light,
  That with long beams the shame-fac't night array'd,
The helmed Cherubim
And sworded Seraphim,
  Are seen in glittering ranks with wings displaid,
Harping in loud and solemn quire,
With unexpressive notes to Heav'ns new-born Heir.

Such musick (as 'tis said)
Before was never made,
  But when of old the sons of morning sung,
While the Creator Great

His constellations set,
  And the well-ballanc't world on hinges hung,
And cast the dark foundations deep,
And bid the weltring waves their oozy channel keep.

Ring out ye Crystall sphears,
Once bless our human ears,
  (If ye have power to touch our senses so)
And let your silver chime
Move in melodious time;
  And let the Base of Heav'ns deep Organ blow
And with your ninefold harmony
Make up full consort to th'Angelike symphony.

For if such holy Song
Enwrap our fancy long,
  Time will run back, and fetch the age of gold,
And speckl'd vanity
Will sicken soon and die,
  And leprous sin will melt from earthly mould,
And Hell it self will pass away,
And leave her dolorous mansions to the peering day.

Yea Truth, and Justice then
Will down return to men,
  Th'enameld Arras of the Rain-bow wearing,
And Mercy set between,
Thron'd in Celestiall sheen,
  With radiant feet the tissued clouds down stearing,
And Heav'n as at som festivall,
Will open wide the Gates of her high Palace Hall.

But wisest Fate sayes no,
This must not yet be so,
  The Babe lies yet in smiling Infancy,
That on the bitter cross
Must redeem our loss;
  So both himself and us to glorifie:
Yet first to those ychain'd in sleep,
The wakefull trump of doom must thunder through the deep,

With such a horrid clang
As on mount Sinai rang
  While the red fire, and smouldring clouds out brake:
The agèd Earth agast
With terrour of that blast,
  Shall from the surface to the center shake;
When at the worlds last session,
The dreadfull Judge in middle Air shall spread his throne.

And then at last our bliss
Full and perfect is,
  But now begins; for from this happy day
Th'old Dragon under ground

In straiter limits bound,
   Not half so far casts his usurped sway,
And wrath to see his Kingdom fail,
Swindges the scaly Horrour of his foulded tail.

The Oracles are dumm,
No voice or hideous humm
   Runs through the arched roof in words deceiving.
Apollo from his shrine
Can no more divine,
   With hollow shreik the steep of Delphos leaving.
No nightly trance, or breathèd spell,
Inspire's the pale-ey'd Priest from the prophetic cell.

The lonely mountains o're,
And the resounding shore,
   A voice of weeping heard, and loud lament;
From haunted spring, and dale
Edg'd with poplar pale,
   The parting Genius is with sighing sent,
With flowre-inwov'n tresses torn
The Nimphs in twilight shade of tangled thickets mourn.

In consecrated Earth,
And on the holy Hearth,
   The Lars, and Lemures moan with midnight plaint,
In Urns, and Altars round,
A drear, and dying sound
   Affrights the Flamins at their service quaint;
And the chill Marble seems to sweat,
While each peculiar power forgoes his wonted seat

Peor, and Baalim,
Forsake their Temples dim,
   With that twise-batter'd god of Palestine,
And moonèd Ashtaroth,
Heav'ns Queen and Mother both,
   Now sits not girt with Tapers holy shine,
The Libyc Hammon shrinks his horn,
In vain the Tyrian Maids their wounded Thamuz mourn.

And sullen Moloch fled,
Hath left in shadows dred,
   His burning Idol all of blackest hue,
In vain with Cymbals ring,
They call the grisly king,
   In dismall dance about the furnace blue;
The brutish gods of Nile as fast,
Isis and Orus, and the Dog Anubis hast.

Nor is Osiris seen
In Memphian Grove, or Green,
   Trampling the unshowr'd Grasse with lowings loud:
Nor can he be at rest

Within his sacred chest,
   Naught but profoundest Hell can be his shroud,
In vain with Timbrel'd Anthems dark
The sable-stolèd Sorcerers bear his worshipt Ark.

He feels from Juda's Land
The dredded Infants hand,
   The rayes of Bethlehem blind his dusky eyn;
Nor all the gods beside,
Longer dare abide,
   Not Typhon huge ending in snaky twine:
Our Babe to shew his Godhead true,
Can in his swadling bands controul the damned crew.

So when the Sun in bed,
Curtain'd with cloudy red,
   Pillows his chin upon an Orient wave,
The flocking shadows pale,
Troop to th'infernall jail,
   Each fetter'd Ghost slips to his severall grave,
And the yellow-skirted Fayes,
Fly after the Night-steeds, leaving their Moon-lov'd maze.

But see the Virgin blest,
Hath laid her Babe to rest.
   Time is our tedious Song should here have ending,
Heav'ns youngest teemed Star,
Hath fixt her polisht Car,
   Her sleeping Lord with Handmaid Lamp attending:
And all about the Courtly Stable,
Bright-harnest Angels sit in order serviceable.

JOHN MILTON (1608–1674)

ON TIME   290

Fly envious Time, till thou run out thy race,
Call on the lazy leaden-stepping hours,
Whose speed is but the heavy Plummets pace;
And glut thy self with what thy womb devours,
Which is no more then what is false and vain,
And meerly mortal dross;
So little is our loss,
So little is thy gain.
For when as each thing bad thou hast entomb'd,
And last of all, thy greedy self consum'd,
Then long Eternity shall greet our bliss
With an individual kiss;
And Joy shall overtake us as a flood,
When every thing that is sincerely good
And perfectly divine,
With Truth, and Peace, and Love shall ever shine

About the supreme Throne
Of him, t'whose happy-making sight alone,
When once our heav'nly-guided soul shall clime,
Then all this Earthy grosnes quit,
Attir'd with Stars, we shall for ever sit,
  Triumphing over Death, and Chance, and thee O Time.
JOHN MILTON (1608–1674)

291   AT A SOLEMN MUSICK

Blest pair of Sirens, pledges of Heav'ns joy,
Sphear-born harmonious Sisters, Voice, and Vers,
Wed your divine sounds, and mixt power employ
Dead things with inbreath'd sense able to pierce,
And to our high-rais'd phantasie present,
That undisturbèd Song of pure content,
Ay sung before the saphire-colour'd throne
To him that sits theron
With Saintly shout, and solemn Jubily,
Where the bright Seraphim in burning row
Their loud up-lifted Angel trumpets blow,
And the Cherubick host in thousand quires
Touch their immortal Harps of golden wires,
With those just Spirits that wear victorious Palms,
Hymns devout and holy Psalms
Singing everlastingly;
That we on Earth with undiscording voice
May rightly answer that melodious noise;
As once we did, till disproportion'd sin
Jarr'd against natures chime, and with harsh din
Broke the fair musick that all creatures made
To their great Lord, whose love their motion sway'd
In perfect Diapason, whilst they stood
In first obedience, and their state of good.
O may we soon again renew that Song,
And keep in tune with Heav'n, till God ere long
To his celestial consort us unite,
To live with him, and sing in endles morn of light.
JOHN MILTON (1608–1674)

292   L'ALLEGRO

Hence loathèd Melancholy
  Of Cerberus and blackest midnight born,
In Stygian Cave forlorn
  'Mongst horrid shapes, and shreiks, and sights unholy.
Find out som uncouth cell,
  Where brooding darknes spreads his jealous wings,
And the night-Raven sings;
  There, under Ebon shades, and low-brow'd Rocks,
As ragged as thy Locks,
  In dark Cimmerian desert ever dwell.
But com thou Goddes fair and free,
In Heav'n ycleap'd Euphrosyne,

And by men, heart-easing Mirth,
Whom lovely Venus, at a birth
With two sister Graces more
To Ivy-crowned Bacchus bore;
Or whether (as som Sager sing)
The frolick Wind that breathes the Spring,
Zephir with Aurora playing,
As he met her once a Maying,
There on Beds of Violets blew,
And fresh-blown Roses washt in dew,
Fill'd her with thee a daughter fair,
So bucksom, blith, and debonair.
  Haste thee nymph, and bring with thee
Jest and youthful Jollity,
Quips and Cranks, and wanton Wiles,
Nods, and Becks, and Wreathèd Smiles,
Such as hang on Hebe's cheek,
And love to live in dimple sleek;
Sport that wrincled Care derides,
And Laughter holding both his sides.
Com, and trip it as ye go
On the light fantastick toe,
And in thy right hand lead with thee,
The Mountain Nymph, sweet Liberty;
And if I give thee honour due,
Mirth, admit me of thy crue
To live with her, and live with thee,
In unreproved pleasures free;
To hear the Lark begin his flight,
And singing startle the dull night,
From his watch-towre in the skies,
Till the dappled dawn doth rise;
Then to com in spight of sorrow,
And at my window bid good morrow,
Through the Sweet-Briar, or the Vine,
Or the twisted Eglantine.
While the Cock with lively din,
Scatters the rear of darknes thin,
And to the stack, or the Barn dore,
Stoutly struts his Dames before,
Oft list'ning how the Hounds and horn
Chearly rouse the slumbring morn,
From the side of som Hoar Hill,
Through the high wood echoing shrill.
Som time walking not unseen
By Hedge-row Elms, on Hillocks green,
Right against the Eastern gate,
Wher the great Sun begins his state,
Rob'd in flames, and Amber light,
The clouds in thousand Liveries dight.
While the Plowman neer at hand,
Whistles ore the Furrow'd Land,

And the Milkmaid singeth blithe,
And the Mower whets his sithe,
And every Shepherd tells his tale
Under the Hawthorn in the dale.
Streit mine eye hath caught new pleasures
Whilst the Lantskip round it measures,
Russet Lawns, and Fallows Gray,
Where the nibling flocks do stray,
Mountains on whose barren brest
The labouring clouds do often rest:
Meadows trim with Daisies pide,
Shallow Brooks, and Rivers wide.
Towers, and Battlements it sees
Boosom'd high in tufted Trees,
Wher perhaps som beauty lies,
The Cynosure of neighbouring eyes.
Hard by, a Cottage chimney smokes,
From betwixt two aged Okes,
Where Corydon and Thyrsis met,
Are at their savory dinner set
Of Hearbs, and other Country Messes,
Which the neat-handed Phillis dresses;
And then in haste her Bowre she leaves,
With Thestylis to bind the Sheaves;
Or if the earlier season lead
To the tann'd Haycock in the Mead,
Som times with secure delight
The up-land Hamlets will invite,
When the merry Bells ring round,
And the jocond rebecks sound
To many a youth, and many a maid,
Dancing in the Chequer'd shade;
And young and old com forth to play
On a Sunshine Holyday,
Till the live-long day-light fail,
Then to the Spicy Nut-brown Ale,
With stories told of many a feat,
How Faery Mab the junkets eat,
She was pincht, and pull'd the sed,
And he by Friars Lanthorn led
Tells how the drudging Goblin swet,
To ern his Cream-bowle duly set,
When in one night, ere glimps of morn,
His shadowy Flale hath thresh'd the Corn
That ten day-labourers could not end,
Then lies him down the Lubbar Fend,
And stretch'd out all the Chimney's length,
Basks at the fire his hairy strength;
And Crop-full out of dores he flings,
Ere the first Cock his Mattin rings.
Thus don the Tales, to bed they creep,
By whispering Windes soon lull'd asleep.

Towred Cities please us then,
And the busie humm of men,
Where throngs of Knights and Barons bold,
In weeds of Peace high triumphs hold,
With store of Ladies, whose bright eies
Rain influence, and judge the prise
Of Wit, or Arms, while both contend
To win her Grace, whom all commend.
There let Hymen oft appear
In Saffron robe, with Taper clear,
And pomp, and feast, and revelry,
With mask, and antique Pageantry,
Such sights as youthfull Poets dream
On Summer eeves by haunted stream.
Then to the well-trod stage anon,
If Jonsons learnèd Sock be on,
Or sweetest Shakespear fancies childe,
Warble his native Wood-notes wilde,
And ever against eating Cares,
Lap me in soft Lydian Aires,
Married to immortal verse
Such as the meeting soul may pierce
In notes, with many a winding bout
Of linckèd sweetnes long drawn out,
With wanton heed, and giddy cunning,
The melting voice through mazes running;
Untwisting all the chains that ty
The hidden soul of harmony.
That Orpheus self may heave his head
From golden slumber on a bed
Of heapt Elysian flowres, and hear
Such streins as would have won the ear
Of Pluto, to have quite set free
His half regain'd Eurydice.
These delights, if thou canst give,
Mirth with thee, I mean to live.

JOHN MILTON (1608–1674)

IL PENSEROSO 293

Hence vain deluding joyes,
   The brood of folly without father bred,
How little you bested,
   Or fill the fixèd mind with all your toyes;
Dwell in som idle brain,
   And fancies fond with gaudy shapes possess,
As thick and numberless
   As the gay motes that people the Sun Beams,
Or likest hovering dreams
   The fickle Pensioners of Morpheus train.
But hail thou Goddes, sage and holy,
Hail divinest Melancholy,

Whose Saintly visage is too bright
To hit the Sense of human sight;
And therfore to our weaker view,
Ore laid with black staid Wisdoms hue.
Black, but such as in esteem,
Prince Memnons sister might beseem,
Or that Starr'd Ethiope Queen that strove
To set her beauties praise above
The Sea Nymphs, and their powers offended.
Yet thou art higher far descended,
Thee bright-hair'd Vesta long of yore,
To solitary Saturn bore;
His daughter she (in Saturns raign,
Such mixture was not held a stain)
Oft in glimmering Bowres, and glades
He met her, and in secret shades
Of woody Ida's inmost grove,
Whilst yet there was no fear of Jove.
Com pensive Nun, devout and pure,
Sober, stedfast, and demure,
All in a robe of darkest grain,
Flowing with majestick train,
And sable stole of Cipres Lawn,
Over thy decent shoulders drawn.
Com, but keep thy wonted state,
With eev'n step, and musing gate,
And looks commercing with the skies,
Thy rapt soul sitting in thine eyes:
There held in holy passion still,
Forget thy self to Marble, till
With a sad Leaden downward cast,
Thou fix them on the earth as fast.
And joyn with thee calm Peace, and Quiet,
Spare Fast, that oft with gods doth diet,
And hears the Muses in a ring,
Ay round about Joves Altar sing.
And adde to these retired Leasure,
That in trim Gardens takes his pleasure;
But first, and chiefest, with thee bring,
Him that yon soars on golden wing,
Guiding the fiery-wheeled throne,
The Cherub Contemplation,
And the mute Silence hist along,
'Less Philomel will daign a Song,
In her sweetest, saddest plight,
Smoothing the rugged brow of night,
While Cynthia checks her Dragon yoke,
Gently o're th'accustom'd Oke;
Sweet Bird that shunn'st the noise of folly,
Most musicall, most melancholy!
Thee Chauntress oft the Woods among,
I woo to hear thy eeven-Song;

And missing thee, I walk unseen
On the dry smooth-shaven Green.
To behold the wandring Moon,
Riding neer her highest noon,
Like one that had bin led astray
Through the Heav'ns wide pathles way;
And oft, as if her head she bow'd,
Stooping through a fleecy cloud.
Oft on a Plat of rising ground,
I hear the far-off Curfeu sound,
Over som wide-water'd shoar,
Swinging slow with sullen roar;
Or if the Ayr will not permit,
Som still removèd place will fit,
Where glowing Embers through the room
Teach light to counterfeit a gloom,
Far from all resort of mirth,
Save the Cricket on the hearth,
Or the Belmans drousie charm,
To bless the dores from nightly harm:
Or let my Lamp at midnight hour,
Be seen in som high lonely Towr,
Where I may oft out-watch the Bear,
With thrice great Hermes, or unsphear
The spirit of Plato to unfold
What Worlds, or what vast Regions hold
The immortal mind that hath forsook
Her mansion in this fleshly nook:
And of those Dæmons that are found
In fire, air, flood, or under ground,
Whose power hath a true consent
With Planet, or with Element.
Som time let Gorgeous Tragedy
In Scepter'd Pall com sweeping by,
Presenting Thebs, or Pelops line,
Or the tale of Troy divine.
Or what (though rare) of later age,
Ennoblèd hath the Buskind stage.
  But, O sad Virgin, that thy power
Might raise Musaeus from his bower
Or bid the soul of Orpheus sing
Such notes as warbled to the string,
Drew Iron tears down Pluto's cheek,
And made Hell grant what Love did seek.
Or call up him that left half told
The story of Cambuscan bold,
Of Camball, and of Algarsife,
And who had Canace to wife,
That own'd the vertuous Ring and Glass,
And of the wondrous Hors of Brass,
On which the Tartar King did ride;
And if ought els, great Bards beside,

In sage and solemn tunes have sung,
Of Turneys and of Trophies hung;
Of Forests, and inchantments drear,
Where more is meant then meets the ear.
Thus night oft see me in thy pale career,
Till civil-suited Morn appeer,
Not trickt and frounc't as she was wont,
With the Attick Boy to hunt,
But Cherchef't in a comly Cloud,
While rocking Winds are Piping loud,
Or usher'd with a shower still,
When the gust hath blown his fill,
Ending on the russling Leaves,
With minute drops from off the Eaves.
And when the Sun begins to fling
His flaring beams, me Goddes bring
To archèd walks of twilight groves,
And shadows brown that Sylvan loves,
Of Pine, or monumental Oake,
Where the rude Ax with heaved stroke,
Was never heard the Nymphs to daunt,
Or fright them from their hallow'd haunt.
There in close covert by som Brook,
Where no profaner eye may look,
Hide me from Day's garish eie,
While the Bee with Honied thie,
That at her flowry work doth sing,
And the Waters murmuring
With such consort as they keep,
Entice the dewy-feather'd Sleep;
And let som strange mysterious dream,
Wave at his Wings in Airy stream,
Of lively portrature display'd,
Softly on my eye-lids laid.
And as I wake, sweet musick breath
Above, about, or underneath,
Sent by som spirit to mortals good,
Or th'unseen Genius of the Wood.
  But let my due feet never fail,
To walk the studious Cloysters pale,
And love the high embowed Roof,
With antick Pillars massy proof,
And storied Windows richly dight,
Casting a dimm religious light.
There let the pealing Organ blow,
To the full voic'd Quire below,
In Service high, and Anthems cleer,
As may with sweetnes, through mine ear,
Dissolve me into extasies,
And bring all Heav'n before mine eyes.
And may at last my weary age
Find out the peacefull hermitage,

The Hairy Gown and Mossy Cell,
Where I may sit and rightly spell
Of every Star that Heav'n doth shew,
And every Herb that sips the dew;
Till old experience do attain
To somthing like Prophetic strain.
These pleasures Melancholy give,
And I with thee will choose to live.

JOHN MILTON (1608–1674)

FROM "ARCADES" 294

O're the smooth enameld green
    Where no print of step hath been,
    Follow me as I sing,
    And touch the warbled string.
Under the shady roof
Of branching Elm Star-proof,
    Follow me,
I will bring you where she sits
Clad in splendor as befits
    Her deity.
Such a rural Queen
All Arcadia hath not seen.

JOHN MILTON (1608–1674)

THE STAR THAT BIDS THE SHEPHERD FOLD 295

The Star that bids the Shepherd fold,
Now the top of Heav'n doth hold,
And the gilded Car of Day,
His glowing Axle doth allay
In the steep Atlantick stream,
And the slope Sun his upward beam
Shoots against the dusky Pole,
Pacing toward the other gole
Of his Chamber in the East.
Mean while welcom Joy, and Feast,
Midnight shout, and revelry,
Tipsie dance, and Jollity.
Braid your Locks with rosie Twine
Dropping odours, dropping Wine.
Rigor now is gon to bed,
And Advice with scrupulous head,
Strict Age, and sowre Severity,
With their grave Saws in slumber ly.
We that are of purer fire
Imitate the Starry Quire,
Who in their nightly watchfull Sphears,
Lead in swift round the Months and Years.
The Sounds, and Seas with all their finny drove
Now to the Moon in wavering Morrice move,
And on the Tawny Sands and Shelves,
Trip the pert Fairies and the dapper Elves;
By dimpled Brook, and Fountain brim,
The Wood-Nymphs deckt with Daisies trim,

Their merry wakes and pastimes keep:
What hath night to do with sleep?
Night hath better sweets to prove,
Venus now wakes, and wak'ns Love....
Com, knit hands, and beat the ground,
In a light fantastick round.

JOHN MILTON (1608–1674)
from "Comus"

296   SWEET ECHO

Sweet Echo, sweetest Nymph that liv'st unseen
    Within thy airy shell
  By slow Meander's margent green,
And in the violet imbroider'd vale
  Where the love-lorn Nightingale
Nightly to thee her sad Song mourneth well.
Canst thou not tell me of a gentle Pair
    That likest thy Narcissus are?
      O if thou have
    Hid them in som flowry Cave,
      Tell me but where
Sweet Queen of Parly, Daughter of the Sphear!
So maist thou be translated to the skies,
And give resounding grace to all Heav'ns Harmonies!

JOHN MILTON (1608–1674)
from "Comus"

297   SABRINA FAIR

The Spirit sings:
Sabrina fair
  Listen where thou art sitting
Under the glassie, cool, translucent wave,
  In twisted braids of Lillies knitting
The loose train of thy amber-dropping hair,
  Listen for dear honour's sake,
  Goddess of the silver lake,
      Listen and save!

Listen and appear to us,
In name of great Oceanus,
By the earth-shaking Neptune's mace,
And Tethys grave majestick pace,
By hoary Nereus wrincled look,
And the Carpathian wisards hook,
By scaly Tritons winding shell,
And old sooth-saying Glaucus spell,
By Leucothea's lovely hands,
And her son that rules the strands,
By Thetis tinsel-slipper'd feet,
And the Songs of Sirens sweet,
By dead Parthenope's dear tomb,
And fair Ligea's golden comb,
  Wherwith she sits on diamond rocks
  Sleeking her soft alluring locks,

By all the Nymphs that nightly dance
Upon thy streams with wily glance,
Rise, rise, and heave thy rosie head
From thy coral-pav'n bed,
And bridle in thy headlong wave,
Till thou our summons answered have.
                Listen and save!

Sabrina replies:
  By the rushy-fringèd bank,
Where grows the Willow and the Osier dank,
  My sliding Chariot stayes,
Thick set with Agat, and the azurn sheen
Of Turkis blew, and Emrauld green
  That in the channell strayes,
Whilst from off the waters fleet
Thus I set my printless feet
O're the Cowslips Velvet head,
  That bends not as I tread,
Gentle swain at thy request
  I am here.

JOHN MILTON (1608–1674)
from "Comus"

TO THE OCEAN NOW I FLY   298

The Spirit epiloguizes:
To the Ocean now I fly,
And those happy climes that ly
Where day never shuts his eye,
Up in the broad fields of the sky:
There I suck the liquid ayr
All amidst the Gardens fair
Of Hesperus, and his daughters three
That sing about the golden tree:
Along the crispèd shades and bowres
Revels the spruce and jocond Spring,
The Graces, and the rosie-boosom'd Howres,
Thither all their bounties bring,
That there eternal Summer dwels,
And West winds, with musky wing
About the cedar'n alleys fling
Nard, and Cassia's balmy smels.
Iris there with humid bow,
Waters the odorous banks that blow
Flowers of more mingled hew
Than her purfl'd scarf can shew,
And drenches with Elysian dew
(List mortals, if your ears be true)
Beds of Hyacinth, and roses
Where young Adonis oft reposes,
Waxing well of his deep wound
In slumber soft, and on the ground

Sadly sits th' Assyrian Queen;
But far above in spangled sheen
Celestial Cupid her fam'd son advanc't,
Holds his dear Psyche sweet intranc't
After her wandring labours long,
Till free consent the gods among
Make her his eternal Bride,
And from her fair unspotted side
Two blissful twins are to be born,
Youth and Joy; so Jove hath sworn.
   But now my task is smoothly don,
I can fly, or I can run
Quickly to the green earths end,
Where the bow'd welkin slow doth bend,
And from thence can soar as soon
To the corners of the Moon.
   Mortals that would follow me,
Love vertue, she alone is free.
She can teach ye how to clime
Higher then the Spheary chime;
Or if Vertue feeble were,
Heav'n it self would stoop to her.

JOHN MILTON (1608–1674)
from "Comus"

299   LYCIDAS
A LAMENT FOR A FRIEND DROWNED

Yet once more, O ye Laurels, and once more
Ye Myrtles brown, with Ivy never-sear,
I com to pluck your Berries harsh and crude,
And with forc'd fingers rude,
Shatter your leaves before the mellowing year.
Bitter constraint, and sad occasion dear,
Compels me to disturb your season due:
For Lycidas is dead, dead ere his prime
Young Lycidas, and hath not left his peer:
Who would not sing for Lycidas? he knew
Himself to sing, and build the lofty rhyme.
He must not flote upon his watry bear
Unwept, and welter to the parching wind,
Without the meed of som melodious tear.

   Begin, then, Sisters of the sacred well,
That from beneath the seat of Jove doth spring,
Begin, and somwhat loudly sweep the string.
Hence with denial vain, and coy excuse,
So may som gentle Muse
With lucky words favour my destin'd Urn,
And as he passes turn,
And bid fair peace be to my sable shrowd.

For we were nurst upon the self-same hill,
Fed the same flock, by fountain, shade, and rill.
Together both, ere the high Lawns appear'd
Under the opening eye-lids of the morn,
We drove a field, and both together heard
What time the Gray-fly winds her sultry horn,
Batt'ning our flocks with the fresh dews of night,
Oft till the Star that rose, at Ev'ning, bright
Toward Heav'ns descent had slop'd his westering wheel.
Mean while the Rural ditties were not mute,
Temper'd to th'Oaten Flute;
Rough Satyrs danc'd, and Fauns with clov'n heel,
From the glad sound would not be absent long,
And old Damaetas lov'd to hear our song.

   But O the heavy change, now thou art gon,
Now thou art gon, and never must return!
Thee Shepherd, thee the Woods, and desert Caves,
With wilde Thyme and the gadding Vine o'regrown,
And all their echoes mourn.
The Willows, and the Hazle Copses green,
Shall now no more be seen,
Fanning their joyous Leaves to thy soft layes.
As killing as the Canker to the Rose,
Or Taint-worm to the weanling Herds that graze,
Or Frost to Flowers, that their gay wardrop wear,
When first the White thorn blows;
Such, Lycidas, thy loss to Shepherds ear.

   Where were ye Nymphs when the remorseless deep
Clos'd o're the head of your lov'd Lycidas?
For neither were ye playing on the steep,
Where your old Bards, the famous Druids ly,
Nor on the shaggy top of Mona high,
Nor yet where Deva spreads her wisard stream:
Ay me, I fondly dream!
Had ye bin there—for what could that have don?
What could the Muse her self that Orpheus bore,
The Muse her self, for her inchanting son
Whom Universal nature did lament,
When by the rout that made the hideous roar,
His goary visage down the stream was sent,
Down the swift Hebrus to the Lesbian shore.

   Alas! what boots it with uncessant care
To tend the homely slighted Shepherds trade,
And strictly meditate the thankles Muse,
Were it not better don as others use,
To sport with Amaryllis in the shade,
Or with the tangles of Neæra's hair?
Fame is the spur that the clear spirit doth raise
(That last infirmity of Noble mind)

To scorn delights, and live laborious dayes;
But the fair Guerdon when we hope to find,
And think to burst out into sudden blaze,
Comes the blind Fury with th'abhorrèd shears,
And slits the thin spun life. But not the praise,
Phœbus repli'd, and touch'd my trembling ears;
Fame is no plant that grows on mortal soil,
Nor in the glistering foil
Set off to th'world, nor in broad rumour lies,
But lives and spreds aloft by those pure eyes,
And perfet witnes of all judging Jove;
As he pronounces lastly on each deed,
Of so much fame in Heav'n expect thy meed.

  O fountain Arethuse, and thou honour'd floud,
Smooth-sliding Mincius, crown'd with vocall reeds,
That strain I heard was of a higher mood:
But now my Oate proceeds,
And listens to the Herald of the Sea
That came in Neptune's plea,
He ask'd the Waves, and ask'd the Fellon winds,
What hard mishap hath doom'd this gentle swain?
And question'd every gust of rugged wings
That blows from off each beaked Promontory,
They knew not of his story,
And sage Hippotades their answer brings,
That not a blast was from his dungeon stray'd,
The Ayr was calm, and on the level brine,
Sleek Panope with all her sisters play'd.
It was that fatall and perfidious Bark
Built in th'eclipse, and rigg'd with curses dark,
That sunk so low that sacred head of thine.

  Next Camus, reverend Sire, went footing slow,
His Mantle hairy, and his Bonnet sedge,
Inwrought with figures dim, and on the edge
Like to that sanguine flower inscrib'd with woe.
Ah; Who hath reft (quoth he) my dearest pledge?
Last came, and last did go,
The Pilot of the Galilean lake,
Two massy Keyes he bore of metals twain,
(The Golden opes, the Iron shuts amain)
He shook his Miter'd locks, and stern bespake,
How well could I have spar'd for thee, young swain,
Anow of such as for their bellies sake,
Creep and intrude, and climb into the fold?
Of other care they little reck'ning make,
Then how to scramble at the shearers feast,
And shove away the worthy bidden guest.
Blind mouthes! that scarce themselves know how to hold
A Sheep-hook, or have learn'd ought els the least
That to the faithfull Herdmans art belongs!
What recks it them? What need they? They are sped;

And when they list, their lean and flashy songs
Grate on their scrannel Pipes of wretched straw,
The hungry Sheep look up, and are not fed,
But swoln with wind, and the rank mist they draw,
Rot inwardly, and foul contagion spread:
Besides what the grim Woolf with privy paw
Daily devours apace, and nothing sed,
But that two-handed engine at the door,
Stands ready to smite once, and smite no more.

   Return Alpheus, the dread voice is past,
That shrunk thy streams; Return Sicilian Muse,
And call the Vales, and bid them hither cast
Their Bels, and Flourets of a thousand hues.
Ye valleys low where the milde whispers use,
Of shades and wanton winds, and gushing brooks,
On whose fresh lap the swart Star sparely looks,
Throw hither all your quaint enameld eyes,
That on the green terf suck the honied showres,
And purple all the ground with vernal flowres.
Bring the rathe Primrose that forsaken dies.
The tufted Crow-toe, and pale Gessamine,
The white Pink, and the Pansie freakt with jeat,
The glowing Violet.
The Musk-rose, and the well attir'd Woodbine.
With Cowslips wan that hang the pensive hed,
And every flower that sad embroidery wears:
Bid Amaranthus all his beauty shed,
And Daffadillies fill their cups with tears,
To strew the Laureat Herse where Lycid lies.
For so to interpose a little ease,
Let our frail thoughts dally with false surmise.
Ay me! Whilst thee the shores, and sounding Seas
Wash far away, where ere thy bones are hurld,
Whether beyond the stormy Hebrides,
Where thou perhaps under the whelming tide
Visit'st the bottom of the monstrous world;
Or whether thou to our moist vows deny'd,
Sleep'st by the fable of Bellerus old,
Where the great vision of the guarded Mount
Looks toward Namancos and Bayona's hold;
Look homeward Angel now, and melt with ruth.
And, O ye Dolphins, waft the haples youth.

   Weep no more, woful Shepherds weep no more,
For Lycidas your sorrow is not dead,
Sunk though he be beneath the watry floar,
So sinks the day-star in the Ocean bed,
And yet anon repairs his drooping head,
And tricks his beams, and with new spangled Ore,
Flames in the forehead of the morning sky:
So Lycidas sunk low, but mounted high,

Through the dear might of him that walk'd the waves
Where other groves, and other streams along,
With Nectar pure his oozy Lock's he laves,
And hears the unexpressive nuptiall Song,
In the blest Kingdoms meek of joy and love.
There entertain him all the Saints above,
In solemn troops, and sweet Societies
That sing, and singing in their glory move,
And wipe the tears for ever from his eyes.
Now Lycidas the Shepherds weep no more;
Hence forth thou art the Genius of the shore,
In thy large recompense, and shalt be good
To all that wander in that perilous flood.

   Thus sang the uncouth Swain to th'Okes and rills,
While the still morn went out with Sandals gray,
He touch'd the tender stops of various Quills,
With eager thought warbling his Dorick lay:
And now the Sun had stretch'd out all the hills,
And now was dropt into the Western bay;
At last he rose, and twitch'd his Mantle blew:
To morrow to fresh Woods, and Pastures new.

JOHN MILTON (1608–1674)

300   ON HIS BLINDNESS

When I consider how my light is spent
  E're half my days, in this dark world and wide,
  And that one Talent which is death to hide,
Lodg'd with me useless, though my Soul more bent
To serve therewith my Maker, and present
  My true account, least he returning chide,
  Doth God exact day-labour, light deny'd,
I fondly ask; But patience to prevent
That murmur, soon replies, God doth not need
  Either man's work or his own gifts, who best
  Bear his milde yoak, they serve him best, his State
Is Kingly. Thousands at his bidding speed
  And post o're Land and Ocean without rest:
  They also serve who only stand and waite.

JOHN MILTON (1608–1674)

301   TO MR. LAWRENCE

Lawrence of vertuous Father vertuous Son,
  Now that the Fields are dank, and ways are mire,
  Where shall we sometimes meet, and by the fire
Help wast a sullen day; what may be won

From the hard Season gaining: time will run
  On smoother, till Favonius re-inspire
  The frozen earth; and cloth in fresh attire
The Lillie and Rose, that neither sow'd nor spun.

What neat repast shall feast us, light and choice,
  Of Attick tast, with Wine, whence we may rise
  To hear the Lute well toucht, or artfull voice
Warble immortal Notes and Tuskan Ayre?

  He who of those delights can judge, and spare
  To interpose them oft, is not unwise.
JOHN MILTON (1608–1674)

TO CYRIACK SKINNER   302

Cyriack, whose Grandsire on the Royal Bench
  Of Brittish Themis, with no mean applause
  Pronounc't and in his volumes taught our Lawes,
  Which others at their Barr so often wrench:
To day deep thoughts resolve with me to drench
  In mirth, that after no repenting drawes;
  Let Euclid rest and Archimedes pause,
  And what the Swede intend, and what the French.
To measure life, learn thou betimes, and know
  Toward solid good what leads the nearest way;
  For other things mild Heav'n a time ordains,
And disapproves that care, though wise in show,
  That with superfluous burden loads the day,
  And when God sends a cheerful hour, refrains.
JOHN MILTON (1608–1674)

ON HIS DECEASED WIFE   303

[The last couplet comprises the most poignant string of words in the English language. – Ed.]

Methought I saw my late espoused Saint
  Brought to me like Alcestis from the grave,
  Whom Joves great Son to her glad Husband gave,
  Rescu'd from death by force though pale and faint.
Mine as whom washt from spot of child-bed taint,
  Purification in the old Law did save,
  And such, as yet once more I trust to have
  Full sight of her in Heaven without restraint,
Came vested all in white, pure as her mind:
  Her face was vail'd, yet to my fancied sight,
  Love, sweetness, goodness, in her person shin'd
So clear, as in no face with more delight.
  But O as to embrace me she enclin'd
  I wak'd, she fled, and day brought back my night.
JOHN MILTON (1608–1674)

LIGHT   304

Hail holy light, ofspring of Heav'n first-born,
Or of th' Eternal Coeternal beam
May I express thee unblam'd? since God is light,
And never but in unapproachèd light
Dwelt from Eternitie, dwelt then in thee,
Bright effluence of bright essence increate.
Or hear'st thou rather pure Ethereal stream,
Whose Fountain who shall tell? before the Sun,

Before the Heavens thou wert, and at the voice
Of God, as with a Mantle didst invest
The rising world of waters dark and deep,
Won from the void and formless infinite.
Thee I re-visit now with bolder wing,
Escap't the Stygian Pool, though long detain'd
In that obscure sojourn, while in my flight
Through utter and through middle darkness borne
With other notes then to th' Orphean Lyre
I sung of Chaos and Eternal Night,
Taught by the heav'nly Muse to venture down
The dark descent, and up to reascend,
Though hard and rare: thee I revisit safe,
And feel thy sovran vital Lamp; but thou
Revisit'st not these eyes, that rowle in vain
To find thy piercing ray, and find no dawn;
So thick a drop serene hath quencht thir Orbs,
Or dim suffusion veild. Yet not the more
Cease I to wander where the Muses haunt
Cleer Spring, or shadie Grove, or Sunnie Hill,
Smit with the love of sacred song; but chief
Thee *Sion* and the flowrie Brooks beneath
That wash thy hallowd feet, and warbling flow,
Nightly I visit: nor somtimes forget
Those other two equal'd with me in Fate,
So were I equal'd with them in renown,
Blind Thamyris and blind Maeonides,
And Tiresias and Phineus Prophets old.
Then feed on thoughts, that voluntarie move
Harmonious numbers; as the wakeful Bird
Sings darkling, and in shadiest Covert hid
Tunes her nocturnal Note. Thus with the Year
Seasons return, but not to me returns
Day, or the sweet approach of Ev'n or Morn,
Or sight of vernal bloom, or Summers Rose,
Or flocks, or herds, or human face divine;
But cloud in stead, and ever-during dark
Surrounds me, from the chearful waies of men
Cut off, and for the Book of knowledg fair
Presented with a Universal blanc
Of Natures works to mee expung'd and ras'd,
And wisdome at one entrance quite shut out.
So much the rather thou Celestial light
Shine inward, and the mind through all her powers
Irradiate, there plant eyes, all mist from thence
Purge and disperse, that I may see and tell
Of things invisible to mortal sight.

JOHN MILTON (1608–1674)

Invincible Might 305

Oh how comely it is and how reviving
To the Spirits of just men long opprest!
When God into the hands of thir deliverer
Puts invincible might
To quell the mighty of the Earth, th' oppressour,
The brute and boist'rous force of violent men
Hardy and industrious to support
Tyrannic power, but raging to pursue
The righteous and all such as honour Truth;
He all thir Ammunition
And feats of War defeats
With plain Heroic magnitude of mind
And celestial vigour arm'd,
Thir Armories and Magazins contemns,
Renders them useless, while
With wingèd expedition
Swift as the lightning glance he executes
His errand on the wicked, who surpris'd
Lose thir defence distracted and amaz'd.

JOHN MILTON (1608–1674)
from "Samson Agonistes"

His Uncontroulable Intent 306

All is best, though we oft doubt,
What th' unsearchable dispose
Of highest wisdom brings about,
And ever best found in the close.
Oft he seems to hide his face,
But unexpectedly returns
And to his faithful Champion hath in place
Bore witness gloriously; whence Gaza mourns
And all that band them to resist
His uncontroulable intent.
His servants he with new acquist
Of true experience from this great event
With peace and consolation hath dismist,
And calm of mind all passion spent.

JOHN MILTON (1608–1674)
from "Samson Agonistes"

A Doubt of Martyrdom 307

O for some honest lover's ghost,
  Some kind unbodied post
    Sent from the shades below!
    I strangely long to know
Whether the noble chaplets wear
Those that their mistress' scorn did bear
  Or those that were used kindly.

For whatsoe'er they tell us here
  To make those sufferings dear,
    'Twill there, I fear, be found
    That to the being crown'd
T' have loved alone will not suffice,
Unless we also have been wise
    And have our loves enjoy'd.

What posture can we think him in
  That, here unloved, again
    Departs, and's thither gone
    Where each sits by his own?
Or how can that Elysium be
Where I my mistress still must see
    Circled in other's arms?

For there the judges all are just,
  And Sophonisba must
    Be his whom she held dear,
    Not his who loved her here.
The sweet Philoclea, since she died,
Lies by her Pirocles his side,
    Not by Amphialus.

Some bays, perchance, or myrtle bough
  For difference crowns the brow
    Of those kind souls that were
    The noble martyrs here:
And if that be the only odds
(As who can tell?), ye kinder gods,
    Give me the woman here!

                    Sir John Suckling (1609–1642)

308   The Constant Lover

Out upon it, I have loved
  Three whole days together!
And am like to love three more,
  If it prove fair weather.

Time shall moult away his wings
  Ere he shall discover
In the whole wide world again
  Such a constant lover.

But the spite on't is, no praise
  Is due at all to me:
Love with me had made no stays,
  Had it any been but she.

Had it any been but she,
  And that very face,
There had been at least ere this
  A dozen dozen in her place.

                    Sir John Suckling (1609–1642)

Why so Pale and Wan? 309

Why so pale and wan, fond lover?
    Prithee, why so pale?
Will, when looking well can't move her,
    Looking ill prevail?
    Prithee, why so pale?

Why so dull and mute, young sinner?
    Prithee, why so mute?
Will, when speaking well can't win her,
    Saying nothing do 't?
    Prithee, why so mute?

Quit, quit for shame! This will not move;
    This cannot take her.
If of herself she will not love,
    Nothing can make her:
    The devil take her!

                      SIR JOHN SUCKLING (1609–1642)

When, Dearest, I but think of Thee 310

When, dearest, I but think of thee,
Methinks all things that lovely be
  Are present, and my soul delighted:
For beauties that from worth arise
Are like the grace of deities,
  Still present with us, tho' unsighted.

Thus while I sit and sigh the day
With all his borrow'd lights away,
  Till night's black wings do overtake me,
Thinking on thee, thy beauties then,
As sudden lights do sleepy men,
  So they by their bright rays awake me.

Thus absence dies, and dying proves
No absence can subsist with loves
  That do partake of fair perfection:
Since in the darkest night they may
By love's quick motion find a way
  To see each other by reflection.

The waving sea can with each flood
Bathe some high promont that hath stood
  Far from the main up in the river:
O think not then but love can do
As much! for that's an ocean too,
  Which flows not every day, but ever!

                      SIR JOHN SUCKLING (1609–1642)

A Rose 311

Blown in the morning, thou shalt fade ere noon.
What boots a life which in such haste forsakes thee?
Thou'rt wondrous frolic, being to die so soon,
And passing proud a little colour makes thee.

If thee thy brittle beauty so deceives,
Know then the thing that swells thee is thy bane;
For the same beauty doth, in bloody leaves,
The sentence of thy early death contain.
Some clown's coarse lungs will poison thy sweet flower,
If by the careless plough thou shalt be torn;
And many Herods lie in wait each hour
To murder thee as soon as thou art born—
   Nay, force thy bud to blow—their tyrant breath
   Anticipating life, to hasten death!
SIR RICHARD FANSHAWE (1608–1666)

312   **TO CHLOE**
          WHO FOR HIS SAKE WISHED HERSELF YOUNGER

There are two births; the one when light
   First strikes the new awaken'd sense;
The other when two souls unite,
   And we must count our life from thence:
When you loved me and I loved you
Then both of us were born anew.

Love then to us new souls did give
   And in those souls did plant new powers;
Since when another life we live,
   The breath we breathe is his, not ours:
Love makes those young whom age doth chill,
And whom he finds young keeps young still.
WILLIAM CARTWRIGHT (1611–1643)

313   **FALSEHOOD**

Still do the stars impart their light
To those that travel in the night;
Still time runs on, nor doth the hand
Or shadow on the dial stand;
The streams still glide and constant are:
     Only thy mind
     Untrue I find,
     Which carelessly
     Neglects to be
Like stream or shadow, hand or star.

Fool that I am! I do recall
My words, and swear thou'rt like them all,
Thou seem'st like stars to nourish fire,
But O how cold is thy desire!
And like the hand upon the brass
     Thou point'st at me
     In mockery;
     If I come nigh
     Shade-like thou'lt fly,
And as the stream with murmur pass.
WILLIAM CARTWRIGHT (1611–1643)

On the Queen's Return from the Low Countries 314
    Hallow the threshold, crown the posts anew!
        The day shall have its due.
    Twist all our victories into one bright wreath,
        On which let honour breathe;
    Then throw it round the temples of our Queen!
    'Tis she that must preserve those glories green.

    When greater tempests than on sea before
        Received her on the shore;
    When she was shot at "for the King's own good"
        By legions hired to blood;
    How bravely did she do, how bravely bear!
    And show'd, though they durst rage, she durst not fear.

    Courage was cast about her like a dress
        Of solemn comeliness:
    A gather'd mind and an untroubled face
        Did give her dangers grace:
    Thus, arm'd with innocence, secure they move
    Whose highest "treason" is but highest love.
                          WILLIAM CARTWRIGHT (1611–1643)

On a Virtuous Young Gentlewoman 315
That Died Suddenly
    She who to Heaven more Heaven doth annex,
    Whose lowest thought was above all our sex,
    Accounted nothing death but t' be repriev'd,
    And died as free from sickness as she lived.
    Others are dragg'd away, or must be driven,
    She only saw her time and stept to Heaven;
    Where seraphims view all her glories o'er,
    As one return'd that had been there before.
    For while she did this lower world adorn,
    Her body seem'd rather assumed than born;
    So rarified, advanced, so pure and whole,
    That body might have been another's soul;
    And equally a miracle it were
    That she could die, or that she could live here.
                          WILLIAM CARTWRIGHT (1611–1643)

I'll never love Thee more 316
    My dear and only Love, I pray
        That little world of thee
    Be govern'd by no other sway
        Than purest monarchy;
    For if confusion have a part
        (Which virtuous souls abhor),
    And hold a synod in thine heart,
        I'll never love thee more.

    Like Alexander I will reign,
        And I will reign alone;
    My thoughts did evermore disdain
        A rival on my throne.

He either fears his fate too much,
　　Or his deserts are small,
That dares not put it to the touch,
　　To gain or lose it all.

And in the empire of thine heart,
　　Where I should solely be,
If others do pretend a part
　　Or dare to vie with me,
Or if *Committees* thou erect,
　　And go on such a score,
I'll laugh and sing at thy neglect,
　　And never love thee more.

But if thou wilt prove faithful then,
　　And constant of thy word,
I'll make thee glorious by my pen
　　And famous by my sword;
I'll serve thee in such noble ways
　　Was never heard before;
I'll crown and deck thee all with bays,
　　And love thee more and more.
　　　　JAMES GRAHAM, MARQUIS OF MONTROSE (1612–1650)

317　CORONEMUS NOS ROSIS ANTEQUAM MARCESCANT

Let us drink and be merry, dance, joke, and rejoice,
With claret and sherry, theorbo and voice!
The changeable world to our joy is unjust,
　　All treasure's uncertain,
　　Then down with your dust!
In frolics dispose your pounds, shillings, and pence,
For we shall be nothing a hundred years hence.

We'll sport and be free with Moll, Betty, and Dolly,
Have oysters and lobsters to cure melancholy:
Fish-dinners will make a man spring like a flea,
　　Dame Venus, love's lady,
　　Was born of the sea;
With her and with Bacchus we'll tickle the sense,
For we shall be past it a hundred years hence.

Your most beautiful bride who with garlands is crown'd
And kills with each glance as she treads on the ground,
Whose lightness and brightness doth shine in such splendour
　　That none but the stars
　　Are thought fit to attend her,
Though now she be pleasant and sweet to the sense,
Will be damnable mouldy a hundred years hence.

Then why should we turmoil in cares and in fears,
Turn all our tranquill'ty to sighs and to tears?
Let's eat, drink, and play till the worms do corrupt us,
    'Tis certain, *Post mortem*
    Nulla voluptas.
For health, wealth and beauty, wit, learning and sense,
Must all come to nothing a hundred years hence.

THOMAS JORDAN (1612?–1685)

WISHES TO HIS SUPPOSED MISTRESS   318

Whoe'er she be—
That not impossible She
That shall command my heart and me:

Where'er she lie,
Lock'd up from mortal eye
In shady leaves of destiny:

Till that ripe birth
Of studied Fate stand forth,
And teach her fair steps to our earth:

Till that divine
Idea take a shrine
Of crystal flesh, through which to shine:

Meet you her, my Wishes,
Bespeak her to my blisses,
And be ye call'd my absent kisses.

I wish her Beauty,
That owes not all its duty
To gaudy tire, or glist'ring shoe-tie:

Something more than
Taffata or tissue can,
Or rampant feather, or rich fan.

A Face, that's best
By its own beauty drest,
And can alone commend the rest.

A Face, made up
Out of no other shop
Than what Nature's white hand sets ope.

A Cheek, where youth
And blood, with pen of truth,
Write what the reader sweetly ru'th.

A Cheek, where grows
More than a morning rose,
Which to no box his being owes.

Lips, where all day
A lover's kiss may play,
Yet carry nothing thence away.

Looks, that oppress
Their richest tires, but dress
And clothe their simplest nakedness.

Eyes, that displace
The neighbour diamond, and outface
That sunshine by their own sweet grace.

Tresses, that wear
Jewels but to declare
How much themselves more precious are:

Whose native ray
Can tame the wanton day
Of gems that in their bright shades play.

Each ruby there,
Or pearl that dare appear,
Be its own blush, be its own tear.

A well-tamed Heart,
For whose more noble smart
Love may be long choosing a dart.

Eyes, that bestow
Full quivers on love's bow,
Yet pay less arrows than they owe.

Smiles, that can warm
The blood, yet teach a charm,
That chastity shall take no harm.

Blushes, that bin
The burnish of no sin,
Nor flames of aught too hot within.

Joys, that confess
Virtue their mistress,
And have no other head to dress.

Fears, fond and slight
As the coy bride's, when night
First does the longing lover right.

Days, that need borrow
No part of their good-morrow
From a fore-spent night of sorrow.

Days, that in spite
Of darkness, by the light
Of a clear mind, are day all night.

Nights, sweet as they,
Made short by lovers' play,
Yet long by th' absence of the day.

Life, that dares send
A challenge to his end,
And when it comes, say, "Welcome, friend!"

Sydneian showers
Of sweet discourse, whose powers
Can crown old Winter's head with flowers.

Soft silken hours,
Open suns, shady bowers;
'Bove all, nothing within that lowers.

Whate'er delight
Can make Day's forehead bright,
Or give down to the wings of Night.

I wish her store
Of worth may leave her poor
Of wishes; and I wish—no more.

Now, if Time knows
That Her, whose radiant brows
Weave them a garland of my vows;

Her, whose just bays
My future hopes can raise,
A trophy to her present praise;

Her, that dares be
What these lines wish to see;
I seek no further, it is She.

'Tis She, and here,
Lo! I unclothe and clear
My Wishes' cloudy character.

May she enjoy it
Whose merit dare apply it,
But modesty dares still deny it!

Such worth as this is
Shall fix my flying Wishes,
And determine them to kisses.

Let her full glory,
My fancies, fly before ye;
Be ye my fictions—but her story.
RICHARD CRASHAW (1613?–1649)

THE WEEPER

Hail, sister springs,
Parents of silver-footed rills!
Ever bubbling things,
Thawing crystal, snowy hills!
Still spending, never spent; I mean
Thy fair eyes, sweet Magdalene.

Heavens thy fair eyes be;
Heavens of ever-falling stars;
  'Tis seed-time still with thee,
And stars thou sow'st whose harvest dares
    Promise the earth to countershine
    Whatever makes Heaven's forehead fine.

Every morn from hence
A brisk cherub something sips
  Whose soft influence
Adds sweetness to his sweetest lips;
    Then to his music: and his song
    Tastes of this breakfast all day long.

When some new bright guest
Takes up among the stars a room,
  And Heaven will make a feast,
Angels with their bottles come,
    And draw from these full eyes of thine
    Their Master's water, their own wine.

The dew no more will weep
The primrose's pale cheek to deck;
  The dew no more will sleep
Nuzzled in the lily's neck:
    Much rather would it tremble here,
    And leave them both to be thy tear.

When sorrow would be seen
In her brightest majesty,
  —For she is a Queen—
Then is she drest by none but thee:
    Then and only then she wears
    Her richest pearls—I mean thy tears.

Not in the evening's eyes,
When they red with weeping are
  For the Sun that dies,
Sits Sorrow with a face so fair.
    Nowhere but here did ever meet
    Sweetness so sad, sadness so sweet.

Does the night arise?
Still thy tears do fall and fall.
  Does night lose her eyes?
Still the fountain weeps for all.
    Let day and night do what they will,
    Thou hast thy task, thou weepest still.

Not *So long she lived*
Will thy tomb report of thee;
But *So long she grieved*:
Thus must we date thy memory.
    Others by days, by months, by years,
    Measure their ages, thou by tears.

    Say, ye bright brothers,
The fugitive sons of those fair eyes
    Your fruitful mothers,
What make you here? What hopes can 'tice
    You to be born? What cause can borrow
    You from those nests of noble sorrow?

    Whither away so fast
For sure the sordid earth
    Your sweetness cannot taste,
Nor does the dust deserve your birth.
    Sweet, whither haste you then? O say,
    Why you trip so fast away?

We go not to seek
The darlings of Aurora's bed,
*   The rose's modest cheek,*
Nor the violet's humble head.
    No such thing: we go to meet
    A worthier object—our Lord's feet.
RICHARD CRASHAW (1613?–1649)

A HYMN TO THE NAME AND HONOUR OF THE ADMIRABLE SAINT TERESA   320

Love, thou are absolute, sole Lord
Of life and death. To prove the word,
We'll now appeal to none of all
Those thy old soldiers, great and tall,
Ripe men of martyrdom, that could reach down
With strong arms their triumphant crown:
Such as could with lusty breath
Speak loud, unto the face of death,
Their great Lord's glorious name; to none
Of those whose spacious bosoms spread a throne
For love at large to fill. Spare blood and sweat:
We'll see Him take a private seat,
And make His mansion in the mild
And milky soul of a soft child.
Scarce has she learnt to lisp a name
Of martyr, yet she thinks it shame
Life should so long play with that breath
Which spent can buy so brave a death.
She never undertook to know
What death with love should have to do.

Nor has she e'er yet understood
Why, to show love, she should shed blood;
Yet, though she cannot tell you why,
She can love, and she can die.
Scarce has she blood enough to make
A guilty sword blush for her sake;
Yet has a heart dares hope to prove
How much less strong is death than love....

Since 'tis not to be had at home,
She'll travel for a martyrdom.
No home for her, confesses she,
But where she may a martyr be.
She'll to the Moors, and trade with them
For this unvalued diadem;
She offers them her dearest breath,
With Christ's name in 't, in charge for death:
She'll bargain with them, and will give
Them God, and teach them how to live
In Him; or, if they this deny,
For Him she'll teach them how to die.
So shall she leave amongst them sown
Her Lord's blood, or at least her own.

Farewell then, all the world, adieu!
Teresa is no more for you.
Farewell all pleasures, sports, and joys,
Never till now esteemed toys!

Farewell whatever dear may be—
Mother's arms, or father's knee!
Farewell house, and farewell home!
She's for the Moors and Martyrdom.

Sweet, not so fast; lo! thy fair spouse,
Whom thou seek'st with so swift vows,
Calls thee back, and bids thee come
T' embrace a milder martyrdom....

O how oft shalt thou complain
Of a sweet and subtle pain!
Of intolerable joys!
Of a death, in which who dies
Loves his death, and dies again,
And would for ever so be slain;
And lives and dies, and knows not why
To live, but that he still may die!
How kindly will thy gentle heart
Kiss the sweetly-killing dart!
And close in his embraces keep
Those delicious wounds, that weep

Balsam, to heal themselves with thus,
When these thy deaths, so numerous,
Shall all at once die into one,
And melt thy soul's sweet mansion;
Like a soft lump of incense, hasted
By too hot a fire, and wasted
Into perfuming clouds, so fast
Shalt thou exhale to heaven at last
In a resolving sigh, and then,—
O what? Ask not the tongues of men.

Angels cannot tell; suffice,
Thyself shalt feel thine own full joys,
And hold them fast for ever there.
So soon as thou shalt first appear,
The moon of maiden stars, thy white
Mistress, attended by such bright
Souls as thy shining self, shall come,
And in her first ranks make thee room;
Where, 'mongst her snowy family,
Immortal welcomes wait for thee.
O what delight, when she shall stand
And teach thy lips heaven, with her hand,
On which thou now may'st to thy wishes
Heap up thy consecrated kisses!
What joy shall seize thy soul, when she,
Bending her blessèd eyes on thee,
Those second smiles of heaven, shall dart
Her mild rays through thy melting heart!

Angels, thy old friends, there shall greet thee,
Glad at their own home now to meet thee.
All thy good works which went before,
And waited for thee at the door,
Shall own thee there; and all in one
Weave a constellation
Of crowns, with which the King, thy spouse,
Shall build up thy triumphant brows.
All thy old woes shall now smile on thee,
And thy pains sit bright upon thee:
All thy sorrows here shall shine,
And thy sufferings be divine.
Tears shall take comfort, and turn gems,
And wrongs repent to diadems.
Even thy deaths shall live, and new
Dress the soul which late they slew.
Thy wounds shall blush to such bright scars
As keep account of the Lamb's wars.

Those rare works, where thou shalt leave writ
Love's noble history, with wit
Taught thee by none but Him, while here
They feed our souls, shall clothe thine there.

Each heavenly word by whose hid flame
Our hard hearts shall strike fire, the same
Shall flourish on thy brows, and be
Both fire to us and flame to thee;
Whose light shall live bright in thy face
By glory, in our hearts by grace.
Thou shalt look round about, and see
Thousands of crown'd souls throng to be
Themselves thy crown, sons of thy vows,
The virgin-births with which thy spouse
Made fruitful thy fair soul; go now,
And with them all about thee bow
To Him; put on, He'll say, put on,
My rosy Love, that thy rich zone,
Sparkling with the sacred flames
Of thousand souls, whose happy names
Heaven keeps upon thy score: thy bright
Life brought them first to kiss the light
That kindled them to stars; and so
Thou with the Lamb, thy Lord, shalt go.
And, wheresoe'er He sets His white
Steps, walk with Him those ways of light,
Which who in death would live to see,
Must learn in life to die like thee.
                    RICHARD CRASHAW (1613?–1649)

321 UPON THE BOOK AND PICTURE OF THE SERAPHICAL SAINT TERESA

O thou undaunted daughter of desires!
By all thy dower of lights and fires;
By all the eagle in thee, all the dove;
By all thy lives and deaths of love;
By thy large draughts of intellectual day,
And by thy thirsts of love more large than they;
By all thy brim-fill'd bowls of fierce desire,
By thy last morning's draught of liquid fire;
By the full kingdom of that final kiss
That seized thy parting soul, and seal'd thee His;
By all the Heav'n thou hast in Him
(Fair sister of the seraphim!);
By all of Him we have in thee;
Leave nothing of myself in me.
Let me so read thy life, that I
Unto all life of mine may die!
                    RICHARD CRASHAW (1613?–1649)

322 VERSES FROM THE SHEPHERDS' HYMN

We saw Thee in Thy balmy nest,
  Young dawn of our eternal day;
We saw Thine eyes break from the East,
  And chase the trembling shades away:
We saw Thee, and we blest the sight,
We saw Thee by Thine own sweet light.

Poor world, said I, what wilt thou do
  To entertain this starry stranger?
Is this the best thou canst bestow—
  A cold and not too cleanly manger?
Contend, the powers of heaven and earth,
To fit a bed for this huge birth.

Proud world, said I, cease your contest,
  And let the mighty babe alone;
The phœnix builds the phœnix' nest,
  Love's architecture is His own.
The babe, whose birth embraves this morn,
Made His own bed ere He was born.

I saw the curl'd drops, soft and slow,
  Come hovering o'er the place's head,
Off'ring their whitest sheets of snow,
  To furnish the fair infant's bed.
Forbear, said I, be not too bold;
Your fleece is white, but 'tis too cold.

I saw th' obsequious seraphim
  Their rosy fleece of fire bestow,
For well they now can spare their wings,
  Since Heaven itself lies here below.
Well done, said I; but are you sure
Your down, so warm, will pass for pure?

No, no, your King's not yet to seek
  Where to repose His royal head;
See, see how soon His new-bloom'd cheek
  'Twixt mother's breasts is gone to bed!
Sweet choice, said we; no way but so,
Not to lie cold, you sleep in snow!

She sings Thy tears asleep, and dips
  Her kisses in Thy weeping eye;
She spreads the red leaves of Thy lips,
  That in their buds yet blushing lie.
She 'gainst those mother diamonds tries
The points of her young eagle's eyes.

Welcome—tho' not to those gay flies,
  Gilded i' th' beams of earthly kings,
Slippery souls in smiling eyes—
  But to poor shepherds, homespun things,
Whose wealth's their flocks, whose wit's to be
Well read in their simplicity.

Yet, when young April's husband show'rs
  Shall bless the fruitful Maia's bed,
We'll bring the first-born of her flowers,
  To kiss Thy feet and crown Thy head.
To Thee, dread Lamb! whose love must keep
The shepherds while they feed their sheep.

To Thee, meek Majesty, soft King
  Of simple graces and sweet loves!
Each of us his lamb will bring,
  Each his pair of silver doves!
At last, in fire of Thy fair eyes,
Ourselves become our own best sacrifice!
RICHARD CRASHAW (1613?–1649)

323   CHRIST CRUCIFIED
Thy restless feet now cannot go
  For us and our eternal good,
As they were ever wont. What though
  They swim, alas! in their own flood?

Thy hands to give Thou canst not lift,
  Yet will Thy hand still giving be;
It gives, but O, itself's the gift!
  It gives tho' bound, tho' bound 'tis free!
RICHARD CRASHAW (1613?–1649)

324   AN EPITAPH UPON HUSBAND AND WIFE
  WHO DIED AND WERE BURIED TOGETHER
To these whom death again did wed
This grave's the second marriage-bed.
For though the hand of Fate could force
'Twixt soul and body a divorce,
It could not sever man and wife,
Because they both lived but one life.
Peace, good reader, do not weep;
Peace, the lovers are asleep.
They, sweet turtles, folded lie
In the last knot that love could tie.
Let them sleep, let them sleep on,
Till the stormy night be gone,
And the eternal morrow dawn;
Then the curtains will be drawn,
And they wake into a light
Whose day shall never die in night.
RICHARD CRASHAW (1613?–1649)

325   TO LUCASTA, GOING TO THE WARS
Tell me not, Sweet, I am unkind,
  That from the nunnery
Of thy chaste breast and quiet mind
  To war and arms I fly.

True, a new mistress now I chase,
    The first foe in the field;
And with a stronger faith embrace
    A sword, a horse, a shield.

Yet this inconstancy is such
    As thou too shalt adore;
I could not love thee, Dear, so much,
    Loved I not Honour more.
              RICHARD LOVELACE (1618–1658)

326. To Lucasta, going beyond the Seas

If to be absent were to be
    Away from thee;
  Or that when I am gone
  You or I were alone;
Then, my Lucasta, might I crave
Pity from blustering wind or swallowing wave.

But I'll not sigh one blast or gale
    To swell my sail,
  Or pay a tear to 'suage
  The foaming blue god's rage;
For whether he will let me pass
Or no, I'm still as happy as I was.

Though seas and land betwixt us both,
    Our faith and troth,
  Like separated souls,
  All time and space controls:
Above the highest sphere we meet
Unseen, unknown; and greet as Angels greet.

So then we do anticipate
    Our after-fate,
  And are alive i' the skies,
  If thus our lips and eyes
Can speak like spirits unconfined
In Heaven, their earthy bodies left behind.
              RICHARD LOVELACE (1618–1658)

327. Gratiana Dancing

She beat the happy pavèment—
By such a star made firmament,
  Which now no more the roof envies!
    But swells up high, with Atlas even,
    Bearing the brighter nobler heaven,
And, in her, all the deities.

Each step trod out a Lover's thought,
And the ambitious hopes he brought
  Chain'd to her brave feet with such arts,
    Such sweet command and gentle awe,
    As, when she ceased, we sighing saw
  The floor lay paved with broken hearts.

       RICHARD LOVELACE (1618–1658)

328   TO AMARANTHA, THAT SHE WOULD
      DISHEVEL HER HAIR

Amarantha sweet and fair,
Ah, braid no more that shining hair!
As my curious hand or eye
Hovering round thee, let it fly!

Let it fly as unconfined
As its calm ravisher the wind,
Who hath left his darling, th' East,
To wanton o'er that spicy nest.

Every tress must be confest,
But neatly tangled at the best;
Like a clew of golden thread
Most excellently ravelled.

Do not then wind up that light
In ribbands, and o'ercloud in night,
Like the Sun in's early ray;
But shake your head, and scatter day!

       RICHARD LOVELACE (1618–1658)

329   THE GRASSHOPPER

O thou that swing'st upon the waving hair
 Of some well-filled oaten beard,
Drunk every night with a delicious tear
 Dropt thee from heaven, where thou wert rear'd!

The joys of earth and air are thine entire,
 That with thy feet and wings dost hop and fly;
And when thy poppy works, thou dost retire
 To thy carved acorn-bed to lie.

Up with the day, the Sun thou welcom'st then,
 Sport'st in the gilt plaits of his beams,
And all these merry days mak'st merry men,
 Thyself, and melancholy streams.

       RICHARD LOVELACE (1618–1658)

330   TO ALTHEA, FROM PRISON

When Love with unconfinèd wings
 Hovers within my gates,
And my divine Althea brings
 To whisper at the grates;

When I lie tangled in her hair
  And fetter'd to her eye,
The birds that wanton in the air
  Know no such liberty.

When flowing cups run swiftly round
  With no allaying Thames,
Our careless heads with roses bound,
  Our hearts with loyal flames;
When thirsty grief in wine we steep,
  When healths and draughts go free—
Fishes that tipple in the deep
  Know no such liberty.

When, like committed linnets, I
  With shriller throat shall sing
The sweetness, mercy, majesty,
  And glories of my King;
When I shall voice aloud how good
  He is, how great should be,
Enlargèd winds, that curl the flood,
  Know no such liberty.

Stone walls do not a prison make,
  Nor iron bars a cage;
Minds innocent and quiet take
  That for an hermitage;
If I have freedom in my love
  And in my soul am free,
Angels alone, that soar above,
  Enjoy such liberty.

                RICHARD LOVELACE (1618–1658)

DRINKING   331

The thirsty earth soaks up the rain,
And drinks and gapes for drink again;
The plants suck in the earth, and are
With constant drinking fresh and fair;
The sea itself (which one would think
Should have but little need of drink)
Drinks twice ten thousand rivers up,
So fill'd that they o'erflow the cup.
The busy Sun (and one would guess
By's drunken fiery face no less)
Drinks up the sea, and when he's done,
The Moon and Stars drink up the Sun:
They drink and dance by their own light,
They drink and revel all the night:
Nothing in Nature's sober found,
But an eternal health goes round.

Fill up the bowl, then, fill it high,
Fill all the glasses there—for why
Should every creature drink but I?
Why, man of morals, tell me why?

ABRAHAM COWLEY (1618–1667)
from Anacreontics

332
THE EPICURE
Underneath this myrtle shade,
On flowerly beds supinely laid,
With odorous oils my head o'erflowing,
And around it roses growing,
What should I do but drink away
The heat and troubles of the day?
In this more than kingly state
Love himself on me shall wait.
Fill to me, Love! nay, fill it up!
And mingled cast into the cup
Wit and mirth and noble fires,
Vigorous health and gay desires.
The wheel of life no less will stay
In a smooth than rugged way:
Since it equally doth flee,
Let the motion pleasant be.
Why do we precious ointments shower?—
Nobler wines why do we pour?—
Beauteous flowers why do we spread
Upon the monuments of the dead?
Nothing they but dust can show,
Or bones that hasten to be so.
Crown me with roses while I live,
Now your wines and ointments give:
After death I nothing crave,
Let me alive my pleasures have:
All are Stoics in the grave.

ABRAHAM COWLEY (1618–1667)
from Anacreontics

333
THE SWALLOW
Foolish prater, what dost thou
So early at my window do?
Cruel bird, thou'st ta'en away
A dream out of my arms to-day;
A dream that ne'er must equall'd be
By all that waking eyes may see.
Thou this damage to repair
Nothing half so sweet and fair,
Nothing half so good, canst bring,
Tho' men say thou bring'st the Spring.

ABRAHAM COWLEY (1618–1667)
from Anacreontics

The Wish 334

Well then! I now do plainly see
    This busy world and I shall ne'er agree.
The very honey of all earthly joy
Does of all meats the soonest cloy;
    And they, methinks, deserve my pity
Who for it can endure the stings,
The crowd and buzz and murmurings,
    Of this great hive, the city.

Ah, yet, ere I descend to the grave
May I a small house and large garden have;
And a few friends, and many books, both true,
Both wise, and both delightful too!
    And since love ne'er will from me flee,
A Mistress moderately fair,
And good as guardian angels are,
    Only beloved and loving me.

O fountains! when in you shall I
Myself eased of unpeaceful thoughts espy?
O fields! O woods! when, when shall I be made
Thy happy tenant of your shade?
    Here's the spring-head of Pleasure's flood:
Here's wealthy Nature's treasury,
Where all the riches lie that she
    Has coin'd and stamp'd for good.

Pride and ambition here
Only in far-fetch'd metaphors appear;
Here nought but winds can hurtful murmurs scatter,
And nought but Echo flatter.
    The gods, when they descended, hither
From heaven did always choose their way:
And therefore we may boldly say
    That 'tis the way too thither.

Hoe happy here should I
And one dear She live, and embracing die!
She who is all the world, and can exclude
In deserts solitude.
    I should have then this only fear:
Lest men, when they my pleasures see,
Should hither throng to live like me,
    And so make a city here.

                      Abraham Cowley (1618–1667)

The Resolve 335

    Tell me not of a face that's fair,
      Nor lip and cheek that's red,
    Nor of the tresses of her hair,
      Nor curls in order laid,

        Nor of a rare seraphic voice
          That like an angel sings;
        Though if I were to take my choice
          I would have all these things:
        But if that thou wilt have me love,
          And it must be a she,
        The only argument can move
          Is that she will love me.

        The glories of your ladies be
          But metaphors of things,
        And but resemble what we see
          Each common object brings.
        Roses out-red their lips and cheeks,
          Lilies their whiteness stain;
        What fool is he that shadows seeks
          And may the substance gain?
        Then if thou'lt have me love a lass,
          Let it be one that's kind:
        Else I'm a servant to the glass
          That's with Canary lined.
                        ALEXANDER BROME (1620–1666)

336   AN HORATIAN ODE
       UPON CROMWELL'S RETURN FROM IRELAND
        The forward youth that would appear
        Must now forsake his Muses dear,
          Nor in the shadows sing
          His numbers languishing.

        'Tis time to leave the books in dust,
        And oil the unused armour's rust,
          Removing from the wall
          The corslet of the hall.

        So restless Cromwell could not cease
        In the inglorious arts of peace,
          But through adventurous war
          Urgèd his active star:

        And like the three-fork'd lightning, first
        Breaking the clouds where it was nurst,
          Did thorough his own side
          His fiery way divide:

        For 'tis all one to courage high,
        The emulous, or enemy;
          And with such, to enclose
          Is more than to oppose.

        Then burning through the air he went
        And palaces and temples rent;
          And Cæsar's head at last
          Did through his laurels blast.

'Tis madness to resist or blame
The face of angry Heaven's flame;
    And if we would speak true,
    Much to the man is due,

Who, from his private gardens, where
He lived reserved and austere
    (As if his highest plot
    To plant the bergamot),

Could by industrious valour climb
To ruin the great work of time,
    And cast the Kingdoms old
    Into another mould;

Though Justice against Fate complain,
And plead the ancient rights in vain—
    But those do hold or break
    As men are strong or weak—

Nature, that hateth emptiness,
Allows of penetration less,
    And therefore must make room
    Where greater spirits come.

What field of all the civil war
Where his were not the deepest scar?
    And Hampton shows what part
    He had of wiser art;

Where, twining subtle fears with hope,
He wove a net of such a scope
    That Charles himself might chase
    To Caresbrooke's narrow case;

That thence the Royal actor borne
The tragic scaffold might adorn:
    While round the armed bands
    Did clap their bloody hands.

He nothing common did or mean
Upon that memorable scene,
    But with his keener eye
    The axe's edge did try;

Nor call'd the gods, with vulgar spite,
To vindicate his helpless right;
    But bow'd his comely head
    Down, as upon a bed.

This was that memorable hour
Which first assured the forced power:
    So when they did design
    The Capitol's first line,

A Bleeding Head, where they begun,
Did fright the architects to run;
    And yet in that the State
    Foresaw its happy fate!

And now the Irish are ashamed
To see themselves in one year tamed:
    So much one man can do
    That does both act and know.

They can affirm his praises best,
And have, though overcome, confest
    How good he is, how just
    And fit for highest trust.

Nor yet grown stiffer with command,
But still in the republic's hand—
    How fit he is to sway
    That can so well obey!

He to the Commons' feet presents
A Kingdom for his first year's rents,
    And, what he may, forbears
    His fame, to make it theirs:

And has his sword and spoils ungirt
To lay them at the public's skirt.
    So when the falcon high
    Falls heavy from the sky,

She, having kill'd, no more doth search
But on the next green bough to perch;
    Where, when he first does lure,
    The falconer has her sure.

What may not then our Isle presume
While victory his crest does plume?
    What may not others fear,
    If thus he crowns each year?

As Cæsar he, ere long, to Gaul,
To Italy an Hannibal,
    And to all States not free
    Shall climacteric be.

The Pict no shelter now shall find
Within his particolour'd mind,
    But, from this valour, sad
    Shrink underneath the plaid;

Happy, if in the tufted brake
The English hunter him mistake,
    Nor lay his hounds in near
    The Caledonian deer.

But thou, the war's and fortune's son,
March indefatigably on;
   And for the last effect,
   Still keep the sword erect:

Besides the force it has to fright
The spirits of the shady night,
   The same arts that did gain
   A power, must it maintain.
ANDREW MARVELL (1621–1678)

A GARDEN   337
WRITTEN AFTER THE CIVIL WARS
See how the flowers, as at parade,
Under their colours stand display'd:
Each regiment in order grows,
That of the tulip, pink, and rose.
But when the vigilant patrol
Of stars walks round about the pole,
Their leaves, that to the stalks are curl'd,
Seem to their staves the ensigns furl'd.
Then in some flower's beloved hut
Each bee, as sentinel, is shut,
And sleeps so too; but if once stirr'd,
She runs you through, nor asks the word.
O thou, that dear and happy Isle,
The garden of the world erewhile,
Thou Paradise of the four seas
Which Heaven planted us to please,
But, to exclude the world, did guard
With wat'ry if not flaming sword;
What luckless apple did we taste
To make us mortal and thee waste!
Unhappy! shall we never more
That sweet militia restore,
When gardens only had their towers,
And all the garrisons were flowers;
When roses only arms might bear,
And men did rosy garlands wear?
ANDREW MARVELL (1621–1678)

TO HIS COY MISTRESS   338
Had we but world enough, and time,
This coyness, Lady, were no crime
We would sit down and think which way
To walk and pass our long love's day.
Thou by the Indian Ganges' side
Shouldst rubies find: I by the tide
Of Humber would complain. I would
Love you ten years before the Flood,
And you should, if you please, refuse
Till the conversion of the Jews.
My vegetable love should grow
Vaster than empires, and more slow;

An hundred years should go to praise
Thine eyes and on thy forehead gaze;
Two hundred to adore each breast,
But thirty thousand to the rest;
An age at least to every part,
And the last age should show your heart.
For, Lady, you deserve this state,
Nor would I love at lower rate.
  But at my back I always hear
Time's wingèd chariot hurrying near;
And yonder all before us lie
Deserts of vast eternity.
Thy beauty shall no more be found,
Nor, in thy marble vault, shall sound
My echoing song: then worms shall try
That long preserved virginity,
And your quaint honour turn to dust,
And into ashes all my lust:
The grave's a fine and private place,
But none, I think, do there embrace.
  Now therefore, while the youthful hue
Sits on thy skin like morning dew,
And while thy willing soul transpires
At every pore with instant fires,
Now let us sport us while we may,
And now, like amorous birds of prey,
Rather at once our time devour
Than languish in his slow-chapt power.
Let us roll all our strength and all
Our sweetness up into one ball,
And tear our pleasures with rough strife
Thorough the iron gates of life:
Thus, though we cannot make our sun
Stand still, yet we will make him run.
                              ANDREW MARVELL (1621–1678)

slow-chapt: *slow-jawed, slowly devouring*

339   THE PICTURE OF LITTLE T. C. IN A PROSPECT OF FLOWERS

See with what simplicity
  This nymph begins her golden days!
    In the green grass she loves to lie,
And there with her fair aspect tames
The wilder flowers, and gives them names;
  But only with the roses plays,
        And them does tell
What colour best becomes them, and what smell.

    Who can foretell for what high cause
  This darling of the gods was born?
    Yet this is she whose chaster laws
The wanton Love shall one day fear,

    And, under her command severe,
      See his bow broke and ensigns torn.
          Happy who can
Appease this virtuous enemy of man!

    O then let me in time compound
      And parley with those conquering eyes,
        Ere they have tried their force to wound;
    Ere with their glancing wheels they drive
    In triumph over hearts that strive,
      And them that yield but more despise:
          Let me be laid,
Where I may see the glories from some shade.

    Meantime, whilst every verdant thing
      Itself does at thy beauty charm,
        Reform the errors of the Spring;
    Make that the tulips may have share
    Of sweetness, seeing they are fair,
      And roses of their thorns disarm;
          But most procure
That violets may a longer age endure.

    But O, young beauty of the woods,
      Whom Nature courts with fruits and flowers,
        Gather the flowers, but spare the buds;
    Lest Flora, angry at thy crime
    To kill her infants in their prime,
      Do quickly make th' example yours;
          And ere we see,
Nip in the blossom all our hopes and thee.

ANDREW MARVELL (1621–1678)

THOUGHTS IN A GARDEN   *340*

How vainly men themselves amaze
To win the palm, the oak, or bays,
And their uncessant labours see
Crown'd from some single herb or tree,
Whose short and narrow-verged shade
Does prudently their toils upbraid;
While all the flowers and trees do close
To weave the garlands of repose!

Fair Quiet, have I found thee here,
And Innocence thy sister dear?
Mistaken long, I sought you then
In busy companies of men:
Your sacred plants, if here below,
Only among the plants will grow:
Society is all but rude
To this delicious solitude.

No white nor red was ever seen
So amorous as this lovely green.
Fond lovers, cruel as their flame,
Cut in these trees their mistress' name:
Little, alas! they know or heed
How far these beauties hers exceed!
Fair trees! wheres'e'er your barks I wound,
No name shall but your own be found.

When we have run our passions' heat,
Love hither makes his best retreat:
The gods, that mortal beauty chase,
Still in a tree did end their race;
Apollo hunted Daphne so
Only that she might laurel grow;
And Pan did after Syrinx speed
Not as a nymph, but for a reed.

What wondrous life in this I lead!
Ripe apples drop about my head;
The luscious clusters of the vine
Upon my mouth do crush their wine;
The nectarine and curious peach
Into my hands themselves do reach;
Stumbling on melons, as I pass,
Ensnared with flowers, I fall on grass.

Meanwhile the mind from pleasure less
Withdraws into its happiness;
The mind, that ocean where each kind
Does straight its own resemblance find;
Yet it creates, transcending these,
Far other worlds, and other seas;
Annihilating all that's made
To a green thought in a green shade.

Here at the fountain's sliding foot,
Or at some fruit-tree's mossy root,
Casting the body's vest aside,
My soul into the boughs does glide;
There, like a bird, it sits and sings,
Then whets and combs its silver wings,
And, till prepared for longer flight,
Waves in its plumes the various light.

Such was that happy Garden-state
While man there walk'd without a mate:
After a place so pure and sweet,
What other help could yet be meet!
But 'twas beyond a mortal's share
To wander solitary there:
Two paradises 'twere in one,
To live in Paradise alone.

How well the skilful gard'ner drew
Of flowers and herbs this dial new!
Where, from above, the milder sun
Does through a fragrant zodiac run:
And, as it works, th' industrious bee
Computes its time as well as we.
How could such sweet and wholesome hours
Be reckon'd, but with herbs and flowers!
ANDREW MARVELL (1621–1678)

SONGS OF THE EMIGRANTS IN BERMUDA   341
Where the remote Bermudas ride
In the ocean's bosom unespied,
From a small boat that row'd along
The listening woods received this song:

"What should we do but sing His praise
That led us through the watery maze
Unto an isle so long unknown,
And yet far kinder than our own?
Where He the huge sea-monsters wracks,
That lift the deep upon their backs,
He lands us on a grassy stage,
Safe from the storms' and prelates' rage:
He gave us this eternal Spring
Which here enamels everything,
And sends the fowls to us in care
On daily visits through the air:
He hangs in shades the orange bright
Like golden lamps in a green night,
And does in the pomegranates close
Jewels more rich than Ormus shows:
He makes the figs our mouths to meet
And throws the melons at our feet;
But apples plants of such a price,
No tree could ever bear them twice.
With cedars chosen by His hand
From Lebanon He stores the land;
And makes the hollow seas that roar
Proclaim the ambergris on shore.
He cast (of which we rather boast)
The Gospel's pearl upon our coast;
And in these rocks for us did frame
A temple where to sound His name.
O, let our voice His praise exalt
Till it arrive at Heaven's vault,
Which thence (perhaps) rebounding may
Echo beyond the Mexique bay!"

Thus sung they in the English boat
A holy and a cheerful note:
And all the way, to guide their chime,
With falling oars they kept the time.
ANDREW MARVELL (1621–1678)

342   An Epitaph

Enough; and leave the rest to Fame!
'Tis to commend her, but to name.
Courtship which, living, she declined,
When dead, to offer were unkind:
Nor can the truest wit, or friend,
Without detracting, her commend.

To say—she lived a virgin chaste
In this age loose and all unlaced;
Nor was, when vice is so allowed,
Of virtue or ashamed or proud;
That her soul was on Heaven so bent,
No minute but it came and went;
That, ready her last debt to pay,
She summ'd her life up every day;
Modest as morn, as mid-day bright,
Gentle as evening, cool as night:
—'Tis true; but all too weakly said.
'Twas more significant, she's dead.
                          ANDREW MARVELL (1621–1678)

343   The Retreat

Happy those early days, when I
Shin'd in my Angel-infancy!
Before I understood this place
Appointed for my second race,
Or taught my soul to fancy aught
But a white celestial thought:
When yet I had not walk'd above
A mile or two from my first Love,

And looking back—at that short space—
Could see a glimpse of His bright face:
When on some gilded cloud, or flow'r,
My gazing soul would dwell an hour,
And in those weaker glories spy
Some shadows of eternity:
Before I taught my tongue to wound
My Conscience with a sinful sound,
Or had the black art to dispense
A several sin to ev'ry sense,
But felt through all this fleshly dress
Bright shoots of everlastingness.

  O how I long to travel back,
And tread again that ancient track!
That I might once more reach that plain
Where first I left my glorious train;
From whence th' enlightned spirit sees
That shady City of Palm-trees.
But ah! my soul with too much stay
Is drunk, and staggers in the way!

Some men a forward motion love,
But I by backward steps would move;
And when this dust falls to the urn,
In that state I came, return.

HENRY VAUGHAN (1621–1695)

PEACE 344

  My soul, there is a country
    Far beyond the stars,
  Where stands a winged sentry
    All skilful in the wars:
  There, above noise and danger,
    Sweet Peace sits crown'd with smiles,
  And One born in a manger
    Commands the beauteous files.
  He is thy gracious Friend,
    And—O my soul, awake!—
  Did in pure love descend
    To die here for thy sake.
  If thou canst get but thither,
    There grows the flower of Peace,
  The Rose that cannot wither,
    Thy fortress, and thy ease.
  Leave then thy foolish ranges;
    For none can thee secure
  But One who never changes—
    Thy God, thy life, thy cure.

HENRY VAUGHAN (1621–1695)

THE TIMBER 345

Sure thou didst flourish once! and many springs,
  Many bright mornings, much dew, many showers,
Pass'd o'er thy head; many light hearts and wings,
  Which now are dead, lodg'd in thy living bowers.

And still a new succession sings and flies;
  Fresh groves grow up, and their green branches shoot
Towards the old and still enduring skies,
  While the low violet thrives at their root.

But thou beneath the sad and heavy line
  Of death, doth waste all senseless, cold, and dark;
Where not so much as dreams of light may shine,
  Nor any thought of greenness, leaf, or bark.

And yet—as if some deep hate and dissent,
  Bred in thy growth betwixt high winds and thee,
Were still alive—thou dost great storms resent
  Before they come, and know'st how near they be.

Else all at rest thou liest, and the fierce breath
  Of tempests can no more disturb thy ease;
But this thy strange resentment after death
  Means only those who broke—in life—thy peace.

HENRY VAUGHAN (1621–1695)

346   FRIENDS DEPARTED

They are all gone into the world of light!
    And I alone sit ling'ring here;
Their very memory is fair and bright,
    And my sad thoughts doth clear.

It glows and glitters in my cloudy breast,
    Like stars upon some gloomy grove,
Or those faint beams in which this hill is drest
    After the sun's remove.

I see them walking in an air of glory,
    Whose light doth trample on my days:
My days, which are at best but dull and hoary,
    Mere glimmering and decays.

O holy Hope! and high Humility,
    High as the heavens above!
These are your walks, and you have show'd them me,
    To kindle my cold love.

Dear, beauteous Death! the jewel of the Just,
    Shining nowhere, but in the dark;
What mysteries do lie beyond thy dust,
    Could man outlook that mark!

He that hath found some fledg'd bird's nest may know,
    At first sight, if the bird be flown;
But what fair well or grove he sings in now,
    That is to him unknown.

And yet as Angels in some brighter dreams
    Call to the soul, when man doth sleep:
So some strange thoughts transcend our wonted themes,
    And into glory peep.

If a star were confin'd into a tomb,
    Her captive flames must needs burn there;
But when the hand that lock'd her up gives room,
    She'll shine through all the sphere.

O Father of eternal life, and all
    Created glories under Thee!
Resume Thy spirit from this world of thrall
    Into true liberty.

Either disperse these mists, which blot and fill
    My perspective still as they pass:
Or else remove me hence unto that hill,
    Where I shall need no glass.
                                        HENRY VAUGHAN (1621–1695)

The Shepherd Boy Sings in the Valley of Humiliation 347

He that is down needs fear no fall,
  He that is low, no pride;
He that is humble ever shall
  Have God to be his guide.

I am content with what I have,
  Little be it or much:
And, Lord, contentment still I crave,
  Because Thou savest such.

Fullness to such a burden is
  That go on pilgrimage:
Here little, and hereafter bliss,
  Is best from age to age.

JOHN BUNYAN (1628–1688)

Sir Patrick Spens 348
I. The Sailing

The king sits in Dunfermline town
  Drinking the blude-red wine;
"O whare will I get a skeely skipper
  To sail this new ship o' mine?"

O up and spak an eldern knight,
  Sat at the king's right knee;
"Sir Patrick Spens is the best sailor
  That ever sail'd the sea."

Our king has written a braid letter,
  And seal'd it with his hand,
And sent it to Sir Patrick Spens,
  Was walking on the strand.

"To Noroway, to Noroway,
  To Noroway o'er the faem;
The king's daughter o' Noroway,
  'Tis thou must bring her hame."

The first word that Sir Patrick read
  So loud, loud laugh'd he;
The neist word that Sir Patrick read
  The tear blinded his e'e.

'O wha is this has done this deed
  And tauld the king o' me,
To send us out, at this time o' year,
  To sail upon the sea?

"Be it wind, be it weet, be it hail, be it sleet,
  Our ship must sail the faem;
The king's daughter o' Noroway,
  'Tis we must fetch her hame."

They hoysed their sails on Monenday morn
    Wi' a' the speed they may;
They hae landed in Noroway
    Upon a Wodensday.

II. The Return

"Mak ready, mak ready, my merry men a'!
    Our gude ship sails the morn."
"Now ever alack, my master dear,
    I fear a deadly storm.

"I saw the new moon late yestreen
    Wi' the auld moon in her arm;
And if we gang to sea, master,
    I fear we'll come to harm."

They hadna sail'd a league, a league,
    A league but barely three,
When the lift grew dark, and the wind blew loud,
    And gurly grew the sea.

The ankers brak, and the topmast lap,
    It was sic a deadly storm:
And the waves cam owre the broken ship
    Till a' her sides were torn.

"Go fetch a web o' the silken claith,
    Another o' the twine,
And wap them into our ship's side,
    And let nae the sea come in."

They fetch'd a web o' the silken claith,
    Another o' the twine,
And they wapp'd them round that gude ship's side,
    But still the sea came in.

O laith, laith were our gude Scots lords
    To wet their cork-heel'd shoon;
But lang or a' the play was play'd
    They wat their hats aboon.

And mony was the feather bed
    That flatter'd on the faem;
And mony was the gude lord's son
    That never mair cam hame.

O lang, lang may the ladies sit,
    Wi' their fans into their hand,
Before they see Sir Patrick Spens
    Come sailing to the strand!

And lang, lang may the maidens sit
    Wi' their gowd kames in their hair,
A-waiting for their ain dear loves!
    For them they'll see nae mair.

> Half-owre, half-owre to Aberdour,
>   'Tis fifty fathoms deep;
> And there lies gude Sir Patrick Spens,
>   Wi' the Scots lords at his feet!
>   BALLADS AND SONGS BY UNKNOWN AUTHORS (17th Cent.)

skeely: *skilful*; lift: *sky*; lap: *sprang*; flatter'd: *tossed afloat*; kames: *combs*

THE DOWIE HOUMS OF YARROW   349

> Late at een, drinkin' the wine,
>   And ere they paid the lawin',
> They set a combat them between,
>   To fight it in the dawin'.
>
> "O stay at hame, my noble lord!
>   O stay at hame, my marrow!
> My cruel brother will you betray,
>   On the dowie houms o' Yarrow."
>
> "O fare ye weel, my lady gay!
>   O fare ye weel, my Sarah!
> For I maun gae, tho' I ne'er return
>   Frae the dowie banks o' Yarrow."
>
> She kiss'd his cheek, she kamed his hair,
>   As she had done before, O;
> She belted on his noble brand,
>   An' he's awa to Yarrow.
>
> O he's gane up yon high, high hill—
>   I wat he gaed wi' sorrow—
> An' in a den spied nine arm'd men,
>   I' the dowie houms o' Yarrow.
>
> "O are ye come to drink the wine,
>   As ye hae doon before, O?
> Or are ye come to wield the brand,
>   On the dowie banks o' Yarrow?"
>
> "I am no come to drink the wine,
>   As I hae don before, O,
> But I am come to wield the brand,
>   On the dowie houms o' Yarrow."
>
> Four he hurt, an' five he slew,
>   On the dowie houms o' Yarrow,
> Till that stubborn knight came him behind,
>   An' ran his body thorrow.
>
> "Gae hame, gae hame, good brother John,
>   An' tell your sister Sarah
> To come an' lift her noble lord,
>   Who's sleepin' sound on Yarrow."

"Yestreen I dream'd a dolefu' dream;
  I ken'd there wad be sorrow;
I dream'd I pu'd the heather green,
  On the dowie banks o' Yarrow."

She gaed up yon high, high hill—
  I wat she gaed wi' sorrow—
An' in a den spied nine dead men,
  On the dowie houms o' Yarrow.

She kiss'd his cheek, she kamed his hair,
  As oft she did before, O;
She drank the red blood frae him ran,
  On the dowie houms o' Yarrow.

"O haud your tongue, my douchter dear,
  For what needs a' this sorrow?
I'll wed you on a better lord
  Than him you lost on Yarrow."

"O haud your tongue, my father dear,
  An' dinna grieve your Sarah;
A better lord was never born
  Than him I lost on Yarrow.

"Tak hame your ousen, tak hame your kye,
  For they hae bred our sorrow;
I wiss that they had a' gane mad
  When they cam first to Yarrow."
      BALLADS AND SONGS BY UNKNOWN AUTHORS (17th Cent.)

lawin': *reckoning*; marrow: *mate, husband or wife*; dowie: *doleful*; houms: *water-meads*

350   CLERK SAUNDERS

Clerk Saunders and may Margaret
  Walk'd owre yon garden green;
And deep and heavy was the love
  That fell thir twa between.

"A bed, a bed," Clerk Saunders said,
  "A bed for you and me!"
"Fye na, fye na," said may Margaret,
  "Till anes we married be!"

"Then I'll take the sword frae my scabbard
  And slowly lift the pin;
And you may swear, and save your aith,
  Ye ne'er let Clerk Saunders in.

"Take you a napkin in your hand,
  And tie up baith your bonnie e'en,
And you may swear, and save your aith,
  Ye saw me na since late yestreen."

It was about the midnight hour,
   When they asleep were laid,
When in and came her seven brothers,
   Wi' torches burning red:

When in and came her seven brothers,
   Wi' torches burning bright:
They said, "We hae but one sister,
   And behold her lying with a knight!"

Then out and spake the first o' them,
   "I bear the sword shall gar him die."
And out and spake the second o' them,
   "His father has nae mair but he."

And out and spake the third o' them,
   "I wot that they are lovers dear."
And out and spake the fourth o' them,
   "They hae been in love this mony a year."

Then out and spake the fifth o' them,
   "It were great sin true love to twain."
And out and spake the sixth o' them,
   "It were shame to slay a sleeping man."

Then up and gat the seventh o' them,
   And never a word spake he;
But he has striped his bright brown brand
   Out through Clerk Saunders' fair bodye.

Clerk Saunders he started, and Margaret she turn'd
   Into his arms as asleep she lay;
And sad and silent was the night
   That was atween thir twae.

And they lay still and sleepit sound
   Until the day began to daw';
And kindly she to him did say,
   "It is time, true love, you were awa'."

But he lay still, and sleepit sound,
   Albeit the sun began to sheen;
She look'd atween her and the wa',
   And dull and drowsie were his e'en.

Then in and came her father dear;
   Said, "Let a' your mourning be;
I'll carry the dead corse to the clay,
   And I'll come back and comfort thee."

"Comfort weel your seven sons,
   For comforted I will never be:
I ween 'twas neither knave nor loon
   Was in the bower last night wi' me."

The clinking bell gaed through the town,
    To carry the dead corse to the clay;
And Clerk Saunders stood at may Margaret's window,
    I wot, an hour before the day.

"Are ye sleeping, Marg'ret?" he says,
    "Or are ye waking presentlie?
Give me my faith and troth again,
    I wot, true love, I gied to thee."

"Your faith and troth ye sall never get,
    Nor our true love sall never twin,
Until ye come within my bower,
    And kiss me cheik and chin."

"My mouth it is full cold, Marg'ret;
    It has the smell, now, of the ground;
And if I kiss thy comely mouth,
    Thy days of life will not be lang.

"O cocks are crowing a merry midnight;
    I wot the wild fowls are boding day;
Give me my faith and troth again,
    And let me fare me on my way."

"Thy faith and troth thou sallna get,
    And our true love sall never twin,
Until ye tell what comes o' women,
    I wot, who die in strong traivelling?"

"Their beds are made in the heavens high,
    Down at the foot of our good Lord's knee,
Weel set about wi' gillyflowers;
    I wot, sweet company for to see.

"O cocks are crowing a merry midnight;
    I wot the wild fowls are boding day;
The psalms of heaven will soon be sung,
    And I, ere now, will be miss'd away."

Then she has taken a crystal wand,
    And she has stroken her troth thereon;
She has given it him out at the shot-window,
    Wi' mony a sad sigh and heavy groan.

"I thank ye, Marg'ret; I thank ye, Marg'ret;
    And ay I thank ye heartilie;
Gin ever the dead come for the quick,
    Be sure, Marg'ret, I'll come for thee."

It's hosen and shoon, and gown alone,
    She climb'd the wall, and follow'd him,
Until she came to the green forest,
    And there she lost the sight o' him.

"Is there ony room at your head, Saunders?
　　Is there ony room at your feet?
　Or ony room at your side, Saunders,
　　Where fain, fain, I wad sleep?"

"There's nae room at my head, Marg'ret,
　　There's nae room at my feet;
　My bed it is fu' lowly now,
　　Amang the hungry worms I sleep.

"Cauld mould is my covering now,
　　But and my winding-sheet;
　The dew it falls nae sooner down
　　Than my resting-place is weet.

"But plait a wand o' bonny birk,
　　And lay it on my breast;
　And shed a tear upon my grave,
　　And wish my saul gude rest."

Then up and crew the red, red cock,
　　And up and crew the gray:
"'Tis time, 'tis time, my dear Marg'ret,
　　That you were going away.

"And fair Marg'ret, and rare Marg'ret,
　　And Marg'ret o' veritie,
　Gin e'er ye love another man,
　　Ne'er love him as ye did me."
　　　　BALLADS AND SONGS BY UNKNOWN AUTHORS (17th Cent.)

striped: *thrust*; twin: *part in two*

EDWARD, EDWARD 351

"Why does your brand sae drop wi' blude,
　　Edward, Edward?
Why does your brand sae drop wi' blude,
　　And why sae sad gang ye, O?"
"O I hae kill'd my hawk sae gude,
　　Mither, mither;
O I hae kill'd my hawk sae gude,
　　And I had nae mair but he, O."

"Your hawk's blude was never sae red,
　　Edward, Edward;
Your hawk's blude was never sae red,
　　My dear son, I tell thee, O."
"O I hae kill'd my red-roan steed,
　　Mither, mither;
O I hae kill'd my red-roan steed,
　　That erst was sae fair and free, O."

"Your steed was auld, and ye hae got mair,
　　Edward, Edward;
Your steed was auld, and ye hae got mair;
　　Some other dule ye dree, O."

"O I hae kill'd my father dear,
    Mither, mither;
O I hae kill'd my father dear,
    Alas, and wae is me, O!"

"And whatten penance will ye dree for that,
    Edward, Edward?
Whatten penance will ye dree for that?
    My dear son, now tell me, O."
"I'll set my feet in yonder boat,
    Mither, mither;
I'll set my feet in yonder boat,
    And I'll fare over the sea, O."

"And what will ye do wi' your tow'rs and your ha',
    Edward, Edward?
And what will ye do wi' your tow'rs and your ha',
    That were sae fair to see, O?"
"I'll let them stand till they doun fa',
    Mither, mither;
I'll let them stand till they doun fa',
    For here never mair maun I be, O."

"And what will ye leave to your bairns and your wife,
    Edward, Edward?
And what will ye leave to your bairns and your wife,
    When ye gang owre the sea, O?"
"The warld's room: let them beg through life,
    Mither, mither;
The warld's room: let them beg through life;
    For them never mair will I see, O."

"And what will ye leave to your ain mither dear,
    Edward, Edward?
And what will ye leave to your ain mither dear,
    My dear son, now tell me, O?"

"The curse of hell frae me sall ye bear,
    Mither, mither;
The curse of hell frae me sall ye bear:
    Sic counsels ye gave to me, O!"
                BALLADS AND SONGS BY UNKNOWN AUTHORS (17th Cent.)
dule ye dree: *grief you suffer*

352   THE QUEEN'S MARIE
Marie Hamilton's to the kirk gane,
    Wi' ribbons in her hair;
The King thought mair o' Marie Hamilton
    Than ony that were there.

Marie Hamilton's to the kirk gane
    Wi' ribbons on her breast;
The King thought mair o' Marie Hamilton
    Than he listen'd to the priest.

Marie Hamilton's to the kirk gane,
  Wi' gloves upon her hands;
The King thought mair o' Marie Hamilton
  Than the Queen and a' her lands.

She hadna been about the King's court
  A month, but barely one,
Till she was beloved by a' the King's court
  And the King the only man.

She hadna been about the King's court
  A month, but barely three,
Till frae the King's court Marie Hamilton,
  Marie Hamilton durstna be.

The King is to the Abbey gane,
  To pu' the Abbey tree,
To scale the babe frae Marie's heart;
  But the thing it wadna be.

O she has row'd it in her apron,
  And set it on the sea—
"Gae sink ye or swim ye, bonny babe,
  Ye'se get nae mair o' me."

Word is to the kitchen gane,
  And word is to the ha',
And word is to the noble room
  Amang the ladies a',
That Marie Hamilton's brought to bed,
  And the bonny babe's miss'd and awa'.

Scarcely had she lain down again,
  And scarcely fa'en asleep,
When up and started our gude Queen
  Just at her bed-feet;
Saying—"Marie Hamilton, where's your babe?
  For I am sure I heard it greet."

"O no, O no, my noble Queen!
  Think no sic thing to be;
'Twas but a stitch into my side,
  And sair it troubles me!"

"Get up, get up, Marie Hamilton:
  Get up and follow me;
For I am going to Edinburgh town,
  A rich wedding for to see."

O slowly, slowly rase she up,
  And slowly put she on;
And slowly rade she out the way
  Wi' mony a weary groan.

The Queen was clad in scarlet,
  Her merry maids all in green;
And every town that they cam to,
  They took Marie for the Queen.

"Ride hooly, hooly, gentlemen,
  Ride hooly now wi' me!
For never, I am sure, a wearier burd
  Rade in your companie."—

But little wist Marie Hamilton,
  When she rade on the brown,
That she was gaen to Edinburgh town,
  And a' to be put down.

"Why weep ye so, ye burgess wives,
  Why look ye so on me?
O I am going to Edinburgh town,
  A rich wedding to see."

When she gaed up the tolbooth stairs,
  The corks frae her heels did flee;
And lang or e'er she cam down again,
  She was condemn'd to die.

When she cam to the Netherbow port,
  She laugh'd loud laughters three;
But when she came to the gallows foot
  The tears blinded her e'e.

"Yestreen the Queen had four Maries,
  The night she'll hae but three;
There was Marie Seaton, and Marie Beaton,
  And Marie Carmichael, and me.

"O often have I dress'd my Queen
  And put gowd upon her hair;
But now I've gotten for my reward
  The gallows to be my share.

"Often have I dress'd my Queen
  And often made her bed;
But now I've gotten for my reward
  The gallows tree to tread.

"I charge ye all, ye mariners,
  When ye sail owre the faem,
Let neither my father nor mother get wit
  But that I'm coming hame.

"I charge ye all, ye mariners,
  That sail upon the sea,
That neither my father nor mother get wit
  The dog's death I'm to die.

"For if my father and mother got wit,
   And my bold brethren three,
O mickle wad be the gude red blude
   This day wad be spilt for me!

"O little did my mother ken,
   The day she cradled me,
The lands I was to travel in
   Or the death I was to die!"
      BALLADS AND SONGS BY UNKNOWN AUTHORS (17th Cent.)

wroken: avenged; row'd: rolled, wrapped; greet: cry; hooly: gently

BINNORIE 353

There were twa sisters sat in a bour;
   Binnorie, O Binnorie!
There cam a knight to be their wooer,
   By the bonnie milldams o' Binnorie.

He courted the eldest with glove and ring,
But he lo'ed the youngest abune a thing.

The eldest she was vexèd sair,
And sair envied her sister fair.

Upon a morning fair and clear,
She cried upon her sister dear:

"O sister, sister tak my hand,
And let's go down to the river-strand."

She's ta'en her by the lily hand,
And led her down to the river-strand.

The youngest stood upon a stane,
The eldest cam and push'd her in.

"O sister, sister reach your hand!
And ye sall be heir o' half my land:

"O sister, reach me but your glove!
And sweet William sall be your love."

Sometimes she sank, sometimes she swam,
Until she cam to the miller's dam.

Out then cam the miller's son,
And saw the fair maid soummin' in.

"O father, father draw your dam!
There's either a mermaid or a milk-white swan."

The miller hasted and drew his dam,
And there he found a drown'd women.

You couldna see her middle sma',
Her gowden girdle was sae braw.

You couldna see her lily feet,
Her gowden fringes were sae deep.

All amang her yellow hair
A string o' pearls was twisted rare.

You couldna see her fingers sma',
Wi' diamond rings they were cover'd a'.

And by there cam a harper fine,
That harpit to the king at dine.

And when he look'd that lady on,
He sigh'd and made a heavy moan.

He's made a harp of her breast-bane,
Whose sound wad melt a heart of stane.

He's ta'en three locks o' her yellow hair,
And wi' them strung his harp sae rare.

He went into her father's hall,
And there was the court assembled all.

He laid his harp upon a stane,
And straight it began to play by lane.

"O yonder sits my father, the King,
And yonder sits my mother, the Queen;

"And yonder stands my brother Hugh,
And by him my William, sweet and true."

But the last tune that the harp play'd then—
  Binnorie, O Binnorie!
Was, "Woe to my sister, false Helèn!"
  By the bonnie milldams o' Binnorie.
      BALLADS AND SONGS BY UNKNOWN AUTHORS (17th Cent.)
soummin': *swimming*

354   THE WIFE OF USHER'S WELL
There lived a wife at Usher's well,
  And a wealthy wife was she;
She had three stout and stalwart sons,
  And sent them o'er the sea.

They hadna been a week from her,
  A week but barely ane,
When word came to the carline wife
  That her three sons were gane.

They hadna been a week from her,
  A week but barely three,
When word came to the carline wife
  That her sons she'd never see.

"I wish the wind may never cease.
    Nor fashes in the flood,
Till my three sons come hame to me,
    In earthly flesh and blood!"

It fell about the Martinmas,
    When nights are lang and mirk,
The carline wife's three sons came hame,
    And their hats were o' the birk.

It neither grew in syke nor ditch,
    Nor yet in ony sheugh;
But at the gates o' Paradise
    That birk grew fair eneugh.

"Blow up the fire, my maidens!
    Bring water from the well!
For a' my house shall feast this night,
    Since my three sons are well."

And she has made to them a bed,
    She's made it large and wide;
And she's ta'en her mantle her about,
    Sat down at the bedside.

Up then crew the red, red cock,
    And up and crew the gray;
The eldest to the youngest said,
    "'Tis time we were away."

The cock he hadna craw'd but once,
    And clapp'd his wings at a',
When the youngest to the eldest said,
    "Brother, we must awa'.

"The cock doth craw, the day doth daw,
    The channerin' worm doth chide;
Gin we be miss'd out o' our place,
    A sair pain we maun bide."

"Lie still, lie still but a little wee while,
    Lie still but if we may;
Gin my mother should miss us when she wakes,
    She'll go mad ere it be day."

"Fare ye weel, my mother dear!
    Fareweel to barn and byre!
And fare ye weel, the bonny lass
    That kindles my mother's fire!"
    BALLADS AND SONGS BY UNKNOWN AUTHORS (17th Cent.)

fashes: *troubles*; syke: *marsh*; sheugh: *trench*; channerin': *fretting*

THE THREE RAVENS   355

There were three ravens sat on a tree,
    They were as black as they might be.

The one of them said to his make,
"Where shall we our breakfast take?"

"Down in yonder greenè field
There lies a knight slain under his shield;

"His hounds they lie down at his feet,
So well they can their master keep;

"His hawks they flie so eagerly,
There's no fowl dare come him nigh.

"Down there comes a fallow doe
As great with young as she might goe.

"She lift up his bloudy head
And kist his wounds that were so red.

"She gat him up upon her back
And carried him to earthen lake.

"She buried him before the prime,
She was dead herself ere evensong time.

"God send every gentleman
Such hounds, such hawks, and such a leman."
  BALLADS AND SONGS BY UNKNOWN AUTHORS (17th Cent.)

make: *mate*

356
THE TWA CORBIES
(SCOTTISH VERSION)

As I was walking all alane
I heard twa corbies making a mane:
The tane unto the tither did say,
"Whar sall we gang and dine the day?"

"—In behint yon auld fail dyke
I wot there lies a new-slain knight;
And naebody kens that he lies there
But his hawk, his hound, and his lady fair.

"His hound is to the hunting gane,
His hawk to fetch the wild-fowl hame,
His lady's ta'en anither mate,
So we may mak our dinner sweet.

"Ye'll sit on his white hause-bane,
And I'll pike out his bonny blue e'en:
Wi' ae lock o' his gowden hair
We'll theek our nest when it grows bare.

"Mony a one for him maks mane,
But nane sall ken whar he is gane:
O'er his white banes, when they are bare,
The wind sall blaw for evermair."
  BALLADS AND SONGS BY UNKNOWN AUTHORS (17th Cent.)

corbies: *ravens*; fail: *turf*; hause: *neck*; theek: *thatch*

A Lyke-Wake Dirge 357

This ae nighte, this ae nighte,
  —*Every nighte and alle,*
Fire and fleet and candle-lighte,
  And Christe receive thy saule.

When thou from hence away art past,
  —*Every nighte and alle,*
To Whinny-muir thou com'st at last;
  And Christe receive thy saule.

If ever thou gavest hosen and shoon,
  —*Every nighte and alle,*
Sit thee down and put them on;
  And Christe receive thy saule.

If hosen and shoon thou ne'er gav'st nane
  —*Every nighte and alle,*
The whinnes sall prick thee to the bare bane;
  And Christe receive thy saule.

From Whinny-muir when thou may'st pass,
  —*Every nighte and alle,*
To Brig o' Dread thou com'st at last;
  And Christe receive thy saule.

From Brig o' Dread when thou may'st pass,
  —*Every nighte and alle,*
To Purgatory fire thou com'st at last;
  And Christe receive thy saule.

If ever thou gavest meat or drink,
  —*Every nighte and alle,*
The fire sall never make thee shrink;
  And Christe receive thy saule.

If meat or drink thou ne'er gav'st nane,
  —*Every nighte and alle,*
The fire will burn thee to the bare bane;
  And Christe receive thy saule.

This ae nighte, this ae nighte,
  —*Every nighte and alle,*
Fire and fleet and candle-lighte,
  And Christe receive thy saule.
      BALLADS AND SONGS BY UNKNOWN AUTHORS (17th Cent.)

fleet: *house-room*

The Seven Virgins. 358
A CAROL

All under the leaves and the leaves of life
  I met with virgins seven,
And one of them was Mary mild,
  Our Lord's mother of Heaven.

"O what are you seeking, you seven fair maids,
  All under the leaves of life?
Come tell, come tell, what seek you
  All under the leaves of life?"

"We're seeking for no leaves, Thomas,
  But for a friend of thine;
We're seeking for sweet Jesus Christ,
  To be our guide and thine."

"Go down, go down, to yonder town,
  And sit in the gallery,
And there you'll see sweet Jesus Christ
  Nail'd to a big yew-tree."

So down they went to yonder town
  As fast as foot could fall,
And many a grievous bitter tear
  From the virgins' eyes did fall.

"O peace, Mother, O peace, Mother,
  Your weeping doth me grieve:
I must suffer this," He said,
  "For Adam and for Eve.

"O Mother, take you John Evangelist
  All for to be your son,
And he will comfort you sometimes,
  Mother, as I have done."

"O come, thou John Evangelist,
  Thou'rt welcome unto me;
But more welcome my own dear Son,
  Whom I nursed on my knee."

Then He laid His head on His right shoulder,
  Seeing death it struck Him nigh—
"The Holy Ghost be with your soul,
  I die, Mother dear, I die."

O the rose, the gentle rose,
  And the fennel that grows so green!
God give us grace in every place
  To pray for our king and queen.

Furthermore for our enemies all
  Our prayers they should be strong:
Amen, good Lord; your charity
  Is the ending of my song.
          BALLADS AND SONGS BY UNKNOWN AUTHORS (17th Cent.)

Two Rivers   359

   Says Tweed to Till—
"What gars ye rin sae still?"
   Says Till to Tweed—
"Though ye rin with speed
   And I rin slaw,
For ae man that ye droon
   I droon twa."
   BALLADS AND SONGS BY UNKNOWN AUTHORS (17th Cent.)

Cradle Song   360

O my deir hert, young Jesus sweit,
Prepare thy creddil in my spreit,
And I sall rock thee in my hert
And never mair from thee depart.

But I sall praise thee evermoir
With sangis sweit unto thy gloir;
The knees of my hert sall I bow,
And sing that richt *Balulalow!*
   BALLADS AND SONGS BY UNKNOWN AUTHORS (17th Cent.)

The Call   361

  My blood so red
  For thee was shed,
Come home again, come home again;
My own sweet heart, come home again!
  You've gone astray
  Out of your way,
Come home again, come home again!
   BALLADS AND SONGS BY UNKNOWN AUTHORS (17th Cent.)

The Bonny Earl of Murray   362

Ye Highlands and ye Lawlands,
  O where hae ye been?
They hae slain the Earl of Murray,
  And hae laid him on the green.

Now wae be to thee, Huntley!
  And whairfore did ye sae!
I bade you bring him wi' you,
  But forbade you him to slay.

He was a braw gallant,
  And he rid at the ring;
Ana the bonny Earl of Murray,
  O he might hae been a king!

He was a braw gallant,
  And he play'd at the ba';
And the bonny Earl of Murray
  Was the flower amang them a'!

He was a braw gallant,
   And he play'd at the gluve;
And the bonny Earl of Murray,
   O he was the Queen's luve!

O lang will his Lady
   Look owre the Castle Downe,
Ere she see the Earl of Murray
   Come sounding through the town!
     Ballads and Songs By Unknown Authors (17th Cent.)

363   Helen of Kirconnell

I wish I were where Helen lies,
   Night and day on me she cries;
O that I were where Helen lies,
   On fair Kirconnell lea!

Curst be the heart that thought the thought,
And curst the hand that fired the shot,
When in my arms burd Helen dropt,
   And died to succour me!

O think na ye my heart was sair,
When my Love dropp'd and spak nae mair!
There did she swoon wi' meikle care,
   On fair Kirconnell lea.

As I went down the water side,
None but my foe to be my guide,
None but my foe to be my guide,
   On fair Kirconnell lea;

I lighted down my sword to draw,
I hacked him in pieces sma',
I hacked him in pieces sma',
   For her sake that died for me.

O Helen fair, beyond compare!
I'll mak a garland o' thy hair,
Shall bind my heart for evermair,
   Until the day I die!

O that I were where Helen lies!
Night and day on me she cries;
Out of my bed she bids me rise,
   Says, "Haste, and come to me!"

O Helen fair! O Helen chaste!
If I were with thee, I'd be blest,
Where thou lies low and taks thy rest,
   On fair Kirconnell lea.

I wish my grave were growing green,
A winding-sheet drawn owre my e'en,
And I in Helen's arms lying,
   On fair Kirconnell lea.

I wish I were where Helen lies!
Night and day on me she cries;
And I am weary of the skies,
  For her sake that died for me.
      BALLADS AND SONGS BY UNKNOWN AUTHORS (17th Cent.)

WALY, WALY   364
O Waly, waly, up the bank,
  And waly, waly, doun the brae,
And waly, waly, yon burn-side,
  Where I and my Love wont to gae!
I lean'd my back unto an aik,
  I thocht it was a trustie tree;
But first it bow'd and syne it brak—
  Sae my true love did lichtlie me.

O waly, waly, gin love be bonnie
  A little time while it is new!
But when 'tis auld it waxeth cauld,
  And fades awa' like morning dew.
O wherefore should I busk my heid,
  Or wherefore should I kame my hair?
For my true Love has me forsook,
  And says he'll never lo'e me mair.

Now Arthur's Seat sall be my bed,
  The sheets sall ne'er be 'filed by me;
Saint Anton's well sall be my drink;
  Since my true Love has forsaken me.
Marti'mas wind, when wilt thou blaw,
  And shake the green leaves aff the tree?
O gentle Death, when wilt thou come?
  For of my life I am wearie.

'Tis not the frost, that freezes fell,
  Nor blawing snaw's inclemencie,
'Tis not sic cauld that makes me cry;
  But my Love's heart grown cauld to me.
When we cam in by Glasgow toun,
  We were a comely sicht to see;
My Love was clad in the black velvet,
  And I mysel in cramasie.

But had I wist, before I kist,
  That love had been sae ill to win,
I had lock'd my heart in a case o' gowd,
  And pinn'd it wi' a siller pin.
And O! if my young babe were born,
  And set upon the nurse's knee;
And I mysel were dead and gane,
  And the green grass growing over me!
      BALLADS AND SONGS BY UNKNOWN AUTHORS (17th Cent.)

cramasie: *crimson*

365   Barbara Allen's Cruelty

In Scarlet town, where I was born,
  There was a fair maid dwellin',
Made every youth cry *Well-a-way!*
  Her name was Barbara Allen.

All in the merry month of May,
  When green buds they were swellin',
Young Jemmy Grove on his death-bed lay,
  For love of Barbara Allen.

He sent his man in to her then,
  To the town where she was dwellin',
"O haste and come to my master dear,
  If your name be Barbara Allen."

So slowly, slowly rase she up,
  And slowly she came nigh him,
And when she drew the curtain by—
  "Young man, I think you're dyin'."

"O it's I am sick and very very sick,
  And it's all for Barbara Allen."
"O the better for me ye'se never be,
  Tho' your heart's blood were a-spillin'!

"O dinna ye mind, young man," says she,
  "When the red wine ye were fillin',
That ye made the healths go round and round,
  And slighted Barbara Allen?"

He turn'd his face unto the wall,
  And death was with him dealin':
"Adieu, adieu, my dear friends all,
  And be kind to Barbara Allen!"

As she was walking o'er the fields,
  She heard the dead-bell knellin';
And every jow the dead-bell gave
  Cried "Woe to Barbara Allen."

"O mother, mother, make my bed,
  O make it saft and narrow:
My love has died for me to-day,
  I'll die for him to-morrow.

"Farewell," she said, "ye virgins all,
  And shun the fault I fell in:
Henceforth take warning by the fall
  Of cruel Barbara Allen."

        Ballads and Songs By Unknown Authors (17th Cent.)

jow: *beat, toll*

PIPE AND CAN

I

The Indian weed witherèd quite;
Green at morn, cut down at night;
Shows thy decay: all flesh is hay:
    Thus think, then drink Tobacco.

And when the smoke ascends on high,
Think thou behold'st the vanity
Of worldly stuff, gone with a puff:
    Thus think, then drink Tobacco.

But when the pipe grows foul within,
Think of thy soul defiled with sin,
And that the fire doth it require:
    Thus think, then drink Tobacco.

The ashes, that are left behind,
May serve to put thee still in mind
That unto dust return thou must:
    Thus think, then drink Tobacco.

II

WHEN as the chill Charokko blows,
  And Winter tells a heavy tale;
When pyes and daws and rooks and crows
Sit cursing of the frosts and snows;
    Then give me ale.

Ale in a Saxon rumkin then,
  Such as will make grimalkin prate;
Bids valour burgeon in tall men,
Quickens the poet's wit and pen,
    Despises fate.

Ale, that the absent battle fights,
  And frames the march of Swedish drum,
Disputes with princes, laws, and rights,
What's done and past tells mortal wights,
    And what's to come.

Ale, that the plowman's heart up-keeps
  And equals it with tyrants' thrones,
That wipes the eye that over-weeps,
And lulls in sure and dainty sleeps
    Th' o'er-wearied bones.

Grandchild of Ceres, Bacchus' daughter,
  Wine's emulous neighbour, though but stale,
Ennobling all the nymphs of water,
And filling each man's heart with laughter—
    Ha! give me ale!

    BALLADS AND SONGS BY UNKNOWN AUTHORS (17th Cent.)

Charokko: *Scirocco*

367   LOVE WILL FIND OUT THE WAY

Over the mountains
  And over the waves,
Under the fountains
  And under the graves;
Under floods that are deepest,
  Which Neptune obey,
Over rocks that are steepest,
  Love will find out the way.

When there is no place
  For the glow-worm to lie,
When there is no space
  For receipt of a fly;
When the midge dares not venture
  Lest herself fast she lay,
If Love come, he will enter
  And will find out the way.

You may esteem him
  A child for his might;
Or you may deem him
  A coward for his flight;
But if she whom Love doth honour
  Be conceal'd from the day—
Set a thousand guards upon her,
  Love will find out the way.

Some think to lose him
  By having him confined;
And some do suppose him,
  Poor heart! to be blind;
But if ne'er so close ye wall him,
  Do the best that ye may,
Blind Love, if so ye call him,
  He will find out his way.

You may train the eagle
  To stoop to your fist;
Or you may inveigle
  The Phœnix of the east;
The lioness, you may move her
  To give over her prey;
But you'll ne'er stop a lover—
  He will find out the way.

If the earth it should part him,
  He would gallop it o'er;
If the seas should o'erthwart him,
  He would swim to the shore;
Should his Love become a swallow,
  Through the air to stray,
Love will lend wings to follow,
  And will find out the way.

There is no striving
  To cross his intent;
There is no contriving
  His plots to prevent;
But if once the message greet him
  That his True Love doth stay,
If Death should come and meet him,
  Love will find out the way!
    BALLADS AND SONGS BY UNKNOWN AUTHORS (17th Cent.)

PHILLADA FLOUTS ME   368

O what a plague is love!
  How shall I bear it?
She will inconstant prove,
  I greatly fear it.
She so torments my mind
  That my strength faileth,
And wavers with the wind
  As a ship saileth.
Please her the best I may,
She loves still to gainsay;
Alack and well-a-day!
  Phillada flouts me.

At the fair yesterday
  She did pass by me;
She look'd another way
  And would not spy me:
I woo'd her for to dine,
  But could not get her;
Will had her to the wine—
  He might entreat her.
With Daniel she did dance,
On me she look'd askance:
O thrice unhappy chance!
  Phillada flouts me.

Fair maid, be not so coy,
  Do not disdain me!
I am my mother's joy:
  Sweet, entertain me!
She'll give me, when she dies,
  All that is fitting:
Her poultry and her bees,
  And her goose sitting,
A pair of mattrass beds,
And a bag full of shreds;
And yet, for all this guedes,
  Phillada flouts me!

She hath a clout of mine
   Wrought with blue coventry,
Which she keeps for a sign
   Of my fidelity:
But i' faith, if she flinch
   She shall not wear it;
To Tib, my t'other wench,
   I mean to bear it.
And yet it grieves my heart
So soon from her to part:
Death strike me with his dart!
   Phillada flouts me.

Thou shalt eat crudded cream
   All the year lasting,
And drink the crystal stream
   Pleasant in tasting;
Whig and whey whilst thou lust,
   And bramble-berries,
Pie-lid and pastry-crust,
   Pears, plums, and cherries.
Thy raiment shall be thin,
Made of a weevil's skin—
Yet all's not worth a pin!
   Phillada flouts me.

In the last month of May
   I made her posies;
I heard her often say
   That she loved roses.
Cowslips and gillyflowers
   And the white lily
I brought to deck the bowers
   For my sweet Philly.
But she did all disdain,
And threw them back again;
Therefore 'tis flat and plain
   Phillada flouts me.

Fair maiden, have a care,
   And in time take me;
I can have those as fair
   If you forsake me:
For Doll the dairy-maid
   Laugh'd at me lately,
And wanton Winifred
   Favours me greatly.
One throws milk on my clothes,
T'other plays with my nose;
What wanting signs are those?
   Phillada flouts me.

I cannot work nor sleep
   At all in season:
Love wounds my heart so deep
   Without all reason.
I 'gin to pine away
   In my love's shadow,
Like as a fat beast may,
   Penn'd in a meadow.
I shall be dead, I fear,
   Within this thousand year:
And all for that my dear
   Phillada flouts me.
BALLADS AND SONGS BY UNKNOWN AUTHORS (17th Cent.)

guedes: *goods, property of any kind*

CHLORIS IN THE SNOW 369
I saw fair Chloris walk alone,
When feather'd rain came softly down,
As Jove descending from his Tower
To court her in a silver shower:
The wanton snow flew to her breast,
Like pretty birds into their nest,
But, overcome with whiteness there,
For grief it thaw'd into a tear:
   Thence falling on her garments' hem,
   To deck her, froze into a gem.
WILLIAM STRODE (1602–1645)

THE RELAPSE 370
O turn away those cruel eyes,
   The stars of my undoing!
Or death, in such a bright disguise,
   May tempt a second wooing.

Punish their blind and impious pride,
   Who dare contemn thy glory;
It was my fall that deified
   Thy name, and seal'd thy story.

Yet no new sufferings can prepare
   A higher praise to crown thee;
Though my first death proclaim thee fair,
   My second will unthrone thee.

Lovers will doubt thou canst entice
   No other for thy fuel,
And if thou burn one victim twice,
   Both think thee poor and cruel.
THOMAS STANLEY (1625–1678)

TO COELIA 371
When, Coelia, must my old day set,
   And my young morning rise
In beams of joy so bright as yet
   Ne'er bless'd a lover's eyes?

My state is more advanced than when
  I first attempted thee:
I sued to be a servant then,
  But now to be made free.

I've served my time faithful and true,
  Expecting to be placed
In happy freedom, as my due,
  To all the joys thou hast:
Ill husbandry in love is such
  A scandal to love's power,
We ought not to misspend so much
  As one poor short-lived hour.

Yet think not, sweet! I'm weary grown,
  That I pretend such haste;
Since none to surfeit e'er was known
  Before he had a taste:
My infant love could humbly wait
  When, young, it scarce knew how
To plead; but grown to man's estate,
  He is impatient now.

                    CHARLES COTTON (1630–1687)

372   TO ONE PERSUADING A LADY TO MARRIAGE

Forbear, bold youth; all's heaven here,
  And what you do aver
To others courtship may appear,
  'Tis sacrilege to her.
She is a public deity;
  And were't not very odd
She should dispose herself to be
  A petty household god?

First make the sun in private shine
  And bid the world adieu,
That so he may his beams confine
  In compliment to you:
But if of that you do despair,
  Think how you did amiss
To strive to fix her beams which are
  More bright and large than his.

                    KATHERINE PHILIPS ("ORINDA") (1631–1664)

373   A SONG FOR ST. CECILIA'S DAY, 1687

From harmony, from heavenly harmony,
  This universal frame began:
When nature underneath a heap
  Of jarring atoms lay,
And could not heave her head,
The tuneful voice was heard from high,
  "Arise, ye more than dead!"
Then cold, and hot, and moist, and dry,

In order to their stations leap,
  And Music's power obey.
From harmony, from heavenly harmony,
  This universal frame began:
  From harmony to harmony
Through all the compass of the notes it ran,
The diapason closing full in Man.

What passion cannot Music raise and quell?
    When Jubal struck the chorded shell,
  His listening brethren stood around,
    And, wondering, on their faces fell
  To worship that celestial sound:
Less than a God they thought there could not dwell
    Within the hollow of that shell,
    That spoke so sweetly, and so well.
What passion cannot Music raise and quell?

    The trumpet's loud clangour
      Excites us to arms,
    With shrill notes of anger,
      And mortal alarms.
    The double double double beat
      Of the thundering drum
        Cries Hark! the foes come;
  Charge, charge, 'tis too late to retreat!

    The soft complaining flute,
    In dying notes, discovers
    The woes of hopeless lovers,
Whose dirge is whisper'd by the warbling lute.

    Sharp violins proclaim
  Their jealous pangs and desperation,
  Fury, frantic indignation,
  Depth of pains, and height of passion,
    For the fair, disdainful dame.

    But O, what art can teach,
    What human voice can reach,
      The sacred organ's praise?
    Notes inspiring holy love,
  Notes that wing their heavenly ways
    To mend the choirs above.

  Orpheus could lead the savage race;
  And trees unrooted left their place,
    Sequacious of the lyre;
But bright Cecilia rais'd the wonder higher:
When to her organ vocal breath was given,
  An angel heard, and straight appear'd
    Mistaking Earth for Heaven.

GRAND CHORUS

As from the power of sacred lays
  The spheres began to move,
And sung the great Creator's praise
  To all the Blest above;
So when the last and dreadful hour
This crumbling pageant shall devour,
The trumpet shall be heard on high,
The dead shall live, the living die,
And Music shall untune the sky!

JOHN DRYDEN (1631–1700)

374   AH, HOW SWEET IT IS TO LOVE!

Ah, how sweet it is to love!
  Ah, how gay is young Desire!
And what pleasing pains we prove
  When we first approach Love's fire!
Pains of love be sweeter far
Than all other pleasures are.

Sighs which are from lovers blown
  Do but gently heave the heart:
Ev'n the tears they shed alone
  Cure, like trickling balm, their smart:
Lovers, when they lose their breath,
Bleed away in easy death.

Love and Time with reverence use,
  Treat them like a parting friend;
Nor the golden gifts refuse
  Which in youth sincere they send:
For each year their price is more,
And they less simple than before.

Love, like spring-tides full and high,
  Swells in every youthful vein;
But each tide does less supply,
  Till they quite shrink in again:
If a flow in age appear,
'Tis but rain, and runs not clear.

JOHN DRYDEN (1631–1700)

375   HIDDEN FLAME

I feed a flame within, which so torments me
That it both pains my heart, and yet contents me:
'Tis such a pleasing smart, and I so love it,
That I had rather die than once remove it.

Yet he, for whom I grieve, shall never know it;
My tongue does not betray, nor my eyes show it.
Not a sigh, nor a tear, my pain discloses,
But they fall silently, like dew on roses.

Thus, to prevent my Love from being cruel,
My heart's the sacrifice, as 'tis the fuel;
And while I suffer this to give him quiet,
My faith rewards my love, though he deny it.

On his eyes will I gaze, and there delight me;
While I conceal my love no frown can fright me.
To be more happy I dare not aspire,
Nor can I fall more low, mounting no higher.

JOHN DRYDEN (1631–1700)

376. Song to a Fair Young Lady, Going Out of the Town in the Spring

Ask not the cause why sullen Spring
  So long delays her flowers to bear;
Why warbling birds forget to sing,
  And winter storms invert the year:
Chloris is gone; and fate provides
To make it Spring where she resides.

Chloris is gone, the cruel fair;
  She cast not back a pitying eye:
But left her lover in despair
To sigh, to languish, and to die:
Ah! how can those fair eyes endure
To give the wounds they will not cure?

Great God of Love, why hast thou made
  A face that can all hearts command,
That all religions can invade,
  And change the laws of every land?
Where thou hadst plac'd such power before,
  Thou shouldst have made her mercy more.

When Chloris to the temple comes,
  Adoring crowds before her fall;
She can restore the dead from tombs
  And every life but mine recall.
I only am by Love design'd
To be the victim for mankind.

JOHN DRYDEN (1631–1700)

377. Song

Ladies, though to your conquering eyes
Love owes his chiefest victories,
And borrows those bright arms from you
With which he does the world subdue,
Yet you yourselves are not above
The empire nor the griefs of love.

Then rack not lovers with disdain,
Lest Love on you revenge their pain:
You are not free because you're fair:
The Boy did not his Mother spare.
Beauty's but an offensive dart:
It is no armour for the heart.

                    Sir George Etherege (1635–1691)

378   How Long he Would Love

It is not, Celia, in our power
  To say how long our love will last;
It may be we within this hour
  May lose those joys we now do taste;
The Blessèd, that immortal be,
From change in love are only free.

Then since we mortal lovers are,
  Ask not how long our love will last;
But while it does, let us take care
  Each minute be with pleasure past:
Were it not madness to deny
To live because we're sure to die?

                    Sir George Etherege (1635–1691)

379   News

News from a foreign country came
As if my treasure and my wealth lay there;
  So much it did my heart inflame,
'Twas wont to call my Soul into mine ear;
     Which thither went to meet
       The approaching sweet,
    And on the threshold stood
  To entertain the unknown Good.
       It hover'd there
     As if 'twould leave mine ear,
And was so eager to embrace
  The joyful tidings as they came,
'Twould almost leave its dwelling-place
  To entertain that same.

As if the tidings were the things,
My very joys themselves, my foreign treasure—
  Or else did bear them on their wings—
With so much joy they came, with so much pleasure.
     My Soul stood at that gate
       To recreate
    Itself with bliss, and to
Be pleased with speed. A fuller view
      It fain would take,
    Yet journeys back would make
Unto my heart; as if 'twould fain
  Go out to meet, yet stay within
To fit a place to entertain
  And bring the tidings in.

What sacred instinct did inspire
My soul in childhood with a hope so strong?
What secret force moved my desire
To expect my joys beyond the seas, so young?
      Felicity I knew
          Was out of view,
     And being here alone,
 I saw that happiness was gone
         From me! For this
     I thirsted absent bliss,
And thought that sure beyond the seas,
  Or else in something near at hand—
I knew not yet—since naught did please
    I knew—my Bliss did stand.

But little did the infant dream
That all the treasures of the world were by:
  And that himself was so the cream
And crown of all which round about did lie.
      Yet thus it was: the Gem,
         The Diadem,
     The ring enclosing all
 That stood upon this earthly ball,
       The Heavenly eye,
     Much wider than the sky,
Wherein they all included were,
  The glorious Soul, that was the King
 Made to possess them, did appear
    A small and little thing!
               THOMAS TRAHERNE (1637?–1674)

THE SAD DAY   380

O the sad day!
When friends shall shake their heads, and say
Of miserable me—
"Hark, how he groans!
Look, how he pants for breath!
See how he struggles with the pangs of death!"
When they shall say of these dear eyes—
"How hollow, O how dim they be!
Mark how his breast doth rise and swell
Against his potent enemy!"
When some old friend shall step to my bedside,
Touch my chill face, and thence shall gently slide.

But—when his next companions say
"How does he do? What hopes?"—shall turn away,
Answering only, with a lift-up hand—
"Who can his fate withstand?"

Then shall a gasp or two do more
Than e'er my rhetoric could before:
Persuade the world to trouble me no more!

THOMAS FLATMAN (1637–1688)

381   SONG
WRITTEN AT SEA, IN THE FIRST DUTCH WAR (1665),
THE NIGHT BEFORE AN ENGAGEMENT

To all you ladies now at land
  We men at sea indite;
But first would have you understand
  How hard it is to write:
The Muses now, and Neptune too,
We must implore to write to you—
  With a fa, la, la, la, la.

For though the Muses should prove kind,
  And fill our empty brain,
Yet if rough Neptune rouse the wind
  To wave the azure main,
Our paper, pen, and ink, and we,
Roll up and down our ships at sea—
  With a fa, la, la, la, la.

Then if we write not by each post,
  Think not we are unkind;
Nor yet conclude our ships are lost
  By Dutchmen or by wind:
Our tears we'll send a speedier way,
The tide shall bring them twice a day—
  With a fa, la, la, la, la.

The King with wonder and surprise
  Will swear the seas grow bold,
Because the tides will higher rise
  Than e'er they did of old:
But let him know it is our tears
Bring floods of grief to Whitehall stairs—
  With a fa, la, la, la, la.

Should foggy Opdam chance to know
  Our sad and dismal story,
The Dutch would scorn so weak a foe,
  And quit their fort at Goree:
For what resistance can they find
From men who've left their hearts behind?—
  With a fa, la, la, la, la.

Let wind and weather do its worst,
  Be you to us but kind;
Let Dutchmen vapour, Spaniards curse,
  No sorrow we shall find:
'Tis then no matter how things go,
Or who's our friend, or who's our foe—
  With a fa, la, la, la, la.

To pass our tedious hours away
  We throw a merry main,
Or else at serious ombre play;
  But why should we in vain
Each other's ruin thus pursue?
We were undone when we left you—
    With a fa, la, la, la, la.

But now our fears tempestuous grow
  And cast our hopes away;
Whilst you, regardless of our woe,
  Sit careless at a play:
Perhaps permit some happier man
To kiss your hand, or flirt your fan—
    With a fa, la, la, la, la.

When any mournful tune you hear,
  That dies in every note
As if it sigh'd with each man's care
  For being so remote,
Think then how often love we've made
To you, when all those tunes were play'd—
    With a fa, la, la, la, la.

In justice you cannot refuse
  To think of our distress,
When we for hopes of honour lose
  Our certain happiness:
All those designs are but to prove
Ourselves more worthy of your love—
    With a fa, la, la, la, la.

And now we've told you all our loves,
  And likewise all our fears,
In hopes this declaration moves
  Some pity for our tears:
Let's hear of no inconstancy—
We have too much of that at sea—
    With a fa, la, la, la, la.
        CHARLES SACKVILLE, EARL OF DORSET (1638–1706)

TO CHLORIS   382

Ah, Chloris! that I now could sit
  As unconcern'd as when
Your infant beauty could beget
  No pleasure, nor no pain!
When I the dawn used to admire,
  And praised the coming day,
I little thought the growing fire
  Must take my rest away.

Your charms in harmless childhood lay
    Like metals in the mine;
Age from no face took more away
    Than youth conceal'd in thine.
But as your charms insensibly
    To their perfection prest,
Fond love as unperceived did fly,
    And in my bosom rest.

My passion with your beauty grew,
    And Cupid at my heart,
Still as his mother favour'd you,
    Threw a new flaming dart:
Each gloried in their wanton part;
    To make a lover, he
Employ'd the utmost of his art—
    To make a beauty, she.

                            SIR CHARLES SEDLEY (1639–1701)

383   TO CELIA

Not, Celia, that I juster am
    Or better than the rest!
For I would change each hour, like them,
    Were not my heart at rest.

But I am tied to very thee
    By every thought I have;
Thy face I only care to see,
    Thy heart I only crave.

All that in woman is adored
    In thy dear self I find—
For the whole sex can but afford
    The handsome and the kind.

Why then should I seek further store,
    And still make love anew?
When change itself can give no more,
    'Tis easy to be true!

                            SIR CHARLES SEDLEY (1639–1701)

384   SONG

Love in fantastic triumph sate
    Whilst bleeding hearts around him flow'd,
For whom fresh pains he did create
    And strange tyrannic power he show'd:
From thy bright eyes he took his fires,
    Which round about in sport he hurl'd;
But 'twas from mine he took desires
    Enough t' undo the amorous world.

From me he took his sighs and tears,
    From thee his pride and cruelty;
From me his languishments and fears,
    And every killing dart from thee.

Thus thou and I the god have arm'd
  And set him up a deity;
But my poor heart alone is harm'd,
  Whilst thine the victor is, and free!
                                APHRA BEHN (1640–1689)

THE LIBERTINE   385

A thousand martyrs I have made,
  All sacrificed to my desire,
A thousand beauties have betray'd
  That languish in resistless fire:
The untamed heart to hand I brought,
And fix'd the wild and wand'ring thought.

I never vow'd nor sigh'd in vain,
  But both, tho' false, were well received;
The fair are pleased to give us pain,
  And what they wish is soon believed:
And tho' I talk'd of wounds and smart,
Love's pleasures only touch'd my heart.

Alone the glory and the spoil
  I always laughing bore away;
The triumphs without pain or toil,
  Without the hell the heaven of joy;
And while I thus at random rove
Despise the fools that whine for love.
                                APHRA BEHN (1640–1689)

RETURN   386

Absent from thee, I languish still;
  Then ask me not, When I return?
The straying fool 'twill plainly kill
  To wish all day, all night to mourn.

Dear, from thine arms then let me fly,
  That my fantastic mind may prove
The torments it deserves to try,
  That tears my fix'd heart from my love.

When, wearied with a world of woe,
  To thy safe bosom I retire,
Where love, and peace, and truth does flow,
  May I contented there expire!

Lest, once more wandering from that heaven,
  I fall on some base heart unblest;
Faithless to thee, false, unforgiven—
  And lose my everlasting rest.
                JOHN WILMOT, EARL OF ROCHESTER (1647–1680)

387 ## Love and Life
All my past life is mine no more;
   The flying hours are gone,
Like transitory dreams given o'er,
Whose images are kept in store
   By memory alone.

The time that is to come is not;
   How can it then be mine?
The present moment's all my lot;
And that, as fast as it is got,
   Phillis, is only thine.

Then talk not of inconstancy,
   False hearts, and broken vows;
If I by miracle can be
This live-long minute true to thee,
   'Tis all that Heaven allows.
      JOHN WILMOT, EARL OF ROCHESTER (1647–1680)

388 ## Constancy
I cannot change as others do,
   Though you unjustly scorn;
Since that poor swain that sighs for you
   For you alone was born.
No, Phillis, no; your heart to move
   A surer way I'll try;
And, to revenge my slighted love,
   Will still love on and die.

When kill'd with grief Amyntas lies,
   And you to mind shall call
The sighs that now unpitied rise,
   The tears that vainly fall—
That welcome hour, that ends this smart,
   Will then begin your pain;
For such a faithful tender heart
   Can never break in vain.
      JOHN WILMOT, EARL OF ROCHESTER (1647–1680)

389 ## To His Mistress
(After Quarles)
Why dost thou shade thy lovely face? O why
Does that eclipsing hand of thine deny
The sunshine of the Sun's enlivening eye?

Without thy light what light remains in me?
Thou art my life; my way, my light's in thee;
I live, I move, and by thy beams I see.

Thou art my life—if thou but turn away
My life's a thousand deaths. Thou art my way—
Without thee, Love, I travel not but stray.

My light thou art—without thy glorious sight
My eyes are darken'd with eternal night.
My Love, thou art my way, my life, my light.

Thou art my way; I wander if thou fly.
Thou art my light; if hid, how blind am I!
Thou art my life; if thou withdraw'st, I die.

My eyes are dark and blind, I cannot see:
To whom or whither should my darkness flee,
But to that light?—and who's that light but thee?

If I have lost my path, dear lover, say,
Shall I still wander in a doubtful way?
Love, shall a lamb of Israel's sheepfold stray?

My path is lost, my wandering steps do stray;
I cannot go, nor can I safely stay;
Whom should I seek but thee, my path, my way?

And yet thou turn'st thy face away and fly'st me!
And yet I sue for grace and thou deny'st me!
Speak, art thou angry, Love, or only try'st me?

Thou art the pilgrim's path, the blind man's eye,
The dead man's life. On thee my hopes rely:
If I but them remove, I surely die.

Dissolve thy sunbeams, close thy wings and stay!
See, see how I am blind, and dead, and stray!
—O thou that art my life, my light, my way!

Then work thy will! If passion bid me flee,
My reason shall obey, my wings shall be
Stretch'd out no farther than from me to thee!
    JOHN WILMOT, EARL OF ROCHESTER (1647–1680)

THE RECONCILEMENT   390

Come, let us now resolve at last
 To live and love in quiet;
We'll tie the knot so very fast
 That Time shall ne'er untie it.

The truest joys they seldom prove
 Who free from quarrels live:
'Tis the most tender part of love
 Each other to forgive.

When least I seem'd concern'd, I took
 No pleasure nor no rest;
And when I feign'd an angry look,
 Alas! I loved you best.

Own but the same to me—you'll find
  How blest will be our fate.
O to be happy—to be kind—
  Sure never is too late!
    JOHN SHEFFIELD, DUKE OF BUCKINGHAMSHIRE (1649–1720)

391   ON ONE WHO DIED DISCOVERING HER KINDNESS
Some vex their souls with jealous pain,
While others sigh for cold disdain:
Love's various slaves we daily see—
Yet happy all compared with me!

Of all mankind I loved the best
A nymph so far above the rest
That we outshined the Blest above;
In beauty she, as I in love.

And therefore They, who could not bear
To be outdone by mortals here,
Among themselves have placed her now,
And left me wretched here below.

All other fate I could have borne,
And even endured her very scorn;
But oh! thus all at once to find
That dread account—both dead and kind!
What heart can hold? If yet I live,
'Tis but to show how much I grieve.
    JOHN SHEFFIELD, DUKE OF BUCKINGHAMSHIRE (1649–1720)

392   ON THE LATE MASSACRE IN PIEMONT
Avenge, O Lord! Thy slaughter'd Saints, whose bones
Lie scatter'd on the Alpine mountains cold;
Even them who kept Thy truth so pure of old
When all our fathers worshipt stocks and stones.

Forget not: In Thy book record their groans
Who were Thy sheep, and in their ancient fold
Slain by the bloody Piemontese, that roll'd
Mother with infant down the rocks. Their moans

The vales redoubled to the hills, and they
To Heaven. Their martyr'd blood and ashes sow
O'er all the Italian field, where still doth sway
The triple tyrant, that from these may grow
A hundred-fold, who, having learnt Thy way,
Early may fly the Babylonian woe.
    JOHN MILTON (1608–1674)

393   WHEN THE ASSAULT WAS INTENDED TO THE CITY
Captain, or Colonel, or Knight in arms,
Whose chance on these defenceless doors may seize,
If deed of honour did thee ever please;
Guard them, and him within protect from harms.

He can requite thee; for he knows the charms
That call fame on such gentle acts as these.
And he can spread thy name o'er lands and seas,
Whatever clime the sun's bright circle warms.

Lift not thy spear against the Muses' bower:
The great Emathian conqueror bid spare
The house of Pindarus, when temple and tower
Went to the ground: and the repeated air
Of sad Electra's poet had the power
To save the Athenian walls from ruin bare.

JOHN MILTON (1608–1674)

THE LOVLINESS OF LOVE 394

It is not Beauty I demand,
A crystal brow, the moon's despair,
Nor the snow's daughter, a white hand,
Nor mermaid's yellow pride of hair:

Tell me not of your starry eyes,
Your lips that seem on roses fed,
Your breasts, where Cupid tumbling lies,
Nor sleeps for kissing of his bed:—

A bloomy pair of vermeil cheeks
Like Hebe's in her ruddiest hours,
A breath that softer music speaks
Than summer winds a-wooing flowers,

These are but gauds: nay what are lips?
Coral beneath the ocean-stream,
Whose brink when your adventurer slips
Full oft he perisheth on them.

And what are cheeks, but ensigns oft
That wave hot youth to fields of blood?
Did Helen's breast, though ne'er so soft,
Do Greece or Ilium any good?

Eyes can with baleful ardour burn;
Poison can breathe, that erst perfumed;
There's many a white hand holds an urn
With lovers hearts to dust consumed.

For crystal brows there's nought within;
They are but empty cells for pride;
He who the Syren's hair would win
Is mostly strangled in the tide.

Give me, instead of Beauty's bust,
A tender heart, a loyal mind
Which with temptation I would trust,
Yet never link'd with error find,—

> One in whose gentle bosom I
> Could pour my secret heart of woes,
> Like the care-burthen'd honey-fly
> That hides his murmurs in the rose,—
>
> My earthly Comforter! whose love
> So indefeasible might be
> That, when my spirit wonn'd above,
> Hers could not stay, for sympathy.
>
> ANONYMOUS (c. 17th Cent.)

395   A SUPPLICATION

> Awake, awake, my Lyre!
> And tell thy silent master's humble tale
>   In sounds that may prevail;
> Sounds that gentle thoughts inspire:
>   Though so exalted she
>   And I so lowly be
> Tell her, such different notes make all thy harmony.
>
> Hark! how the strings awake:
> And, though the moving hand approach not near,
>   Themselves with awful fear
> A kind of numerous trembling make.
>   Now all thy forces try;
>   Now all thy charms apply;
> Revenge upon her ear the conquests of her eye.
>
> Weak Lyre! thy virtue sure
> Is useless here, since thou art only found
>   To cure, but not to wound,
> And she to wound, but not to cure.
>   Too weak too wilt thou prove
>   My passion to remove;
> Physic to other ills, thou'rt nourishment to love.
>
> Sleep, sleep again my Lyre!
> For thou canst never tell my humble tale
>   In sounds that will prevail,
> Nor gentle thoughts in her inspire;
>   All thy vain mirth lay by,
>   Bid thy strings silent lie,
> Sleep, sleep again, my Lyre, and let thy master die.
>
> ABRAHAM COWLEY (1618–1667)

396   THE FAIR SINGER

> To make a final conquest of all me,
> Love did compose so sweet an enemy,
> In whom both beauties to my death agree,
> Joining themselves in fatal harmony,
> That, while she with her eyes my heart does bind,
> She with her voice might captivate my mind.

I could have fled from one but singly fair;
My disentangled soul itself might save,
Breaking the curlèd trammels of her hair;
But how should I avoid to be her slave,
Whose subtle art invisibly can wreathe
My fetters of the very air I breathe?

It had been easy fighting in some plain,
Where victory might hang in equal choice,
But all resistance against her is vain,
Who has the advantage both of eyes and voice;
And all my forces needs must be undone,
She having gainèd both the wind and sun.

        ANDREW MARVELL (1621–1678)

WHEN ON MINE EYES HER EYES FIRST SHONE   397
When on mine eyes her eyes first shone,
  I all amazèd
  Steadily gazèd,
And she to make me more amazèd,
So caught, so wove, four eyes in one
As who had with advisement seen us
Would have admired love's equal force between us.

But treason in those friend-like eyes,
  My heart first charming
  And then disarming,
So maimed it, e'er it dreamed of harming,
As at her mercy now it lies,
And shews me, to my endless smart,
She loved but with her eyes, I with my heart.

        JOHN WILSON (1595–1674)

THE PASTIME OF THE QUEEN OF FAIRIES   398
Queen Mab and all her Fairy fry,
Dance on a pleasant molehill high:
With fine straw pipes sweet music's pleasure,
They make and keep just time and measure.
All hand in hand, around, around,
They dance upon the Fairy ground.
And when she leaves her dancing-hall
She doth for her attendants call,
To wait upon her to a bower,
Where she doth sit beneath a flower,
To shade her from the moonshine bright;
And gnats do sing for her delight.
The whilst the bat doth fly about
To keep in order all the rout.
She on a dewy leaf doth bathe,
And as she sits the leaf doth wave:
Like a new fallen flake of snow
All her white limbs in beauty show.
Her garments fair her maids put on,
Made of the pure light from the sun,

From whence such colours she inshades
In every object she invades.
Then to her dinner she goes straight,
Where all her imps in order wait.
Upon a mushroom there is spread
A cover fine of spiders web;
And for her stool a thistle-down;
And for her cup an acorn's crown,
Wherein strong nectar there is filled,
That from sweet flower is distilled.
Flies of all sorts both fat and good,
For snipe, quail, partridge are her food.
Omelettes made of ant eggs new—
Of such high meats she eats but few.
Her milk is from the dormouse udder,
Which makes her cheese and cream and butter:
This they do mix in many a knack,
And fresh laid ants' eggs therein crack:—
Both pudding, custard and seed-cake,
Her skilled cook well knows how to bake.
To sweeten them the bee doth bring
Pure honey gathered by her sting:
But for her guard serves grosser meat—
They of the stall-fed dormouse eat.
When dined she calls, to take the air,
Her coach which is a nutshell fair;
Lined soft it is and rich within,
Made of a glistening adders skin,
And there six crickets draw her fast,
When she a journey takes in haste:
Or else two serve to pace a round,
And trample on the Fairy ground.
To hawk sometimes she takes delight,
Her bird a hornet swift for flight,
Whose horns do serve for talons strong,
To gripe the partridge-fly among.
But if she will a hunting go,
The lizard answers for a doe;
It is so swift and fleet in chase,
That her slow coach cannot keep pace;
Then on the grasshopper she'll ride
And gallop in the forest wide.
Her bow is of a willow branch,
To shoot the lizard on the haunch:
Her arrow sharp, much like a blade,
Of a rosemary leaf is made.
Then home she's summoned by the cock,
Who gives her warning what's o'clock,
And when the moon doth hide her head,
Her day is done, she goes to bed.
Meteors do serve, when they are bright,
As torches do, to give her light,

Glow-worms for candles are lit up,
Set on the table while she sup.
But women, the inconstant kind,
Ne'er in one place content their mind,
She calls her chariot and away
To upper earth—impatient of long stay.

The stately palace in which the Queen dwells
Is a fabric built of hodmandod shells:
The hangings thereof a rainbow that's thin,
Which shew wondrous fine as you enter in;
The chambers are made of amber that's clear
Which gives a sweet smell when fire is near:
Her bed is a cherry-stone carvèd throughout
And with a bright butterfly's wing hung about:
Her sheets are made of dove's eyes skin—
Her pillow's a violet bud laid therein:
The doors of her chamber are transparent glass,
Where the Queen may be seen as within she doth pass.
The doors are locked fast with silver pins;
The Queen is asleep and now man's day begins.
MARGARET CAVENDISH, DUCHESS OF NEWCASTLE (1624–1674)

LET DOGS DELIGHT TO BARK AND BITE 399

    Let dogs delight to bark and bite,
        For God hath made them so;
    Let bears and lions growl and fight,
        For 'tis their nature too.

    But, children, you should never let
        Such angry passions rise;
    Your little hands were never made
        To tear each other's eyes.
ISAAC WATTS (1674–1748)

SOLITUDE 400

Happy the man, whose wish and care
A few paternal acres bound,
Content to breathe his native air
    In his own ground.

Whose herds with milk, whose fields with bread,
Whose flocks supply him with attire;
Whose trees in summer yield him shade,
    In winter fire.

Blest, who can unconcern'dly find
Hours, days, and years slide soft away
In health of body, peace of mind,
    Quiet by day,

Sound sleep by night; study and ease
Together mixt, sweet recreation,
And innocence, which most does please
    With meditation.

Thus let me live, unseen, unknown;
Thus unlamented let me die;
Steal from the world, and not a stone
    Tell where I lie.

ALEXANDER POPE (1688–1744)

401   CHLOE DIVINE

Chloe's a Nymph in flowery groves,
    A Nereid in the streams;
Saint-like she in the temple moves,
    A woman in my dreams.

Love steals artillery from her eyes,
    The Graces point her charms;
Orpheus is rivall'd in her voice,
    And Venus in her arms.

Never so happily in one
    Did heaven and earth combine:
And yet 'tis flesh and blood alone
    That makes her so divine.

THOMAS D'URFEY (1653–1723)

402   AGAINST INDIFFERENCE

More love or more disdain I crave;
    Sweet, be not still indifferent:
O send me quickly to my grave,
    Or else afford me more content!
Or love or hate me more or less,
For love abhors all lukewarmness.

Give me a tempest if 'twill drive
    Me to the place where I would be;
Or if you'll have me still alive,
    Confess you will be kind to me.
Give hopes of bliss or dig my grave:
More love or more disdain I crave.

CHARLES WEBBE (*floruit* c. 1678)

403   THE ENCHANTMENT

I did but look and love awhile,
    'Twas but for one half-hour;
Then to resist I had no will,
    And now I have no power.

To sigh and wish is all my ease;
    Sighs which do heat impart
Enough to melt the coldest ice,
    Yet cannot warm your heart.

O would your pity give my heart
    One corner of your breast,
'Twould learn of yours the winning art,
    And quickly steal the rest.

THOMAS OTWAY (1652–1685)

A QUIET SOUL 404

Thy soul within such silent pomp did keep,
  As if humanity were lull'd asleep;
So gentle was thy pilgrimage beneath,
  Time's unheard feet scarce make less noise,
  Or the soft journey which a planet goes:
Life seem'd all calm as its last breath.
  A still tranquillity so hush'd thy breast,
    As if some Halcyon were its guest,
    And there had built her nest;
  It hardly now enjoys a greater rest.

JOHN OLDHAM (1653–1683)

SONG 405

Only tell her that I love:
  Leave the rest to her and Fate:
Some kind planet from above
May perhaps her pity move:
  Lovers on their stars must wait.—
Only tell her that I love!

Why, O why should I despair!
  Mercy's pictured in her eye:
If she once vouchsafe to hear,
Welcome Hope and farewell Fear!
  She's too good to let me die.—
Why, O why should I despair?

JOHN CUTTS, LORD CUTTS (1661–1707)

THE QUESTION TO LISETTA 406

What nymph should I admire or trust,
But Chloe beauteous, Chloe just?
What nymph should I desire to see,
But her who leaves the plain for me?
To whom should I compose the lay,
But her who listens when I play?
To whom in song repeat my cares,
But her who in my sorrow shares?
For whom should I the garland make,
But her who joys the gift to take,
And boasts she wears it for my sake?
In love am I not fully blest?
Lisetta, prithee tell the rest.

LISETTA'S REPLY

Sure Chloe just, and Chloe fair,
Deserves to be your only care;
But, when you and she to-day
Far into the wood did stray,
And I happen'd to pass by,
Which way did you cast your eye?

But, when your cares to her you sing,
You dare not tell her whence they spring:
Does it not more afflict your heart,
That in those cares she bears a part?
When you the flowers for Chloe twine,
Why do you to her garland join
The meanest bud that falls from mine?
Simplest of swains! the world may see
Whom Chloe loves, and who loves me.

MATTHEW PRIOR (1664–1721)

407   TO A CHILD OF QUALITY
SAID CHILD BEING FIVE YEARS OLD AND THE AUTHER THEN FORTY

Lords, knights, and squires, the numerous band
  That wear the fair Miss Mary's fetters,
Were summoned by her high command
  To show their passions by their letters.

My pen amongst the rest I took,
  Lest those bright eyes, that cannot read,
Should dart their kindling fire, and look
  The power they have to be obey'd.

Nor quality, nor reputation,
  Forbid me yet my flame to tell;
Dear Five-years-old befriends my passion,
  And I may write till she can spell.

For, while she makes her silkworms beds
  With all the tender things I swear;
Whilst all the house my passion reads,
  In papers round her baby's hair;

She may receive and own my flame;
  For, though the strictest prudes should know it,
She'll pass for a most virtuous dame,
  And I for an unhappy poet.

Then too, alas! when she shall tear
  The rhymes some younger rival sends,
She'll give me leave to write, I fear,
  And we shall still continue friends.

For, as our different ages move,
  'Tis so ordain'd (would Fate but mend it!),
That I shall be past making love
  When she begins to comprehend it.

MATTHEW PRIOR (1664–1721)

408   SONG

The merchant, to secure his treasure,
  Conveys it in a borrow'd name:
Euphelia serves to grace my measure;
  But Chloe is my real flame.

My softest verse, my darling lyre,
  Upon Euphelia's toilet lay;
When Chloe noted her desire
  That I should sing, that I should play.

My lyre I tune, my voice I raise;
  But with my numbers mix my sighs:
And while I sing Euphelia's praise,
  I fix my soul on Chloe's eyes.

Fair Chloe blush'd: Euphelia frown'd:
  I sung, and gazed: I play'd, and trembled:
And Venus to the Loves around
  Remark'd, how ill we all dissembled.

MATTHEW PRIOR (1664–1721)

ON MY BIRTHDAY, JULY 21   409

I, my dear, was born to-day—
So all my jolly comrades say:
They bring me music, wreaths, and mirth,
And ask to celebrate my birth:
Little, alas! my comrades know
That I was born to pain and woe;
To thy denial, to thy scorn,
Better I had ne'er been born:
I wish to die, even whilst I say—
"I, my dear, was born to-day."

I, my dear, was born to-day:
Shall I salute the rising ray,
Well-spring of all my joy and woe?
Clotilda, thou alone dost know.
Shall the wreath surround my hair?
Or shall the music please my ear?
Shall I my comrades' mirth receive,
And bless my birth, and wish to live?
Then let me see great Venus chase
Imperious anger from thy face;
Then let me hear thee smiling say—
"Thou, my dear, wert born to-day."

MATTHEW PRIOR (1664–1721)

THE LADY WHO OFFERS HER   410
LOOKING-GLASS TO VENUS

Venus, take my votive glass:
Since I am not what I was,
What from this day I shall be,
Venus, let me never see.

MATTHEW PRIOR (1664–1721)

411 **To Lady Margaret Cavendish Holles-Harley, When a Child**

My noble, lovely, little Peggy,
Let this my First Epistle beg ye,
At dawn of morn, and close of even,
To lift your heart and hands to Heaven.
In double duty say your prayer:
Our Father first, then *Notre Père*.

And, dearest child, along the day,
In every thing you do and say,
Obey and please my lord and lady,
So God shall love and angels aid ye.

If to these precepts you attend,
No second letter need I send,
And so I rest your constant friend.

MATTHEW PRIOR (1664–1721)

412 **For my own Monument**

As doctors give physic by way of prevention,
   Mat, alive and in health, of his tombstone took care;
For delays are unsafe, and his pious intention
   May haply be never fulfill'd by his heir.

Then take Mat's word for it, the sculptor is paid;
   That the figure is fine, pray believe your own eye;
Yet credit but lightly what more may be said,
   For we flatter ourselves, and teach marble to lie.

Yet counting as far as to fifty his years,
   His virtues and vices were as other men's are;
High hopes he conceived, and he smother'd great fears,
   In a life parti-colour'd, half pleasure, half care.

Nor to business a drudge, nor to faction a slave,
   He strove to make int'rest and freedom agree;
In public employments industrious and grave,
   And alone with his friends, Lord! how merry was he!

Now in equipage stately, now humbly on foot,
   Both fortunes he tried, but to neither would trust;
And whirl'd in the round as the wheel turn'd about,
   He found riches had wings, and knew man was but dust.

This verse, little polish'd, tho' mighty sincere,
   Sets neither his titles nor merit to view;
It says that his relics collected lie here,
   And no mortal yet knows too if this may be true.

Fierce robbers there are that infest the highway,
   So Mat may be kill'd, and his bones never found;
False witness at court, and fierce tempests at sea,
   So Mat may yet chance to be hang'd or be drown'd.

If his bones lie in earth, roll in sea, fly in air,
  To Fate we must yield, and the thing is the same;
And if passing thou giv'st him a smile or a tear,
  He cares not—yet, prithee, be kind to his fame.
MATTHEW PRIOR (1664–1721)

RIVALS   413

Of all the torments, all the cares,
  With which our lives are curst;
Of all the plagues a lover bears,
  Sure rivals are the worst!
By partners in each other kind
  Afflictions easier grow;
In love alone we hate to find
  Companions of our woe.

Sylvia, for all the pangs you see
  Are labouring in my breast,
I beg not you would favour me,
  Would you but slight the rest!
How great soe'er your rigours are,
  With them alone I'll cope;
I can endure my own despair,
  But not another's hope.
WILLIAM WALSH (1663–1708)

WERENA MY HEART'S LICHT I WAD DEE   414

There ance was a may, and she lo'ed na men;
She biggit her bonnie bow'r doun in yon glen;
But now she cries, Dool and a well-a-day!
Come doun the green gait and come here away!

When bonnie young Johnnie cam owre the sea,
He said he saw naething sae lovely as me;
He hecht me baith rings and mony braw things—
And werena my heart's licht, I wad dee.

He had a wee titty that lo'ed na me,
Because I was twice as bonnie as she;
She raised sic a pother 'twixt him and his mother
That werena my heart's licht, I wad dee.

The day it was set, and the bridal to be:
The wife took a dwam and lay doun to dee;
She maned and she graned out o' dolour and pain,
Till he vow'd he never wad see me again.

His kin was for ane of a higher degree,
Said—What had he do wi' the likes of me?
Appose I was bonnie, I wasna for Johnnie—
And werena my heart's licht, I wad dee.

They said I had neither cow nor calf,
Nor dribbles o' drink rins thro' the draff,
Nor pickles o' meal rins thro' the mill-e'e—
And werena my heart's licht, I wad dee.

His titty she was baith wylie and slee:
She spied me as I cam owre the lea;
And then she ran in and made a loud din—
Believe your ain e'en, an ye trow not me.

His bonnet stood ay fu' round on his brow,
His auld ane look'd ay as well as some's new:
But now he lets't wear ony gait it will hing,
And casts himsel dowie upon the corn bing.

And now he gaes daund'ring about the dykes,
And a' he dow do is to hund the tykes:
The live-lang nicht he ne'er steeks his e'e—
And werena my heart's licht, I wad dee.

Were I but young for thee, as I hae been,
We should hae been gallopin' doun in yon green,
And linkin' it owre the lily-white lea—
And wow, gin I were but young for thee!
Lady Grisel Baillie (1665–1746)

may: *maid*; biggit: *built*; gait: *way, path*; hecht: *promised*; titty: *sister*; dwam: *sudden illness*; appose: *suppose*; pickles: *small quantities*; hing: *hang*; dowie: *dejectedly*; hund the tykes: *direct the dogs*; steeks: *closes*; linkin': *tripping*

415   False though She be

False though she be to me and love,
  I'll ne'er pursue revenge;
For still the charmer I approve,
  Though I deplore her change.

In hours of bliss we oft have met:
  They could not always last;
And though the present I regret,
  I'm grateful for the past.
William Congreve (1670–1729)

416   A Hue and Cry after Fair Amoret

Fair Amoret is gone astray—
  Pursue and seek her, ev'ry lover;
I'll tell the signs by which you may
  The wand'ring Shepherdess discover.

Coquette and coy at once her air,
  Both studied, tho' both seem neglected;
Careless she is, with artful care,
  Affecting to seem unaffected.

With skill her eyes dart ev'ry glance,
  Yet change so soon you'd ne'er suspect them,
For she'd persuade they wound by chance,
  Tho' certain aim and art direct them.

She likes herself, yet others hates
   For that which in herself she prizes;
And, while she laughs at them, forgets
   She is the thing hat she despises.
                          WILLIAM CONGREVE (1670–1729)

HYMN 417

The spacious firmament on high,
With all the blue ethereal sky,
And spangled heavens, a shining frame,
Their great Original proclaim.
Th' unwearied Sun from day to day
Does his Creator's power display;
And publishes to every land
The work of an Almighty hand.

Soon as the evening shades prevail,
The Moon takes up the wondrous tale;
And nightly to the listening Earth
Repeats the story of her birth:
Whilst all the stars that round her burn,
And all the planets in their turn,
Confirm the tidings as they roll,
And spread the truth from pole to pole.

What though in solemn silence all
Move round the dark terrestrial ball;
What though nor real voice nor sound
Amidst their radiant orbs be found?
In Reason's ear they all rejoice,
And utter forth a glorious voice;
For ever singing as they shine,
"The Hand that made us is divine."
                          JOSEPH ADDISON (1672–1719)

THE DAY OF JUDGEMENT 418

When the fierce North-wind with his airy forces
Rears up the Baltic to a foaming fury;
And the red lightning with a storm of hail comes
           Rushing amain down;

How the poor sailors stand amazed and tremble,
While the hoarse thunder, like a bloody trumpet,
Roars a loud onset to the gaping waters
           Quick to devour them.

Such shall the noise be, and the wild disorder
(If things eternal may be like these earthly),
Such the dire terror when the great Archangel
           Shakes the creation;

Tears the strong pillars of the vault of Heaven,
Breaks up old marble, the repose of princes,
Sees the graves open, and the bones arising,
           Flames all around them.

Hark, the shrill outcries of the guilty wretches!
Lively bright horror and amazing anguish
Stare thro' their eyelids, while the living worm lies
        Gnawing within them.

Thoughts, like old vultures, prey upon their heart-strings,
And the smart twinges, when the eye beholds the
Lofty Judge frowning, and a flood of vengeance
        Rolling afore him.

Hopeless immortals! how they scream and shiver,
While devils push them to the pit wide-yawning
Hideous and gloomy, to receive them headlong
        Down to the centre!

Stop here, my fancy: (all away, ye horrid
Doleful ideas!) come, arise to Jesus,
How He sits God-like! and the saints around Him
        Throned, yet adoring!

O may I sit there when He comes triumphant,
Dooming the nations! then ascend to glory,
While our Hosannas all along the passage
        Shout the Redeemer.

                              ISAAC WATTS (1674–1748)

419   A CRADLE HYMN
    Hush! my dear, lie still and slumber,
      Holy angels guard thy bed!
    Heavenly blessings without number
      Gently falling on thy head.

    Sleep, my babe; thy food and raiment,
      House and home, thy friends provide;
    All without thy care or payment:
      All thy wants are well supplied.

    How much better thou'rt attended
      Than the Son of God could be,
    When from heaven He descended
      And became a child like thee!

    Soft and easy is thy cradle:
      Coarse and hard thy Saviour lay,
    When His birthplace was a stable
      And His softest bed was hay.

    Blessèd babe! what glorious features—
      Spotless fair, divinely bright!
    Must He dwell with brutal creatures?
      How could angels bear the sight?

Was there nothing but a manger
   Cursèd sinners could afford
To receive the heavenly stranger?
   Did they thus affront their Lord?

Soft, my child: I did not chide thee,
   Though my song might sound too hard;
'Tis thy mother sits beside thee,
   And her arms shall be thy guard.

Yet to read the shameful story
   How the Jews abused their King,
How they served the Lord of Glory,
   Makes me angry while I sing.

See the kinder shepherds round Him,
   Telling wonders from the sky!
Where they sought Him, there they found Him,
   With His Virgin mother by.

See the lovely babe a-dressing;
   Lovely infant, how He smiled!
When He wept, the mother's blessing
   Soothed and hush'd the holy child.

Lo, He slumbers in His manger,
   Where the hornèd oxen fed:
Peace, my darling; here's no danger,
   Here's no ox anear thy bed.

'Twas to save thee, child, from dying,
   Save my dear from burning flame,
Bitter groans and endless crying,
   That thy blest Redeemer came.

May'st thou live to know and fear Him,
   Trust and love Him all thy days;
Then go dwell for ever near Him,
   See His face, and sing His praise!

Isaac Watts (1674–1748)

Song   420

When thy beauty appears
   In its graces and airs
All bright as an angel new dropp'd from the sky,
At distance I gaze and am awed by my fears:
   So strangely you dazzle my eye!

But when without art
   Your kind thoughts you impart,
When your love runs in blushes through every vein;
When it darts from your eyes, when it pants in your heart,
   Then I know you're a woman again.

There's a passion and pride
    In our sex (she replied),
And thus, might I gratify both, I would do:
Still an angel appear to each lover beside,
    But still be a woman to you.
                                THOMAS PARNELL (1670–1718)

421   PEGGY
My Peggy is a young thing,
    Just enter'd in her teens
Fair as the day, and sweet as May,
Fair as the day, and always gay;
    My Peggy is a young thing,
        And I'm not very auld,
    Yet well I like to meet her at
        The wawking of the fauld.

My Peggy speaks sae sweetly
    Whene'er we meet alane,
I wish nae mair to lay my care,
I wish nae mair of a' that's rare;
    My Peggy speaks sae sweetly,
        To a' the lave I'm cauld,
    But she gars a' my spirits glow
        At wawking of the fauld.

My Peggy smiles sae kindly
    Whene'er I whisper love,
That I look down on a' the town,
That I look down upon a crown;
    My Peggy smiles sae kindly,
        It makes me blyth and bauld,
    And naething gi'es me sic delight
        As wawking of the fauld.

My Peggy sings sae saftly
    When on my pipe I play,
By a' the rest it is confest,
By a' the rest, that she sings best;
    My Peggy sings sae saftly,
        And in her sangs are tauld
    With innocence the wale of sense,
        At wawking of the fauld.
                                ALLAN RAMSAY (1686–1758)

wawking: *watching*; lave: *rest*; wale: *choice, best*

422   ON A FLY DRINKING OUT OF HIS CUP
Busy, curious, thirsty fly!
Drink with me and drink as I:
Freely welcome to my cup,
Couldst thou sip and sip it up:
Make the most of life you may,
Life is short and wears away.

Both alike are mine and thine
Hastening quick to their decline:
Thine's a summer, mine's no more,
Though repeated to threescore.
Threescore summers, when they're gone,
Will appear as short as one!

WILLIAM OLDYS (1687–1761)

SONG 423

O ruddier than the cherry!
O sweeter than the berry!
   O nymph more bright
   Than moonshine night,
Like kidlings blithe and merry!
Ripe as the melting cluster!
No lily has such lustre;
   Yet hard to tame
   As raging flame,
And fierce as storms that bluster!

JOHN GAY (1688–1732)

ON A CERTAIN LADY AT COURT 424

I know a thing that's most uncommon;
  (Envy, be silent and attend!)
I know a reasonable woman,
  Handsome and witty, yet a friend.

Not warp'd by passion, awed by rumour;
  Not grave through pride, nor gay through folly;
An equal mixture of good-humour
  And sensible soft melancholy.

"Has she no faults then (Envy says), Sir?"
  Yes, she has one, I must aver:
When all the world conspires to praise her,
  The woman's deaf, and does not hear.

ALEXANDER POPE (1688–1744)

ELEGY TO THE MEMORY OF AN UNFORTUNATE LADY 425

What beck'ning ghost, along the moonlight shade
Invites my steps, and points to yonder glade?
'Tis she!—but why that bleeding bosom gored,
Why dimly gleams the visionary sword?
O, ever beauteous, ever friendly! tell,
Is it, in Heav'n, a crime to love too well?
To bear too tender or too firm a heart,
To act a lover's or a Roman's part?
Is there no bright reversion in the sky
For those who greatly think, or bravely die?

  Why bade ye else, ye Pow'rs! her soul aspire
Above the vulgar flight of low desire?
Ambition first sprung from your blest abodes;
The glorious fault of angels and of gods;
Thence to their images on earth it flows,
And in the breasts of kings and heroes glows.

Most souls, 'tis true, but peep out once an age,
Dull sullen pris'ners in the body's cage:
Dim lights of life, that burn a length of years,
Useless, unseen, as lamps in sepulchres;
Like Eastern kings a lazy state they keep,
And close confined to their own palace, sleep.
  From these perhaps (ere Nature bade her die)
Fate snatch'd her early to the pitying sky.
As into air the purer spirits flow,
And sep'rate from their kindred dregs below,
So flew the soul to its congenial place,
Nor left one virtue to redeem her race.
  But thou, false guardian of a charge too good!
Thou, mean deserter of thy brother's blood!
See on these ruby lips the trembling breath,
These cheeks now fading at the blast of Death:
Cold is that breast which warm'd the world before,
And those love-darting eyes must roll no more.
Thus, if eternal Justice rules the ball,
Thus shall your wives, and thus your children fall;
On all the line a sudden vengeance waits,
And frequent herses shall besiege your gates.
There passengers shall stand, and pointing say
(While the long fun'rals blacken all the way),
"Lo! these were they whose souls the Furies steel'd
And cursed with hearts unknowing how to yield."
Thus unlamented pass the proud away,
The gaze of fools, and pageant of a day!
So perish all whose breast ne'er learn'd to glow
For others' good, or melt at others' woe!
  What can atone (O ever-injured shade!)
Thy fate unpitied, and thy rites unpaid?
No friend's complaint, no kind domestic tear
Pleased thy pale ghost, or graced thy mournful bier.
By foreign hands thy dying eyes were closed,
By foreign hands thy decent limbs composed,
By foreign hands thy humble grave adorn'd,
By strangers honour'd, and by strangers mourn'd!
What tho' no friends in sable weeds appear,
Grieve for an hour, perhaps, then mourn a year,
And bear about the mockery of woe
To midnight dances, and the public show?
What tho' no weeping Loves thy ashes grace,
Nor polish'd marble emulate thy face?
What tho' no sacred earth allow thee room,
Nor hallow'd dirge be mutter'd o'er thy tomb?
Yet shall thy grave with rising flow'rs be drest,
And the green turf lie lightly on thy breast:
There shall the morn her earliest tears bestow,
There the first roses of the year shall blow;
While angels with their silver wings o'ershade
The ground now sacred by thy reliques made.

So peaceful rests, without a stone, a name,
What once had beauty, titles, wealth, and fame.
How loved, how honour'd once, avails thee not,
To whom related, or by whom begot;
A heap of dust alone remains of thee,
'Tis all thou art, and all the proud shall be!
  Poets themselves must fall, like those they sung,
Deaf the praised ear, and mute the tuneful tongue.
Ev'n he, whose soul now melts in mournful lays,
Shall shortly want the gen'rous tear he pays;
Then from this closing eyes thy form shall part,
And the last pang shall tear thee from his heart;
Life's idle business at one gasp be o'er,
The Muse forgot, and thou beloved no more!
                              ALEXANDER POPE (1688–1744)

THE DYING CHRISTIAN TO HIS SOUL   426
Vital spark of heav'nly flame!
  Quit, O quit this mortal frame:
  Trembling, hoping, ling'ring, flying,
  O the pain, the bliss of dying!
Cease, fond Nature, cease thy strife,
And let me languish into life.

  Hark! they whisper; angels say,
  Sister Spirit, come away!
  What is this absorbs me quite?
  Steals my senses, shuts my sight,
Drowns my spirits, draws my breath?
Tell me, my soul, can this be death?

The world recedes; it disappears!
Heav'n opens on my eyes! my ears
  With sounds seraphic ring!
Lend, lend your wings! I mount! I fly!
O Grave! where is thy victory?
O Death! where is thy sting?
                              ALEXANDER POPE (1688–1744)

SHORTEN SAIL   427
Love thy country, wish it well,
  Not with too intense a care;
'Tis enough that, when it fell,
  Thou its ruin didst not share.

Envy's censure, Flattery's praise,
  With unmoved indifference view:
Learn to tread Life's dangerous maze
  With unerring Virtue's clue.

Void of strong desire and fear,
  Life's wide ocean trust no more;
Strive thy little bark to steer
  With the tide, but near the shore.

Thus prepared, thy shorten'd sail
  Shall, whene'er the winds increase,
Seizing each propitious gale,
  Waft thee to the port of Peace.

Keep thy conscience from offence
  And tempestuous passions free,
So, when thou art call'd from hence,
  Easy shall thy passage be.

—Easy shall thy passage be,
  Cheerful thy allotted stay,
Short the account 'twixt God and thee,
  Hope shall meet thee on thy way.
    GEORGE BUBB DODINGTON, LORD MELCOMBE (1691?–1762)

SALLY IN OUR ALLEY

Of all the girls that are so smart
  There's none like pretty Sally;
She is the darling of my heart,
  And she lives in our alley.
There is no lady in the land
  Is half so sweet as Sally;
She is the darling of my heart,
  And she lives in our alley.

Her father he makes cabbage-nets,
  And through the streets does cry 'em;
Her mother she sells laces long
  To such as please to buy 'em;
But sure such folks could ne'er beget
  So sweet a girl as Sally!
She is the darling of my heart,
  And she lives in our alley.

When she is by, I leave my work,
  I love her so sincerely;
My master comes like any Turk,
  And bangs me most severely:
But let him bang his bellyful,
  I'll bear it all for Sally;
She is the darling of my heart,
  And she lives in our alley.

Of all the days that's in the week
  I dearly love but one day—
And that's the day that comes betwixt
  A Saturday and Monday;
For then I'm drest all in my best
  To walk abroad with Sally;
She is the darling of my heart,
  And she lives in our alley.

My master carries me to church,
   And often am I blamèd
Because I leave him in the lurch
   As soon as text is namèd;
I leave the church in sermon-time
   And slink away to Sally;
She is the darling of my heart,
   And she lives in our alley.

When Christmas comes about again,
   O, then I shall have money;
I'll hoard it up, and box it all,
   I'll give it to my honey:
I would it were ten thousand pound,
   I'd give it all to Sally;
She is the darling of my heart,
   And she lives in our alley.

My master and the neighbors all
   Make gave of me and Sally,
And, but for her, I'd better be
   A slave and row a galley;
But when my seven long years are out,
   O, then I'll marry Sally;
O, then we'll wed, and then we'll bed—
   But not in our alley!

Henry Carey (1693?–1743)

A Drinking-Song   429

Bacchus must now his power resign—
I am the only God of Wine!
It is not fit the wretch should be
In competition set with me,
Who can drink ten times more than he.

Make a new world, ye powers divine!
Stock'd with nothing else but Wine:
Let Wine its only product be,
Let Wine be earth, and air, and sea—
And let that Wine be all for me!

Henry Carey (1693?–1743)

To Miss Charlotte Pulteney   430

Timely blossom, Infant fair,
Fondling of a happy pair,
Every morn and every night
Their solicitous delight,
Sleeping, waking, still at ease,
Pleasing, without skill to please,
Little gossip, blithe and hale,
Tattling many a broken tale,
Singing many a tuneless song.
Lavish of a heedless tongue;
Simple maiden, void of art,
Babbling out the very heart,

Yet abandon'd to thy will,
Yet imagining no ill,
Yet too innocent to blush,
Like the linnet in the bush
To the mother-linnet's note
Moduling her slender throat;
Chirping forth thy petty joys,
Wanton in the change of toys,
Like the linnet green, in May
Flitting to each bloomy spray;
Wearied then and glad of rest,
Like the linnet in the nest:—
This thy present happy lot
This, in time will be forgot:
Other pleasures, other cares,
Ever-busy Time prepares;
And thou shalt in thy daughter see,
This picture, once, resembled thee.

AMBROSE PHILIPS (1675–1749)

431   BLACK-EYED SUSAN

All in the Downs the fleet was moor'd,
  The streamers waving in the wind,
When black-eyed Susan came aboard;
  "O! where shall I my true-love find?
Tell me, ye jovial sailors, tell me true
If my sweet William sails among the crew."

William, who high upon the yard
  Rock'd with the billow to and fro,
Soon as her well-known voice he heard
  He sigh'd, and cast his eyes below;
The cord slides swiftly through his glowing hands,
And quick as lightning on the deck he stands.

So the sweet lark, high poised in air,
  Shuts close his pinions to his breast
If chance his mate's shrill call he hear,
  And drops at once into her nest:—
The noblest captain in the British fleet
Might envy William's lip those kisses sweet

"O Susan, Susan, lovely dear,
  My vows shall ever true remain
Let me kiss off that falling tear;
  We only part to meet again.
Change as ye list, ye winds; my heart shall be
The faithful compass that still points to thee.

"Believe not what the landmen say
   Who tempt with doubts thy constant mind:
They'll tell thee, sailors, when away,
   In every port a mistress find:
Yes, yes, believe them when they tell thee so,
For Thou art present wheresoe'er I go.

"If to fair India's coast we sail,
   Thy eyes are seen in diamonds bright,
Thy breath is Afric's spicy gale,
   Thy skin is ivory so white.
Thus every beauteous object that I view
Wakes in my soul some charm of lovely Sue.

"Though battle call me from thy arms
   Let not my pretty Susan mourn;
Though cannons roar, yet safe from harms
   William shall to his Dear return.
Love turns aside the balls that round me fly,
Lest precious tears should drop from Susan's eye."

The boatswain gave the dreadful word,
   The sails their swelling bosom spread;
No longer must she stay aboard;
   They kiss'd, she sigh'd, he hung his head.
Her lessening boat unwilling rows to land;
   "Adieu!" she cries; and waved her lily hand.

                          JOHN GAY (1685–1732)

What is Love?   432

'Tis a child of phansies getting,
   Brought up between Hope and Fear;
Fed with smiles, grown by uniting
   Strong, and so kept by Desire.
'Tis a perpetual vestal fire
   Never dying,
Whose smoke like incense doth aspire,
   Upwards flying.

It is a soft magnetic stone,
   Attracting hearts by sympathy,
Binding up close two souls in one,
   Both discoursing secretly.
'Tis the true Gordian knot that ties
   Yet ne'er unbinds,
Fixing thus two lovers' eyes
   As well as minds.

'Tis the sphere's heavenly harmony
   When two skilful hands do strike;
And every sound expressively
   Marries sweetly with the like:

'Tis the world's everlasting chain
    That all things tied,
And bid them like the fixed wain
    Unmoved to bide.

'Tis Nature's law inviolate,
    Confirmed by mutual consent
Where two dislike, like, love, and hate,
    Each to the other's full content:
'Tis the caress of every thing;
    The turtle-dove;
Both birds and beasts do offering bring
    To Mighty Love.

'Tis th' angels' joy: the gods' delight, man's bliss,
'Tis all in all: without Love nothing is.
                                                   ROBERT HEATH (*flor.* 1650)

433   HUMILITY

Nor Love nor Fate dare I accuse
For that my love did me refuse,
But O! mine own unworthiness
That durst presume so mickle bliss.
It was too much for me to love
A man so like the gods above:
An angel's shape, a saint-like voice,
Are too divine for human choice.

O had I wisely given my heart
For to have loved him but in part;
Sought only to enjoy his face,
Or any one peculiar grace
Of foot, of hand, of lip, or eye,—
I might have lived where now I die:
But I, presuming all to choose,
Am now condemnèd all to lose.
                                           RICHARD BROME (*flor.* 1652)

434   THE NIGHTINGALE AND THE GLOW-WORM

A nightingale, that all day long
Had cheered the village with his song,
Nor yet at eve his note suspended,
Nor yet when eventide was ended,
Began to feel, as well he might,
The keen demands of appetite;
When, looking eagerly around,
He spied far off, upon the ground,
A something shining in the dark,
And knew the glow-worm by his spark;
So, stooping down from hawthorn top,
He thought to put him in his crop.
The worm, aware of his intent,
Harangued him thus, right eloquent:
"Did you admire my lamp," quoth he,
"As much as I your minstrelsy,

You would abhor to do me wrong,
As much as I to spoil your song;
For 'twas the self-same power divine,
Taught you to sing and me to shine;
That you with music, I with light,
Might beautify and cheer the night."
The songster heard his short oration,
And warbling out his approbation,
Released him, as my story tells,
And found a supper somewhere else.

WILLIAM COWPER (1731–1800)

THE SOLITUDE OF ALEXANDER SELKIRK   435

[A. Selkirk was a Royal Navy officer, marooned on a South Pacific island for over four years. His widely-publicized story inspired Defoe's *Robinson Crusoe*. – Ed.]

I am monarch of all I survey,
  My right there is none to dispute,
From the center all round to the sea,
  I am lord of the fowl and the brute.
O Solitude! where are the charms
  That sages have seen in thy face?
Better dwell in the midst of alarms
  Than reign in this horrible place.

I am out of humanity's reach,
  I must finish my journey alone,
Never hear the sweet music of speech,—
  I start at the sound of my own.
The beasts that roam over the plain
  My form with indifference see;
They are so unacquainted with man,
  Their tameness is shocking to me.

Society, Friendship, and Love,
  Divinely bestow'd upon man,
Oh, had I the wings of a dove,
  How soon would I taste you again!
My sorrows I then might assuage
  In the ways of religion and truth,
Might learn from the wisdom of age,
  And be cheer'd by the sallies of youth.

Ye winds that have made me your sport,
  Convey to this desolate shore
Some cordial endearing report
  Of a land I shall visit no more!

My friends—do they now and then send
  A wish or a thought after me?
Oh, tell me I yet have a friend,
  Though a friend I am never to see.

How fleet is a glance of the mind!
    Compared with the speed of its flight,
The tempest itself lags behind,
    And the swift-wingèd arrows of light.
When I think of my own native land,
    In a moment I seem to be there;
But alas! recollection at hand
    Soon hurries me back to despair.

But the seafowl is gone to her nest,
    The beast is laid down in his lair,
Even here is a season of rest,
    And I to my cabin repair.
There's mercy in every place,
    And mercy, encouraging thought!
Gives even affliction a grace,
    And reconciles man to his lot.

WILLIAM COWPER (1731–1800)

436   THE LANDING OF THE PILGRIMS

The breaking waves dashed high
    On a stern and rock-bound coast,
And the woods against a stormy sky
    Their giant branches tossed.

And the heavy night hung dark
    The hills and waters o'er,
When a band of exiles moored their bark
    On the wild New England shore.

Not as the conqueror comes,
    They, the true-hearted, came;
Not with the roll of the stirring drums,
    And the trumpet that sings of fame.

Not as the flying come,
    In silence and in fear;
They shook the depths of the desert gloom
    With their hymns of lofty cheer.

Amid the storm they sang,
    And the stars heard, and the sea,
And the sounding aisles of the dim woods rang
    To the anthem of the free!

The ocean eagle soared
    From his nest by the white wave's foam;
And the rocking pines of the forest roared,—
    This was their welcome home!

There were men with hoary hair,
    Amid that pilgrim band;
Why had *they* come to wither there,
    Away from their childhood's land?

There was woman's fearless eye,
  Lit by her deep love's truth;
There was manhood's brow serenely high,
  And the fiery heart of youth.

What sought they thus afar?
  Bright jewels of the mine?
The wealth of seas, the spoils of war?—
  They sought a faith's pure shrine!

Ay! call it holy ground,
  The soil where first they trod:
They have left unstained what there they found,
  Freedom to worship God.
FELICIA DOROTHEA HEMANS (1749–1835)

THE VOICE OF SPRING   437

I come, I come! ye have called me long;
I come o'er the mountains, with light and song.
Ye may trace my step o'er the waking earth
By the winds which tell of the violet's birth,
By the primrose stars in the shadowy grass,
By the green leaves opening as I pass.

I have breathed on the South, and the chestnut-flowers
By thousands have burst from the forest bowers,
And the ancient graves and the fallen fanes
Are veiled with wreaths on Italian plains;
But it is not for me, in my hour of bloom,
To speak of the ruin or the tomb!

I have looked o'er the hills of the stormy North,
And the larch has hung all his tassels forth;
The fisher is out on the sunny sea,
And the reindeer bounds o'er the pastures free,
And the pine has a fringe of softer green,
And the moss looks bright, where my step has been.

I have sent through the wood-paths a glowing sigh,
And called out each voice of the deep blue sky,
From the night-bird's lay through the starry time,
In the groves of the soft Hesperian clime,
To the swan's wild note by the Iceland lakes,
When the dark fir-branch into verdure breaks.

From the streams and founts I have loosed the chain;
They are sweeping on to the silvery main,
They are flashing down from the mountain brows,
They are flinging spray o'er the forest boughs,
They are bursting fresh from their sparry caves,
And the earth resounds with the joy of waves.
FELICIA DOROTHEA HEMANS (1749–1835)

438   ELEGY WRITTEN IN
                 A COUNTRY CHURCHYARD

The curfew tolls the knell of parting day,
    The lowing herd winds slowly o'er the lea,
The plowman homeward plods his weary way,
    And leaves the world to darkness and to me.

Now fades the glimmering landscape on the sight,
    And all the air a solemn stillness holds,
Save where the beetle wheels his droning flight,
    And drowsy tinklings lull the distant folds.

Save that from yonder ivy-mantled tow'r
    The moping owl does to the moon complain
Of such as, wandering near her secret bow'r,
    Molest her ancient solitary reign.

Beneath those rugged elms, that yew-tree's shade,
    Where heaves the turf in many a mould'ring heap,
Each in his narrow cell forever laid,
    The rude Forefathers of the hamlet sleep.

The breezy call of incense-breathing morn,
    The swallow twitt'ring from the straw-built shed,
The cock's shrill clarion, or the echoing horn,
    No more shall rouse them from their lowly bed.

For them no more the blazing hearth shall burn,
    Or busy housewife ply her evening care:
No children run to lisp their sire's return,
    Or climb his knees the envied kiss to share.

Oft did the harvest to their sickle yield,
    Their furrow oft the stubborn glebe has broke;
How jocund did they drive their team afield!
    How bow'd the woods beneath their sturdy stroke!

Let not Ambition mock their useful toil,
    Their homely joys, and destiny obscure;
Nor Grandeur hear with a disdainful smile,
    The short and simple annals of the Poor.

The boast of heraldry, the pomp of pow'r,
    And all that beauty, all that wealth e'er gave,
Await alike th' inevitable hour.
    The paths of glory lead but to the grave.

Forgive, ye Proud, th' involuntary fault
    If Memory to these no trophies raise,
Where thro' the long-drawn aisle and fretted vault
    The pealing anthem swells the note of praise.

Can storied urn or animated bust
  Back to its mansion call the fleeting breath?
Can Honour's voice provoke the silent dust,
  Or Flatt'ry soothe the dull cold ear of Death?

Perhaps in this neglected spot is laid
  Some heart once pregnant with celestial fire,
Hands that the rod of empire might have sway'd,
  Or waked to ecstasy the living lyre.

But Knowledge to their eyes her ample page
  Rich with the spoils of time did ne'er unroll;
Chill Penury repress'd their noble rage,
  And froze the genial current of the soul.

Full many a gem of purest ray serene,
  The dark unfathom'd caves of ocean bear:
Full many a flower is born to blush unseen,
  And waste its sweetness on the desert air.

Some village-Hampden, that with dauntless breast
  The little tyrant of his fields withstood;
Some mute inglorious Milton here may rest,
  Some Cromwell guiltless of his country's blood.

Th' applause of listening senates to command,
  The threats of pain and ruin to despise,
To scatter plenty o'er a smiling land,
  And read their history in a nation's eyes,

Their lot forbad: nor circumscribed alone
  Their growing virtues, but their crimes confined
Forbad to wade through slaughter to a throne,
  And shut the gates of mercy on mankind,

The struggling pangs of conscious truth to hide,
  To quench the blushes of ingenuous shame,
Or heap the shrine of Luxury and Pride
  With incense, kindled at the Muse's flame.

Far from the madding crowd's ignoble strife,
  Their sober wishes never learn'd to stray;
Along the cool sequester'd vale of life
  They kept the noiseless tenour of their way.

Yet e'en those bones from insult to protect
  Some frail memorial still erected nigh,
With uncouth rhimes and shapeless sculpture deck'd,
  Implores the passing tribute of a sigh.

Their name, their years, spelt by th' unlettered Muse,
  The place of fame and elegy supply.
And many a holy text around she strews
  That teach the rustic moralist to die.

For who to dumb forgetfulness a prey,
  This pleasing anxious being e'er resigned,
Left the warm precincts of the cheerful day,
  Nor cast one longing, ling'ring look behind?

On some fond breast the parting soul relies,
  Some pious drops the closing eye requires;
E'en from the tomb the voice of Nature cries,
  E'en in our ashes live their wonted fires.

For thee, who, mindful of th' unhonour'd dead,
  Dost in these lines their artless tale relate;
If chance, by lonely Contemplation led,
  Some kindred spirit shall inquire thy fate,

Haply some hoary-headed swain may say,
  "Oft have we seen him at the peep of dawn
Brushing with hasty steps the dews away,
  To meet the sun upon the upland lawn.

"There at the foot of yonder nodding beech
  That wreathes its old fantastic roots so high,
His listless length at noon-tide would he stretch,
  And pore upon the brook that babbles by.

"Hard by yon wood, now smiling as in scorn,
  Muttering his wayward fancies he would rove;
Now drooping, woeful wan, like one forlorn,
  Or crazed with care, or crossed in hopeless love.

"One morn I miss'd him on the custom'd hill,
  Along the heath, and near his favourite tree;
Another came; nor yet beside the rill,
  Nor up the lawn, nor at the wood was he.

"The next with dirges due in sad array
  Slow thro' the church-way path we saw him borne.
Approach and read (for thou canst read) the lay,
  Graved on the stone beneath yon agèd thorn."

THE EPITAPH
Here rests his head upon the lap of Earth
  A Youth to Fortune and to Fame unknown;
Fair Science frown'd not on his humble birth,
  And Melancholy mark'd him for her own.

Large was his bounty, and his soul sincere,
  Heaven did a recompense as largely send:
He gave to Mis'ry all he had, a tear:
  He gain'd from Heav'n ('twas all he wish'd) a friend.

No farther seek his merits to disclose,
  Or draw his frailties from their dread abode,
(There they alike in trembling hope repose,)
  The bosom of his Father and his God.

THOMAS GRAY (1716–1771)

On the Death of a Particular Friend 439

As those we love decay, we die in part,
String after string is sever'd from the heart;
Till loosen'd life, at last but breathing clay,
Without one pang is glad to fall away.

Unhappy he who latest feels the blow!
Whose eyes have wept o'er every friend laid low,
Dragg'd ling'ring on from partial death to death,
Till, dying, all he can resign is—breath.

JAMES THOMSON (1700–1748)

Tell Me, My Heart, If This Be Love 440

When Delia on the plain appears,
  Awed by a thousand tender fears
  I would approach, but dare not move:
Tell me, my heart, if this be love?

Whene'er she speaks, my ravish'd ear
  No other voice than hers can hear,
  No other wit but hers approve:
Tell me, my heart, if this be love?

If she some other youth commend,
  Though I was once his fondest friend,
  His instant enemy I prove:
Tell me, my heart, if this be love?

When she is absent, I no more
  Delight in all that pleased before—
  The clearest spring, or shadiest grove:
Tell me, my heart, if this be love?

When fond of power, of beauty vain,
  Her nets she spread for every swain,
  I strove to hate, but vainly strove:
Tell me, my heart, if this be love?

GEORGE LYTTELTON, LORD LYTTELTON (1709–1773)

One-and-Twenty 441

Long-expected one-and-twenty,
  Ling'ring year, at length is flown:
Pride and pleasure, pomp and plenty,
          Great — — , are now your own.

Loosen'd from the minor's tether,
  Free to mortgage or to sell,
Wild as wind, and light as feather,
  Bid the sons of thrift farewell.

Call the Betsies, Kates, and Jennies,
  All the names that banish care;
Lavish of your grandsire's guineas,
  Show the spirit of an heir.

All that prey on vice and folly
  Joy to see their quarry fly:
There the gamester, light and jolly,
  There the lender, grave and sly.

Wealth, my lad, was made to wander,
  Let it wander as it will;
Call the jockey, call the pander,
  Bid them come and take their fill.

When the bonny blade carouses,
  Pockets full, and spirits high—
What are acres? What are houses?
  Only dirt, or wet or dry.

Should the guardian friend or mother
  Tell the woes of wilful waste,
Scorn their counsel, scorn their pother;—
  You can hang or drown at last!
                      SAMUEL JOHNSON (1709–1784)

442   ON THE DEATH OF MR. ROBERT LEVET,
           A PRACTISER IN PHYSIC
Condemn'd to Hope's delusive mine,
  As on we toil from day to day,
By sudden blasts or slow decline
  Our social comforts drop away.

Well tried through many a varying year,
  See Levet to the grave descend,
Officious, innocent, sincere,
  Of every friendless name the friend.

Yet still he fills affection's eye,
  Obscurely wise and coarsely kind;
Nor, letter'd Arrogance, deny
  Thy praise to merit unrefined.

When fainting nature call'd for aid,
  And hov'ring death prepared the blow,
His vig'rous remedy display'd
  The power of art without the show.

In Misery's darkest cavern known,
  His useful care was ever nigh,
Where hopeless Anguish pour'd his groan,
  And lonely Want retired to die.

No summons mock'd by chill delay,
  No petty gain disdained by pride;
The modest wants of every day
  The toil of every day supplied.

His virtues walk'd their narrow round,
  Nor made a pause, nor left a void;
And sure th' Eternal Master found
  The single talent well employ'd.

The busy day, the peaceful night,
  Unfelt, uncounted, glided by;
His frame was firm—his powers were bright,
  Though now his eightieth year was nigh.

Then with no fiery throbbing pain,
  No cold gradations of decay,
Death broke at once the vital chain,
  And freed his soul the nearest way.
SAMUEL JOHNSON (1709–1784)

ABSENCE   443
With leaden foot Time creeps along
  While Delia is away:
With her, nor plaintive was the song,
  Nor tedious was the day.

Ah, envious Pow'r! reverse my doom;
  Now double thy career,
Strain ev'ry nerve, stretch ev'ry plume,
  And rest them when she's here!
RICHARD JAGO (1715–1781)

THE CURSE UPON EDWARD   444
Weave the warp, and weave the woof,
The winding-sheet of Edward's race.
  Give ample room, and verge enough
The characters of hell to trace.
Mark the year, and mark the night,
When Severn shall re-echo with affright
The shrieks of death, thro' Berkley's roofs that ring,
Shrieks of an agonizing King!
  She-wolf of France, with unrelenting fangs,
That tear'st the bowels of thy mangled mate,
  From thee be born, who o'er thy country hangs
The scourge of Heav'n. What terrors round him wait!
Amazement in his van, with Flight combined,
And Sorrow's faded form, and Solitude behind.

  Mighty Victor, mighty Lord!
Low on his funeral couch he lies!
  No pitying heart, no eye, afford
A tear to grace his obsequies.
Is the sable warrior fled?
Thy son is gone. He rests among the dead.
The swarm that in thy noon tide beam were born?
Gone to salute the rising morn.

Fair laughs the morn, and soft the zephyr blows,
While proudly riding o'er the azure realm
In gallant trim the gilded vessel goes;
   Youth on the prow, and Pleasure at the helm;
Regardless of the sweeping whirlwind's sway,
That, hush'd in grim repose, expects his evening prey.

  Fill high the sparkling bowl,
The rich repast prepare;
  Reft of a crown, he yet may share the feast:
Close by the regal chair
  Fell Thirst and Famine scowl
  A baleful smile upon their baffled guest.
Heard ye the din of battle bray,
  Lance to lance, and horse to horse?
  Long years of havoc urge their destined course,
And thro' the kindred squadrons mow their way.
  Ye Towers of Julius, London's lasting shame,
With many a foul and midnight murder fed,
  Revere his consort's faith, his father's fame,
And spare the meek usurper's holy head.
Above, below, the rose of snow,
  Twined with her blushing foe, we spread:
The bristled boar in infant-gore
  Wallows beneath the thorny shade.
Now, brothers, bending o'er th' accursed loom
Stamp we our vengeance deep, and ratify his doom.

  Edward, lo! to sudden fate
(Weave we the woof. The thread is spun)
  Half of thy heart we consecrate.
(The web is wove. The work is done.)
THOMAS GRAY (1716–1771)

445   THE PROGRESS OF POESY
A PINDARIC ODE

  Awake, Æolian lyre, awake,
And give to rapture all thy trembling strings,
From Helicon's harmonious springs
  A thousand rills their mazy progress take:
The laughing flowers, that round them blow,
Drink life and fragrance as they flow.
Now the rich stream of music winds along
Deep, majestic, smooth, and strong,
Thro' verdant vales, and Ceres' golden reign:
Now rolling down the steep amain,
Headlong, impetuous, see it pour;
The rocks and nodding groves rebellow to the roar.

  O Sovereign of the willing soul,
Parent of sweet and solemn-breathing airs,
Enchanting shell! the sullen Cares
  And frantic Passions hear thy soft controul.

On Thracia's hills the Lord of War
Has curb'd the fury of his car,
And dropp'd his thirsty lance at thy command.
Perching on the sceptred hand
Of Jove, thy magic lulls the feather'd king
With ruffled plumes and flagging wing:
Quench'd in dark clouds of slumber lie
The terror of his beak, and lightnings of his eye.

Thee the voice, the dance, obey,
Temper'd to thy warbled lay.
  O'er Idalia's velvet-green
  The rosy-crowned Loves are seen
On Cytherea's day
  With antic Sports, and blue-eyed Pleasures,
  Frisking light in frolic measures;
Now pursuing, now retreating,
  Now in circling troops they meet:
To brisk notes in cadence beating,
  Glance their many-twinkling feet.
Slow melting strains their Queen's approach declare:
  Where'er she turns the Graces homage pay.
With arms sublime, that float upon the air,
  In gliding state she wins her easy way:
O'er her warm cheek and rising bosom move
The bloom of young Desire and purple light of Love.

  Man's feeble race what ills await,
Labour, and Penury, the racks of Pain,
  Disease, and Sorrow's weeping train,
  And Death, sad refuge from the storms of fate!
The fond complaint, my song, disprove,
And justify the laws of Jove.
Say, has he giv'n in vain the heav'nly Muse?
Night, and all her sickly dews,
Her sceptres wan, and birds of boding cry,
He gives to range the dreary sky:
Till down the eastern cliffs afar
Hyperion's march they spy, and glitt'ring shafts of war.

  In climes beyond the solar road,
Where shaggy forms o'er ice-built mountains roam,
The Muse has broke the twilight gloom
  To cheer the shiv'ring native's dull abode,
And oft, beneath the od'rous shade
Of Chili's boundless forests laid,
She deigns to hear the savage youth repeat
In loose numbers wildly sweet
Their feather-cinctured chiefs, and dusky loves.
Her track, where'er the Goddess roves,
Glory pursue, and generous Shame,
Th' unconquerable Mind, and Freedom's holy flame.

Woods, that wave o'er Delphi's steep,
Isles, that crown th' Ægean deep,
  Fields, that cool Ilissus laves,
  Or where Mæander's amber waves
In lingering lab'rinths creep,
  How do your tuneful echoes languish,
  Mute, but to the voice of anguish?
Where each old poetic mountain
  Inspiration breathed around:
Ev'ry shade and hallow'd fountain
  Murmur'd deep a solemn sound:
Till the sad Nine, in Greece's evil hour,
  Left their Parnassus for the Latian plains.
Alike they scorn the pomp of tyrant Power,
  And coward Vice, that revels in her chains.
When Latium had her lofty spirit lost,
They sought, O Albion! next, thy sea-encircled coast.

  Far from the sun and summer gale,
In thy green lap was Nature's darling laid,
What time, where lucid Avon stray'd,
  To Him the mighty mother did unveil
Her awful face: the dauntless child
Stretch'd forth his little arms, and smiled.
This pencil take (she said), whose colours clear
Richly paint the vernal year:
Thine too these golden keys, immortal boy!
This can unlock the gates of joy;
Of horror that, and thrilling fears,
Or ope the sacred source of sympathetic tears.

  Nor second he, that rode sublime
Upon the seraph-wings of Ecstasy,
The secrets of th' abyss to spy.
  He pass'd the flaming bounds of place and time:
The living Throne, the sapphire-blaze,
Where Angels tremble while they gaze,
He saw; but blasted with excess of light,
Closed his eyes in endless night.
Behold, where Dryden's less presumptuous car,
Wide o'er the fields of glory bear
Two coursers of ethereal race,
With necks in thunder clothed, and long-resounding pace.

Hark, his hands the lyre explore!
Bright-eyed Fancy hovering o'er
  Scatters from her pictured urn
  Thoughts that breathe, and words that burn.
But ah! 'tis heard no more—
  O Lyre divine! what daring Spirit
  Wakes thee now? Tho' he inherit
Nor the pride, nor ample pinion,

   That the Theban eagle bear
Sailing with supreme dominion
  Thro' the azure deep of air:
Yet oft before his infant eyes would run
  Such forms as glitter in the Muse's ray,
With orient hues, unborrow'd of the Sun:
  Yet shall he mount, and keep his distant way
Beyond the limits of a vulgar fate,
Beneath the Good how far—but far above the Great.

THOMAS GRAY (1716–1771)

ON A FAVOURITE CAT, 446
DROWNED IN A TUB OF GOLD FISHES

  Twas on a lofty vase's side,
  Where China's gayest art had dyed
    The azure flowers that blow;
  Demurest of the tabby kind,
  The pensive Selima reclined,
    Gazed on the lake below.

Her conscious tail her joy declared;
The fair round face, the snowy beard,
    The velvet of her paws,
Her coat, that with the tortoise vies,
Her ears of jet, and emerald eyes,
    She saw; and purr'd applause.

Still had she gazed; but 'midst the tide
Two angel forms were seen to glide,
    The Genii of the stream:
Their scaly armour's Tyrian hue
Thro' richest purple to the view
    Betray'd a golden gleam.

The hapless Nymph with wonder saw:
A whisker first and then a claw,
    With many an ardent wish,
She stretch'd in vain to reach the prize.
What female heart can gold despise?
What Cat's averse to fish?

Presumptuous Maid! with looks intent
Again she stretch'd, again she bent,
    Nor knew the gulf between.
(Malignant Fate sat by, and smiled.)
The slipp'ry verge her feet beguiled,
    She tumbled headlong in.

Eight times emerging from the flood
She mew'd to ev'ry wat'ry god,
    Some speedy aid to send.
No Dolphin came, no Nereid stirr'd:
Nor cruel *Tom*, nor *Susan* heard.
    A Fav'rite has no friend!

From hence, ye Beauties, undeceived,
Know, one false step is ne'er retrieved,
  And be with caution bold.
Not all that tempts your wand'ring eyes
And heedless hearts, is lawful prize;
  Nor all that glisters, gold.

THOMAS GRAY (1716–1771)

447   ODE TO SIMPLICITY

  O thou, by Nature taught
  To breathe her genuine thought
In numbers warmly pure and sweetly strong:
  Who first on mountains wild,
  In Fancy, loveliest child,
Thy babe and Pleasure's, nursed the pow'rs of song!

  Thou, who with hermit heart
  Disdain'st the wealth of art,
And gauds, and pageant weeds, and trailing pall:
  But com'st a decent maid,
  In Attic robe array'd,
O chaste, unboastful nymph, to thee I call!

  By all the honey'd store
  On Hybla's thymy shore,
By all her blooms and mingled murmurs dear,
  By her whose love-lorn woe,
  In evening musings slow,
Soothed sweetly sad Electra's poet's ear:

  By old Cephisus deep,
  Who spread his wavy sweep
In warbled wand'rings round thy green retreat;
  On whose enamell'd side,
  When holy Freedom died,
No equal haunt allured thy future feet!

  O sister meek of Truth,
  To my admiring youth
Thy sober aid and native charms infuse!
  The flow'rs that sweetest breathe,
  Though beauty cull'd the wreath,
Still ask thy hand to range their order'd hues.

  While Rome could none esteem,
  But virtue's patriot theme,
You loved her hills, and led her laureate band;
  But stay'd to sing alone
  To one distinguish'd throne,
And turn'd thy face, and fled her alter'd land.

No more, in hall or bow'r,
The passions own thy pow'r.
Love, only Love her forceless numbers mean;
   For thou hast left her shrine,
   Nor olive more, nor vine,
Shall gain thy feet to bless the servile scene.

Though taste, though genius bless
To some divine excess,
Faint's the cold work till thou inspire the whole;
   What each, what all supply,
   May court, may charm our eye,
Thou, only thou, canst raise the meeting soul!

Of these let others ask,
To aid some mighty task,
I only seek to find thy temperate vale;
   Where oft my reed might sound
   To maids and shepherds round,
And all thy sons, O Nature, learn my tale.
WILLIAM COLLINS (1721–1759)

HOW SLEEP THE BRAVE   448
How sleep the brave, who sink to rest
By all their country's wishes blest!
When Spring, with dewy fingers cold,
Returns to deck their hallow'd mould,
She there shall dress a sweeter sod
Than Fancy's feet have ever trod.

By fairy hands their knell is rung;
By forms unseen their dirge is sung;
There Honour comes, a pilgrim grey,
To bless the turf that wraps their clay;
And Freedom shall awhile repair
To dwell, a weeping hermit, there!
WILLIAM COLLINS (1721–1759)

ODE TO EVENING   449
If aught of oaten stop, or pastoral song,
May hope, chaste Eve, to soothe thy modest ear,
   Like thy own solemn springs,
   Thy springs and dying gales;

O nymph reserved, while now the bright-hair'd sun
Sits in yon western tent, whose cloudy skirts,
   With brede ethereal wove,
   O'erhang his wavy bed:

Now air is hush'd, save where the weak-eyed bat
With short shrill shriek flits by on leathern wing,
   Or where the beetle winds
   His small but sullen horn,

As oft he rises, 'midst the twilight path
Against the pilgrim borne in heedless hum:
    Now teach me, maid composed,
    To breathe some soften'd strain,

Whose numbers, stealing through thy darkening vale,
May not unseemly with its stillness suit,
    As musing slow, I hail
    Thy genial loved return!

For when thy folding-star arising shows
His paly circlet, at his warning lamp
    The fragrant hours, and elves
    Who slept in buds the day,

And many a nymph who wreathes her brows with sedge,
And sheds the freshening dew, and, lovelier still,
    The pensive pleasures sweet,
    Prepare thy shadowy car:

Then lead, calm votaress, where some sheety lake
Cheers the lone heath, or some time-hallow'd pile,
    Or upland fallows grey
    Reflect its last cool gleam.

Or if chill blustering winds, or driving rain,
Prevent my willing feet, be mine the hut
    That from the mountain's side
    Views wilds and swelling floods,

And hamlets brown, and dim-discover'd spires,
And hears their simple bell, and marks o'er all
    Thy dewy fingers draw
    The gradual dusky veil.

While Spring shall pour his show'rs, as oft he wont,
And bathe thy breathing tresses, meekest Eve!
    While Summer loves to sport
    Beneath thy lingering light;

While sallow Autumn fills thy lap with leaves,
Or Winter, yelling through the troublous air,
    Affrights thy shrinking train,
    And rudely rends thy robes:

So long, regardful of thy quiet rule,
Shall Fancy, Friendship, Science, rose-lipp'd Health
    Thy gentlest influence own,
    And hymn thy favourite name!

                      WILLIAM COLLINS (1721–1759)

450   FIDELE

    To fair Fidele's grassy tomb
      Soft maids and village hinds shall bring
    Each opening sweet of earliest bloom,
      And rifle all the breathing Spring.

No wailing ghost shall dare appear
  To vex with shrieks this quiet grove;
But shepherd lads assemble here,
  And melting virgins own their love.

No wither'd witch shall here be seen,
  No goblins lead their nightly crew;
The female fays shall haunt the green,
  And dress thy grave with pearly dew.

The redbreast oft at evening hours
  Shall kindly lend his little aid,
With hoary moss, and gather'd flowers,
  To deck the ground where thou art laid.

When howling winds, and beating rain,
  In tempests shake the sylvan cell;
Or 'midst the chase, on every plain,
  The tender thought on thee shall dwell;

Each lonely scene shall thee restore,
  For thee the tear be duly shed;
Beloved, till life can charm no more;
  And mourn'd till Pity's self be dead.
WILLIAM COLLINS (1721–1759)

451 AMORET

If rightly tuneful bards decide,
  If it be fix'd in Love's decrees,
That Beauty ought not to be tried
  But by its native power to please,
Then tell me, youths and lovers, tell—
What fair can Amoret excel?

Behold that bright unsullied smile,
  And wisdom speaking in her mien:
Yet—she so artless all the while,
  So little studious to be seen—
We naught but instant gladness know,
Nor think to whom the gift we owe.

But neither music, nor the powers
  Of youth and mirth and frolic cheer,
Add half the sunshine to the hours,
  Or make life's prospect half so clear,
As memory brings it to the eye
From scenes where Amoret was by.

This, sure, is Beauty's happiest part;
  This gives the most unbounded sway;
This shall enchant the subject heart
  When rose and lily fade away;
And she be still, in spite of Time,
Sweet Amoret in all her prime.
MARK AKENSIDE (1721–1770)

452 THE COMPLAINT

Away! away!
Tempt me no more, insidious Love:
   Thy soothing sway
Long did my youthful bosom prove:
At length thy treason is discern'd,
At length some dear-bought caution earn'd:
Away! nor hope my riper age to move.

   I know, I see
Her merit. Needs it now be shown,
   Alas! to me?
How often, to myself unknown,
The graceful, gentle, virtuous maid
Have I admired! How often said—
What joy to call a heart like hers one's own!

   But, flattering god,
O squanderer of content and ease
   In thy abode
Will care's rude lesson learn to please?
O say, deceiver, hast thou won
Proud Fortune to attend thy throne,
Or placed thy friends above her stern decrees?

MARK AKENSIDE (1721–1770)

453 THE NIGHTINGALE

To-night retired, the queen of heaven
   With young Endymion stays;
And now to Hesper it is given
Awhile to rule the vacant sky,
Till she shall to her lamp supply
   A stream of brighter rays.

Propitious send thy golden ray,
   Thou purest light above!
Let no false flame seduce to stray
Where gulf or steep lie hid for harm;
But lead where music's healing charm
   May soothe afflicted love.

To them, by many a grateful song
   In happier seasons vow'd,
These lawns, Olympia's haunts, belong:
Oft by yon silver stream we walk'd,
Or fix'd, while Philomela talk'd,
   Beneath yon copses stood.

Nor seldom, where the beechen boughs
   That roofless tower invade,
We came, while her enchanting Muse
The radiant moon above us held:
Till, by a clamorous owl compell'd,
   She fled the solemn shade.

But hark! I hear her liquid tone!
  Now Hesper guide my feet!
Down the red marl with moss o'ergrown,
Through yon wild thicket next the plain,
Whose hawthorns choke the winding lane
  Which leads to her retreat.

See the green space: on either hand
  Enlarged it spreads around:
See, in the midst she takes her stand,
Where one old oak his awful shade
Extends o'er half the level mead,
  Enclosed in woods profound.

Hark! how through many a melting note
  She now prolongs her lays:
How sweetly down the void they float!
The breeze their magic path attends;
The stars shine out; the forest bends;
  The wakeful heifers graze.

Whoe'er thou art whom chance may bring
  To this sequester'd spot,
If then the plaintive Siren sing,
O softly tread beneath her bower
And think of Heaven's disposing power,
  Of man's uncertain lot.

O think, o'er all this mortal stage
  What mournful scenes arise:
What ruin waits on kingly rage;
How often virtue dwells with woe;
How many griefs from knowledge flow;
  How swiftly pleasure flies!

O sacred bird! let me at eve,
  Thus wandering all alone,
Thy tender counsel oft receive,
Bear witness to thy pensive airs,
And pity Nature's common cares,
  Till I forget my own.

                    MARK AKENSIDE (1721–1770)

454 To Leven Water

Pure stream, in whose transparent wave
My youthful limbs I wont to lave;
No torrents stain thy limpid source,
No rocks impede thy dimpling course
Devolving from thy parent lake
A charming maze thy waters make
By bowers of birch and groves of pine
And edges flower'd with eglantine.

Still on thy banks so gaily green
May numerous herds and flocks be seen,
And lasses chanting o'er the pail,
And shepherds piping in the dale,
And ancient faith that knows no guile,
And industry embrown'd with toil,
And hearts resolved and hands prepared
The blessings they enjoy to guard.
TOBIAS GEORGE SMOLLETT (1721–1771)

455   A LAMENT FOR FLODDEN

I've heard them lilting at our ewe-milking,
   Lasses a' lilting before dawn o' day;
But now they are moaning on ilka green loaning—
   The Flowers of the Forest are a' wede away.

At bughts, in the morning, nae blythe lads are scorning,
   Lasses are lonely and dowie and wae;
Nae daffing, nae gabbing, but sighing and sabbing,
   Ilk ane lifts her leglin and hies her away.

In hairst, at the shearing, nae youths now are jeering,
   Bandsters are lyart, and runkled, and gray:
At fair or at preaching, nae wooing, nae fleeching—
   The Flowers of the Forest are a' wede away.

At e'en, in the gloaming, nae swankies are roaming
   'Bout stacks wi' the lasses at bogle to play;
But ilk ane sits eerie, lamenting her dearie—
   The Flowers of the Forest are a' wede away.

Dool and wae for the order sent our lads to the Border!
   The English, for ance, by guile wan the day;
The Flowers of the Forest, that fought aye the foremost,
   The prime of our land, lie cauld in the clay.

We'll hear nae mair lilting at our ewe-milking;
   Women and bairns are heartless and wae;
Sighing and moaning on ilka green loaning—
   The Flowers of the Forest are a' wede away.
JANE ELLIOT (1727–1805)

loaning: *lane, field-track*; wede: *weeded*; bughts: *sheep-folds*;
daffing: *joking*; leglin: *milk-pail*; hairst: *harvest*; bandsters: *binders*;
lyart: *gray-haired*; runkled: *wrinkled*; fleeching: *coaxing*;
swankies: *lusty lads*; bogle: *bogy, hide-and-seek*; dool: *mourning*

456   WOMAN

When lovely woman stoops to folly,
   And finds too late that men betray,
What charm can soothe her melancholy?
   What art can wash her tears away?

    The only art her guilt to cover,
      To hide her shame from ev'ry eye,
    To give repentance to her lover,
      And wring his bosom is—to die.
                          OLIVER GOLDSMITH (1728–1774)

MEMORY   457

O Memory, thou fond deceiver,
  Still importunate and vain,
To former joys recurring ever,
  And turning all the past to pain:

Thou, like the world, th' oppress'd oppressing,
  Thy smiles increase the wretch's woe:
And he who wants each other blessing
  In thee must ever find a foe.
                          OLIVER GOLDSMITH (1728–1774)

IF DOUGHTY DEEDS   458

  If doughty deeds my lady please,
    Right soon I'll mount my steed;
  And strong his arm and fast his seat,
    That bears frae me the meed.
  I'll wear thy colours in my cap,
    Thy picture in my heart;
  And he that bends not to thine eye
    Shall rue it to his smart!
      Then tell me how to woo thee, Love;
        O tell me how to woo thee!
      For thy dear sake nae care I'll take,
        Tho' ne'er another trow me.

  If gay attire delight thine eye
    I'll dight me in array;
  I'll tend thy chamber door all night,
    And squire thee all the day.
  If sweetest sounds can win thine ear,
    These sounds I'll strive to catch;
  Thy voice I'll steal to woo thysel',
    That voice that nane can match.
      Then tell me how to woo thee, Love...

  But if fond love thy heart can gain,
    I never broke a vow;
  Nae maiden lays her skaith to me,
    I never loved but you.
  For you alone I ride the ring,
    For you I wear the blue;
  For you alone I strive to sing,
    O tell me how to woo!
      Then tell me how to woo thee, Love;
        O tell me how to woo thee!
      For thy dear sake nae care I'll take
        Tho' ne'er another trow me.
    ROBERT CUNNINGHAME-GRAHAM OF GARTMORE (1735–1797)

459   TO MARY UNWIN

Mary! I want a lyre with other strings,
Such aid from Heaven as some have feign'd they drew,
An eloquence scarce given to mortals, new
And undebased by praise of meaner things;
That ere through age or woe I shed my wings,
I may record thy worth with honour due,
In verse as musical as thou art true,
And that immortalizes whom it sings:
But thou hast little need. There is a Book
By seraphs writ with beams of heavenly light,
On which the eyes of God not rarely look,
A chronicle of actions just and bright—
  There all thy deeds, my faithful Mary, shine;
  And since thou own'st that praise, I spare thee mine.
                           WILLIAM COWPER (1731–1800)

460   MY MARY

The twentieth year is wellnigh past
Since first our sky was overcast;
Ah, would that this might be the last!
        My Mary!

Thy spirits have a fainter flow,
I see thee daily weaker grow;
'Twas my distress that brought thee low,
        My Mary!

Thy needles, once a shining store,
For my sake restless heretofore,
Now rust disused, and shine no more;
        My Mary!

For though thou gladly wouldst fulfil
The same kind office for me still,
Thy sight now seconds not thy will,
        My Mary!

But well thou play'dst the housewife's part,
And all thy threads with magic art
Have wound themselves about this heart,
        My Mary!

Thy indistinct expressions seem
Like language utter'd in a dream;
Yet me they charm, whate'er the theme,
        My Mary!

Thy silver locks, once auburn bright,
Are still more lovely in my sight
Than golden beams of orient light,
        My Mary!

For could I view nor them nor thee,
What sight worth seeing could I see?
The sun would rise in vain for me.
      My Mary!

Partakers of thy sad decline,
Thy hands their little force resign;
Yet, gently press'd, press gently mine,
      My Mary!

Such feebleness of limbs thou prov'st,
That now at every step thou mov'st
Upheld by two; yet still thou lov'st,
      My Mary!

And still to love, though press'd with ill,
In wintry age to feel no chill,
With me is to be lovely still,
      My Mary!

But ah! by constant heed I know
How oft the sadness that I show
Transforms thy smiles to looks of woe,
      My Mary!

And should my future lot be cast
With much resemblance of the past,
Thy worn-out heart will break at last—
      My Mary!
            WILLIAM COWPER (1731–1800)

AN EPITAPH   461

Like thee I once have stemm'd the sea of life,
  Like thee have languish'd after empty joys,
Like thee have labour'd in the stormy strife,
  Been grieved for trifles, and amused with toys.

Forget my frailties; thou art also frail:
  Forgive my lapses; for thyself may'st fall:
Nor read unmoved my artless tender tale—
  I was a friend, O man, to thee, to all.
            JAMES BEATTIE (1735–1803)

CA' THE YOWES TO THE KNOWES   462

  Ca' the yowes to the knowes,
    Ca' them where the heather grows,
    Ca' them where the burnie rows,
      My bonnie dearie.

As I gaed down the water side,
There I met my shepherd lad;
He row'd me sweetly in his plaid,
  And he ca'd me his dearie.

> "Will ye gang down the water side,
> And see the waves sae sweetly glide
> Beneath the hazels spreading wide?
> The moon it shines fu' clearly."
>
> "I was bred up at nae sic school,
> My shepherd lad, to play the fool,
> And a' the day to sit in dool,
> And naebody to see me."
>
> "Ye sall get gowns and ribbons meet,
> Cauf-leather shoon upon your feet,
> And in my arms ye'se lie and sleep,
> And ye sall be my dearie."
>
> "If ye'll but stand to what ye've said,
> I'se gang wi' you, my shepherd lad,
> And ye may row me in your plaid,
> And I sall be your dearie."
>
> "While waters wimple to the sea,
> While day blinks in the lift sae hie,
> Till clay-cauld death sall blin' my e'e,
> Ye aye sall be my dearie!"
>
> ISOBEL PAGAN (1740–1821)

yowes: *ewes*; knowes: *knolls, little hills*; rows: *rolls*; row'd: *rolled, wrapped*; dool: *dule, sorrow*; lift: *sky*

463   LIFE

Life! I know not what thou art,
But know that thou and I must part;
And when, or how, or where we met,
I own to me's a secret yet.
But this I know, when thou art fled,
Where'er they lay these limbs, this head,
No clod so valueless shall be
As all that then remains of me.

O whither, whither dost thou fly?
Where bend unseen thy trackless course?
   And in this strange divorce,
Ah, tell where I must seek this compound I?
To the vast ocean of empyreal flame
   From whence thy essence came
Dost thou thy flight pursue, when freed
From matter's base encumbering weed?
   Or dost thou, hid from sight,
   Wait, like some spell-bound knight,
Through blank oblivious years th' appointed hour
To break thy trance and reassume thy power?
Yet canst thou without thought or feeling be?
O say, what art thou, when no more thou'rt thee?

Life! we have been long together,
Through pleasant and through cloudy weather;
  'Tis hard to part when friends are dear;
  Perhaps 'twill cost a sigh, a tear;—
Then steal away, give little warning,
      Choose thine own time;
Say not Good-night, but in some brighter clime
      Bid me Good-morning!
ANNA LÆTITIA BARBAULD (1743–1825)

PRAYER FOR INDIFFERENCE   464
I ask no kind return of love,
  No tempting charm to please;
Far from the heart those gifts remove,
  That sighs for peace and ease.

Nor peace nor ease the heart can know,
  That, like the needle true,
Turns at the touch of joy or woe,
  But turning, trembles too.

Far as distress the soul can wound,
  'Tis pain in each degree:
'Tis bliss but to a certain bound,
  Beyond is agony.
FANNY GREVILLE (18th Cent.)

TO THE CUCKOO   465
Hail, beauteous stranger of the grove!
  Thou messenger of Spring!
Now Heaven repairs thy rural seat,
  And woods thy welcome ring.

What time the daisy decks the green,
  Thy certain voice we hear:
Hast thou a star to guide thy path,
  Or mark the rolling year?

Delightful visitant! with thee
  I hail the time of flowers,
And hear the sound of music sweet
  From birds among the bowers.

The schoolboy, wand'ring through the wood
  To pull the primrose gay,
Starts, the new voice of Spring to hear,
  And imitates thy lay.

What time the pea puts on the bloom,
  Thou fli'st thy vocal vale,
An annual guest in other lands,
  Another Spring to hail.

Sweet bird! thy bower is ever green,
  Thy sky is ever clear;
Thou hast no sorrow in thy song,
  No Winter in thy year!

O could I fly, I'd fly with thee!
  We'd make, with joyful wing,
Our annual visit o'er the globe,
  Companions of the Spring.

JOHN LOGAN (1748–1788)

466   Epigram

On parent knees, a naked new-born child,
Weeping thou sat'st while all around thee smiled:
So live, that sinking to thy life's last sleep,
Calm thou may'st smile, whilst all around thee weep.

SIR WILLIAM JONES (1746–1794)

467   Ode on the Pleasure Arising From Vicissitude

  Now the golden Morn aloft
  Waves her dew-bespangled wing,
  With vermeil cheek and whisper soft
  She woos the tardy Spring:
  Till April starts, and calls around
  The sleeping fragrance from the ground,
  And lightly o'er the living scene
  Scatters his freshest, tenderest green.

  New-born flocks, in rustic dance,
  Frisking ply their feeble feet;
  Forgetful of their wintry trance
  The birds his presence greet:
  But chief, the sky-lark warbles high
  His trembling thrilling ecstasy;
  And lessening from the dazzled sight,
  Melts into air and liquid light.

  Yesterday the sullen year
  Saw the snowy whirlwind fly;
  Mute was the music of the air,
  The herd stood drooping by:
  Their raptures now that wildly flow
  No yesterday nor morrow know;
  'Tis Man alone that joy descries
  With forward and reverted eyes.

  Smiles on past Misfortune's brow
  Soft Reflection's hand can trace,
  And o'er the cheek of Sorrow throw
  A melancholy grace;
  While Hope prolongs our happier hour,
  Or deepest shades, that dimly lour
  And blacken round our weary way,
  Gilds with a gleam of distant day.

Still, where rosy Pleasure leads,
See a kindred Grief pursue;
Behind the steps that Misery treads
Approaching Comfort view:
The hues of bliss more brightly glow
Chastised by sabler tints of woe,
And blended form, with artful strife,
The strength and harmony of life.

See the wretch that long has tost
On the thorny bed of pain,
At length repair his vigour lost
And breathe and walk again:
The meanest floweret of the vale,
The simplest note that swells the gale,
The common sun, the air, the skies,
To him are opening Paradise.

THOMAS GRAY (1716–1771)

THE BLIND BOY   468

O say what is that thing call'd Light,
Which I must ne'er enjoy;
What are the blessings of the sight,
O tell your poor blind boy!

You talk of wondrous things you see,
You say the sun shines bright;
I feel him warm, but how can he
Or make it day or night?

My day or night myself I make
Whene'er I sleep or play;
And could I ever keep awake
With me 'twere always day.

With heavy sighs I often hear
You mourn my hapless woe;
But sure with patience I can bear
A loss I ne'er can know.

Then let not what I cannot have
My cheer of mind destroy;
Whilst thus I sing, I am a king,
Although a poor blind boy.

COLLEY CIBBER (1701–1757)

RULE BRITANNIA   469

When Britain first at Heaven's command
  Arose from out the azure main,
This was the charter of her land,
  And guardian angels sung the strain:
Rule Brittania! Brittania rules the waves!
Britons never shall be slaves.

The nations not so blest as thee
  Must in their turn to tyrants fall,
Whilst thou shalt flourish great and free
  The dread and envy of them all.

Still more majestic shalt thou rise,
  More dreadful from each foreign stroke;
As the loud blast that tears the skies
  Serves but to root thy native oak.

Thee haughty tyrants ne'er shall tame;
  All their attempts to bend thee down
Will but arouse thy generous flame,
  And work their woe and thy renown.

To thee belongs the rural reign;
  Thy cities shall with commerce shine;
All thine shall be the subject main,
  And every shore it circles thine!

The Muses, still with Freedom found,
  Shall to thy happy coast repair;
Blest Isle, with matchless beauty crown'd,
  And manly hearts to guard the fair:—
Rule Britannia! Brittania rules the waves!
Britons never shall be slaves!
JAMES THOMSON (1700–1748)

470   THE POPLAR FIELD

The poplars are fell'd, farewell to the shade
  And the whispering sound of the cool colonnade;
The winds play no longer and sing in the leaves,
  Nor Ouse on his bosom their image receives.

Twelve years have elapsed since I last took a view
  Of my favourite field, and the bank where they grew:
And now in the grass behold they are laid,
  And the tree is my seat that once lent me a shade.

The blackbird has fled to another retreat
  Where the hazels afford him a screen from the heat;
And the scene where his melody charm'd me before
  Resounds with his sweet-flowing ditty no more.

My fugitive years are all hasting away,
  And I must ere long lie lowly as they,
With a turf on my breast and a stone at my head,
  Ere another such grove shall arise in its stead.

'Tis a sight to engage me, if anything can,
  To muse on the perishing pleasures of man;
Short-lived as we are, our enjoyments, I see,
  Have a still shorter date, and die sooner than we.
WILLIAM COWPER (1731–1800)

To A Young Lady 471
Sweet stream, that winds through yonder glade,
Apt emblem of a virtuous maid—
Silent and chaste she steals along,
Far from the world's gay busy throng:
With gentle yet prevailing force,
Intent upon her destined course;
Graceful and useful all she does,
Blessing and blest where'er she goes;
Pure-bosom'd as that watery glass,
And Heaven reflected in her face.
                    WILLIAM COWPER (1731–1800)

Hymn to Adversity 472
Daughter of Jove, relentless power,
Thou tamer of the human breast,
Whose iron scourge and torturing hour
The bad affright, afflict the best!
Bound in thy adamantine chain
The proud are taught to taste of pain,
And purple tyrants vainly groan
With pangs unfelt before, unpitied and alone.

When first thy Sire to send on earth
Virtue, his darling child, design'd,
To thee he gave the heavenly birth
And bade to form her infant mind.
Stern rugged Nurse! thy rigid lore
With patience many a year she bore:
What sorrow was, thou bad'st her know,
And from her own she learn'd to melt at others' woe.

Scared at thy frown terrific, fly
Self-pleasing Folly's idle brood,
Wild Laughter, Noise, and thoughtless Joy,
And leave us leisure to be good.
Light they disperse, and with them go
The summer Friend, the flattering Foe;
By vain Prosperity received
To her they vow their truth, and are again believed.

And Melancholy, silent maid,
With leaden eye, that loves the ground,
Still on thy solemn steps attend:
Warm Charity, the general friend,
With Justice, to herself severe,
And Pity dropping soft the sadly-pleasing tear.

Oh, gently on thy suppliant's head,
Dread Goddess, lay thy chastening hand!
Not in thy Gorgon terrors clad,
Not circled with the vengeful band

(As by the impious thou art seen)
With thundering voice, and threatening mien,
With screaming Horror's funeral cry,
Despair, and fell Disease, and ghastly Poverty:

Thy form benign, O Goddess, wear,
Thy milder influence impart,
Thy philosophic train be there
To soften, not to wound my heart.
The generous spark extinct revive,
Teach me to love and to forgive,
Exact my own defects to scan,
What others are to feel, and know myself a Man.
Thomas Gray (1716–1771)

473   THE DYING MAN IN HIS GARDEN

Why, Damon, with the forward day
Dost thou thy little spot survey,
From tree to tree, with doubtful cheer,
Pursue the progress of the year,
What winds arise, what rains descend,
When thou before that year shalt end?

What do thy noontide walks avail,
To clear the leaf, and pick the snail,
Then wantonly to death decree
An insect usefuller than thee?
Thou and the worm are brother-kind,
As low, as earthy, and as blind.

Vain wretch! canst thou expect to see
The downy peach make court to thee?
Or that thy sense shall ever meet
The bean-flower's deep-embosom'd sweet
Exhaling with an evening blast?
Thy evenings then will all be past!

Thy narrow pride, thy fancied green
(For vanity's in little seen),
All must be left when Death appears,
In spite of wishes, groans, and tears;
Nor one of all thy plants that grow
But Rosemary will with thee go.
George Sewel (1687–1726)

474   TO MORROW

In the downhill of life, when I find I'm declining,
May my lot no less fortunate be
Than a snug elbow-chair can afford for reclining,
And a cot that o'erlooks the wide sea;
With an ambling pad-pony to pace o'er the lawn,
While I carol away idle sorrow,
And blithe as the lark that each day hails the dawn
Look forward with hope for to-morrow.

With a porch at my door, both for shelter and shade too,
As the sunshine or rain may prevail;
And a small spot of ground for the use of the spade too,
With a barn for the use of the flail:
A cow for my dairy, a dog for my game,
And a purse when a friend wants to borrow;
I'll envy no nabob his riches or fame,
Nor what honours await him to-morrow.

From the bleak northern blast may my cot be completely
Secured by a neighbouring hill;
And at night may repose steal upon me more sweetly
By the sound of a murmuring rill:
And while peace and plenty I find at my board,
With a heart free from sickness and sorrow,
With my friends may I share what to-day may afford,
And let them spread the table to-morrow.

And when I at last must throw off this frail covering
Which I've worn for three-score years and ten,
On the brink of the grave I'll not seek to keep hovering,
Nor my thread wish to spin o'er again:
But my face in the glass I'll serenely survey,
And with smiles count each wrinkle and furrow;
As this old worn-out stuff, which is threadbare to-day
May become everlasting to-morrow.

WILLIAM COLLINS (1721–1759)

TWINKLE, TWINKLE, LITTLE STAR   475

Twinkle, twinkle, little star!
How I wonder what you are,
Up above the world so high,
Like a diamond in the sky.

When the glorious sun is set,
When the grass with dew is wet,
Then you show your little light,
Twinkle, twinkle all the night.

In the dark-blue sky you keep,
And often through my curtains peep,
For you never shut your eye,
Till the sun is in the sky.

As your bright and tiny spark
Guides the traveller in the dark,
Though I know not what you are,
Twinkle, twinkle, little star!

JANE TAYLOR (1783–1824)

476 CASABIANCA

["Casabianca" commemorates an actual incident that occurred in 1798 during the Battle of the Nile aboard the French ship *Orient* involving Giocante, the young son of the commander Louis de Casabianca. – Ed.]

> The boy stood on the burning deck,
>   Whence all but him had fled;
> The flame that lit the battle's wreck
>   Shone round him o'er the dead.
>
> Yet beautiful and bright he stood,
>   As born to rule the storm;
> A creature of heroic blood,
>   A proud though childlike form.
>
> The flames rolled on—he would not go
>   Without his father's word;
> That father, faint in death below,
>   His voice no longer heard.
>
> He called aloud, "Say, father, say
>   If yet my task is done?"
> He knew not that the chieftain lay
>   Unconscious of his son.
>
> "Speak, father!" once again he cried,
>   "If I may yet be gone!"
> And but the booming shots replied,
>   And fast the flames rolled on.
>
> Upon his brow he felt their breath,
>   And in his waving hair;
> And looked from that lone post of death
>   In still, yet brave despair.
>
> And shouted but once more aloud
>   "My father! must I stay?"
> While o'er him fast, through sail and shroud,
>   The wreathing fires made way.
>
> They wrapt the ship in splendour wild,
>   They caught the flag on high,
> And streamed above the gallant child
>   Like banners in the sky.
>
> Then came a burst of thunder sound—
>   The boy—oh! where was he?
> —Ask of the winds that far around
>   With fragments strew the sea;

With mast, and helm, and pennon fair.
  That well had borne their part—
But the noblest thing that perished there
  Was that young, faithful heart.

FELICIA DOROTHEA HEMANS (1793–1835)

THE VIOLET 477

Down in a green and shady bed
  A modest violet grew;
Its stalk was bent, it hung its head,
  As if to hide from view.

And yet it was a lovely flower,
  No colours bright and fair;
It might have graced a rosy bower,
  Instead of hiding there.

Yet there it was content to bloom,
  In modest tints arrayed;
And there diffused its sweet perfume,
  Within the silent shade.

Then let me to the valley go,
  This pretty flower to see;
That I may also learn to grow
  In sweet humility.

JANE TAYLOR (1783–1824)

A VISIT FROM ST. NICHOLAS 478

'Twas the night before Christmas, when all through the house
Not a creature was stirring, not even a mouse;
The stockings were hung by the chimney with care,
In hopes that St. Nicholas soon would be there;
The children were nestled all snug in their beds,
While visions of sugar-plums danced in their heads;
And mamma in her 'kerchief, and I in my cap,
Had just settled our brains for a long winter's nap,
When out on the lawn there arose such a clatter,
I sprang from the bed to see what was the matter.
Away to the window I flew like a flash,
Tore open the shutters and threw up the sash.
The moon on the breast of the new-fallen snow
Gave the luster of mid-day to objects below,
When, what to my wondering eyes should appear,
But a miniature sleigh, and eight tiny reindeer.
With a little old driver, so lively and quick,
I knew in a moment it must be St. Nick.
More rapid than eagles his coursers they came,
And he whistled, and shouted, and called them by name:
"Now, *Dasher*! now, *Dancer*! now, *Prancer* and *Vixen*!
On, *Comet*! on, *Cupid*! on, *Donder* and *Blitzen*!
To the top of the porch! to the top of the wall!
Now dash away! dash away! dash away all!"

As dry leaves that before the wild hurricane fly,
When they meet with an obstacle, mount to the sky;
So up to the house-top the coursers they flew,
With the sleigh full of toys, and St. Nicholas, too.
And then, in a twinkling, I heard on the roof
The prancing and pawing of each little hoof.
As I drew in my head, and was turning around,
Down the chimney St. Nicholas came with a bound.
He was dressed all in fur, from his head to his foot,
And his clothes were all tarnished with ashes and soot;
A bundle of toys he had flung on his back,
And he looked like a peddler just opening his pack.
His eyes—how they twinkled! his dimples how merry!
His cheeks were like roses, his nose like a cherry!
His droll little mouth was drawn up like a bow,
And the beard of his chin was as white as the snow;
The stump of a pipe he held tight in his teeth,
And the smoke it encircled his head like a wreath;
He had a broad face and a little round belly,
That shook when he laughed, like a bowlful of jelly.
He was chubby and plump, a right jolly old elf,
And I laughed when I saw him, in spite of myself;
A wink of his eye and a twist of his head,
Soon gave me to know I had nothing to dread;
He spoke not a word, but went straight to his work,
And filled all the stockings; then turned with a jerk,
And laying his finger aside of his nose,
And giving a nod, up the chimney he rose;
He sprang to his sleigh, to his team gave a whistle,
And away they all flew like the down on a thistle.
But I heard him exclaim, ere he drove out of sight,
"*Happy Christmas to all, and to all a good-night.*"
CLEMENT CLARKE MOORE (1779–1863)

479   THE STAR-SPANGLED BANNER

O! say, can you see, by the dawn's early light,
  What so proudly we hailed at the twilight's last gleaming—
Whose broad stripes and bright stars, through the perilous fight,
  O'er the ramparts we watched were so gallantly streaming!
And the rocket's red glare, the bombs bursting in air,
Gave proof through the night that our flag was still there;
O! say, does that star-spangled banner yet wave
O'er the land of the free, and the home of the brave?

On that shore dimly seen through the mists of the deep,
  Where the foe's haughty host in dread silence reposes,
What is that which the breeze, o'er the towering steep,
  As it fitfully blows, now conceals, now discloses?
Now it catches the gleam of the morning's first beam,
In full glory reflected now shines on the stream;
'Tis the star-spangled banner; O long may it wave
O'er the land of the free, and the home of the brave!

And where is that band who so vauntingly swore
   That the havoc of war and the battle's confusion
A home and a country should leave us no more?
   Their blood has washed out their foul footsteps, pollution.
No refuge could save the hireling and slave
From the terror of flight, or the gloom of the grave;
And the star-spangled banner in triumph doth wave
O'er the land of the free, and the home of the brave.

O! thus be it ever, when freemen shall stand
   Between their loved homes and the war's desolation!
Blest with victory and peace, may the heav'n-rescued land
   Praise the power that hath made and preserved us a nation.
Then conquer we must, for our cause it is just,
And this be our motto—"*In God is our trust*":
And the star-spangled banner in triumph shall wave
O'er the land of the free, and the home of the brave.
                         FRANCIS SCOTT KEY (1779–1843)

THE BUTTERFLY AND THE BEE   480
Methought I heard a butterfly
   Say to a labouring bee:
"Thou hast no colours of the sky
   On painted wings like me."

"Poor child of vanity! those dyes,
   And colours bright and rare,"
With mild reproof, the bee replies,
   "Are all beneath my care.

"Content I toil from morn to eve,
   And scorning idleness,
To tribes of gaudy sloth I leave
   The vanity of dress."
                      WILLIAM LISLE BOWLES (1762–1850)

THE SPIDER AND THE FLY   481
"Will you walk into my parlour?" said the Spider to the Fly,
'Tis the prettiest little parlour that ever you did spy;
The way into my parlour is up a winding stair,
And I've a many curious things to show when you are there."
  "Oh no, no," said the little Fly, "to ask me is in vain,
  For who goes up your winding stair can ne'er come down again."

"I'm sure you must be weary, dear, with soaring up so high;
Will you rest upon my little bed?" said the Spider to the Fly.
"There are pretty curtains drawn around; the sheets are fine and thin,
And if you like to rest awhile, I'll snugly tuck you in!"
  "Oh no, no," said the little Fly, "for I've often heard it said,
  They *never, never wake* again, who sleep upon *your* bed!"

Said the cunning Spider to the Fly, "Dear friend what can I do,
To prove the warm affection I've always felt for you?
I have within my pantry, good store of all that's nice;
I'm sure you're very welcome — will you please to take a slice?"
 "Oh no, no," said the little Fly, "kind Sir, that cannot be,
 I've heard what's in your pantry, and I do not wish to see!"

"Sweet creature!" said the Spider, "you're witty and you're wise,
 How handsome are your gauzy wings, how brilliant are your eyes!
 I've a little looking-glass upon my parlour shelf,
 If you'll step in one moment, dear, you shall behold yourself.
 "I thank you, gentle sir," she said, "for what you're pleased to say,
 And bidding you good morning *now*, I'll call *another* day."

The Spider turned him round about, and went into his den,
For well he knew the silly Fly would soon come back again:
So he wove a subtle web, in a little corner sly,
And set his table ready, to dine upon the Fly.

Then he came out to his door again, and merrily did sing,
"Come hither, hither, pretty Fly, with the pearl and silver wing;
 Your robes are green and purple — there's a crest upon your head;
 Your eyes are like the diamond bright, but mine are dull as lead!"

Alas, alas! how very soon this silly little Fly,
Hearing his wily, flattering words, came slowly flitting by;
With buzzing wings she hung aloft, then near and nearer drew,
Thinking only of her brilliant eyes, and green and purple hue —
Thinking only of her crested head — *poor foolish thing!* At last,
Up jumped the cunning Spider, and fiercely held her fast.
He dragged her up his winding stair, into his dismal den,
Within his little parlour — but she ne'er came out again!

And now dear little children, who may this story read,
To idle, silly flattering words, I pray you ne'er give heed:
Unto an evil counsellor, close heart and ear and eye,
And take a lesson from this tale, of the Spider and the Fly.
Mary Howitt (1799–1888)

482 Warren's Address To The American Soldiers
(before the Battle of Bunker Hill, June 17, 1775)

Stand! the ground's your own, my braves!
Will ye give it up to slaves?
Will ye look for greener graves?
 Hope ye mercy still?
What's the mercy despots feel?
Hear it in that battle-peal!
Read it on yon bristling steel!
 Ask it,—ye who will.

Fear ye foes who kill for hire?
Will ye to your homes retire?
Look behind you! they're afire!
 And, before you, see

Who have done it!—From the vale
On they come!—And will ye quail?—
Leaden rain and iron hail
  Let their welcome be!

In the God of battles trust!
Die we may,—and die we must;
But, O, where can dust to dust
  Be consigned so well,
As where Heaven its dews shall shed
On the martyred patriot's bed,
And the rocks shall raise their head,
  Of his deeds to tell!

JOHN PIERPONT (1785–1866)

I Wandered Lonely As A Cloud 483

I wandered lonely as a cloud
  That floats on high o'er vales and hills,
When all at once I saw a crowd,
  A host of golden daffodils:
Beside the lake, beneath the trees,
Fluttering and dancing in the breeze.

Continuous as the stars that shine
  And twinkle on the milky way,
They stretched in never-ending line
  Along the margin of a bay;
Ten thousand saw I at a glance,
Tossing their heads in sprightly dance.

The waves beside them danced, but they
  Outdid the sparkling waves in glee:—
A poet could not but be gay
  In such a jocund company;
I gazed—and gazed—but little thought
What wealth the show to me had brought.

For oft, when on my couch I lie
  In vacant or in pensive mood,
They flash upon that inward eye
  Which is the bliss of solitude;
And then my heart with pleasure fills,
And dances with the daffodils.
          WILLIAM WORDSWORTH (1770–1850)

John Barleycorn 484

There were three kings into the East,
  Three kings both great and high;
And they ha'e sworn a solemn oath
  John Barleycorn should die.

They took a plow and plowed him down,
  Put clods upon his head;
And they ha'e sworn a solemn oath
  John Barleycorn was dead.

But the cheerful spring came kindly on,
  And showers began to fall;
John Barleycorn got up again,
  And sore surprised them all.

The sultry suns of summer came,
  And he grew thick and strong;
His head well arm'd wi' pointed spears,
  That no one should him wrong.

The sober autumn entered mild,
   And he grew wan and pale;
His bending joints and drooping head
   Showed he began to fail.

His colour sickened more and more,
   He faded into age;
And then his enemies began
   To show their deadly rage.

They took a weapon long and sharp,
   And cut him by the knee,
Then tied him fast upon a cart,
   Like a rogue for forgery.

They laid him down upon his back,
   And cudgelled him full sore;
They hung him up before the storm,
   And turn'd him o'er and o'er.

They filled up then a darksome pit
   With water to the brim,
And heaved in poor John Barleycorn,
   To let him sink or swim.

They laid him out upon the floor,
   To work him further woe;
And still as signs of life appeared,
   They tossed him to and fro.

They wasted o'er a scorching flame
   The marrow of his bones;
But a miller used him worst of all—
   He crushed him 'tween two stones.

And they have taken his very heart's blood,
   And drunk it round and round;
And still the more and more they drank,
   Their joy did more abound.

                ROBERT BURNS (1759–1796)

485   ABOU BEN ADHEM

Abou Ben Adhem (may his tribe increase!)
Awoke one night from a deep dream of peace,
And saw within the moonlight in his room,
Making it rich and like a lily in bloom,
An angel writing in a book of gold.
Exceeding peace had made Ben Adhem bold;
And to the presence in the room he said,
"What writest thou?" The vision raised its head,
And, with a look made of all sweet accord,
Answered, "The names of those who love the Lord."
"And is mine one?" said Abou. "Nay, not so,"
Replied the angel. Abou spoke more low,
But cheerly still; and said, "I pray thee, then,
Write me as one that loves his fellow-men."

The angel wrote, and vanished. The next night
It came again, with a great wakening light,
And showed the names whom love of God had blessed;
And, lo! Ben Adhem's name led all the rest.
      JAMES HENRY LEIGH HUNT (1784–1859)

TO A MOUSE, 486
ON TURNING UP HER NEST WITH THE PLOW, NOVEMBER, 1785

 Wee, sleekit, cow'rin', tim'rous beastie,
 Oh, what a panic's in thy breastie!
 Thou needna start awa' sae hasty,
  Wi' bickering brattle!
 I wad be laith to rin and chase thee,
  Wi' murd'ring pattle!

 I'm truly sorry man's dominion
 Has broken Nature's social union,
 And justifies that ill opinion,
  Which makes thee startle
 At me, thy poor earth-born companion
  And fellow-mortal!

 I doubtna, whiles, but thou may thieve;
 What then? poor beastie, thou maun live!
 A daimen icker in a thrave
  'S a sma' request:
 I'll get a blessin' wi' the lave,
  And never miss 't!

 Thy wee bit housie, too, in ruin!
 Its silly wa's the win's are strewin'!
 And naething now to big a new ane
  O' foggage green,
 And bleak December's winds ensuin',
  Baith snell and keen!

 Thou saw the fields laid bare and waste,
 And weary winter comin' fast,
 And cozie here, beneath the blast,
  Thou thought to dwell,
 Till, crash! the cruel coulter passed
  Out through thy cell.

 That wee bit heap o' leaves and stibble
 Has cost thee monie a weary nibble!
 Now thou's turned out for a' thy trouble,
  But house or hald,
 To thole the winter's sleety dribble,
  And cranreuch cauld!

But, Mousie, thou art no thy lane,
In proving foresight may be vain:
The best-laid schemes o' mice and men
    Gang aft a-gley,
And lea'e us naught but grief and pain,
    For promised joy.

Still thou art blest, compared wi' me!
The present only toucheth thee:
But, och! I backward cast my e'e
    On prospects drear!
And forward, though I canna see,
    I guess and fear.

                    ROBERT BURNS (1759–1796)

487   TO A MOUNTAIN DAISY,
ON TURNING ONE DOWN WITH THE PLOW IN APRIL, 1786

Wee, modest, crimson-tipped flower,
Thou's met me in an evil hour;
For I maun crush amang the stoure
    Thy slender stem:
To spare thee now is past my power,
    Thou bonny gem.

Alas! it's no thy neebor sweet,
The bonny lark, companion meet,
Bending thee 'mang the dewy weet,
    Wi' speckled breast,
When upward-springing, blithe, to greet
    The purpling east!

Cauld blew the bitter biting north
Upon thy early, humble birth;
Yet cheerfully thou glinted forth
    Amid the storm,
Scarce reared above the parent earth
    Thy tender form.

The flaunting flowers our gardens yield,
High sheltering woods and wa's maun shield,
But thou, beneath the random bield
    O' clod or stane,
Adorns the histie stibble-field,
    Unseen, alane.

There, in thy scanty mantle clad,
Thy snawie bosom sunward spread,
Thou lifts thy unassuming head
    In humble guise;
But now the share uptears thy bed,
    And low thou lies!

Such is the fate of artless maid,
Sweet floweret of the rural shade!
By love's simplicity betrayed,
    And guileless trust,
Till she, like thee, all soiled, is laid
    Low i' the dust.

Such is the fate of simple bard,
On life's rough ocean luckless starr'd!
Unskilful he to note the card
    Of prudent lore,
Till billows rage, and gales blow hard,
    And whelm him o'er!

Such fate to suffering worth is given,
Who long with wants and woes has striven,
By human pride or cunning driven
    To misery's brink,
Till wrenched of every stay but Heaven,
    He, ruined, sink!

Even thou who mourn'st the Daisy's fate,
That fate is thine—no distant date;
Stern Ruin's plowshare drives, elate,
    Full on thy bloom,
Till crushed beneath the furrow's weight
    Shall be thy doom.

ROBERT BURNS (1759–1796)

LOCHINVAR   488

Oh, young Lochinvar is come out of the west.
Through all the wide Border his steed was the best,
And save his good broadsword he weapons had none;
He rode all unarmed, and he rode all alone.
So faithful in love, and so dauntless in war,
There never was knight like the young Lochinvar.

He stayed not for brake, and he stopped not for stone,
He swam the Eske River where ford there was none;
But ere he alighted at Netherby gate
The bride had consented, the gallant came late:
For a laggard in love, and a dastard in war
Was to wed the fair Ellen of brave Lochinvar.

So boldly he entered the Netherby Hall,
Among bridesmen and kinsmen and brothers and all:
Then spoke the bride's father, his hand on his sword
(For the poor craven bridegroom said never a word),
"Oh, come ye in peace here, or come ye in war,
Or to dance at our bridal, young Lord Lochinvar?"

"I long woo'd your daughter, my suit you denied;—
Love swells like the Solway, but ebbs like its tide—
And now am I come, with this lost love of mine,
To lead but one measure, drink one cup of wine.
There are maidens in Scotland more lovely by far,
That would gladly be bride to the young Lochinvar."

The bride kissed the goblet; the knight took it up;
He quaffed of the wine, and he threw down the cup.
She looked down to blush, and she looked up to sigh,
With a smile on her lips and a tear in her eye.
He took her soft hand ere her mother could bar,—
"Now tread we a measure!" said young Lochinvar.

So stately his form, and so lovely her face,
That never a hall such a galliard did grace;
While her mother did fret, and her father did fume,
And the bridegroom stood dangling his bonnet and plume,
And the bridemaidens whispered, "'Twere better by far
To have matched our fair cousin with young Lochinvar."

One touch to her hand, and one word in her ear,
When they reached the hall door, and the charger stood near;
So light to the croupe the fair lady he swung,
So light to the saddle before her he sprung!
"She is won! we are gone, over bank, bush, and scaur;
They'll have fleet steeds that follow," quoth young Lochinvar.

There was mounting 'mong Græmes of the Netherby clan;
Forsters, Fenwicks, and Musgraves, they rode and they ran:
There was racing and chasing, on Cannobie Lee,
But the lost bride of Netherby ne'er did they see.
So daring in love, and so dauntless in war,
Have ye e'er heard of gallant like young Lochinvar?

                              Sir Walter Scott (1771–1832)

489   Lord Ullin's Daughter

  A chieftain, to the Highlands bound,
    Cries, "Boatman, do not tarry!
  And I'll give thee a silver pound,
    To row us o'er the ferry."

  "Now who be ye, would cross Lochgyle,
    This dark and stormy water?"
  "O, I'm the chief of Ulva's isle,
    And this Lord Ullin's daughter.

  "And fast before her father's men
    Three days we've fled together,
  For should he find us in the glen,
    My blood would stain the heather.

"His horsemen hard behind us ride;
  Should they our steps discover,
Then who will cheer my bonny bride
  When they have slain her lover?"

Outspoke the hardy Highland wight,
  "I'll go, my chief—I'm ready;
It is not for your silver bright,
  But for your winsome lady:

"And by my word! the bonny bird
  In danger shall not tarry;
So though the waves are raging white,
  I'll row you o'er the ferry."

By this the storm grew loud apace,
  The water-wraith was shrieking;
And in the scowl of heaven each face
  Grew dark as they were speaking.

But still as wilder blew the wind,
  And as the night grew drearer,
Adown the glen rode armèd men,
  Their trampling sounded nearer.

"O haste thee, haste!" the lady cries,
  "Though tempests round us gather;
I'll meet the raging of the skies,
  But not an angry father."

The boat has left a stormy land,
  A stormy sea before her,—
When, oh! too strong for human hand,
  The tempest gathered o'er her.

And still they row'd amid the roar
  Of waters fast prevailing:
Lord Ullin reach'd that fatal shore,
  His wrath was changed to wailing.

For sore dismay'd through storm and shade,
  His child he did discover:—
One lovely hand she stretch'd for aid,
  And one was round her lover.

"Come back! come back!" he cried in grief,
  "Across this stormy water:
And I'll forgive your Highland chief,
  My daughter!—oh my daughter!"

'Twas vain the loud waves lashed the shore,
  Return or aid preventing;—
The waters wild went o'er his child,—
  And he was left lamenting.

THOMAS CAMPBELL (1774–1844)

490   A DREAM

Once a dream did wave a shade
O'er my angel-guarded bed,
That an emmet lost its way
When on grass methought I lay.

Troubled, 'wildered, and forlorn,
Dark, benighted, travel-worn,
Over many a tangled spray,
All heart-broke, I heard her say:

"Oh, my children! do they cry?
Do they hear their father sigh?
Now they look abroad to see.
Now return and weep for me."

Pitying, I dropped a tear;
But I saw a glow-worm near,
Who replied, "What wailing wight
Calls the watchman of the night?

"I am set to light the ground
While the beetle goes his round.
Follow now the beetle's hum—
Little wanderer, hie thee home!"
                         WILLIAM BLAKE (1757–1827)

491   THE BATTLE OF BLENHEIM

It was a summer's evening,
  Old Kaspar's work was done,
And he before his cottage door
  Was sitting in the sun;
And by him sported on the green
His little grandchild Wilhelmine.

She saw her brother Peterkin
  Roll something large and round,
Which he, beside the rivulet,
  In playing there, had found.
He came to ask what he had found,
That was so large, and smooth, and round.

Old Kaspar took it from the boy,
  Who stood expectant by;
And then the old man shook his head,
  And, with a natural sigh,
"'Tis some poor fellow's skull," said he,
"Who fell in the great victory!

"I find them in the garden,
  For there's many hereabout;
And often when I go to plow,
  The plowshare turns them out;
For many thousand men," said he,
"Were slain in that great victory!"

"Now tell us what 'twas all about,"
   Young Peterkin he cries;
And little Wilhelmine looks up
   With wonder-waiting eyes;
"Now tell us all about the war,
And what they killed each other for."

"It was the English," Kaspar cried,
   "Who put the French to rout;
But what they killed each other for
   I could not well make out.
But everybody said," quoth he,
"That 'twas a famous victory!

"My father lived at Blenheim then,
   Yon little stream hard by:
They burned his dwelling to the ground
   And he was forced to fly;
So with his wife and child he fled,
Nor had he where to rest his head.

"With fire and sword the country round
   Was wasted far and wide;
And many a childing mother then
   And new-born baby died.
But things like that, you know, must be
At every famous victory.

"They say it was a shocking sight
   After the field was won;
For many thousand bodies here
   Lay rotting in the sun.
But things like that, you know, must be
After a famous victory.

"Great praise the Duke of Marlborough won,
   And our good Prince Eugene."
"Why, 'twas a very wicked thing!"
   Said little Wilhelmine.
"Nay, nay, my little girl," quoth he,
"It was a famous victory!

"And everybody praised the Duke
   Who this great fight did win."
"But what good came of it at last?"
   Quoth little Peterkin.
"Why, that I cannot tell," said he,
"But 'twas a famous victory."

ROBERT SOUTHEY (1774–1843)

492				FIDELITY
A barking sound the Shepherd hears,
A cry as of a dog or fox;
He halts—and searches with his eyes
Among the scattered rocks;
And now at distance can discern
A stirring in a brake of fern;
And instantly a Dog is seen,
Glancing through that covert green.

The Dog is not of mountain breed;
Its motions, too, are wild and shy;
With something, as the Shepherd thinks,
Unusual in its cry:
Nor is there any one in sight
All round, in hollow or on height;
Nor shout, nor whistle strikes his ear;
What is the Creature doing here?

It was a cove, a huge recess,
That keeps, till June, December's snow.
A lofty precipice in front,
A silent tarn below!
Far in the bosom of Helvellyn,
Remote from public road or dwelling,
Pathway, or cultivated land;
From trace of human foot or hand.

There sometimes doth a leaping fish
Send through the tarn a lonely cheer;
The crags repeat the raven's croak,
In symphony austere;
Thither the rainbow comes—the cloud—
And mists that spread the flying shroud;
And sunbeams; and the sounding blast,
That, if it could, would hurry past,
But that enormous barrier binds it fast.

Not free from boding thoughts, a while
The Shepherd stood: then makes his way
Toward the Dog, o'er rocks and stones,
As quickly as he may;
Nor far had gone, before he found
A human skeleton on the ground;
The appalled discoverer with a sigh
Looks round, to learn the history.

From those abrupt and perilous rocks
The Man had fallen, that place of fear!
At length upon the Shepherd's mind
It breaks, and all is clear:

He instantly recalled the name,
And who he was, and whence he came;
Remembered, too, the very day
On which the traveller passed this way.

But hear a wonder, for whose sake
This lamentable tale I tell!
A lasting monument of words
This wonder merits well.
The Dog, which still was hovering nigh,
Repeating the same timid cry,
This Dog had been through three months space
A dweller in that savage place.

Yes, proof was plain that, since the day
When this ill-fated traveller died,
The Dog had watched about the spot,
Or by his master's side:
How nourished here through such long time
He knows, who gave that love sublime;
And gave that strength of feeling, great
Above all human estimate.

WILLIAM WORDSWORTH (1770–1850)

GATHERING SONG OF DONALD DHU 493
  Pibroch of Donuil Dhu,
    Pibroch of Donuil,
  Wake thy wild voice anew,
    Summon Clan Conuil.
  Come away, come away,
    Hark to the summons!
  Come in your war-array,
    Gentles and commons.

  Come from deep glen, and
    From mountain so rocky,
  The war-pipe and pennon
    Are at Inverlochy.
  Come every hill-plaid, and
    True heart that wears one,
  Come every steel blade, and
    Strong hand that bears one.

  Leave untended the herd,
    The flock without shelter;
  Leave the corpse uninterr'd,
    The bride at the altar;
  Leave the deer, leave the steer,
    Leave nets and barges:
  Come with your fighting gear,
    Broadswords and targes.

Come as the winds come, when
  Forests are rended;
Come as the waves come, when
  Navies are stranded:
Faster come, faster come,
  Faster and faster,
Chief, vassal, page, and groom,
  Tenant and master.

Fast they come, fast they come;
  See how they gather!
Wide waves the eagle plume
  Blended with heather,
Cast your plaids, draw your blades,
  Forward each man set!
Pibroch of Donuil Dhu
  Knell for the onset!

SIR WALTER SCOTT (1771–1832)

494   MARCO BOZZARIS

At midnight, in his guarded tent,
  The Turk was dreaming of the hour
When Greece, her knee in suppliance bent,
  Should tremble at his power:
In dreams, through camp and court, he bore
The trophies of a conqueror;
  In dreams his song of triumph heard;
Then wore his monarch's signet ring:
Then pressed that monarch's throne—a king;
As wild his thoughts, and gay of wing,
  As Eden's garden bird.

At midnight, in the forest shades,
  Bozzaris ranged his Suliote band,
True as the steel of their tried blades,
  Heroes in heart and hand.
There had the Persian's thousands stood,
There had the glad earth drunk their blood
  On old Platæa's day;
And now there breathed that haunted air
The sons of sires who conquered there,
With arm to strike and soul to dare,
  As quick, as far as they.

An hour passed on—the Turk awoke;
  That bright dream was his last;
He woke—to hear his sentries shriek,
  "To arms! they come! the Greek! the Greek!"
He woke—to die midst flame, and smoke,
And shout, and groan, and sabre-stroke,
  And death-shots falling thick and fast
As lightnings from the mountain-cloud;

And heard, with voice as trumpet loud,
   Bozzaris cheer his band:
"Strike—till the last armed foe expires;
  Strike—for your altars and your fires;
  Strike—for the green graves of your sires;
   God—and your native land!"

They fought—like brave men, long and well;
   They piled that ground with Moslem slain,
They conquered—but Bozzaris fell,
   Bleeding at every vein.
His few surviving comrades saw
His smile when rang their proud hurrah,
   And the red field was won;
Then saw in death his eyelids close
Calmly, as to a night's repose,
   Like flowers at set of sun.

Come to the bridal-chamber, Death!
   Come to the mother's, when she feels,
For the first time, her first-born's breath;
   Come when the blessed seals
That close the pestilence are broke,
And crowded cities wail its stroke;
Come in consumption's ghastly form,
The earthquake shock, the ocean storm;
Come when the heart beats high and warm
   With banquet-song, and dance, and wine;
And thou art terrible—the tear,
The groan, the knell, the pall, the bier,
And all we know, or dream, or fear
   Of agony, are thine.

But to the hero, when his sword
   Has won the battle for the free,
Thy voice sounds like a prophet's word;
And in its hollow tones are heard
   The thanks of millions yet to be.
Come, when his task of fame is wrought—
Come, with her laurel-leaf, blood-bought—
   Come in her crowning hour—and then
Thy sunken eye's unearthly light
To him is welcome as the sight
   Of sky and stars to prisoned men;
Thy grasp is welcome as the hand
Of brother in a foreign land;
Thy summons welcome as the cry
That told the Indian isles were nigh
   To the world-seeking Genoese,
When the land wind, from woods of palm,
And orange-groves, and fields of balm,
   Blew o'er the Haytian seas.

Bozzaris! with the storied brave
  Greece nurtured in her glory's time,
Rest thee—there is no prouder grave,
  Even in her own proud clime.
She wore no funeral-weeds for thee,
  Nor bade the dark hearse wave its plume
Like torn branch from death's leafless tree
In sorrow's pomp and pageantry,
  The heartless luxury of the tomb;
But she remembers thee as one
Long loved and for a season gone;
For thee her poet's lyre is wreathed,
Her marble wrought, her music breathed;
For thee she rings the birthday bells;
Of thee her babe's first lisping tells;
For thine her evening prayer is said
At palace-couch and cottage-bed;
Her soldier, closing with the foe,
Gives for thy sake a deadlier blow,
His plighted maiden, when she fears
For him the joy of her young years,
Thinks of thy fate, and checks her tears;
  And she, the mother of thy boys,
Though in her eye and faded cheek
Is read the grief she will not speak,
  The memory of her buried joys,
And even she who gave thee birth,
Will, by their pilgrim-circled hearth,
  Talk of thy doom without a sigh;
For thou art Freedom's now, and Fame's:
One of the few, the immortal names,
  That were not born to die.

                          FITZ-GREENE HALLECK (1790–1867)

495   HOHENLINDEN
  On Linden, when the sun was low,
  All bloodless lay th' untrodden snow;
  And dark as winter was the flow
    Of Iser, rolling rapidly.

  But Linden saw another sight,
  When the drum beat, at dead of night,
  Commanding fires of death to light
    The darkness of her scenery.

  By torch and trumpet fast array'd
  Each horseman drew his battle-blade,
  And furious every charger neigh'd
    To join the dreadful revelry.

  Then shook the hills with thunder riven,
  Then rush'd the steed to battle driven,
  And louder than the bolts of Heaven,
    Far flashed the red artillery.

But redder yet that light shall glow
On Linden's hills or stainèd snow;
And bloodier yet the torrent flow
   Of Iser, rolling rapidly.

'Tis morn, but scarce yon level sun
Can pierce the war-clouds, rolling dun,
Where furious Frank, and fiery Hun,
   Shout in their sulphurous canopy.

The combat deepens. On, ye brave
Who rush to glory or the grave!
Wave, Munich! all thy banners wave,
   And charge with all thy chivalry!

Few, few shall part, where many meet!
The snow shall be their winding-sheet,
And every turf beneath their feet
   Shall be a soldier's sepulcher.
                THOMAS CAMPBELL (1774–1844)

BANNOCKBURN   496
ROBERT BRUCE'S ADDRESS TO HIS ARMY

[You can look down on the battle-field of Bannockburn from Stirling Castle, Scotland, near which stands a magnificent statue of Robert, the Bruce. – Ed.]

Scots, wha hae wi' Wallace bled,
Scots, wham Bruce has aften led;
Welcome to your gory bed,
   Or to victorie.

Now's the day, and now's the hour;
See the front o' battle lower;
See approach proud Edward's power—
   Chains and slaverie!

Wha will be a traitor knave?
Wha can fill a coward's grave?
Wha sae base as be a slave?
   Let him turn and flee!

Wha for Scotland's King and law
Freedom's sword will strongly draw,
Freeman stand, or freeman fa'?
   Let him follow me!

By oppression's woes and pains!
By your sons in servile chains!
We will drain our dearest veins,
   But they shall be free!

Lay the proud usurpers low!
Tyrants fall in every foe!
Liberty's in every blow!
Let us do, or die!

ROBERT BURNS (1759–1796)

497   THE DESTRUCTION OF SENNACHERIB

The Assyrian came down like a wolf on the fold,
And his cohorts were gleaming in purple and gold;
And the sheen of their spears was like stars on the sea,
When the blue wave rolls nightly on deep Galilee.

Like the leaves of the forest when the Summer is green,
That host with their banners at sunset were seen:
Like the leaves of the forest when Autumn hath blown,
That host on the morrow lay withered and strown.

For the Angel of Death spread his wings on the blast,
And breathed in the face of the foe as he passed;
And the eyes of the sleepers waxed deadly and chill,
And their hearts but once heaved, and forever grew still!

And there lay the steed with his nostril all wide,
But through it there rolled not the breath of his pride;
And the foam of his gasping lay white on the turf,
And cold as the spray of the rock-beating surf.

And there lay the rider distorted and pale,
With the dew on his brow, and the rust on his mail,
And the tents were all silent, the banners alone,
The lances unlifted, the trumpet unblown.

And the widows of Ashur are loud in their wail,
And the idols are broke in the temple of Baal;
And the might of the Gentile, unsmote by the sword,
Hath melted like snow in the glance of the Lord!

GEORGE GORDON BYRON, LORD BYRON (1788–1824)

498   I REMEMBER, I REMEMBER

I remember, I remember
The house where I was born,
The little window where the sun
Came peeping in at morn;
He never came a wink too soon
Nor brought too long a day;
But now, I often wish the night
Had borne my breath away.

I remember, I remember
The roses, red and white,
The violets, and the lily-cups—
Those flowers made of light!
The lilacs where the robin built,
And where my brother set
The laburnum on his birthday,—
The tree is living yet!

I remember, I remember
Where I was used to swing,
And thought the air must rush as fresh
To swallows on the wing;
My spirit flew in feathers then
That is so heavy now,
And summer pools could hardly cool
The fever on my brow.

I remember, I remember
The fir trees dark and high;
I used to think their slender tops
Were close against the sky:
It was a childish ignorance,
But now 'tis little joy
To know I'm farther off from Heaven
Than when I was a boy.
       Thomas Hood (1798–1845)

A Modest Wit   499

A supercilious nabob of the East—
 Haughty, being great—purse-proud, being rich—
A governor, or general, at the least,
 I have forgotten which—
Had in his family a humble youth,
 Who went from England in his patron's suit,
An unassuming boy, in truth
 A lad of decent parts, and good repute.

This youth had sense and spirit;
 But yet with all his sense,
  Excessive diffidence
Obscured his merit.

One day, at table, flushed with pride and wine,
 His honour, proudly free, severely merry,
Conceived it would be vastly fine
 To crack a joke upon his secretary.

"Young man," he said, "by what art, craft, or trade,
 Did your good father gain a livelihood?"—
"He was a saddler, sir," Modestus said,
 "And in his time was reckon'd good."

"A saddler, eh! and taught you Greek,
 Instead of teaching you to sew!
Pray, why did not your father make
 A saddler, sir, of you?"

Each parasite, then, as in duty bound,
The joke applauded, and the laugh went round.
 At length Modestus, bowing low,
Said (craving pardon, if too free he made),
 "Sir, by your leave, I fain would know
Your father's trade!"

"My father's trade! by heaven, that's too bad!
My father's trade? Why, blockhead, are you mad?
My father, sir, did never stoop so low—
He was a gentleman, I'd have you know."

"Excuse the liberty I take,"
  Modestus said, with archness on his brow,
"Pray, why did not your father make
  A gentleman of you?"

                                  SELLECK OSBORNE (1783–1826)

500   THE LEGEND OF BISHOP HATTO

The summer and autumn had been so wet,
That in winter the corn was growing yet:
'Twas a piteous sight to see, all around,
The grain lie rotting on the ground.

Every day the starving poor
Crowded around Bishop Hatto's door;
For he had a plentiful last-year's store,
And all the neighbourhood could tell
His granaries were furnished well.

At last Bishop Hatto appointed a day
To quiet the poor without delay:
He bade them to his great barn repair,
And they should have food for winter there.

Rejoiced such tidings good to hear,
The poor folk flocked from far and near;
The great barn was full as it could hold
Of women and children, and young and old.

Then, when he saw it could hold no more,
Bishop Hatto, he made fast the door;
And while for mercy on Christ they call,
He set fire to the barn and burned them all.

"I' faith, 'tis an excellent bonfire!" quoth he;
"And the country is greatly obliged to me
For ridding it in these times forlorn
Of Rats that only consume the corn."

So then to his palace returnèd he,
And he sat down to supper merrily,
And he slept that night like an innocent man;
But Bishop Hatto never slept again.

In the morning as he entered the hall,
Where his picture hung against the wall,
A sweat-like death all over him came;
For the Rats had eaten it out of the frame.

As he looked, there came a man from his farm;
He had a countenance white with alarm:
"My Lord, I opened your granaries this morn,
And the Rats had eaten all your corn."

Another came running presently,
And he was pale as pale could be:
"Fly, my Lord Bishop, fly!" quoth he,
"Ten thousand Rats are coming this way;
The Lord forgive you yesterday!"

"I'll go to my town on the Rhine," replied he;
"'Tis the safest place in Germany;
The walls are high, and the shores are steep,
And the stream is strong, and the water deep."

Bishop Hatto fearfully hastened away,
And he crossed the Rhine without delay,
And reached his tower, and barred with care
All windows, doors, and loop-holes there.

He laid him down, and closed his eyes;
But soon a scream made him arise:
He started and saw two eyes of flame
On his pillow, from whence the screaming came.

He listened and looked; it was only the cat:
But the Bishop he grew more fearful for that;
For she sat screaming, mad with fear
At the army of Rats that was drawing near.

For they have swum over the river so deep,
And they have climbed the shore so steep;
And up the tower their way is bent,
To do the work for which they were sent.

They are not to be told by the dozen or score;
By thousands they come, and by myriads and more;
Such numbers had never been heard of before,
Such a judgment had never been witnessed of yore.

Down on his knees the Bishop fell,
And faster and faster his beads did tell,
As, louder and louder drawing near,
The gnawing of their teeth he could hear.

And in at the windows and in at the door,
And through the walls, helter-skelter they pour,
And down from the ceiling and up through the floor,
From the right and the left, from behind and before,
And all at once to the Bishop they go.

They have whetted their teeth against the stones;
And now they pick the Bishop's bones:
They gnawed the flesh from every limb;
For they were sent to do judgment on him!

                                                                                     ROBERT SOUTHEY (1774–1843)

501   THE EVE OF WATERLOO

There was a sound of revelry by night,
  And Belgium's capital had gathered then
Her beauty and her chivalry, and bright
  The lamps shone o'er fair women and brave men.
A thousand hearts beat happily; and when
  Music arose with its voluptuous swell,
Soft eyes looked love to eyes which spake again,
  And all went merry as a marriage-bell:
  But hush! hark! a deep sound strikes like a rising knell!

Did ye not hear it? No; 'twas but the wind,
  Or the car rattling o'er the stony street.
On with the dance! let joy be unconfined!
  No sleep till morn, when Youth and Pleasure meet
To chase the glowing hours with flying feet!
  But hark!—that heavy sound breaks in once more,
As if the clouds its echo would repeat;
  And nearer, clearer, deadlier, than before!
  Arm! arm! it is—it is the cannon's opening roar!

Ah! then and there was hurrying to and fro,
  And gathering tears, and tremblings of distress
And cheeks all pale, which, but an hour ago,
  Blushed at the praise of their own loveliness;
And there were sudden partings, such as press
  The life from out young hearts, and choking sighs
Which ne'er might be repeated: who could guess
  If ever more should meet those mutual eyes,
  Since upon night so sweet such awful morn could rise?

And there was mounting in hot haste: the steed,
  The mustering squadron, and the clattering car,
Went pouring forward with impetuous speed,
  And swiftly forming in the ranks of war;
And the deep thunder peal on peal afar;
  And near, the beat of the alarming drum
Roused up the soldier ere the morning star;
  While thronged the citizens with terror dumb,
  Or whispering with white lips, "The foe! They come! They come!"

And Ardennes waves above them her green leaves,
  Dewy with Nature's tear-drops, as they pass,
Grieving, if aught inanimate e'er grieves,
  Over the unreturning brave—alas!

Ere evening to be trodden like the grass
  Which, now beneath them, but above shall grow
In its next verdure, when this fiery mass
  Of living valour, rolling on the foe,
  And burning with high hope, shall moulder cold and low.

Last noon beheld them full of lusty life,
  Last eve in Beauty's circle proudly gay;
The midnight brought the signal-sound of strife,
  The morn the marshalling in arms,—the day,
Battle's magnificently stern array!
  The thunder-clouds close o'er it, which, when rent,
The earth is covered thick with other clay,
  Which her own clay shall cover, heaped and pent,
  Rider, and horse—friend, foe—in one red burial blent!
GEORGE GORDON BYRON, LORD BYRON (1788–1824)

THE GLOVE AND THE LIONS   502

King Francis was a hearty king, and loved a royal sport,
And one day as his lions fought, sat looking on the court;
The nobles filled the benches, with the ladies in their pride,
And 'mong them sat the Count de Lorge with one for whom he sighed:
And truly 'twas a gallant thing to see that crowning show,
Valour, and love, and a king above, and the royal beasts below.

Ramp'd and roar'd the lions, with horrid laughing jaws;
They bit, they glared, gave blows like beams, a wind
     went with their paws;
With wallowing might and stifled roar they rolled on one another,
Till all the pit with sand and mane was in a thunderous smother;
The bloody foam above the bars came whisking through the air;
Said Francis then, "Faith, gentlemen, we're better here than there."

De Lorge's love o'erheard the King,—a beauteous lively dame
With smiling lips and sharp, bright eyes, which always seem'd the same:
She thought, "The Count, my lover, is brave as brave can be;
He surely would do wondrous things to show his love of me;
King, ladies, lovers, all look on; the occasion is divine;
I'll drop my glove, to prove his love; great glory will be mine."

She dropped her glove, to prove his love, then look'd
    at him and smiled;
He bowed, and in a moment leapt among the lions wild:
His leap was quick, return was quick, he has regain'd his place,
Then threw the glove, but not with love, right in the lady's face.
"Well done!" cried Francis, "bravely done!" and he rose
    from where he sat:
"No love," quoth he, "but vanity, sets love a task like that."
JAMES HENRY LEIGH HUNT (1784–1859)

503   HOME, SWEET HOME!
'Mid pleasures and palaces though we may roam,
Be it ever so humble, there's no place like home;
A charm from the sky seems to hallow us there,
Which, seek through the world, is ne'er met with elsewhere.
    Home! Home! sweet, sweet Home!
There's no place like Home! there's no place like Home!

An exile from Home, splendour dazzles in vain;
O, give me my lowly thatched cottage again!
The birds singing gaily, that came at my call,—
Give me them,—and the peace of mind, dearer than all!
    Home! Home! sweet, sweet Home!
There's no place like Home! there's no place like Home!

How sweet 'tis to sit 'neath a fond father's smile,
And the cares of a mother to soothe and beguile!
Let others delight 'mid new pleasures to roam,
But give me, oh, give me, the pleasures of Home!
    Home! Home! sweet, sweet Home!
There's no place like Home! there's no place like Home!

To thee I'll return, overburdened with care;
The heart's dearest solace will smile on me there;
No more from that cottage again will I roam;
Be it ever so humble, there's no place like Home.
    Home! Home! sweet, sweet Home!
There's no place like Home! there's no place like Home!
                    JOHN HOWARD PAYNE (1791–1852)

504   ABIDE WITH ME
Abide with me! fast falls the eventide;
The darkness deepens; Lord, with me abide!
When other helpers fail, and comforts flee,
Help of the helpless, O abide with me.

Swift to its close ebbs out life's little day;
Earth's joys grow dim, its glories pass away;
Change and decay in all around I see:
O Thou who changest not, abide with me!
                    HENRY FRANCIS LYTE (1793–1847)

505   THE LAST ROSE OF SUMMER
'Tis the last rose of summer
    Left blooming alone;
All her lovely companions
    Are faded and gone;
No flower of her kindred,
    No rose-bud is nigh,
To reflect back her blushes,
    Or give sigh for sigh.

I'll not leave thee, thou lone one!
   To pine on the stem;
Since the lovely are sleeping,
   Go, sleep thou with them.
Thus kindly I scatter
   Thy leaves o'er the bed
Where thy mates of the garden
   Lie scentless and dead.

So soon may I follow,
   When friendships decay,
And from Love's shining circle
   The gems drop away.
When true hearts lie withered,
   And fond ones are flown,
O! who would inhabit
   This bleak world alone?
                      THOMAS MOORE (1779–1852)

CUPID DROWNED   506

T'other day as I was twining
Roses, for a crown to dine in,
What, of all things, 'mid the heap,
Should I light on, fast asleep,
But the little desperate elf,
The tiny traitor, Love, himself!
By the wings I picked him up
Like a bee, and in a cup
Of my wine I plunged and sank him,
Then what d'ye think I did?—I drank him.
Faith, I thought him dead. Not he!
There he lives with tenfold glee;
And now this moment with his wings
I feel him tickling my heart-strings.
              JAMES HENRY LEIGH HUNT (1779–1852)

CUPID STUNG   507

Cupid once upon a bed
Of roses laid his weary head;
Luckless urchin, not to see
Within the leaves a slumbering bee.
The bee awak'd—with anger wild
The bee awak'd, and stung the child.
Loud and piteous are his cries;
To Venus quick he runs, he flies;
"Oh, Mother! I am wounded through—
I die with pain—in sooth I do!
Stung by some little angry thing,
Some serpent on a tiny wing—
A bee it was—for once, I know,
I heard a rustic call it so."
Thus he spoke, and she the while
Heard him with a soothing smile;

Then said, "My infant, if so much
Thou feel the little wild bee's touch,
How must the heart, ah, Cupid! be,
The hapless heart that's stung by thee!"

THOMAS MOORE (1779–1852)

508

A NAME IN THE SAND

Alone I walked the ocean strand;
A pearly shell was in my hand:
I stooped and wrote upon the sand
   My name—the year—the day.
As onward from the spot I passed,
One lingering look behind I cast;
A wave came rolling high and fast,
   And washed my lines away.

And so, methought, 'twill shortly be
With every mark on earth from me:
A wave of dark oblivion's sea
   Will sweep across the place
Where I have trod the sandy shore
Of time, and been, to be no more,
Of me—my day—the name I bore,
   To leave nor track nor trace.

And yet, with Him who counts the sands
And holds the waters in His hands,
I know a lasting record stands
   Inscribed against my name,
Of all this mortal part has wrought,
Of all this thinking soul has thought,
And from these fleeting moments caught
   For glory or for shame.

HANNAH FLAGG GOULD (1789–1856)

509

A WISH

Mine be a cot beside the hill;
   A bee-hive's hum shall soothe my ear;
A willowy brook that turns a mill
   With many a fall shall linger near.

The swallow, oft, beneath my thatch
   Shall twitter from her clay-built nest;
Oft shall the pilgrim lift the latch,
   And share my meal, a welcome guest.

Around my ivied porch shall spring
   Each fragrant flower that drinks the dew;
And Lucy, at her wheel, shall sing
   In russet gown and apron blue.

The village church among the trees,
   Where first our marriage-vows were given,
With merry peals shall swell the breeze
   And point with taper spire to Heaven.
SAMUEL ROGERS (1763–1855)

THE HARP THAT ONCE THROUGH TARA'S HALLS   510

The harp that once through Tara's halls
   The soul of music shed,
Now hangs as mute on Tara's walls
   As if that soul were fled.
So sleeps the pride of former days,
   So glory's thrill is o'er,
And hearts, that once beat high for praise,
   Now feel that pulse no more.

No more to chiefs and ladies bright
   The harp of Tara swells;
The chord alone, that breaks at night,
   Its tale of ruin tells.
Thus Freedom now so seldom wakes,
   The only throb she gives
Is when some heart indignant breaks,
   To show that still she lives.
THOMAS MOORE (1779–1852)

THE OLD OAKEN BUCKET   511

How dear to this heart are the scenes of my childhood,
   When fond recollection presents them to view!
The orchard, the meadow, the deep-tangled wild-wood,
   And every loved spot which my infancy knew!
The wide-spreading pond, and the mill that stood by it,
   The bridge, and the rock where the cataract fell,
The cot of my father, the dairy-house nigh it,
   And e'en the rude bucket that hung in the well—
The old oaken bucket, the iron-bound bucket,
The moss-covered bucket which hung in the well.

That moss-covered vessel I hailed as a treasure,
   For often at noon, when returned from the field,
I found it the source of an exquisite pleasure,
   The purest and sweetest that nature can yield.
How ardent I seized it, with hands that were glowing,
   And quick to the white-pebbled bottom it fell;
Then soon, with the emblem of truth overflowing,
   And dripping with coolness, it rose from the well—
The old oaken bucket, the iron-bound bucket,
The moss-covered bucket arose from the well.

How sweet from the green mossy brim to receive it
   As poised on the curb it inclined to my lips!
Not a full blushing goblet could tempt me to leave it,
   The brightest that beauty or revelry sips.

And now, far removed from the loved habitation,
  The tear of regret will intrusively swell.
As fancy reverts to my father's plantation,
  And sighs for the bucket that hangs in the well—
The old oaken bucket, the iron-bound bucket,
The moss-covered bucket that hangs in the well!
                              SAMUEL WOODWORTH (1785–1848)

512   ARNOLD VON WINKLERIED
  "Make way for liberty!" he cried,
  Make way for liberty, and died.
  In arms the Austrian phalanx stood,
  A living wall, a human wood,—
  A wall, where every conscious stone
  Seemed to its kindred thousands grown.
  A rampart all assaults to bear,
  Till time to dust their frames should wear;
  So still, so dense the Austrians stood,
  A living wall, a human wood.

  Impregnable their front appears,
  All horrent with projected spears.
  Whose polished points before them shine,
  From flank to flank, one brilliant line,
  Bright as the breakers' splendours run
  Along the billows to the sun.

  Opposed to these a hovering band
  Contended for their fatherland;
  Peasants, whose new-found strength had broke
  From manly necks the ignoble yoke,
  And beat their fetters into swords,
  On equal terms to fight their lords;
  And what insurgent rage had gained,
  In many a mortal fray maintained;
  Marshalled, once more, at Freedom's call,
  They came to conquer or to fall,
  Where he who conquered, he who fell,
  Was deemed a dead or living Tell,
  Such virtue had that patriot breathed,
  So to the soil his soul bequeathed,
  That wheresoe'er his arrows flew,
  Heroes in his own likeness grew,
  And warriors sprang from every sod,
  Which his awakening footstep trod.

  And now the work of life and death
  Hung on the passing of a breath;
  The fire of conflict burned within,
  The battle trembled to begin;
  Yet, while the Austrians held their ground,
  Point for attack was nowhere found;
  Where'er the impatient Switzers gazed,
  The unbroken line of lances blazed;

That line 'twere suicide to meet,
And perish at their tyrant's feet;
How could they rest within their graves,
And leave their homes, the homes of slaves!
Would not they feel their children tread,
With clanging chains, above their head?

It must not be; this day, this hour,
Annihilates the invader's power;
All Switzerland is in the field;
She will not fly,—she cannot yield,—
She must not fall; her better fate
Here gives her an immortal date.
Few were the numbers she could boast,
But every freeman was a host,
And felt as 'twere a secret known
That one should turn the scale alone,
While each unto himself was he
On whose sole arm hung victory.

It did depend on one indeed;
Behold him,—Arnold Winkelried;
There sounds not to the trump of fame
The echo of a nobler name.
Unmarked he stood amid the throng,
In rumination deep and long,
Till you might see, with sudden grace,
The very thought come o'er his face;
And, by the motion of his form,
Anticipate the bursting storm,
And, by the uplifting of his brow,
Tell where the bolt would strike, and how.

But 'twas no sooner thought than done!
The field was in a moment won;
"Make way for liberty!" he cried,
Then ran, with arms extended wide,
As if his dearest friend to clasp;
Ten spears he swept within his grasp.
"Make way for liberty!" he cried.
Their keen points crossed from side to side;
He bowed amidst them like a tree,
And thus made way for liberty.

Swift to the breach his comrades fly,
"Make way for liberty!" they cry,
And through the Austrian phalanx dart,
As rushed the spears through Arnold's heart.
While instantaneous as his fall,
Rout, ruin, panic, seized them all;
An earthquake could not overthrow
A city with a surer blow.

Thus Switzerland again was free;
Thus Death made way for Liberty!
JAMES MONTGOMERY (1771–1854)

513 THE SKYLARK

    Bird of the wilderness,
    Blithesome and cumberless,
Sweet be thy matin o'er moorland and lea!
    Emblem of happiness,
    Blest is thy dwelling-place—
Oh, to abide in the desert with thee!

    Wild is thy lay and loud,
    Far in the downy cloud,
Love gives it energy, love gave it birth.
    Where, on thy dewy wing,
    Where art thou journeying?
Thy lay is in heaven, thy love is on earth.

    O'er fell and fountain sheen,
    O'er moor and mountain green,
O'er the red streamer that heralds the day,
    Over the cloudlet dim,
    Over the rainbow's rim,
Musical cherub, soar, singing, away!

    Then, when the gloaming comes,
    Low in the heather blooms
Sweet will thy welcome and bed of love be!
    Emblem of happiness,
    Blest is thy dwelling-place—
Oh, to abide in the desert with thee!
THOMAS JEFFERSON HOGG (1792–1827)

514 OZYMANDIAS OF EGYPT

I met a traveller from an antique land
Who said: "Two vast and trunkless legs of stone
Stand in the desert. Near them on the sand,
Half sunk, a shattered visage lies, whose frown
And wrinkled lip and sneer of cold command
Tell that its sculptor well those passions read
Which yet survive, stamped on these lifeless things,
The hand that mock'd them and the heart that fed;
And on the pedestal these words appear:
'My name is Ozymandias, king of kings:
Look on my works, ye Mighty, and despair!'
Nothing beside remains. Round the decay
Of that colossal wreck, boundless and bare,
The lone and level sands stretch far away."
PERCY BYSSHE SHELLEY (1792–1822)

515 MORTALITY

O why should the spirit of mortal be proud?
Like a fast-flitting meteor, a fast-flying cloud,
A flash of the lightning, a break of the wave,
He passes from life to his rest in the grave.

The leaves of the oak and the willow shall fade,
Be scattered around and together be laid;
And the young and the old, and the low and the high,
Shall moulder to dust and together shall lie.

The child that a mother attended and loved,
The mother that infant's affection that proved,
The husband that mother and infant that blessed,
Each, all, are away to their dwelling of rest.

The maid on whose cheek, on whose brow, in whose eye,
Shone beauty and pleasure,—her triumphs are by;
And the memory of those that beloved her and praised
Are alike from the minds of the living erased.

The hand of the king that the scepter hath borne,
The brow of the priest that the miter hath worn,
The eye of the sage, and the heart of the brave,
Are hidden and lost in the depths of the grave.

The peasant whose lot was to sow and to reap,
The herdsman who climbed with his goats to the steep,
The beggar that wandered in search of his bread,
Have faded away like the grass that we tread.

The saint that enjoyed the communion of heaven,
The sinner that dared to remain unforgiven,
The wise and the foolish, the guilty and just,
Have quietly mingled their bones in the dust.

So the multitude goes, like the flower and the weed
That wither away to let others succeed;
So the multitude comes, even those we behold,
To repeat every tale that hath often been told.

For we are the same that our fathers have been;
We see the same sights that our fathers have seen,—
We drink the same stream, and we feel the same sun,
And we run the same course that our fathers have run.

The thoughts we are thinking, our fathers would think;
From the death we are shrinking from, they too would shrink;
To the life we are clinging to, they too would cling;
But it speeds from the earth like a bird on the wing.

They loved, but their story we cannot unfold;
They scorned, but the heart of the haughty is cold;
They grieved, but no wail from their slumbers may come;
They enjoyed, but the voice of their gladness is dumb.

They died, ay! they died! and we things that are now,
Who walk on the turf that lies over their brow,
Who make in their dwellings a transient abode,
Meet the changes they met on their pilgrimage road.

Yea! hope and despondence, and pleasure and pain,
Are mingled together like sunshine and rain;
And the smile and the tear, and the song and the dirge,
Still follow each other, like surge upon surge.

'Tis the wink of an eye, 'tis the draught of a breath,
From the blossom of health to the paleness of death,
From the gilded saloon to the bier and the shroud,—
O why should the spirit of mortal be proud?

WILLIAM KNOX (1789–1825)

516   AULD ROBIN GRAY

When the sheep are in the fauld, and the kye at hame,
And a' the warld to rest are gane,
The waes o' my heart fa' in showers frae my e'e,
While my gudeman lies sound by me.

Young Jamie lo'ed me weel, and sought me for his bride;
But saving a croun he had naething else beside:
To make the croun a pund, young Jamie gaed to sea;
And the croun and the pund were baith for me.

He hadna been awa' a week but only twa,
When my father brak his arm, and the cow was stown awa;
My mother she fell sick,—and my Jamie at the sea—
And auld Robin Gray came a-courtin' me.

My father couldna work, and my mother couldna spin;
I toil'd day and night, but their bread I couldna win;
Auld Rob maintain'd them baith, and wi' tears in his e'e
Said, "Jennie, for their sakes, O, marry me!"

My heart it said nay; I look'd for Jamie back;
But the wind it blew high, and the ship it was a wrack;
His ship it was a wrack—Why didna Jamie dee?
Or why do I live to cry, Wae's me?

My father urged me sair: my mother didna speak;
But she look'd in my face till my heart was like to break:
They gi'ed him my hand, tho' my heart was in the sea;
Sae auld Robin Gray he was gudeman to me.

I hadna been a wife a week but only four,
When mournfu' as I sat on the stane at the door,
I saw my Jamie's wraith,—for I couldna think it he,
Till he said, "I'm come hame to marry thee."

O sair, sair did we greet, and muckle did we say;
We took but ae kiss, and we tore ourselves away:
I wish that I were dead, but I'm no like to dee;
And why was I born to say, Wae's me!

I gang like a ghaist, and I carena to spin;
I daurna think on Jamie, for that wad be a sin;
But I'll do my best a gude wife aye to be,
For auld Robin Gray he is kind unto me.

LADY ANNE LINDSAY (1750–1825)

SONG FROM AELLA 517

O Sing unto my roundelay,
O drop the briny tear with me;
Dance no more at holyday,
Like a running river be:
   My love is dead,
    Gone to his death-bed
All under the willow-tree.

Black his cryne as the winter night,
White his rode as the summer snow,
Red his face as the morning light,
Cold he lies in the grave below:
   My love is dead,
    Gone to his death-bed
All under the willow-tree.

Sweet his tongue as the throstle's note,
Quick in dance as thought can be,
Deft his tabor, cudgel stout;
O he lies by the willow-tree!
   My love is dead,
    Gone to his death-bed
All under the willow-tree.

Hark! the raven flaps his wing
In the brier'd dell below;
Hark! the death-owl loud doth sing
To the nightmares, as they go:
   My love is dead,
    Gone to his death-bed
All under the willow-tree.

See! the white moon shines on high;
Whiter is my true-love's shroud:
Whiter than the morning sky,
Whiter than the evening cloud:
   My love is dead,
    Gone to his death-bed
All under the willow-tree.

Here upon my true-love's grave
Shall the barren flowers be laid;
Not one holy saint to save
All the coldness of a maid:
   My love is dead,
    Gone to his death-bed
All under the willow-tree.

With my hands I'll dent the briers
Round his holy corse to gre:
Ouph and fairy, light your fires,
Here my body still shall be:
   My love is dead,
    Gone to his death-bed
All under the willow-tree.

Come, with acorn-cup and thorn,
Drain my heartès blood away;
Life and all its good I scorn,
Dance by night, or feast by day:
   My love is dead,
    Gone to his death-bed
All under the willow-tree.
                           THOMAS CHATTERTON (1752–1770)
cryne: hair; rode: complexion; dent: fasten; gre: grow; ouph: elf

518   MEETING
My Damon was the first to wake
   The gentle flame that cannot die;
My Damon is the last to take
   The faithful bosom's softest sigh:
The life between is nothing worth,
   O cast it from thy thought away!
Think of the day that gave it birth,
   And this its sweet returning day.

Buried be all that has been done,
   Or say that naught is done amiss;
For who the dangerous path can shun
   In such bewildering world as this?
But love can every fault forgive,
   Or with a tender look reprove;
And now let naught in memory live
   But that we meet, and that we love.
                            GEORGE CRABBE (1754–1832)

519   LATE WISDOM
We've trod the maze of error round,
   Long wandering in the winding glade;
And now the torch of truth is found,
   It only shows us where we strayed:
By long experience taught, we know—
   Can rightly judge of friends and foes;
Can all the worth of these allow,
   And all the faults discern in those.

Now, 'tis our boast that we can quell
   The wildest passions in their rage,
Can their destructive force repel,
   And their impetuous wrath assuage.—

Ah, Virtue! dost thou arm when now
  This bold rebellious race are fled?
When all these tyrants rest, and thou
  Art warring with the mighty dead?
GEORGE CRABBE (1754–1832)

A MARRIAGE RING 520
The ring, so worn as you behold,
So thin, so pale, is yet of gold:
The passion such it was to prove—
Worn with life's care, love yet was love.
GEORGE CRABBE (1754–1832)

TO THE MUSES 521
Whether on Ida's shady brow
  Or in the chambers of the East,
The chambers of the Sun, that now
  From ancient melody have ceased;

Whether in heaven ye wander fair,
  Or the green corners of the earth,
Or the blue regions of the air
  Where the melodious winds have birth;

Whether on crystal rocks ye rove,
  Beneath the bosom of the sea,
Wandering in many a coral grove;
  Fair Nine, forsaking Poetry;

How have you left the ancient love
  That bards of old enjoy'd in you!
The languid strings do scarcely move,
  The sound is forced, the notes are few.
WILLIAM BLAKE (1757–1827)

TO SPRING 522
O thou with dewy locks, who lookest down
Through the clear windows of the morning, turn
Thine angel eyes upon our western isle,
Which in full choir hails thy approach, O Spring!

The hills tell one another, and the listening
Valleys hear; all our longing eyes are turn'd
Up to thy bright pavilions: issue forth
And let thy holy feet visit our clime!

Come o'er the eastern hills, and let our winds
Kiss thy perfumed garments; let us taste
Thy morn and evening breath; scatter thy pearls
Upon our lovesick land that mourns for thee.

O deck her forth with thy fair fingers; pour
Thy soft kisses on her bosom; and put
Thy golden crown upon her languish'd head,
Whose modest tresses are bound up for thee.
WILLIAM BLAKE (1757–1827)

523   SONG

My silks and fine array,
  My smiles and languish'd air,
By Love are driven away;
  And mournful lean Despair
Brings me yew to deck my grave:
Such end true lovers have.

His face is fair as heaven
  When springing buds unfold:
O why to him was't given,
  Whose heart is wintry cold?
His breast is Love's all-worshipp'd tomb,
Where all Love's pilgrims come.

Bring me an axe and spade,
  Bring me a winding-sheet;
When I my grave have made,
  Let winds and tempests beat:
Then down I'll lie, as cold as clay:
True love doth pass away!

                                               WILLIAM BLAKE (1757–1827)

524   REEDS OF INNOCENCE

Piping down the valleys wild,
  Piping songs of pleasant glee,
On a cloud I saw a child,
  And he laughing said to me:

"Pipe a song about a Lamb!"
  So I piped with merry cheer.
"Piper, pipe that song again;"
  So I piped: he wept to hear.

"Drop thy pipe, thy happy pipe;
  Sing thy songs of happy cheer!"
So I sung the same again,
  While he wept with joy to hear.

"Piper, sit thee down and write
  In a book that all may read."
So he vanish'd from my sight;
  And I pluck'd a hollow reed,

And I made a rural pen,
  And I stain'd the water clear,
And I wrote my happy songs
  Every child may joy to hear.

                                               WILLIAM BLAKE (1757–1827)

525   THE LITTLE BLACK BOY

My mother bore me in the southern wild,
  And I am black, but O, my soul is white!
White as an angel is the English child,
  But I am black, as if bereaved of light.

My mother taught me underneath a tree,
    And, sitting down before the heat of day,
She took me on her lap and kissèd me,
    And, pointing to the East, began to say:

"Look at the rising sun: there God does live,
    And gives His light, and gives His heat away,
And flowers and trees and beasts and men receive
    Comfort in morning, joy in the noonday.

"And we are put on earth a little space,
    That we may learn to bear the beams of love;
And these black bodies and this sunburnt face
    Are but a cloud, and like a shady grove.

"For when our souls have learn'd the heat to bear,
    The cloud will vanish; we shall hear His voice,
Saying, 'Come out from the grove, my love and care,
    And round my golden tent like lambs rejoice.'"

Thus did my mother say, and kissèd me,
    And thus I say to little English boy.
When I from black and he from white cloud free,
    And round the tent of God like lambs we joy,

I'll shade him from the heat till he can bear
    To lean in joy upon our Father's knee;
And then I'll stand and stroke his silver hair,
    And be like him, and he will then love me.
                              WILLIAM BLAKE (1757–1827)

HEAR THE VOICE   526

Hear the voice of the Bard,
Who present, past, and future, sees;
Whose ears have heard
The Holy Word
That walk'd among the ancient trees;

Calling the lapsèd soul,
And weeping in the evening dew;
That might control
The starry pole,
And fallen, fallen light renew!

"O Earth, O Earth, return!
Arise from out the dewy grass!
Night is worn,
And the morn
Rises from the slumbrous mass.

"Turn away no more;
Why wilt thou turn away?
The starry floor,
The watery shore,
Is given thee till the break of day."

WILLIAM BLAKE (1757–1827)

527   THE TIGER

Tiger, tiger, burning bright
In the forests of the night,
What immortal hand or eye
Could frame thy fearful symmetry?

In what distant deeps or skies
Burnt the fire of thine eyes?
On what wings dare he aspire?
What the hand dare seize the fire?

And what shoulder and what art
Could twist the sinews of thy heart?
And when thy heart began to beat,
What dread hand and what dread feet?

What the hammer? what the chain?
In what furnace was thy brain?
What the anvil? What dread grasp
Dare its deadly terrors clasp?

When the stars threw down their spears,
And water'd heaven with their tears,
Did He smile His work to see?
Did He who made the lamb make thee?

Tiger, tiger, burning bright
In the forests of the night,
What immortal hand or eye
Dare frame thy fearful symmetry?

WILLIAM BLAKE (1757–1827)

528   CRADLE SONG

Sleep, sleep, beauty bright,
Dreaming in the joys of night;
Sleep, sleep; in thy sleep
Little sorrows sit and weep.

Sweet babe, in thy face
Soft desires I can trace,
Secret joys and secret smiles,
Little pretty infant wiles.

As thy softest limbs I feel
Smiles as of the morning steal
O'er thy cheek, and o'er thy breast
Where thy little heart doth rest.

O the cunning wiles that creep
In thy little heart asleep!
When thy little heart doth wake,
Then the dreadful night shall break.
                    WILLIAM BLAKE (1757–1827)

529   NIGHT

The sun descending in the west,
  The evening star does shine;
The birds are silent in their nest.
  And I must seek for mine.
    The moon, like a flower
    In heaven's high bower,
    With silent delight
    Sits and smiles on the night.

Farewell, green fields and happy grove,
  Where flocks have took delight:
Where lambs have nibbled, silent move
  The feet of angels bright;
    Unseen they pour blessing
    And joy without ceasing
    On each bud and blossom,
    And each sleeping bosom.

They look in every thoughtless nest
  Where birds are cover'd warm;
They visit caves of every beast,
  To keep them all from harm:
    If they see any weeping
    That should have been sleeping,
    They pour sleep on their head,
    And sit down by their bed.

When wolves and tigers howl for prey,
  They pitying stand and weep,
Seeking to drive their thirst away
  And keep them from the sheep.
    But, if they rush dreadful,
    The angels, most heedful,
    Receive each mild spirit,
    New worlds to inherit.

And there the lion's ruddy eyes
  Shall flow with tears of gold:
And pitying the tender cries,
  And walking round the fold:
    Saying, "Wrath, by His meekness,
    And, by His health, sickness,
    Are driven away
    From our immortal day.

"And now beside thee, bleating lamb,
  I can lie down and sleep,
Or think on Him who bore thy name,
  Graze after thee, and weep.
    For, wash'd in life's river,
    My bright mane for ever
    Shall shine like the gold
    As I guard o'er the fold."

WILLIAM BLAKE (1757–1827)

530   LOVE'S SECRET

Never seek to tell thy love,
  Love that never told can be;
For the gentle wind doth move
  Silently, invisibly.

I told my love, I told my love,
  I told her all my heart,
Trembling, cold, in ghastly fears.
  Ah! she did depart!

Soon after she was gone from me,
  A traveller came by,
Silently, invisibly:
  He took her with a sigh.

WILLIAM BLAKE (1757–1827)

531   MARY MORISON

O Mary, at thy window be,
  It is the wish'd, the trysted hour!
Those smiles and glances let me see,
  That make the miser's treasure poor:
How blythely wad I bide the stour
  A weary slave frae sun to sun,
Could I the rich reward secure,
  The lovely Mary Morison!

Yestreen, when to the trembling string
  The dance gaed thro' the lighted ha',
To thee my fancy took its wing,
  I sat, but neither heard nor saw:
Tho' this was fair, and that was braw,
  And yon the toast of a' the town,
I sigh'd, and said amang them a',
  "Ye arena Mary Morison."

O Mary, canst thou wreck his peace,
  Wha for thy sake wad gladly die?
Or canst thou break that heart of his,
  Whase only faut is loving thee?

If love for love thou wiltna gie,
  At least be pity to me shown;
A thought ungentle canna be
  The thought o' Mary Morison.
ROBERT BURNS (1759–1796)

stour: *dust, turmoil*

JEAN 532

Of a' the airts the wind can blaw,
  I dearly like the west,
For there the bonnie lassie lives,
  The lassie I lo'e best:
There wild woods grow, and rivers row,
  And monie a hill between;
But day and night my fancy's flight
  Is ever wi' my Jean.

I see her in the dewy flowers,
  I see her sweet and fair:
I hear her in the tunefu' birds,
  I hear her charm the air:
There's not a bonnie flower that springs
  By fountain, shaw, or green;
There's not a bonnie bird that sings,
  But minds me o' my Jean.
ROBERT BURNS (1759–1796)

airts: *points of the compass*; row: *roll*

AULD LANG SYNE 533

Should auld acquaintance be forgot,
  And never brought to min'?
Should auld acquaintance be forgot,
  And days o' lang syne?

We twa hae rin about the braes,
  And pu'd the gowans fine;
But we've wander'd monie a weary fit
  Sin' auld lang syne.

We twa hae paidl't i' the burn,
  Frae mornin' sun till dine;
But seas between us braid hae roar'd
  Sin' auld lang syne.

And here's a hand, my trusty fiere,
  And gie's a hand o' thine;
And we'll tak a right guid-willie waught
  For auld lang syne.

And surely ye'll be your pint-stowp,
  And surely I'll be mine;
And we'll tak a cup o' kindness yet
  For auld lang syne!

> For auld lang syne, my dear,
>   For auld lang syne,
> We'll tak a cup o' kindness yet
>   For auld lang syne.
>   ROBERT BURNS (1759–1796)

gowans: *daisies*; fit: *foot*; dine: *dinner-time*; fiere: *partner*; guid-willie waught: *friendly draught*

534   MY BONNIE MARY

> Go fetch to me a pint o' wine,
>   An' fill it in a silver tassie,
> That I may drink, before I go,
>   A service to my bonnie lassie.
> The boat rocks at the pier o' Leith,
>   Fu' loud the wind blaws frae the ferry,
> The ship rides by the Berwick-law,
>   And I maun leave my bonnie Mary.
>
> The trumpets sound, the banners fly,
>   The glittering spears are ranked ready;
> The shouts o' war are heard afar,
>   The battle closes thick and bloody;
> But it's no the roar o' sea or shore
>   Wad mak me langer wish to tarry;
> Nor shout o' war that's heard afar—
>   It's leaving thee, my bonnie Mary!
>   ROBERT BURNS (1759–1796)

tassie: *cup*

535   JOHN ANDERSON, MY JO

> John Anderson, my jo, John,
>   When we were first acquent,
> Your locks were like the raven,
>   Your bonnie brow was brent;
> But now your brow is beld, John,
>   Your locks are like the snow;
> But blessings on your frosty pow,
>   John Anderson, my jo!
>
> John Anderson, my jo, John,
>   We clamb the hill thegither;
> And monie a canty day, John,
>   We've had wi' ane anither:
> Now we maun totter down, John,
>   But hand in hand we'll go,
> And sleep thegither at the foot,
>   John Anderson, my jo.
>   ROBERT BURNS (1759–1796)

jo: *sweetheart*; brent: *smooth, unwrinkled*; beld: *bald*; pow: *pate*; canty: *cheerful*

536   THE BANKS O' DOON

> Ye flowery banks o' bonnie Doon,
>   How can ye blume sae fair!
> How can ye chant, ye little birds,
>   And I sae fu' o' care!

Thou'll break my heart, thou bonnie bird,
   That sings upon the bough;
Thou minds me o' the happy days
   When my fause luve was true.

Thou'll break my heart, thou bonnie bird,
   That sings beside thy mate;
For sae I sat, and sae I sang,
   And wistna o' my fate.

Aft hae I roved by bonnie Doon,
   To see the woodbine twine;
And ilka bird sang o' its luve,
   And sae did I o' mine.

Wi' lightsome heart I pu'd a rose
   Upon a morn in June;
And sae I flourish'd on the morn,
   And sae was pu'd or' noon.

Wi' lightsome heart I pu'd a rose
   Upon its thorny tree;
But my fause luver staw my rose,
   And left the thorn wi' me.

                             ROBERT BURNS (1759–1796)

or': *ere*; staw: *stole*

AE FOND KISS   537

Ae fond kiss, and then we sever;
Ae fareweel, alas, for ever!
Deep in heart-wrung tears I'll pledge thee,
Warring sighs and groans I'll wage thee!

Who shall say that Fortune grieves him
While the star of hope she leaves him?
Me, nae cheerfu' twinkle lights me,
Dark despair around benights me.

I'll ne'er blame my partial fancy;
Naething could resist my Nancy;
But to see her was to love her,
Love but her, and love for ever.

Had we never loved sae kindly,
Had we never loved sae blindly,
Never met—or never parted,
We had ne'er been broken-hearted.

Fare thee weel, thou first and fairest!
Fare thee weel, thou best and dearest!
Thine be ilka joy and treasure,
Peace, enjoyment, love, and pleasure!

Ae fond kiss, and then we sever!
Ae fareweel, alas, for ever!
Deep in heart-wrung tears I'll pledge thee,
Warring sighs and groans I'll wage thee!
ROBERT BURNS (1759–1796)

wage: *stake, plight*

538   BONNIE LESLEY

O saw ye bonnie Lesley
  As she gaed o'er the Border?
She's gane, like Alexander,
  To spread her conquests farther.

To see her is to love her,
  And love but her for ever;
For Nature made her what she is,
  And ne'er made sic anither!

Thou art a queen, fair Lesley,
  Thy subjects we, before thee:
Thou art divine, fair Lesley,
  The hearts o' men adore thee.

The Deil he couldna scaith thee,
  Or aught that wad belang thee;
He'd look into thy bonnie face
  And say, "I canna wrang thee!"

The Powers aboon will tent thee,
  Misfortune sha'na steer thee:
Thou'rt like themsel' sae lovely,
  That ill they'll ne'er let near thee.

Return again, fair Lesley,
  Return to Caledonie!
That we may brag we hae a lass
  There's nane again sae bonnie!
ROBERT BURNS (1759–1796)

scaith: *harm*; tent: *watch*; steer: *molest*

539   HIGHLAND MARY

Ye banks and braes and streams around
  The castle o' Montgomery,
Green be your woods, and fair your flowers,
  Your waters never drumlie!
There simmer first unfauld her robes,
  And there the langest tarry;
For there I took the last fareweel
  O' my sweet Highland Mary.

How sweetly bloom'd the gay green birk,
  How rich the hawthorn's blossom,
As underneath their fragrant shade
  I clasp'd her to my bosom!

The golden hours on angel wings
  Flew o'er me and my dearie;
For dear to me as light and life
  Was my sweet Highland Mary.

Wi' monie a vow and lock'd embrace
  Our parting was fu' tender;
And, pledging aft to meet again,
  We tore oursels asunder;
But oh! fell Death's untimely frost,
  That nipt my flower sae early!
Now green's the sod, and cauld's the clay,
  That wraps my Highland Mary!

O pale, pale now, those rosy lips
  I aft hae kiss'd sae fondly!
And closed for aye the sparkling glance
  That dwelt on me sae kindly!

And mouldering now in silent dust
  That heart that lo'ed me dearly!
But still within my bosom's core
  Shall live my Highland Mary.

ROBERT BURNS (1759–1796)

drumlie: *miry*

540. O WERE MY LOVE YON LILAC FAIR

O were my Love yon lilac fair,
  Wi' purple blossoms to the spring,
And I a bird to shelter there,
  When wearied on my little wing;
How I wad mourn when it was torn
  By autumn wild and winter rude!
But I wad sing on wanton wing
  When youthfu' May its bloom renew'd.

O gin my Love were yon red rose
  That grows upon the castle wa',
And I mysel a drap o' dew,
  Into her bonnie breast to fa';
O there, beyond expression blest,
  I'd feast on beauty a' the night;
Seal'd on her silk-saft faulds to rest,
  Till fley'd awa' by Phœbus' light.

ROBERT BURNS (1759–1796)

541. A RED, RED ROSE

O my Luve's like a red, red rose
  That's newly sprung in June:
O my Luve's like the melodie
  That's sweetly play'd in tune!

As fair art thou, my bonnie lass,
  So deep in luve am I:
And I will luve thee still, my dear,
  Till a' the seas gang dry:

> Till a' the seas gang dry, my dear,
>   And the rocks melt wi' the sun;
> I will luve thee still, my dear,
>   While the sands o' life shall run.
>
> And fare thee weel, my only Luve,
>   And fare thee weel a while!
> And I will come again, my Luve,
>   Tho' it were ten thousand mile.

ROBERT BURNS (1759–1796)

542   LAMENT FOR CULLODEN

> The lovely lass o' Inverness,
>   Nae joy nor pleasure can she see;
> For e'en and morn she cries, "Alas!"
>   And aye the saut tear blin's her e'e:
> "Drumossie moor, Drumossie day,
>   A waefu' day it was to me!
> For there I lost my father dear,
>   My father dear and brethren three.
>
> "Their winding-sheet the bluidy clay,
>   Their graves are growing green to see;
> And by them lies the dearest lad
>   That ever blest a woman's e'e!
> Now wae to thee, thou cruel lord,
>   A bluidy man I trow thou be;
> For monie a heart thou hast made sair,
>   That ne'er did wrang to thine or thee."

ROBERT BURNS (1759–1796)

543   THE FAREWELL

> It was a' for our rightfu' King
>   We left fair Scotland's strand;
> It was a' for our rightfu' King
>   We e'er saw Irish land,
>   My dear—
>   We e'er saw Irish land.
>
> Now a' is done that men can do,
>   And a' is done in vain;
> My love and native land, farewell,
>   For I maun cross the main,
>   My dear—
>   For I maun cross the main.
>
> He turn'd him right and round about
>   Upon the Irish shore;
> And gae his bridle-reins a shake,
>   With, Adieu for evermore,
>   My dear—
>   With, Adieu for evermore!

The sodger frae the wars returns,
   The sailor frae the main;
But I hae parted frae my love,
   Never to meet again,
      My dear—
   Never to meet again.

When day is gane, and night is come,
   And a' folk bound to sleep,
I think on him that's far awa',
   The lee-lang night, and weep,
      My dear—
   The lee-lang night, and weep.
ROBERT BURNS (1759–1796)

lee-lang: *livelong*

HARK! THE MAVIS

Ca' the yowes to the knowes,
   Ca' them where the heather grows,
Ca' them where the burnie rows,
   My bonnie dearie.

Hark! the mavis' evening sang
Sounding Clouden's woods amang,
Then a-faulding let us gang,
   My bonnie dearie.

We'll gae down by Clouden side,
Through the hazels spreading wide,
O'er the waves that sweetly glide
   To the moon sae clearly.

Yonder Clouden's silent towers,
Where at moonshine midnight hours
O'er the dewy bending flowers
   Fairies dance sae cheery.

Ghaist nor bogle shalt thou fear;
Thou'rt to Love and Heaven sae dear,
Nocht of ill may come thee near,
   My bonnie dearie.

Fair and lovely as thou art,
Thou hast stown my very heart;
I can die—but canna part,
   My bonnie dearie.

While waters wimple to the sea;
While day blinks in the lift sae hie;
Till clay-cauld death shall blin' my e'e,
   Ye shall be my dearie.

   Ca' the yowes to the knowes...
ROBERT BURNS (1759–1796)

lift: *sky*

545   SUN

Angel, king of streaming morn;
Cherub, call'd by Heav'n to shine;
T' orient tread the waste forlorn;
Guide ætherial, pow'r divine;
   Thou, Lord of all within!

Golden spirit, lamp of day,
Host, that dips in blood the plain,
Bids the crimson'd mead be gay,
Bids the green blood burst the vein;
   Thou, Lord of all within!

Soul, that wraps the globe in light;
Spirit, beckoning to arise;
Drives the frowning brow of night,
Glory bursting o'er the skies;
   Thou, Lord of all within!

                                    HENRY ROWE (1750–1819)

546   MOON

Thee too, modest tressed maid,
   When thy fallen stars appear;
When in lawn of fire array'd
   Sov'reign of yon powder'd sphere;
To thee I chant at close of day,
Beneath, O maiden Moon! thy ray.

Throned in sapphired ring supreme,
   Pregnant with celestial juice,
On silver wing thy diamond stream
   Gives what summer hours produce;
While view'd impearl'd earth's rich inlay,
Beneath, O maiden Moon! thy ray.

Glad, pale Cynthian wine I sip,
   Breathed the flow'ry leaves among;
Draughts delicious wet my lip;
   Drown'd in nectar drunk my song;
While tuned to Philomel the lay,
Beneath, O maiden Moon! thy ray.

Dew, that od'rous ointment yields,
   Sweets, that western winds disclose,
Bathing spring's more purpled fields,
   Soft's the band that winds the rose;
While o'er thy myrtled lawns I stray
Beneath, O maiden Moon! thy ray.

                                    HENRY ROWE (1750–1819)

547   TIME AND GRIEF

O Time! who know'st a lenient hand to lay
Softest on sorrow's wound, and slowly thence
(Lulling to sad repose the weary sense)
The faint pang stealest unperceived away;

On thee I rest my only hope at last,
And think, when thou hast dried the bitter tear
That flows in vain o'er all my soul held dear,
I may look back on every sorrow past,
And meet life's peaceful evening with a smile:
As some lone bird, at day's departing hour,
Sings in the sunbeam, of the transient shower
Forgetful, though its wings are wet the while:—
   Yet ah! how much must this poor heart endure,
   Which hopes from thee, and thee alone, a cure!
WILLIAM LISLE BOWLES (1762–1850)

THE OUTLAW'S SONG 548

The chough and crow to roost are gone,
  The owl sits on the tree,
The hush'd wind wails with feeble moan,
  Like infant charity.
The wild-fire dances on the fen,
  The red star sheds its ray;
Uprouse ye then, my merry men!
  It is our op'ning day.

Both child and nurse are fast asleep,
  And closed is every flower,
And winking tapers faintly peep
  High from my lady's bower;
Bewilder'd hinds with shorten'd ken
  Shrink on their murky way;
Uprouse ye then, my merry men!
  It is our op'ning day.

Nor board nor garner own we now,
  Nor roof nor latchèd door,
Nor kind mate, bound by holy vow
  To bless a good man's store;
Noon lulls us in a gloomy den,
  And night is grown our day;
Uprouse ye then, my merry men!
  And use it as ye may.
JOANNA BAILLIE (1762–1851)

A CHILD 549

A child's a plaything for an hour;
  Its pretty tricks we try
For that or for a longer space—
  Then tire, and lay it by.

But I knew one that to itself
  All seasons could control;
That would have mock'd the sense of pain
  Out of a grievèd soul.

    Thou straggler into loving arms,
        Young climber-up of knees,
    When I forget thy thousand ways
        Then life and all shall cease.
                                MARY LAMB (1765–1847)

550   THE LAND O' THE LEAL
    I'm wearin' awa', John
    Like snaw-wreaths in thaw, John,
    I'm wearin' awa'
        To the land o' the leal.
    There's nae sorrow there, John,
    There's neither cauld nor care, John,
    The day is aye fair
        In the land o' the leal.

    Our bonnie bairn's there, John,
    She was baith gude and fair, John;
    And O! we grudged her sair
        To the land o' the leal.
    But sorrow's sel' wears past, John,
    And joy's a-coming fast, John,
    The joy that's aye to last
        In the land o' the leal.

    Sae dear's the joy was bought, John,
    Sae free the battle fought, John,
    That sinfu' man e'er brought
        To the land o' the leal.
    O, dry your glistening e'e, John!
    My saul langs to be free, John,
    And angels beckon me
        To the land o' the leal.

    O, haud ye leal and true, John!
    Your day it's wearin' through, John,
    And I'll welcome you
        To the land o' the leal.
    Now fare-ye-weel, my ain John,
    This warld's cares are vain, John,
    We'll meet, and we'll be fain,
        In the land o' the leal.
                CAROLINA NAIRNE, LADY NAIRNE (1766–1845)

551   A BOY'S SONG
    Where the pools are bright and deep,
    Where the grey trout lies asleep,
    Up the river and over the lea,
    That's the way for Billy and me.

    Where the blackbird sings the latest,
    Where the hawthorn blooms the sweetest,
    Where the nestlings chirp and flee,
    That's the way for Billy and me.

Where the mowers mow the cleanest,
Where the hay lies thick and greenest,
There to track the homeward bee,
That's the way for Billy and me.

Where the hazel bank is steepest,
Where the shadow falls the deepest,
Where the clustering nuts fall free,
That's the way for Billy and me.

Why the boys should drive away
Little sweet maidens from the play,
Or love to banter and fight so well,
That's the thing I never could tell.

But this I know, I love to play
Through the meadow, among the hay;
Up the water and over the lea,
That's the way for Billy and me.

James Hogg (1770–1835)

Strange Fits of Passion Have I Known
from the "Lucy" poems

Strange fits of passion have I known:
  And I will dare to tell,
But in the lover's ear alone,
  What once to me befell.

When she I loved look'd every day
  Fresh as a rose in June,
I to her cottage bent my way,
  Beneath an evening moon.

Upon the moon I fix'd my eye,
All over the wide lea;
With quickening pace my horse drew nigh
Those paths so dear to me.

And now we reach'd the orchard-plot;
And, as we climb'd the hill,
The sinking moon to Lucy's cot
Came near and nearer still.

In one of those sweet dreams I slept,
Kind Nature's gentlest boon!
And all the while my eyes I kept
On the descending moon.

My horse moved on; hoof after hoof
He raised, and never stopp'd:
When down behind the cottage roof,
At once, the bright moon dropp'd.

What fond and wayward thoughts will slide
  Into a lover's head!
"O mercy!" to myself I cried,
  "If Lucy should be dead!"

WILLIAM WORDSWORTH (1770–1850)

553   SHE DWELT AMONG THE UNTRODDEN WAYS
FROM THE "LUCY" POEMS
She dwelt among the untrodden ways
  Beside the springs of Dove,
A Maid whom there were none to praise
  And very few to love:

A violet by a mossy stone
  Half hidden from the eye!
Fair as a star, when only one
  Is shining in the sky.

She lived unknown, and few could know
  When Lucy ceased to be;
But she is in her grave, and oh,
  The difference to me!

WILLIAM WORDSWORTH (1770–1850)

554   I TRAVELL'D AMONG UNKNOWN MEN
FROM THE "LUCY" POEMS
I travell'd among unknown men,
  In lands beyond the sea;
Nor, England! did I know till then
  What love I bore to thee.

'Tis past, that melancholy dream!
  Nor will I quit thy shore
A second time; for still I seem
  To love thee more and more.

Among thy mountains did I feel
  The joy of my desire;
And she I cherish'd turn'd her wheel
  Beside an English fire.

Thy mornings showed, thy nights conceal'd,
  The bowers where Lucy played;
And thine too is the last green field
  That Lucy's eyes survey'd.

WILLIAM WORDSWORTH (1770–1850)

555   THREE YEARS SHE GREW IN SUN AND SHOWER
FROM THE "LUCY" POEMS
Three years she grew in sun and shower;
Then Nature said, "A lovelier flower
  On earth was never sown;
This child I to myself will take;
She shall be mine, and I will make
  A lady of my own.

"Myself will to my darling be
Both law and impulse: and with me
  The girl, in rock and plain,
In earth and heaven, in glade and bower,
Shall feel an overseeing power
  To kindle or restrain.

"She shall be sportive as the fawn
That wild with glee across the lawn
  Or up the mountain springs;
And hers shall be the breathing balm,
And hers the silence and the calm
  Of mute insensate things.

"The floating clouds their state shall lend
To her; for her the willow bend;
  Nor shall she fail to see
Even in the motions of the storm
Grace that shall mould the maiden's form
  By silent sympathy.

"The stars of midnight shall be dear
To her; and she shall lean her ear
  In many a secret place
Where rivulets dance their wayward round,
And beauty born of murmuring sound
  Shall pass into her face.

"And vital feelings of delight
Shall rear her form to stately height,
  Her virgin bosom swell;
Such thoughts to Lucy I will give
While she and I together live
  Here in this happy dell."

Thus Nature spake—The work was done—
How soon my Lucy's race was run!
  She died, and left to me
This heath, this calm, and quiet scene;
The memory of what has been,
  And never more will be.

WILLIAM WORDSWORTH (1770–1850)

A SLUMBER DID MY SPIRIT SEAL 556
FROM THE "LUCY" POEMS

A slumber did my spirit seal;
  I had no human fears:
She seem'd a thing that could not feel
  The touch of earthly years.

No motion has she now, no force;
  She neither hears nor sees;
Roll'd round in earth's diurnal course,
  With rocks, and stones, and trees.

WILLIAM WORDSWORTH (1770–1850)

557   Upon Westminster Bridge

Earth has not anything to show more fair:
  Dull would he be of soul who could pass by
  A sight so touching in its majesty:
This City now doth like a garment wear
The beauty of the morning; silent, bare,
  Ships, towers, domes, theatres, and temples lie
  Open unto the fields, and to the sky;
All bright and glittering in the smokeless air.
Never did sun more beautifully steep
  In his first splendour valley, rock, or hill;
Ne'er saw I, never felt, a calm so deep!
  The river glideth at his own sweet will:
Dear God! the very houses seem asleep;
  And all that mighty heart is lying still!
William Wordsworth (1770–1850)

558   Evening on Calais Beach

It is a beauteous evening, calm and free,
  The holy time is quiet as a Nun
  Breathless with adoration; the broad sun
Is sinking down in its tranquillity;
The gentleness of heaven broods o'er the sea:
  Listen! the mighty Being is awake,
  And doth with his eternal motion make
A sound like thunder—everlastingly.
Dear Child! dear Girl! that walkest with me here,
  If thou appear untouch'd by solemn thought,
  Thy nature is not therefore less divine:
Thou liest in Abraham's bosom all the year;
  And worshipp'st at the Temple's inner shrine,
  God being with thee when we know it not.
William Wordsworth (1770–1850)

559   On the Extinction of
The Venetian Republic, 1802

Once did she hold the gorgeous East in fee;
  And was the safeguard of the West: the worth
  Of Venice did not fall below her birth,
Venice, the eldest Child of Liberty.

She was a maiden City, bright and free;
  No guile seduced, no force could violate;
  And, when she took unto herself a mate,
She must espouse the everlasting Sea.

And what if she had seen those glories fade,
  Those titles vanish, and that strength decay;
  Yet shall some tribute of regret be paid
When her long life hath reach'd its final day:

Men are we, and must grieve when even the Shade
Of that which once was great is pass'd away.
William Wordsworth (1770–1850)

O Friend! I Know Not Which Way I Must Look 560
  O Friend! I know not which way I must look
    For comfort, being, as I am, opprest,
    To think that now our life is only drest
  For show; mean handy-work of craftsman, cook,
  Or groom!—We must run glittering like a brook
    In the open sunshine, or we are unblest:
    The wealthiest man among us is the best:
  No grandeur now in nature or in book
  Delights us. Rapine, avarice, expense,
    This is idolatry; and these we adore:
    Plain living and high thinking are no more:
    The homely beauty of the good old cause
  Is gone; our peace, our fearful innocence,
    And pure religion breathing household laws.
                      WILLIAM WORDSWORTH (1770–1850)

Milton! Thou Shouldst be Living at this Hour 561
  Milton! thou shouldst be living at this hour:
    England hath need of thee: she is a fen
    Of stagnant waters: altar, sword, and pen,
  Fireside, the heroic wealth of hall and bower,
  Have forfeited their ancient English dower
    Of inward happiness. We are selfish men;
    O raise us up, return to us again,
  And give us manners, virtue, freedom, power!
  Thy soul was like a Star, and dwelt apart;
    Thou hadst a voice whose sound was like the sea:
    Pure as the naked heavens, majestic, free,
    So didst thou travel on life's common way,
  In cheerful godliness; and yet thy heart
    The lowliest duties on herself did lay.
                      WILLIAM WORDSWORTH (1770–1850)

Great Men Have Been Among Us 562
  Great men have been among us; hands that penn'd
    And tongues that utter'd wisdom—better none:
    The later Sidney, Marvel, Harrington,
  Young Vane, and others who call'd Milton friend.
  These moralists could act and comprehend:
    They knew how genuine glory was put on;
    Taught us how rightfully a nation shone
  In splendour: what strength was, that would not bend
  But in magnanimous meekness. France, 'tis strange,
    Hath brought forth no such souls as we had then.
  Perpetual emptiness! unceasing change!
    No single volume paramount, no code,
    No master spirit, no determined road;
    But equally a want of books and men!
                      WILLIAM WORDSWORTH (1770–1850)

563   **BRITISH FREEDOM**

It is not to be thought of that the flood
  Of British freedom, which, to the open sea
  Of the world's praise, from dark antiquity
Hath flow'd, "with pomp of waters, unwithstood,"
Roused though it be full often to a mood
  Which spurns the check of salutary bands,—
  That this most famous stream in bogs and sands
Should perish; and to evil and to good
Be lost for ever. In our halls is hung
  Armoury of the invincible Knights of old:
We must be free or die, who speak the tongue
  That Shakespeare spake; the faith and morals hold
Which Milton held.—In everything we are sprung
  Of Earth's first blood, have titles manifold.
                          WILLIAM WORDSWORTH (1770–1850)

564   **WHEN MEN CHANGE SWORDS FOR LEDGERS**

When I have borne in memory what has tamed
  Great Nations, how ennobling thoughts depart
  When men change swords for ledgers, and desert
The student's bower for gold, some fears unnamed
I had, my Country!—am I to be blamed?
  Now, when I think of thee, and what thou art,
  Verily, in the bottom of my heart,
Of those unfilial fears I am ashamed.
For dearly must we prize thee; we who find
  In thee a bulwark for the cause of men;
  And I by my affection was beguiled:
What wonder if a Poet now and then,
Among the many movements of his mind,
  Felt for thee as a lover or a child!
                          WILLIAM WORDSWORTH (1770–1850)

565   **THE SOLITARY REAPER**

Behold her, single in the field,
  Yon solitary Highland Lass!
Reaping and singing by herself;
  Stop here, or gently pass!
Alone she cuts and binds the grain,
And sings a melancholy strain;
O listen! for the Vale profound
Is overflowing with the sound.

No Nightingale did ever chaunt
  More welcome notes to weary bands
Of travellers in some shady haunt,
  Among Arabian sands:
A voice so thrilling ne'er was heard
In spring-time from the Cuckoo-bird,
Breaking the silence of the seas
Among the farthest Hebrides.

Will no one tell me what she sings?—
　　Perhaps the plaintive numbers flow
For old, unhappy, far-off things,
　　And battles long ago:
Or is it some more humble lay,
Familiar matter of to-day?
Some natural sorrow, loss, or pain,
That has been, and may be again?

Whate'er the theme, the Maiden sang
　　As if her song could have no ending;
I saw her singing at her work,
　　And o'er the sickle bending;—
I listen'd, motionless and still;
And, as I mounted up the hill,
The music in my heart I bore,
Long after it was heard no more.
　　　　　　　　WILLIAM WORDSWORTH (1770–1850)

PERFECT WOMAN 566

She was a phantom of delight
When first she gleam'd upon my sight;
A lovely apparition, sent
To be a moment's ornament;
Her eyes as stars of twilight fair;
Like twilight's, too, her dusky hair;
But all things else about her drawn
From May-time and the cheerful dawn;
A dancing shape, an image gay,
To haunt, to startle, and waylay.

I saw her upon nearer view,
A Spirit, yet a Woman too!
Her household motions light and free,
And steps of virgin liberty;
A countenance in which did meet
Sweet records, promises as sweet;
A creature not too bright or good
For human nature's daily food;
For transient sorrows, simple wiles,
Praise, blame, love, kisses, tears, and smiles.

And now I see with eye serene
The very pulse of the machine;
A being breathing thoughtful breath,
A traveller between life and death;
The reason firm, the temperate will,
Endurance, foresight, strength, and skill;
A perfect Woman, nobly plann'd,
To warn, to comfort, and command;
And yet a Spirit still, and bright
With something of angelic light.
　　　　　　　　WILLIAM WORDSWORTH (1770–1850)

567   ODE TO DUTY

Stern Daughter of the Voice of God!
O Duty! if that name thou love,
Who art a light to guide, a rod
To check the erring and reprove;
Thou, who art victory and law
When empty terrors overawe;
From vain temptations dost set free;
And calm'st the weary strife of frail humanity!

There are who ask not if thine eye
Be on them; who, in love and truth,
Where no misgiving is, rely
Upon the genial sense of youth:
Glad hearts! without reproach or blot;
Who do thy work, and know it not:
O, if through confidence misplaced
They fail, thy saving arms, dread Power! around them cast.

Serene will be our days and bright,
And happy will our nature be,
When love is an unerring light,
And joy its own security.
And they a blissful course may hold
Even now, who, not unwisely bold,
Live in the spirit of this creed;
Yet seek thy firm support, according to their need.

I, loving freedom, and untried;
No sport of every random gust,
Yet being to myself a guide,
Too blindly have reposed my trust:
And oft, when in my heart was heard
Thy timely mandate, I deferr'd
The task, in smoother walks to stray;
But thee I now would serve more strictly, if I may.

Through no disturbance of my soul,
Or strong compunction in me wrought,
I supplicate for thy control;
But in the quietness of thought.
Me this uncharter'd freedom tires;
I feel the weight of chance-desires;
My hopes no more must change their name,
I long for a repose that ever is the same.

Yet not the less would I throughout
Still act according to the voice
Of my own wish; and feel past doubt
That my submissiveness was choice:
Not seeking in the school of pride
For "precepts over dignified,"
Denial and restraint I prize
No farther than they breed a second Will more wise.

Stern Lawgiver! yet thou dost wear
The Godhead's most benignant grace;
Nor know we anything so fair
As is the smile upon thy face:
Flowers laugh before thee on their beds,
And fragrance in thy footing treads;
Thou dost preserve the stars from wrong;
And the most ancient heavens, through Thee, are fresh and strong.

To humbler functions, awful Power!
I call thee: I myself commend
Unto thy guidance from this hour;
O, let my weakness have an end!
Give unto me, made lowly wise,
The spirit of self-sacrifice;
The confidence of reason give;
And in the light of truth thy bondman let me live!
WILLIAM WORDSWORTH (1770–1850)

THE RAINBOW 568
(A FRAGMENT)
My heart leaps up when I behold
A rainbow in the sky:
So was it when my life began;
So is it now I am a man;
So be it when I shall grow old,
    Or let me die!
The Child is father of the Man;
I could wish my days to be
Bound each to each by natural piety.
WILLIAM WORDSWORTH (1770–1850)

THE SONNET 569
Nuns fret not at their convent's narrow room,
  And hermits are contented with their cells,
  And students with their pensive citadels;
Maids at the wheel, the weaver at his loom,
Sit blithe and happy; bees that soar for bloom,
  High as the highest peak of Furness fells,
  Will murmur by the hour in foxglove bells:
In truth the prison unto which we doom
Ourselves no prison is: and hence for me,
  In sundry moods, 'twas pastime to be bound
  Within the Sonnet's scanty plot of ground;
Pleased if some souls (for such there needs must be)
Who have felt the weight of too much liberty,
  Should find brief solace there, as I have found.
WILLIAM WORDSWORTH (1770–1850)

SCORN NOT THE SONNET 570
Scorn not the Sonnet; Critic, you have frown'd,
  Mindless of its just honours; with this key
  Shakespeare unlock'd his heart; the melody
Of this small lute gave ease to Petrarch's wound;

A thousand times this pipe did Tasso sound;
  With it Camöens sooth'd an exile's grief;
  The Sonnet glitter'd a gay myrtle leaf
Amid the cypress with which Dante crown'd
His visionary brow: a glow-worm lamp,
  It cheer'd mild Spenser, call'd from Faery-land
To struggle through dark ways; and when a damp
  Fell round the path of Milton, in his hand
The Thing became a trumpet; whence he blew
  Soul-animating strains—alas, too few!
WILLIAM WORDSWORTH (1770–1850)

571   THE WORLD

The world is too much with us; late and soon,
  Getting and spending, we lay waste our powers:
  Little we see in Nature that is ours;
We have given our hearts away, a sordid boon!
This sea that bares her bosom to the moon;
  The winds that will be howling at all hours,
  And are up-gather'd now like sleeping flowers;
For this, for everything, we are out of tune;
  It moves us not.—Great God! I'd rather be
A Pagan suckled in a creed outworn;
So might I, standing on this pleasant lea,
  Have glimpses that would make me less forlorn;
Have sight of Proteus rising from the sea;
Or hear old Triton blow his wreathed horn.
WILLIAM WORDSWORTH (1770–1850)

572   ODE

INTIMATIONS OF IMMORTALITY FROM RECOLLECTIONS OF EARLY CHILDHOOD

There was a time when meadow, grove, and stream,
  The earth, and every common sight,
    To me did seem
  Apparell'd in celestial light,
The glory and the freshness of a dream.
It is not now as it hath been of yore;—
    Turn wheresoe'er I may,
      By night or day,
The things which I have seen I now can see no more.

    The rainbow comes and goes,
    And lovely is the rose;
    The moon doth with delight
  Look round her when the heavens are bare;
    Waters on a starry night
    Are beautiful and fair;
  The sunshine is a glorious birth;
  But yet I know, where'er I go,
That there hath pass'd away a glory from the earth.

Now, while the birds thus sing a joyous song,
    And while the young lambs bound
      As to the tabor's sound,
To me alone there came a thought of grief:
A timely utterance gave that thought relief,
    And I again am strong:
The cataracts blow their trumpets from the steep;
No more shall grief of mine the season wrong;
I hear the echoes through the mountains throng,
The winds come to me from the fields of sleep,
    And all the earth is gay;
      Land and sea
   Give themselves up to jollity,
    And with the heart of May
   Doth every beast keep holiday;—
      Thou Child of Joy,
Shout round me, let me hear thy shouts, thou happy
   Shepherd-boy!

Ye blessèd creatures, I have heard the call
    Ye to each other make; I see
The heavens laugh with you in your jubilee;
    My heart is at your festival,
    My head hath its coronal,
The fulness of your bliss, I feel—I feel it all.
     O evil day! if I were sullen
      While Earth herself is adorning,
        This sweet May-morning,
     And the children are culling
       On every side,
    In a thousand valleys far and wide,
    Fresh flowers; while the sun shines warm,
And the babe leaps up on his mother's arm:—
    I hear, I hear, with joy I hear!
    —But there's a tree, of many, one,
A single field which I have look'd upon,
Both of them speak of something that is gone:
      The pansy at my feet
      Doth the same tale repeat:
Whither is fled the visionary gleam?
Where is it now, the glory and the dream?

Our birth is but a sleep and a forgetting:
The Soul that rises with us, our life's Star,
    Hath had elsewhere its setting,
      And cometh from afar:
    Not in entire forgetfulness,
    And not in utter nakedness,
But trailing clouds of glory do we come
    From God, who is our home:

Heaven lies about us in our infancy!
Shades of the prison-house begin to close
    Upon the growing Boy,
But he beholds the light, and whence it flows,
    He sees it in his joy;
The Youth, who daily farther from the east
  Must travel, still is Nature's priest,
    And by the vision splendid
    Is on his way attended;
At length the Man perceives it die away,
And fade into the light of common day.

Earth fills her lap with pleasures of her own;
Yearnings she hath in her own natural kind,
And, even with something of a mother's mind,
    And no unworthy aim,
  The homely nurse doth all she can
To make her foster-child, her Inmate Man,
  Forget the glories he hath known,
And that imperial palace whence he came.

Behold the Child among his new-born blisses,
A six years' darling of a pigmy size!
See, where 'mid work of his own hand he lies,
Fretted by sallies of his mother's kisses,
With light upon him from his father's eyes!
See, at his feet, some little plan or chart,
Some fragment from his dream of human life,
Shaped by himself with newly-learned art;
    A wedding or a festival,
    A mourning or a funeral;
      And this hath now his heart,
    And unto this he frames his song:
      Then will he fit his tongue
To dialogues of business, love, or strife;
    But it will not be long
    Ere this be thrown aside,
    And with new joy and pride
The little actor cons another part;
Filling from time to time his "humorous stage"
With all the Persons, down to palsied Age,
That Life brings with her in her equipage;
    As if his whole vocation
    Were endless imitation.

Thou, whose exterior semblance doth belie
    Thy soul's immensity;
Thou best philosopher, who yet dost keep
Thy heritage, thou eye among the blind,
That, deaf and silent, read'st the eternal deep,
Haunted for ever by the eternal mind,—
    Mighty prophet! Seer blest!
    On whom those truths do rest,

Which we are toiling all our lives to find,
In darkness lost, the darkness of the grave;
Thou, over whom thy Immortality
Broods like the Day, a master o'er a slave,
A presence which is not to be put by;
      To whom the grave
Is but a lonely bed without the sense or sight
      Of day or the warm light,
A place of thought where we in waiting lie;
Thou little Child, yet glorious in the might
Of heaven-born freedom on thy being's height,
Why with such earnest pains dost thou provoke
The years to bring the inevitable yoke,
Thus blindly with thy blessedness at strife?
Full soon thy soul shall have her earthly freight,
And custom lie upon thee with a weight,
Heavy as frost, and deep almost as life!

      O joy! that in our embers
      Is something that doth live,
      That nature yet remembers
      What was so fugitive!
The thought of our past years in me doth breed
Perpetual benediction: not indeed
For that which is most worthy to be blest—
Delight and liberty, the simple creed
Of childhood, whether busy or at rest,
With new-fledged hope still fluttering in his breast:—
      Not for these I raise
      The song of thanks and praise;
    But for those obstinate questionings
    Of sense and outward things,
    Fallings from us, vanishings;
    Blank misgivings of a Creature
Moving about in worlds not realized,
High instincts before which our mortal Nature
Did tremble like a guilty thing surprised:
      But for those first affections,
      Those shadowy recollections,
    Which, be they what they may,
Are yet the fountain-light of all our day,
Are yet a master-light of all our seeing;
  Uphold us, cherish, and have power to make
Our noisy years seem moments in the being
Of the eternal Silence: truths that wake,
      To perish never:
Which neither listlessness, nor mad endeavour,
      Nor Man nor Boy,
Nor all that is at enmity with joy,
Can utterly abolish or destroy!

Hence in a season of calm weather
            Though inland far we be,
Our souls have sight of that immortal sea
            Which brought us hither,
    Can in a moment travel thither,
And see the children sport upon the shore,
And hear the mighty waters rolling evermore.

Then sing, ye birds, sing, sing a joyous song!
            And let the young lambs bound
            As to the tabor's sound!
We in thought will join your throng,
        Ye that pipe and ye that play,
        Ye that through your hearts to-day
        Feel the gladness of the May!
What though the radiance which was once so bright
Be now for ever taken from my sight,
        Though nothing can bring back the hour
Of splendour in the grass, of glory in the flower;
        We will grieve not, rather find
        Strength in what remains behind;
        In the primal sympathy
        Which having been must ever be;
        In the soothing thoughts that spring
        Out of human suffering;
        In the faith that looks through death,
In years that bring the philosophic mind.

And O ye Fountains, Meadows, Hills, and Groves,
Forebode not any severing of our loves!
Yet in my heart of hearts I feel your might;
I only have relinquish'd one delight
To live beneath your more habitual sway.
I love the brooks which down their channels fret,
Even more than when I tripp'd lightly as they;
The innocent brightness of a new-born Day
            Is lovely yet;
The clouds that gather round the setting sun
Do take a sober colouring from an eye
That hath kept watch o'er man's mortality;
Another race hath been, and other palms are won.
Thanks to the human heart by which we live,
Thanks to its tenderness, its joys, and fears,
To me the meanest flower that blows can give
Thoughts that do often lie too deep for tears.
                    WILLIAM WORDSWORTH (1770–1850)

573   DESIDERIA
Surprised by joy—impatient as the Wind
  I turned to share the transport—O! with whom
  But Thee, deep buried in the silent tomb,
That spot which no vicissitude can find?

Love, faithful love, recall'd thee to my mind—
  But how could I forget thee? Through what power,
  Even for the least division of an hour,
Have I been so beguiled as to be blind
To my most grievous loss?—That thought's return
  Was the worst pang that sorrow ever bore,
Save one, one only, when I stood forlorn,
  Knowing my heart's best treasure was no more;
That neither present time, nor years unborn
  Could to my sight that heavenly face restore.
William Wordsworth (1770–1850)

Valedictory Sonnet to the River Duddon 574
I thought of Thee, my partner and my guide,
  As being pass'd away.—Vain sympathies!
  For, backward, Duddon! as I cast my eyes,
I see what was, and is, and will abide;
Still glides the Stream, and shall for ever glide;
  The Form remains, the Function never dies;
  While we, the brave, the mighty, and the wise,
We Men, who in our morn of youth defied
The elements, must vanish;—be it so!
  Enough, if something from our hands have power
  To live, and act, and serve the future hour;
And if, as toward the silent tomb we go,
  Through love, through hope, and faith's transcendent dower,
We feel that we are greater than we know.
William Wordsworth (1770–1850)

Mutability 575
From low to high doth dissolution climb,
  And sink from high to low, along a scale
  Of awful notes, whose concord shall not fail;
A musical but melancholy chime,
Which they can hear who meddle not with crime,
  Nor avarice, nor over-anxious care.
  Truth fails not; but her outward forms that bear
The longest date do melt like frosty rime,
That in the morning whiten'd hill and plain
And is no more; drop like the tower sublime
  Of yesterday, which royally did wear
His crown of weeds, but could not even sustain
  Some casual shout that broke the silent air,
  Or the unimaginable touch of Time.
William Wordsworth (1770–1850)

The Trosachs 576
There's not a nook within this solemn Pass,
  But were an apt confessional for one
  Taught by his summer spent, his autumn gone,
That Life is but a tale of morning grass
Wither'd at eve. From scenes of art which chase
  That thought away, turn, and with watchful eyes
  Feed it 'mid Nature's old felicities,
Rocks, rivers, and smooth lakes more clear than glass

Untouch'd, unbreathed upon. Thrice happy quest,
  If from a golden perch of aspen spray
  (October's workmanship to rival May)
The pensive warbler of the ruddy breast
  That moral sweeten by a heaven-taught lay,
Lulling the year, with all its cares, to rest!
WILLIAM WORDSWORTH (1770–1850)

577   SPEAK!

Why art thou silent! Is thy love a plant
  Of such weak fibre that the treacherous air
  Of absence withers what was once so fair?
Is there no debt to pay, no boon to grant?
Yet have my thoughts for thee been vigilant—
  Bound to thy service with unceasing care,
The mind's least generous wish a mendicant
  For nought but what thy happiness could spare.
Speak—though this soft warm heart, once free to hold
  A thousand tender pleasures, thine and mine,
Be left more desolate, more dreary cold
  Than a forsaken bird's-nest filled with snow
  'Mid its own bush of leafless eglantine—
Speak, that my torturing doubts their end may know!
WILLIAM WORDSWORTH (1770–1850)

578   PROUD MAISIE

Proud Maisie is in the wood,
  Walking so early;
Sweet Robin sits on the bush,
  Singing so rarely.

"Tell me, thou bonny bird,
  When shall I marry me?"
—"When six braw gentlemen
  Kirkward shall carry ye."

"Who makes the bridal bed,
  Birdie, say truly?"
—"The grey-headed sexton
  That delves the grave duly.

"The glow-worm o'er grave and stone
  Shall light thee steady;
The owl from the steeple sing
  Welcome, proud lady!"
SIR WALTER SCOTT (1771–1832)

579   BRIGNALL BANKS

O, Brignall banks are wild and fair,
  And Greta woods are green,
And you may gather garlands there,
  Would grace a summer queen:
And as I rode by Dalton Hall,
  Beneath the turrets high,
A Maiden on the castle wall
  Was singing merrily:—

"O, Brignall banks are fresh and fair,
   And Greta woods are green!
I'd rather rove with Edmund there
   Than reign our English Queen."

"If, Maiden, thou wouldst wend with me
   To leave both tower and town,
Thou first must guess what life lead we,
   That dwell by dale and down:
And if thou canst that riddle read,
   As read full well you may,
Then to the green-wood shalt thou speed
   As blithe as Queen of May."

Yet sung she, "Brignall banks are fair,
   And Greta woods are green!
I'd rather rove with Edmund there
   Than reign our English Queen.

"I read you by your bugle horn
   And by your palfrey good,
I read you for a Ranger sworn
   To keep the King's green-wood."
"A Ranger, Lady, winds his horn,
   And 'tis at peep of light;
His blast is heard at merry morn,
   And mine at dead of night."

Yet sung she, "Brignall banks are fair,
   And Greta woods are gay!
I would I were with Edmund there,
   To reign his Queen of May!

"With burnish'd brand and musketoon
   So gallantly you come,
I read you for a bold Dragoon,
   That lists the tuck of drum."
"I list no more the tuck of drum,
   No more the trumpet hear;
But when the beetle sounds his hum,
   My comrades take the spear.

"And O! though Brignall banks be fair,
   And Greta woods be gay,
Yet mickle must the maiden dare,
   Would reign my Queen of May!

"Maiden! a nameless life I lead,
   A nameless death I'll die;
The fiend whose lantern lights the mead
   Were better mate than I!

And when I'm with my comrades met
   Beneath the green-wood bough,
What once we were we all forget,
   Nor think what we are now."

Chorus. Yet Brignall banks are fresh and fair,
   And Greta woods are green,
And you may gather flowers there
   Would grace a summer queen.
                Sir Walter Scott (1771–1832)

580   Lucy Ashton's Song

Look not thou on beauty's charming;
Sit thou still when kings are arming;
Taste not when the wine-cup glistens;
Speak not when the people listens;
Stop thine ear against the singer;
From the red gold keep thy finger;
Vacant heart and hand and eye,
Easy live and quiet die.
                Sir Walter Scott (1771–1832)

581   Answer

Sound, sound the clarion, fill the fife!
   To all the sensual world proclaim,
One crowded hour of glorious life
   Is worth an age without a name.
                Sir Walter Scott (1771–1832)

582   The Rover's Adieu

A weary lot is thine, fair maid,
   A weary lot is thine!
To pull the thorn thy brow to braid,
   And press the rue for wine.
A lightsome eye, a soldier's mien,
   A feather of the blue,
A doublet of the Lincoln green—
   No more of me ye knew,
      My Love!
No more of me ye knew.

"This morn is merry June, I trow,
   The rose is budding fain;
But she shall bloom in winter snow
   Ere we two meet again."
—He turn'd his charger as he spake
   Upon the river shore,
He gave the bridle-reins a shake,
   Said "Adieu for evermore,
      My Love!
And adieu for evermore."
                Sir Walter Scott (1771–1832)

Breathes There The Man   583
(EXCERPT)

Breathes there the man with soul so dead,
Who never to himself hath said,
    "This is my own, my native land!"
Whose heart hath ne'er within him burn'd
As home his footsteps he hath turn'd
    From wandering on a foreign strand?
If such there breathe, go, mark him well;
For him no Minstrel raptures swell;
High though his titles, proud his name,
Boundless his wealth as wish can claim;
Despite those titles, power, and pelf,
The wretch, concentred all in self,
Living, shall forfeit fair renown,
And, doubly dying, shall go down
To the vile dust from whence he sprung,
Unwept, unhonour'd, and unsung.
                    SIR WALTER SCOTT (1771–1832)

The Rime of the Ancient Mariner   584
PART I

An ancient Mariner meeteth three gallants bidden to a wedding feast, and detaineth one.

It is an ancient Mariner,
And he stoppeth one of three.
"By thy long beard and glittering eye,
Now wherefore stopp'st thou me?

The Bridegroom's doors are opened wide,
And I am next of kin;
The guests are met, the feast is set:
May'st hear the merry din."

He holds him with his skinny hand,
"There was a ship," quoth he.
"Hold off! unhand me, grey-beard loon!"
Eftsoons his hand dropt he.

He holds him with his glittering eye—
The Wedding-Guest stood still,
And listens like a three years' child:
The Mariner hath his will.

The Wedding-Guest sat on a stone:
He cannot choose but hear;
And thus spake on that ancient man,
The bright-eyed Mariner.

"The ship was cheer'd, the harbour clear'd,
Merrily did we drop
Below the kirk, below the hill,
Below the lighthouse top.

The Mariner tells how the ship sailed southward with a

The Sun came up upon the left,
Out of the sea came he!

good wind and fair weather, till it reached the Line.

And he shone bright, and on the right
Went down into the sea.

Higher and higher every day,
Till over the mast at noon—"
The Wedding-Guest here beat his breast,
For he heard the loud bassoon.

The Wedding-Guest heareth the bridal music; but the Mariner continueth his tale.

The bride hath paced into the hall,
Red as a rose is she;
Nodding their heads before her goes
The merry minstrelsy.

The Wedding-Guest he beat his breast,
Yet he cannot choose but hear;
And thus spake on that ancient man,
The bright-eyed Mariner.

The ship drawn by a storm toward the South Pole.

"And now the Storm-blast came, and he
Was tyrannous and strong:
He struck with his o'ertaking wings,
And chased us south along.

With sloping masts and dipping prow,
As who pursued with yell and blow
Still treads the shadow of his foe,
And forward bends his head,
The ship drove fast, loud roar'd the blast,
The southward aye we fled.

And now there came both mist and snow,
And it grew wondrous cold:
And ice, mast-high, came floating by,
As green as emerald.

The land of ice, and of fearful sounds, where no living thing was to be seen.

And through the drifts the snowy clifts
Did send a dismal sheen:
Nor shapes of men nor beasts we ken—
The ice was all between.

The ice was here, the ice was there,
The ice was all around:
It crack'd and growl'd, and roar'd and howl'd,
Like noises in a swound!

Till a great sea-bird, called the Albatross, came through the snow-fog, and was received with great joy and hospitality.

At length did cross an Albatross,
Thorough the fog it came;
As if it had been a Christian soul,
We hail'd it in God's name.

It ate the food it ne'er had eat,
And round and round it flew.
The ice did split with a thunder-fit;
The helmsman steer'd us through!

And lo! the Albatross proveth a bird of good omen, and followeth the ship as it returned northward through fog and floating ice.	And a good south wind sprung up behind; The Albatross did follow, And every day, for food or play, Came to the mariners' hollo! In mist or cloud, on mast or shroud, It perch'd for vespers nine; Whiles all the night, through fog-smoke white, Glimmer'd the white moonshine."
The ancient Mariner inhospitably killeth the pious bird of good omen.	"God save thee, ancient Mariner! From the fiends, that plague thee thus!— Why look'st thou so?" — "With my crossbow I shot the Albatross."

PART II

"The Sun now rose upon the right:
Out of the sea came he,
Still hid in mist, and on the left
Went down into the sea.

And the good south wind still blew behind,
But no sweet bird did follow,
Nor any day for food or play
Came to the mariners' hollo!

His shipmates cry out against the ancient Mariner for killing the bird of good luck.	And I had done an hellish thing, And it would work 'em woe: For all averr'd, I had kill'd the bird That made the breeze to blow. Ah wretch! said they, the bird to slay, That made the breeze to blow!
But when the fog cleared off, they justify the same, and thus make themselves accomplices in the crime.	Nor dim nor red, like God's own head, The glorious Sun uprist: Then all averr'd, I had kill'd the bird That brought the fog and mist. 'Twas right, said they, such birds to slay, That bring the fog and mist.
The fair breeze continues; the ship enters the Pacific Ocean, and sails northward, even till it reaches the Line.	The fair breeze blew, the white foam flew, The furrow follow'd free; We were the first that ever burst Into that silent sea.
The ship hath been suddenly becalmed.	Down dropt the breeze, the sails dropt down, 'Twas sad as sad could be; And we did speak only to break The silence of the sea!

All in a hot and copper sky,
The bloody Sun, at noon,
Right up above the mast did stand,
No bigger than the Moon.

>Day after day, day after day,
>We stuck, nor breath nor motion;
>As idle as a painted ship
>Upon a painted ocean.

And the Albatross begins to be avenged.

>Water, water, everywhere,
>And all the boards did shrink;
>Water, water, everywhere,
>Nor any drop to drink.

>The very deep did rot: O Christ!
>That ever this should be!
>Yea, slimy things did crawl with legs
>Upon the slimy sea.

>About, about, in reel and rout
>The death-fires danced at night;
>The water, like a witch's oils,
>Burnt green, and blue, and white.

A Spirit had followed them; one of the invisible inhabitants of this planet, neither departed souls nor angels; concerning whom the learned Jew, Josephus, and the Platonic Constantinopolitan, Michael Psellus, may be consulted. They are very numerous, and There is no climate or element without one or more.

>And some in dreams assurèd were
>Of the Spirit that plagued us so;
>Nine fathom deep he had followed us
>From the land of mist and snow.

>And every tongue, through utter drought,
>Was wither'd at the root;
>We could not speak, no more than if
>We had been choked with soot.

The Shipmates in their sore distress, would fain throw the whole guilt on the ancient Mariner: in sign whereof they hang the dead sea-bird round his neck.

>Ah! well a-day! what evil looks
>Had I from old and young!
>Instead of the cross, the Albatross
>About my neck was hung."

PART III

>"There passed a weary time. Each throat
>Was parch'd, and glazed each eye.
>A weary time! a weary time!

The ancient Mariner beholdeth a sign in the element afar off.

>How glazed each weary eye!
>When looking westward, I beheld
>A something in the sky.

>At first it seem'd a little speck,
>And then it seem'd a mist;
>It moved and moved, and took at last
>A certain shape, I wist.

	A speck, a mist, a shape, I wist!
	And still it near'd and near'd:
	As if it dodged a water-sprite,
	It plunged, and tack'd, and veer'd.

As its nearer approach, it seemeth him to be a ship; and at a dear ransom he freeth his speech from the bonds of thirst.

With throats unslaked, with black lips baked,
We could nor laugh nor wail;
Through utter drought all dumb we stood!
I bit my arm, I suck'd the blood,
And cried, A sail! a sail!

A flash of joy;

With throats unslaked, with black lips baked,
Agape they heard me call:
Gramercy! they for joy did grin,
And all at once their breath drew in,
As they were drinking all.

And horror follows. For can it be a ship that comes onward without wind or tide?

See! see! (I cried) she tacks no more!
Hither to work us weal—
Without a breeze, without a tide,
She steadies with upright keel!

The western wave was all aflame,
The day was wellnigh done!
Almost upon the western wave
Rested the broad, bright Sun;
When that strange shape drove suddenly
Betwixt us and the Sun.

It seemeth him but the skeleton of a ship.

And straight the Sun was fleck'd with bars
(Heaven's Mother send us grace!),
As if through a dungeon-grate he peer'd
With broad and burning face.

Alas! (thought I, and my heart beat loud)
How fast she nears and nears!
Are those *her* sails that glance in the Sun,
Like restless gossameres?

And its ribs are seen as bars on the face of the setting Sun. The Spectre-Woman and her Death-mate, and no other on board the skeleton ship. Like vessel, like crew!

Are those her *ribs* through which the Sun
Did peer, as through a grate?
And is that Woman all her crew?
Is that a DEATH? and are there two?
Is DEATH that Woman's mate?

Her lips were red, *her* looks were free,
Her locks were yellow as gold:
Her skin was as white as leprosy,
The Nightmare LIFE-IN-DEATH was she,
Who thicks man's blood with cold.

Death and Life-in-Death have diced for the ship's crew, and she (the latter) winneth the ancient Mariner.

The naked hulk alongside came,
And the twain were casting dice;
'The game is done! I've won! I've won!'
Quoth she, and whistles thrice.

No twilight within the courts of the Sun.	The Sun's rim dips; the stars rush out: At one stride comes the dark; With far-heard whisper, o'er the sea, Off shot the spectre-bark.
	We listen'd and look'd sideways up! Fear at my heart, as at a cup, My life-blood seem'd to sip! The stars were dim, and thick the night, The steersman's face by his lamp gleam'd white;
	From the sails the dew did drip—
At the rising of the Moon.	Till clomb above the eastern bar The hornèd Moon, with one bright star Within the nether tip.
One after another,	One after one, by the star-dogg'd Moon, Too quick for groan or sigh, Each turn'd his face with a ghastly pang, And cursed me with his eye.
His shipmates dop down dead.	Four times fifty living men (And I heard nor sigh nor groan), With heavy thump, a lifeless lump, They dropp'd down one by one.
But Life-in-Death begins her work on the ancient Mariner.	The souls did from their bodies fly— They fled to bliss or woe! And every soul, it pass'd me by Like the whizz of my crossbow!"

                              PART IV

The Wedding-Guest feareth that a spirit is talking to him;	"I fear thee, ancient Mariner! I fear thy skinny hand! And thou art long, and lank, and brown, As is the ribb'd sea-sand.
But the ancient Mariner assureth him of his bodily life, and proceedeth to relate his horrible penance.	I fear thee and thy glittering eye, And thy skinny hand so brown." — "Fear not, fear not, thou Wedding-Guest! This body dropt not down.
	Alone, alone, all, all alone, Alone on a wide, wide sea! And never a saint took pity on My soul in agony.
He despiseth the creatures of the calm.	The many men, so beautiful! And they all dead did lie: And a thousand thousand slimy things Lived on; and so did I.

And envieth that they should live, and so many lie dead.	I look'd upon the rotting sea, And drew my eyes away; I look'd upon the rotting deck, And there the dead men lay.
	I look'd to heaven, and tried to pray; But or ever a prayer had gusht, A wicked whisper came, and made My heart as dry as dust.
	I closed my lids, and kept them close, And the balls like pulses beat; For the sky and the sea, and the sea and the sky, Lay like a load on my weary eye, And the dead were at my feet.
But the curse liveth for him in the eye of the dead men.	The cold sweat melted from their limbs, Nor rot nor reek did they: The look with which they look'd on me Had never pass'd away.
	An orphan's curse would drag to hell A spirit from on high; But oh! more horrible than that Is the curse in a dead man's eye! Seven days, seven nights, I saw that curse, And yet I could not die.
In his lonliness and fixedness he yearneth towards the journeying Moon, and the stars that still sojourn, yet still move onward; and everywhere the blue sky belongs to the them, and is their appointed rest and their native country and their own natural homes, which they enter unannounced, as lords that are certainly expected, and yet there is a silent joy at their arrival. By the light of the Moon he beholdeth God's creatures of the great calm.	The moving Moon went up the sky, And nowhere did abide; Softly she was going up, And a star or two beside—
	Her beams bemock'd the sultry main, Like April hoar-frost spread; But where the ship's huge shadow lay, The charmed water burnt alway A still and awful red.
	Beyond the shadow of the ship, I watch'd the water-snakes: They moved in tracks of shining white, And when they rear'd, the elfish light Fell off in hoary flakes.
	Within the shadow of the ship I watch'd their rich attire: Blue, glossy green, and velvet black, They coil'd and swam; and every track Was a flash of golden fire.
Their beauty and their happiness.	O happy living things! no tongue Their beauty might declare:

	A spring of love gush'd from my heart,
He blesseth them in his heart.	And I bless'd them unaware: Sure my kind saint took pity on me, And I bless'd them unaware.
The spell begins to break.	The selfsame moment I could pray; And from my neck so free The Albatross fell off, and sank Like lead into the sea."

PART V

"O sleep! it is a gentle thing,
Beloved from pole to pole!
To Mary Queen the praise be given!
She sent the gentle sleep from Heaven,
That slid into my soul.

By the grace of the holy Mother the ancient Mariner is refreshed with rain.	The silly buckets on the deck, That had so long remain'd, I dreamt that they were fill'd with dew; And when I awoke, it rain'd.

My lips were wet, my throat was cold,
My garments all were dank;
Sure I had drunken in my dreams,
And still my body drank.

I moved, and could not feel my limbs:
I was so light—almost
I thought that I had died in sleep,
And was a blessed ghost.

He heareth sounds and seeth strange sights and commotions in the sky and the element.	And soon I heard a roaring wind: It did not come anear; But with its sound it shook the sails, That were so thin and sere.

The upper air burst into life;
And a hundred fire-flags sheen;
To and fro they were hurried about!
And to and fro, and in and out,
The wan stars danced between.

And the coming wind did roar more loud,
And the sails did sigh like sedge;
And the rain pour'd down from one black cloud;
The Moon was at its edge.

The thick black cloud was cleft, and still
The Moon was at its side;
Like waters shot from some high crag,
The lightning fell with never a jag,
A river steep and wide.

The bodies of the ship's crew are inspired, and the ship moves on;	The loud wind never reach'd the ship, Yet now the ship moved on! Beneath the lightning and the Moon The dead men gave a groan.

They groan'd, they stirr'd, they all uprose,
Nor spake, nor moved their eyes;
It had been strange, even in a dream,
To have seen those dead men rise.

The helmsman steer'd, the ship moved on;
Yet never a breeze up-blew;
The mariners all 'gan work the ropes,
Where they were wont to do;
They raised their limbs like lifeless tools—
We were a ghastly crew.

The body of my brother's son
Stood by me, knee to knee:
The body and I pull'd at one rope,
But he said naught to me."

But not by the souls of the men, nor by demons of earth or middle air, but by a blessed troop of angelic spirits, sent down by the invocation of the guardian saint.	"I fear thee, ancient Mariner!" "Be calm, thou Wedding-Guest: 'Twas not those souls that fled in pain, Which to their corses came again, But a troop of spirits blest:

For when it dawn'd—they dropp'd their arms,
And cluster'd round the mast;
Sweet sounds rose slowly through their mouths,
And from their bodies pass'd.

Around, around, flew each sweet sound,
Then darted to the Sun;
Slowly the sounds came back again,
Now mix'd, now one by one.

Sometimes a-dropping from the sky
I heard the skylark sing;
Sometimes all little birds that are,
How they seem'd to fill the sea and air
With their sweet jargoning!

And now 'twas like all instruments,
Now like a lonely flute;
And now it is an angel's song,
That makes the Heavens be mute.

It ceased; yet still the sails made on
A pleasant noise till noon,
A noise like of a hidden brook
In the leafy month of June,
That to the sleeping woods all night
Singeth a quiet tune.

Till noon we quietly sail'd on,
Yet never a breeze did breathe:
Slowly and smoothly went the ship,
Moved onward from beneath.

The lonesome Spirit from the South Pole carries on the ship as far as the Line, in obedience to the angelic troop, but still requireth vengeance.

Under the keel nine fathom deep,
From the land of mist and snow,
The Spirit slid: and it was he
That made the ship to go.
The sails at noon left off their tune,
And the ship stood still also.

The Sun, right up above the mast,
Had fix'd her to the ocean:
But in a minute she 'gan stir,
With a short uneasy motion—
Backwards and forwards half her length
With a short uneasy motion.

Then like a pawing horse let go,
She made a sudden bound:
It flung the blood into my head,
And I fell down in a swound.

The Polar Spirit's fellow-demons, the invisible inhabitants of the element take part in his wrong; and two of them relate, one to the other, that penance long and heavy for the ancient Mariner hath been accorded to the Polar Spirit, who returneth southward.

How long in that same fit I lay,
I have not to declare;
But ere my living life return'd,
I heard, and in my soul discern'd
Two voices in the air.

'Is it he?' quoth one, 'is this the man?
By Him who died on cross,
With his cruel bow he laid full low
The harmless Albatross.

The Spirit who bideth by himself
In the land of mist and snow,
He loved the bird that loved the man
Who shot him with his bow.'

The other was a softer voice,
As soft as honey-dew:
Quoth he, 'The man hath penance done,
And penance more will do."'

PART VI

The Mariner hath been cast into a trance; for the angelic power causesth the vessel to drive northward faster than human life could endure.

First Voice
'But tell me, tell me! speak again,
Thy soft response renewing—
What makes that ship drive on so fast?
What is the Ocean doing?'

Second Voice
'Still as a slave before his lord,
The Ocean hath no blast;
His great bright eye most silently
Up to the Moon is cast—

If he may know which way to go;
For she guides him smooth or grim.
See, brother, see! how graciously
She looketh down on him.'

First Voice
'But why drives on that ship so fast,
Without or wave or wind?'

Second Voice
'The air is cut away before,
And closes from behind.

Fly, brother, fly! more high, more high!
Or we shall be belated:
For slow and slow that ship will go,
When the Mariner's trance is abated.'

<small>The supernatural motion is retarded; the Mariner awakes, and his penance begins anew.</small>

I woke, and we were sailing on
As in a gentle weather:
'Twas night, calm night, the Moon was high;
The dead men stood together.

All stood together on the deck,
For a charnel-dungeon fitter:
All fix'd on me their stony eyes,
That in the Moon did glitter.

The pang, the curse, with which they died,
Had never pass'd away:
I could not draw my eyes from theirs,
Nor turn them up to pray.

<small>The curse is finally expiated.</small>

And now this spell was snapt: once more
I viewed the ocean green,
And look'd far forth, yet little saw
Of what had else been seen—

Like one that on a lonesome road
Doth walk in fear and dread,
And having once turn'd round, walks on,
And turns no more his head;
Because he knows a frightful fiend
Doth close behind him tread.

But soon there breathed a wind on me,
Nor sound nor motion made:
Its path was not upon the sea,
In ripple or in shade.

It raised my hair, it fann'd my cheek
Like a meadow-gale of spring—
It mingled strangely with my fears,
Yet it felt like a welcoming.

Swiftly, swiftly flew the ship,
Yet she sail'd softly too:
Sweetly, sweetly blew the breeze—
On me alone it blew.

And the ancient Mariner beholdeth his native country.

O dream of joy! is this indeed
The lighthouse top I see?
Is this the hill? is this the kirk?
Is this mine own countree?

We drifted o'er the harbour-bar,
And I with sobs did pray—
O let me be awake, my God!
Or let me sleep alway.

The harbour-bay was clear as glass,
So smoothly it was strewn!
And on the bay the moonlight lay,
And the shadow of the Moon.

The rock shone bright, the kirk no less
That stands above the rock:
The moonlight steep'd in silentness
The steady weathercock.

The angelic spirits leave the dead bodies,

And the bay was white with silent light
Till rising from the same,
Full many shapes, that shadows were,
In crimson colours came.

And appear in their own forms of light.

A little distance from the prow
Those crimson shadows were:
I turn'd my eyes upon the deck—
O Christ! what saw I there!

Each corse lay flat, lifeless and flat,
And, by the holy rood!
A man all light, a seraph-man,
On every corse there stood.

This seraph-band, each waved his hand:
It was a heavenly sight!
They stood as signals to the land,
Each one a lovely light;

This seraph-band, each waved his hand,
No voice did they impart—
No voice; but O, the silence sank
Like music on my heart.

But soon I heard the dash of oars,
I heard the Pilot's cheer;
My head was turn'd perforce away,
And I saw a boat appear.

The Pilot and the Pilot's boy,
I heard them coming fast:
Dear Lord in Heaven! it was a joy
The dead men could not blast.

I saw a third—I heard his voice:
It is the Hermit good!
He singeth loud his godly hymns
That he makes in the wood.
He'll shrieve my soul, he'll wash away
The Albatross's blood."

PART VII

The Hermit of the Wood

"This Hermit good lives in that wood
Which slopes down to the sea.
How loudly his sweet voice he rears!
He loves to talk with marineres
That come from a far countree.

He kneels at morn, and noon, and eve—
He hath a cushion plump:
It is the moss that wholly hides
The rotted old oak-stump.

The skiff-boat near'd: I heard them talk,
'Why, this is strange, I trow!
Where are those lights so many and fair,
That signal made but now?'

Approacheth the ship with wonder.

'Strange, by my faith!' the Hermit said—
'And they answer'd not our cheer!
The planks looked warp'd! and see those sails,
How thin they are and sere!
I never saw aught like to them,
Unless perchance it were

Brown skeletons of leaves that lag
My forest-brook along;
When the ivy-tod is heavy with snow,
And the owlet whoops to the wolf below,
That eats the she-wolf's young.'

'Dear Lord! it hath a fiendish look—'
(The Pilot made reply)
'I am a-fear'd' — 'Push on, push on!'
Said the Hermit cheerily.

                                The boat came closer to the ship,
                                But I nor spake nor stirr'd;
                                The boat came close beneath the ship,
                                And straight a sound was heard.

The ship suddenly sinketh   Under the water it rumbled on,
                                Still louder and more dread:
                                It reach'd the ship, it split the bay;
                                The ship went down like lead.

The ancient Mariner is saved Stunn'd by that loud and dreadful sound,
in the Pilot's boat.   Which sky and ocean smote,
                                Like one that hath been seven days drown'd
                                My body lay afloat;
                                But swift as dreams, myself I found
                                Within the Pilot's boat.

                                Upon the whirl, where sank the ship,
                                The boat spun round and round;
                                And all was still, save that the hill
                                Was telling of the sound.

                                I moved my lips—the Pilot shriek'd
                                And fell down in a fit;
                                The holy Hermit raised his eyes,
                                And pray'd where he did sit.

                                I took the oars: the Pilot's boy,
                                Who now doth crazy go,
                                Laugh'd loud and long, and all the while
                                His eyes went to and fro.
                                'Ha! ha!' quoth he, 'full plain I see
                                The Devil knows how to row.'

                                And now, all in my own countree,
                                I stood on the firm land!
                                The Hermit stepp'd forth from the boat,
                                And scarcely he could stand.

The ancient Mariner   'O shrieve me, shrieve me, holy man!'
earnestly entreateth the   The Hermit cross'd his brow.
Hermit to shrieve him; and   'Say quick,' quoth he, 'I bid thee say—
the penance of life falls on What manner of man art thou?'
him.

                                Forthwith this frame of mine was wrench'd
                                With a woful agony,
                                Which forced me to begin my tale;
                                And then it left me free.

And ever and anon   Since then, at an uncertain hour,
throughout his future life an That agony returns:
agony constraineth him to   And till my ghastly tale is told,
travel from land to land;   This heart within me burns.

I pass, like night, from land to land;
I have strange power of speech;
That moment that his face I see,
I know the man that must hear me:
To him my tale I teach.

What loud uproar bursts from that door!
The wedding-guests are there:
But in the garden-bower the bride
And bride-maids singing are:
And hark the little vesper bell,
Which biddeth me to prayer!

O Wedding-Guest! this soul hath been
Alone on a wide, wide sea:
So lonely 'twas, that God Himself
Scarce seemèd there to be.

O sweeter than the marriage-feast,
'Tis sweeter far to me,
To walk together to the kirk
With a goodly company!—

To walk together to the kirk,
And all together pray,
While each to his great Father bends,
Old men, and babes, and loving friends,
And youths and maidens gay!

<small>And to teach, by his own exampled, love and reverance to all things that God made and loveth.</small>

Farewell, farewell! but this I tell
To thee, thou Wedding-Guest!
He prayeth well, who loveth well
Both man and bird and beast.

He prayeth best, who loveth best
All things both great and small;
For the dear God who loveth us,
He made and loveth all."

The Mariner, whose eye is bright,
Whose beard with age is hoar,
Is gone: and now the Wedding-Guest
Turn'd from the bridegroom's door.

He went like one that hath been stunn'd,
And is of sense forlorn:
A sadder and a wiser man
He rose the morrow morn.

Samuel Taylor Coleridge (1772–1834)

Kubla Khan   585

In Xanadu did Kubla Khan
  A stately pleasure-dome decree:
Where Alph, the sacred river, ran
Through caverns measureless to man

       Down to a sunless sea.
    So twice five miles of fertile ground
    With walls and towers were girdled round:
And there were gardens bright with sinuous rills
Where blossom'd many an incense-bearing tree;
And here were forests ancient as the hills,
Enfolding sunny spots of greenery.

But O, that deep romantic chasm which slanted
Down the green hill athwart a cedarn cover!
A savage place! as holy and enchanted
As e'er beneath a waning moon was haunted
By woman wailing for her demon-lover!
And from this chasm, with ceaseless turmoil seething,
As if this earth in fast thick pants were breathing,
A mighty fountain momently was forced;
Amid whose swift half-intermitted burst
Huge fragments vaulted like rebounding hail,
Or chaffy grain beneath the thresher's flail:
And 'mid these dancing rocks at once and ever
It flung up momently the sacred river.
Five miles meandering with a mazy motion
Through wood and dale the sacred river ran,
Then reach'd the caverns measureless to man,
And sank in tumult to a lifeless ocean:
And 'mid this tumult Kubla heard from far
Ancestral voices prophesying war!

   The shadow of the dome of pleasure
      Floated midway on the waves;
   Where was heard the mingled measure
      From the fountain and the caves.
It was a miracle of rare device,
A sunny pleasure-dome with caves of ice!

   A damsel with a dulcimer
      In a vision once I saw:
   It was an Abyssinian maid,
      And on her dulcimer she play'd,
   Singing of Mount Abora.
   Could I revive within me,
      Her symphony and song,
To such a deep delight 'twould win me,
That with music loud and long,
I would build that dome in air,
That sunny dome! those caves of ice!
And all who heard should see them there,

And all should cry, Beware! Beware!
His flashing eyes, his floating hair!
Weave a circle round him thrice,
  And close your eyes with holy dread,
  For he on honey-dew hath fed,
And drunk the milk of Paradise.
                SAMUEL TAYLOR COLERIDGE (1772–1834)

LOVE   586

All thoughts, all passions, all delights,
Whatever stirs this mortal frame,
All are but ministers of Love,
  And feed his sacred flame.

Oft in my waking dreams do I
Live o'er again that happy hour,
When midway on the mount I lay,
  Beside the ruin'd tower.

The moonshine, stealing o'er the scene,
Had blended with the lights of eve;
And she was there, my hope, my joy,
  My own dear Genevieve!

She lean'd against the armèd man,
The statue of the armèd Knight;
She stood and listen'd to my lay,
  Amid the lingering light.

Few sorrows hath she of her own,
My hope! my joy! my Genevieve!
She loves me best whene'er I sing
  The songs that make her grieve.

I play'd a soft and doleful air;
I sang an old and moving story—
An old rude song, that suited well
  That ruin wild and hoary.

She listen'd with a flitting blush,
With downcast eyes and modest grace;
For well she knew I could not choose
  But gaze upon her face.

I told her of the Knight that wore
Upon his shield a burning brand;
And that for ten long years he woo'd
  The Lady of the Land.

I told her how he pined: and ah!
The deep, the low, the pleading tone
With which I sang another's love,
  Interpreted my own.

She listen'd with a flitting blush,
With downcast eyes, and modest grace;
And she forgave me, that I gazed
   Too fondly on her face!

But when I told the cruel scorn
That crazed that bold and lovely Knight,
And that he cross'd the mountain-woods,
   Nor rested day nor night;

That sometimes from the savage den,
And sometimes from the darksome shade,
And sometimes starting up at once
   In green and sunny glade—

There came and look'd him in the face
An angel beautiful and bright;
And that he knew it was a Fiend,
   This miserable Knight!

And that, unknowing what he did,
He leap'd amid a murderous band,
And saved from outrage worse than death
   The Lady of the Land;—

And how she wept and clasp'd his knees;
And how she tended him in vain—
And ever strove to expiate
   The scorn that crazed his brain;—

And that she nursed him in a cave;
And how his madness went away,
When on the yellow forest leaves
   A dying man he lay;—

His dying words—but when I reach'd
That tenderest strain of all the ditty,
My faltering voice and pausing harp
   Disturb'd her soul with pity!

All impulses of soul and sense
Had thrill'd my guileless Genevieve;
The music and the doleful tale,
   The rich and balmy eve;

And hopes, and fears that kindle hope,
An undistinguishable throng,
And gentle wishes long subdued,
   Subdued and cherish'd long!

She wept with pity and delight,
She blush'd with love and virgin shame;
And like the murmur of a dream,
   I heard her breathe my name.

Her bosom heaved—she stepp'd aside,
As conscious of my look she stept—
Then suddenly, with timorous eye
    She fled to me and wept.

She half enclosed me with her arms,
She press'd me with a meek embrace;
And bending back her head, look'd up,
    And gazed upon my face.

'Twas partly love, and partly fear,
And partly 'twas a bashful art,
That I might rather feel, than see.
    The swelling of her heart.

I calm'd her fears, and she was calm,
And told her love with virgin pride;
And so I won my Genevieve,
    My bright and beauteous Bride.
          SAMUEL TAYLOR COLERIDGE (1772–1834)

YOUTH AND AGE   587

Verse, a breeze 'mid blossoms straying,
Where Hope clung feeding, like a bee—
Both were mine! Life went a-maying
With Nature, Hope, and Poesy,
            When I was young!
When I was young?—Ah, woful When!
Ah! for the change 'twixt Now and Then!
This breathing house not built with hands,
This body that does me grievous wrong,
O'er aery cliffs and glittering sands,
How lightly then it flash'd along—
Like those trim skiffs, unknown of yore,
On winding lakes and rivers wide,
That ask no aid of sail or oar,
That fear no spite of wind or tide!
Naught cared this body for wind or weather
When Youth and I lived in't together.

Flowers are lovely! Love is flower-like;
Friendship is a sheltering tree;
O the joys, that came down shower-like,
Of Friendship, Love, and Liberty,
            Ere I was old!
Ere I was old? Ah, woful Ere,
Which tells me, Youth's no longer here!
O Youth! for years so many and sweet,
'Tis known that thou and I were one;
I'll think it but a fond conceit—
It cannot be that thou art gone!
Thy vesper-bell hath not yet toll'd—

And thou wert aye a masker bold!
What strange disguise hast now put on,
To make believe that thou art gone?
I see these locks in silvery slips,
This drooping gait, this alter'd size:
But springtide blossoms on thy lips,
And tears take sunshine from thine eyes!
Life is but thought: so think I will
That Youth and I are housemates still.

Dewdrops are the gems of morning,
But the tears of mournful eve!
Where no hope is, life's a warning
That only serves to make us grieve,
                      When we are old!
That only serves to make us grieve
With oft and tedious taking-leave,
Like some poor nigh-related guest
That may not rudely be dismist.
Yet hath outstay'd his welcome while,
And tells the jest without the smile.
                    SAMUEL TAYLOR COLERIDGE (1772–1834)

588   TIME, REAL AND IMAGINARY
                      AN ALLEGORY
On the wide level of a mountain's head
(I knew not where, but 'twas some faery place),
Their pinions, ostrich-like, for sails outspread,
Two lovely children run an endless race,
    A sister and a brother!
    This far outstripp'd the other;
Yet ever runs she with reverted face,
And looks and listens for the boy behind:
    For he, alas! is blind!
O'er rough and smooth with even step he pass'd,
And knows not whether he be first or last.
                    SAMUEL TAYLOR COLERIDGE (1772–1834)

589   WORK WITHOUT HOPE
All Nature seems at work. Slugs leave their lair—
The bees are stirring—birds are on the wing—
And Winter, slumbering in the open air,
Wears on his smiling face a dream of Spring!
And I, the while, the sole unbusy thing,
Nor honey make, nor pair, nor build, nor sing.

Yet well I ken the banks where amaranths blow,
Have traced the fount whence streams of nectar flow.
Bloom, O ye amaranths! bloom for whom ye may,
For me ye bloom not! Glide, rich streams, away!

With lips unbrighten'd, wreathless brow, I stroll:
And would you learn the spells that drowse my soul?
Work without Hope draws nectar in a sieve,
And Hope without an object cannot live.
SAMUEL TAYLOR COLERIDGE (1772–1834)

GLYCINE'S SONG 590

A sunny shaft did I behold,
  From sky to earth it slanted:
And poised therein a bird so bold—
  Sweet bird, thou wert enchanted!

He sank, he rose, he twinkled, he troll'd
  Within that shaft of sunny mist;
His eyes of fire, his beak of gold,
  All else of amethyst!

And thus he sang: "Adieu! adieu!
Love's dreams prove seldom true.
The blossoms, they make no delay:
The sparking dew-drops will not stay.
    Sweet month of May,
      We must away;
    Far, far away!
      To-day! to-day!"
SAMUEL TAYLOR COLERIDGE (1772–1834)

HIS BOOKS 591

My days among the Dead are past;
  Around me I behold,
Where'er these casual eyes are cast,
  The mighty minds of old:
My never-failing friends are they,
With whom I converse day by day.

With them I take delight in weal
  And seek relief in woe;
And while I understand and feel
  How much to them I owe,
My cheeks have often been bedew'd
With tears of thoughtful gratitude.

My thoughts are with the Dead; with them
  I live in long-past years,
Their virtues love, their faults condemn,
  Partake their hopes and fears;
And from their lessons seek and find
Instruction with an humble mind.

My hopes are with the Dead; anon
   My place with them will be,
And I with them shall travel on
   Through all Futurity;
Yet leaving here a name, I trust,
That will not perish in the dust.
                                       ROBERT SOUTHEY (1774–1843)

592   THE MAID'S LAMENT

I loved him not; and yet now he is gone,
   I feel I am alone.
I check'd him while he spoke; yet, could he speak,
   Alas! I would not check.
For reasons not to love him once I sought,
   And wearied all my thought
To vex myself and him; I now would give
   My love, could he but live
Who lately lived for me, and when he found
   'Twas vain, in holy ground
He hid his face amid the shades of death.
   I waste for him my breath
Who wasted his for me; but mine returns,
   And this lorn bosom burns
With stifling heat, heaving it up in sleep,
   And waking me to weep
Tears that had melted his soft heart: for years
   Wept he as bitter tears.
"Merciful God!" such was his latest prayer,
   "These may she never share!"
Quieter is his breath, his breast more cold
   Than daisies in the mould,
Where children spell, athwart the churchyard gate,
   His name and life's brief date.
Pray for him, gentle souls, whoe'er you be,
   And, O, pray too for me!
                          WALTER SAVAGE LANDOR (1775–1864)

593   ROSE AYLMER

Ah, what avails the sceptred race!
   Ah, what the form divine!
What every virtue, every grace!
   Rose Aylmer, all were thine.

Rose Aylmer, whom these wakeful eyes
   May weep, but never see,
A night of memories and sighs
   I consecrate to thee.
                          WALTER SAVAGE LANDOR (1775–1864)

594   IANTHE

From you, Ianthe, little troubles pass
   Like little ripples down a sunny river;
Your pleasures spring like daisies in the grass,
   Cut down, and up again as blithe as ever.
                          WALTER SAVAGE LANDOR (1775–1864)

Twenty Years Hence 595

Twenty years hence my eyes may grow,
If not quite dim, yet rather so;
Yet yours from others they shall know,
    Twenty years hence.

Twenty years hence, though it may hap
That I be call'd to take a nap
In a cool cell where thunder-clap
    Was never heard,

There breathe but o'er my arch of grass
A not too sadly sigh'd "Alas!"
And I shall catch, ere you can pass,
    That wingèd word.
        WALTER SAVAGE LANDOR (1775–1864)

Verse 596

Past ruin'd Ilion Helen lives,
  Alcestis rises from the shades;
Verse calls them forth; 'tis verse that gives
  Immortal youth to mortal maids.

Soon shall Oblivion's deepening veil
  Hide all the peopled hills you see,
The gay, the proud, while lovers hail
  These many summers you and me.
        WALTER SAVAGE LANDOR (1775–1864)

Proud Word You Never Spoke 597

Proud word you never spoke, but you will speak
Four not exempt from pride some future day.
Resting on one white hand a warm wet cheek,
  Over my open volume you will say,
"This man loved *me*"—then rise and trip away.
        WALTER SAVAGE LANDOR (1775–1864)

Resignation 598

Why, why repine, my pensive friend,
  At pleasures slipp'd away?
Some the stern Fates will never lend,
  And all refuse to stay.

I see the rainbow in the sky,
  The dew upon the grass;
I see them, and I ask not why
  They glimmer or they pass.

With folded arms I linger not
  To call them back; 'twere vain:
In this, or in some other spot,
  I know they'll shine again.
        WALTER SAVAGE LANDOR (1775–1864)

599   MOTHER, I CANNOT MIND MY WHEEL

Mother, I cannot mind my wheel;
  My fingers ache, my lips are dry:
O, if you felt the pain I feel!
  But O, who ever felt as I?

No longer could I doubt him true—
  All other men may use deceit;
He always said my eyes were blue,
  And often swore my lips were sweet.
WALTER SAVAGE LANDOR (1775–1864)

600   AUTUMN

Mild is the parting year, and sweet
  The odour of the falling spray;
Life passes on more rudely fleet,
  And balmless is its closing day.

I wait its close, I court its gloom,
  But mourn that never must there fall
Or on my breast or on my tomb
  The tear that would have soothed it all.
WALTER SAVAGE LANDOR (1775–1864)

601   REMAIN!

Remain, ah not in youth alone!
  —Tho' youth, where you are, long will stay—
But when my summer days are gone,
  And my autumnal haste away.
"Can I be always by your side?"
  No; but the hours you can, you must,
Nor rise at Death's approaching stride,
  Nor go when dust is gone to dust.
WALTER SAVAGE LANDOR (1775–1864)

602   ABSENCE

Here, ever since you went abroad,
  If there be change no change I see:
I only walk our wonted road,
  The road is only walk'd by me.

Yes; I forgot; a change there is—
  Was it of *that* you bade me tell?
I catch at times, at times I miss
  The sight, the tone, I know so well.

Only two months since you stood here?
  Two shortest months? Then tell me why
Voices are harsher than they were,
  And tears are longer ere they dry.
WALTER SAVAGE LANDOR (1775–1864)

603   OF CLEMENTINA

In Clementina's artless mien
  Lucilla asks me what I see,
And are the roses of sixteen
  Enough for me?

Lucilla asks, if that be all,
  Have I not cull'd as sweet before:
Ah yes, Lucilla! and their fall
    I still deplore.

I now behold another scene,
  Where Pleasure beams with Heaven's own light,
More pure, more constant, more serene,
    And not less bright.

Faith, on whose breast the Loves repose,
  Whose chain of flowers no force can sever,
And Modesty who, when she goes,
    Is gone for ever.
              WALTER SAVAGE LANDOR (1775–1864)

IANTHE'S QUESTION   604

"Do you remember me? or are you proud?"
Lightly advancing thro' her star-trimm'd crowd,
  Ianthe said, and look'd into my eyes.
"A *yes*, a *yes* to both: for Memory
Where you but once have been must ever be,
  And at your voice Pride from his throne must rise."
              WALTER SAVAGE LANDOR (1775–1864)

ON CATULLUS   605

Tell me not what too well I know
About the bard of Sirmio.
  Yes, in Thalia's son
Such stains there are—as when a Grace
Sprinkles another's laughing face
  With nectar, and runs on.
              WALTER SAVAGE LANDOR (1775–1864)

DIRCE   606

Stand close around, ye Stygian set,
  With Dirce in one boat convey'd!
Or Charon, seeing, may forget
  That he is old and she a shade.
              WALTER SAVAGE LANDOR (1775–1864)

YEARS   607

Years, many parti-colour'd years,
  Some have crept on, and some have flown
Since first before me fell those tears
  I never could see fall alone.

Years, not so many, are to come,
  Years not so varied, when from you
One more will fall: when, carried home,
  I see it not, nor hear *Adieu.*
              WALTER SAVAGE LANDOR (1775–1864)

608   SEPARATION
There is a mountain and a wood between us,
Where the lone shepherd and late bird have seen us
    Morning and noon and eventide repass.
Between us now the mountain and the wood
Seem standing darker than last year they stood,
    And say we must not cross—alas! alas!
                    WALTER SAVAGE LANDOR (1775–1864)

609   LATE LEAVES
The leaves are falling; so am I;
The few late flowers have moisture in the eye;
    So have I too.
Scarcely on any bough is heard
Joyous, or even unjoyous, bird
    The whole wood through.

Winter may come: he brings but nigher
His circle (yearly narrowing) to the fire
    Where old friends meet.
Let him; now heaven is overcast,
And spring and summer both are past,
    And all things sweet.
                    WALTER SAVAGE LANDOR (1775–1864)

610   FINIS
I strove with none, for none was worth my strife.
Nature I loved and, next to Nature, Art:
I warm'd both hands before the fire of life;
It sinks, and I am ready to depart.
                    WALTER SAVAGE LANDOR (1775–1864)

611   THE OLD FAMILIAR FACES
I have had playmates, I have had companions,
In my days of childhood, in my joyful school-days—
All, all are gone, the old familiar faces.

I have been laughing, I have been carousing,
Drinking late, sitting late, with my bosom cronies—
All, all are gone, the old familiar faces.

I loved a Love once, fairest among women:
Closed are her doors on me, I must not see her—
All, all are gone, the old familiar faces.

I have a friend, a kinder friend has no man:
Like an ingrate, I left my friend abruptly;
Left him, to muse on the old familiar faces.

Ghost-like I paced round the haunts of my childhood,
Earth seem'd a desert I was bound to traverse,
Seeking to find the old familiar faces.

Friend of my bosom, thou more than a brother,
Why wert not thou born in my father's dwelling?
So might we talk of the old familiar faces—

How some they have died, and some they have left me,
And some are taken from me; all are departed—
All, all are gone, the old familiar faces.

CHARLES LAMB (1775–1834)

HESTER 612

When maidens such as Hester die
Their place ye may not well supply,
Though ye among a thousand try
    With vain endeavour.

A month or more hath she been dead,
Yet cannot I by force be led
To think upon the wormy bed
    And her together.

A springy motion in her gait,
A rising step, did indicate
Of pride and joy no common rate,
    That flush'd her spirit:

I know not by what name beside
I shall it call: if 'twas not pride,
It was a joy to that allied,
    She did inherit.

Her parents held the Quaker rule,
Which doth the human feeling cool;
But she was train'd in Nature's school;
    Nature had blest her.

A waking eye, a prying mind;
A heart that stirs, is hard to bind;
A hawk's keen sight ye cannot blind;
    Ye could not Hester.

My sprightly neighbour! gone before
To that unknown and silent shore,
Shall we not meet, as heretofore,
    Some summer morning—

When from thy cheerful eyes a ray
Hath struck a bliss upon the day,
A bliss that would not go away,
    A sweet forewarning?

CHARLES LAMB (1775–1834)

ON AN INFANT DYING AS SOON AS BORN 613

I saw where in the shroud did lurk
A curious frame of Nature's work;
A floweret crush'd in the bud,
A nameless piece of Babyhood,
Was in her cradle-coffin lying;
Extinct, with scarce the sense of dying:
So soon to exchange the imprisoning womb
For darker closets of the tomb!

She did but ope an eye, and put
A clear beam forth, then straight up shut
For the long dark: ne'er more to see
Through glasses of mortality.
  Riddle of destiny, who can show
What thy short visit meant, or know
What thy errand here below?
Shall we say that Nature blind
Check'd her hand, and changed her mind,
Just when she had exactly wrought
A finish'd pattern without fault?
Could she flag, or could she tire,
Or lack'd she the Promethean fire
(With her nine moons' long workings sicken'd)
That should thy little limbs have quicken'd?
Limbs so firm, they seem'd to assure
Life of health, and days mature:
Woman's self in miniature!
Limbs so fair, they might supply
(Themselves now but cold imagery)
The sculptor to make Beauty by.
Or did the stern-eyed Fate descry
That babe or mother, one must die;
So in mercy left the stock
And cut the branch; to save the shock
Of young years widow'd, and the pain
When single state comes back again
To the lone man who, reft of wife,
Thenceforward drags a maimed life?
The economy of Heaven is dark,
And wisest clerks have miss'd the mark,
Why human buds, like this, should fall,
More brief than fly ephemeral
That has his day; while shrivell'd crones
Stiffen with age to stocks and stones;
And crabbèd use the conscience sears
In sinners of an hundred years.
  Mother's prattle, mother's kiss,
Baby fond, thou ne'er wilt miss:
Rites, which custom does impose,
Silver bells, and baby clothes;
Coral redder than those lips
Which pale death did late eclipse;
Music framed for infants' glee,
Whistle never tuned for thee;
Though thou want'st not, thou shalt have them,
Loving hearts were they which gave them.
Let not one be missing; nurse,
See them laid upon the hearse
Of infant slain by doom perverse.
Why should kings and nobles have
Pictured trophies to their grave,

And we, churls, to thee deny
Thy pretty toys with thee to lie—
A more harmless vanity?

CHARLES LAMB (1775–1834)

YE MARINERS OF ENGLAND   614

Ye Mariners of England
  That guard our native seas!
Whose flag has braved a thousand years
  The battle and the breeze!
Your glorious standard launch again
  To match another foe;
And sweep through the deep,
  While the stormy winds do blow!
While the battle rages loud and long
  And the stormy winds do blow.

The spirits of your fathers
  Shall start from every wave—
For the deck it was their field of fame,
  And Ocean was their grave:
Where Blake and mighty Nelson fell
  Your manly hearts shall glow,
As ye sweep through the deep,
  While the stormy winds do blow!
While the battle rages loud and long
  And the stormy winds do blow.

Britannia needs no bulwarks,
  No towers along the steep;
Her march is o'er the mountain-waves,
  Her home is on the deep.
The thunders from her native oak
  She quells the floods below,
As they roar on the shore,
  When the stormy winds do blow!
When the battle rages loud and long,
  And the stormy winds do blow.

The meteor flag of England
  Shall yet terrific burn;
Till danger's troubled night depart
  And the star of peace return.
Then, then, ye ocean-warriors!
  Our song and feast shall flow
To the fame of your name,
  When the storm has ceased to blow!
When the fiery fight is heard no more,
  And the storm has ceased to blow.

THOMAS CAMPBELL (1774–1844)

615   THE BATTLE OF THE BALTIC

Of Nelson and the North
Sing the glorious day's renown,
When to battle fierce came forth
All the might of Denmark's crown,
And her arms along the deep proudly shone;
By each gun the lighted brand
In a bold determined hand,
And the Prince of all the land
Led them on.

Like leviathans afloat
Lay their bulwarks on the brine,
While the sign of battle flew
On the lofty British line:
It was ten of April morn by the chime:
As they drifted on their path
There was silence deep as death,
And the boldest held his breath
For a time.

But the might of England flush'd
To anticipate the scene;
And her van the fleeter rush'd
O'er the deadly space between:
"Hearts of oak!" our captains cried, when each gun
From its adamantine lips
Spread a death-shade round the ships,
Like the hurricane eclipse
Of the sun.

Again! again! again!
And the havoc did not slack,
Till a feeble cheer the Dane
To our cheering sent us back;—
Their shots along the deep slowly boom:—
Then ceased—and all is wail,
As they strike the shatter'd sail,
Or in conflagration pale
Light the gloom.

Out spoke the victor then
As he hail'd them o'er the wave:
"Ye are brothers! ye are men!
And we conquer but to save:—
So peace instead of death let us bring:
But yield, proud foe, thy fleet,
With the crews, at England's feet,
And make submission meet
To our King."...

Now joy, old England, raise!
For the tidings of thy might,
By the festal cities' blaze,
Whilst the wine-cup shines in light!
And yet amidst that joy and uproar,
Let us think of them that sleep
Full many a fathom deep,
By thy wild and stormy steep,
Elsinore!

       THOMAS CAMPBELL (1774–1844)

THE YOUNG MAY MOON   616

The young May moon is beaming, love,
The glow-worm's lamp is gleaming, love;
  How sweet to rove
  Through Morna's grove,
When the drowsy world is dreaming, love!
Then awake!—the heavens look bright, my dear,
'Tis never too late for delight, my dear;
  And the best of all ways
  To lengthen our days
Is to steal a few hours from the night, my dear!

Now all the world is sleeping, love,
But the Sage, his star-watch keeping, love,
  And I, whose star
  More glorious far
Is the eye from that casement peeping, love.
Then awake!—till rise of sun, my dear,
The Sage's glass we'll shun, my dear,
  Or in watching the flight
  Of bodies of light
He might happen to take thee for one, my dear!

       THOMAS MOORE (1779–1852)

THE IRISH PEASANT TO HIS MISTRESS   617

Through grief and through danger thy smile hath cheer'd my way,
Till hope seem'd to bud from each thorn that round me lay;
The darker our fortune, the brighter our pure love burn'd,
Till shame into glory, till fear into zeal was turn'd:
Yes, slave as I was, in thy arms my spirit felt free,
And bless'd even the sorrows that made me more dear to thee.

Thy rival was honour'd, while thou wert wrong'd and scorn'd;
Thy crown was of briers, while gold her brows adorn'd;
She woo'd me to temples, whilst thou lay'st hid in caves;
Her friends were all masters, while thine, alas! were slaves;
Yet cold in the earth, at thy feet, I would rather be
Than wed what I loved not, or turn one thought from thee.

They slander thee sorely, who say thy vows are frail—
Hadst thou been a false one, thy cheek had look'd less pale!
They say, too, so long thou hast worn those lingering chains,
That deep in thy heart they have printed their servile stains:
O, foul is the slander!—no chain could that soul subdue—
Where shineth thy spirit, there Liberty shineth too!
        THOMAS MOORE (1779–1852)

618   THE LIGHT OF OTHER DAYS
  Oft, in the stilly night,
   Ere slumber's chain has bound me,
  Fond Memory brings the light
   Of other days around me:
    The smiles, the tears
    Of boyhood's years,
   The words of love then spoken;
    The eyes that shone,
     Now dimm'd and gone,
   The cheerful hearts now broken!
  Thus, in the stilly night,
   Ere slumber's chain has bound me,
  Sad Memory brings the light
   Of other days around me.

  When I remember all
   The friends, so link'd together,
  I've seen around me fall
   Like leaves in wintry weather,
    I feel like one
    Who treads alone
   Some banquet-hall deserted,
    Whose lights are fled,
    Whose garlands dead,
   And all but he departed!
  Thus, in the stilly night,
   Ere slumber's chain has bound me.
  Sad Memory brings the light
   Of other days around me.
        THOMAS MOORE (1779–1852)

619   AT THE MID HOUR OF NIGHT
At the mid hour of night, when stars are weeping, I fly
To the lone vale we loved, when life shone warm in thine eye;
 And I think oft, if spirits can steal from the regions of air
 To revisit past scenes of delight, thou wilt come to me there,
And tell me our love is remember'd even in the sky.

Then I sing the wild song it once was rapture to hear,
When our voices commingling breathed like one on the ear;
 And as Echo far off through the vale my sad orison rolls,
 I think, O my love! 'tis thy voice from the Kingdom of Souls
Faintly answering still the notes that once were so dear.
        THOMAS MOORE (1779–1852)

MAY   620

    May! queen of blossoms,
      And fulfilling flowers,
    With what pretty music
      Shall we charm the hours?
    Wilt thou have pipe and reed,
    Blown in the open mead?
    Or to the lute give heed
      In the green bowers?

    Thou hast no need of us,
      Or pipe or wire;
    Thou hast the golden bee
      Ripen'd with fire;
    And many thousand more
    Songsters, that thee adore,
    Filling earth's grassy floor
      With new desire.

    Thou hast thy mighty herds,
      Tame and free-livers;
    Doubt not, thy music too
      In the deep rivers;
    And the whole plumy flight
    Warbling the day and night—
    Up at the gates of light,
      See, the lark quivers!

        EDWARD THURLOW, LORD THURLOW (1781–1829)

BATTLE SONG   621

Day, like our souls, is fiercely dark;
    What then? 'Tis day!
We sleep no more; the cock crows—hark!
    To arms! away!
They come! they come! the knell is rung
    Of us or them;
Wide o'er their march the pomp is flung
    Of gold and gem.
What collar'd hound of lawless sway,
    To famine dear—
What pension'd slave of Attila,
    Leads in the rear?
Come they from Scythian wilds afar,
    Our blood to spill?
Wear they the livery of the Czar?
    They do his will.
Nor tassell'd silk, nor epaulet,
    Nor plume, nor torse—
No splendour gilds, all sternly met,
    Our foot and horse.
But, dark and still, we inly glow,
    Condensed in ire!
Strike, tawdry slaves, and ye shall know
    Our gloom is fire.

In vain your pomp, ye evil powers,
    Insults the land;
Wrongs, vengeance, and the Cause are ours,
    And God's right hand!
Madmen! they trample into snakes
    The wormy clod!
Like fire, beneath their feet awakes
    The sword of God!
Behind, before, above, below,
    They rouse the brave;
Where'er they go, they make a foe,
    Or find a grave.
EBENEZER ELLIOTT (1781–1849)

622   PLAINT

Dark, deep, and cold the current flows
Unto the sea where no wind blows,
Seeking the land which no one knows.

O'er its sad gloom still comes and goes
The mingled wail of friends and foes,
Borne to the land which no one knows.

Why shrieks for help yon wretch, who goes
With millions, from a world of woes,
Unto the land which no one knows?

Though myriads go with him who goes,
Alone he goes where no wind blows,
Unto the land which no one knows.

For all must go where no wind blows,
And none can go for him who goes;
None, none return whence no one knows.

Yet why should he who shrieking goes
With millions, from a world of woes,
Reunion seek with it or those?

Alone with God, where no wind blows,
And Death, his shadow—doom'd, he goes.
That God is there the shadow shows.

O shoreless Deep, where no wind blows!
And thou, O Land which no one knows!
That God is All, His shadow shows.
EBENEZER ELLIOTT (1781–1849)

623   THE SUN RISES BRIGHT IN FRANCE

The sun rises bright in France,
    And fair sets he;
But he has tint the blythe blink he had
    In my ain countree.

O, it's nae my ain ruin
  That saddens aye my e'e,
But the dear Marie I left behin'
  Wi' sweet bairnies three.

My lanely hearth burn'd bonnie,
  And smiled my ain Marie;
I've left a' my heart behin'
  In my ain countree.

The bud comes back to summer,
  And the blossom to the bee;
But I'll win back, O never,
  To my ain countree.

O, I am leal to high Heaven,
  Where soon I hope to be,
An' there I'll meet ye a' soon
  Frae my ain countree!
                  ALLAN CUNNINGHAM (1784–1842)

tint: *lost*

HAME, HAME, HAME 624

Hame, hame, hame, O hame fain wad I be—
O hame, hame, hame, to my ain countree!

When the flower is i' the bud and the leaf is on the tree,
The larks shall sing me hame in my ain countree;
Hame, hame, hame, O hame fain wad I be—
O hame, hame, hame, to my ain countree!

The green leaf o' loyaltie's beginning for to fa',
The bonnie White Rose it is withering an' a';
But I'll water 't wi' the blude of usurping tyrannie,
An' green it will graw in my ain countree.

O, there's nocht now frae ruin my country can save,
But the keys o' kind heaven, to open the grave;
That a' the noble martyrs wha died for loyaltie
May rise again an' fight for their ain countree.

The great now are gane, a' wha ventured to save,
The new grass is springing on the tap o' their grave;
But the sun through the mirk blinks blythe in my e'e,
"I'll shine on ye yet in your ain countree."

Hame, hame, hame, O hame fain wad I be—
O hame, hame, hame, to my ain countree!
                  ALLAN CUNNINGHAM (1784–1842)

THE SPRING OF THE YEAR 625

  Gone were but the winter cold,
    And gone were but the snow,
  I could sleep in the wild woods
    Where primroses blow.

Cold's the snow at my head,
  And cold at my feet;
And the finger of death's at my e'en,
  Closing them to sleep.

Let none tell my father
  Or my mother so dear,—
I'll meet them both in heaven
  At the spring of the year.
         ALLAN CUNNINGHAM (1784–1842)

626   JENNY KISS'D ME
Jenny kiss'd me when we met,
  Jumping from the chair she sat in;
Time, you thief, who love to get
  Sweets into your list, put that in!
Say I'm weary, say I'm sad,
  Say that health and wealth have miss'd me,
Say I'm growing old, but add,
    Jenny kiss'd me.
         JAMES HENRY LEIGH HUNT (1784–1859)

627   LOVE AND AGE
I play'd with you 'mid cowslips blowing,
  When I was six and you were four;
When garlands weaving, flower-balls throwing,
  Were pleasures soon to please no more.
Through groves and meads, o'er grass and heather,
  With little playmates, to and fro,
We wander'd hand in hand together;
  But that was sixty years ago.

You grew a lovely roseate maiden,
  And still our early love was strong;
Still with no care our days were laden,
  They glided joyously along;
And I did love you very dearly,
  How dearly words want power to show;
I thought your heart was touch'd as nearly;
  But that was fifty years ago.

Then other lovers came around you,
  Your beauty grew from year to year,
And many a splendid circle found you
  The centre of its glimmering sphere.
I saw you then, first vows forsaking,
  On rank and wealth your hand bestow;
O, then I thought my heart was breaking!—
  But that was forty years ago.

And I lived on, to wed another:
  No cause she gave me to repine;
And when I heard you were a mother,
  I did not wish the children mine.

My own young flock, in fair progression,
  Made up a pleasant Christmas row:
My joy in them was past expression;
  But that was thirty years ago.

You grew a matron plump and comely,
  You dwelt in fashion's brightest blaze;
My earthly lot was far more homely;
  But I too had my festal days.
No merrier eyes have ever glisten'd
  Around the hearth-stone's wintry glow,
Than when my youngest child was christen'd;
  But that was twenty years ago.

Time pass'd. My eldest girl was married,
  And I am now a grandsire gray;
One pet of four years old I've carried
  Among the wild-flower'd meads to play.
In our old fields of childish pleasure,
  Where now, as then, the cowslips blow,
She fills her basket's ample measure;
  And that is not ten years ago.

But though first love's impassion'd blindness
  Has pass'd away in colder light,
I still have thought of you with kindness,
  And shall do, till our last good-night.
The ever-rolling silent hours
  Will bring a time we shall not know,
When our young days of gathering flowers
  Will be an hundred years ago.
              THOMAS LOVE PEACOCK (1785–1866)

THE GRAVE OF LOVE   628
I dug, beneath the cypress shade,
  What well might seem an elfin's grave;
And every pledge in earth I laid,
  That erst thy false affection gave.

I press'd them down the sod beneath;
  I placed one mossy stone above;
And twined the rose's fading wreath
  Around the sepulchre of love.

Frail as thy love, the flowers were dead
  Ere yet the evening sun was set:
But years shall see the cypress spread,
  Immutable as my regret.
              THOMAS LOVE PEACOCK (1785–1866)

629

Three Men of Gotham

Seamen three! What men be ye?
Gotham's three wise men we be.
Whither in your bowl so free?
To rake the moon from out the sea.
The bowl goes trim. The moon doth shine.
And our ballast is old wine.—
And your ballast is old wine.

Who art thou, so fast adrift?
I am he they call Old Care.
Here on board we will thee lift.
No: I may not enter there.
Wherefore so? 'Tis Jove's decree,
In a bowl Care may not be.—
In a bowl Care may not be.

Fear ye not the waves that roll?
No: in charmèd bowl we swim.
What the charm that floats the bowl?
Water may not pass the brim.
The bowl goes trim. The moon doth shine.
And our ballast is old wine.—
And your ballast is old wine.

Thomas Love Peacock (1785–1866)

630

To Death

Come not in terrors clad, to claim
    An unresisting prey:
Come like an evening shadow, Death!
    So stealthily, so silently!
And shut mine eyes, and steal my breath;
    Then willingly, O willingly,
      With thee I'll go away!

What need to clutch with iron grasp
    What gentlest touch may take?
What need with aspect dark to scare,
    So awfully, so terribly,
The weary soul would hardly care,
    Call'd quietly, call'd tenderly,
      From thy dread power to break?

'Tis not as when thou markest out
    The young, the blest, the gay,
The loved, the loving—they who dream
    So happily, so hopefully;
Then harsh thy kindest call may seem,
    And shrinkingly, reluctantly,
      The summon'd may obey.

But I have drunk enough of life—
    The cup assign'd to me
Dash'd with a little sweet at best,
    So scantily, so scantily—
To know full well that all the rest
    More bitterly, more bitterly,
      Drugg'd to the last will be.

And I may live to pain some heart
    That kindly cares for me:
To pain, but not to bless. O Death!
    Come quietly—come lovingly—
And shut mine eyes, and steal my breath;
    Then willingly, O willingly,
      I'll go away with thee!
                CAROLINE SOUTHEY (1787–1854)

WHEN WE TWO PARTED   631

When we two parted
    In silence and tears,
Half broken-hearted
    To sever for years,
Pale grew thy cheek and cold,
    Colder thy kiss;
Truly that hour foretold
    Sorrow to this.

The dew of the morning
    Sunk chill on my brow—
It felt like the warning
    Of what I feel now.
Thy vows are all broken,
    And light is thy fame:
I hear thy name spoken,
    And share in its shame.

They name thee before me,
    A knell to mine ear;
A shudder comes o'er me—
    Why wert thou so dear?
They know not I knew thee,
    Who knew thee too well:
Long, long shall I rue thee,
    Too deeply to tell.

In secret we met—
    In silence I grieve,
That thy heart could forget,
    Thy spirit deceive.
If I should meet thee
    After long years,
How should I greet thee?
    With silence and tears.
        GEORGE GORDON BYRON, LORD BYRON (1788–1824)

632   FOR MUSIC

There be none of Beauty's daughters
  With a magic like thee;
And like music on the waters
  Is thy sweet voice to me:
When, as if its sound were causing
The charmed ocean's pausing,
The waves lie still and gleaming,
And the lull'd winds seem dreaming:

And the midnight moon is weaving
  Her bright chain o'er the deep;
Whose breast is gently heaving,
  As an infant's asleep:
So the spirit bows before thee,
To listen and adore thee;
With a full but soft emotion,
Like the swell of Summer's ocean.
              GEORGE GORDON BYRON, LORD BYRON (1788–1824)

633   WE'LL GO NO MORE A-ROVING

So, we'll go no more a-roving
  So late into the night,
Though the heart be still as loving,
  And the moon be still as bright.

For the sword outwears its sheath,
  And the soul wears out the breast,
And the heart must pause to breathe,
  And love itself have rest.

Though the night was made for loving,
  And the day returns too soon,
Yet we'll go no more a-roving
  By the light of the moon.
              GEORGE GORDON BYRON, LORD BYRON (1788–1824)

634   SHE WALKS IN BEAUTY

She walks in beauty, like the night
  Of cloudless climes and starry skies;
And all that's best of dark and bright
  Meet in her aspect and her eyes:
Thus mellow'd to that tender light
  Which heaven to gaudy day denies.
One shade the more, one ray the less,
  Had half impair'd the nameless grace
Which waves in every raven tress,
  Or softly lightens o'er her face;
Where thoughts serenely sweet express
  How pure, how dear their dwelling-place.

And on that cheek, and o'er that brow,
  So soft, so calm, yet eloquent,
The smiles that win, the tints that glow,
  But tell of days in goodness spent,
A mind at peace with all below,
  A heart whose love is innocent!
          GEORGE GORDON BYRON, LORD BYRON (1788–1824)

THE ISLES OF GREECE 635
The isles of Greece! the isles of Greece
  Where burning Sappho loved and sung,
Where grew the arts of war and peace,
  Where Delos rose, and Phœbus sprung!
Eternal summer gilds them yet,
But all, except their sun, is set.

The Scian and the Teian muse,
  The hero's harp, the lover's lute,
Have found the fame your shores refuse:
  Their place of birth alone is mute
To sounds which echo further west
Than your sires' "Islands of the Blest."

The mountains look on Marathon—
  And Marathon looks on the sea;
And musing there an hour alone,
  I dream'd that Greece might still be free;
For standing on the Persians' grave,
I could not deem myself a slave.

A king sate on the rocky brow
  Which looks o'er sea-born Salamis;
And ships, by thousands, lay below,
  And men in nations;—all were his!
He counted them at break of day—
And when the sun set, where were they?

And where are they? and where art thou,
  My country? On thy voiceless shore
The heroic lay is tuneless now—
  The heroic bosom beats no more!
And must thy lyre, so long divine,
Degenerate into hands like mine?

'Tis something in the dearth of fame,
  Though link'd among a fetter'd race,
To feel at least a patriot's shame,
  Even as I sing, suffuse my face;
For what is left the poet here?
For Greeks a blush—for Greece a tear.

Must *we* but weep o'er days more blest?
  Must *we* but blush?—Our fathers bled.
Earth! render back from out thy breast
  A remnant of our Spartan dead!
Of the three hundred grant but three,
To make a new Thermopylae!

What, silent still? and silent all?
  Ah! no;—the voices of the dead
Sound like a distant torrent's fall,
  And answer, "Let one living head,
But one, arise,—we come, we come!"
'Tis but the living who are dumb.

In vain—in vain: strike other chords;
  Fill high the cup with Samian wine!
Leave battles to the Turkish hordes,
  And shed the blood of Scio's vine:
Hark! rising to the ignoble call—
How answers each bold Bacchanal!

You have the Pyrrhic dance as yet;
  Where is the Pyrrhic phalanx gone?
Of two such lessons, why forget
  The nobler and the manlier one?
You have the letters Cadmus gave—
Think ye he meant them for a slave?

Fill high the bowl with Samian wine!
  We will not think of themes like these!
It made Anacreon's song divine:
  He served—but served Polycrates—
A tyrant; but our masters then
Were still, at least, our countrymen.

The tyrant of the Chersonese
  Was freedom's best and bravest friend;
That tyrant was Miltiades!
  O that the present hour would lend
Another despot of the kind!
Such chains as his were sure to bind.

Fill high the bowl with Samian wine!
  On Suli's rock, and Parga's shore,
Exists the remnant of a line
  Such as the Doric mothers bore;
And there, perhaps, some seed is sown,
The Heracleidan blood might own.

Trust not for freedom to the Franks—
  They have a king who buys and sells;
In native swords and native ranks
  The only hope of courage dwells:
But Turkish force and Latin fraud
Would break your shield, however broad.

Fill high the bowl with Samian wine!
   Our virgins dance beneath the shade—
I see their glorious black eyes shine;
   But gazing on each glowing maid,
My own the burning tear-drop laves,
To think such breasts must suckle slaves.

Place me on Sunium's marbled steep,
   Where nothing, save the waves and I,
May hear our mutual murmurs sweep;
   There, swan-like, let me sing and die:
A land of slaves shall ne'er be mine—
Dash down yon cup of Samian wine!
               GEORGE GORDON BYRON, LORD BYRON (1788–1824)

THE CHILDREN BAND   636

All holy influences dwell within
The breast of Childhood: instincts fresh from God
  Inspire it, ere the heart beneath the rod
Of grief hath bled, or caught the plague of sin.
How mighty was that fervour which could win
  Its way to infant souls!—and was the sod
  Of Palestine by infant Croises trod?
Like Joseph went they forth, or Benjamin,
In all their touching beauty to redeem?
  And did their soft lips kiss the Sepulchre?
Alas! the lovely pageant as a dream
  Faded! They sank not through ignoble fear;
They felt not Moslem steel. By mountain, stream,
  In sands, in fens, they died—no mother near!
               SIR AUBREY DE VERE (1788–1846)

THE BURIAL OF SIR JOHN MOORE AFTER CORUNNA   637

Not a drum was heard, not a funeral note,
  As his corse to the rampart we hurried;
Not a soldier discharged his farewell shot
  O'er the grave where our hero we buried.

We buried him darkly at dead of night,
  The sods with our bayonets turning,
By the struggling moonbeam's misty light
  And the lanthorn dimly burning.

No useless coffin enclosed his breast,
  Not in sheet or in shroud we wound him;
But he lay like a warrior taking his rest
  With his martial cloak around him.

Few and short were the prayers we said,
  And we spoke not a word of sorrow;
But we steadfastly gazed on the face that was dead,
  And we bitterly thought of the morrow.

We thought, as we hollow'd his narrow bed
  And smooth'd down his lonely pillow,
That the foe and the stranger would tread o'er his head,
  And we far away on the billow!

Lightly they'll talk of the spirit that's gone,
  And o'er his cold ashes upbraid him—
But little he'll reck, if they let him sleep on
  In the grave where a Briton has laid him.

But half of our heavy task was done
  When the clock struck the hour for retiring;
And we heard the distant and random gun
  That the foe was sullenly firing.

Slowly and sadly we laid him down,
  From the field of his fame fresh and gory;
We carved not a line, and we raised not a stone,
  But we left him alone with his glory.

                        CHARLES WOLFE (1791–1823)

638
To Mary

If I had thought thou couldst have died,
  I might not weep for thee;
But I forgot, when by thy side,
  That thou couldst mortal be:
It never through my mind had past
  The time would e'er be o'er,
And I on thee should look my last,
  And thou shouldst smile no more!

And still upon that face I look,
  And think 'twill smile again;
And still the thought I will not brook,
  That I must look in vain.
But when I speak—thou dost not say
  What thou ne'er left'st unsaid;
And now I feel, as well I may,
  Sweet Mary, thou art dead!

If thou wouldst stay, e'en as thou art,
  All cold and all serene—
I still might press thy silent heart,
  And where thy smiles have been.
While e'en thy chill, bleak corse I have,
  Thou seemest still mine own;
But there—I lay thee in thy grave,
  And I am now alone!

I do not think, where'er thou art,
  Thou hast forgotten me;
And I, perhaps, may soothe this heart
  In thinking too of thee:

Yet there was round thee such a dawn
  Of light ne'er seen before,
As fancy never could have drawn,
  And never can restore!

CHARLES WOLFE (1791–1823)

HYMN OF PAN   639

From the forests and highlands
  We come, we come;
From the river-girt islands,
  Where loud waves are dumb,
    Listening to my sweet pipings.
  The wind in the reeds and the rushes,
    The bees on the bells of thyme,
  The birds on the myrtle bushes,
    The cicale above in the lime,
And the lizards below in the grass,
Were as silent as ever old Tmolus was,
  Listening to my sweet pipings.

Liquid Peneus was flowing,
  And all dark Tempe lay
In Pelion's shadow, outgrowing
  The light of the dying day,
    Speeded by my sweet pipings.
  The Sileni and Sylvans and Fauns,
    And the Nymphs of the woods and waves,
  To the edge of the moist river-lawns,
    And the brink of the dewy caves,
And all that did then attend and follow,
Were silent with love, as you now, Apollo,
  With envy of my sweet pipings.

I sang of the dancing stars,
  I sang of the daedal earth,
And of heaven, and the giant wars,
  And love, and death, and birth.
    And then I changed my pipings—
  Singing how down the vale of Maenalus
    I pursued a maiden, and clasp'd a reed:
  Gods and men, we are all deluded thus!
    It breaks in our bosom, and then we bleed.
All wept—as I think both ye now would,
If envy or age had not frozen your blood—
  At the sorrow of my sweet pipings.

PERCY BYSSHE SHELLEY (1792–1822)

THE INVITATION   640

Best and brightest, come away!
Fairer far than this fair Day,
Which, like thee to those in sorrow,
Comes to bid a sweet good-morrow

To the rough Year just awake
In its cradle on the brake.
The brightest hour of unborn Spring,
Through the winter wandering,
Found, it seems, the halcyon Morn
To hoar February born.
Bending from heaven, in azure mirth,
It kiss'd the forehead of the Earth;
And smiled upon the silent sea;
And bade the frozen streams be free;
And waked to music all their fountains;
And breathed upon the frozen mountains;
And like a prophetess of May
Strew'd flowers upon the barren way,
Making the wintry world appear
Like one on whom thou smilest, dear.

Away, away, from men and towns,
To the wild wood and the downs—
To the silent wilderness
Where the soul need not repress
Its music lest it should not find
An echo in another's mind,
While the touch of Nature's art
Harmonizes heart to heart.
I leave this notice on my door
For each accustom'd visitor:—
"I am gone into the fields
To take what this sweet hour yields.
Reflection, you may come to-morrow;
Sit by the fireside with Sorrow.
You with the unpaid bill, Despair,—
You, tiresome verse-reciter, Care,—
I will pay you in the grave,—
Death will listen to your stave.
Expectation too, be off!
To-day is for itself enough.
Hope, in pity mock not Woe
With smiles, nor follow where I go;
Long having lived on your sweet food,
At length I find one moment's good
After long pain: with all your love,
This you never told me of."

Radiant Sister of the Day,
Awake! arise! and come away!
To the wild woods and the plains;
And the pools where winter rains
Image all their roof of leaves;
Where the pine its garland weaves
Of sapless green and ivy dun
Round stems that never kiss the sun;

Where the lawns and pastures be,
And the sandhills of the sea;
Where the melting hoar-frost wets
The daisy-star that never sets,
And wind-flowers, and violets
Which yet join not scent to hue,
Crown the pale year weak and new;
When the night is left behind
In the deep east, dun and blind,
And the blue noon is over us,
And the multitudinous
Billows murmur at our feet
Where the earth and ocean meet,
And all things seem only one
In the universal sun.

PERCY BYSSHE SHELLEY (1792–1822)

HELLAS 641

The world's great age begins anew,
  The golden years return,
The earth doth like a snake renew
  Her winter weeds outworn;
Heaven smiles, and faiths and empires gleam
Like wrecks of a dissolving dream.

A brighter Hellas rears its mountains
  From waves serener far;
A new Peneus rolls his fountains
  Against the morning star;
Where fairer Tempes bloom, there sleep
Young Cyclads on a sunnier deep.

A loftier Argo cleaves the main,
  Fraught with a later prize;
Another Orpheus sings again,
  And loves, and weeps, and dies;
A new Ulysses leaves once more
Calypso for his native shore.

O write no more the tale of Troy,
  If earth Death's scroll must be—
Nor mix with Laian rage the joy
  Which dawns upon the free,
Although a subtler Sphinx renew
Riddles of death Thebes never knew.

Another Athens shall arise,
  And to remoter time
Bequeath, like sunset to the skies,
  The splendour of its prime;
And leave, if naught so bright may live,
All earth can take or Heaven can give.

       Saturn and Love their long repose
         Shall burst, more bright and good
       Than all who fell, than One who rose,
         Than many unsubdued:
    Not gold, not blood, their altar dowers,
    But votive tears and symbol flowers.

       O cease! must hate and death return?
         Cease! must men kill and die?
       Cease! drain not to its dregs the urn
         Of bitter prophecy!
       The world is weary of the past—
       O might it die or rest at last!
                        PERCY BYSSHE SHELLEY (1792–1822)

642   TO A SKYLARK

       Hail to thee, blithe spirit!
         Bird thou never wert—
     That from heaven or near it
        Pourest thy full heart
In profuse strains of unpremeditated art.

       Higher still and higher
         From the earth thou springest,
     Like a cloud of fire;
         The blue deep thou wingest,
And singing still dost soar, and soaring ever singest.

       In the golden light'ning
         Of the sunken sun,
     O'er which clouds are bright'ning,
        Thou dost float and run,
Like an unbodied joy whose race is just begun.

       The pale purple even
         Melts around thy flight;
     Like a star of heaven,
        In the broad daylight
Thou art unseen, but yet I hear thy shrill delight—

       Keen as are the arrows
         Of that silver sphere
     Whose intense lamp narrows
        In the white dawn clear,
Until we hardly see, we feel that it is there.

       All the earth and air
         With thy voice is loud,
     As when night is bare,
        From one lonely cloud
The moon rains out her beams, and heaven is overflow'd.

What thou art we know not;
   What is most like thee?
From rainbow clouds there flow not
   Drops so bright to see,
As from thy presence showers a rain of melody:—

   Like a poet hidden
     In the light of thought,
   Singing hymns unbidden,
     Till the world is wrought
To sympathy with hopes and fears it heeded not:

   Like a high-born maiden
     In a palace tower,
   Soothing her love-laden
     Soul in secret hour
With music sweet as love, which overflows her bower:

   Like a glow-worm golden
     In a dell of dew,
   Scattering unbeholden
     Its aërial hue
Among the flowers and grass which screen it from the view:

   Like a rose embower'd
     In its own green leaves,
   By warm winds deflower'd,
     Till the scent it gives
Makes faint with too much sweet those heavy-winged thieves.

   Sound of vernal showers
     On the twinkling grass,
   Rain-awaken'd flowers—
     All that ever was
Joyous and clear and fresh—thy music doth surpass.

   Teach us, sprite or bird,
     What sweet thoughts are thine:
   I have never heard
     Praise of love or wine
That panted forth a flood of rapture so divine.

   Chorus hymeneal,
     Or triumphal chant,
   Match'd with thine would be all
     But an empty vaunt—
A thin wherein we feel there is some hidden want.

   What objects are the fountains
     Of thy happy strain?
   What fields, or waves, or mountains?
     What shapes of sky or plain?
What love of thine own kind? what ignorance of pain?

With thy clear keen joyance
   Languor cannot be:
Shadow of annoyance
   Never came near thee:
Thou lovest, but ne'er knew love's sad satiety.

Waking or asleep,
   Thou of death must deem
Things more true and deep
   Than we mortals dream,
Or how could thy notes flow in such a crystal stream?

We look before and after,
   And pine for what is not:
Our sincerest laughter
   With some pain is fraught;
Our sweetest songs are those that tell of saddest thought.

Yet, if we could scorn
   Hate and pride and fear,
If we were things born
   Not to shed a tear,
I know not how thy joy we ever should come near.

Better than all measures
   Of delightful sound,
Better than all treasures
   That in books are found,
Thy skill to poet were, thou scorner of the ground!

Teach me half the gladness
   That thy brain must know;
Such harmonious madness
   From my lips would flow,
The world should listen then, as I am listening now.

              PERCY BYSSHE SHELLEY (1792–1822)

THE MOON

I

And, like a dying lady lean and pale,
Who totters forth, wrapp'd in a gauzy veil,
Out of her chamber, led by the insane
And feeble wanderings of her fading brain,
The moon arose up in the murky east,
A white and shapeless mass.

II

Art thou pale for weariness
Of climbing heaven and gazing on the earth,
   Wandering companionless
Among the stars that have a different birth,
And ever changing, like a joyless eye
That finds no object worth its constancy?

              PERCY BYSSHE SHELLEY (1792–1822)

ODE TO THE WEST WIND

I

O wild West Wind, thou breath of Autumn's being
   Thou from whose unseen presence the leaves dead
Are driven like ghosts from an enchanter fleeing,

   Yellow, and black, and pale, and hectic red,
Pestilence-stricken multitudes! O thou
   Who chariotest to their dark wintry bed

The winged seeds, where they lie cold and low,
   Each like a corpse within its grave, until
Thine azure sister of the Spring shall blow

   Her clarion o'er the dreaming earth, and fill
(Driving sweet buds like flocks to feed in air)
   With living hues and odours plain and hill;

Wild Spirit, which art moving everywhere;
Destroyer and preserver; hear, O hear!

II

Thou on whose stream, 'mid the steep sky's commotion,
   Loose clouds like earth's decaying leaves are shed,
Shook from the tangled boughs of heaven and ocean,

   Angels of rain and lightning! there are spread
On the blue surface of thine airy surge,
   Like the bright hair uplifted from the head

Of some fierce Maenad, even from the dim verge
   Of the horizon to the zenith's height,
The locks of the approaching storm. Thou dirge

   Of the dying year, to which this closing night
Will be the dome of a vast sepulchre,
   Vaulted with all thy congregated might

Of vapours, from whose solid atmosphere
Black rain, and fire, and hail, will burst: O hear!

III

Thou who didst waken from his summer dreams
   The blue Mediterranean, where he lay,
Lull'd by the coil of his crystalline streams,

   Beside a pumice isle in Baiae's bay,
And saw in sleep old palaces and towers
   Quivering within the wave's intenser day,

All overgrown with azure moss, and flowers
   So sweet, the sense faints picturing them! Thou
For whose path the Atlantic's level powers

  Cleave themselves into chasms, while far below
 The sea-blooms and the oozy woods which wear
  The sapless foliage of the ocean, know

Thy voice, and suddenly grow gray with fear,
And tremble and despoil themselves: O hear!

IV

If I were a dead leaf thou mightest bear;
 If I were a swift cloud to fly with thee;
A wave to pant beneath thy power, and share

 The impulse of thy strength, only less free
Than thou, O uncontrollable! if even
 I were as in my boyhood, and could be

The comrade of thy wanderings over heaven,
 As then, when to outstrip thy skiey speed
Scarce seem'd a vision—I would ne'er have striven

 As thus with thee in prayer in my sore need.
O! lift me as a wave, a leaf, a cloud!
 I fall upon the thorns of life! I bleed!

A heavy weight of hours has chain'd and bow'd
One too like thee—tameless, and swift, and proud.

V

Make me thy lyre, even as the forest is:
 What if my leaves are falling like its own?
The tumult of thy mighty harmonies

 Will take from both a deep autumnal tone,
Sweet though in sadness. Be thou, Spirit fierce,
 My spirit! Be thou me, impetuous one!

Drive my dead thoughts over the universe,
 Like wither'd leaves, to quicken a new birth;
And, by the incantation of this verse,

 Scatter, as from an unextinguish'd hearth
Ashes and sparks, my words among mankind!
 Be through my lips to unawaken'd earth

The trumpet of a prophecy! O Wind,
If Winter comes, can Spring be far behind?
Percy Bysshe Shelley (1792–1822)

645   THE INDIAN SERENADE

I arise from dreams of thee
 In the first sweet sleep of night,
When the winds are breathing low,
 And the stars are shining bright.

I arise from dreams of thee,
    And a spirit in my feet
Hath led me—who knows how?
    To thy chamber window, Sweet!

The wandering airs they faint
    On the dark, the silent stream—
And the champak's odours [pine]
    Like sweet thoughts in a dream;
The nightingale's complaint,
    It dies upon her heart,
As I must on thine,
    O belovèd as thou art!

O lift me from the grass!
    I die! I faint! I fail!
Let thy love in kisses rain
    On my lips and eyelids pale.
My cheek is cold and white, alas!
    My heart beats loud and fast:
O press it to thine own again,
    Where it will break at last!

                  PERCY BYSSHE SHELLEY (1792–1822)

NIGHT

Swiftly walk o'er the western wave,
    Spirit of Night!
Out of the misty eastern cave,—
Where, all the long and lone daylight,
Thou wovest dreams of joy and fear
Which make thee terrible and dear,—
    Swift be thy flight!

Wrap thy form in a mantle grey,
    Star-inwrought!
Blind with thine hair the eyes of Day;
Kiss her until she be wearied out.
Then wander o'er city and sea and land,
Touching all with thine opiate wand—
    Come, long-sought!

When I arose and saw the dawn,
    I sigh'd for thee;
When light rode high, and the dew was gone,
And noon lay heavy on flower and tree,
And the weary Day turn'd to his rest,
Lingering like an unloved guest,
    I sigh'd for thee.

    Thy brother Death came, and cried,
        "Wouldst thou me?"
    Thy sweet child Sleep, the filmy-eyed,
    Murmur'd like a noontide bee,
   "Shall I nestle near thy side?
    Wouldst thou me?"—And I replied,
        "No, not thee!"

    Death will come when thou art dead,
        Soon, too soon—
    Sleep will come when thou art fled.
    Of neither would I ask the boon
   I ask of thee, belovèd Night—
    Swift be thine approaching flight,
        Come soon, soon!
              PERCY BYSSHE SHELLEY (1792–1822)

647
FROM THE ARABIC
AN IMITATION

My faint spirit was sitting in the light
    Of thy looks, my love;
  It panted for thee like the hind at noon
    For the brooks, my love.
Thy barb, whose hoofs outspeed the tempest's flight,
    Bore thee far from me;
My heart, for my weak feet were weary soon,
    Did companion thee.

Ah! fleeter far than fleetest storm or steed,
    Or the death they bear,
The heart which tender thought clothes like a dove
    With the wings of care;
In the battle, in the darkness, in the need,
    Shall mine cling to thee,
Nor claim one smile for all the comfort, love,
    It may bring to thee.
        PERCY BYSSHE SHELLEY (1792–1822)

648
LINES

   When the lamp is shatter'd,
  The light in the dust lies dead;
   When the cloud is scatter'd,
  The rainbow's glory is shed;
   When the lute is broken,
  Sweet tones are remember'd not
   When the lips have spoken,
  Loved accents are soon forgot.

   As music and splendour
  Survive not the lamp and the lute,
   The heart's echoes render
  No song when the spirit is mute—

No song but sad dirges,
Like the wind through a ruin'd cell,
  Or the mournful surges
That ring the dead seaman's knell.

When hearts have once mingled,
Love first leaves the well-built nest;
  The weak one is singled
To endure what it once possest.
  O Love, who bewailest
The frailty of all things here,
  Why choose you the frailest
For your cradle, your home, and your bier?

Its passions will rock thee,
As the storms rock the ravens on high:
  Bright reason will mock thee,
Like the sun from a wintry sky.
  From thy nest every rafter
Will rot, and thine eagle home
  Leave thee naked to laughter,
When leaves fall and cold winds come.

Percy Bysshe Shelley (1792–1822)

To —   649

One word is too often profaned
  For me to profane it;
One feeling too falsely disdain'd
  For thee to disdain it;
One hope is too like despair
  For prudence to smother;
And pity from thee more dear
  Than that from another.

I can give not what men call love:
  But wilt thou accept not
The worship the heart lifts above
  And the heavens reject not,
The desire of the moth for the star,
  Of the night for the morrow,
The devotion to something afar
  From the sphere of our sorrow?

Percy Bysshe Shelley (1792–1822)

The Question   650

I dream'd that, as I wander'd by the way,
  Bare Winter suddenly was changed to Spring;
And gentle odours led my steps astray,
  Mix'd with a sound of waters murmuring
Along a shelving bank of turf, which lay
  Under a copse, and hardly dared to fling
Its green arms round the bosom of the stream,
But kiss'd it and then fled, as thou mightest in dream.

There grew pied wind-flowers and violets;
   Daisies, those pearl'd Arcturi of the earth,
The constellated flower that never sets;
   Faint oxlips; tender bluebells, at whose birth
The sod scarce heaved; and that tall flower that wets—
   Like a child, half in tenderness and mirth—
Its mother's face with heaven-collected tears
When the low wind, its playmate's voice, it hears.

And in the warm hedge grew lush eglantine,
   Green cowbind and the moonlight-colour'd May,
And cherry-blossoms, and white cups whose wine
   Was the bright dew yet drain'd not by the day;
And wild roses, and ivy serpentine,
   With its dark buds and leaves wandering astray;
And flowers, azure, black, and streak'd with gold,
Fairer than any waken'd eyes behold.

And nearer to the river's trembling edge
   There grew broad flag-flowers, purple prank'd with white,
And starry river-buds among the sedge,
   And floating water-lilies, broad and bright,
Which lit the oak that overhung the hedge
   With moonlight beams of their own watery light;
And bulrushes, and reeds of such deep green
As soothed the dazzled eye with sober sheen.

Methought that of these visionary flowers
   I made a nosegay, bound in such a way
That the same hues which in their natural bowers
   Were mingled or opposed, the like array
Kept these imprison'd children of the Hours
   Within my hand;—and then, elate and gay,
I hasten'd to the spot whence I had come,
That I might there present it—O! to whom?
                         PERCY BYSSHE SHELLEY (1792–1822)

651   REMORSE

Away! the moor is dark beneath the moon,
   Rapid clouds have drunk the last pale beam of even:
Away! the gathering winds will call the darkness soon,
   And profoundest midnight shroud the serene lights of heaven.
Pause not! the time is past! Every voice cries, "Away!"
   Tempt not with one last tear thy friend's ungentle mood:
Thy lover's eye, so glazed and cold, dares not entreat thy stay:
   Duty and dereliction guide thee back to solitude.

Away, away! to thy sad and silent home;
   Pour bitter tears on its desolated hearth;
Watch the dim shades as like ghosts they go and come,
   And complicate strange webs of melancholy mirth.

The leaves of wasted autumn woods shall float around thine head,
   The blooms of dewy Spring shall gleam beneath thy feet:
But thy soul or this world must fade in the frost that binds the dead,
   Ere midnight's frown and morning's smile, ere thou and peace, may meet.

The cloud shadows of midnight possess their own repose,
   For the weary winds are silent, or the moon is in the deep;
Some respite to its turbulence unresting ocean knows;
   Whatever moves or toils or grieves hath its appointed sleep.
Thou in the grave shalt rest:—yet, till the phantoms flee,
   Which that house and heath and garden made dear to thee erewhile,
Thy remembrance and repentance and deep musings are not free
   From the music of two voices, and the light of one sweet smile.
                      PERCY BYSSHE SHELLEY (1792–1822)

MUSIC, WHEN SOFT VOICES DIE   652

Music, when soft voices die,
Vibrates in the memory;
Odours, when sweet violets sicken,
Live within the sense they quicken.

Rose leaves, when the rose is dead,
Are heap'd for the belovèd's bed;
And so thy thoughts, when thou art gone,
Love itself shall slumber on.
          PERCY BYSSHE SHELLEY (1792–1822)

WILLIE AND HELEN   653

"Wharefore sou'd ye talk o' love,
   Unless it be to pain us?
Wharefore sou'd ye talk o' love
   Whan ye say the sea maun twain us?"

"It's no because my love is light,
   Nor for your angry deddy;
It's a' to buy ye pearlins bright,
   An' to busk ye like a leddy."

"O Willy, I can caird an' spin,
   Se ne'er can want for cleedin';
An' gin I hae my Willy's heart,
   I hae a' the pearls I'm heedin'.

"Will it be time to praise this cheek
   Whan years an' tears has blench'd it?
Will it be time to talk o' love
   Whan cauld an' care has quench'd it?"

He's laid ae han' about her waist—
   The ither's held to heaven;
An' his luik was like the luik o' man
   Wha's heart in twa is riven.
              HEW AINSLIE (1792–1878)

cleedin': *clothing*

654 BURIAL OF THE DEAD

I thought to meet no more, so dreary seem'd
Death's interposing veil, and thou so pure,
    Thy place in Paradise
    Beyond where I could soar;

Friend of this worthless heart! but happier thoughts
Spring like unbidden violets from the sod,
    Where patiently thou tak'st
    Thy sweet and sure repose.

The shadows fall more soothing: the soft air
Is full of cheering whispers like thine own;
    While Memory, by thy grave,
    Lives o'er thy funeral day;

The deep knell dying down, the mourners' pause,
Waiting their Saviour's welcome at the gate.—
    Sure with the words of Heaven
    Thy spirit met us there,

And sought with us along th' accustom'd way
The hallow'd porch, and entering in, beheld
    The pageant of sad joy
    So dear to Faith and Hope.

O! hadst thou brought a strain from Paradise
To cheer us, happy soul, thou hadst not touch'd
    The sacred springs of grief
    More tenderly and true,

Than those deep-warbled anthems, high and low,
Low as the grave, high as th' Eternal Throne,
    Guiding through light and gloom
    Our mourning fancies wild,

Till gently, like soft golden clouds at eve
Around the western twilight, all subside
    Into a placid faith,
    That even with beaming eye

Counts thy sad honours, coffin, bier, and pall;
So many relics of a frail love lost,
    So many tokens dear
    Of endless love begun.

Listen! it is no dream: th' Apostles' trump
Gives earnest of th' Archangel's;—calmly now,
    Our hearts yet beating high
    To that victorious lay

(Most like a warrior's, to the martial dirge
Of a true comrade), in the grave we trust
    Our treasure for awhile:
    And if a tear steal down,

If human anguish o'er the shaded brow
Pass shuddering, when the handful of pure earth
    Touches the coffin-lid;
    If at our brother's name,

Once and again the thought, "for ever gone,"
Come o'er us like a cloud; yet, gentle spright,
    Thou turnest not away,
    Thou know'st us calm at heart.

One look, and we have seen our last of thee,
Till we too sleep and our long sleep be o'er.
    O cleanse us, ere we view
    That countenance pure again,

Thou, who canst change the heart, and raise the dead!
As Thou art by to soothe our parting hour,
    Be ready when we meet,
    With Thy dear pardoning words.
                         JOHN KEBLE (1792–1866)

WRITTEN IN NORTHAMPTON COUNTY ASYLUM   655

I am! yet what I am who cares, or knows?
  My friends forsake me like a memory lost.
I am the self-consumer of my woes;
  They rise and vanish, an oblivious host,
Shadows of life, whose very soul is lost.
And yet I am—I live—though I am toss'd

Into the nothingness of scorn and noise,
  Into the living sea of waking dream,
Where there is neither sense of life, nor joys,
  But the huge shipwreck of my own esteem
And all that's dear. Even those I loved the best
Are strange—nay, they are stranger than the rest.

I long for scenes where man has never trod—
  For scenes where woman never smiled or wept—
There to abide with my Creator, God,
  And sleep as I in childhood sweetly slept,
Full of high thoughts, unborn. So let me lie,—
The grass below; above, the vaulted sky.
                         JOHN CLARE (1793–1864)

DIRGE   656

Calm on the bosom of thy God,
  Fair spirit, rest thee now!
E'en while with ours thy footsteps trod,
  His seal was on thy brow.

Dust, to its narrow house beneath!
  Soul, to its place on high!
They that have seen thy look in death
  No more may fear to die.
                    FELICIA DOROTHEA HEMANS (1793–1835)

657   ODE TO A NIGHTINGALE
My heart aches, and a drowsy numbness pains
  My sense, as though of hemlock I had drunk,
Or emptied some dull opiate to the drains
  One minute past, and Lethe-wards had sunk:
'Tis not through envy of thy happy lot,
  But being too happy in thine happiness,
    That thou, light-wingèd Dryad of the trees,
      In some melodious plot
  Of beechen green, and shadows numberless,
    Singest of summer in full-throated ease.

O for a draught of vintage! that hath been
  Cool'd a long age in the deep-delvèd earth,
Tasting of Flora and the country-green,
  Dance, and Provençal song, and sunburnt mirth!
O for a beaker full of the warm South!
  Full of the true, the blushful Hippocrene,
    With beaded bubbles winking at the brim,
      And purple-stainèd mouth;
  That I might drink, and leave the world unseen,
    And with thee fade away into the forest dim:

Fade far away, dissolve, and quite forget
  What thou among the leaves hast never known,
The weariness, the fever, and the fret
  Here, where men sit and hear each other groan;
Where palsy shakes a few, sad, last grey hairs,
  Where youth grows pale, and spectre-thin, and dies;
    Where but to think is to be full of sorrow
      And leaden-eyed despairs;
  Where beauty cannot keep her lustrous eyes,
    Or new Love pine at them beyond to-morrow.

Away! away! for I will fly to thee,
  Not charioted by Bacchus and his pards,
But on the viewless wings of Poesy,
  Though the dull brain perplexes and retards:
Already with thee! tender is the night,
  And haply the Queen-Moon is on her throne,
    Cluster'd around by all her starry Fays
      But here there is no light,
  Save what from heaven is with the breezes blown
    Through verdurous glooms and winding mossy ways.

I cannot see what flowers are at my feet,
  Nor what soft incense hangs upon the boughs,
But, in embalmèd darkness, guess each sweet
  Wherewith the seasonable month endows

The grass, the thicket, and the fruit-tree wild;
  White hawthorn, and the pastoral eglantine;
    Fast-fading violets cover'd up in leaves;
      And mid-May's eldest child,
  The coming musk-rose, full of dewy wine,
    The murmurous haunt of flies on summer eves.

Darkling I listen; and, for many a time
  I have been half in love with easeful Death,
Call'd him soft names in many a musèd rhyme,
  To take into the air my quiet breath;
Now more than ever seems it rich to die,
  To cease upon the midnight with no pain,
    While thou art pouring forth thy soul abroad
      In such an ecstasy!
  Still wouldst thou sing, and I have ears in vain—
    To thy high requiem become a sod.

Thou wast not born for death, immortal Bird!
  No hungry generations tread thee down;
The voice I hear this passing night was heard
  In ancient days by emperor and clown:
Perhaps the self-same song that found a path
  Through the sad heart of Ruth, when, sick for home,
    She stood in tears amid the alien corn;
      The same that ofttimes hath
  Charm'd magic casements, opening on the foam
    Of perilous seas, in faery lands forlorn.

Forlorn! the very word is like a bell
  To toll me back from thee to my sole self!
Adieu! the fancy cannot cheat so well
  As she is famed to do, deceiving elf.
Adieu! adieu! thy plaintive anthem fades
  Past the near meadows, over the still stream,
    Up the hill-side; and now 'tis buried deep
      In the next valley-glades:
  Was it a vision, or a waking dream?
    Fled is that music:—do I wake or sleep?
                              JOHN KEATS (1795–1821)

ODE ON A GRECIAN URN 658
Thou still unravish'd bride of quietness,
  Thou foster-child of Silence and slow Time,
Sylvan historian, who canst thus express
  A flowery tale more sweetly than our rhyme:
What leaf-fringed legend haunts about thy shape
  Of deities or mortals, or of both,
    In Tempe or the dales of Arcady?
  What men or gods are these? What maidens loth?
  What mad pursuit? What struggle to escape?
    What pipes and timbrels? What wild ecstasy?

Heard melodies are sweet, but those unheard
  Are sweeter; therefore, ye soft pipes, play on;
Not to the sensual ear, but, more endear'd,
  Pipe to the spirit ditties of no tone:
Fair youth, beneath the trees, thou canst not leave
  Thy song, nor ever can those trees be bare;
    Bold Lover, never, never canst thou kiss,
Though winning near the goal—yet, do not grieve;
    She cannot fade, though thou hast not thy bliss,
  For ever wilt thou love, and she be fair!

Ah, happy, happy boughs! that cannot shed
  Your leaves, nor ever bid the Spring adieu;
And, happy melodist, unwearièd,
  For ever piping songs for ever new;
More happy love! more happy, happy love!
  For ever warm and still to be enjoy'd,
    For ever panting, and for ever young;
All breathing human passion far above,
    That leaves a heart high-sorrowful and cloy'd,
  A burning forehead, and a parching tongue.

Who are these coming to the sacrifice?
  To what green altar, O mysterious priest,
Lead'st thou that heifer lowing at the skies,
  And all her silken flanks with garlands drest?
What little town by river or sea-shore,
  Or mountain-built with peaceful citadel,
    Is emptied of its folk, this pious morn?
And, little town, thy streets for evermore
  Will silent be; and not a soul, to tell
    Why thou art desolate, can e'er return.

O Attic shape! fair attitude! with brede
  Of marble men and maidens overwrought,
With forest branches and the trodden weed;
  Thou, silent form! dost tease us out of thought
As doth eternity: Cold Pastoral!
  When old age shall this generation waste,
    Thou shalt remain, in midst of other woe
Than ours, a friend to man, to whom thou say'st,
  "Beauty is truth, truth beauty,—that is all
    Ye know on earth, and all ye need to know."
JOHN KEATS (1795–1821)

659   TO AUTUMN

Season of mists and mellow fruitfulness!
  Close bosom-friend of the maturing sun;
Conspiring with him how to load and bless
  With fruit the vines that round the thatch-eaves run;
To bend with apples the moss'd cottage-trees,
  And fill all fruit with ripeness to the core;
    To swell the gourd, and plump the hazel shells
With a sweet kernel; to set budding more,

And still more, later flowers for the bees,
Until they think warm days will never cease,
   For Summer has o'er-brimm'd their clammy cells.

Who hath not seen thee oft amid thy store?
   Sometimes whoever seeks abroad may find
Thee sitting careless on a granary floor,
   Thy hair soft-lifted by the winnowing wind;
Or on a half-reap'd furrow sound asleep,
   Drowsed with the fume of poppies, while thy hook
     Spares the next swath and all its twinèd flowers;
And sometimes like a gleaner thou dost keep
   Steady thy laden head across a brook;
   Or by a cider-press, with patient look,
     Thou watchest the last oozings hours by hours.

Where are the songs of Spring? Ay, where are they?
   Think not of them, thou hast thy music too,—
While barrèd clouds bloom the soft-dying day,
   And touch the stubble-plains with rosy hue;
Then in a wailful choir the small gnats mourn
   Among the river sallows, borne aloft
     Or sinking as the light wind lives or dies;
And full-grown lambs loud bleat from hilly bourn;
   Hedge-crickets sing; and now with treble soft
   The redbreast whistles from a garden-croft;
     And gathering swallows twitter in the skies.

JOHN KEATS (1795–1821)

ODE ON MELANCHOLY   660

No, no! go not to Lethe, neither twist
   Wolf's-bane, tight-rooted, for its poisonous wine;
Nor suffer thy pale forehead to be kist
   By nightshade, ruby grape of Proserpine;
Make not your rosary of yew-berries,
   Nor let the beetle, nor the death-moth be
     Your mournful Psyche, nor the downy owl
A partner in your sorrow's mysteries;
   For shade to shade will come too drowsily,
     And drown the wakeful anguish of the soul.

But when the melancholy fit shall fall
   Sudden from heaven like a weeping cloud,
That fosters the droop-headed flowers all,
   And hides the green hill in an April shroud;
Then glut thy sorrow on a morning rose,
   Or on the rainbow of the salt sand-wave,
     Or on the wealth of globed peonies;
Or if thy mistress some rich anger shows,
   Emprison her soft hand, and let her rave,
     And feed deep, deep upon her peerless eyes.

She dwells with Beauty—Beauty that must die;
    And Joy, whose hand is ever at his lips
  Bidding adieu; and aching Pleasure nigh,
    Turning to poison while the bee-mouth sips:
  Ay, in the very temple of Delight
    Veil'd Melancholy has her sovran shrine,
      Though seen of none save him whose strenuous tongue
  Can burst Joy's grape against his palate fine;
    His soul shall taste the sadness of her might,
      And be among her cloudy trophies hung.
JOHN KEATS (1795–1821)

661   FRAGMENT OF AN ODE TO MAIA
(WRITTEN ON MAY-DAY, 1818)

  Mother of Hermes! and still youthful Maia!
    May I sing to thee
  As thou wast hymned on the shores of Baiae?
    Or may I woo thee
  In earlier Sicilian? or thy smiles
  Seek as they once were sought, in Grecian isles,
  By bards who died content on pleasant sward,
    Leaving great verse unto a little clan?
  O give me their old vigour! and unheard
    Save of the quiet primrose, and the span
      Of heaven, and few ears,
  Rounded by thee, my song should die away
        Content as theirs,
  Rich in the simple worship of a day.
JOHN KEATS (1795–1821)

662   BARDS OF PASSION AND OF MIRTH

  Bards of Passion and of Mirth,
  Ye have left your souls on earth!
  Have ye souls in heaven too,
  Doubled-lived in regions new?
  Yes, and those of heaven commune
  With the spheres of sun and moon;
  With the noise of fountains wondrous,
  And the parle of voices thund'rous;
  With the whisper of heaven's trees
  And one another, in soft ease
  Seated on Elysian lawns
  Browsed by none but Dian's fawns;
  Underneath large blue-bells tented,
  Where the daisies are rose-scented,
  And the rose herself has got
  Perfume which on earth is not;
  Where the nightingale doth sing
  Not a senseless, trancèd thing,
  But divine melodious truth;
  Philosophic numbers smooth;
  Tales and golden histories
  Of heaven and its mysteries.

    Thus ye live on high, and then
On the earth ye live again;
And the souls ye left behind you
Teach us, here, the way to find you,
Where your other souls are joying,
Never slumber'd, never cloying.
Here, your earth-born souls still speak
To mortals, of their little week;
Of their sorrows and delights;
Of their passions and their spites;
Of their glory and their shame;
What doth strengthen and what maim.
Thus ye teach us, every day,
Wisdom, though fled far away.

    Bards of Passion and of Mirth,
Ye have left your souls on earth!
Ye have souls in heaven too,
Double-lived in regions new!
JOHN KEATS (1795–1821)

FANCY 663

Ever let the Fancy roam,
Pleasure never is at home:
At a touch sweet Pleasure melteth,
Like to bubbles when rain pelteth;
Then let wingèd Fancy wander
Through the thought still spread beyond her:
Open wide the mind's cage-door,
She'll dart forth, and cloudward soar.
O sweet Fancy! let her loose;
Summer's joys are spoilt by use,
And the enjoying of the Spring
Fades as does its blossoming;
Autumn's red-lipp'd fruitage too,
Blushing through the mist and dew,
Cloys with tasting: What do then?
Sit thee by the ingle, when
The sear faggot blazes bright,
Spirit of a winter's night;
When the soundless earth is muffled,
And the cakèd snow is shuffled
From the ploughboy's heavy shoon;
When the Night doth meet the Noon
In a dark conspiracy
To banish Even from her sky.
Sit thee there, and send abroad,
With a mind self-overawed,
Fancy, high-commission'd:—send her!
She has vassals to attend her:

She will bring, in spite of frost,
Beauties that the earth hath lost;
She will bring thee, all together,
All delights of summer weather;
All the buds and bells of May,
From dewy sward or thorny spray;
All the heapèd Autumn's wealth,
With a still, mysterious stealth:
She will mix these pleasures up
Like three fit wines in a cup,
And thou shalt quaff it:—thou shalt hear
Distant harvest-carols clear;
Rustle of the reapèd corn;
Sweet birds antheming the morn:
And, in the same moment—hark!
'Tis the early April lark,
Or the rooks, with busy caw,
Foraging for sticks and straw.
Thou shalt, at one glance, behold
The daisy and the marigold;
White-plumed lilies, and the first
Hedge-grown primrose that hath burst;
Shaded hyacinth, alway
Sapphire queen of the mid-May;
And every leaf, and every flower
Pearled with the self-same shower.
Thou shalt see the fieldmouse peep
Meagre from its cellèd sleep;
And the snake all winter-thin
Cast on sunny bank its skin;
Freckled nest-eggs thou shalt see
Hatching in the hawthorn-tree,
When the hen-bird's wing doth rest
Quiet on her mossy nest;
Then the hurry and alarm
When the beehive casts its swarm;
Acorns ripe down-pattering
While the autumn breezes sing.

O sweet Fancy! let her loose;
Every thing is spoilt by use:
Where's the cheek that doth not fade,
Too much gazed at? Where's the maid
Whose lip mature is ever new?
Where's the eye, however blue,
Doth not weary? Where's the face
One would meet in every place?
Where's the voice, however soft,
One would hear so very oft?
At a touch sweet Pleasure melteth
Like to bubbles when rain pelteth.

Let, then, wingèd Fancy find
Thee a mistress to thy mind:
Dulcet-eyed as Ceres' daughter,
Ere the God of Torment taught her
How to frown and how to chide;
With a waist and with a side
White as Hebe's, when her zone
Slipt its golden clasp, and down
Fell her kirtle to her feet,
While she held the goblet sweet,
And Jove grew languid.—Break the mesh
Of the Fancy's silken leash;
Quickly break her prison-string,
And such joys as these she'll bring.—
Let the wingèd Fancy roam,
Pleasure never is at home.

JOHN KEATS (1795–1821)

STANZAS 664

In a drear-nighted December,
  Too happy, happy tree,
Thy branches ne'er remember
  Their green felicity:
The north cannot undo them,
With a sleety whistle through them;
Nor frozen thawings glue them
  From budding at the prime.

In a drear-nighted December,
  Too happy, happy brook,
Thy bubblings ne'er remember
  Apollo's summer look;
But with a sweet forgetting,
They stay their crystal fretting,
Never, never petting
  About the frozen time.

Ah! would 'twere so with many
  A gentle girl and boy!
But were there ever any
  Writhed not at passèd joy?
To know the change and feel it,
When there is none to heal it,
Nor numbèd sense to steal it,
  Was never said in rhyme.

JOHN KEATS (1795–1821)

LAS BELLE DAME SANS MERCI 665

"O what can ail thee, knight-at-arms,
  Alone and palely loitering?
The sedge is wither'd from the lake,
  And no birds sing.

"O what can ail thee, knight-at-arms,
   So haggard and so woe-begone?
The squirrel's granary is full,
   And the harvest's done.

"I see a lily on thy brow
   With anguish moist and fever dew;
And on thy cheeks a fading rose
   Fast withereth too."

"I met a lady in the meads,
   Full beautiful—a faery's child,
Her hair was long, her foot was light,
   And her eyes were wild.

"I made a garland for her head,
   And bracelets too, and fragrant zone;
She look'd at me as she did love,
   And made sweet moan.

"I set her on my pacing steed
   And nothing else saw all day long,
For sideways would she lean, and sing
   A faery's song.

"She found me roots of relish sweet,
   And honey wild and manna dew,
And sure in language strange she said,
   'I love thee true!'

"She took me to her elfin grot,
   And there she wept and sigh'd full sore;
And there I shut her wild, wild eyes
   With kisses four.

"And there she lullèd me asleep,
   And there I dream'd—Ah! woe betide!
The latest dream I ever dream'd
   On the cold hill's side.

"I saw pale kings and princes too,
   Pale warriors, death-pale were they all;
They cried—'La belle Dame sans Merci
   Hath thee in thrall!'

"I saw their starved lips in the gloam
   With horrid warning gapèd wide,
And I awoke and found me here,
   On the cold hill's side.

"And this is why I sojourn here
   Alone and palely loitering,
Though the sedge is wither'd from the lake,
   And no birds sing."

JOHN KEATS (1795–1821)

On First Looking into Chapman's Homer 666

Much have I travell'd in the realms of gold,
  And many goodly states and kingdoms seen;
  Round many western islands have I been
Which bards in fealty to Apollo hold.
Oft of one wide expanse had I been told
  That deep-brow'd Homer ruled as his demesne:
  Yet did I never breathe its pure serene
Till I heard Chapman speak out loud and bold:
Then felt I like some watcher of the skies
  When a new planet swims into his ken;
Or like stout Cortez, when with eagle eyes
  He stared at the Pacific—and all his men
Look'd at each other with a wild surmise—
  Silent, upon a peak in Darien.
JOHN KEATS (1795–1821)

When I have Fears that I may Cease to Be 667

When I have fears that I may cease to be
  Before my pen has glean'd my teeming brain,
  Before high-pilèd books, in charact'ry,
  Hold like rich garners the full-ripen'd grain;
When I behold, upon the night's starr'd face,
  Huge cloudy symbols of a high romance,
  And feel that I may never live to trace
  Their shadows, with the magic hand of chance;
And when I feel, fair creature of an hour!
  That I shall never look upon thee more,
  Never have relish in the faery power
Of unreflecting love;—then on the shore
  Of the wide world I stand alone, and think,
  Till Love and Fame to nothingness do sink.
JOHN KEATS (1795–1821)

To Sleep 668

O soft embalmer of the still midnight!
  Shutting with careful fingers and benign
Our gloom-pleased eyes, embower'd from the light,
  Enshaded in forgetfulness divine;
O soothest Sleep! if so it please thee, close,
  In midst of this thine hymn, my willing eyes,
Or wait the amen, ere thy poppy throws
  Around my bed its lulling charities;
  Then save me, or the passed day will shine
Upon my pillow, breeding many woes;
Save me from curious conscience, that still lords
  Its strength for darkness, burrowing like a mole;
Turn the key deftly in the oiled wards,
  And seal the hushed casket of my soul.
JOHN KEATS (1795–1821)

669   Last Sonnet

Bright Star, would I were steadfast as thou art—
Not in lone splendour hung aloft the night,
And watching, with eternal lids apart,
Like Nature's patient sleepless Eremite,

The moving waters at their priest-like task
Of pure ablution round earth's human shores,
Or gazing on the new soft-fallen mask
Of snow upon the mountains and the moors—

No—yet still steadfast, still unchangeable,
Pillow'd upon my fair love's ripening breast,
To feel for ever its soft fall and swell,
Awake for ever in a sweet unrest,

  Still, still to hear her tender-taken breath,
  And so live ever—or else swoon to death.
JOHN KEATS (1795–1821)

670   The Outlaw of Loch Lene
From the Irish

O many a day have I made good ale in the glen,
That came not of stream or malt, like the brewing of men:
My bed was the ground; my roof, the green-wood above;
And the wealth that I sought, one far kind glance from my Love.

Alas! on that night when the horses I drove from the field,
That I was not near from terror my angel to shield!
She stretch'd forth her arms; her mantle she flung to the wind,
And swam o'er Loch Lene, her outlaw'd lover to find.

O would that a freezing sleet-wing'd tempest did sweep,
And I and my love were alone, far off on the deep;
I'd ask not a ship, or a bark, or a pinnace, to save—
With her hand round my waist, I'd fear not the wind or the wave.

'Tis down by the lake where the wild tree fringes its sides,
The maid of my heart, my fair one of Heaven resides:
I think, as at eve she wanders its mazes among,
The birds go to sleep by the sweet wild twist of her song.
JEREMIAH JOSEPH CALLANAN (1795–1839)

671   Too Solemn for Day, Too Sweet for Night

Too solemn for day, too sweet for night,
  Come not in darkness, come not in light;
But come in some twilight interim,
  When the gloom is soft, and the light is dim.
WILLIAM SIDNEY WALKER (1795–1846)

672   Song

Sweet in her green dell the flower of beauty slumbers,
  Lull'd by the faint breezes sighing through her hair;
Sleeps she and hears not the melancholy numbers
  Breathed to my sad lute 'mid the lonely air.

Down from the high cliffs the rivulet is teeming
  To wind round the willow banks that lure him from above:
O that in tears, from my rocky prison streaming,
  I too could glide to the bower of my love!

Ah! where the woodbines with sleepy arms have wound her,
  Opes she her eyelids at the dream of my lay,
Listening, like the dove, while the fountains echo round her,
  To her lost mate's call in the forests far away.

Come then, my bird! For the peace thou ever bearest,
  Still Heaven's messenger of comfort to me—
Come—this fond bosom, O faithfullest and fairest,
  Bleeds with its death-wound, its wound of love for thee!
                                GEORGE DARLEY (1795–1846)

To Helene 673
On a Gift-ring Carelessly Lost

I sent a ring—a little band
  Of emerald and ruby stone,
And bade it, sparkling on thy hand,
  Tell thee sweet tales of one
    Whose constant memory
    Was full of loveliness, and thee.

A shell was graven on its gold,—
  'Twas Cupid fix'd without his wings—
To Helene once it would have told
  More than was ever told by rings:
    But now all's past and gone,
    Her love is buried with that stone.

Thou shalt not see the tears that start
  From eyes by thoughts like these beguiled;
Thou shalt not know the beating heart,
  Ever a victim and a child:
    Yet Helene, love, believe
    The heart that never could deceive.

I'll hear thy voice of melody
  In the sweet whispers of the air;
I'll see the brightness of thine eye
  In the blue evening's dewy star;
    In crystal streams thy purity;
    And look on Heaven to look on thee.
                                GEORGE DARLEY (1795–1846)

The Fallen Star 674

A star is gone! a star is gone!
  There is a blank in Heaven;
One of the cherub choir has done
  His airy course this even.

He sat upon the orb of fire
  That hung for ages there,
And lent his music to the choir
  That haunts the nightly air.

But when his thousand years are pass'd,
  With a cherubic sigh
He vanish'd with his car at last,
  For even cherubs die!

Hear how his angel-brothers mourn—
  The minstrels of the spheres—
Each chiming sadly in his turn
  And dropping splendid tears.

The planetary sisters all
  Join in the fatal song,
And weep this hapless brother's fall,
  Who sang with them so long.

But deepest of the choral band
  The Lunar Spirit sings,
And with a bass-according hand
  Sweeps all her sullen strings.

From the deep chambers of the dome
  Where sleepless Uriel lies,
His rude harmonic thunders come
  Mingled with mighty sighs.

The thousand car-bourne cherubim,
  The wandering eleven,
All join to chant the dirge of him
  Who fell just now from Heaven.

GEORGE DARLEY (1795–1846)

675   THE SOLITARY-HEARTED
She was a queen of noble Nature's crowning,
A smile of hers was like an act of grace;
She had no winsome looks, no pretty frowning,
Like daily beauties of the vulgar race:
But if she smiled, a light was on her face,
A clear, cool kindliness, a lunar beam
Of peaceful radiance, silvering o'er the stream
Of human thought with unabiding glory;
Not quite a waking truth, not quite a dream,
A visitation, bright and transitory.

But she is changed,—hath felt the touch of sorrow,
No love hath she, no understanding friend;
O grief! when Heaven is forced of earth to borrow
What the poor niggard earth has not to lend;

But when the stalk is snapt, the rose must bend.
The tallest flower that skyward rears its head
Grows from the common ground, and there must shed
Its delicate petals. Cruel fate, too surely,
That they should find so base a bridal bed,
Who lived in virgin pride, so sweet and purely.

She had a brother, and a tender father,
And she was loved, but not as others are
From whom we ask return of love,—but rather
As one might love a dream; a phantom fair
Of something exquisitely strange and rare,
Which all were glad to look on, men and maids,
Yet no one claim'd—as oft, in dewy glades,
The peering primrose, like a sudden gladness,
Gleams on the soul, yet unregarded fades;—
The joy is ours, but all its own the sadness.

'Tis vain to say—her worst of grief is only
The common lot, which all the world have known;
To her 'tis more, because her heart is lonely,
And yet she hath no strength to stand alone,—
Once she had playmates, fancies of her own,
And she did love them. They are past away
As Fairies vanish at the break of day;
And like a spectre of an age departed,
Or unsphered Angel wofully astray,
She glides along—the solitary-hearted.
HARTLEY COLERIDGE (1796–1849)

Song 676

She is not fair to outward view
As many maidens be,
Her loveliness I never knew
  Until she smiled on me;
O, then I saw her eye was bright,
A well of love, a spring of light!

But now her looks are coy and cold,
To mine they ne'er reply,
And yet I cease not to behold
  The love-light in her eye:
Her very frowns are fairer far
Than smiles of other maidens are.
HARTLEY COLERIDGE (1796–1849)

Early Death 677

She pass'd away like morning dew
  Before the sun was high;
So brief her time, she scarcely knew
  The meaning of a sigh.

As round the rose its soft perfume,
  Sweet love around her floated;
Admired she grew—while mortal doom
  Crept on, unfear'd, unnoted.

Love was her guardian Angel here,
  But Love to Death resign'd her;
Tho' Love was kind, why should we fear
  But holy Death is kinder?
HARTLEY COLERIDGE (1796–1849)

678   FRIENDSHIP

When we were idlers with the loitering rills,
The need of human love we little noted:
  Our love was nature; and the peace that floated
On the white mist, and dwelt upon the hills,
To sweet accord subdued our wayward wills:
  One soul was ours, one mind, one heart devoted,
  That, wisely doting, ask'd not why it doted,
And ours the unknown joy, which knowing kills.
But now I find how dear thou wert to me;
  That man is more than half of nature's treasure,
Of that fair beauty which no eye can see,
  Of that sweet music which no ear can measure;
  And now the streams may sing for others' pleasure,
The hills sleep on in their eternity.
HARTLEY COLERIDGE (1796–1849)

679   AUTUMN

I saw old Autumn in the misty morn
Stand shadowless like Silence, listening
To silence, for no lonely bird would sing
Into his hollow ear from woods forlorn,
Nor lowly hedge nor solitary thorn;—
Shaking his languid locks all dewy bright
With tangled gossamer that fell by night,
  Pearling his coronet of golden corn.

Where are the songs of Summer?—With the sun,
Oping the dusky eyelids of the south,
Till shade and silence waken up as one,
And Morning sings with a warm odorous mouth.
Where are the merry birds?—Away, away,
On panting wings through the inclement skies,
    Lest owls should prey
    Undazzled at noonday,
And tear with horny beak their lustrous eyes.

Where are the blooms of Summer?—In the west,
Blushing their last to the last sunny hours,
When the mild Eve by sudden Night is prest
Like tearful Proserpine, snatch'd from her flow'rs

    To a most gloomy breast.
Where is the pride of Summer,—the green prime,—
The many, many leaves all twinkling?—Three
On the moss'd elm; three on the naked lime
Trembling,—and one upon the old oak-tree!
    Where is the Dryad's immortality?—
Gone into mournful cypress and dark yew,
Or wearing the long gloomy Winter through
    In the smooth holly's green eternity.

The squirrel gloats on his accomplish'd hoard,
The ants have brimm'd their garners with ripe grain,
    And honey bees have stored
The sweets of Summer in their luscious cells;
The swallows all have wing'd across the main;
But here the Autumn melancholy dwells,
    And sighs her tearful spells
Amongst the sunless shadows of the plain.
    Alone, alone,
    Upon a mossy stone,
She sits and reckons up the dead and gone
With the last leaves for a love-rosary,
Whilst all the wither'd world looks drearily,
Like a dim picture of the drowned past
In the hush'd mind's mysterious far away,
Doubtful what ghostly thing will steal the last
Into that distance, gray upon the gray.

O go and sit with her, and be o'ershaded
Under the languid downfall of her hair:
She wears a coronal of flowers faded
Upon her forehead, and a face of care;—
There is enough of wither'd everywhere
To make her bower,—and enough of gloom;
There is enough of sadness to invite,
If only for the rose that died, whose doom
Is Beauty's,—she that with the living bloom
Of conscious cheeks most beautifies the light:
There is enough of sorrowing, and quite
Enough of bitter fruits the earth doth bear,—
Enough of chilly droppings for her bowl;
Enough of fear and shadowy despair,
To frame her cloudy prison for the soul!
                            THOMAS HOOD (1798–1845)

SILENCE

There is a silence where hath been no sound,
There is a silence where no sound may be,
  In the cold grave—under the deep, deep sea,
Or in wide desert where no life is found,
Which hath been mute, and still must sleep profound;
  No voice is hush'd—no life treads silently,
  But clouds and cloudy shadows wander free,
That never spoke, over the idle ground:

But in green ruins, in the desolate walls
  Of antique palaces, where Man hath been,
Though the dun fox or wild hyaena calls,
  And owls, that flit continually between,
Shriek to the echo, and the low winds moan—
There the true Silence is, self-conscious and alone.

THOMAS HOOD (1798–1845)

681   DEATH

It is not death, that sometime in a sigh
  This eloquent breath shall take its speechless flight;
That sometime these bright stars, that now reply
  In sunlight to the sun, shall set in night;
That this warm conscious flesh shall perish quite,
  And all life's ruddy springs forget to flow;
That thoughts shall cease, and the immortal sprite
Be lapp'd in alien clay and laid below;
It is not death to know this—but to know
  That pious thoughts, which visit at new graves
In tender pilgrimage, will cease to go
  So duly and so oft—and when grass waves
Over the pass'd-away, there may be then
No resurrection in the minds of men.

THOMAS HOOD (1798–1845)

682   FAIR INES

  O saw ye not fair Ines?
    She's gone into the West,
To dazzle when the sun is down,
    And rob the world of rest:
She took our daylight with her,
    The smiles that we love best,
With morning blushes on her cheek,
    And pearls upon her breast.

O turn again, fair Ines,
    Before the fall of night,
For fear the Moon should shine alone,
    And stars unrivall'd bright;
And blessèd will the lover be
    That walks beneath their light,
And breathes the love against thy cheek
    I dare not even write!

Would I had been, fair Ines,
    That gallant cavalier,
Who rode so gaily by thy side,
    And whisper'd thee so near!
Were there no bonny dames at home,
    Or no true lovers here,
That he should cross the seas to win
    The dearest of the dear?

I saw thee, lovely Ines,
  Descend along the shore,
With bands of noble gentlemen,
  And banners waved before;
And gentle youth and maidens gay,
  And snowy plumes they wore:
It would have been a beauteous dream,—
  If it had been no more!

Alas, alas! fair Ines,
  She went away with song,
With Music waiting on her steps,
  And shoutings of the throng;
But some were sad, and felt no mirth,
  But only Music's wrong,
In sounds that sang Farewell, farewell,
  To her you've loved so long.

Farewell, farewell, fair Ines!
  That vessel never bore
So fair a lady on its deck,
  Nor danced so light before,—
Alas for pleasure on the sea,
  And sorrow on the shore!
The smile that bless'd one lover's heart
  Has broken many more!

                  THOMAS HOOD (1798–1845)

TIME OF ROSES   683

It was not in the Winter
  Our loving lot was cast;
It was the time of roses—
  We pluck'd them as we pass'd!

That churlish season never frown'd
  On early lovers yet:
O no—the world was newly crown'd
  With flowers when first we met!

'Twas twilight, and I bade you go,
  But still you held me fast;
It was the time of roses—
  We pluck'd them as we pass'd!

                  THOMAS HOOD (1798–1845)

RUTH   684

She stood breast-high amid the corn,
Clasp'd by the golden light of morn,
Like the sweetheart of the sun,
Who many a glowing kiss had won.

On her cheek an autumn flush,
Deeply ripen'd;—such a blush
In the midst of brown was born,
Like red poppies grown with corn.

Round her eyes her tresses fell,
Which were blackest none could tell,
But long lashes veil'd a light,
That had else been all too bright.

And her hat, with shady brim,
Made her tressy forehead dim;
Thus she stood amid the stooks,
Praising God with sweetest looks:—

Sure, I said, Heav'n did not mean,
Where I reap thou shouldst but glean,
Lay thy sheaf adown and come,
Share my harvest and my home.
Thomas Hood (1798–1845)

685   **The Death-bed**

We watch'd her breathing thro' the night,
  Her breathing soft and low,
As in her breast the wave of life
  Kept heaving to and fro.

So silently we seem'd to speak,
  So slowly moved about,
As we had lent her half our powers
  To eke her living out.

Our very hopes belied our fears,
  Our fears our hopes belied—
We thought her dying when she slept,
  And sleeping when she died.

For when the morn came dim and sad,
  And chill with early showers,
Her quiet eyelids closed—she had
  Another morn than ours.
Thomas Hood (1798–1845)

686   **The Bridge of Sighs**

One more Unfortunate,
  Weary of breath,
Rashly importunate,
  Gone to her death!

Take her up tenderly,
  Lift her with care;
Fashion'd so slenderly
  Young, and so fair!

Look at her garments
Clinging like cerements;
Whilst the wave constantly
  Drips from her clothing;
Take her up instantly,
  Loving, not loathing.

Touch her not scornfully;
Think of her mournfully,
　Gently and humanly;
Not of the stains of her,
All that remains of her
　Now is pure womanly.

Make no deep scrutiny
Into her mutiny
　Rash and undutiful:
Past all dishonour,
Death has left on her
　Only the beautiful.

Still, for all slips of hers,
　One of Eve's family—
Wipe those poor lips of hers
　Oozing so clammily.

Loop up her tresses
　Escaped from the comb,
Her fair auburn tresses;
　Whilst wonderment guesses
　Where was her home?

Who was her father?
　Who was her mother?
Had she a sister?
　Had she a brother?
Or was there a dearer one
Still, and a nearer one
　Yet, than all other?

Alas! for the rarity
Of Christian charity
　Under the sun!
O, it was pitiful!
Near a whole city full,
　Home she had none.

Sisterly, brotherly,
Fatherly, motherly
　Feelings had changed:
Love, by harsh evidence,
Thrown from its eminence;
Even God's providence
　Seeming estranged.

Where the lamps quiver
So far in the river,
  With many a light
From window and casement,
From garret to basement,
She stood, with amazement,
  Houseless by night.

The bleak wind of March
  Made her tremble and shiver;
But not the dark arch,
Or the black flowing river:
Mad from life's history,
Glad to death's mystery,
  Swift to be hurl'd—
Anywhere, anywhere
  Out of the world!

In she plunged boldly—
No matter how coldly
  The rough river ran—
Over the brink of it,
Picture it—think of it,
  Dissolute Man!
Lave in it, drink of it,
  Then, if you can!

Take her up tenderly,
  Lift her with care;
Fashion'd so slenderly,
  Young, and so fair!

Ere her limbs frigidly
Stiffen too rigidly,
  Decently, kindly,
Smooth and compose them;
And her eyes, close them,
  Staring so blindly!

Dreadfully staring
  Thro' muddy impurity,
As when with the daring
Last look of despairing
  Fix'd on futurity.

Perishing gloomily,
Spurr'd by contumely,
Cold inhumanity,
Burning insanity,
  Into her rest.—
Cross her hands humbly
As if praying dumbly,
  Over her breast!

Owning her weakness,
   Her evil behaviour,
And leaving, with meekness,
   Her sins to her Saviour!

THOMAS HOOD (1798–1845)

TO A LOCK OF HAIR   687

Thy hue, dear pledge, is pure and bright
As in that well-remember'd night
When first thy mystic braid was wove,
And first my Agnes whisper'd love.

   Since then how often hast thou prest
The torrid zone of this wild breast,
Whose wrath and hate have sworn to dwell
With the first sin that peopled hell;
A breast whose blood's a troubled ocean,
Each throb the earthquake's wild commotion!
O if such clime thou canst endure
Yet keep thy hue unstain'd and pure,
What conquest o'er each erring thought
Of that fierce realm had Agnes wrought!
I had not wander'd far and wide
With such an angel for my guide;
Nor heaven nor earth could then reprove me
If she had lived, and lived to love me.

   Not then this world's wild joys had been
To me one savage hunting scene,
My sole delight the headlong race,
And frantic hurry of the chase;
To start, pursue, and bring to bay,
Rush in, drag down, and rend my prey,
Then—from the carcase turn away!
Mine ireful mood had sweetness tamed,
And soothed each wound which pride inflamed:—
Yes, God and man might now approve me
If thou hadst lived, and lived to love me!

SIR WALTER SCOTT (1771–1832)

THE SLEEPING BEAUTY   688

Sleep on, and dream of Heaven awhile—
Tho' shut so close thy laughing eyes,
Thy rosy lips still wear a smile
And move, and breathe delicious sighs!

Ah, now soft blushes tinge her cheeks
And mantle o'er her neck of snow:
Ah, now she murmurs, now she speaks
What most I wish—and fear to know!

She starts, she trembles, and she weeps!
Her fair hands folded on her breast:
—And now, how like a saint she sleeps!
A seraph in the realms of rest!

Sleep on secure! Above controul
Thy thoughts belong to Heaven and thee:
And may the secret of thy soul
Remain within its sanctuary!
                      SAMUEL ROGERS (1763–1855)

689   ALL FOR LOVE

O talk not to me of a name great in story;
The days of our youth are the days of our glory;
And the myrtle and ivy of sweet two-and-twenty
Are worth all your laurels, though ever so plenty.

What are garlands and crowns to the brow that is wrinkled?
'Tis but as a dead flower with May-dew besprinkled:
Then away with all such from the head that is hoary—
What care I for the wreaths that can only give glory?

O Fame!—if I e'er took delight in thy praises,
'Twas less for the sake of thy high-sounding phrases,
Than to see the bright eyes of the dear one discover
She thought that I was not unworthy to love her.

There chiefly I sought thee, there only I found thee;
Her glance was the best of the rays that surround thee;
When it sparkled o'er aught that was bright in my story,
I knew it was love, and I felt it was glory.
                GEORGE GORDON BYRON, LORD BYRON (1788–1824)

690   ELEGY

O snatch'd away in beauty's bloom!
On thee shall press no ponderous tomb;
But on thy turf shall roses rear
Their leaves, the earliest of the year,
And the wild cypress wave in tender gloom:

And oft by yon blue gushing stream
Shall Sorrow lean her drooping head,
And feed deep thought with many a dream,
And lingering pause and lightly tread;
Fond wretch! as if her step disturb'd the dead!

Away! we know that tears are vain,
That Death nor heeds nor hears distress:
Will this unteach us to complain?
Or make one mourner weep the less?
And thou, who tell'st me to forget,
Thy looks are wan, thine eyes are wet.
                GEORGE GORDON BYRON, LORD BYRON (1788–1824)

691   THY KISSES

I fear thy kisses, gentle maiden;
Thou needest not fear mine;
My spirit is too deeply laden
Ever to burthen thine.

I fear thy mien, thy tones, thy motion;
Thou needest not fear mine;
Innocent is the heart's devotion
With which I worship thine.
                    PERCY BYSSHE SHELLEY (1792–1822)

FREEDOM AND LOVE 692

How delicious is the winning
Of a kiss at love's beginning,
When two mutual hearts are sighing
For the knot there's no untying!

Yet remember, 'midst your wooing,
Love has bliss, but Love has ruing;
Other smiles may make you fickle,
Tears for other charms may trickle.

Love he comes, and Love he tarries,
Just as fate or fancy carries;
Longest stays, when sorest chidden;
Laughs and flies, when press'd and bidden.

Bind the sea to slumber stilly,
Bind its odour to the lily,
Bind the aspen ne'er to quiver,
Then bind Love to last for ever.

Love's a fire that needs renewal
Of fresh beauty for its fuel:
Love's wing moults when caged and captured,
Only free, he soars enraptured.

Can you keep the bee from ranging
Or the ringdove's neck from changing?
No! nor fetter'd Love from dying
In the knot there's no untying.
                    THOMAS CAMPBELL (1774–1844)

LOVE'S PHILOSOPHY 693

The fountains mingle with the river
And the rivers with the ocean,
The winds of heaven mix for ever
With a sweet emotion;
Nothing in the world is single,
All things by a law divine
In one another's being mingle—
Why not I with thine?

See the mountains kiss high heaven
And the waves clasp one another;
No sister-flower would be forgiven
If it disdain'd its brother:

    And the sunlight clasps the earth,
    And the moonbeams kiss the sea—
    What are all these kissings worth,
    If thou kiss not me?
                               PERCY BYSSHE SHELLEY (1792–1822)

694   HOW SWEET THE ANSWER ECHO MAKES
    How sweet the answer Echo makes
    To Music at night
    When, roused by lute or horn, she wakes,
    And far away o'er lawns and lakes
    Goes answering light!

    Yet Love hath echoes truer far
    And far more sweet
    Than e'er, beneath the moonlight's star,
    Of horn or lute or soft guitar
    The songs repeat.

    'Tis when the sigh,—in youth sincere
    And only then,
    The sigh that's breathed for one to hear—
    Is by that one, that only Dear
    Breathed back again.
                                    THOMAS MOORE (1779–1852)

695   THE JOURNEY ONWARDS
    As slow our ship her foamy track
    Against the wind was cleaving,
    Her trembling pennant still look'd back
    To that dear isle 'twas leaving.
    So loth we part from all we love,
    From all the links that bind us;
    So turn our hearts, as on we rove,
    To those we've left behind us!

    When, round the bowl, of vanish'd years
    We talk with joyous seeming—
    With smiles that might as well be tears,
    So faint, so sad their beaming;
    While memory brings us back again
    Each early tie that twined us,
    Oh, sweet's the cup that circles then
    To those we've left behind us!

    And when in other climes, we meet
    Some isle or vale enchanting,
    Where all looks flowery wild and sweet,
    And nought but love is wanting;
    We think how great had been our bliss
    If Heaven had but assign'd us
    To live and die in scenes like this,
    With some we've left behind us!

As travellers oft look back at eve
When eastward darkly going,
To gaze upon that light they leave
Still faint behind them glowing,—
So, when the close of pleasure's day
To gloom hath near consign'd us,
We turn to catch our fading ray
Of joy that's left behind us.

THOMAS MOORE (1779–1852)

Eleu loro 696
Where shall the lover rest
Whom the fates sever
From his true maiden's breast
Parted for ever?
Where, through groves deep and high
Sounds the far billow,
Where early violets die
Under the willow.
   Eleu loro
Soft shall be his pillow.

There, through the summer day
Cool streams are laving:
There, while the tempests sway,
Scarce are boughs waving;
There thy rest shalt thou take,
Parted for ever,
Never again to wake
Never, O never!
   Eleu loro
Never, O never!

Where shall the traitor rest,
He, the deceiver,
Who would win maiden's breast,
Ruin, and leave her?
In the lost battle,
Borne down by the flying,
Where mingles war's rattle
With groans of the dying;
   Eleu loro
There shall he be lying.

Her wing shall the eagle flap
O'er the falsehearted;
His warm blood the wolf shall lap
Ere life be parted:

Shame and dishonour sit
By his grave ever;
Blessing shall hallow it
Never, O never!
  Eleu loro
Never, O never!

                                SIR WALTER SCOTT (1771–1832)

Eleu loro: *similar in meaning to* Alas, for them!

697 THE MAID OF NEIDPATH

O lovers' eyes are sharp to see,
And lovers' ears in hearing;
And love, in life's extremity
Can lend an hour of cheering.
Disease had been in Mary's bower
And slow decay from mourning,
Though now she sits on Neidpath's tower
To watch her Love's returning.

All sunk and dim her eyes so bright,
Her form decay'd by pining,
Till through her wasted hand, at night,
You saw the taper shining.
By fits a sultry hectic hue
Across her cheek was flying;
By fits so ashy pale she grew
Her maidens thought her dying.

Yet keenest powers to see and hear
Seem'd in her frame residing;
Before the watch-dog prick'd his ear
She heard her lover's riding;
Ere scarce a distant form was kenn'd
She knew and waved to greet him,
And o'er the battlement did bend
As on the wing to meet him.

He came—he pass'd—an heedless gaze
As o'er some stranger glancing;
Her welcome, spoke in faltering phrase,
Lost in his courser's prancing—

The castle-arch, whose hollow tone
Returns each whisper spoken,
Could scarcely catch the feeble moan
Which told her heart was broken.

                                SIR WALTER SCOTT (1771–1832)

698 THE SEA

A wet sheet and a flowing sea,
A wind that follows fast
And fills the white and rustling sail
And bends the gallant mast;

And bends the gallant mast, my boys,
While like the eagle free
Away the good ship flies, and leaves
Old England on the lee.

O for a soft and gentle wind!
I heard a fair one cry;
But give to me the snoring breeze
And white waves heaving high;
And white waves heaving high, my lads,
The good ship tight and free—
The world of waters is our home,
And merry men are we.

There's tempest in yon hornèd moon,
And lightning in yon cloud;
But hark the music, mariners!
The wind is piping loud;
The wind is piping loud, my boys,
The lightning flashes free—
While the hollow oak our palace is,
Our heritage the sea.
     ALLAN CUNNINGHAM (1784–1842)

ON THE CASTLE OF CHILLON 699

Eternal Spirit of the chainless Mind!
Brightest in dungeons, Liberty, thou art—
For there thy habitation is the heart—
The heart which love of Thee alone can bind;

And when thy sons to fetters are consign'd,
To fetters, and the damp vault's dayless gloom,
Their country conquers with their martyrdom
And Freedom's fame finds wings on every wind.

Chillon! thy prison is a holy place
And thy sad floor an altar, for 'twas trod
Until his very steps have left a trace

Worn as if thy cold pavement were a sod,
By Bonnivard! May none those marks efface!
For they appeal from tyranny to God.
   GEORGE GORDON BYRON, LORD BYRON (1788–1824)

PRO PATRIA MORI 700

When he who adores thee has left but the name
 Of his fault and his sorrows behind,
O! say wilt thou weep, when they darken the fame
 Of a life that for thee was resign'd!
Yes, weep, and however my foes may condemn,
 Thy tears shall efface their decree;
For, Heaven can witness, though guilty to them,
 I have been but too faithful to thee.

With thee were the dreams of my earliest love;
    Every thought of my reason was thine;
In my last humble prayer to the Spirit above
    Thy name shall be mingled with mine!
O! blest are the lovers and friends who shall live
    The days of thy glory to see;
But the next dearest blessing that Heaven can give
    Is the pride of thus dying for thee.
                                           THOMAS MOORE (1779–1852)

701   YOUTH AND AGE

There's not a joy the world can give like that it takes away
When the glow of early thought declines in feeling's dull decay;
'Tis not on youth's smooth cheek the blush alone which fades so fast,
But the tender bloom of heart is gone, ere youth itself be past.

Then the few whose spirits float above the wreck of happiness
Are driven o'er the shoals of guilt or ocean of excess:
The magnet of their course is gone, or only points in vain
The shore to which their shiver'd sail shall never stretch again.

Then the mortal coldness of the soul like death itself comes down;
It cannot feel for others' woes, it dare not dream its own;
That heavy chill has frozen o'er the fountain of our tears,
And though the eye may sparkle still, 'tis where the ice appears.

Though wit may flash from fluent lips, and mirth distract the breast,
Through midnight hours that yield no more their former hope of rest;
'Tis but as ivy-leaves around the ruin'd turret wreathe,
All green and wildly fresh without, but worn and gray beneath.

O could I feel as I have felt, or be what I have been,
Or weep as I could once have wept o'er many a vanish'd scene,—
As springs in deserts found seem sweet, all brackish though they be,
So midst the wither'd waste of life, those tears would flow to me!
                    GEORGE GORDON BYRON, LORD BYRON (1788–1824)

702   ADMONITION TO A TRAVELLER

Yes, there is holy pleasure in thine eye!
—The lovely cottage in the guardian nook
Hath stirr'd thee deeply; with its own dear brook,
Its own small pasture, almost its own sky!

But covet not the abode—O do not sigh
As many do, repining while they look;
Intruders who would tear from Nature's book
This precious leaf with harsh impiety:

—Think what the home would be if it were thine,
Even thine, though few thy wants!—Roof, window, door,
The very flowers are sacred to the Poor,

The roses to the porch which they entwine:
Yea, all that now enchants thee, from the day
On which it should be touch'd would melt away!
                                    WILLIAM WORDSWORTH (1770–1850)

To Sleep   703

A flock of sheep that leisurely pass by
One after one; the sound of rain, and bees
Murmuring; the fall of rivers, winds and seas,
Smooth fields, white sheets of water, and pure sky;—

I've thought of all by turns, and still I lie
Sleepless; and soon the small birds' melodies
Must hear, first utter'd from my orchard trees,
And the first cuckoo's melancholy cry.

Even thus last night, and two nights more I lay,
And could not win thee, Sleep! by any stealth:
So do not let me wear to-night away:

Without Thee what is all the morning's wealth?
Come, blessèd barrier between day and day,
Dear mother of fresh thoughts and joyous health!
                    WILLIAM WORDSWORTH (1770–1850)

A Lesson   704

There is a flower, the Lesser Celandine,
That shrinks like many more from cold and rain,
And the first moment that the sun may shine,
Bright as the sun himself, 'tis out again!

When hailstones have been falling, swarm on swarm,
Or blasts the green field and the trees distrest,
Oft have I seen it muffled up from harm
In close self-shelter, like a thing at rest.

But lately, one rough day, this flower I past,
And recognised it, though an alter'd form,
Now standing forth an offering to the blast,
And buffeted at will by rain and storm.

I stopp'd and said with inly-mutter'd voice,
"It doth not love the shower, nor seek the cold;
This neither is its courage nor its choice,
But its necessity in being old.

"The sunshine may not cheer it, nor the dew;
It cannot help itself in its decay;
Stiff in its members, wither'd, changed of hue."
And, in my spleen, I smiled that it was gray.

To be a prodigal's favourite—then, worse truth,
A miser's pensioner—behold our lot!
O Man! that from thy fair and shining youth
Age might but take the things Youth needed not!
                    WILLIAM WORDSWORTH (1770–1850)

705   THE SOLIDER'S DREAM

Our bugles sang truce, for the night-cloud had lower'd,
And the sentinel stars set their watch in the sky;
And thousands had sunk on the ground overpower'd,
The weary to sleep, and the wounded to die.

When reposing that night on my pallet of straw
By the wolf-scaring faggot that guarded the slain,
At the dead of the night a sweet Vision I saw;
And thrice ere the morning I dreamt it again.

Methought from the battle-field's dreadful array
Far, far, I had roam'd on a desolate track:
'Twas Autumn,—and sunshine arose on the way
To the home of my fathers, that welcomed me back.

I flew to the pleasant fields traversed so oft
In life's morning march, when my bosom was young;
I heard my own mountain-goats bleating aloft,
And knew the sweet strain that the corn-reapers sung.

Then pledged we the wine-cup, and fondly I swore
From my home and my weeping friends never to part;
My little ones kiss'd me a thousand times o'er,
And my wife sobb'd aloud in her fulness of heart.

"Stay—stay with us!—rest!—thou art weary and worn!"—
And fain was their war-broken soldier to stay;—
But sorrow return'd with the dawning of morn,
And the voice in my dreaming ear melted away.
                              THOMAS CAMPBELL (1774–1844)

706   THE POET'S DREAM

On a Poet's lips I slept
Dreaming like a love-adept
In the sound his breathing kept;
Nor seeks nor finds he mortal blisses,
But feeds on the aerial kisses
Of shapes that haunt Thought's wildernesses.
He will watch from dawn to gloom
The lake-reflected sun illume
The yellow bees in the ivy-bloom,
Nor heed nor see, what things they be—
But from these create he can
Forms more real than living Man,
Nurslings of immortality!
                            PERCY BYSSHE SHELLEY (1792–1822)

707   THE RIVER OF LIFE

The more we live, more brief appear
Our life's succeeding stages:
A day to childhood seems a year,
And years like passing ages.

The gladsome current of our youth
Ere passion yet disorders,
Steals lingering like a river smooth
Along its grassy borders.

But as the careworn cheek grows wan,
And sorrow's shafts fly thicker,
Ye Stars, that measure life to man,
Why seem your courses quicker?

When joys have lost their bloom and breath
And life itself is vapid,
Why, as we reach the Falls of Death,
Feel we its tide more rapid?

It may be strange—yet who would change
Time's course to lower speeding,
When one by one our friends have gone
And left our bosoms bleeding?

Heaven gives our years of fading strength
Indemnifying fleetness;
And those of youth, a seeming length,
Proportion'd to their sweetness.

THOMAS CAMPBELL (1774–1844)

THE HUMAN SEASONS 708

Four Seasons fill the measure of the year;
There are four seasons in the mind of Man:
He has his lusty Spring, when fancy clear
Takes in all beauty with an easy span:

He has his summer, when luxuriously
Spring's honey'd cud of youthful thought he loves
To ruminate, and by such dreaming high
Is nearest unto heaven: quiet coves

His soul has in its Autumn, when his wings
He furleth close; contented so to look
On mists in idleness—to let fair things
Pass by unheeded as a threshold brook:—

He has his Winter too of pale misfeature,
Or else he would forego his mortal nature.

JOHN KEATS (1795–1821)

HER NAME 709

[So long as there be anthologies, let them include this verse as a testament to the immortal power of poetry. – Ed.]

Well I remember how you smiled
  To see me write your name upon
The soft sea-sand... "O, what a child!
  You think you're writing upon stone!"

  I have since written what no tide
   Shall ever wash away; what men
  Unborn shall read o'er ocean wide
   And find Ianthe's name again.
      WALTER SAVAGE LANDOR (1775–1864)

710   ON HIS OWN DEATH
  Death stands above me, whispering low
   I know not what into my ear;
  Of his strange language all I know
   Is, there is not a word of fear.
      WALTER SAVAGE LANDOR (1775–1864)

711   LITTLE THINGS
  Little drops of water,
   Little grains of sand,
  Make the mighty ocean
   And the pleasant land.

  Thus the little minutes,
   Humble though they be,
  Make the mighty ages
   Of eternity.
      EBENEZER COBHAM BREWER (1810–1897)

712   LITTLE WHITE LILY
Little White Lily
Sat by a stone,
Drooping and waiting
Till the sun shone.
Little White Lily
Sunshine has fed;
Little White Lily
Is lifting her head.

Little White Lily
Said: "It is good
Little White Lily's
Clothing and food."
Little White Lily
Dressed like a bride!
Shining with whiteness,
And crownèd beside!

Little White Lily
Drooping with pain,
Waiting and waiting
For the wet rain.
Little White Lily
Holdeth her cup;
Rain is fast falling
And filling it up.

Little White Lily
Said: "Good again,
When I am thirsty
To have the nice rain.
Now I am stronger,
Now I am cool;
Heat cannot burn me,
My veins are so full."

Little White Lily
Smells very sweet;
On her head sunshine,
Rain at her feet.
Thanks to the sunshine,
Thanks to the rain,
Little White Lily
Is happy again.

GEORGE MACDONALD (1824–1905)

How The Leaves Came Down

"I'll tell you how the leaves came down,"
  The great Tree to his children said:
"You're getting sleepy, Yellow and Brown,
  Yes, very sleepy, little Red.
  It is quite time to go to bed."

"Ah!" begged each silly, pouting leaf,
  "Let us a little longer stay;
Dear Father Tree, behold our grief!
  'Tis such a very pleasant day,
  We do not want to go away."

So, for just one more merry day
  To the great Tree the leaflets clung,
Frolicked and danced, and had their way,
  Upon the autumn breezes swung,
  Whispering all their sports among—

"Perhaps the great Tree will forget,
  And let us stay until the spring,
If we all beg, and coax, and fret."
  But the great Tree did no such thing;
  He smiled to hear their whispering.

"Come, children, all to bed," he cried;
  And ere the leaves could urge their prayer,
He shook his head, and far and wide,
  Fluttering and rustling everywhere,
  Down sped the leaflets through the air.

I saw them; on the ground they lay,
  Golden and red, a huddled swarm,
Waiting till one from far away,
  White bedclothes heaped upon her arm,
  Should come to wrap them safe and warm.

The great bare Tree looked down and smiled.
"Good-night, dear little leaves," he said.
And from below each sleepy child
  Replied, "Good-night," and murmured,
"It is *so* nice to go to bed!"
Susan Coolidge (1835–1905)

714   Wee Willie Winkie

Wee Willie Winkie rins through the town,
Up-stairs and doon-stairs, in his nicht-gown,
Tirlin' at the window, cryin' at the lock,
"Are the weans in their bed?—for it's now ten o'clock."

Hey, Willie Winkie! are ye comin' ben?
The cat's singin' gay thrums to the sleepin' hen,
The doug's speldered on the floor, and disna gie a cheep;
But here's a waukrife laddie that winna fa' asleep.

Onything but sleep, ye rogue! glow'rin' like the moon,
Rattlin' in an airn jug wi' an airn spoon,
Rumblin' tumblin' roun' about, crowin' like a cock,
Skirlin' like a kenna-what—wauknin' sleepin' folk.

Hey, Willie Winkie! the wean's in a creel!
Waumblin' aff a body's knee like a vera eel,
Ruggin' at the cat's lug, and ravellin' a' her thrums,—
Hey, Willie Winkie!—See, there he comes!

Wearie is the mither that has a storie wean,
A wee stumpie stoussie that canna rin his lane,
That has a battle aye wi' sleep before he'll close an ee;
But a kiss frae aff his rosy lips gies strength anew to me.
William Miller (1810–1872)

715   The Owl And The Pussy-cat

The Owl and the Pussy-Cat went to sea
    In a beautiful pea-green boat;
They took some honey, and plenty of money
    Wrapped up in a five-pound note.
The Owl looked up to the moon above,
    And sang to a small guitar,
"O lovely Pussy! O Pussy, my love!
    What a beautiful Pussy you are,—
        You are,
    What a beautiful Pussy you are!"

Pussy said to the Owl, "You elegant fowl!
    How wonderful sweet you sing!
Oh, let us be married,—too long we have tarried,—
    But what shall we do for a ring?"

They sailed away for a year and a day
    To the land where the Bong-tree grows,
And there in a wood a piggy-wig stood
    With a ring in the end of his nose,—
        His nose,
With a ring in the end of his nose.

"Dear Pig, are you willing to sell for one shilling
    Your ring?" Said the piggy, "I will,"
So they took it away, and were married next day
    By the turkey who lives on the hill.
They dined upon mince and slices of quince,
    Which they ate with a runcible spoon,
And hand in hand on the edge of the sand
    They danced by the light of the moon,—
        The moon,
They danced by the light of the moon.

                        EDWARD LEAR (1812–1888)

A FAREWELL   716

My fairest child, I have no song to give you;
    No lark could pipe to skies so dull and gray;
Yet, ere we part, one lesson I can leave you
    For every day.

Be good, sweet maid, and let who will be clever;
    Do noble things, not dream them all day long:
And so make life, death, and that vast forever
    One grand, sweet song.

                        CHARLES KINGSLEY (1819–1875)

THE CAPTAIN'S DAUGHTER   717

We were crowded in the cabin,
    Not a soul would dare to sleep,—
It was midnight on the waters,
    And a storm was on the deep.

'Tis a fearful thing in winter
    To be shattered by the blast,
And to hear the rattling trumpet
    Thunder, "Cut away the mast!"

So we shuddered there in silence,—
    For the stoutest held his breath,
While the hungry sea was roaring
    And the breakers talked with Death.

As thus we sat in darkness,
    Each one busy with his prayers,
"We are lost!" the captain shouted
    As he staggered down the stairs.

But his little daughter whispered,
    As she took his icy hand,
"Isn't God upon the ocean,
    Just the same as on the land?"

Then we kissed the little maiden,
  And we spoke in better cheer,
And we anchored safe in harbour
  When the morn was shining clear.

JAMES T. FIELDS (1816–1881)

718   THE VILLAGE BLACKSMITH

Under a spreading chestnut-tree
  The village smithy stands;
The smith, a mighty man is he,
  With large and sinewy hands,
And the muscles of his brawny arms
  Are strong as iron bands.

His hair is crisp, and black, and long;
  His face is like the tan;
His brow is wet with honest sweat,
  He earns whate'er he can,
And looks the whole world in the face,
  For he owes not any man.

Week in, week out, from morn till night,
  You can hear his bellows blow;
You can hear him swing his heavy sledge,
  With measured beat and slow,
Like a sexton ringing the village bell,
  When the evening sun is low.

And children coming home from school
  Look in at the open door;
They love to see the flaming forge,
  And hear the bellows roar,
And catch the burning sparks that fly
  Like chaff from a threshing-floor.

He goes on Sunday to the church,
  And sits among his boys;
He hears the parson pray and preach,
  He hears his daughter's voice
Singing in the village choir,
  And it makes his heart rejoice.

It sounds to him like her mother's voice,
  Singing in Paradise!
He needs must think of her once more,
  How in the grave she lies;
And with his hard, rough hand he wipes
  A tear out of his eyes.

Toiling,—rejoicing,—sorrowing,
  Onward through life he goes;
Each morning sees some task begin,
  Each evening sees it close;
Something attempted, something done,
  Has earned a night's repose.

Thanks, thanks to thee, my worthy friend,
  For the lesson thou hast taught!
Thus at the flaming forge of life
  Our fortunes must be wrought;
Thus on its sounding anvil shaped
  Each burning deed and thought.
                HENRY WADSWORTH LONGFELLOW (1807–1882)

Alfred, Lord Tennyson
1809-1892

Sweet And Low 719

Sweet and low, sweet and low,
  Wind of the western sea,
Low, low, breathe and blow,
  Wind of the western sea!
Over the rolling waters go,
Come from the dropping moon and blow,
  Blow him again to me;
While my little one, while my pretty one sleeps.

Sleep and rest, sleep and rest,
  Father will come to thee soon;
Rest, rest, on mother's breast,
  Father will come to thee soon;
Father will come to his babe in the nest,
Silver sails all out of the west
  Under the silver moon:
Sleep, my little one, sleep, my pretty one, sleep.
                ALFRED TENNYSON, LORD TENNYSON (1809–1892)

Father William 720

"You are old, Father William," the young man said,
  "And your hair has become very white;
And yet you incessantly stand on your head—
  Do you think, at your age, it is right?"

"In my youth," Father William replied to his son,
  "I feared it might injure the brain;
But now that I'm perfectly sure I have none,
  Why, I do it again and again."

"You are old," said the youth, "as I mentioned before,
  And have grown most uncommonly fat;
Yet you turned a back-somersault in at the door—
  Pray, what is the reason of that?"

"In my youth," said the sage, as he shook his gray locks,
  "I kept all my limbs very supple
By the use of this ointment—one shilling the box—
  Allow me to sell you a couple."

"You are old," said the youth, "and your jaws are too weak
  For anything tougher than suet;
Yet you finished the goose, with the bones and the beak:
  Pray, how did you manage to do it?"

"In my youth," said his father, "I took to the law,
  And argued each case with my wife;
And the muscular strength which it gave to my jaw
  Has lasted the rest of my life."

"You are old," said the youth; "one would hardly suppose
  That your eye was as steady as ever;
Yet you balanced an eel on the end of your nose—
  What made you so awfully clever?"

"I have answered three questions, and that is enough,"
  Said his father, "don't give yourself airs!
Do you think I can listen all day to such stuff?
  Be off, or I'll kick you down-stairs!"
                              LEWIS CARROLL (1832–1898)

721   JABBERWOCKY

'Twas brillig, and the slithy toves
Did gyre and gimble in the wabe;
All mimsy were the borogoves,
And the mome raths outgrabe.

"Beware the Jabberwock, my son!
The jaws that bite, the claws that catch!
Beware the Jubjub bird, and shun
The frumious Bandersnatch!"

He took his vorpal sword in hand:
Long time the manxome foe he sought—
So rested he by the Tumtum tree,
And stood awhile in thought.

And as in uffish thought he stood,
The Jabberwock, with eyes of flame,
Came whiffling through the tulgey wood,
And burbled as it came!

One, two! One, two! and through and through
The vorpal blade went snicker-snack!
He left it dead, and with its head
He went galumphing back.

"And hast thou slain the Jabberwock?
Come to my arms, my beamish boy!
O frabjous day! Callooh! Callay!"
He chortled in his joy.

'Twas brillig, and the slithy toves
Did gyre and gimble in the wabe;
All mimsy were the borogoves,
And the mome raths outgrabe.
                              LEWIS CARROLL (1832–1898)

722   THE WALRUS AND THE CARPENTER

The sun was shining on the sea,
  Shining with all his might:
He did his very best to make
  The billows smooth and bright—
And this was odd, because it was
  The middle of the night.

The moon was shining sulkily,
Because she thought the sun
Had got no business to be there
After the day was done—
"It's very rude of him," she said,
"To come and spoil the fun!"

The sea was wet as wet could be,
The sands were dry as dry.
You could not see a cloud, because
No cloud was in the sky:
No birds were flying overhead—
There were no birds to fly.

The Walrus and the Carpenter
Were walking close at hand;
They wept like anything to see
Such quantities of sand:
"If this were only cleared away,"
They said, "it would be grand!"

"If seven maids with seven mops
Swept it for half a year.
Do you suppose," the Walrus said,
"That they could get it clear?"
"I doubt it," said the Carpenter,
And shed a bitter tear.

"O Oysters, come and walk with us!"
The Walrus did beseech.
"A pleasant walk, a pleasant talk,
Along the briny beach:
We cannot do with more than four,
To give a hand to each."

The eldest Oyster looked at him,
But never a word he said:
The eldest Oyster winked his eye,
And shook his heavy head—
Meaning to say he did not choose
To leave the oyster-bed.

But four young Oysters hurried up,
All eager for the treat:
Their coats were brushed, their faces washed,
Their shoes were clean and neat—
And this was odd, because, you know,
They hadn't any feet.

Four other Oysters followed them,
And yet another four;
And thick and fast they came at last,
And more, and more, and more—
All hopping through the frothy waves,
And scrambling to the shore.

The Walrus and the Carpenter
Walked on a mile or so,
And then they rested on a rock
Conveniently low:
And all the little Oysters stood
And waited in a row.

"The time has come," the Walrus said,
"To talk of many things:
Of shoes—and ships—and sealing-wax—
Of cabbages—and kings—
And why the sea is boiling hot—
And whether pigs have wings."

"But wait a bit," the Oysters cried,
"Before we have our chat;
For some of us are out of breath,
And all of us are fat!"
"No hurry!" said the Carpenter.
They thanked him much for that.

"A loaf of bread," the Walrus said,
"Is what we chiefly need:
Pepper and vinegar besides
Are very good indeed—
Now if you're ready, Oysters dear,
We can begin to feed."

"But not on us!" the Oysters cried,
Turning a little blue.
"After such kindness, that would be
A dismal thing to do!"
"The night is fine," the Walrus said.
"Do you admire the view?

"It was so kind of you to come!
And you are very nice!"
The Carpenter said nothing but
"Cut us another slice:
I wish you were not quite so deaf—
I've had to ask you twice!"

"It seems a shame," the Walrus said,
"To play them such a trick,
After we've brought them out so far,
And made them trot so quick!"
The Carpenter said nothing but
"The butter's spread too thick!"

"I weep for you," the Walrus said:
"I deeply sympathize."
 With sobs and tears he sorted out
 Those of the largest size,
 Holding his pocket-handkerchief
 Before his streaming eyes.

"O Oysters," said the Carpenter,
"You've had a pleasant run!
 Shall we be trotting home again?"
 But answer came there none—
 And this was scarcely odd, because
 They'd eaten every one.

LEWIS CARROLL (1832–1898)

LITTLE BILLEE   723

There were three sailors of Bristol city
  Who took a boat and went to sea.
But first with beef and captain's biscuits
  And pickled pork they loaded she.

There was gorging Jack and guzzling Jimmy,
  And the youngest he was little Billee.
Now when they got so far as the Equator
  They'd nothing left but one split pea.

Says gorging Jack to guzzling Jimmy,
  "I am extremely hungaree."
To gorging Jack says guzzling Jimmy,
  "We've nothing left, us must eat we."

Says gorging Jack to guzzling Jimmy,
  "With one another, we shouldn't agree!
There's little Bill, he's young and tender,
  We're old and tough, so let's eat he."

"Oh! Billy, we're going to kill and eat you,
  So undo the button of your chemie."
When Bill received this information
  He used his pocket-handkerchie.

"First let me say my catechism,
  Which my poor mammy taught to me."
"Make haste, make haste," says guzzling Jimmy
  While Jack pulled out his snickersnee.

So Billy went up to the main-topgallant mast,
  And down he fell on his bended knee.
He scarce had come to the Twelfth Commandment
  When up he jumps, "There's land I see.

"Jerusalem and Madagascar,
  And North and South Amerikee:
There's the British flag a-riding at anchor,
  With Admiral Napier, K.C.B."

So when they got aboard of the Admiral's
   He hanged fat Jack and flogged Jimmee;
But as for little Bill, he made him
   The Captain of a Seventy-three.
               WILLIAM MAKEPEACE THACKERAY (1811–1863)

724   AN INCIDENT OF THE FRENCH CAMP

You know, we French storm'd Ratisbon:
   A mile or so away
On a little mound, Napoleon
   Stood on our storming-day;
With neck out-thrust, you fancy how,
   Legs wide, arms lock'd behind,
As if to balance the prone brow
   Oppressive with its mind.

Just as perhaps he mus'd "My plans
   That soar, to earth may fall,
Let once my army leader Lannes
   Waver at yonder wall,"—
Out 'twixt the battery smokes there flew
   A rider, bound on bound
Full-galloping; nor bridle drew
   Until he reach'd the mound.

Then off there flung in smiling joy,
   And held himself erect
By just his horse's mane, a boy:
   You hardly could suspect—
(So tight he kept his lips compress'd,
   Scarce any blood came through)
You look'd twice ere you saw his breast
   Was all but shot in two.

"Well," cried he, "Emperor, by God's grace
   We've got you Ratisbon!
The Marshal's in the market-place,
   And you'll be there anon
To see your flag-bird flap his vans
   Where I, to heart's desire,
Perched him!" The chief's eye flashed; his plans
   Soared up again like fire.

The chief's eye flashed; but presently
   Softened itself, as sheathes
A film the mother-eagle's eye
   When her bruised eaglet breathes;
"You're wounded!" "Nay," the soldier's pride
   Touched to the quick, he said:
"I'm killed, Sire!" And his chief beside,
   Smiling the boy fell dead.
               ROBERT BROWNING (1812–1889)

Song Of Life 725

A traveller on a dusty road
  Strewed acorns on the lea;
And one took root and sprouted up,
  And grew into a tree.
Love sought its shade at evening-time,
  To breathe its early vows;
And Age was pleased, in heights of noon,
  To bask beneath its boughs.
The dormouse loved its dangling twigs,
  The birds sweet music bore—
It stood a glory in its place,
  A blessing evermore.

A little spring had lost its way
  Amid the grass and fern;
A passing stranger scooped a well
  Where weary men might turn.
He walled it in, and hung with care
  A ladle on the brink;
He thought not of the deed he did,
  But judged that Toil might drink.
He passed again; and lo! the well,
  By summer never dried,
Had cooled ten thousand parchéd tongues,
  And saved a life beside.

A nameless man, amid the crowd
  That thronged the daily mart,
Let fall a word of hope and love,
  Unstudied from the heart,
A whisper on the tumult thrown,
  A transitory breath,
It raised a brother from the dust,
  It saved a soul from death.
O germ! O fount! O word of love!
  O thought at random cast!
Ye were but little at the first,
  But mighty at the last.

                Charles Mackay (1814–1889)

Sheridan's Ride 726

[The poem describes the Battle of Cedar Creek wherein Union Maj. Gen. Philip Sheridan made a breakneck ride to join and rally his forces against an unexpected Confederate attack. – Ed.]

Up from the South at break of day,
Bringing to Winchester fresh dismay,
The affrighted air with a shudder bore,
Like a herald in haste, to the chieftain's door,
The terrible grumble, and rumble, and roar,
Telling the battle was on once more,
And Sheridan twenty miles away.

And wider still those billows of war
Thundered along the horizon's bar;
And louder yet into Winchester rolled
The roar of that red sea uncontrolled,
Making the blood of the listener cold
As he thought of the stake in that fiery fray,
And Sheridan twenty miles away.

But there is a road from Winchester town,
A good, broad highway leading down;
And there, through the flush of the morning light,
A steed as black as the steeds of night
Was seen to pass as with eagle flight;
As if he knew the terrible need,
He stretched away with his utmost speed;
Hills rose and fell; but his heart was gay,
With Sheridan fifteen miles away.

Still sprung from those swift hoofs, thundering South,
The dust, like smoke from the cannon's mouth;
Or the trail of a comet, sweeping faster and faster,
Foreboding to traitors the doom of disaster.
The heart of the steed and the heart of the master
Were beating like prisoners assaulting their walls,
Impatient to be where the battle-field calls;
Every nerve of the charger was strained to full play,
With Sheridan only ten miles away.

Under his spurning feet the road
Like an arrowy Alpine river flowed,
And the landscape sped away behind
Like an ocean flying before the wind.
And the steed, like a bark fed with furnace fire,
Swept on, with his wild eye full of ire.
But lo! he is nearing his heart's desire;
He is snuffing the smoke of the roaring fray,
With Sheridan only five miles away.

The first that the General saw were the groups
Of stragglers, and then the retreating troops.
What was done—what to do? A glance told him both,
Then striking his spurs, with a terrible oath,
He dashed down the line, mid a storm of huzzas,
And the wave of retreat checked its course there, because
The sight of the master compelled it to pause.
With foam and with dust the black charger was gray;
By the flash of his eye, and the red nostrils' play,
He seemed to the whole great army to say:
"I have brought you Sheridan all the way
From Winchester down to save the day!"

Hurrah! hurrah for Sheridan!
Hurrah! hurrah for horse and man!
And when their statues are placed on high,
Under the dome of the Union sky,
The American soldiers' Temple of Fame,
There with the glorious General's name
Be it said, in letters both bold and bright:
"Here is the steed that saved the day,
By carrying Sheridan into the fight
From Winchester, twenty miles away!"
     THOMAS BUCHANAN READ (1822–1872)

LADY CLARE   727

 It was the time when lilies blow
  And clouds are highest up in air;
 Lord Ronald brought a lily-white doe
  To give his cousin, Lady Clare.

 I trow they did not part in scorn:
  Lovers long-betroth'd were they:
 They too will wed the morrow morn:
  God's blessing on the day!

 "He does not love me for my birth,
  Nor for my lands so broad and fair;
 He loves me for my own true worth,
  And that is well," said Lady Clare.

 In there came old Alice the nurse;
  Said: "Who was this that went from thee?"
 "It was my cousin," said Lady Clare;
  "To-morrow he weds with me."

 "O God be thank'd!" said Alice the nurse,
  "That all comes round so just and fair:
 Lord Ronald is heir of all your lands,
  And you are not the Lady Clare."

 "Are ye out of your mind, my nurse, my nurse,"
  Said Lady Clare, "that ye speak so wild?"
 "As God's above," said Alice the nurse,
  "I speak the truth: you are my child.

 "The old Earl's daughter died at my breast;
  I speak the truth, as I live by bread!
 I buried her like my own sweet child,
  And put my child in her stead."

 "Falsely, falsely have ye done,
  O mother," she said, "if this be true,
 To keep the best man under the sun
  So many years from his due."

"Nay now, my child," said Alice the nurse,
  "But keep the secret for your life,
And all you have will be Lord Ronald's
  When you are man and wife."

"If I'm a beggar born," she said,
  "I will speak out, for I dare not lie.
Pull off, pull off the brooch of gold,
  And fling the diamond necklace by."

"Nay now, my child," said Alice the nurse,
  "But keep the secret all ye can."
She said: "Not so: but I will know
  If there be any faith in man."

"Nay now, what faith?" said Alice the nurse,
  "The man will cleave unto his right,"
"And he shall have it," the lady replied,
  "Tho' I should die to-night."

"Yet give one kiss to your mother dear!
  Alas! my child, I sinn'd for thee."
"O mother, mother, mother," she said,
  "So strange it seems to me.

"Yet here's a kiss for my mother dear,
  My mother dear, if this be so,
And lay your hand upon my head,
  And bless me, mother, ere I go."

She clad herself in a russet gown,
  She was no longer Lady Clare:
She went by dale, and she went by down,
  With a single rose in her hair.

The lily-white doe Lord Ronald had brought
  Leapt up from where she lay,
Dropt her head in the maiden's hand,
  And follow'd her all the way.

Down stept Lord Ronald from his tower:
  "O Lady Clare, you shame your worth!
Why come you drest like a village maid,
  That are the flower of the earth?"

"If I come drest like a village maid,
  I am but as my fortunes are:
I am a beggar born," she said,
  "And not the Lady Clare."

"Play me no tricks," said Lord Ronald,
  "For I am yours in word and in deed.
Play me no tricks," said Lord Ronald,
  "Your riddle is hard to read."

O and proudly stood she up!
  Her heart within her did not fail:
She look'd into Lord Ronald's eyes,
  And told him all her nurse's tale.

He laugh'd a laugh of merry scorn:
  He turn'd and kiss'd her where she stood:
"If you are not the heiress born?
  And I," said he, "the next in blood—

"If you are not the heiress born,
  And I," said he, "the lawful heir,
We two will wed to-morrow morn,
  And you shall still be Lady Clare."
               ALFRED TENNYSON, LORD TENNYSON (1809–1892)

THE LORD OF BURLEIGH   728
In her ear he whispers gaily,
  "If my heart by signs can tell,
Maiden, I have watched thee daily,
  And I think thou lov'st me well."

She replies, in accents fainter,
  "There is none I love like thee."
He is but a landscape-painter,
  And a village maiden she.

He to lips, that fondly falter,
  Presses his without reproof;
Leads her to the village altar,
  And they leave her father's roof.

"I can make no marriage present;
  Little can I give my wife.
Love will make our cottage pleasant,
  And I love thee more than life."

They by parks and lodges going
  See the lordly castles stand;
Summer woods, about them blowing,
  Made a murmur in the land.

From deep thought himself he rouses,
  Says to her that loves him well,
"Let us see these handsome houses
  Where the wealthy nobles dwell."

So she goes by him attended,
  Hears him lovingly converse,
Sees whatever fair and splendid
  Lay betwixt his home and hers.

Parks with oak and chestnut shady,
  Parks and order'd gardens great,
Ancient homes of lord and lady,
  Built for pleasure and for state.

All he shows her makes him dearer;
  Evermore she seems to gaze
On that cottage growing nearer,
  Where they twain will spend their days.

O but she will love him truly!
  He shall have a cheerful home;
She will order all things duly
  When beneath his roof they come.

Thus her heart rejoices greatly
  Till a gateway she discerns
With armorial bearings stately,
  And beneath the gate she turns;

Sees a mansion more majestic
  Than all those she saw before;
Many a gallant gay domestic
  Bows before him at the door.

And they speak in gentle murmur
  When they answer to his call,
While he treads with footstep firmer,
  Leading on from hall to hall.

And while now she wanders blindly,
  Nor the meaning can divine,
Proudly turns he round and kindly,
  "All of this is mine and thine."

Here he lives in state and bounty,
  Lord of Burleigh, fair and free,
Not a lord in all the county
  Is so great a lord as he.

All at once the colour flushes
  Her sweet face from brow to chin;
As it were with same she blushes,
  And her spirit changed within.

Then her countenance all over
  Pale again as death did prove:
But he clasp'd her like a lover,
  And he cheer'd her soul with love.

So she strove against her weakness,
  Tho' at times her spirits sank;
Shaped her heart with woman's meekness
  To all duties of her rank;

And a gentle consort made he,
  And her gentle mind was such
That she grew a noble lady,
  And the people loved her much.

But a trouble weigh'd upon her
    And perplex'd her, night and morn,
With the burden of an honour
    Unto which she was not born.

Faint she grew and ever fainter,
    As she murmur'd, "Oh, that he
Were once more that landscape-painter
    Which did win my heart from me!"

So she droop'd and droop'd before him,
    Fading slowly from his side;
Three fair children first she bore him,
    Then before her time she died.

Weeping, weeping late and early,
    Walking up and pacing down,
Deeply mourn'd the Lord of Burleigh,
    Burleigh-house by Stamford-town.

And he came to look upon her,
    And he look'd at her and said,
"Bring the dress and put it on her
    That she wore when she was wed."

Then her people, softly treading,
    Bore to earth her body, drest
In the dress that she was wed in,
    That her spirit might have rest.
                ALFRED TENNYSON, LORD TENNYSON (1809–1892)

HIAWATHA'S CHILDHOOD   729

By the shores of Gitche Gumee,
By the shining Big-Sea-Water,
Stood the wigwam of Nokomis,
Daughter of the Moon, Nokomis.
Dark behind it rose the forest,
Rose the black and gloomy pine-trees,
Rose the firs with cones upon them;
Bright before it beat the water,
Beat the clear and sunny water,
Beat the shining Big-Sea-Water.

There the wrinkled old Nokomis
Nursed the little Hiawatha,
Rocked him in his linden cradle,
Bedded soft in moss and rushes,
Safely bound with reindeer sinews;
Stilled his fretful wail by saying,
"Hush! the Naked Bear will hear thee!"
Lulled him into slumber, singing,
"Ewa-yea! my little owlet!
Who is this that lights the wigwam?
With his great eyes lights the wigwam?
Ewa-yea! my little owlet!"

Many things Nokomis taught him
Of the stars that shine in heaven;
Showed him Ishkoodah, the comet,
Ishkoodah, with fiery tresses;
Showed the Death-Dance of the spirits,
Warriors with their plumes and war-clubs,
Flaring far away to northward
In the frosty nights of winter;
Showed the broad, white road in heaven,
Pathway of the ghosts, the shadows,
Running straight across the heavens,
Crowded with the ghosts, the shadows.

At the door, on summer evenings,
Sat the little Hiawatha;
Heard the whispering of the pine-trees,
Heard the lapping of the water,
Sounds of music, words of wonder;
"Minnie-wawa!" said the pine-trees,
"Mudway-aushka!" said the water;
Saw the fire-fly, Wah-wah-taysee,
Flitting through the dusk of evening,
With the twinkle of its candle
Lighting up the brakes and bushes,
And he sang the song of children.
Sang the song Nokomis taught him:
"Wah-wah-taysee, little fire-fly,
Little, flitting, white-fire insect,
Little, dancing, white-fire creature,
Light me with your little candle,
Ere upon my bed I lay me,
Ere in sleep I close my eyelids!"

Saw the moon rise from the water
Rippling, rounding from the water,
Saw the flecks and shadows on it,
Whispered, "What is that, Nokomis?"
And the good Nokomis answered:
"Once a warrior, very angry,
Seized his grandmother, and threw her
Up into the sky at midnight;
Right against the moon he threw her;
'Tis her body that you see there."

Saw the rainbow in the heaven,
In the eastern sky, the rainbow,
Whispered, "What is that, Nokomis?"
And the good Nokomis answered:
"'Tis the heaven of flowers you see there;
All the wild-flowers of the forest,
All the lilies of the prairie,
When on earth they fade and perish,
Blossom in that heaven above us."

When he heard the owls at midnight,
Hooting, laughing in the forest,
"What is that?" he cried, in terror;
"What is that," he said, "Nokomis?"
And the good Nokomis answered:
"That is but the owl and owlet,
Talking in their native language,
Talking, scolding at each other."

Then the little Hiawatha
Learned of every bird its language,
Learned their names and all their secrets,
How they built their nests in summer,
Where they hid themselves in winter,
Talked with them whene'er he met them,
Called them "Hiawatha's Chickens."

Of all beasts he learned the language,
Learned their names and all their secrets,
How the beavers built their lodges,
Where the squirrels hid their acorns,
How the reindeer ran so swiftly,
Why the rabbit was so timid,
Talked with them whene'er he met them,
Called them "Hiawatha's Brothers."
    HENRY WADSWORTH LONGFELLOW (1807–1882)

A LIFE ON THE OCEAN WAVE   730

A life on the ocean wave,
 A home on the rolling deep,
Where the scattered waters rave,
 And the winds their revels keep!
Like an eagle caged, I pine
 On this dull, unchanging shore:
Oh! give me the flashing brine,
 The spray and the tempest's roar!

Once more on the deck I stand
 Of my own swift-gliding craft:
Set sail! farewell to the land!
 The gale follows fair abaft.
We shoot through the sparkling foam
 Like an ocean-bird set free;—
Like the ocean-bird, our home
 We'll find far out on the sea.

The land is no longer in view,
 The clouds have begun to frown;
But with a stout vessel and crew,
 We'll say, Let the storm come down!

And the song of our hearts shall be,
  While the winds and the waters rave,
A home on the rolling sea!
A life on the ocean wave!

EPES SARGENT (1813–1880)

731   BARBARA FRIETCHIE

Up from the meadows rich with corn,
Clear in the cool September morn,

The clustered spires of Frederick stand
Green-walled by the hills of Maryland.

Roundabout them orchards sweep,
Apple and peach tree fruited deep,

Fair as the garden of the Lord
To the eyes of the famished rebel horde,

On that pleasant morn of the early fall
When Lee marched over the mountain-wall,

Over the mountains winding down,
Horse and foot, into Frederick town.

Forty flags with their silver stars,
Forty flags with their crimson bars,

Flapped in the morning wind: the sun
Of noon looked down, and saw not one.

Up rose old Barbara Frietchie then,
Bowed with her fourscore years and ten,

Bravest of all in Frederick town,
She took up the flag the men hauled down.

In her attic window the staff she set,
To show that one heart was loyal yet.

Up the street came the rebel tread,
Stonewall Jackson riding ahead.

Under his slouched hat left and right
He glanced: the old flag met his sight.

"Halt!"—the dust-brown ranks stood fast.
"Fire!"—out blazed the rifle-blast.

It shivered the window, pane and sash;
It rent the banner with seam and gash.

Quick, as it fell, from the broken staff
Dame Barbara snatched the silken scarf.

She leaned far out on the window-sill,
And shook it forth with a royal will.

"Shoot, if you must, this old gray head,
But spare your country's flag," she said.

A shade of sadness, a blush of shame,
Over the face of the leader came;

The nobler nature within him stirred
To life at that woman's deed and word:

"Who touches a hair of yon gray head
Dies like a dog! March on!" he said.

All day long through Frederick street
Sounded the tread of marching feet:

All day long that free flag tost
Over the heads of the rebel host.

Even its torn folds rose and fell
On the loyal winds that loved it well;

And through the hill-gaps sunset light
Shone over it with a warm good-night.

Barbara Frietchie's work is o'er,
And the rebel rides on his raids no more.

Honour to her! and let a tear
Fall, for her sake, on Stonewall's bier.

Over Barbara Frietchie's grave,
Flag of Freedom and Union, wave!

Peace and order and beauty draw
Round thy symbol of light and law;

And ever the stars above look down
On thy stars below in Frederick town!
    JOHN GREENLEAF WHITTIER (1807–1892)

THE CHARGE OF THE LIGHT BRIGADE 732
 Half a league, half a league,
  Half a league onward,
 All in the valley of Death
  Rode the six hundred.
 "Forward, the Light Brigade!
  Charge for the guns!" he said:
 Into the valley of Death
  Rode the six hundred.

  "Forward, the Light Brigade!"
  Was there a man dismay'd?
  Not tho' the soldier knew
   Some one had blunder'd:

Theirs not to make reply,
Theirs not to reason why,
Theirs but to do and die:
Into the valley of Death
  Rode the six hundred.

Cannon to right of them,
Cannon to left of them,
Cannon in front of them
  Volley'd and thunder'd;
Storm'd at with shot and shell
Boldly they rode and well,
Into the jaws of Death,
Into the mouth of Hell
  Rode the six hundred.

Flash'd all their sabers bare,
Flash'd as they turn'd in air
Sab'ring the gunners there,
Charging an army, while
  All the world wonder'd:
Plunged in the battery-smoke
Right thro' the line they broke;
Cossack and Russian
Reel'd from the saber-stroke
  Shatter'd and sunder'd.
Then they rode back, but not
  Not the six hundred.

Cannon to right of them,
Cannon to left of them,
Cannon behind them
  Volleyed and thundered:
Stormed at with shot and shell,
While horse and hero fell,
They that had fought so well
Came through the jaws of death
Back from the mouth of hell,
All that was left of them—
  Left of six hundred.

When can their glory fade?
Oh, the wild charge they made!
  All the world wondered.
Honour the charge they made!
Honour the Light Brigade—
  Noble six hundred!

    ALFRED TENNYSON, LORD TENNYSON (1809–1892)

The Tournament 733

I
Bright shone the lists, blue bent the skies,
   And the knights still hurried amain
To the tournament under the ladies' eyes,
   Where the jousters were Heart and Brain.

II
Flourished the trumpets, entered Heart,
   A youth in crimson and gold;
Flourished again; Brain stood apart,
   Steel-armoured, dark and cold.

III
Heart's palfrey caracoled gaily round,
   Heart tra-li-ra'd merrily;
But Brain sat still, with never a sound,
   So cynical-calm was he.

IV
Heart's helmet-crest bore favours three
   From his lady's white hand caught;
While Brain wore a plumeless casque; not he
   Or favour gave or sought.

V
The trumpet blew; Heart shot a glance
   To catch his lady's eye.
But Brain gazed straight ahead, his lance
   To aim more faithfully.

VI
They charged, they struck; both fell, both bled;
   Brain rose again, ungloved;
Heart, dying, smiled and faintly said,
   "My love to my beloved."

                              SIDNEY LANIER (1842–1881)

The Wind And The Moon 734

Said the Wind to the Moon, "I will blow you out,
     You stare
     In the air
     Like a ghost in a chair,
Always looking what I am about—
I hate to be watched; I'll blow you out."

The Wind blew hard, and out went the Moon.
     So, deep
     On a heap
     Of clouds to sleep,
Down lay the Wind, and slumbered soon,
Muttering low, "I've done for that Moon."

He turned in his bed; she was there again!
>   On high
>   In the sky,
>   With her one ghost eye,
The Moon shone white and alive and plain.
Said the Wind, "I will blow you out again."

The Wind blew hard, and the Moon grew dim.
>   "With my sledge,
>   And my wedge,
>   I have knocked off her edge!
If only I blow right fierce and grim,
The creature will soon be dimmer than dim."

He blew and he blew, and she thinned to a thread.
>   "One puff
>   More's enough
>   To blow her to snuff!
One good puff more where the last was bred,
And glimmer, glimmer, glum will go the thread."

He blew a great blast, and the thread was gone
>   In the air
>   Nowhere
>   Was a moonbeam bare;
Far off and harmless the shy stars shone—
Sure and certain the Moon was gone!

The Wind he took to his revels once more;
>   On down,
>   In town,
>   Like a merry-mad clown,
He leaped and hallooed with whistle and roar—
"What's that?" The glimmering thread once more!

He flew in a rage—he danced and blew;
>   But in vain
>   Was the pain
>   Of his bursting brain;
For still the broader the Moon-scrap grew,
The broader he swelled his big cheeks and blew.

Slowly she grew—till she filled the night,
>   And shone
>   On her throne
>   In the sky alone,
A matchless, wonderful silvery light,
Radiant and lovely, the queen of the night.

Said the Wind: "What a marvel of power am I
>   With my breath,
>   Good faith!
>   I blew her to death—
First blew her away right out of the sky—
Then blew her in; what strength have I!"

But the Moon she knew nothing about the affair;
    For high
    In the sky,
    With her one white eye,
Motionless, miles above the air,
She had never heard the great Wind blare.

GEORGE MACDONALD (1824–1905)

JESUS THE CARPENTER

735

"Isn't this Joseph's son?"—ay, it is He;
Joseph the carpenter—same trade as me—
I thought as I'd find it—I knew it was here—
    But my sight's getting queer.

I don't know right where as His shed must ha' stood—
But often, as I've been a-planing my wood,
I've took off my hat, just with thinking of He
    At the same work as me.

He warn't that set up that He couldn't stoop down
And work in the country for folks in the town;
And I'll warrant He felt a bit pride, like I've done,
    At a good job begun.

The parson he knows that I'll not make too free,
But on Sunday I feels as pleased as can be,
When I wears my clean smock, and sits in a pew,
    And has taught a few.

I think of as how not the parson hissen,
As is teacher and father and shepherd o' men,
Not he knows as much of the Lord in that shed,
    Where He earned His own bread.

And when I goes home to my missus, says she,
"Are ye wanting your key?"
For she knows my queer ways, and my love for the shed
    (We've been forty years wed).

So I comes right away by mysen, with the book,
And I turns the old pages and has a good look
For the text as I've found, as tells me as He
    Were the same trade as me.

Why don't I mark it? Ah, many say so,
But I think I'd as lief, with your leaves, let it go:
It do seem that nice when I fall on it sudden—
    Unexpected, you know!

CATHERINE C. LIDDELL (1848–1927)

736 Heaven Is Not Reached At A Single Bound
(A FRAGMENT)

Heaven is not reached at a single bound,
  But we build the ladder by which we rise
  From the lowly earth to the vaulted skies,
And we mount to its summit round by round.

I count this thing to be grandly true:
  That a noble deed is a step toward God,—
  Lifting the soul from the common clod
To a purer air and a broader view.

                                J.G. HOLLAND (1819–1881)

737 The Chambered Nautilus

This is the ship of pearl, which, poets feign,
    Sailed the unshadowed main,—
    The venturous bark that flings
On the sweet summer wind its purpled wings
In gulfs enchanted, where the Siren sings,
    And coral reefs lie bare,
Where the cold sea-maids rise to sun their streaming hair.

Its webs of living gauze no more unfurl;
    Wrecked is the ship of pearl!
    And every chambered cell,
Where its dim dreaming life was wont to dwell,
As the frail tenant shaped his growing shell,
    Before thee lies revealed,—
Its irised ceiling rent, its sunless crypt unsealed!

Year after year beheld the silent toil
    That spread his lustrous coil;
    Still, as the spiral grew,
He left the past year's dwelling for the new,
Stole with soft step its shining archway through,
    Built up its idle door,
Stretched in his last-found home, and knew the old no more.

Thanks for the heavenly message brought by thee,
    Child of the wandering sea,
    Cast from her lap, forlorn!
From thy dead lips a clearer note is born
Than ever Triton blew from wreathed horn!
    While on mine ear it rings,
Through the deep caves of thought I hear a voice that sings:—

Build thee more stately mansions, O my soul,
    As the swift seasons roll!
    Leave thy low-vaulted past!
Let each new temple, nobler than the last,
Shut thee from heaven with a dome more vast,
    Till thou at length art free,
Leaving thine outgrown shell by life's unresting sea!
                  OLIVER WENDELL HOLMES (1841–1935)

CROSSING THE BAR   738

    Sunset and evening star,
      And one clear call for me!
    And may there be no moaning of the bar,
      When I put out to sea,

    But such a tide as moving seems asleep,
      Too full for sound and foam,
    When that which drew from out the boundless deep
      Turns again home.

    Twilight and evening bell,
      And after that the dark!
    And may there be no sadness of farewell,
      When I embark;

    For tho' from out our bourne of Time and Place
      The flood may bear me far,
    I hope to see my Pilot face to face
      When I have cross'd the bar.
            ALFRED TENNYSON, LORD TENNYSON (1809–1892)

THE DEATH OF NAPOLEON   739

Wild was the night, yet a wilder night
  Hung round the soldier's pillow;
In his bosom there waged a fiercer fight
  Than the fight on the wrathful billow.

A few fond mourners were kneeling by,
  The few that his stern heart cherished;
They knew, by his glazed and unearthly eye,
  That life had nearly perished.

They knew by his awful and kingly look,
  By the order hastily spoken,
That he dreamed of days when the nations shook,
  And the nations' hosts were broken.

He dreamed that the Frenchman's sword still slew,
  And triumphed the Frenchman's eagle,
And the struggling Austrian fled anew,
  Like the hare before the beagle.

The bearded Russian he scourged again,
  The Prussian's camp was routed,
And again on the hills of haughty Spain
  His mighty armies shouted.

Over Egypt's sands, over Alpine snows,
  At the pyramids, at the mountain,
Where the wave of the lordly Danube flows,
  And by the Italian fountain,

On the snowy cliffs where mountain streams
  Dash by the Switzer's dwelling,
He led again, in his dying dreams,
  His hosts, the proud earth quelling.

Again Marengo's field was won,
  And Jena's bloody battle;
Again the world was overrun,
  Made pale at his cannon's rattle.

He died at the close of that darksome day,
  A day that shall live in story;
In the rocky land they placed his clay,
  "And left him alone with his glory."

                              Isaac McClellan (1806–1899)

740   The Wreck Of The *Hesperus*

It was the schooner *Hesperus*,
  That sailed the wintry sea;
And the skipper had taken his little daughter,
  To bear him company.

Blue were her eyes as the fairy-flax,
  Her cheeks like the dawn of day,
And her bosom white as the hawthorn buds
  That ope in the month of May.

The skipper he stood beside the helm,
  His pipe was in his mouth,
And he watched how the veering flaw did blow
  The smoke now west, now south.

Then up and spake an old sailor,
  Had sailed the Spanish Main,
"I pray thee put into yonder port,
  For I fear a hurricane.

"Last night the moon had a golden ring,
  And to-night no moon we see!"
The skipper he blew a whiff from his pipe,
  And a scornful laugh laughed he.

Colder and louder blew the wind,
  A gale from the northeast,
The snow fell hissing in the brine,
  And the billows frothed like yeast.

Down came the storm, and smote amain
   The vessel in its strength;
She shuddered and paused, like a frighted steed,
   Then leaped her cable's length.

"Come hither! come hither! my little daughter,
   And do not tremble so;
For I can weather the roughest gale
   That ever wind did blow."

He wrapped her warm in his seaman's coat
   Against the stinging blast;
He cut a rope from a broken spar,
   And bound her to the mast.

"O father! I hear the church-bells ring,
   O say, what may it be?"
"Tis a fog-bell on a rock-bound coast!"—
   And he steered for the open sea.

"O father! I hear the sound of guns,
   O say, what may it be?"
"Some ship in distress, that cannot live
   In such an angry sea!"

"O father! I see a gleaming light,
   O say, what may it be?"
But the father answered never a word,
   A frozen corpse was he.

Lashed to the helm, all stiff and stark,
   With his face turned to the skies,
The lantern gleamed through the gleaming snow
   On his fixed and glassy eyes.

Then the maiden clasped her hands and prayed
   That savèd she might be;
And she thought of Christ, who stilled the wave
   On the Lake of Galilee.

And fast through the midnight dark and drear,
   Through the whistling sleet and snow,
Like a sheeted ghost the vessel swept
   Toward the reef of Norman's Woe.

And ever the fitful gusts between
   A sound came from the land;
It was the sound of the trampling surf
   On the rocks and the hard sea-sand.

The breakers were right beneath her bows,
   She drifted a dreary wreck,
And a whooping billow swept the crew
   Like icicles from her deck.

She struck where the white and fleecy waves
  Looked soft as carded wool,
But the cruel rocks they gored her side
  Like the horns of an angry bull.

Her rattling shrouds all sheathed in ice,
  With the masts went by the board;
Like a vessel of glass she stove and sank,—
  Ho! ho! the breakers roared!

At daybreak on the bleak sea-beach
  A fisherman stood aghast,
To see the form of a maiden fair
  Lashed close to a drifting mast.

The salt sea was frozen on her breast,
  The salt tears in her eyes;
And he saw her hair, like the brown sea-weed,
  On the billows fall and rise.

Such was the wreck of the *Hesperus*,
  In the midnight and the snow!
Christ save us all from a death like this,
  On the reef of Norman's Woe!
          HENRY WADSWORTH LONGFELLOW (1807–1882)

741   THE FINDING OF THE LYRE

There lay upon the ocean's shore
What once a tortoise served to cover;
A year and more, with rush and roar,
The surf had rolled it over,
Had played with it, and flung it by,
As wind and weather might decide it,
Then tossed it high where sand-drifts dry
Cheap burial might provide it.

It rested there to bleach or tan,
The rains had soaked, the sun had burned it;
With many a ban the fisherman
Had stumbled o'er and spurned it;
And there the fisher-girl would stay,
Conjecturing with her brother
How in their play the poor estray
Might serve some use or other.

So there it lay, through wet and dry,
As empty as the last new sonnet,
Till by and by came Mercury,
And, having mused upon it,
"Why, here," cried he, "the thing of things
In shape, material, and dimension!
Give it but strings, and, lo, it sings,
A wonderful invention!"

So said, so done; the chords he strained,
And, as his fingers o'er them hovered,
The shell disdained a soul had gained,
The lyre had been discovered.
O empty world that round us lies,
Dead shell, of soul and thought forsaken,
Brought we but eyes like Mercury's,
In thee what songs should waken!
JAMES RUSSELL LOWELL (1819–1891)

A CHRYSALIS 742

My little Mädchen found one day
A curious something in her play,
That was not fruit, nor flower, nor seed;
It was not anything that grew,
Or crept, or climbed, or swam, or flew;
Had neither legs nor wings, indeed;
And yet she was not sure, she said,
Whether it was alive or dead.

She brought it in her tiny hand
To see if I would understand,
And wondered when I made reply,
"You've found a baby butterfly."
"A butterfly is not like this,"
With doubtful look she answered me.
So then I told her what would be
Some day within the chrysalis:
How, slowly, in the dull brown thing
Now still as death, a spotted wing,
And then another, would unfold,
Till from the empty shell would fly
A pretty creature, by and by,
All radiant in blue and gold.

"And will it, truly?" questioned she—
Her laughing lips and eager eyes
All in a sparkle of surprise—
"And shall your little Mädchen see?"
"She shall!" I said. How could I tell
That ere the worm within its shell
Its gauzy, splendid wings had spread,
My little Mädchen would be dead?

To-day the butterfly has flown,—
She was not here to see it fly,—
And sorrowing I wonder why
The empty shell is mine alone.
Perhaps the secret lies in this:
I too had found a chrysalis,
And Death that robbed me of delight
Was but the radiant creature's flight!
MARY EMILY BRADLEY (1835–1898)

743   THE BROOK

> I chatter, chatter, as I flow
>   To join the brimming river;
> For men may come and men may go,
>   But I go on forever.
>
> I wind about, and in and out,
>   With here a blossom sailing,
> And here and there a lusty trout,
>   And here and there a grayling.
>
> I steal by lawns and grassy plots,
>   I slide by hazel covers;
> I move the sweet forget-me-nots
>   That grow for happy lovers.
>
> I slip, I slide, I gloom, I glance,
>   Among my skimming swallows;
> I make the netted sunbeams dance
>   Against my sandy shallows.
>
> I murmur under moon and stars
>   In brambly wildernesses;
> I linger by my shingly bars;
>   I loiter round my cresses.
>
> And out again I curve and flow
>   To join the brimming river;
> For men may come and men may go,
>   But I go on forever.
>   ALFRED TENNYSON, LORD TENNYSON (1809–1892)

744   THE SHEPHERD OF KING ADMETUS

> There came a youth upon the earth,
>   Some thousand years ago,
> Whose slender hands were nothing worth,
>   Whether to plow, or reap, or sow.
>
> Upon an empty tortoise-shell
>   He stretched some chords, and drew
> Music that made men's bosoms swell
>   Fearless, or brimmed their eyes with dew.
>
> Then King Admetus, one who had
>   Pure taste by right divine,
> Decreed his singing not too bad
>   To hear between the cups of wine:
>
> And so, well pleased with being soothed
>   Into a sweet half-sleep,
> Three times his kingly beard he smoothed,
>   And made him viceroy o'er his sheep.

His words were simple words enough,
   And yet he used them so,
That what in other mouths was rough
   In his seemed musical and low.

Men called him but a shiftless youth,
   In whom no good they saw;
And yet, unwittingly, in truth,
   They made his careless words their law.

They knew not how he learned at all,
   For idly, hour by hour,
He sat and watched the dead leaves fall,
   Or mused upon a common flower.

It seemed the loveliness of things
   Did teach him all their use,
For, in mere weeds, and stones, and springs,
   He found a healing power profuse.

Men granted that his speech was wise,
   But, when a glance they caught
Of his slim grace and woman's eyes,
   They laughed, and called him good-for-naught.

Yet after he was dead and gone,
   And e'en his memory dim,
Earth seemed more sweet to live upon,
   More full of love, because of him.

And day by day more holy grew
   Each spot where he had trod,
Till after-poets only knew
   Their first-born brother as a god.

                  JAMES RUSSELL LOWELL (1819–1891)

HOW THEY BROUGHT THE GOOD NEWS FROM GHENT TO AIX

I sprang to the stirrup, and Joris, and he;
I galloped, Dirck galloped, we galloped all three;
"Good speed!" cried the watch as the gate-bolts undrew;
"Speed!" echoed the wall to us galloping through;
Behind shut the postern, the lights sank to rest,
And into the midnight we galloped abreast.

Not a word to each other; we kept the great pace
Neck by neck, stride by stride, never changing our place;
I turned in my saddle and made its girth tight,
Then shortened each stirrup, and set the pique right,
Rebuckled the cheek-strap, chained slacker the bit,
Nor galloped less steadily Roland a whit.

'Twas moonset at starting; but while we drew near
Lokeren, the cocks crew and twilight dawned clear;
At Boom, a great yellow star came out to see;
At Düffeld, 'twas morning as plain as could be;
And from Mecheln church-steeple we heard the half-chime,
So Joris broke silence with, "Yet there is time!"

At Aershot, up leaped of a sudden the sun,
And against him the cattle stood black every one,
To stare through the mist at us galloping past,
And I saw my stout galloper Roland at last,
With resolute shoulders, each butting away
The haze, as some bluff river headland its spray:

And his low head and crest, just one sharp ear bent back
For my voice, and the other pricked out on his track;
And one eye's black intelligence,—ever that glance
O'er its white edge at me, his own master, askance!
And the thick, heavy spume-flakes which aye and anon
His fierce lips shook upward in galloping on.

By Hasselt, Dirck groaned; and cried Joris, "Stay spur!
Your Roos galloped bravely, the fault's not in her,
We'll remember at Aix"—for one heard the quick wheeze
Of her chest, saw the stretched neck and staggering knees,
And sunk tail, and horrible heave of the flank,
As down on her haunches she shuddered and sank.

So, we were left galloping, Joris and I,
Past Looz and past Tongres, no cloud in the sky;
The broad sun above laughed a pitiless laugh,
'Neath our feet broke the brittle bright stubble like chaff;
Till over by Dalhem a dome-spire sprang white,
And "Gallop," gasped Joris, "for Aix is in sight!"

"How they'll greet us!"—and all in a moment his roan
Rolled neck and croup over, lay dead as a stone;
And there was my Roland to bear the whole weight
Of the news which alone could save Aix from her fate,
With his nostrils like pits full of blood to the brim,
And with circles of red for his eye-sockets' rim.

Then I cast loose my buff-coat, each holster let fall,
Shook off both my jack-boots, let go belt and all,
Stood up in the stirrup, leaned, patted his ear,
Called my Roland his pet-name, my horse without peer;
Clapped my hands, laughed and sang, any noise, bad or good,
Till at length into Aix Roland galloped and stood.

And all I remember is—friends flocking round
As I sat with his head 'twixt my knees on the ground;
And no voice but was praising this Roland of mine,
As I poured down his throat our last measure of wine,
Which (the burgesses voting by common consent)
Was no more than his due who brought the good news from Ghent.
ROBERT BROWNING (1812–1889)

HORATIUS AT THE BRIDGE 746

Lars Porsena of Clusium,
  By the Nine Gods he swore
That the great house of Tarquin
  Should suffer wrong no more.
By the Nine Gods he swore it,
  And named a trysting-day,
And bade his messengers ride forth,
East and west and south and north,
  To summon his array.

East and west and south and north
  The messengers ride fast,
And tower and town and cottage
  Have heard the trumpet's blast.
Shame on the false Etruscan
  Who lingers in his home,
When Porsena of Clusium
  Is on the march for Rome!

The horsemen and the footmen
  Are pouring in amain
From many a stately market-place,
  From many a fruitful plain,
From many a lonely hamlet,
  Which, hid by beech and pine,
Like an eagle's nest hangs on the crest
  Of purple Apennine:

From lordly Volaterræ,
  Where scowls the far-famed hold
Piled by the hands of giants
  For godlike kings of old;
From sea-girt Populonia,
  Whose sentinels descry
Sardinia's snowy mountain-tops
  Fringing the southern sky;

From the proud mart of Pisæ,
  Queen of the western waves,
Where ride Massilia's triremes,
  Heavy with fair-haired slaves;
From where sweet Clanis wanders
  Through corn and vines and flowers,
From where Cortona lifts to heaven
  Her diadem of towers.

Tall are the oaks whose acorns
   Drop in dark Auser's rill;
Fat are the stags that champ the boughs
   Of the Ciminian hill;
Beyond all streams, Clitumnus
   Is to the herdsman dear;
Best of all pools the fowler loves
   The great Volsinian mere.

But now no stroke of woodman
   Is heard by Auser's rill;
No hunter tracks the stag's green path
   Up the Ciminian hill;
Unwatched along Clitumnus
   Grazes the milk-white steer;
Unharmed the water-fowl may dip
   In the Volsinian mere.

The harvests of Arretium,
   This year, old men shall reap;
This year, young boys in Umbro
   Shall plunge the struggling sheep;
And in the vats of Luna,
   This year, the must shall foam
Round the white feet of laughing girls
   Whose sires have marched to Rome.

There be thirty chosen prophets,
   The wisest of the land,
Who always by Lars Porsena
   Both morn and evening stand.
Evening and morn the Thirty
   Have turned the verses o'er,
Traced from the right on linen white
   By mighty seers of yore;

And with one voice the Thirty
   Have their glad answer given:
"Go forth, go forth, Lars Porsena,—
   Go forth, beloved of Heaven!
Go, and return in glory
   To Clusium's royal dome,
And hang round Nurscia's altars
   The golden shields of Rome!"

And now hath every city
   Sent up her tale of men;
The foot are fourscore thousand,
   The horse are thousands ten.
Before the gates of Sutrium
   Is met the great array;
A proud man was Lars Porsena
   Upon the trysting-day.

For all the Etruscan armies
  Were ranged beneath his eye,
And many a banished Roman,
  And many a stout ally;
And with a mighty following,
  To join the muster, came
The Tusculan Mamilius,
  Prince of the Latian name.

But by the yellow Tiber
  Was tumult and affright;
From all the spacious champaign
  To Rome men took their flight.
A mile around the city
  The throng stopped up the ways;
A fearful sight it was to see
  Through two long nights and days.

For aged folk on crutches,
  And women great with child,
And mothers, sobbing over babes
  That clung to them and smiled,
And sick men borne in litters
  High on the necks of slaves,
And troops of sunburned husbandmen
  With reaping-hooks and staves,

And droves of mules and asses
  Laden with skins of wine,
And endless flocks of goats and sheep,
  And endless herds of kine,
And endless trains of wagons,
  That creaked beneath the weight
Of corn-sacks and of household goods,
  Choked every roaring gate.

Now, from the rock Tarpeian,
  Could the wan burghers spy
The line of blazing villages
  Red in the midnight sky.
The Fathers of the City,
  They sat all night and day,
For every hour some horseman came
  With tidings of dismay.

To eastward and to westward
  Have spread the Tuscan bands,
Nor house, nor fence, nor dovecote
  In Crustumerium stands.
Verbenna down to Ostia
  Hath wasted all the plain;
Astur hath stormed Janiculum,
  And the stout guards are slain.

I wis, in all the Senate
  There was no heart so bold
But sore it ached, and fast it beat,
  When that ill news was told.
Forthwith up rose the Consul,
  Up rose the Fathers all;
In haste they girded up their gowns,
  And hied them to the wall.

They held a council, standing
  Before the River-gate;
Short time was there, ye well may guess,
  For musing or debate.
Out spake the Consul roundly:
  "The bridge must straight go down;
For, since Janiculum is lost,
  Naught else can save the town."

Just then a scout came flying,
  All wild with haste and fear:
"To arms! to arms! Sir Consul,—
  Lars Porsena is here."
On the low hills to westward
  The Consul fixed his eye,
And saw the swarthy storm of dust
  Rise fast along the sky.

And nearer fast and nearer
  Doth the red whirlwind come;
And louder still, and still more loud,
From underneath that rolling cloud,
Is heard the trumpets' war-note proud,
  The trampling and the hum.
And plainly and more plainly
  Now through the gloom appears,
Far to left and far to right,
In broken gleams of dark-blue light,
The long array of helmets bright,
  The long array of spears.

And plainly and more plainly,
  Above that glimmering line,
Now might ye see the banners
  Of twelve fair cities shine;
But the banner of proud Clusium
  Was highest of them all,—
The terror of the Umbrian,
  The terror of the Gaul.

And plainly and more plainly
  Now might the burghers know,
By port and vest, by horse and crest,
  Each warlike Lucumo:

There Cilnius of Arretium
  On his fleet roan was seen;
And Astur of the fourfold shield,
  Girt with the brand none else may wield;
Tolumnius with the belt of gold,
And dark Verbenna from the hold
  By reedy Thrasymene.

Fast by the royal standard,
  O'erlooking all the war,
Lars Porsena of Clusium
  Sat in his ivory car.
By the right wheel rode Mamilius,
  Prince of the Latian name;
And by the left false Sextus,
  That wrought the deed of shame.

But when the face of Sextus
  Was seen among the foes,
A yell that rent the firmament
  From all the town arose.
On the house-tops was no woman
  But spat towards him and hissed,
No child but screamed out curses,
  And shook its little fist.

But the Consul's brow was sad,
  And the Consul's speech was low,
And darkly looked he at the wall,
  And darkly at the foe;
"Their van will be upon us
  Before the bridge goes down;
And if they once may win the bridge,
  What hope to save the town?"

Then out spake brave Horatius,
  The Captain of the gate:
"To every man upon this earth
  Death cometh soon or late.
And how can man die better
  Than facing fearful odds
For the ashes of his fathers
  And the temples of his gods,

"And for the tender mother
  Who dandled him to rest,
And for the wife who nurses
  His baby at her breast,
And for the holy maidens
  Who feed the eternal flame,—
To save them from false Sextus
  That wrought the deed of shame?

"Hew down the bridge, Sir Consul,
   With all the speed ye may;
I, with two more to help me,
   Will hold the foe in play.
In yon strait path a thousand
   May well be stopped by three:
Now who will stand on either hand,
   And keep the bridge with me?"

Then out spake Spurius Lartius,—
   A Ramnian proud was he:
"Lo, I will stand at thy right hand,
   And keep the bridge with thee."
And out spake strong Herminius,—
   Of Titian blood was he:
"I will abide on thy left side,
   And keep the bridge with thee."

"Horatius," quoth the Consul,
   "As thou sayest so let it be,"
And straight against that great array
   Went forth the dauntless three.
For Romans in Rome's quarrel
   Spared neither land nor gold,
Nor son nor wife, nor limb nor life,
   In the brave days of old.

Then none was for a party—
   Then all were for the state;
Then the great man helped the poor,
   And the poor man loved the great;
Then lands were fairly portioned!
   Then spoils were fairly sold:
The Romans were like brothers
   In the brave days of old.

Now Roman is to Roman
   More hateful than a foe,
And the tribunes beard the high,
   And the fathers grind the low.
As we wax hot in faction,
   In battle we wax cold;
Wherefore men fight not as they fought
   In the brave days of old.

Now while the three were tightening
   Their harness on their backs,
The Consul was the foremost man
   To take in hand an axe;
And fathers, mixed with commons,
   Seized hatchet, bar, and crow,
And smote upon the planks above,
   And loosed the props below.

Meanwhile the Tuscan army,
   Right glorious to behold,
Came flashing back the noonday light,
Rank behind rank, like surges bright
   Of a broad sea of gold.
Four hundred trumpets sounded
   A peal of warlike glee,
As that great host with measured tread,
And spears advanced, and ensigns spread,
Rolled slowly toward the bridge's head,
   Where stood the dauntless three.

The three stood calm and silent,
   And looked upon the foes,
And a great shout of laughter
   From all the vanguard rose;
And forth three chiefs came spurring
   Before that deep array;
To earth they sprang, their swords they drew,
And lifted high their shields, and flew
   To win the narrow way.

Aunus, from green Tifernum,
   Lord of the Hill of Vines;
And Seius, whose eight hundred slaves
   Sicken in Ilva's mines;
And Picus, long to Clusium
   Vassal in peace and war,
Who led to fight his Umbrian powers
From that gray crag where, girt with towers,
The fortress of Nequinum lowers
   O'er the pale waves of Nar.

Stout Lartius hurled down Aunus
   Into the stream beneath;
Herminius struck at Seius,
   And clove him to the teeth;
At Picus brave Horatius
   Darted one fiery thrust,
And the proud Umbrian's gilded arms
   Clashed in the bloody dust.

Then Ocnus of Falerii
   Rushed on the Roman three;
And Lausulus of Urgo,
   The rover of the sea;
And Aruns of Volsinium,
   Who slew the great wild boar,—
The great wild boar that had his den
Amidst the reeds of Cosa's fen,
And wasted fields, and slaughtered men,
   Along Albinia's shore.

Herminius smote down Aruns;
   Lartius laid Ocnus low;
Right to the heart of Lausulus
   Horatius sent a blow:
"Lie there," he cried, "fell pirate!
   No more, aghast and pale,
From Ostia's walls the crowd shall mark
The track of thy destroying bark;
No more Campania's hinds shall fly
To woods and caverns, when they spy
   Thy thrice-accursèd sail!"

But now no sound of laughter
   Was heard among the foes;
A wild and wrathful clamor
   From all the vanguard rose.
Six spears' length from the entrance,
   Halted that mighty mass,
And for a space no man came forth
   To win the narrow pass.

But, hark! the cry is Astur:
   And lo! the ranks divide;
And the great lord of Luna
   Comes with his stately stride.
Upon his ample shoulders
   Clangs loud the fourfold shield,
And in his hand he shakes the brand
   Which none but he can wield.

He smiled on those bold Romans,
   A smile serene and high;
He eyed the flinching Tuscans,
   And scorn was in his eye.
Quoth he, "The she-wolf's litter
   Stand savagely at bay;
But will ye dare to follow,
   If Astur clears the way?"

Then, whirling up his broadsword
   With both hands to the height,
He rushed against Horatius,
   And smote with all his might.
With shield and blade Horatius
   Right deftly turned the blow.
The blow, though turned, came yet too nigh;
It missed his helm, but gashed his thigh.
The Tuscans raised a joyful cry
   To see the red blood flow.

He reeled, and on Herminius
   He leaned one breathing-space,
Then, like a wild-cat mad with wounds,
   Sprang right at Astur's face.

Through teeth and skull and helmet
  So fierce a thrust he sped,
The good sword stood a handbreadth out
  Behind the Tuscan's head.

And the great lord of Luna
  Fell at that deadly stroke,
As falls on Mount Avernus
  A thunder-smitten oak.
Far o'er the crashing forest
  The giant arms lie spread;
And the pale augurs, muttering low
  Gaze on the blasted head.

On Astur's throat Horatius
  Right firmly pressed his heel,
And thrice and four times tugged amain,
  Ere he wrenched out the steel.
And "See," he cried, "the welcome,
  Fair guests, that waits you here!
What noble Lucumo comes next
  To taste our Roman cheer?"

But at his haughty challenge
  A sullen murmur ran,
Mingled with wrath and shame and dread,
  Along that glittering van.
There lacked not men of prowess,
  Nor men of lordly race,
For all Etruria's noblest
  Were round the fatal place.

But all Etruria's noblest
  Felt their hearts sink to see
On the earth the bloody corpses,
  In the path the dauntless three;
And from the ghastly entrance,
  Where those bold Romans stood,
All shrank,—like boys who, unaware,
Ranging the woods to start a hare,
Come to the mouth of the dark lair
Where, growling low, a fierce old bear
  Lies amidst bones and blood.

Was none who would be foremost
  To lead such dire attack;
But those behind cried "Forward!"
  And those before cried "Back!"
And backward now and forward
  Wavers the deep array;
And on the tossing sea of steel
To and fro the standards reel,
And the victorious trumpet-peal
  Dies fitfully away.

Yet one man for one moment
　　Strode out before the crowd;
Well known was he to all the three,
　　And they gave him greeting loud:
"Now welcome, welcome, Sextus!
　　Now welcome to thy home!
Why dost thou stay, and turn away?
　　Here lies the road to Rome."

Thrice looked he at the city;
　　Thrice looked he at the dead:
And thrice came on in fury,
　　And thrice turned back in dread;
And, white with fear and hatred,
　　Scowled at the narrow way
Where, wallowing in a pool of blood,
　　The bravest Tuscans lay.

But meanwhile axe and lever
　　Have manfully been plied:
And now the bridge hangs tottering
　　Above the boiling tide.
"Come back, come back, Horatius!"
　　Loud cried the Fathers all,—
"Back, Lartius! back, Herminius!
　　Back, ere the ruin fall!"

Back darted Spurius Lartius,—
　　Herminius darted back;
And, as they passed, beneath their feet
　　They felt the timbers crack.
But when they turned their faces,
　　And on the farther shore
Saw brave Horatius stand alone,
　　They would have crossed once more;

But with a crash like thunder
　　Fell every loosened beam,
And, like a dam, the mighty wreck
　　Lay right athwart the stream;
And a long shout of triumph
　　Rose from the walls of Rome,
As to the highest turret-tops
　　Was splashed the yellow foam.

And like a horse unbroken,
　　When first he feels the rein,
The furious river struggled hard,
　　And tossed his tawny mane,

And burst the curb, and bounded,
   Rejoicing to be free;
And whirling down, in fierce career,
Battlement and plank and pier,
   Rushed headlong to the sea.

Alone stood brave Horatius,
   But constant still in mind,—
Thrice thirty thousand foes before,
   And the broad flood behind.
"Down with him!" cried false Sextus,
   With a smile on his pale face;
"Now yield thee," cried Lars Porsena,
   "Now yield thee to our grace!"

Round turned he, as not deigning
   Those craven ranks to see;
Naught spake he to Lars Porsena,
   To Sextus naught spake he;
But he saw on Palatinus
   The white porch of his home;
And he spake to the noble river
   That rolls by the towers of Rome:

"O Tiber! Father Tiber!
   To whom the Romans pray,
A Roman's life, a Roman's arms,
   Take thou in charge this day!"
So he spake, and, speaking, sheathed
   The good sword by his side,
And, with his harness on his back,
   Plunged headlong in the tide.

No sound of joy or sorrow
   Was heard from either bank,
But friends and foes in dumb surprise,
With parted lips and straining eyes,
   Stood gazing where he sank;
And when above the surges
   They saw his crest appear,
All Rome sent forth a rapturous cry,
And even the ranks of Tuscany
   Could scarce forbear to cheer.

But fiercely ran the current,
   Swollen high by months of rain;
And fast his blood was flowing,
   And he was sore in pain,
And heavy with his armor,
   And spent with changing blows;
And oft they thought him sinking,
   But still again he rose.

Never, I ween, did swimmer,
  In such an evil case,
Struggle through such a raging flood
  Safe to the landing-place;
But his limbs were borne up bravely
  By the brave heart within,
And our good Father Tiber
  Bare bravely up his chin.

"Curse on him!" quoth false Sextus,—
  "Will not the villain drown?
But for this stay, ere close of day
  We should have sacked the town!"
"Heaven help him!" quoth Lars Porsena,
  "And bring him safe to shore;
For such a gallant feat of arms
  Was never seen before."

And now he feels the bottom;
  Now on dry earth he stands;
Now round him throng the Fathers
  To press his gory hands;
And now, with shouts and clapping,
  And noise of weeping loud,
He enters through the River-gate,
  Borne by the joyous crowd.

They gave him of the corn-land,
  That was of public right,
As much as two strong oxen
  Could plough from morn till night;
And they made a molten image,
  And set it up on high,—
And there it stands unto this day
  To witness if I lie.

It stands in the Comitium,
  Plain for all folk to see,—
Horatius in his harness,
  Halting upon one knee;
And underneath is written,
  In letters all of gold,
How valiantly he kept the bridge
  In the brave days of old.

And still his name sounds stirring
  Unto the men of Rome,
As the trumpet-blast that cries to them
  To charge the Volscian home;
And wives still pray to Juno
  For boys with hearts as bold
As his who kept the bridge so well
  In the brave days of old.

And in the nights of winter,
   When the cold north-winds blow,
And the long howling of the wolves
   Is heard amidst the snow;
When round the lonely cottage
   Roars loud the tempest's din,
And the good logs of Algidus
   Roar louder yet within;

When the oldest cask is opened,
   And the largest lamp is lit;
When the chestnuts glow in the embers,
   And the kid turns on the spit;
When young and old in circle
   Around the firebrands close;
When the girls are weaving baskets,
   And the lads are shaping bows;

When the goodman mends his armor,
   And trims his helmet's plume;
When the goodwife's shuttle merrily
   Goes flashing through the loom;
With weeping and with laughter
   Still is the story told,
How well Horatius kept the bridge
   In the brave days of old.
      THOMAS BABINGTON MACAULAY, LORD MACAULAY (1800–1859)

JUNE

What is so rare as a day in June?
Then, if ever, come perfect days;
Then Heaven tries the earth if it be in tune,
   And over it softly her warm ear lays:
Whether we look, or whether we listen,
We hear life murmur, or see it glisten;
Every clod feels a stir of might,
   An instinct within it that reaches and towers,
And, groping blindly above it for light,
   Climbs to a soul in grass and flowers;
The flush of life may well be seen
   Thrilling back over hills and valleys;
The cowslip startles in meadows green.
   The buttercup catches the sun in its chalice,
And there's never a leaf nor a blade too mean
   To be some happy creature's palace;
The little bird sits at his door in the sun,
   Atilt like a blossom among the leaves,
And lets his illumined being o'errun
   With the deluge of summer it receives;

His mate feels the eggs beneath her wings,
And the heart in her dumb breast flutters and sings;
He sings to the wide world, and she to her nest,—
In the nice ear of Nature which song is the best?
JAMES RUSSELL LOWELL (1819–1891)
fragment from "The Vision of Sir Launfal"

748   A PSALM OF LIFE
WHAT THE HEART OF THE YOUNG MAN SAID TO THE PSALMIST

Tell me not, in mournful numbers,
  Life is but an empty dream!—
For the soul is dead that slumbers,
  And things are not what they seem.

Life is real! Life is earnest!
  And the grave is not its goal;
Dust thou art, to dust returnest,
  Was not spoken of the soul.

Not enjoyment, and not sorrow,
  Is our destined end or way;
But to act, that each to-morrow
  Find us farther than to-day.

Art is long, and Time is fleeting,
  And our hearts, though stout and brave,
Still, like muffled drums, are beating
  Funeral marches to the grave.

In the world's broad field of battle,
  In the bivouac of Life,
Be not like dumb, driven cattle!
  Be a hero in the strife!

Trust no Future, howe'er pleasant!
  Let the dead Past bury its dead!
Act,—act in the living Present!
  Heart within, and God o'erhead!

Lives of great men all remind us
  We can make our lives sublime,
And, departing, leave behind us
  Footprints on the sands of time;

Footprints, that perhaps another,
  Sailing o'er life's solemn main,
A forlorn and shipwrecked brother,
  Seeing, shall take heart again.

Let us, then, be up and doing,
  With a heart for any fate;
Still achieving, still pursuing,
  Learn to labour and to wait.
HENRY WADSWORTH LONGFELLOW (1807–1882)

Barnacles 749

My soul is sailing through the sea,
But the Past is heavy and hindereth me.
The Past hath crusted cumbrous shells
That hold the flesh of cold sea-mells
    About my soul.
The huge waves wash, the high waves roll,
Each barnacle clingeth and worketh dole
    And hindereth me from sailing!

Old Past, let go, and drop i' the sea
Till fathomless waters cover thee!
For I am living, but thou art dead;
Thou drawest back, I strive ahead
    The Day to find.
Thy shells unbind! Night comes behind;
I needs must hurry with the wind
    And trim me best for sailing.

SIDNEY LANIER (1842–1881)

Woodman, Spare That Tree! 750

Woodman, spare that tree!
  Touch not a single bough!
In youth it sheltered me,
  And I'll protect it now.
'Twas my forefather's hand
  That placed it near his cot;
There, woodman, let it stand,
  Thy ax shall harm it not.

That old familiar tree,
  Whose glory and renown
Are spread o'er land and sea—
  And wouldst thou hew it down?
Woodman, forbear thy stroke!
  Cut not its earth-bound ties;
Oh, spare that agèd oak
  Now towering to the skies!

When but an idle boy,
  I sought its grateful shade;
In all their gushing joy
  Here, too, my sisters played.
My mother kissed me here;
  My father pressed my hand—
Forgive this foolish tear,
  But let that old oak stand.

My heart-strings round thee cling,
  Close as thy bark, old friend!
Here shall the wild-bird sing,
  And still thy branches bend.

  Old tree! the storm still brave!
   And, woodman, leave the spot;
  While I've a hand to save,
   Thy ax shall harm it not.
      GEORGE POPE MORRIS (1802–1864)

751   LEAD, KINDLY LIGHT
Lead, kindly Light, amid th' encircling gloom,
   Lead Thou me on,
The night is dark, and I am far from home,
   Lead Thou me on.
Keep Thou my feet; I do not ask to see
The distant scene; one step enough for me.

I was not ever thus, nor prayed that Thou
   Shouldst lead me on;
I loved to choose and see my path; but now
   Lead Thou me on.
I loved the garish day; and, spite of fears,
Pride ruled my will: remember not past years.

So long Thy power hath blest me, sure it still
   Will lead me on
O'er moor and fen, o'er crag and torrent, till
   The night is gone,
And with the morn those angel faces smile,
Which I have loved long since, and lost a while.
      JOHN HENRY NEWMAN (1801–1890)

752   THE SKELETON IN ARMOUR
 "Speak! speak! thou fearful guest!
 Who, with thy hollow breast
 Still in rude armour drest,
  Comest to daunt me!
 Wrapt not in Eastern balms,
 But with thy fleshless palms
 Stretched, as if asking alms,
  Why dost thou haunt me?"

 Then from those cavernous eyes
 Pale flashes seemed to rise,
 As when the Northern skies
  Gleam in December;
 And, like the water's flow
 Under December's snow,
 Came a dull voice of woe
  From the heart's chamber.

 "I was a Viking old!
 My deeds, though manifold,
 No Skald in song has told,
  No Saga taught thee!

Take heed that in thy verse
Thou dost the tale rehearse,
Else dread a dead man's curse;
   For this I sought thee.

"Far in the Northern Land,
By the wild Baltic's strand,
I, with my childish hand,
   Tamed the gerfalcon;
And, with my skates fast-bound,
Skimmed the half-frozen Sound,
That the poor whimpering hound
   Trembled to walk on.

"Oft to his frozen lair
Tracked I the grizzly bear,
While from my path the hare
   Fled like a shadow;
Oft through the forest dark
Followed the were-wolf's bark,
Until the soaring lark
   Sang from the meadow.

"But when I older grew,
Joining a corsair's crew,
O'er the dark sea I flew
   With the marauders.
Wild was the life we led;
Many the souls that sped,
Many the hearts that bled,
   By our stern orders.

"Many a wassail-bout
Wore the long Winter out;
Often our midnight shout
   Set the cocks crowing,
As we the Berserk's tale
Measured in cups of ale,
Draining the oaken pail
   Filled to overflowing.

"Once as I told in glee
Tales of the stormy sea,
Soft eyes did gaze on me,
   Burning yet tender;
And as the white stars shine
On the dark Norway pine,
On that dark heart of mine
   Fell their soft splendour.

"I wooed the blue-eyed maid,
Yielding, yet half afraid,
And in the forest's shade
   Our vows were plighted.

Under its loosened vest
Fluttered her little breast,
Like birds within their nest
  By the hawk frighted.

"Bright in her father's hall
Shields gleamed upon the wall,
Loud sang the minstrels all,
  Chanting his glory;
When of old Hildebrand
I asked his daughter's hand,
Mute did the minstrels stand
  To hear my story.

"While the brown ale he quaffed,
Loud then the champion laughed,
And as the wind-gusts waft
  The sea-foam brightly,
So the loud laugh of scorn,
Out of those lips unshorn,
From the deep drinking-horn
  Blew the foam lightly.

"She was a Prince's child,
I but a Viking wild,
And though she blushed and smiled,
  I was discarded!
Should not the dove so white
Follow the sea-mew's flight?
Why did they leave that night
  Her nest unguarded?

"Scarce had I put to sea,
Bearing the maid with me,—
Fairest of all was she
  Among the Norsemen!—
When on the white sea-strand,
Waving his armed hand,
Saw we old Hildebrand,
  With twenty horsemen.

"Then launched they to the blast,
Bent like a reed each mast,
Yet we were gaining fast,
  When the wind failed us;
And with a sudden flaw
Came round the gusty Skaw,
So that our foe we saw
  Laugh as he hailed us.

"And as to catch the gale
Round veered the flapping sail,
'Death!' was the helmsman's hail,
  'Death without quarter!'

Midships with iron keel
Struck we her ribs of steel;
Down her black hulk did reel
   Through the black water!

"As with his wings aslant,
Sails the fierce cormorant,
Seeking some rocky haunt,
   With his prey laden,
So toward the open main,
Beating to sea again,
Through the wild hurricane,
   Bore I the maiden.

"Three weeks we westward bore,
And when the storm was o'er,
Cloud-like we saw the shore
   Stretching to leeward;
There for my lady's bower
Built I the lofty tower
Which to this very hour
   Stands looking seaward.

"There lived we many years;
Time dried the maiden's tears;
She had forgot her fears,
   She was a mother;
Death closed her mild blue eyes;
Under that tower she lies;
Ne'er shall the sun arise
   On such another.

"Still grew my bosom then,
Still as a stagnant fen!
Hateful to me were men,
   The sunlight hateful!
In the vast forest here,
Clad in my warlike gear,
Fell I upon my spear,
   Oh, death was grateful!

"Thus, seamed with many scars,
Bursting these prison bars,
Up to its native stars
   My soul ascended!
There from the flowing bowl
Deep drinks the warrior's soul,
Skoal! to the Northland! *skoal!*"
   Thus the tale ended.
            HENRY WADSWORTH LONGFELLOW (1807–1882)

753   THE REVENGE
                          A BALLAD OF THE FLEET
At Flores in the Azores Sir Richard Grenville lay,
And a pinnace, like a fluttered bird, came flying from away:
"Spanish ships of war at sea! we have sighted fifty-three!"
Then sware Lord Thomas Howard: "'Fore God, I am no coward;
But I cannot meet them here, for my ships are out of gear,
And the half my men are sick. I must fly, but follow quick.
We are six ships of the line; can we fight with fifty-three?"

Then spake Sir Richard Grenville: "I know you are no coward;
You fly them for a moment, to fight with them again.
But I've ninety men and more that are lying sick ashore.
I should count myself the coward if I left them, my Lord Howard,
To these Inquisition dogs and the devildoms of Spain."

So Lord Howard passed away with five ships of war that day,
Till he melted like a cloud in the silent summer heaven;
But Sir Richard bore in hand all his sick men from the land
Very carefully and slow,
Men of Bideford in Devon,
And we laid them on the ballast down below;
For we brought them all aboard,
And they blest him in their pain that they were not left to Spain,
To the thumbscrew and the stake, for the glory of the Lord.

He had only a hundred seamen to work the ship and to fight,
And he sail'd away from Flores till the Spaniard came in sight,
With his huge sea-castles heaving upon the weather bow.
"Shall we fight or shall we fly?
Good Sir Richard, tell us now,
For to fight is but to die!

"There'll be little of us left by the time this sun be set"
And Sir Richard said again: "We be all good Englishmen.
Let us bang these dogs ofr Seville, the children of the devil,
For I never turn'd my back upon Don or devil yet."

Sir Richard spoke and he laugh'd, and we roar'd a hurrah, and so
The little *Revenge* ran on sheer into the heart of the foe,
With her hundred fighters on deck, and her ninety sick below;
For half of their fleet to the right and half to the left were seen,
And the little *Revenge* ran on thro' the long sea-lane between.

Thousands of their soldiers looked down from their decks and laugh'd,
Thousands of their seamen made mock at the mad little craft
Running on and on, till delay'd
By their mountain-like *San Philip* that, of fifteen hundred tons,
And up-shadowing high above us with her yawning tiers of guns,
Took the breath from our sails, and we stay'd.

And while now the great *San Philip* hung above us like a cloud
Whence the thunderbolt will fall
Long and loud.
Four galleons drew away
From the Spanish fleet that day,
And two upon the larboard and two upon the starboard lay,
And the battle-thunder broke from them all.

But anon the great *San Philip*, she bethought herself and went,
Having that within her womb that had left her ill content;
And the rest they came aboard us, and they fought us hand to hand,
For a dozen times they came with their pikes and musqueteers,
And a dozen times we shook 'em off as a dog that shakes his ears
When he leaps from the water to the land.

And the sun went down, and the stars came out far over the summer sea,
But never a moment ceased the fight of the one and the fifty-three;
Ship after ship, the whole night long, their high-built galleons came,
Ship after ship, the whole night long, with her battle-thunder
      and flame;
Ship after ship, the whole night long, drew back with her dead
      and her shame.
For some were sunk and many were shatter'd, and so could
      fight us no more—
God of battles, was ever a battle like this in the world before?

For he said, "Fight on! fight on!"
Tho' his vessel was all but a wreck;
And it chanced that, when half of the short summer night was gone,
With a grisly wound to be drest he had left the deck,
But a bullet struck him that was dressing it suddenly dead,
And himself he was wounded again in the side and the head,
And he said, "Fight on! Fight on!"

And the night went down, and the sun smiled out far
      over the summer sea,
And the Spanish fleet with broken sides lay round us all in a ring;
But they dared not touch us again, for they fear'd that
      we still could sting,
So they watched what the end would be.
And we had not fought them in vain,
But in perilous plight were we,
Seeing forty of our poor hundred were slain,
And half of the rest of us maim'd for life
In the crash of the cannonades and the desperate strife;
And the sick men down in the hold were most of them stark and cold,
And the pikes were all broken or bent, and the powder was
      all of it spent;
And the masts and the rigging were lying over the side;
But Sir Richard cried in his English pride:
"We have fought such a fight for a day and a night
As may never be fought again!
We have won great glory, my men!
And a day less or more

>   At sea or ashore,
>   We die—does it matter when?
>   Sink me the ship, Master Gunner—sink her, split her in twain!
>   Fall into the hands of God, not into the hands of Spain!"
>
>   And the gunner said. "Ay, ay," but the seamen made reply:
>   "We have children, we have wives,
>   And the Lord hath spared our lives.
>   We will make the Spaniard promise, if we yield, to let us go;
>   We shall live to fight again, and to strike another blow."
>   And the lion there lay dying, and they yielded to the foe.
>   And the stately Spanish men to their flagship bore him then,
>   Where they laid him by the mast, old Sir Richard caught at last,
>   And they praised him to his face with their courtly foreign grace;
>   But he rose upon their decks, and he cried:
>   "I have fought for Queen and Faith like a valiant man and true;
>   I have only done my duty as a man is bound to do.
>   With a joyful spirit I, Sir Richard Grenville, die!"
>   And he fell upon their decks, and he died.
>
>   And they stared at the dead that had been so valiant and true,
>   And had holden the power and glory of Spain so cheap
>   That he dared her with one little ship and his English few.
>   Was he devil or man? He was devil for aught they knew,
>   But they sank his body with honour down into the deep,
>   And they mann'd the *Revenge* with a swarthier alien crew,
>   And away she sail'd with her loss and long'd for her own;
>   When a wind from the lands they had ruin'd awoke from sleep,
>   And the water began to heave and the weather to moan,
>   And or ever that evening ended a great gale blew,
>   And a wave like the wave that is raised by an earthquake grew,
>   Till it smote on their hulls, and their sails, and their masts,
>   and their flags,
>   And the whole sea plunged and fell on the shot-shatter'd navy of Spain,
>   And the little *Revenge* herself went down by the island crags,
>   To be lost evermore in the main.

ALFRED TENNYSON, LORD TENNYSON (1809–1892)

754   SIR GALAHAD

> My good blade carves the casques of men,
>   My tough lance thrusteth sure,
> My strength is as the strength of ten,
>   Because my heart is pure.
> The shattering trumpet shrilleth high,
>   The hard brands shiver on the steel,
> The splintered spear-shafts crack and fly,
>   The horse and rider reel:
> They reel, they roll in clanging lists,
>   And when the tide of combat stands,
> Perfume and flowers fall in showers,
>   That lightly rain from ladies' hands.

How sweet are looks that ladies bend
  On whom their favours fall!
For them I battle till the end,
  To save from shame and thrall:
But all my heart is drawn above,
  My knees are bow'd in crypt and shrine:
I never felt the kiss of love,
  Nor maiden's hand in mine.
More bounteous aspects on me beam,
  Me mightier transports move and thrill;
So keep I fair thro' faith and prayer
  A virgin heart in work and will.

When down the stormy crescent goes,
  A light before me swims,
Between dark stems the forest glows,
  I hear a noise of hymns:
Then by some secret shrine I ride;
  I hear a voice, but none are there;
The stalls are void, the doors are wide,
  The tapers burning fair.
Fair gleams the snowy altar-cloth,
  The silver vessels sparkle clean,
The shrill bell rings, the censer swings,
  And solemn chaunts resound between.

Sometimes on lonely mountain-meres
  I find a magic bark;
I leap on board: no helmsman steers,
  I float till all is dark.
A gentle sound, an awful light!
  Three angels bear the holy Grail:
With folded feet, in stoles of white,
  On sleeping wings they sail.
Ah, blessèd vision! blood of God!
  My spirit beats her mortal bars,
As down dark tides the glory slides,
  And star-like mingles with the stars.

When on my goodly charger borne
  Thro' dreaming towns I go,
The cock crows ere the Christmas morn,
  The streets are dumb with snow.
The tempest crackles on the leads,
  And, ringing, springs from brand and mail;
But o'er the dark a glory spreads,
  And gilds the driving hail.
I leave the plain, I climb the height;
  No branchy thicket shelter yields;
But blessèd forms in whistling storms
  Fly o'er waste fens and windy fields.

A maiden knight—to me is given
  Such hope, I know not fear;
I yearn to breathe the airs of heaven
  That often meet me here.
I muse on joy that will not cease,
  Pure spaces cloth'd in living beams,
Pure lilies of eternal peace,
  Whose odours haunt my dreams;
And, stricken by an angel's hand,
  This mortal armour that I wear,
This weight and size, this heart and eyes,
  Are touch'd, are turn'd to finest air.

The clouds are broken in the sky,
  And thro' the mountain-walls
A rolling organ-harmony
  Swells up, and shakes and falls.
Then move the trees, the copses nod,
  Wings flutter, voices hover clear:
"O just and faithful knight of God!
  Ride on! the prize is near."
So pass I hostel, hall, and grange;
  By bridge and ford, by park and pale,
All-arm'd I ride, whate'er betide,
  Until I find the holy Grail.
        ALFRED TENNYSON, LORD TENNYSON (1809–1892)

755   MY OWN SHALL COME TO ME

Serene I fold my hands and wait,
  Nor care for wind, nor tide, nor sea.
I rave no more 'gainst time or fate,
  For lo! my own shall come to me.

I stay my haste, I make delays,
  For what avails this eager pace?
I stand amid the eternal ways,
  And what is mine shall know my face.

Asleep, awake, by night or day
  The friends I seek are seeking me;
No wind can drive my bark astray,
  Nor change the tide of destiny.

What matter if I stand alone?
  I wait with joy the coming years;
My heart shall reap when it has sown,
  And gather up its fruit of tears.

The stars come nightly to the sky;
  The tidal wave comes to the sea;
Nor time, nor space, nor deep, nor high,
  Can keep my own away from me.

> The waters know their own and draw
>   The brook that springs in yonder heights;
> So flows the good with equal law
>   Unto the soul of pure delights.
>
> JOHN BURROUGHS (1837–1921)

THE BRIDES OF ENDERBY   756

The old mayor climb'd the belfry tower,
  The ringers ran by two, by three;
"Pull, if ye never pull'd before;
  Good ringers, pull your best," quoth he.
"Play uppe, play uppe, O Boston bells!
Ply all your changes, all your swells,
  Play uppe, 'The Brides of Enderby.'"

Men say it was a stolen tyde—
  The Lord that sent it, He knows all;
But in myne ears doth still abide
  The message that the bells let fall:
And there was naught of strange, beside
The flight of mews and peewits pied
  By millions crouch'd on the old sea wall.

I sat and spun within the doore,
  My thread brake off, I raised myne eyes;
The level sun, like ruddy ore,
  Lay sinking in the barren skies;
And dark against day's golden death
She moved where Lindis wandereth,
My sonne's faire wife, Elizabeth.

"Cusha! Cusha! Cusha!" calling,
Ere the early dews were falling,
Farre away I heard her song,
"Cusha! Cusha!" all along;
Where the reedy Lindis floweth,
    Floweth, floweth,
From the meads where melick groweth
Faintly came her milking song—

"Cusha! Cusha! Cusha!" calling,
"For the dews will soone be falling;
Leave your meadow grasses mellow,
    Mellow, mellow;
Quit your cowslips, cowslips yellow;
Come uppe, Whitefoot, come uppe, Lightfoot;
Quit the stalks of parsley hollow,
    Hollow, hollow;
Come uppe, Jetty, rise and follow,
From the clovers lift your head;
Come uppe, Whitefoot, come uppe, Lightfoot,
Come uppe, Jetty, rise and follow,
Jetty, to the milking shed."

If it be long ay, long ago,
  When I beginne to think howe long,
Againe I hear the Lindis flow,
  Swift as an arrowe, sharpe and strong;
And all the aire, it seemeth mee,
Bin full of floating bells (sayth shee),
That ring the tune of Enderby.

Alle fresh the level pasture lay,
  And not a shadowe mote be seene,
Save where full fyve good miles away
  The steeple tower'd from out the greene;
And lo! the great bell farre and wide
Was heard in all the country side
That Saturday at eventide.

The swanherds where their sedges are
  Mov'd on in sunset's golden breath,
The shepherde lads I heard afarre,
  And my sonne's wife, Elizabeth;
Till floating o'er the grassy sea
Came downe that kyndly message free,
The "Brides of Mavis Enderby."

Then some look'd uppe into the sky,
  And all along where Lindis flows
To where the goodly vessels lie,
  And where the lordly steeple shows.
They sayde, "And why should this thing be?
What danger lowers by land or sea?
They ring the tune of Enderby!

"For evil news from Mablethorpe,
  Of pyrate galleys warping down;
For shippes ashore beyond the scorpe,
  They have not spar'd to wake the towne:
But while the west bin red to see,
And storms be none, and pyrates flee,
Why ring 'The Brides of Enderby'?"

I look'd without, and lo! my sonne
  Came riding downe with might and main;
He rais'd a shout as he drew on,
  Till all the welkin rang again,
"Elizabeth! Elizabeth!"
(A sweeter woman ne'er drew breath
Than my sonne's wife, Elizabeth.)

"The olde sea wall," he cried, "is downe,
   The rising tide comes on apace,
And boats adrift in yonder towne
   Go sailing uppe the market-place."
He shook as one that looks on death:
"God save you, mother!" straight he saith
"Where is my wife, Elizabeth?"

"Good sonne, where Lindis winds her way
   With her two bairns I marked her long;
And ere yon bells beganne to play
   Afar I heard her milking song."
He looked across the grassy lea,
To right, to left, "Ho, Enderby!"
They rang "The Brides of Enderby!"

With that he cried and beat his breast;
   For, lo! along the river's bed
A mighty eygre rear'd his crest,
   And uppe the Lindis raging sped.
It swept with thunderous noises loud;
Shap'd like a curling snow-white cloud,
Or like a demon in a shroud.

And rearing Lindis backward press'd
   Shook all her trembling bankes amaine;
Then madly at the eygre's breast
   Flung uppe her weltering walls again.
Then bankes came downe with ruin and rout—
Then beaten foam flew round about—
Then all the mighty floods were out.

So farre, so fast the eygre drave,
   The heart had hardly time to beat
Before a shallow seething wave
   Sobb'd in the grasses at oure feet:
The feet had hardly time to flee
Before it brake against the knee,
And all the world was in the sea.

Upon the roofe we sate that night,
   The noise of bells went sweeping by;
I mark'd the lofty beacon light
   Stream from the church tower, red and high—
A lurid mark and dread to see;
And awsome bells they were to mee,
That in the dark rang "Enderby."

They rang the sailor lads to guide
  From roofe to roofe who fearless row'd;
And I—my sonne was at my side,
  And yet the ruddy beacon glow'd:
And yet he moan'd beneath his breath,
"O come in life, or come in death!
O lost! my love, Elizabeth."

And didst thou visit him no more?
  Thou didst, thou didst, my daughter deare
The waters laid thee at his doore,
  Ere yet the early dawn was clear.
Thy pretty bairns in fast embrace,
The lifted sun shone on thy face,
Downe drifted to thy dwelling-place.

That flow strew'd wrecks about the grass,
  That ebbe swept out the flocks to sea;
A fatal ebbe and flow, alas!
  To manye more than myne and mee;
But each will mourn his own (she saith);
And sweeter woman ne'er drew breath
Than my sonne's wife, Elizabeth.

I shall never hear her more
By the reedy Lindis shore,
"Cusha! Cusha! Cusha!" calling,
Ere the early dews be falling;
I shall never hear her song,
"Cusha! Cusha!" all along
Where the sunny Lindis floweth,
    Goeth, floweth;
From the meads where melick groweth,
  When the water winding down,
  Onward floweth to the town.

I shall never see her more
Where the reeds and rushes quiver,
    Shiver, quiver;
Stand beside the sobbing river,
Sobbing, throbbing, in its falling
To the sandy lonesome shore;
I shall never hear her calling,
"Leave your meadow grasses mellow,
    Mellow, mellow;
Quit your cowslips, cowslips yellow;

"Come uppe, Whitefoot, come uppe, Lightfoot;
Quit your pipes of parsley hollow,
    Hollow, hollow;
Come uppe, Lightfoot, rise and follow;

>   Lightfoot, Whitefoot,
>   From your clovers lift the head;
>   Come uppe, Jetty, follow, follow,
>   Jetty, to the milking shed."

JEAN INGELOW (1830–1897)

THE RAVEN   757

Once upon a midnight dreary, while I pondered, weak and weary,
Over many a quaint and curious volume of forgotten lore—
While I nodded, nearly napping, suddenly there came a tapping,
As of some one gently rapping, rapping at my chamber door"
'Tis some visitor," I muttered, "tapping at my chamber door—
    Only this, and nothing more."

Ah! distinctly I remember, it was in the bleak December,
And each separate dying ember wrought its ghost upon the floor;
Eagerly I wished the morrow; vainly I had sought to borrow
From my books surcease of sorrow—sorrow for the lost Lenore—
For the rare and radiant maiden whom the angels name Lenore—
    Nameless here for evermore.

And the silken, sad, uncertain rustling of each purple curtain
Thrilled me—filled me with fantastic terrors never felt before;
So that now, to still the beating of my heart, I stood repeating,
"Tis some visitor entreating entrance at my chamber door—
Some late visitor entreating entrance at my chamber door:
    This it is, and nothing more."

Presently my soul grew stronger; hesitating then no longer,
"Sir," said I, "or madam, truly your forgiveness I implore;
But the fact is, I was napping, and so gently you came rapping,
And so faintly you came tapping, tapping at my chamber door,
That I scarce was sure I heard you." Here I opened wide the door:
    Darkness there, and nothing more.

Deep into that darkness peering, long I stood there, wondering,
    fearing,
Doubting, dreaming dreams no mortal ever dared to dream before;
But the silence was unbroken, and the stillness gave no token,
And the only word there spoken was the whispered word, "Lenore!"
This I whispered, and an echo murmured back the word, "Lenore!"
    Merely this, and nothing more.

Back into my chamber turning, all my soul within me burning,
Soon again I heard a rapping, something louder than before:
"Surely," said I, "surely that is something at my window lattice;
Let me see, then, what thereat is, and this mystery explore—
Let my heart be still a moment, and this mystery explore.
    'Tis the wind, and nothing more."

Open here I flung the shutter, when, with many a flirt and flutter,
In there stepped a stately Raven, of the saintly days of yore;
Not the least obeisance made he, not a minute stopped or stayed he;
But with mien of lord or lady, perched above my chamber door—
Perched above a bust of Pallas, just above my chamber door—
    Perched, and sat, and nothing more.

Then this ebony bird beguiling my sad fancy into smiling,
By the grave and stern decorum of the countenance it wore;
"Though thy crest be shorn and shaven, thou," I said, "art
      sure, no craven;
Ghastly, grim, and ancient Raven, wandering from the nightly shore,
Tell me what thy lordly name is on the night's Plutonian shore?"
    Quoth the Raven, "Nevermore."

Much I marvelled this ungainly fowl to hear discourse so plainly,
Though its answer, little meaning, little relevancy bore;
For we cannot help agreeing that no living human being
Ever yet was blessed with seeing bird above his chamber door—
Bird or beast upon the sculptured bust above his chamber door
    With such a name as "Nevermore."

But the Raven, sitting lonely on that placid bust, spoke only
That one word, as if his soul in that one word he did outpour;
Nothing further then he uttered, not a feather then he fluttered,
Till I scarcely more than muttered—"Other friends have flown before,
On the morrow he will leave me, as my hopes have flown before."
    Then the bird said, "Nevermore."

Startled by the stillness broken by reply so aptly spoken,
"Doubtless," said I, "what it utters is its only stock and store,
Caught from some unhappy master, whom unmerciful disaster
Followed fast and followed faster, till his songs one burden bore—
Till the dirges of his hope this melancholy burden bore—
    Of 'Never, nevermore.'"

But the Raven still beguiling all my sad soul into smiling,
Straight I wheeled a cushioned seat in front of bird, and
      bust, and door;
Then upon the velvet sinking, I betook myself to linking
Fancy into fancy, thinking what this ominous bird of yore—
What this grim, ungainly, ghastly, gaunt, and ominous bird of yore
    Meant in croaking "Nevermore."

Thus I sat engaged in guessing, but no syllable expressing
To the fowl whose fiery eyes now burned into my bosom's core;
This and more I sat divining, with my head at ease reclining
On the cushion's velvet lining, that the lamp-light gloated o'er,
But whose velvet violet lining, with the lamp-light gloating o'er,
    She shall press, ah, nevermore!

Then methought the air grew denser, perfumed from an unseen censer
Swung by seraphim, whose footfalls twinkled on the tufted floor.
"Wretch," I cried, "thy God hath lent thee—by these angels He
    hath sent thee
Respite—respite and nepenthe from my memories of Lenore!
Quaff, oh, quaff this kind nepenthe, and forget this lost Lenore!"
    Quoth the Raven, "Nevermore."

"Prophet," said I, "thing of evil—prophet still, if bird or devil!
Whether tempter sent, or whether tempest tossed thee here ashore
Desolate, yet all undaunted, on this desert land enchanted,
On this home by horror haunted—tell me truly, I implore,
Is there—*is* there balm in Gilead?—tell me, tell me, I implore!"
    Quoth the Raven, "Nevermore."

"Prophet," said I, "thing of evil!—prophet still if bird or devil!
By that heaven that bends above us—by that God we both adore—
Tell this soul, with sorrow laden, if, within the distant Aiden
It shall clasp a sainted maiden, whom the angels name Lenore!
Clasp a rare and radiant maiden, whom the angels name Lenore?"
    Quoth the Raven, "Nevermore."

"Be that our sign of parting, bird or fiend," I shrieked, upstarting—
"Get thee back into the tempest and the night's Plutonian shore;
Leave no black plume as a token of that lie thy soul hath spoken,
Leave my loneliness unbroken—quit the bust above my door,
Take thy beak from out my heart and take thy form from off my door!"
    Quoth the Raven, "Nevermore."

And the Raven, never flitting, still is sitting, still is sitting,
On the pallid bust of Pallas, just above my chamber door;
And his eyes have all the seeming of a demon's that is dreaming,
And the lamp-light o'er him streaming, throws his shadow on the floor;
And my soul from out that shadow, that lies floating on the floor,
    Shall be lifted—nevermore!

EDGAR ALLAN POE (1809–1849)

THE CHOIR INVISIBLE   758

O, may I join the choir invisible
Of those immortal dead who live again
In minds made better by their presence; live
In pulses stirred to generosity,
In deeds of daring rectitude, in scorn
Of miserable aims that end with self,
In thoughts sublime that pierce the night like stars,
And with their mild persistence urge man's search
To vaster issues.   So to live is heaven:
To make undying music in the world,
Breathing as beauteous order that controls
With growing sway the growing life of man.
So we inherit that sweet purity
For which we struggled, fail'd, and agoniz'd
With widening retrospect that bred despair.

Rebellious flesh that would not be subdued,
A vicious parent shaming still its child,
Poor anxious penitence, is quick dissolv'd;
Its discords, quench'd by meeting harmonies,
Die in the large and charitable air.
And all our rarer, better, truer self,
That sobb'd religiously in yearning song,
That watch'd to ease the burthen of the world,
Laboriously tracing what must be,
And what may yet be better,—saw within
A worthier image for the sanctuary,
And shap'd it forth before the multitude,
Divinely human, raising worship so
To higher reverence more mix'd with love,—
That better self shall live till human Time
Shall fold its eyelids, and the human sky
Be gather'd like a scroll within the tomb Unread forever.
    This is life to come,
Which martyr'd men have made more glorious
For us who strive to follow. May I reach
That purest heaven,—be to other souls
The cup of strength in some great agony,
Enkindle generous ardour, feed pure love,
Beget the smiles that have no cruelty,
Be the sweet presence of good diffused,
And in diffusion ever more intense!
So shall I join the choir invisible,
Whose music is the gladness of the world.
       GEORGE ELIOT (1819–1890)

759   RABBI BEN EZRA

  Grow old along with me!
  The best is yet to be,
The last of life, for which the first was made:
  Our times are in His hand
  Who saith, "A whole I plann'd,
Youth shows but half; trust God: see all nor be afraid!"

  Not that, amassing flowers,
  Youth sigh'd, "Which rose make ours,
Which lily leave and then as best recall?"
  Not that, admiring stars,
  It yearn'd, "Nor Jove, nor Mars;
Mine be some figured flame which blends, transcends them all!"

  Not for such hopes and fears
  Annulling youth's brief years,
Do I remonstrate: folly wide the mark!
  Rather I prize the doubt
  Low kinds exist without,
Finish'd and finite clods, untroubled by a spark.

       Poor vaunt of life indeed,
       Were man but formed to feed
On joy, to solely seek and find and feast:
       Such feasting ended, then
       As sure an end to men;
Irks care the crop-full bird? Frets doubt the maw-cramm'd beast?

       Rejoice we are allied
       To That which doth provide
And not partake, effect and not receive!
       A spark disturbs our clod;
       Nearer we hold of God
Who gives, than of His tribes that take, I must believe.

       Then, welcome each rebuff
       That turns earth's smoothness rough,
Each sting, that bids nor sit nor stand, but go!
       Be our joys three parts pain!
       Strive, and hold cheap the strain;
Learn, nor account the pang; dare, never grudge the throe!

       For thence,—a paradox
       Which comforts while it mocks,—
Shall life succeed in that it seems to fail:
       What I aspired to be,
       And was not, comforts me:
A brute I might have been, but would not sink i' the scale.

       What is he but a brute
       Whose flesh has soul to suit,
Whose spirit works lest arms and legs want play?
       To man, propose this test—
       Thy body at its best,
How far can that project thy soul on its lone way?

       Yet gifts should prove their use:
       I own the Past profuse
Of power each side, perfection every turn:
       Eyes, ears took in their dole,
       Brain treasured up the whole:
Should not the heart beat once "How good to live and learn?"

       Not once beat "Praise be Thine!
       I see the whole design,
I, who saw power, see now love perfect too:
       Perfect I call Thy plan:
       Thanks that I was a man!
Maker, remake, complete,—I trust what Thou shalt do!"

       For pleasant is this flesh,
       Our soul, in its rose-mesh
Pull'd ever to the earth, still yearns for rest;
       Would we some prize might hold
       To match those manifold
Possessions of the brute,—gain most, as we did best!

Let us not always say,
    "Spite of this flesh to-day
I strove, made head, gained ground upon the whole!"
    As the bird wings and sings,
    Let us cry, "All good things
Are ours, nor soul helps flesh more, now, than flesh helps soul!"

    Therefore I summon age
    To grant youth's heritage,
Life's struggle having so far reached its term:
    Thence shall I pass, approved
    A man, for aye removed
From the developed brute; a god though in the germ.

    And I shall thereupon
    Take rest, ere I be gone
Once more on my adventure brave and new:
    Fearless and unperplex'd,
    When I wage battle next,
What weapons to select, what armour to indue.

    Youth ended, I shall try
    My gain or loss thereby;
Leave the fire ashes, what survives is gold:
    And I shall weigh the same,
    Give life its praise or blame:
Young, all lay in dispute; I shall know, being old.

    For note, when evening shuts,
    A certain moment cuts
The deed off, calls the glory from the gray:
    A whisper from the west
    Shoots—"Add this to the rest,
Take it and try its worth: here dies another day."

    So, still within this life,
    Though lifted o'er its strife,
Let me discern, compare, pronounce at last,
    "This rage was right i' the main,
    That acquiescence vain:
The Future I may face now I have proved the Past"

    For more is not reserved
    To man, with soul just nerved
To act to-morrow what he learns to-day:
    Here, work enough to watch
    The Master work, and catch
Hints of the proper craft, tricks of the tool's true play.

        As it was better, youth
        Should strive, through acts uncouth,
Toward making, than repose on aught found made:
        So, better, age, exempt
        From strife, should know, than tempt
Further. Thou waitedest age: wait death nor be afraid!

        Enough now, if the Right
        And Good and Infinite
Be named here, as thou callest thy hand thine own,
        With knowledge absolute,
        Subject to no dispute
From fools that crowded youth, nor let thee feel alone.

        Be there, for once and all,
        Sever'd great minds from small,
Announced to each his station in the Past!
        Was I, the world arraigned,
        Were they, my soul disdain'd,
Right? Let age speak the truth and give us peace at last!

        Now, who shall arbitrate?
        Ten men love what I hate,
Shun what I follow, slight what I receive;
        Ten, who in ears and eyes
        Match me: we all surmise,
They this thing, and I that: whom shall my soul believe?

        Not on the vulgar mass
        Call'd "work," must sentence pass,
Things done, that took the eye and had the price;
        O'er which, from level stand,
        The low world laid its hand,
Found straightway to its mind, could value in a trice:

        But all, the world's coarse thumb
        And finger fail'd to plumb,
So pass'd in making up the main account;
        All instincts immature,
        All purposes unsure,
That weigh'd not as his work, yet swell'd the man's amount:

        Thoughts hardly to be pack'd
        Into a narrow act,
Fancies that broke through language and escaped,
        All I could never be,
        All, men ignored in me,
This, I was worth to God, whose wheel the pitcher shaped.

        Ay, note that Potter's wheel,
        That metaphor! and feel
Why time spins fast, why passive lies our clay,—
        Thou, to whom fools propound,
        When the wine makes its round,
"Since life fleets, all is change; the Past gone, seize to-day!"

    Fool! All that is, at all,
    Lasts ever, past recall;
Earth changes, but thy soul and God stand sure;
    What enter'd into thee,
    That was, is, and shall be:
Time's wheel runs back or stops: Potter and clay endure.

    He fix'd thee 'mid this dance
    Of plastic circumstance,
This Present, thou, forsooth, wouldst fain arrest
    Machinery just meant
    To give thy soul its bent,
Try thee and turn thee forth, sufficiently impress'd.

    What though the earlier grooves
    Which ran the laughing loves
Around thy base, no longer pause and press?
    What though, about thy rim,
    Scull-things in order grim
Grow out, in graver mood, obey the sterner stress?

    Look not thou down but up!
    To uses of a cup,
The festal board, lamp's flash and trumpet's peal,
    The new wine's foaming flow,
    The master's lips aglow!
Thou, heaven's consummate cup, what need'st thou with earth's wheel?

    But I need, now as then,
    Thee, God, who mouldest men;
And since, not even while the whirl was worst
    Did I,—to the wheel of life
    With shapes and colours rife,
Bound dizzily,—mistake my end, to slake Thy thirst:

    So, take and use Thy work:
    Amend what flaws may lurk,
What strain o' the stuff, what warpings past the aim!
    My times be in Thy hand!
    Perfect the cup as plann'd!
Lest age approve of youth, and death complete the same!
                                             Robert Browning (1812–1889)

760   PROSPICE

    Fear death?—to feel the fog in my throat,
        The mist in *my* face,
    When the snows begin, and the blasts denote
        I am nearing the place,
    The power of the night, the press of the storm,
        The post of the foe;
    Where he stands, the Arch Fear in a visible form,
        Yet the strong man must go:

For the journey is done and the summit attained,
    And the barriers fall,
Though a battle's to fight ere a guerdon be gained,
    The reward of it all.
I was ever a fighter, so—one fight more,
    The best and the last!
I would hate that death bandaged my eyes, and forebore,
    And bade me creep past.
No! let me taste the whole of it, fare like my peers
    The heroes of old,
Bear the brunt, in a minute pay glad life's arrears
    Of pain, darkness, and cold.
For sudden the worst turns the best to the brave,
    The black minute's at end,
And the elements' rage, the fiend-voices that rave
    Shall dwindle, shall blend,
Shall change, shall become first a peace out of pain,
    Then a light, then thy breast,
O thou soul of my soul! I shall clasp thee again,
    And with God be the rest!

                                          Robert Browning (1812–1889)

Hervé Riel   761

On the sea and at the Hogue, sixteen hundred ninety-two,
  Did the English fight the French—woe to France!
And, the thirty-first of May, helter-skelter through the blue,
Like a crowd of frightened porpoises a shoal of sharks pursue,
    Came crowding ship on ship to St. Malo on the Rance,
        With the English fleet in view.

'Twas the squadron that escaped, with the victor in full chase;
    First and foremost of the drove, in his great ship, Damfreville;
        Close on him fled, great and small,
        Twenty-two good ships in all;
        And they signalled to the place,
        "Help the winners of a race!
    Get us guidance, give us harbour, take us quick—or, quicker still,
        Here's the English can and will!"

Then the pilots of the place put out brisk and leaped on board:
  "Why, what hope or chance have ships like these to pass?"
        laughed they:
  "Rocks to starboard, rocks to port, all the passage scarred
        and scored,
Shall the *Formidable* here, with her twelve and eighty guns,
  Think to make the river-mouth by the single narrow way,
Trust to enter where 'tis ticklish for a craft of twenty tons,
And with flow at full beside?
        Now 'tis slackest ebb of tide.
        Reach the mooring! Rather say,
        While rock stands or water runs,
        Not a ship will leave the bay!"

   Then was called a council straight;
    Brief and bitter the debate:
"Here's the English at our heels; would you have them take in tow
All that's left us of the fleet, linked together stern and bow,
   For a prize to Plymouth Sound?—
   Better run the ships aground!"
   (Ended Damfreville his speech.)
   "Not a minute more to wait!
   Let the captains all and each
Shove ashore, then blow up, burn the vessels on the beach!
   France must undergo her fate.

   "Give the word!"—But no such word
    Was ever spoke or heard;
For up stood, for out stepped, for in struck amid all these—
A captain? A lieutenant? A mate—first, second, third?
   No such man of mark, and meet
   With his betters to compete!
But a simple Breton sailor pressed by Tourville for the fleet—
A poor coasting pilot he, Hervé Riel, the Croisiekese.

And "What mockery or malice have we here?" cries Hervé Riel:
"Are you mad, you Malouins? Are you cowards, fools, or rogues?
Talk to me of rocks and shoals, me who took the soundings, tell
On my fingers every bank, every shallow, every swell,
 'Twixt the offing here and Grève where the river disembogues?
Are you bought by English gold? Is it love the lying's for?
   Morn and eve, night and day.
   Have I piloted your bay,
Entered free and anchored fast at the foot of Solidor.
 Burn the fleet and ruin France? That were worse than fifty Hogues!
Sirs, they know I speak the truth! Sirs, believe me there's a way!
   Only let me lead the line,
    Have the biggest ship to steer,
    Get this *Formidable* clear,
   Make the others follow mine,
And I lead them, most and least, by a passage I know well,
   Right to Solidor past Grève,
    And there lay them safe and sound;
   And if one ship misbehave,
    —Keel so much as grate the ground,
Why, I've nothing but my life,—here's my head!" cries Hervé Riel.

Not a minute more to wait
   "Steer us in, then, small and great!
Take the helm, lead the line, save the squadron!" cried its chief.
   Captains, give the sailor place!
    He is Admiral, in brief.
   Still the north wind, by God's grace!
   See the noble fellow's face
   As the big ship, with a bound,

    Clears the entry like a hound,
Keeps the passage as its inch of way were the wide sea's profound!
    See, safe through shoal and rock,
    How they follow in a flock,
Not a ship that misbehaves, not a keel that grates the ground,
    Not a spar that comes to grief!
    The peril, see, is past,
    All are harboured to the last,
And just as Hervé Riel hollas "Anchor!"—sure as fate,
    Up the English come—too late!

    So, the storm subsides to calm:
     They see the green trees wave
    On the heights o'erlooking Grève.
    Hearts that bled are stanched with balm,
    "Just our rapture to enhance,
     Let the English rake the bay,
    Gnash their teeth and glare askance
     As they cannonade away!
'Neath rampired Solidor pleasant riding on the Rance!"
How hope succeeds despair on each Captain's countenance!
    Out burst all with one accord,
     "This is Paradise for Hell!
     Let France, let France's King
     Thank the man that did the thing!"
    What a shout, and all one word,
     "Hervé Riel!"
    As he stepped in front once more,
     Not a symptom of surprise
     In the frank blue Breton eyes,
    Just the same man as before.

    Then said Damfreville, "My friend,
    I must speak out at the end,
     Though I find the speaking hard.
    Praise is deeper than the lips:
    You have saved the King his ships,
     You must name your own reward.
    'Faith, our sun was near eclipse!
    Demand whate'er you will,
    France remains your debtor still.
Ask to heart's content and have! or my name's not Damfreville."

    Then a beam of fun outbroke
    On the bearded mouth that spoke,
    As the honest heart laughed through
    Those frank eyes of Breton blue:
    "Since I needs must say my say,
    Since on board the duty's done,
And from Malo Roads to Croisic Point, what is it but a run?—
    Since 'tis ask and have, I may—

Since the others go ashore—
  Come! A good whole holiday!
Leave to go and see my wife, whom I call the Belle Aurore!"
That he asked and that he got,—nothing more.

   Name and deed alike are lost:
   Not a pillar nor a post
In his Croisic keeps alive the feat as it befell;
   Not a head in white and black
   On a single fishing smack,
In memory of the man but for whom had gone to wrack
 All that France saved from the fight whence England bore the bell.
   Go to Paris: rank on rank
     Search the heroes flung pell-mell
   On the Louvre, face and flank!
You shall look long enough ere you come to Hervé Riel.
   So, for better and for worse,
   Hervé Riel, accept my verse!
In my verse, Hervé Riel, do thou once more
Save the squadron, honour France, love thy wife the Belle Aurore!
                                    ROBERT BROWNING (1812–1889)

762   THE PROBLEM
        I like a church; I like a cowl;
        I love a prophet of the soul;
        And on my heart monastic aisles
        Fall like sweet strains, or pensive smiles:
        Yet not for all his faith can see
        Would I that cowlèd churchman be.
        Why should the vest on him allure,
        Which I could not on me endure?

        Not from a vain or shallow thought
        His awful Jove young Phidias brought;
        Never from lips of cunning fell
        The thrilling Delphic oracle;
        Out from the heart of nature rolled
        The burdens of the Bible old;
        The litanies of nations came,
        Like the volcano's tongue of flame,
        Up from the burning core below,—
        The canticles of love and woe:
        The hand that rounded Peter's dome
        And groined the aisles of Christian Rome
        Wrought in a sad sincerity;
        Himself from God he could not free;
        He builded better than he knew;
        The conscious stone to beauty grew.

        Knowst thou what wove yon woodbird's nest
        Of leaves and feathers from her breast?
        Or how the fish outbuilt her shell,
        Painting with morn each annual cell?

Or how the sacred pine-tree adds
To her old leaves new myriads?
Such and so grew these holy piles,
While love and terror laid the tiles.
Earth proudly wears the Parthenon,
As the best gem upon her zone,
And Morning opes with haste her lids
To gaze upon the Pyramids;
O'er England's abbeys bends the sky,
As on its friends, with kindred eye;
For out of Thought's interior sphere
These wonders rose to upper air;
And Nature gladly gave them place,
Adopted them into her race,
And granted them an equal date
With Andes and with Ararat.

These temples grew as grows the grass;
Art might obey, but not surpass.
The passive Master lent his hand
To the vast soul that o'er him planned;
And the same power that reared the shrine
Bestrode the tribes that knelt within.
Ever the fiery Pentecost
Girds with one flame the countless host,
Trances the heart through chanting choirs,
And through the priest the mind inspires.
The word unto the prophet spoken
Was writ on tables yet unbroken;
The word by seers or sibyls told,
In groves of oak, or fanes of gold.
Still floats upon the morning wind,
Still whispers to the willing mind.
One accent of the Holy Ghost
The heedless world hath never lost.
I know what say the fathers wise,—
The Book itself before me lies,
Old Chrysostom, best Augustine,
And he who blent both in his line,
The younger Golden Lips or mines,
Taylor, the Shakespeare of divines.
His words are music in my ear,
I see his cowlèd portrait dear;
And yet, for all his faith could see,
I would not the good bishop be.
                    RALPH WALDO EMERSON (1803–1860)

763   To America

[Alfred Austin, an English poet, was appointed Poet Lauraeate in 1896. – Ed.]

What is the voice I hear
   On the winds of the western sea?
Sentinel, listen from out Cape Clear
   And say what the voice may be.
'Tis a proud free people calling loud to a people proud and free.

And it says to them: "Kinsmen, hail!
   We severed have been too long.
Now let us have done with a worn-out tale—
   The tale of an ancient wrong—
And our friendship last long as our love doth and be stronger than death is strong."

Answer them, sons of the self-same race,
   And blood of the self-same clan;
Let us speak with each other face to face
   And answer as man to man,
And loyally love and trust each other as none but free men can.

Now fling them out to the breeze,
   Shamrock, Thistle, and Rose,
And the Star-spangled Banner unfurl with these—
   A message to friends and foes
Wherever the sails of peace are seen and wherever the war-wind blows—

A message to bond and thrall to wake,
   For wherever we come, we twain,
The throne of the tyrant shall rock and quake,
   And his menace be void and vain;
For you are lords of a strong land and we are lords of the main.

Yes, this is the voice of the bluff March gale;
   We severed have been too long,
But now we have done with a worn-out tale—
   The tale of an ancient wrong—
And our friendship last long as love doth last and stronger than death is strong.

                                                                                                                 ALFRED AUSTIN (1835–1913)

764   Song Of Myself

I celebrate myself, and sing myself,
And what I assume you shall assume,
For every atom belonging to me as good belongs to you.
I loafe and invite my soul,
I lean and loafe at my ease observing a spear of summer grass.
My tongue, every atom of my blood, form'd from this soil, this air,
Born here of parents born here from parents the same, and their parents the same,
I, now thirty-seven years old in perfect health begin,
Hoping to cease not till death.

I harbor for good or bad, I permit to speak at every hazard,
Nature without check with original energy.

Have you reckoned a thousand acres much? have you reckon'd the
    earth much?
Have you practised so long to learn to read?
Have you felt so proud to get at the meaning of poems?

Stop this day and night with me and you shall possess the origin
    of all poems,
You shall possess the good of the earth and sun (there are
    millions of suns left),
You shall no longer take things at second or third hand, nor look
    through the eyes of the dead, nor feed on the specters in books,
You shall not look through my eyes either, nor take things from me,
You shall listen to all sides and filter them from yourself.

A child said, "*What is the grass?*" fetching it to me with full hands;
How could I answer the child? I do not know what it is any more
    than he.
I guess it must be the flag of my disposition, out of hopeful green
    stuff woven.
Or, I guess it is the handkerchief of the Lord,
A scented gift and remembrance designedly dropt,
Bearing the owner's name some way in the corners,
   that we may see and remark, and say,
"Whose?"

Alone far in the wilds and mountains I hunt,
Wandering amazed at my own lightness and glee,
In the late afternoon choosing a safe spot to pass the night,
Kindling a fire and broiling the fresh-kill'd game,
Falling asleep on the gathered leaves with my dog and gun by my side.
The Yankee clipper is under her sky-sails, she cuts the sparkle
    and scud,
My eyes settle the land, I bend at her prow or shout joyously from
    the deck.
The boatman and clam-diggers arose early and stopt for me,
I tucked my trouser-ends in my boots and went and had a good time;
You should have been with us that day round the chowder-kettle.

The runaway slave came to my house and stopt outside,
I heard his motions crackling the twigs of the woodpile,
Through the swung half-door of the kitchen I saw him limpsy and weak,
And went where he sat on a log and led him in and assured him,
And brought water and fill'd a tub for his sweated body and
    bruis'd feet,
And gave him a room that entered from my own, and gave him some
    coarse clean clothes,
And remember perfectly well his revolving eyes and his awkwardness,
And remember putting plasters on the galls of his neck and ankles;
He staid with me a week before he was recuperated and passed north,
I had him sit next me at table, my firelock lean'd in the corner.

I am the poet of the woman the same as the man,
And I say it is as great to be a woman as to be a man,
And I say there is nothing greater than the mother of men.

I understand the large hearts of heroes,
The courage of present times and all times,
How the skipper saw the crowded and rudderless wreck of the steamship,
    and Death chasing it up and down the storm,
How he knuckled tight and gave not back an inch and was faithful of
    days and faithful of nights,
And chalked in large letters on a board, "*Be of good cheer, we will
    not desert you*";
How he followed with them and tack'd with them three days and would
    not give it up,
How he saved the drifting company at last,
How the lank loose-gown'd women looked when boated from the side
    of their prepared graves,
How the silent old-faced infants and the lifted sick, and the
    sharp-lipp'd unshaved men;
All this I swallow, it tastes good, I like it well, it becomes mine,
I am the man, I suffered, I was there.
The disdain and calmness of martyrs,
The mother of old, condemned for a witch, burned with dry wood, her
    children gazing on,
The hounded slave that flags in the race, leans by the fence blowing,
    covered with sweat.
I am the hounded slave, I wince at the bite of the dogs,
Hell and despair are upon me, crack and again crack the marksmen,
I clutch the rails of the fence, my gore dribs, thinn'd with the
    ooze of my skin,
I fall on the weeds and stones,
The riders spur their unwilling horses, haul close,
Taunt my dizzy ears and beat me violently over the head with
    whip-stocks.

Old age superbly rising! O welcome, ineffable grace of dying days!
See ever so far, there is limitless space outside of that,
Count ever so much, there is limitless time around that.
My rendezvous is appointed, it is certain,
The Lord will be there and wait till I come on perfect terms.
The great Camerado, the lover true for whom I pine will be there.

And whoever walks a furlong without sympathy walks to his own
    funeral drest in his shroud.

And to glance with an eye or show a bean in its pod confounds
    the learning of all times,
And there is no trade or employment but the young man following
    it may become a hero,
And there is no object so soft but it makes a hub for the wheel'd
    universe.
And I say to any man or woman, "Let your soul stand cool and composed
    before a million universes."

I see something of God each hour of the twenty-four, and each
    moment then,
In the faces of men and women I see God, and in my own face in
    the glass,
I find letters from God dropt in the street, and every one is
    sign'd by God's name,
And I leave them where they are, for I know that wheresoe'er I go,
Others will punctually come forever and ever.

Listener up there! What have you to confide in me?
Look in my face while I snuff the sidle of evening.
(Talk honestly, no one else hears you, and I stay only a minute
    longer.)
Who has done his day's work? Who will soonest be through with
    his supper?
Who wishes to walk with me?

I too am not a bit tamed, I too am untranslatable,
I sound my barbaric yawp over the roofs of the world.
                           WALT WHITMAN (1819–1892)

ELENA'S SONG 765
Quoth tongue of neither maid nor wife
    To heart of neither wife nor maid—
Lead we not here a jolly life
    Betwixt the shine and shade?

Quoth heart of neither maid nor wife
    To tongue of neither wife nor maid—
Thou wagg'st, but I am worn with strife,
    And feel like flowers that fade.
                           SIR HENRY TAYLOR (1800–1866)

A JACOBITE'S EPITAPH 766
To my true king I offer'd free from stain
Courage and faith; vain faith, and courage vain.
For him I threw lands, honours, wealth, away,
And one dear hope, that was more prized than they.
For him I languish'd in a foreign clime,
Gray-hair'd with sorrow in my manhood's prime;
Heard on Lavernia Scargill's whispering trees,
And pined by Arno for my lovelier Tees;
Beheld each night my home in fever'd sleep,
Each morning started from the dream to weep;
Till God, who saw me tried too sorely, gave
The resting-place I ask'd, an early grave.
O thou, whom chance leads to this nameless stone,
From that proud country which was once mine own,
By those white cliffs I never more must see,
By that dear language which I spake like thee,
Forget all feuds, and shed one English tear
O'er English dust. A broken heart lies here.
            THOMAS BABINGTON MACAULAY, LORD MACAULAY (1800–1859)

767   MATER DOLOROSA

    I'd a dream to-night
      As I fell asleep,
    O! the touching sight
      Makes me still to weep:
    Of my little lad,
    Gone to leave me sad,
    Ay, the child I had,
      But was not to keep.

    As in heaven high,
      I my child did seek,
    There in train came by
      Children fair and meek,
    Each in lily white,
    With a lamp alight;
    Each was clear to sight,
      But they did not speak.

    Then, a little sad,
    Came my child in turn,
    But the lamp he had,
      O it did not burn!
    He, to clear my doubt,
    Said, half turn'd about,
    "Your tears put it out;
      Mother, never mourn."
                      WILLIAM BARNES (1801–1886)

768   THE WIFE A-LOST

    Since I noo mwore do zee your feäce,
      Up steärs or down below,
    I'll zit me in the lwonesome pleäce,
      Where flat-bough'd beech do grow;
    Below the beeches' bough, my love,
      Where you did never come,
    An' I don't look to meet ye now,
      As I do look at hwome.

    Since you noo mwore be at my zide,
      In walks in zummer het,
    I'll goo alwone where mist do ride,
      Droo trees a-drippèn wet;
    Below the raïn-wet bough, my love,
      Where you did never come,
    An' I don't grieve to miss ye now,
      As I do grieve at hwome.

    Since now bezide my dinner-bwoard
      Your vaïce do never sound,
    I'll eat the bit I can avword
      A-vield upon the ground;

Below the darksome bough, my love,
  Where you did never dine,
An' I don't grieve to miss ye now,
  As I at hwome do pine.

Since I do miss your vaïce an' feäce
  In praÿer at eventide,
I'll pray wi' woone sad vaïce vor greäce
  To goo where you do bide;
Above the tree an' bough, my love,
  Where you be gone avore,
An' be a-waïtèn vor me now,
  To come vor evermwore.
                    WILLIAM BARNES (1801–1886)

FAIRY SONG 769
He has conn'd the lesson now;
  He has read the book of pain:
There are furrows on his brow;
  I must make it smooth again.

Lo! I knock the spurs away;
  Lo! I loosen belt and brand;
Hark! I hear the courser neigh
  For his stall in Fairy-land.

Bring the cap, and bring the vest;
  Buckle on his sandal shoon;
Fetch his memory from the chest
  In the treasury of the moon.

I have taught him to be wise
  For a little maiden's sake;—
Lo! he opens his glad eyes,
  Softly, slowly: Minstrel, wake!
                    WINTHROP MACKWORTH PRAED (1802–1839)

O SLEEP, MY BABE 770
O sleep, my babe, hear not the rippling wave,
Nor feel the breeze that round thee ling'ring strays
    To drink thy balmy breath,
    And sigh one long farewell.

Soon shall it mourn above thy wat'ry bed,
And whisper to me, on the wave-beat shore,
    Deep murm'ring in reproach,
    Thy sad untimely fate.

Ere those dear eyes had open'd on the light,
In vain to plead, thy coming life was sold,
    O waken'd but to sleep,
    Whence it can wake no more!

A thousand and a thousand silken leaves
The tufted beech unfolds in early spring,
    All clad in tenderest green,
    All of the self-same shape:

A thousand infant faces, soft and sweet,
Each year sends forth, yet every mother views
    Her last not least beloved
    Like its dear self alone.

No musing mind hath ever yet foreshaped
The face to-morrow's sun shall first reveal,
    No heart hath e'er conceived
    What love that face will bring.

O sleep, my babe, nor heed how mourns the gale
To part with thy soft locks and fragrant breath,
    As when it deeply sighs
    O'er autumn's latest bloom.
            SARA COLERIDGE (1802–1850)

771   THE CHILD

See yon blithe child that dances in our sight!
Can gloomy shadows fall from one so bright?
    Fond mother, whence these fears?
While buoyantly he rushes o'er the lawn,
Dream not of clouds to stain his manhood's dawn,
    Nor dim that sight with tears.

No cloud he spies in brightly glowing hours,
But feels as if the newly vested bowers
    For him could never fade:
Too well we know that vernal pleasures fleet,
But having him, so gladsome, fair, and sweet,
    Our loss is overpaid.

Amid the balmiest flowers that earth can give
Some bitter drops distil, and all that live
    A mingled portion share;
But, while he learns these truths which we lament,
Such fortitude as ours will sure be sent,
    Such solace to his care.
            SARA COLERIDGE (1802–1850)

772   DARK ROSALEEN

    O my Dark Rosaleen,
      Do not sigh, do not weep!
The priests are on the ocean green,
    They march along the deep.
There's wine from the royal Pope,
    Upon the ocean green;
And Spanish ale shall give you hope,
    My Dark Rosaleen!

My own Rosaleen!
Shall glad your heart, shall give you hope,
Shall give you health, and help, and hope,
  My Dark Rosaleen!

Over hills, and thro' dales,
  Have I roam'd for your sake;
All yesterday I sail'd with sails
  On river and on lake.
The Erne, at its highest flood,
  I dash'd across unseen,
For there was lightning in my blood,
  My Dark Rosaleen!
  My own Rosaleen!
O, there was lightning in my blood,
Red lightning lighten'd thro' my blood.
  My Dark Rosaleen!

All day long, in unrest,
  To and fro, do I move.
The very soul within my breast
  Is wasted for you, love!
The heart in my bosom faints
  To think of you, my Queen,
My life of life, my saint of saints,
  My Dark Rosaleen!
  My own Rosaleen!
To hear your sweet and sad complaints,
My life, my love, my saint of saints,
  My Dark Rosaleen!

Woe and pain, pain and woe,
  Are my lot, night and noon,
To see your bright face clouded so,
  Like to the mournful moon.
But yet will I rear your throne
  Again in golden sheen;
'Tis you shall reign, shall reign alone,
  My Dark Rosaleen!
  My own Rosaleen!
'Tis you shall have the golden throne,
'Tis you shall reign, and reign alone,
  My Dark Rosaleen!

Over dews, over sands,
  Will I fly, for your weal:
Your holy delicate white hands
  Shall girdle me with steel.
At home, in your emerald bowers,
  From morning's dawn till e'en,
You'll pray for me, my flower of flowers,
  My Dark Rosaleen!

My fond Rosaleen!
You'll think of me through daylight hours,
My virgin flower, my flower of flowers,
  My Dark Rosaleen!

I could scale the blue air,
  I could plough the high hills,
O, I could kneel all night in prayer,
  To heal your many ills!
And one beamy smile from you
  Would float like light between
My toils and me, my own, my true,
  My Dark Rosaleen!
  My fond Rosaleen!
Would give me life and soul anew,
A second life, a soul anew,
  My Dark Rosaleen!

O, the Erne shall run red,
  With redundance of blood,
The earth shall rock beneath our tread,
  And flames wrap hill and wood,
And gun-peal and slogan-cry
  Wake many a glen serene,
Ere you shall fade, ere you shall die,
  My Dark Rosaleen!
  My own Rosaleen!
The Judgement Hour must first be nigh,
Ere you can fade, ere you can die,
  My Dark Rosaleen!

        JAMES CLARENCE MANGAN (1803–1849)

773   THE NAMELESS ONE

Roll forth, my song, like the rushing river,
  That sweeps along to the mighty sea;
God will inspire me while I deliver
    My soul of thee!

Tell thou the world, when my bones lie whitening
  Amid the last homes of youth and eld,
That once there was one whose veins ran lightning
    No eye beheld.

Tell how his boyhood was one drear night-hour,
  How shone for him, through his griefs and gloom,
No star of all heaven sends to light our
    Path to the tomb.

Roll on, my song, and to after ages
  Tell how, disdaining all earth can give,
He would have taught men, from wisdom's pages,
    The way to live.

And tell how trampled, derided, hated,
  And worn by weakness, disease, and wrong,
He fled for shelter to God, who mated
      His soul with song.

—With song which alway, sublime or vapid,
  Flow'd like a rill in the morning beam,
Perchance not deep, but intense and rapid—
      A mountain stream.

Tell how this Nameless, condemn'd for years long
  To herd with demons from hell beneath,
Saw things that made him, with groans and tears, long
      For even death.

Go on to tell how, with genius wasted,
  Betray'd in friendship, befool'd in love,
With spirit shipwreck'd, and young hopes blasted,
      He still, still strove;

Till, spent with toil, dreeing death for others
  (And some whose hands should have wrought for him,
If children live not for sires and mothers),
      His mind grew dim;

And he fell far through that pit abysmal,
  The gulf and grave of Maginn and Burns,
And pawn'd his soul for the devil's dismal
      Stock of returns.

But yet redeem'd it in days of darkness,
  And shapes and signs of the final wrath,
When death, in hideous and ghastly starkness,
      Stood on his path.

And tell how now, amid wreck and sorrow,
  And want, and sickness, and houseless nights,
He bides in calmness the silent morrow,
      That no ray lights.

And lives he still, then? Yes! Old and hoary
  At thirty-nine, from despair and woe,
He lives, enduring what future story
      Will never know.

Him grant a grave to, ye pitying noble,
  Deep in your bosoms: there let him dwell!
He, too, had tears for all souls in trouble,
      Here and in hell.
                    JAMES CLARENCE MANGAN (1803–1849)

WOLFRAM'S DIRGE   774
If thou wilt ease thine heart
Of love and all its smart,
  Then sleep, dear, sleep;
And not a sorrow

Hang any tear on your eyelashes;
   Lie still and deep,
Sad soul, until the sea-wave washes
The rim o' the sun to-morrow,
   In eastern sky.

But wilt thou cure thine heart
Of love and all its smart,
   Then die, dear, die;
'Tis deeper, sweeter,
   Than on a rose-bank to lie dreaming
    With folded eye;
  And there alone, amid the beaming
Of Love's stars, thou'lt meet her
    In eastern sky.
          THOMAS LOVELL BEDDOES (1803–1849)

775   DREAM-PEDLARY

If there were dreams to sell,
   What would you buy?
Some cost a passing bell;
   Some a light sigh,
That shakes from Life's fresh crown
Only a rose-leaf down.
If there were dreams to sell,
Merry and sad to tell,
And the crier rang the bell,
   What would you buy?

A cottage lone and still,
   With bowers nigh,
Shadowy, my woes to still,
   Until I die.
Such pearl from Life's fresh crown
Fain would I shake me down.
Were dreams to have at will,
This would best heal my ill,
   This would I buy.
          THOMAS LOVELL BEDDOES (1803–1849)

776   SONG

How many times do I love thee, dear?
  Tell me how many thoughts there be
    In the atmosphere
    Of a new-fall'n year,
Whose white and sable hours appear
  The latest flake of Eternity:
So many times do I love thee, dear.

How many times do I love again?
  Tell me how many beads there are
      In a silver chain
      Of evening rain,
Unravell'd from the tumbling main,
  And threading the eye of a yellow star:
So many times do I love again.
                    THOMAS LOVELL BEDDOES (1803–1849)

GIVE ALL TO LOVE

Give all to love;
Obey thy heart;
Friends, kindred, days,
Estate, good fame,
Plans, credit, and the Muse—
Nothing refuse.

'Tis a brave master;
Let it have scope:
Follow it utterly,
Hope beyond hope:
High and more high
It dives into noon,
With wing unspent,
Untold intent;
But it is a god,
Knows its own path,
And the outlets of the sky.

It was never for the mean;
It requireth courage stout,
Souls above doubt,
Valour unbending:
Such 'twill reward;—
They shall return
More than they were,
And ever ascending.

Leave all for love;
Yet, hear me, yet,
One word more thy heart behoved,
One pulse more of firm endeavour—
Keep thee to-day,
To-morrow, for ever,
Free as an Arab
Of thy beloved.

Cling with life to the maid;
But when the surprise,
First vague shadow of surmise,
Flits across her bosom young,

Of a joy apart from thee,
Free be she, fancy-free;
Nor thou detain her vesture's hem,
Nor the palest rose she flung
From her summer diadem.

Though thou loved her as thyself,
As a self of purer clay;
Though her parting dims the day,
Stealing grace from all alive;
Heartily know,
When half-gods go
The gods arrive.

RALPH WALDO EMERSON (1803–1882)

778   URIEL

It fell in the ancient periods
  Which the brooding soul surveys,
Or ever the wild Time coin'd itself
  Into calendar months and days.

This was the lapse of Uriel,
Which in Paradise befell.
Once, among the Pleiads walking,
Sayd overheard the young gods talking;
And the treason, too long pent,
To his ears was evident.
The young deities discuss'd
Laws of form, and metre just,
Orb, quintessence, and sunbeams,
What subsisteth, and what seems.
One, with low tones that decide,
And doubt and reverend use defied,
With a look that solved the sphere,
And stirr'd the devils everywhere,
Gave his sentiment divine
Against the being of a line.
"Line in nature is not found;
Unit and universe are round;
In vain produced, all rays return;
Evil will bless, and ice will burn."
As Uriel spoke with piercing eye,
A shudder ran around the sky;
The stern old war-gods shook their heads;
The seraphs frown'd from myrtle-beds;
Seem'd to the holy festival
The rash word boded ill to all;
The balance-beam of Fate was bent;
The bounds of good and ill were rent;
Strong Hades could not keep his own,
But all slid to confusion.

A sad self-knowledge withering fell
On the beauty of Uriel;
In heaven once eminent, the god
Withdrew that hour into his cloud;
Whether doom'd to long gyration
In the sea of generation,
Or by knowledge grown too bright
To hit the nerve of feebler sight.
Straightway a forgetting wind
Stole over the celestial kind,
And their lips the secret kept,
If in ashes the fire-seed slept.
But, now and then, truth-speaking things
Shamed the angels' veiling wings;
And, shrilling from the solar course,
Or from fruit of chemic force,
Procession of a soul in matter,
Or the speeding change of water,
Or out of the good of evil born,
Came Uriel's voice of cherub scorn,
And a blush tinged the upper sky,
And the gods shook, they knew not why.
                    RALPH WALDO EMERSON (1803–1882)

BACCHUS 779

Bring me wine, but wine which never grew
In the belly of the grape,
Or grew on vine whose tap-roots, reaching through
Under the Andes to the Cape,
Suffer'd no savour of the earth to 'scape.

Let its grapes the morn salute
From a nocturnal root,
Which feels the acrid juice
Of Styx and Erebus;
And turns the woe of Night,
By its own craft, to a more rich delight.

We buy ashes for bread;
We buy diluted wine;
Give me of the true,
Whose ample leaves and tendrils curl'd
Among the silver hills of heaven
Draw everlasting dew;
Wine of wine,
Blood of the world,
Form of forms, and mould of statures,
That I intoxicated,
And by the draught assimilated,
May float at pleasure through all natures;
The bird-language rightly spell,
And that which roses say so well:

Wine that is shed
Like the torrents of the sun
Up the horizon walls,
Or like the Atlantic streams, which run
When the South Sea calls.

Water and bread,
Food which needs no transmuting,
Rainbow-flowering, wisdom-fruiting,
Wine which is already man,
Food which teach and reason can.

Wine which Music is,—
Music and wine are one,—
That I, drinking this,
Shall hear far Chaos talk with me;
Kings unborn shall walk with me;
And the poor grass shall plot and plan
What it will do when it is man.
Quicken'd so, will I unlock
Every crypt of every rock.

I thank the joyful juice
For all I know;
Winds of remembering
Of the ancient being blow,
And seeming-solid walls of use
Open and flow.

Pour, Bacchus! the remembering wine;
Retrieve the loss of me and mine!
Vine for vine be antidote,
And the grape requite the lote!
Haste to cure the old despair;
Reason in Nature's lotus drench'd—
The memory of ages quench'd—
Give them again to shine;
Let wine repair what this undid;
And where the infection slid,
A dazzling memory revive;
Refresh the faded tints,
Recut the agèd prints,
And write my old adventures with the pen
Which on the first day drew,
Upon the tablets blue,
The dancing Pleiads and eternal men.

RALPH WALDO EMERSON (1803–1882)

BRAHMA

If the red slayer think he slays,
  Or if the slain think he is slain,
They know not well the subtle ways
  I keep, and pass, and turn again.

Far or forgot to me is near;
   Shadow and sunlight are the same;
The vanish'd gods to me appear;
   And one to me are shame and fame.

They reckon ill who leave me out;
   When me they fly, I am the wings;
I am the doubter and the doubt,
   And I the hymn the Brahmin sings.

The strong gods pine for my abode,
   And pine in vain the sacred Seven;
But thou, meek lover of the good!
   Find me, and turn thy back on heaven.
                    RALPH WALDO EMERSON (1803–1882)

THE PLOUGH 781
A LANDSCAPE IN BERKSHIRE
Above yon sombre swell of land
   Thou see'st the dawn's grave orange hue,
With one pale streak like yellow sand,
   And over that a vein of blue.

The air is cold above the woods;
   All silent is the earth and sky,
Except with his own lonely moods
   The blackbird holds a colloquy.

Over the broad hill creeps a beam,
   Like hope that gilds a good man's brow;
And now ascends the nostril-stream
   Of stalwart horses come to plough.

Ye rigid Ploughmen, bear in mind
   Your labour is for future hours:
Advance—spare not—nor look behind—
   Plough deep and straight with all your powers!
                    RICHARD HENRY HORNE (1803–1884)

KING ARTHUR'S WAES-HAEL 782
Waes-hael for knight and dame!
   O merry be their dole!
Drink-hael! in Jesu's name
   We fill the tawny bowl;
But cover down the curving crest,
Mould of the Orient Lady's breast.

Waes-hael! yet lift no lid:
   Drain ye the reeds for wine.
Drink-hael! the milk was hid
   That soothed that Babe divine;
Hush'd, as this hollow channel flows,
He drew the balsam from the rose.

> Waes-hael! thus glow'd the breast
>   Where a God yearn'd to cling;
> Drink-hael! so Jesu press'd
>   Life from its mystic spring;
> Then hush and bend in reverent sign
> And breathe the thrilling reeds for wine.
>
> Waes-hael! in shadowy scene
>   Lo! Christmas children we:
> Drink-hael! behold we lean
>   At a far Mother's knee;
> To dream that thus her bosom smiled,
> And learn the lip of Bethlehem's Child.
> ROBERT STEPHEN HAWKER (1804–1875)

Waes-hael: *Old Saxon drinking toast; "Be Well!" or "Cheers!"*

783   ARE THEY NOT ALL MINISTERING SPIRITS?

> We see them not—we cannot hear
>   The music of their wing—
> Yet know we that they sojourn near,
>   The Angels of the spring!
>
> They glide along this lovely ground
>   When the first violet grows;
> Their graceful hands have just unbound
>   The zone of yonder rose.
>
> I gather it for thy dear breast,
>   From stain and shadow free:
> That which an Angel's touch hath blest
>   Is meet, my love, for thee!
> ROBERT STEPHEN HAWKER (1804–1875)

784   THE HALF-ASLEEP

> O for the mighty wakening that aroused
>   The old-time Prophets to their missions high;
>   And to blind Homer's inward sunlike eye
> Show'd the heart's universe where he caroused
> Radiantly; the Fishers poor unhoused,
>   And sent them forth to preach divinity;
>   And made our Milton his great dark defy,
> To the light of one immortal theme espoused!
> But half asleep are those now most awake;
>   And save calm-thoughted Wordsworth, we have none
> Who for eternity put time at stake,
>   And hold a constant course as doth the sun:
> We yield but drops that no deep thirstings slake;
>   And feebly cease ere we have well begun.
> THOMAS WADE (1805–1875)

785   THE BELLS OF SHANDON

> With deep affection,
>   And recollection,
> I often think of
>   Those Shandon bells,

Whose sounds so wild would,
In the days of childhood,
Fling around my cradle
　Their magic spells.
On this I ponder
Where'er I wander,
And thus grow fonder,
　Sweet Cork, of thee;
With thy bells of Shandon,
That sound so grand on
The pleasant waters
　Of the River Lee.

I've heard bells chiming
Full many a clime in,
Tolling sublime in
　Cathedral shrine,
While at a glib rate
Brass tongues would vibrate—
But all their music
　Spoke naught like thine;
For memory, dwelling
On each proud swelling
Of the belfry knelling
　Its bold notes free,
Made the bells of Shandon
Sound far more grand on
The pleasant waters
　Of the River Lee.

I've heard bells tolling
Old Adrian's Mole in,
Their thunder rolling
　From the Vatican,
And cymbals glorious
Swinging uproarious
In the gorgeous turrets
　Of Notre Dame;
But thy sounds were sweeter
Than the dome of Peter
Flings o'er the Tiber,
　Pealing solemnly—
O, the bells of Shandon
Sound far more grand on
The pleasant waters
　Of the River Lee.

There's a bell in Moscow,
While on tower and kiosk O!
In Saint Sophia
　The Turkman gets,

        And loud in air
        Calls men to prayer
        From the tapering summits
          Of tall minarets.
        Such empty phantom
        I freely grant them;
        But there's an anthem
          More dear to me,—
        'Tis the bells of Shandon,
        That sound so grand on
        The pleasant waters
          Of the River Lee.

                              FRANCIS MAHONY (1805–1866)

786   ROSALIND'S SCROLL

I left thee last, a child at heart,
   A woman scarce in years:
I come to thee, a solemn corpse
   Which neither feels nor fears.
I have no breath to use in sighs;
They laid the dead-weights on mine eyes
   To seal them safe from tears.

Look on me with thine own calm look:
   I meet it calm as thou.
No look of thine can change this smile,
   Or break thy sinful vow:
I tell thee that my poor scorn'd heart
Is of thine earth—thine earth—a part:
   It cannot vex thee now.

I have pray'd for thee with bursting sob
   When passion's course was free;
I have pray'd for thee with silent lips
   In the anguish none could see;
They whisper'd oft, "She sleepeth soft"—
   But I only pray'd for thee.

Go to! I pray for thee no more:
   The corpse's tongue is still;
Its folded fingers point to heaven,
   But point there stiff and chill:
No farther wrong, no farther woe
Hath licence from the sin below
   Its tranquil heart to thrill.

I charge thee, by the living's prayer,
   And the dead's silentness,
To wring from out thy soul a cry
   Which God shall hear and bless!
Lest Heaven's own palm droop in my hand,
And pale among the saints I stand,
   A saint companionless.

                        ELIZABETH BARRETT BROWNING (1806–1861)

The Deserted Garden

I mind me in the days departed,
How often underneath the sun
With childish bounds I used to run
   To a garden long deserted.

The beds and walks were vanish'd quite;
And wheresoe'er had struck the spade,
The greenest grasses Nature laid,
   To sanctify her right.

I call'd the place my wilderness,
For no one enter'd there but I.
The sheep look'd in, the grass to espy,
   And pass'd it ne'ertheless.

The trees were interwoven wild,
And spread their boughs enough about
To keep both sheep and shepherd out,
   But not a happy child.

Adventurous joy it was for me!
I crept beneath the boughs, and found
A circle smooth of mossy ground
   Beneath a poplar-tree.

Old garden rose-trees hedged it in,
Bedropt with roses waxen-white,
Well satisfied with dew and light,
   And careless to be seen.

Long years ago, it might befall,
When all the garden flowers were trim,
The grave old gardener prided him
   On these the most of all.

Some Lady, stately overmuch,
Here moving with a silken noise,
Has blush'd beside them at the voice
   That liken'd her to such.

Or these, to make a diadem,
She often may have pluck'd and twined;
Half-smiling as it came to mind,
   That few would look at *them*.

O, little thought that Lady proud,
A child would watch her fair white rose,
When buried lay her whiter brows,
   And silk was changed for shroud!—

Nor thought that gardener (full of scorns
For men unlearn'd and simple phrase)
A child would bring it all its praise,
   By creeping through the thorns!

To me upon my low moss seat,
Though never a dream the roses sent
Of science or love's compliment,
   I ween they smelt as sweet.

It did not move my grief to see
The trace of human step departed:
Because the garden was deserted,
   The blither place for me!

Friends, blame me not! a narrow ken
Hath childhood 'twixt the sun and sward:
We draw the moral afterward—
   We feel the gladness then.

And gladdest hours for me did glide
In silence at the rose-tree wall:
A thrush made gladness musical
   Upon the other side.

Nor he nor I did e'er incline
To peck or pluck the blossoms white:—
How should I know but that they might
   Lead lives as glad as mine?

To make my hermit-home complete,
I brought clear water from the spring
Praised in its own low murmuring,
   And cresses glossy wet.

And so, I thought, my likeness grew
(Without the melancholy tale)
To "gentle hermit of the dale,"
   And Angelina too.

For oft I read within my nook
Such minstrel stories; till the breeze
Made sounds poetic in the trees,
   And then I shut the book.

If I shut this wherein I write,
I hear no more the wind athwart
Those trees, nor feel that childish heart
   Delighting in delight.

My childhood from my life is parted,
My footstep from the moss which drew
Its fairy circle round: anew
   The garden is deserted.

Another thrush may there rehearse
The madrigals which sweetest are;
No more for me!—myself afar
   Do sing a sadder verse.

Ah me! ah me! when erst I lay
In that child's-nest so greenly wrought,
I laugh'd unto myself and thought,
  "The time will pass away."

And still I laugh'd, and did not fear
But that, whene'er was pass'd away
The childish time, some happier play
  My womanhood would cheer.

I knew the time would pass away;
And yet, beside the rose-tree wall,
Dear God, how seldom, if at all,
  Did I look up to pray!

The time is past: and now that grows
The cypress high among the trees,
And I behold white sepulchres
  As well as the white rose,—

When wiser, meeker thoughts are given,
And I have learnt to lift my face,
Reminded how earth's greenest place
  The colour draws from heaven,—

It something saith for earthly pain,
But more for heavenly promise free,
That I who was, would shrink to be
  That happy child again.
                ELIZABETH BARRETT BROWNING (1806–1861)

CONSOLATION 788

All are not taken; there are left behind
  Living Belovèds, tender looks to bring
  And make the daylight still a happy thing,
And tender voices, to make soft the wind:
But if it were not so—if I could find
  No love in all this world for comforting,
  Nor any path but hollowly did ring
Where "dust to dust" the love from life disjoin'd;
And if, before those sepulchres unmoving
  I stood alone (as some forsaken lamb
Goes bleating up the moors in weary dearth)
Crying "Where are ye, O my loved and loving?"—
  I know a voice would sound, "Daughter, I AM.
Can I suffice for Heaven and not for earth?"
                ELIZABETH BARRETT BROWNING (1806–1861)

GRIEF 789

I tell you, hopeless grief is passionless;
  That only men incredulous of despair,
  Half-taught in anguish, through the midnight air
Beat upward to God's throne in loud access

Of shrieking and reproach. Full desertness
  In souls as countries lieth silent-bare
  Under the blanching, vertical eye-glare
Of the absolute Heavens. Deep-hearted man, express
Grief for thy Dead in silence like to death—
  Most like a monumental statue set
In everlasting watch and moveless woe
Till itself crumble to the dust beneath.
  Touch it; the marble eyelids are not wet:
If it could weep, it could arise and go.
ELIZABETH BARRETT BROWNING (1806–1861)

790   SONNETS FROM THE PORTUGUESE, No. 1

I thought once how Theocritus had sung
  Of the sweet years, the dear and wish'd-for years,
  Who each one in a gracious hand appears
To bear a gift for mortals old or young:
And, as I mused it in his antique tongue,
  I saw in gradual vision through my tears
  The sweet, sad years, the melancholy years—
Those of my own life, who by turns had flung
A shadow across me. Straightway I was 'ware,
  So weeping, how a mystic Shape did move
Behind me, and drew me backward by the hair;
  And a voice said in mastery, while I strove,
"Guess now who holds thee?"—"Death," I said. But there
  The silver answer rang—"Not Death, but Love."
ELIZABETH BARRETT BROWNING (1806–1861)

791   SONNETS FROM THE PORTUGUESE, No. 3

Unlike are we, unlike, O princely Heart!
  Unlike our uses and our destinies.
  Our ministering two angels look surprise
On one another, as they strike athwart
Their wings in passing. Thou, bethink thee, art
  A guest for queens to social pageantries,
  With gages from a hundred brighter eyes
Than tears even can make mine, to play thy part
Of chief musician. What hast thou to do
  With looking from the lattice-lights at me—
A poor, tired, wandering singer, singing through
  The dark, and leaning up a cypress tree?
The chrism is on thine head—on mine the dew—
  And Death must dig the level where these agree.
ELIZABETH BARRETT BROWNING (1806–1861)

792   SONNETS FROM THE PORTUGUESE, No. 6

Go from me. Yet I feel that I shall stand
  Henceforward in thy shadow. Nevermore
  Alone upon the threshold of my door
Of individual life I shall command
The uses of my soul, nor lift my hand
  Serenely in the sunshine as before,
  Without the sense of that which I forbore—
Thy touch upon the palm. The widest land

Doom takes to part us, leaves thy heart in mine
  With pulses that beat double. What I do
And what I dream include thee, as the wine
  Must taste of its own grapes. And when I sue
God for myself, He hears that name of thine,
  And sees within my eyes the tears of two.
                    ELIZABETH BARRETT BROWNING (1806–1861)

SONNETS FROM THE PORTUGUESE, NO. 14   793
If thou must love me, let it be for naught
  Except for love's sake only. Do not say,
"I love her for her smile—her look—her way
Of speaking gently,—for a trick of thought
That falls in well with mine, and certes brought
  A sense of pleasant ease on such a day"—
  For these things in themselves, Beloved, may
Be changed, or change for thee—and love, so wrought,
May be unwrought so. Neither love me for
  Thine own dear pity's wiping my cheeks dry:
A creature might forget to weep, who bore
  Thy comfort long, and lose thy love thereby!
But love me for love's sake, that evermore
  Thou mayst love on, through love's eternity.
                    ELIZABETH BARRETT BROWNING (1806–1861)

SONNETS FROM THE PORTUGUESE, NO. 22   794
  When our two souls stand up erect and strong,
    Face to face, silent, drawing nigh and nigher,
    Until the lengthening wings break into fire
  At either curving point,—what bitter wrong
  Can the earth do us, that we should not long
    Be here contented? Think! In mounting higher,
    The angels would press on us, and aspire
  To drop some golden orb of perfect song
  Into our deep, dear silence. Let us stay
    Rather on earth, Beloved—where the unfit
  Contrarious moods of men recoil away
    And isolate pure spirits, and permit
  A place to stand and love in for a day,
    With darkness and the death-hour rounding it.
                    ELIZABETH BARRETT BROWNING (1806–1861)

A MUSICAL INSTRUMENT   795
What was he doing, the great god Pan,
  Down in the reeds by the river?
Spreading ruin and scattering ban,
Splashing and paddling with hoofs of a goat,
And breaking the golden lilies afloat
  With the dragon-fly on the river.

He tore out a reed, the great god Pan,
   From the deep cool bed of the river;
The limpid water turbidly ran,
And the broken lilies a-dying lay,
And the dragon-fly had fled away,
   Ere he brought it out of the river.

High on the shore sat the great god Pan,
   While turbidly flow'd the river;
And hack'd and hew'd as a great god can
With his hard bleak steel at the patient reed,
Till there was not a sign of the leaf indeed
   To prove it fresh from the river.

He cut it short, did the great god Pan
   (How tall it stood in the river!),
Then drew the pith, like the heart of a man,
Steadily from the outside ring,
And notch'd the poor dry empty thing
   In holes, as he sat by the river.

"This is the way," laugh'd the great god Pan
   (Laugh'd while he sat by the river),
"The only way, since gods began
To make sweet music, they could succeed."
Then dropping his mouth to a hole in the reed,
   He blew in power by the river.

Sweet, sweet, sweet, O Pan!
   Piercing sweet by the river!
Blinding sweet, O great god Pan!
The sun on the hill forgot to die,
And the lilies revived, and the dragon-fly
   Came back to dream on the river.

Yet half a beast is the great god Pan,
   To laugh as he sits by the river,
Making a poet out of a man:
The true gods sigh for the cost and pain—
For the reed which grows nevermore again
   As a reed with the reeds of the river.
               ELIZABETH BARRETT BROWNING (1806–1861)

796   THE HOLY TIDE

The days are sad, it is the Holy tide:
   The Winter morn is short, the Night is long;
So let the lifeless Hours be glorified
   With deathless thoughts and echo'd in sweet song:
And through the sunset of this purple cup
   They will resume the roses of their prime,
And the old Dead will hear us and wake up,
   Pass with dim smiles and make our hearts sublime!

The days are sad, it is the Holy tide:
  Be dusky mistletoes and hollies strown,
Sharp as the spear that pierced His sacred side,
  Red as the drops upon His thorny crown;
No haggard Passion and no lawless Mirth
  Fright off the solemn Muse,—tell sweet old tales,
Sing songs as we sit brooding o'er the hearth,
  Till the lamp flickers, and the memory fails.
                              FREDERICK TENNYSON (1807–1898)

MY LOST YOUTH

Often I think of the beautiful town
  That is seated by the sea;
Often in thought go up and down
The pleasant streets of that dear old town,
  And my youth comes back to me.
    And a verse of a Lapland song
    Is haunting my memory still:
  "A boy's will is the wind's will,
And the thoughts of youth are long, long thoughts."

I can see the shadowy lines of its trees,
  And catch, in sudden gleams,
The sheen of the far-surrounding seas,
And islands that were the Hesperides
  Of all my boyish dreams.
    And the burden of that old song,
    It murmurs and whispers still:
  "A boy's will is the wind's will,
And the thoughts of youth are long, long thoughts."

I remember the black wharves and the slips,
  And the sea-tides tossing free;
And Spanish sailors with bearded lips,
And the beauty and mystery of the ships,
  And the magic of the sea.
    And the voice of that wayward song
    Is singing and saying still:
  "A boy's will is the wind's will,
And the thoughts of youth are long, long thoughts."

I remember the bulwarks by the shore,
  And the fort upon the hill;
The sunrise gun with its hollow roar,
The drum-beat repeated o'er and o'er,
  And the bugle wild and shrill.
    And the music of that old song
    Throbs in my memory still:
  "A boy's will is the wind's will,
And the thoughts of youth are long, long thoughts."

I remember the sea-fight far away,
  How it thunder'd o'er the tide!
And the dead sea-captains, as they lay
In their graves o'erlooking the tranquil bay
  Where they in battle died.
    And the sound of that mournful song
    Goes through me with a thrill:
  "A boy's will is the wind's will,
And the thoughts of youth are long, long thoughts."

I can see the breezy dome of groves,
  The shadows of Deering's woods;
And the friendships old and the early loves
Come back with a Sabbath sound, as of doves
  In quiet neighbourhoods.
    And the verse of that sweet old song,
    It flutters and murmurs still:
  "A boy's will is the wind's will,
And the thoughts of youth are long, long thoughts."

I remember the gleams and glooms that dart
  Across the schoolboy's brain;
The song and the silence in the heart,
That in part are prophecies, and in part
  Are longings wild and vain.
    And the voice of that fitful song
    Sings on, and is never still:
  "A boy's will is the wind's will,
And the thoughts of youth are long, long thoughts."

There are things of which I may not speak;
  There are dreams that cannot die;
There are thoughts that make the strong heart weak,
And bring a pallor into the cheek,
  And a mist before the eye.
    And the words of that fatal song
    Come over me like a chill:
  "A boy's will is the wind's will,
And the thoughts of youth are long, long thoughts."

Strange to me now are the forms I meet
  When I visit the dear old town;
But the native air is pure and sweet,
And the trees that o'ershadow each well-known street,
  As they balance up and down,
    Are singing the beautiful song,
    Are sighing and whispering still:
  "A boy's will is the wind's will,
And the thoughts of youth are long, long thoughts."

And Deering's woods are fresh and fair,
  And with joy that is almost pain
My heart goes back to wander there,
And among the dreams of the days that were

I find my lost youth again.
  And the strange and beautiful song,
  The groves are repeating it still:
  "A boy's will is the wind's will,
And the thoughts of youth are long, long thoughts."
                    HENRY WADSWORTH LONGFELLOW (1807–1882)

VESTA   798
O Christ of God! whose life and death
  Our own have reconciled,
Most quietly, most tenderly
  Take home thy star-named child!

Thy grace is in her patient eyes,
  Thy words are on her tongue;
The very silence round her seems
  As if the angels sung.

Her smile is as a listening child's
  Who hears its mother's call;
The lilies of Thy perfect peace
  About her pillow fall.

She leans from out our clinging arms
  To rest herself in Thine;
Alone to Thee, dear Lord, can we
  Our well-beloved resign.

O, less for her than for ourselves
  We bow our heads and pray;
Her setting star, like Bethlehem's,
  To Thee shall point the way!
                    JOHN GREENLEAF WHITTIER (1807–1892)

LAMENT OF THE IRISH EMIGRANT   799
I'm sittin' on the stile, Mary,
  Where we sat side by side
On a bright May mornin' long ago,
  When first you were my bride;
The corn was springin' fresh and green,
  And the lark sang loud and high—
And the red was on your lip, Mary,
  And the love-light in your eye.

The place is little changed, Mary,
  The day is bright as then,
The lark's loud song is in my ear,
  And the corn is green again;
But I miss the soft clasp of your hand,
  And your breath warm on my cheek,
And I still keep list'ning for the words
  You never more will speak.

'Tis but a step down yonder lane,
  And the little church stands near,
The church where we were wed, Mary,
  I see the spire from here.
But the graveyard lies between, Mary,
  And my step might break your rest—
For I've laid you, darling! down to sleep,
  With your baby on your breast.

I'm very lonely now, Mary,
  For the poor make no new friends,
But, O, they love the better still,
  The few our Father sends!
And you were all *I* had, Mary,
  My blessin' and my pride:
There's nothin' left to care for now,
  Since my poor Mary died.

Yours was the good, brave heart, Mary,
  That still kept hoping on,
When the trust in God had left my soul,
  And my arm's young strength was gone:
There was comfort ever on your lip,
  And the kind look on your brow—
I bless you, Mary, for that same,
  Though you cannot hear me now.

I thank you for the patient smile
  When your heart was fit to break,
When the hunger pain was gnawin' there,
  And you hid it, for my sake!
I bless you for the pleasant word,
  When your heart was sad and sore—
O, I'm thankful you are gone, Mary,
  Where grief can't reach you more!

I'm biddin' you a long farewell,
  My Mary—kind and true!
But I'll not forget you, darling!
  In the land I'm goin' to;
They say there's bread and work for all,
  And the sun shines always there—
But I'll not forget old Ireland,
  Were it fifty times as fair!

And often in those grand old woods
  I'll sit, and shut my eyes,
And my heart will travel back again
  To the place where Mary lies;
And I'll think I see the little stile
  Where we sat side by side:
And the springin' corn, and the bright May morn,
  When first you were my bride.

        HELEN SELINA, LADY DUFFERIN (1807–1867)

I DO NOT LOVE THEE 800

I do not love thee!—no! I do not love thee!
And yet when thou art absent I am sad;
  And envy even the bright blue sky above thee,
Whose quiet stars may see thee and be glad.

  I do not love thee!—yet, I know not why,
Whate'er thou dost seems still well done, to me:
  And often in my solitude I sigh
That those I do love are not more like thee!

  I do not love thee!—yet, when thou art gone,
I hate the sound (though those who speak be dear)
  Which breaks the lingering echo of the tone
Thy voice of music leaves upon my ear.

  I do not love thee!—yet thy speaking eyes,
With their deep, bright, and most expressive blue,
  Between me and the midnight heaven arise,
Oftener than any eyes I ever knew.

  I know I do not love thee! yet, alas!
Others will scarcely trust my candid heart;
  And oft I catch them smiling as they pass,
Because they see me gazing where thou art.

        CAROLINE ELIZABETH SARAH NORTON (1808–1876)

LETTY'S GLOBE 801

When Letty had scarce pass'd her third glad year,
  And her young artless words began to flow,
One day we gave the child a colour'd sphere
  Of the wide earth, that she might mark and know,
By tint and outline, all its sea and land.
  She patted all the world; old empires peep'd
Between her baby fingers; her soft hand
  Was welcome at all frontiers. How she leap'd,
And laugh'd and prattled in her world-wide bliss;
But when we turn'd her sweet unlearnèd eye
On our own isle, she raised a joyous cry—
"Oh! yes, I see it, Letty's home is there!"
  And while she hid all England with a kiss,
Bright over Europe fell her golden hair.

        CHARLES TENNYSON TURNER (1808–1879)

TO HELEN 802

  Helen, thy beauty is to me
    Like those Nicèan barks of yore
  That gently, o'er a perfumed sea,
    The weary way-worn wanderer bore
    To his own native shore.

On desperate seas long wont to roam,
   Thy hyacinth hair, thy classic face,
Thy Naiad airs have brought me home
   To the glory that was Greece,
And the grandeur that was Rome.

Lo, in yon brilliant window-niche
   How statue-like I see thee stand,
   The agate lamp within thy hand,
Ah! Psyche, from the regions which
   Are holy land!

EDGAR ALLAN POE (1809–1849)

803   ANNABEL LEE

It was many and many a year ago,
   In a kingdom by the sea,
That a maiden there lived whom you may know
   By the name of Annabel Lee.
And this maiden she lived with no other thought
   Than to love and be loved by me.

I was a child and she was a child
   In this kingdom by the sea:
But we loved with a love that was more than love—
   I and my Annabel Lee,
With a love that the wingèd seraphs of heaven
   Coveted her and me.

And this was the reason that, long ago,
   In this kingdom by the sea,
A wind blew out of a cloud, chilling
   My beautiful Annabel Lee,
So that her high-born kinsmen came
   And bore her away from me,
To shut her up in a sepulchre
   In this kingdom by the sea.

The angels, not half so happy in heaven,
   Went envying her and me—
Yes! that was the reason (as all men know,
   In this kingdom by the sea)
That the wind came out of the cloud one night,
   Chilling and killing my Annabel Lee.

But our love it was stronger by far than the love
   Of those who were older than we—
   Of many far wiser than we—
And neither the angels in heaven above,
   Nor the demons down under the sea,
Can ever dissever my soul from the soul
   Of the beautiful Annabel Lee:

For the moon never beams without bringing me dreams
   Of the beautiful Annabel Lee;
And the stars never rise, but I feel the bright eyes
   Of the beautiful Annabel Lee;
And so, all the night-tide, I lie down by the side
Of my darling—my darling—my life and my bride,
   In the sepulchre there by the sea,
   In her tomb by the sounding sea.

                         EDGAR ALLAN POE (1809–1849)

FOR ANNIE

Thank Heaven! the crisis—
   The danger is past,
And the lingering illness
   Is over at last—
And the fever called "Living"
   Is conquer'd at last.

Sadly, I know
   I am shorn of my strength,
And no muscle I move
   As I lie at full length:
But no matter—I feel
   I am better at length.

And I rest so composedly
   Now, in my bed,
That any beholder
   Might fancy me dead—
Might start at beholding me,
   Thinking me dead.

The moaning and groaning,
   The sighing and sobbing,
Are quieted now,
   With that horrible throbbing
At heart—ah, that horrible,
   Horrible throbbing!

The sickness—the nausea—
   The pitiless pain—
Have ceased, with the fever
   That madden'd my brain—
With the fever called "Living"
   That burn'd in my brain.

And O! of all tortures
   That torture the worst
Has abated—the terrible
   Torture of thirst
For the naphthaline river
   Of Passion accurst—
I have drunk of a water
   That quenches all thirst.

—Of a water that flows,
  With a lullaby sound,
From a spring but a very few
  Feet under ground—
From a cavern not very far
  Down under ground.

And ah! let it never
  Be foolishly said
That my room it is gloomy,
  And narrow my bed;
For man never slept
  In a different bed—
And, to *sleep*, you must slumber
  In just such a bed.

My tantalized spirit
  Here blandly reposes,
Forgetting, or never
  Regretting its roses—
Its old agitations
  Of myrtles and roses:

For now, while so quietly
  Lying, it fancies
A holier odour
  About it, of pansies—
A rosemary odour,
  Commingled with pansies—
With rue and the beautiful
  Puritan pansies.

And so it lies happily,
  Bathing in many
A dream of the truth
  And the beauty of Annie—
Drown'd in a bath
  Of the tresses of Annie.

She tenderly kiss'd me,
  She fondly caress'd,
And then I fell gently
  To sleep on her breast—
Deeply to sleep
  From the heaven of her breast.

When the light was extinguish'd,
  She cover'd me warm,
And she pray'd to the angels
  To keep me from harm—
To the queen of the angels
  To shield me from harm.

And I lie so composedly,
  Now, in my bed
(Knowing her love),
  That you fancy me dead—
And I rest so contentedly,
  Now, in my bed
(With her love at my breast),
  That you fancy me dead—
That you shudder to look at me,
  Thinking me dead.

But my heart it is brighter
  Than all of the many
Stars in the sky,
  For it sparkles with Annie—
It glows with the light
  Of the love of my Annie—
With the thought of the light
  Of the eyes of my Annie.

          EDGAR ALLAN POE (1809–1849)

OLD SONG

Tis a dull sight
  To see the year dying,
When winter winds
  Set the yellow wood sighing:
    Sighing, O sighing!

When such a time cometh
  I do retire
Into an old room
  Beside a bright fire:
    O, pile a bright fire!

And there I sit
  Reading old things,
Of knights and lorn damsels,
  While the wind sings—
    O, drearily sings!

I never look out
  Nor attend to the blast;
For all to be seen
  Is the leaves falling fast:
    Falling, falling!

But close at the hearth,
  Like a cricket, sit I,
Reading of summer
  And chivalry—
    Gallant chivalry!

Then with an old friend
  I talk of our youth—
How 'twas gladsome, but often
  Foolish, forsooth:
    But gladsome, gladsome!

Or, to get merry,
  We sing some old rhyme
That made the wood ring again
  In summer time—
    Sweet summer time!

Then go we smoking,
  Silent and snug:
Naught passes between us,
  Save a brown jug—
    Sometimes!

And sometimes a tear
  Will rise in each eye,
Seeing the two old friends
  So merrily—
    So merrily!

And ere to bed
  Go we, go we,
Down on the ashes
  We kneel on the knee,
    Praying together!

Thus, then, live I
  Till, 'mid all the gloom,
By Heaven! the bold sun
  Is with me in the room
    Shining, shining!

Then the clouds part,
  Swallows soaring between;
The spring is alive,
  And the meadows are green!

I jump up like mad,
  Break the old pipe in twain,
And away to the meadows,
  The meadows again!

EDWARD FITZGERALD (1809–1883)

From Omar Khayyám

I

A Book of Verses underneath the Bough,
A Jug of Wine, a Loaf of Bread—and Thou
  Beside me singing in the Wilderness—
O, Wilderness were Paradise enow!

Some for the Glories of This World; and some
Sigh for the Prophet's Paradise to come;
   Ah, take the Cash, and let the Credit go,
Nor heed the rumble of a distant Drum!

Look to the blowing Rose about us—"Lo,
Laughing," she says, "into the world I blow,
   At once the silken tassel of my Purse
Tear, and its Treasure on the Garden throw."

And those who husbanded the Golden grain
And those who flung it to the winds like Rain
   Alike to no such aureate Earth are turn'd
As, buried once, Men want dug up again.

II

Think, in this batter'd Caravanserai
Whose Portals are alternate Night and Day,
   How Sultán after Sultán with his Pomp
Abode his destined Hour, and went his way.

They say the Lion and the Lizard keep
The Courts where Jamshyd gloried and drank deep:
   And Bahrám, that great Hunter—the wild Ass
Stamps o'er his Head, but cannot break his Sleep.

I sometimes think that never blows so red
The Rose as where some buried Cæsar bled;
   That every Hyacinth the Garden wears
Dropt in her Lap from some once lovely Head.

And this reviving Herb whose tender Green
Fledges the River-Lip on which we lean—
   Ah, lean upon it lightly! for who knows
From what once lovely Lip it springs unseen!

Ah, my Belovèd, fill the Cup that clears
TO-DAY of past Regrets and Future Fears:
   To-morrow!—Why, To-morrow I may be
Myself with Yesterday's Sev'n thousand Years.

For some we loved, the loveliest and the best
That from his Vintage rolling Time hath prest,
   Have drunk their Cup a Round or two before,
And one by one crept silently to rest.

And we, that now make merry in the Room
They left, and Summer dresses in new bloom,
   Ourselves must we beneath the Couch of Earth
Descend—ourselves to make a Couch—for whom?

Ah, make the most of what we yet may spend,
Before we too into the Dust descend;
   Dust unto Dust, and under Dust to lie,
Sans Wine, sans Song, sans Singer, and—sans End!

III

Ah, with the Grape my fading Life provide,
And wash my Body whence the Life has died,
  And lay me, shrouded in the living Leaf,
By some not unfrequented Garden-side....

Yon rising Moon that looks for us again—
How oft hereafter will she wax and wane;
  How oft hereafter rising look or us
Through this same Garden—and for *one* in vain!

And when like her O Sákí, you shall pass
Among the Guests star-scatter'd on the Grass,
  And in your joyous errand reach the spot
Where I made One—turn down an empty Glass!

EDWARD FITZGERALD (1809–1883)

807   MARIANA

With blackest moss the flower-plots
  Were thickly crusted, one and all:
The rusted nails fell from the knots
  That held the pear to the gable-wall.
The broken sheds look'd sad and strange:
  Unlifted was the clinking latch;
  Weeded and worn the ancient thatch
Upon the lonely moated grange.
    She only said, "My life is dreary,
      He cometh not," she said;
    She said, "I am aweary, aweary,
      I would that I were dead!"

Her tears fell with the dews at even;
  Her tears fell ere the dews were dried;
She could not look on the sweet heaven,
  Either at morn or eventide.
After the flitting of the bats,
  When thickest dark did trance the sky,
  She drew her casement-curtain by,
And glanced athwart the glooming flats.
    She only said, "The night is dreary,
      He cometh not," she said;
    She said, "I am aweary, aweary,
      I would that I were dead!"

Upon the middle of the night,
  Waking she heard the night-fowl crow:
The cock sung out an hour ere light:
  From the dark fen the oxen's low
Came to her: without hope of change,
  In sleep she seem'd to walk forlorn,
  Till cold winds woke the gray-eyed morn
About the lonely moated grange.

    She only said, "The day is dreary,
      He cometh not," she said;
    She said, "I am aweary, aweary,
      I would that I were dead!"

About a stone-cast from the wall
  A sluice with blacken'd waters slept,
And o'er it many, round and small,
  The cluster'd marish-mosses crept.
Hard by a poplar shook alway,
  All silver-green with gnarled bark:
  For leagues no other tree did mark
The level waste, the rounding gray.
    She only said, "My life is dreary,
      He cometh not," she said;
    She said, "I am aweary, aweary,
      I would that I were dead!"

And ever when the moon was low,
  And the shrill winds were up and away,
In the white curtain, to and fro,
  She saw the gusty shadow sway.
But when the moon was very low,
  And wild winds bound within their cell,
  The shadow of the poplar fell
Upon her bed, across her brow.
    She only said, "The night is dreary,
      He cometh not," she said;
    She said, "I am aweary, aweary,
      I would that I were dead!"

All day within the dreamy house,
  The doors upon their hinges creak'd;
The blue fly sung in the pane; the mouse
  Behind the mouldering wainscot shriek'd,
Or from the crevice peer'd about.
  Old faces glimmer'd thro' the doors,
  Old footsteps trod the upper floors,
Old voices call'd her from without.
    She only said, "My life is dreary,
      He cometh not," she said;
    She said, "I am aweary, aweary,
      I would that I were dead!"

The sparrow's chirrup on the roof,
  The slow clock ticking, and the sound
Which to the wooing wind aloof
  The poplar made, did all confound
Her sense; but most she loathed the hour
  When the thick-moted sunbeam lay
  Athwart the chambers, and the day
Was sloping toward his western bower.

Then, said she, "I am very dreary,
  He will not come," she said;
She wept, "I am aweary, aweary,
  O God, that I were dead!"
                    ALFRED TENNYSON, LORD TENNYSON (1809–1892)

808   THE LADY OF SHALOTT
                        PART I
On either side the river lie
Long fields of barley and of rye,
That clothe the wold and meet the sky;
And thro' the field the road runs by
          To many-tower'd Camelot;
And up and down the people go,
Gazing where the lilies blow
Round an island there below,
          The island of Shalott.

Willows whiten, aspens quiver,
Little breezes dusk and shiver
Thro' the wave that runs for ever
By the island in the river
          Flowing down to Camelot.
Four gray walls, and four gray towers,
Overlook a space of flowers,
And the silent isle imbowers
          The Lady of Shalott.

By the margin, willow-veil'd,
Slide the heavy barges trail'd
By slow horses; and unhail'd
The shallop flitteth silken-sail'd
          Skimming down to Camelot:
But who hath seen her wave her hand?
Or at the casement seen her stand?
Or is she known in all the land,
          The Lady of Shalott?

Only reapers, reaping early
In among the bearded barley,
Hear a song that echoes cheerly
From the river winding clearly,
          Down to tower'd Camelot:
And by the moon the reaper weary,
Piling sheaves in uplands airy,
Listening, whispers "Tis the fairy
          Lady of Shalott."

                        PART II
There she weaves by night and day
A magic web with colours gay.

She has heard a whisper say,
A curse is on her if she stay
  To look down to Camelot.
She knows not what the curse may be,
And so she weaveth steadily,
And little other care hath she,
  The Lady of Shalott.

And moving thro' a mirror clear
That hangs before her all the year,
Shadows of the world appear.
There she sees the highway near
  Winding down to Camelot:
There the river eddy whirls,
And there the surly village-churls,
And the red cloaks of market girls,
  Pass onward from Shalott.

Sometimes a troop of damsels glad,
An abbot on an ambling pad,
Sometimes a curly shepherd-lad,
Or long-hair'd page in crimson clad,
  Goes by to tower'd Camelot;
And sometimes thro' the mirror blue
The knights come riding two and two:
She hath no loyal knight and true,
  The Lady of Shalott.

But in her web she still delights
To weave the mirror's magic sights,
For often thro' the silent nights
A funeral, with plumes and lights,
  And music, went to Camelot:
Or when the moon was overhead,
Came two young lovers lately wed;
"I am half sick of shadows," said
  The Lady of Shalott.

  PART III
A bow-shot from her bower-eaves,
He rode between the barley-sheaves,
The sun came dazzling thro' the leaves,
And flamed upon the brazen greaves
  Of bold Sir Lancelot.
A red-cross knight for ever kneel'd
To a lady in his shield,
That sparkled on the yellow field,
  Beside remote Shalott.

The gemmy bridle glitter'd free,
Like to some branch of stars we see
Hung in the golden Galaxy.
The bridle bells rang merrily

> As he rode down to Camelot:
> And from his blazon'd baldric slung
> A mighty silver bugle hung,
> And as he rode his armour rung,
> > Beside remote Shalott.
>
> All in the blue unclouded weather
> Thick-jewell'd shone the saddle-leather,
> The helmet and the helmet-feather
> Burn'd like one burning flame together,
> > As he rode down to Camelot.
> As often thro' the purple night,
> Below the starry clusters bright,
> Some bearded meteor, trailing light,
> > Moves over still Shalott.
>
> His broad clear brow in sunlight glow'd;
> On burnish'd hooves his war-horse trode;
> From underneath his helmet flow'd
> His coal-black curls as on he rode,
> > As he rode down to Camelot.
> From the bank and from the river
> He flash'd into the crystal mirror,
> "Tirra lirra," by the river
> > Sang Sir Lancelot.
>
> She left the web, she left the loom,
> She made three paces thro' the room,
> She saw the water-lily bloom,
> She saw the helmet and the plume,
> > She look'd down to Camelot.
> Out flew the web and floated wide;
> The mirror crack'd from side to side;
> "The curse is come upon me!" cried
> > The Lady of Shalott.
>
> > PART IV
> In the stormy east-wind straining,
> The pale yellow woods were waning,
> The broad stream in his banks complaining,
> Heavily the low sky raining
> > Over tower'd Camelot;
> Down she came and found a boat
> Beneath a willow left afloat,
> And round about the prow she wrote
> > The Lady of Shalott.
>
> And down the river's dim expanse—
> Like some bold seer in a trance,
> Seeing all his own mischance—
> With a glassy countenance

Did she look to Camelot.
And at the closing of the day
She loosed the chain, and down she lay;
The broad stream bore her far away,
    The Lady of Shalott.

Lying, robed in snowy white
That loosely flew to left and right—
The leaves upon her falling light—
Thro' the noises of the night
    She floated down to Camelot:
And as the boat-head wound along
The willowy hills and fields among,
They heard her singing her last song,
    The Lady of Shalott.

Heard a carol, mournful, holy,
Chanted loudly, chanted lowly,
Till her blood was frozen slowly,
And her eyes were darken'd wholly,
    Turn'd to tower'd Camelot;
For ere she reach'd upon the tide
The first house by the water-side,
Singing in her song she died,
    The Lady of Shalott.

Under tower and balcony,
By garden-wall and gallery,
A gleaming shape she floated by,
Dead-pale between the houses high,
    Silent into Camelot.
Out upon the wharfs they came,
Knight and burgher, lord and dame,
And round the prow they read her name,
    The Lady of Shalott.

Who is this? and what is here?
And in the lighted palace near
Died the sound of royal cheer;
And they cross'd themselves for fear,
    All the knights at Camelot:
But Lancelot mused a little space;
He said, "She has a lovely face;
God in His mercy lend her grace,
    The Lady of Shalott."
    ALFRED TENNYSON, LORD TENNYSON (1809–1892)

THE MILLER'S DAUGHTER   809

It is the miller's daughter,
  And she is grown so dear, so dear,
That I would be the jewel
  That trembles in her ear:
For hid in ringlets day and night,
I'd touch her neck so warm and white.

    And I would be the girdle
      About her dainty dainty waist,
    And her heart would beat against me,
      In sorrow and in rest:
    And I should know if it beat right,
    I'd clasp it round so close and tight.

    And I would be the necklace,
      And all day long to fall and rise
    Upon her balmy bosom,
      With her laughter or her sighs:
    And I would lie so light, so light,
    I scarce should be unclasp'd at night.
           ALFRED TENNYSON, LORD TENNYSON (1809–1892)

810   SONG OF THE LOTOS-EATERS

There is sweet music here that softer falls
Than petals from blown roses on the grass,
Or night-dews on still waters between walls
Of shadowy granite, in a gleaming pass;
Music that gentlier on the spirit lies,
Than tired eyelids upon tired eyes;
Music that brings sweet sleep down from the blissful skies.
Here are cool mosses deep,
And thro' the moss the ivies creep,
And in the stream the long-leaved flowers weep,
And from the craggy ledge the poppy hangs in sleep.

Why are we weigh'd upon with heaviness,
And utterly consumed with sharp distress,
While all things else have rest from weariness?
All things have rest: why should we toil alone,
We only toil, who are the first of things,
And make perpetual moan,
Still from one sorrow to another thrown:
Nor ever fold our wings,
And cease from wanderings,
Nor steep our brows in slumber's holy balm;
Nor harken what the inner spirit sings,
"There is no joy but calm!"—
Why should we only toil, the roof and crown of things?

Lo! in the middle of the wood,
The folded leaf is woo'd from out the bud
With winds upon the branch, and there
Grows green and broad, and takes no care,
Sun-steep'd at noon, and in the moon
Nightly dew-fed; and turning yellow
Falls, and floats adown the air.
Lo! sweeten'd with the summer light,

The full-juiced apple, waxing over-mellow,
Drops in a silent autumn night.
All its allotted length of days,
The flower ripens in its place,
Ripens and fades, and falls, and hath no toil,
Fast-rooted in the fruitful soil.

Hateful is the dark-blue sky,
Vaulted o'er the dark-blue sea.
Death is the end of life; ah, why
Should life all labour be?
Let us alone. Time driveth onward fast,
And in a little while our lips are dumb.
Let us alone. What is it that will last?
All things are taken from us, and become
Portions and parcels of the dreadful Past.
Let us alone. What pleasure can we have
To war with evil? Is there any peace
In ever climbing up the climbing wave?
All things have rest, and ripen toward the grave
In silence; ripen, fall and cease:
Give us long rest or death, dark death, or dreamful ease.

How sweet it were, hearing the downward stream,
With half-shut eyes ever to seem
Falling asleep in a half-dream!
To dream and dream, like yonder amber light,
Which will not leave the myrrh-bush on the height;
To hear each other's whisper'd speech;
Eating the Lotos day by day,
To watch the crisping ripples on the beach,
And tender curving lines of creamy spray;
To lend our hearts and spirits wholly
To the influence of mild-minded melancholy;
To muse and brood and live again in memory,
With those old faces of our infancy
Heap'd over with a mound of grass,
Two handfuls of white dust, shut in an urn of brass!

Dear is the memory of our wedded lives,
And dear the last embraces of our wives
And their warm tears: but all hath suffer'd change;
For surely now our household hearts are cold:
Our sons inherit us: our looks are strange:
And we should come like ghosts to trouble joy.
Or else the island princes over-bold
Have eat our substance, and the minstrel sings
Before them of the ten years' war in Troy,
And our great deeds, as half-forgotten things.
Is there confusion in the little isle?
Let what is broken so remain.

The Gods are hard to reconcile:
'Tis hard to settle order once again.
There *is* confusion worse than death,
Trouble on trouble, pain on pain,
Long labour unto aged breath,
Sore task to hearts worn out with many wars
And eyes grown dim with gazing on the pilot-stars.

But, propt on beds of amaranth and moly,
How sweet (while warm airs lull us, blowing lowly)
With half-dropt eyelids still,
Beneath a heaven dark and holy,
To watch the long bright river drawing slowly
His waters from the purple hill—
To hear the dewy echoes calling
From cave to cave thro' the thick-twined vine—
To watch the emerald-colour'd water falling
Thro' many a wov'n acanthus-wreath divine!
Only to hear and see the far-off sparkling brine,
Only to hear were sweet, stretch'd out beneath the pine.

The Lotos blooms below the barren peak:
The Lotos blows by every winding creek:
All day the wind breathes low with mellower tone:
Thro' every hollow cave and alley lone
Round and round the spicy downs the yellow Lotos-dust is blown.
We have had enough of action, and of motion we,
Roll'd to starboard, roll'd to larboard, when the surge was seething free,
Where the wallowing monster spouted his foam-fountains in the sea.
Let us swear an oath, and keep it with an equal mind,
In the hollow Lotos-land to live and lie reclined
On the hills like Gods together, careless of mankind.
For they lie beside their nectar, and the bolts are hurl'd
Far below them in the valleys, and the clouds are lightly curl'd
Round their golden houses, girdled with the gleaming world:
Where the smile in secret, looking over wasted lands,
Blight and famine, plague and earthquake, roaring deeps and fiery sands,
Clanging fights, and flaming towns, and sinking ships, and praying hands.
But they smile, they find a music centred in a doleful song
Steaming up, a lamentation and an ancient tale of wrong,
Like a tale of little meaning tho' the words are strong;
Chanted from an ill-used race of men that cleave the soil,
Sow the seed, and reap the harvest with enduring toil,
Storing yearly little dues of wheat, and wine and oil;
Till they perish and they suffer—some, 'tis whisper'd—down in hell
Suffer endless anguish, others in Elysian valleys dwell,

Resting weary limbs at last on beds of asphodel.
Surely, surely, slumber is more sweet than toil, the shore
Than labour in the deep mid-ocean, wind and wave and oar;
O rest ye, brother mariners, we will not wander more.
     ALFRED TENNYSON, LORD TENNYSON (1809–1892)

ST. AGNES' EVE   811

Deep on the convent-roof the snows
 Are sparkling to the moon:
My breath to heaven like vapour goes:
 May my soul follow soon!
The shadows of the convent-towers
 Slant down the snowy sward,
Still creeping with the creeping hours
 That lead me to my Lord:
Make Thou my spirit pure and clear
 As are the frosty skies,
Or this first snowdrop of the year
 That in my bosom lies.

As these white robes are soil'd and dark,
 To yonder shining ground;
As this pale taper's earthly spark,
 To yonder argent round;
So shows my soul before the Lamb,
 My spirit before Thee;
So in mine earthly house I am,
 To that I hope to be.
Break up the heavens, O Lord! and far,
 Thro' all yon starlight keen,
Draw me, thy bride, a glittering star,
 In raiment white and clean.

He lifts me to the golden doors;
 The flashes come and go;
All heaven bursts her starry floors,
 And strows her lights below,
And deepens on and up! the gates
 Roll back, and far within
For me the Heavenly Bridegroom waits,
 To make me pure of sin.
The sabbaths of Eternity,
 One sabbath deep and wide—
A light upon the shining sea—
 The Bridegroom with his bride!
     ALFRED TENNYSON, LORD TENNYSON (1809–1892)

BLOW, BUGLE, BLOW   812

The splendour falls on castle walls
 And snowy summits old in story:
The long light shakes across the lakes,
 And the wild cataract leaps in glory.
Blow, bugle, blow, set the wild echoes flying,
Blow, bugle; answer, echoes, dying, dying, dying.

O hark, O hear! how thin and clear,
  And thinner, clearer, farther going!
O sweet and far from cliff and scar
  The horns of Elfland faintly blowing!
Blow, let us hear the purple glens replying:
Blow, bugle; answer, echoes, dying, dying, dying.

O love, they die in yon rich sky,
  They faint on hill or field or river:
Our echoes roll from soul to soul,
  And grow for ever and for ever.
Blow, bugle, blow, set the wild echoes flying,
And answer, echoes, answer, dying, dying, dying.
                ALFRED TENNYSON, LORD TENNYSON (1809–1892)

813   SUMMER NIGHT
Now sleeps the crimson petal, now the white;
Nor waves the cypress in the palace walk;
Nor winks the gold fin in the porphyry font:
The firefly wakens: waken thou with me.

  Now droops the milk-white peacock like a ghost,
And like a ghost she glimmers on to me.

  Now lies the Earth all Danaë to the stars,
And all thy heart lies open unto me.

  Now slides the silent meteor on, and leaves
A shining furrow, as thy thoughts in me.

  Now folds the lily all her sweetness up,
And slips into the bosom of the lake:
So fold thyself, my dearest, thou, and slip
Into my bosom and be lost in me.
                ALFRED TENNYSON, LORD TENNYSON (1809–1892)

814   COME DOWN, O MAID
Come down, O maid, from yonder mountain height:
What pleasure lives in height (the shepherd sang),
In height and cold, the splendour of the hills?
But cease to move so near the Heavens, and cease
To glide a sunbeam by the blasted Pine,
To sit a star upon the sparkling spire;
And come, for Love is of the valley, come,
For Love is of the valley, come thou down
And find him; by the happy threshold, he,
Or hand in hand with Plenty in the maize,
Or red with spirted purple of the vats,
Or foxlike in the vine; nor cares to walk
With Death and Morning on the silver horns,
Nor wilt thou snare him in the white ravine,
Nor find him dropt upon the firths of ice,
That huddling slant in furrow-cloven falls

To roll the torrent out of dusky doors:
But follow; let the torrent dance thee down
To find him in the valley; let the wild
Lean-headed Eagles yelp alone, and leave
The monstrous ledges there to slope, and spill
Their thousand wreaths of dangling water-smoke,
That like a broken purpose waste in air:
So waste not thou; but come; for all the vales
Await thee; azure pillars of the hearth
Arise to thee; the children call, and I
Thy shepherd pipe, and sweet is every sound,
Sweeter thy voice, but every sound is sweet;
Myriads of rivulets hurrying thro' the lawn,
The moan of doves in immemorial elms,
And murmuring of innumerable bees.
    ALFRED TENNYSON, LORD TENNYSON (1809–1892)

FROM "IN MEMORIAM"   815
(ARTHUR HENRY HALLAM, MDCCCXXXIII)

I

Fair ship, that from the Italian shore
 Sailest the placid ocean-plains
 With my lost Arthur's loved remains,
Spread thy full wings, and waft him o'er.

So draw him home to those that mourn
 In vain; a favourable speed
 Ruffle thy mirror'd mast, and lead
Thro' prosperous floods his holy urn.

All night no ruder air perplex
 Thy sliding keel, till Phosphor, bright
 As our pure love, thro' early light
Shall glimmer on the dewy decks.

Sphere all your lights around, above;
 Sleep, gentle heavens, before the prow;
 Sleep, gentle winds, as he sleeps now,
My friend, the brother of my love;

My Arthur, whom I shall not see
 Till all my widow'd race be run;
 Dear as the mother to the son,
More than my brothers are to me.

II

I hear the noise about thy keel;
 I hear the bell struck in the night;
 I see the cabin-window bright;
I see the sailor at the wheel.

Thou bring'st the sailor to his wife,
 And travell'd men from foreign lands;
 And letters unto trembling hands;
And, thy dark freight, a vanish'd life.

So bring him: we have idle dreams:
   This look of quiet flatters thus
   Our home-bred fancies: O to us,
The fools of habit, sweeter seems

To rest beneath the clover sod,
   That takes the sunshine and the rains,
   Or where the kneeling hamlet drains
The chalice of the grapes of God;

Than if with thee the roaring wells
   Should gulf him fathom-deep in brine;
   And hands so often clasp'd in mine,
Should toss with tangle and with shells.

III

Calm is the morn without a sound,
   Calm as to suit a calmer grief,
   And only thro' the faded leaf
The chestnut pattering to the ground:

Calm and deep peace on this high wold,
   And on these dews that drench the furze,
   And all the silvery gossamers
That twinkle into green and gold:

Calm and still light on yon great plain
   That sweeps with all its autumn bowers,
   And crowded farms and lessening towers,
To mingle with the bounding main:

Calm and deep peace in this wide air,
   These leaves that redden to the fall;
   And in my heart, if calm at all,
If any calm, a calm despair:

Calm on the seas, and silver sleep,
   And waves that sway themselves in rest,
   And dead calm in that noble breast
Which heaves but with the heaving deep.

IV

To-night the winds begin to rise
   And roar from yonder dropping day:
   The last red leaf is whirl'd away,
The rooks are blown about the skies;

The forest crack'd, the waters curl'd,
   The cattle huddled on the lea;
   And wildly dash'd on tower and tree
The sunbeam strikes along the world:

And but for fancies, which aver
    That all thy motions gently pass
    Athwart a plane of molten glass,
I scarce could brook the strain and stir

That makes the barren branches loud;
    And but for fear it is not so,
    The wild unrest that lives in woe
Would dote and pore on yonder cloud

That rises upward always higher,
    And onward drags a labouring breast,
    And topples round the dreary west,
A looming bastion fringed with fire.

V

Thou comest, much wept for: such a breeze
    Compell'd thy canvas, and my prayer
    Was as the whisper of an air
To breathe thee over lonely seas.

For I in spirit saw thee move
    Thro' circles of the bounding sky,
    Week after week: the days go by:
Come quick, thou bringest all I love.

Henceforth, wherever thou mayst roam
    My blessing, like a line of light,
    Is on the waters day and night,
And like a beacon guards thee home.

So may whatever tempest mars
    Mid-ocean, spare thee, sacred bark;
    And balmy drops in summer dark
Slide from the bosom of the stars.

So kind an office hath been done,
    Such precious relics brought by thee;
    The dust of him I shall not see
Till all my widow'd race be run.

VI

Now, sometimes in my sorrow shut,
    Or breaking into song by fits,
    Alone, alone, to where he sits,
The Shadow cloak'd from head to foot,

Who keeps the keys of all the creeds,
    I wander, often falling lame,
    And looking back to whence I came,
Or on to where the pathway leads;

And crying, How changed from where it ran
    Thro' lands where not a leaf was dumb;
    But all the lavish hills would hum
The murmur of a happy Pan:

When each by turns was guide to each,
    And Fancy light from Fancy caught,
    And Thought leapt out to wed with Thought
Ere Thought could wed itself with Speech;

And all we met was fair and good,
    And all was good that Time could bring,
    And all the secret of the Spring
Moved in the chambers of the blood;

And many an old philosophy
    On Argive heights divinely sang,
    And round us all the thicket rang
To many a flute of Arcady.

VII

How fares it with the happy dead?
    For here the man is more and more;
    But he forgets the days before
God shut the doorways of his head.

The days have vanish'd, tone and tint,
    And yet perhaps the hoarding sense
    Gives out at times (he knows not whence)
A little flash, a mystic hint;

And in the long harmonious years
    (If Death so taste Lethean springs)
    May some dim touch of earthly things
Surprise thee ranging with thy peers.

If such a dreamy touch should fall,
    O turn thee round, resolve the doubt;
    My guardian angel will speak out
In that high place, and tell thee all.

VIII

The wish, that of the living whole
    No life may fail beyond the grave,
    Derives it not from what we have
The likest God within the soul?

Are God and Nature then at strife,
    That Nature lends such evil dreams?
    So careful of the type she seems,
So careless of the single life;

That I, considering everywhere
    Her secret meaning in her deeds,
    And finding that of fifty seeds
She often brings but one to bear,

I falter where I firmly trod,
    And falling with my weight of cares
    Upon the great world's altar-stairs
That slope thro' darkness up to God,

I stretch lame hands of faith, and grope,
    And gather dust and chaff, and call
    To what I feel is Lord of all,
And faintly trust the larger hope.

IX

"So careful of the type?" but no.
    From scarpèd cliff and quarried stone
    She cries, "A thousand types are gone:
I care for nothing, all shall go.

Thou makest thine appeal to me:
    I bring to life, I bring to death:
    The spirit does but mean the breath:
I know no more." And he, shall he,

Man, her last work, who seem'd so fair,
    Such splendid purpose in his eyes,
    Who roll'd the psalm to wintry skies,
Who built him fanes of fruitless prayer,

Who trusted God was love indeed
    And love Creation's final law—
    Tho' Nature, red in tooth and claw
With ravine, shriek'd against his creed—

Who loved, who suffer'd countless ills,
    Who battled for the True, the Just,
    Be blown about the desert dust,
Or seal'd within the iron hills?

No more? A monster then, a dream,
    A discord. Dragons of the prime,
    That tare each other in their slime,
Were mellow music match'd with him.

O life as futile, then, as frail!
    O for thy voice to soothe and bless!
    What hope of answer, or redress?
Behind the veil, behind the veil.

X

Unwatch'd, the garden bough shall sway,
  The tender blossom flutter down;
  Unloved, that beech will gather brown,
This maple burn itself away;

Unloved, the sunflower, shining fair,
  Ray round with flames her disk of seed,
  And many a rose-carnation feed
With summer spice the humming air;

Unloved, by many a sandy bar,
  The brook shall babble down the plain,
  At noon or when the lesser wain
Is twisting round the polar star;

Uncared for, gird the windy grove,
  And flood the haunts of hern and crake;
  Or into silver arrows break
The sailing moon in creek and cove;

Till from the garden and the wild
  A fresh association blow,
  And year by year the landscape grow
Familiar to the stranger's child;

As year by year the labourer tills
  His wonted glebe, or lops the glades;
  And year by year our memory fades
From all the circle of the hills.

XI

Now fades the last long streak of snow,
  Now burgeons every maze of quick
  About the flowering squares, and thick
By ashen roots the violets blow.

Now rings the woodland loud and long,
  The distance takes a lovelier hue,
  And drown'd in yonder living blue
The lark becomes a sightless song.

Now dance the lights on lawn and lea,
  The flocks are whiter down the vale,
  And milkier every milky sail
On winding stream or distant sea;

Where now the seamew pipes, or dives
  In yonder greening gleam, and fly
  The happy birds, that change their sky
To build and brood; that live their lives

From land to land; and in my breast
  Spring wakens too; and my regret
  Becomes an April violet,
And buds and blossoms like the rest.

XII

Love is and was my Lord and King,
   And in his presence I attend
   To hear the tidings of my friend,
Which every hour his couriers bring.

Love is and was my King and Lord,
   And will be, tho' as yet I keep
   Within his court on earth, and sleep
Encompass'd by his faithful guard,

And hear at times a sentinel
   Who moves about from place to place,
   And whispers to the worlds of space,
In the deep night, that all is well.

           ALFRED TENNYSON, LORD TENNYSON (1809–1892)

MAUD   816

Come into the garden, Maud,
   For the black bat, Night, has flown,
Come into the garden, Maud,
   I am here at the gate alone;
And the woodbine spices are wafted abroad,
   And the musk of the roses blown.

For a breeze of morning moves,
   And the planet of Love is on high,
Beginning to faint in the light that she loves
   On a bed of daffodil sky,
To faint in the light of the sun she loves,
   To faint in his light, and to die.

All night have the roses heard
   The flute, violin, bassoon;
All night has the casement jessamine stirr'd
   To the dancers dancing in tune;
Till a silence fell with the waking bird,
   And a hush with the setting moon.

I said to the lily, "There is but one
   With whom she has heart to be gay.
When will the dancers leave her alone?
   She is weary of dance and play."
Now half to the setting moon are gone,
   And half to the rising day;
Low on the sand and loud on the stone
   The last wheel echoes away.

I said to the rose, "The brief night goes
   In babble and revel and wine.
O young lord-lover, what sighs are those
   For one that will never be thine?
But mine, but mine," so I sware to the rose,
   "For ever and ever, mine."

And the soul of the rose went into my blood,
  As the music clash'd in the hall;
And long by the garden lake I stood,
  For I heard your rivulet fall
From the lake to the meadow and on to the wood,
  Our wood, that is dearer than all;

From the meadow your walks have left so sweet
  That whenever a March-wind sighs
He sets the jewel-print of your feet
  In violets blue as your eyes,
To the woody hollows in which we meet
  And the valleys of Paradise.

The slender acacia would not shake
  One long milk-bloom on the tree;
The white lake-blossom fell into the lake,
  As the pimpernel dozed on the lea;
But the rose was awake all night for your sake,
  Knowing your promise to me;
The lilies and roses were all awake,
  They sigh'd for the dawn and thee.

Queen rose of the rosebud garden of girls,
  Come hither, the dances are done,
In gloss of satin and glimmer of pearls,
  Queen lily and rose in one;
Shine out, little head, sunning over with curls.
  To the flowers, and be their sun.

There has fallen a splendid tear
  From the passion-flower at the gate.
She is coming, my dove, my dear;
  She is coming, my life, my fate;
The red rose cries, "She is near, she is near;"
  And the white rose weeps, "She is late;"
The larkspur listens, "I hear, I hear;"
  And the lily whispers, "I wait."

She is coming, my own, my sweet;
  Were it ever so airy a tread,
My heart would hear her and beat,
  Were it earth in an earthy bed;
My dust would hear her and beat,
  Had I lain for a century dead;
Would start and tremble under her feet,
  And blossom in purple and red.
      ALFRED TENNYSON, LORD TENNYSON (1809–1892)

O THAT 'TWERE POSSIBLE

O that 'twere possible
After long grief and pain
To find the arms of my true love
Round me once again!...

A shadow flits before me,
Not thou, but like to thee:
Ah, Christ! that it were possible
For one short hour to see
The souls we loved, that they might tell us
What and where they be!
          ALFRED TENNYSON, LORD TENNYSON (1809–1892)

SHADOWS   818

They seem'd, to those who saw them meet,
  The casual friends of every day;
Her smile was undisturb'd and sweet,
  His courtesy was free and gay.

But yet if one the other's name
  In some unguarded moment heard,
The heart you thought so calm and tame
  Would struggle like a captured bird:

And letters of mere formal phrase
  Were blister'd with repeated tears,—
And this was not the work of days,
  But had gone on for years and years!

Alas, that love was not too strong
  For maiden shame and manly pride!
Alas, that they delay'd so long
  The goal of mutual bliss beside!

Yet what no chance could then reveal,
  And neither would be first to own,
Let fate and courage now conceal,
  When truth could bring remorse alone.
      RICHARD MONCKTON MILNES, LORD HOUGHTON (1809–1885)

THE BRIDE   819

"Rise," said the Master, "come unto the feast."
She heard the call and rose with willing feet;
  But thinking it not otherwise than meet
For such a bidding to put on her best,
She is gone from us for a few short hours
  Into her bridal closet, there to wait
  For the unfolding of the palace gate
That gives her entrance to the blissful bowers.
We have not seen her yet, though we have been
  Full often to her chamber door, and oft
Have listen'd underneath the postern green,
  And laid fresh flowers, and whisper'd short and soft.
But she hath made no answer, and the day
From the clear west is fading fast away.
                         HENRY ALFORD (1810–1871)

820   Cean Dubh Deelish

Put your head, darling, darling, darling,
  Your darling black head my heart above;
O mouth of honey, with thyme for fragrance,
  Who, with heart in breast, could deny you love?

O many and many a young girl for me is pining,
  Letting her locks of gold to the cold wind free,
For me, the foremost of our gay young fellows;
  But I'd leave a hundred, pure love, for thee!

Then put your head, darling, darling, darling,
  Your darling black head my heart above;
O mouth of honey, with thyme for fragrance,
  Who, with heart in breast, could deny you love?
                          Sir Samuel Ferguson (1810–1886)

Cean dubh deelish: *darling black head*

821   Song from "Paracelsus"

Heap cassia, sandal-buds and stripes
  Of labdanum, and aloe-balls,
Smear'd with dull nard an Indian wipes
  From out her hair: such balsam falls
  Down sea-side mountain pedestals,
From tree-tops where tired winds are fain,
Spent with the vast and howling main,
To treasure half their island-gain.

And strew faint sweetness from some old
  Egyptian's fine worm-eaten shroud
Which breaks to dust when once unroll'd;
  Or shredded perfume, like a cloud
  From closet long to quiet vow'd,
With moth'd and dropping arras hung,
Mouldering her lute and books among,
As when a queen, long dead, was young.
                          Robert Browning (1812–1889)

822   The Wanderers

Over the sea our galleys went,
With cleaving prows in order brave
To a speeding wind and a bounding wave—
  A gallant armament:
Each bark built out of a forest-tree
  Left leafy and rough as first it grew,
And nail'd all over the gaping sides,
Within and without, with black bull-hides,
Seethed in fat and suppled in flame,
To bear the playful billows' game;
So, each good ship was rude to see,
Rude and bare to the outward view.
  But each upbore a stately tent
Where cedar pales in scented row
Kept out the flakes of the dancing brine,
And an awning droop'd the mast below,

In fold on fold of the purple fine,
That neither noontide nor star-shine
Nor moonlight cold which maketh mad,
   Might pierce the regal tenement.
When the sun dawn'd, O, gay and glad
We set the sail and plied the oar;
But when the night-wind blew like breath,
For joy of one day's voyage more,
We sang together on the wide sea,
Like men at peace on a peaceful shore;
Each sail was loosed to the wind so free,
Each helm made sure by the twilight star,
And in a sleep as calm as death,
We, the voyagers from afar,
   Lay stretch'd along, each weary crew
In a circle round its wondrous tent
Whence gleam'd soft light and curl'd rich scent,
   And with light and perfume, music too:
So the stars wheel'd round, and the darkness past,
And at morn we started beside the mast,
And still each ship was sailing fast!

Now, one morn, land appear'd—a speck
Dim trembling betwixt sea and sky—
"Avoid it," cried our pilot, "check
   The shout, restrain the eager eye!"
But the heaving sea was black behind
For many a night and many a day,
And land, though but a rock, drew nigh;
So we broke the cedar pales away,
Let the purple awning flap in the wind,
   And a statue bright was on every deck!
We shouted, every man of us,
And steer'd right into the harbour thus,
With pomp and pæan glorious.

A hundred shapes of lucid stone!
   All day we built its shrine for each,
A shrine of rock for ever one,
Nor paused till in the westering sun
   We sat together on the beach
To sing because our task was done;
When lo! what shouts and merry songs!
What laughter all the distance stirs!
A loaded raft with happy throngs
Of gentle islanders!
"Our isles are just at hand," they cried,
   "Like cloudlets faint in even sleeping;
Our temple-gates are open'd wide,
   Our olive-groves thick shade are keeping
For these majestic forms"—they cried.
O, then we awoke with sudden start

From our deep dream, and knew, too late,
How bare the rock, how desolate,
Which had received our precious freight:
   Yet we call'd out—"Depart!
Our gifts, once given, must here abide:
   Our work is done; we have no heart
To mar our work,"—we cried.
                           ROBERT BROWNING (1812–1889)

823   THUS THE MAYNE GLIDETH

Thus the Mayne glideth
Where my Love abideth;
Sleep's no softer: it proceeds
On through lawns, on through meads,
On and on, whate'er befall,
Meandering and musical,
Though the niggard pasturage
Bears not on its shaven ledge
Aught but weeds and waving grasses
To view the river as it passes,
Save here and there a scanty patch
Of primroses too faint to catch
A weary bee.... And scarce it pushes
Its gentle way through strangling rushes
Where the glossy kingfisher
Flutters when noon-heats are near,
Glad the shelving banks to shun,
Red and steaming in the sun,
Where the shrew-mouse with pale throat
Burrows, and the speckled stoat;
Where the quick sandpipers flit
In and out the marl and grit
That seems to breed them, brown as they:
Naught disturbs its quiet way,
Save some lazy stork that springs,
Trailing it with legs and wings,
Whom the shy fox from the hill
Rouses, creep he ne'er so still.
                           ROBERT BROWNING (1812–1889)

824   PIPPA'S SONG

The year's at the spring,
And day's at the morn;
Morning's at seven;
The hill-side's dew-pearl'd;

The lark's on the wing;
The snail's on the thorn;
God's in His heaven—
All's right with the world!
                           ROBERT BROWNING (1812–1889)

You'll Love Me Yet   825

You'll love me yet!—and I can tarry
  Your love's protracted growing:
June rear'd that bunch of flowers you carry,
  From seeds of April's sowing.

I plant a heartful now: some seed
  At least is sure to strike,
And yield—what you'll not pluck indeed,
  Not love, but, may be, like.

You'll look at least on love's remains,
  A grave's one violet:
Your look?—that pays a thousand pains.
  What's death? You'll love me yet!

                    ROBERT BROWNING (1812–1889)

Porphyria's Lover   826

The rain set early in to-night,
  The sullen wind was soon awake,
It tore the elm-tops down for spite,
  And did its worst to vex the lake:
I listen'd with heart fit to break.
When glided in Porphyria; straight
  She shut the cold out and the storm,
And kneel'd and made the cheerless grate
  Blaze up, and all the cottage warm;
  Which done, she rose, and from her form
Withdrew the dripping cloak and shawl,
  And laid her soil'd gloves by, untied
Her hat and let the damp hair fall,
  And, last, she sat down by my side
  And call'd me. When no voice replied,
She put my arm about her waist,
  And made her smooth white shoulder bare,
And all her yellow hair displaced,
  And, stooping, made my cheek lie there,
  And spread, o'er all, her yellow hair,
Murmuring how she loved me—she
  Too weak, for all her heart's endeavour,
To set its struggling passion free
  From pride, and vainer ties dissever,
  And give herself to me for ever.
But passion sometimes would prevail,
  Nor could to-night's gay feast restrain
A sudden thought of one so pale
  For love of her, and all in vain:
  So, she was come through wind and rain.
Be sure I look'd up at her eyes
  Happy and proud; at last I knew
Porphyria worshipp'd me; surprise
  Made my heart swell, and still it grew
  While I debated what to do.
That moment she was mine, mine, fair,

    Perfectly pure and good: I found
  A thing to do, and all her hair
    In one long yellow string I wound
    Three times her little throat around,
  And strangled her. No pain felt she;
    I am quite sure she felt no pain.
  As a shut bud that holds a bee,
    I warily oped her lids: again
    Laugh'd the blue eyes without a stain.
  And I untighten'd next the tress
    About her neck; her cheek once more
  Blush'd bright beneath my burning kiss:
    I propp'd her head up as before,
    Only, this time my shoulder bore
  Her head, which droops upon it still:
    The smiling rosy little head,
  So glad it has its utmost will,
    That all it scorn'd at once is fled,
    And I, its love, am gain'd instead!
  Porphyria's love: she guess'd not how
    Her darling one wish would be heard.
  And thus we sit together now,
    And all night long we have not stirr'd,
    And yet God has not said a word!
                  ROBERT BROWNING (1812–1889)

827   SONG

  Nay but you, who do not love her,
    Is she not pure gold, my mistress?
  Holds earth aught—speak truth—above her?
    Aught like this tress, see, and this tress,
  And this last fairest tress of all,
  So fair, see, ere I let it fall?
  Because, you spend your lives in praising;
    To praise, you search the wide world over:
  Then why not witness, calmly gazing,
    If earth holds aught—speak truth—above her?
  Above this tress, and this, I touch
  But cannot praise, I love so much!
                  ROBERT BROWNING (1812–1889)

828   EARL MERTOUN'S SONG

There's a woman like a dewdrop, she's so purer than the purest;
And her noble heart's the noblest, yes, and her sure faith's the surest:
And her eyes are dark and humid, like the depth on depth of lustre
Hid i' the harebell, while her tresses, sunnier than the wild-grape cluster,
Gush in golden-tinted plenty down her neck's rose-misted marble:
Then her voice's music ... call it the well's bubbling, the bird's warble!

And this woman says, "My days were sunless and my nights were
     moonless,
Parch'd the pleasant April herbage, and the lark's heart's outbreak
     tuneless,
If you loved me not!" And I who (ah, for words of flame!) adore her,
Who am mad to lay my spirit prostrate palpably before her—
I may enter at her portal soon, as now her lattice takes me,
And by noontide as by midnight make her mine, as hers she makes me!
                              ROBERT BROWNING (1812–1889)

IN A GONDOLA   829
The moth's kiss, first!
Kiss me as if you made me believe
You were not sure, this eve,
How my face, your flower, had pursed
Its petals up; so, here and there
You brush it, till I grow aware
Who wants me, and wide ope I burst.

The bee's kiss, now!
Kiss me as if you enter'd gay
My heart at some noonday,
A bud that dares not disallow
The claim, so all is render'd up,
And passively its shatter'd cup
Over your head to sleep I bow.
                              ROBERT BROWNING (1812–1889)

MEETING AT NIGHT   830
The gray sea and the long black land;
And the yellow half-moon large and low;
And the startled little waves that leap
In fiery ringlets from their sleep,
As I gain the cove with pushing prow,
And quench its speed i' the slushy sand.

Then a mile of warm sea-scented beach;
Three fields to cross till a farm appears;
A tap at the pane, the quick sharp scratch
And blue spurt of a lighted match,
And a voice less loud, thro' its joys and fears,
Than the two hearts beating each to each!
                              ROBERT BROWNING (1812–1889)

PARTING AT MORNING   831
Round the cape of a sudden came the sea,
And the sun look'd over the mountain's rim:
And straight was a path of gold for him,
And the need of a world of men for me.
                              ROBERT BROWNING (1812–1889)

THE LOST MISTRESS   832
All's over, then: does truth sound bitter
   As one at first believes?
Hark, 'tis the sparrows' good-night twitter
   About your cottage eaves!

And the leaf-buds on the vine are woolly,
  I noticed that, to-day;
One day more bursts them open fully
  —You know the red turns gray.

To-morrow we meet the same then, dearest?
  May I take your hand in mine?
Mere friends are we,—well, friends the merest
  Keep much that I resign:

For each glance of the eye so bright and black,
  Though I keep with heart's endeavour,—
Your voice, when you wish the snowdrops back,
  Though it stay in my soul for ever!—

Yet I will but say what mere friends say,
  Or only a thought stronger;
I will hold your hand but as long as all may,
  Or so very little longer!
                        ROBERT BROWNING (1812–1889)

833   THE LAST RIDE TOGETHER
I Said—Then, dearest, since 'tis so,
Since now at length my fate I know,
Since nothing all my love avails,
Since all, my life seem'd meant for, fails,
  Since this was written and needs must be—
My whole heart rises up to bless
Your name in pride and thankfulness!
Take back the hope you gave,—I claim
Only a memory of the same,
  —And this beside, if you will not blame;
  Your leave for one more last ride with me.

My mistress bent that brow of hers,
Those deep dark eyes where pride demurs
When pity would be softening through,
Fix'd me a breathing-while or two
  With life or death in the balance: right!
The blood replenish'd me again;
My last thought was at least not vain:
I and my mistress, side by side
Shall be together, breathe and ride,
So, one day more am I deified.
  Who knows but the world may end to-night?

Hush! if you saw some western cloud
All billowy-bosom'd, over-bow'd
By many benedictions—sun's
And moon's and evening-star's at once—
  And so, you, looking and loving best,
Conscious grew, your passion drew
Cloud, sunset, moonrise, star-shine too,
Down on you, near and yet more near,

Till flesh must fade for heaven was here!—
Thus leant she and linger'd—joy and fear!
   Thus lay she a moment on my breast.

Then we began to ride. My soul
Smooth'd itself out, a long-cramp'd scroll
Freshening and fluttering in the wind.
Past hopes already lay behind.
   What need to strive with a life awry?
Had I said that, had I done this,
So might I gain, so might I miss.
Might she have loved me? just as well
She might have hated, who can tell!
Where had I been now if the worst befell?
   And here we are riding, she and I.

Fail I alone, in words and deeds?
Why, all men strive and who succeeds?
We rode; it seem'd my spirit flew,
Saw other regions, cities new,
   As the world rush'd by on either side.
I thought,—All labour, yet no less
Bear up beneath their unsuccess.
Look at the end of work, contrast
The petty done, the undone vast,
This present of theirs with the hopeful past!
   I hoped she would love me; here we ride.

What hand and brain went ever pair'd?
What heart alike conceived and dared?
What act proved all its thought had been?
What will but felt the fleshly screen?
   We ride and I see her bosom heave.
There's many a crown for who can reach.
Ten lines, a statesman's life in each!
The flag stuck on a heap of bones,
A soldier's doing! what atones?
They scratch his name on the Abbey-stones.
   My riding is better, by their leave.

What does it all mean, poet? Well,
Your brains beat into rhythm, you tell
What we felt only; you express'd
You hold things beautiful the best,
   And pace them in rhyme so, side by side.
'Tis something, nay 'tis much: but then,
Have you yourself what's best for men?
Are you—poor, sick, old ere your time—
Nearer one whit your own sublime
Than we who never have turn'd a rhyme?
   Sing, riding's a joy! For me, I ride.

And you, great sculptor—so, you gave
A score of years to Art, her slave,
And that's your Venus, whence we turn
To yonder girl that fords the burn!
   You acquiesce, and shall I repine?
What, man of music, you grown gray
With notes and nothing else to say,
Is this your sole praise from a friend,
"Greatly his opera's strains intend,
But in music we know how fashions end!"
   I gave my youth: but we ride, in fine.

Who knows what's fit for us? Had fate
Proposed bliss here should sublimate
My being—had I sign'd the bond—
Still one must lead some life beyond,
   Have a bliss to die with, dim-descried.
This foot once planted on the goal,
This glory-garland round my soul,
Could I descry such? Try and test!
I sink back shuddering from the quest.
Earth being so good, would heaven seem best?
   Now, heaven and she are beyond this ride.

And yet—she has not spoke so long!
What if heaven be that, fair and strong
At life's best, with our eyes upturn'd
Whither life's flower is first discern'd,
   We, fix'd so, ever should so abide?
What if we still ride on, we two
With life for ever old yet new,
Changed not in kind but in degree,
The instant made eternity,—
And heaven just prove that I and she
   Ride, ride together, for ever ride?

ROBERT BROWNING (1812–1889)

834   MISCONCEPTIONS

   This is a spray the Bird clung to,
     Making it blossom with pleasure,
   Ere the high tree-top she sprung to,
     Fit for her nest and her treasure.
     O, what a hope beyond measure
Was the poor spray's, which the flying feet hung to,—
So to be singled out, built in, and sung to!

   This is a heart the Queen leant on,
     Thrill'd in a minute erratic,
   Ere the true bosom she bent on,
     Meet for love's regal dalmatic.
     O, what a fancy ecstatic
Was the poor heart's, ere the wanderer went on—
Love to be saved for it, proffer'd to, spent on!

ROBERT BROWNING (1812–1889)

Home-Thoughts, from Abroad   835

O, to be in England
Now that April's there,
And whoever wakes in England
Sees, some morning, unaware,
That the lowest boughs and the brushwood sheaf
Round the elm-tree bole are in tiny leaf,
While the chaffinch sings on the orchard bough
In England—now!

And after April, when May follows,
And the whitethroat builds, and all the swallows!
Hark, where my blossom'd pear-tree in the hedge
Leans to the field and scatters on the clover
Blossoms and dewdrops—at the bent spray's edge—
That's the wise thrush; he sings each song twice over,
Lest you should think he never could recapture
The first fine careless rapture!
And though the fields look rough with hoary dew,
All will be gay when noontide wakes anew
The buttercups, the little children's dower
—Far brighter than this gaudy melon-flower!

                                                                ROBERT BROWNING (1812–1889)

Home-Thoughts, from the Sea   836

Nobly, nobly Cape Saint Vincent to the North-west died away;
Sunset ran, one glorious blood-red, reeking into Cadiz Bay;
Bluish 'mid the burning water, full in face Trafalgar lay;
In the dimmest North-east distance dawn'd Gibraltar grand and gray;
"Here and here did England help me: how can I help England?"—say,
Whoso turns as I, this evening, turn to God to praise and pray,
While Jove's planet rises yonder, silent over Africa.

                                                             ROBERT BROWNING (1812–1889)

Serenade   837

   Softly, O midnight Hours!
      Move softly o'er the bowers
Where lies in happy sleep a girl so fair!
      For ye have power, men say,
      Our hearts in sleep to sway,
And cage cold fancies in a moonlight snare.
      Round ivory neck and arm
      Enclasp a separate charm;
Hang o'er her poised, but breathe nor sigh nor prayer:
      Silently ye may smile,
      But hold your breath the while,
And let the wind sweep back your cloudy hair!

      Bend down your glittering urns,
      Ere yet the dawn returns,
And star with dew the lawn her feet shall tread;
      Upon the air rain balm,

    Bid all the woods be calm,
Ambrosial dreams with healthful slumbers wed;
    That so the Maiden may
    With smiles your care repay,
When from her couch she lifts her golden head;
    Waking with earliest birds,
    Ere yet the misty herds
Leave warm 'mid the gray grass their dusky bed.
AUBREY THOMAS DE VERE (1814–1902)

838   Sorrow

Count each affliction, whether light or grave,
  God's messenger sent down to thee; do thou
  With courtesy receive him; rise and bow;
And, ere his shadow pass thy threshold, crave
Permission first his heavenly feet to lave;
  Then lay before him all thou hast; allow
  No cloud of passion to usurp thy brow,
Or mar thy hospitality; no wave
Of mortal tumult to obliterate
  The soul's marmoreal calmness: Grief should be,
Like joy, majestic, equable, sedate;
  Confirming, cleansing, raising, making free;
Strong to consume small troubles; to commend
Great thoughts, grave thoughts, thoughts lasting to the end.
AUBREY THOMAS DE VERE (1814–1902)

839   My Lady's Grave

  The linnet in the rocky dells,
    The moor-lark in the air,
  The bee among the heather bells
    That hide my lady fair:

  The wild deer browse above her breast;
    The wild birds raise their brood;
  And they, her smiles of love caress'd,
    Have left her solitude!

  I ween that when the grave's dark wall
    Did first her form retain,
  They thought their hearts could ne'er recall
    The light of joy again.

  They thought the tide of grief would flow
    Uncheck'd through future years;
  But where is all their anguish now,
    And where are all their tears?

  Well, let them fight for honour's breath,
    Or pleasure's shade pursue—
  The dweller in the land of death
    Is changed and careless too.

And if their eyes should watch and weep
  Till sorrow's source were dry,
She would not, in her tranquil sleep,
  Return a single sigh!

Blow, west wind, by the lonely mound:
  And murmur, summer streams!
There is no need of other sound
  To soothe my lady's dreams.

EMILY BRONTË (1818–1848)

REMEMBRANCE 840

Cold in the earth—and the deep snow piled above thee,
  Far, far removed, cold in the dreary grave!
Have I forgot, my only Love, to love thee,
  Sever'd at last by Time's all-severing wave?

Now, when alone, do my thoughts no longer hover
  Over the mountains, on that northern shore,
Resting their wings where heath and fern-leaves cover
  Thy noble heart for ever, ever more?

Cold in the earth—and fifteen wild Decembers
  From those brown hills have melted into spring:
Faithful, indeed, is the spirit that remembers
  After such years of change and suffering!

Sweet Love of youth, forgive, if I forget thee,
  While the world's tide is bearing me along;
Other desires and other hopes beset me,
  Hopes which obscure, but cannot do thee wrong!

No later light has lighten'd up my heaven,
  No second morn has ever shone for me;
All my life's bliss from thy dear life was given,
  All my life's bliss is in the grave with thee.

But when the days of golden dreams had perish'd,
  And even Despair was powerless to destroy;
Then did I learn how existence could be cherish'd,
  Strengthen'd and fed without the aid of joy.

Then did I check the tears of useless passion—
  Wean'd my young soul from yearning after thine;
Sternly denied its burning wish to hasten
  Down to that tomb already more than mine.

And, even yet, I dare not let it languish,
  Dare not indulge in memory's rapturous pain;
Once drinking deep of that divinest anguish,
  How could I seek the empty world again?

EMILY BRONTË (1818–1848)

841 THE PRISONER

Still let my tyrants know, I am not doom'd to wear
Year after year in gloom and desolate despair;
A messenger of Hope comes every night to me,
And offers for short life, eternal liberty.

He comes with Western winds, with evening's wandering airs,
With that clear dusk of heaven that brings the thickest stars:
Winds take a pensive tone, and stars a tender fire,
And visions rise, and change, that kill me with desire.

Desire for nothing known in my maturer years,
When Joy grew mad with awe, at counting future tears:
When, if my spirit's sky was full of flashes warm,
I knew not whence they came, from sun or thunder-storm.

But first, a hush of peace—a soundless calm descends;
The struggle of distress and fierce impatience ends.
Mute music soothes my breast—unutter'd harmony
That I could never dream, till Earth was lost to me.

Then dawns the Invisible; the Unseen its truth reveals;
My outward sense is gone, my inward essence feels;
Its wings are almost free—its home, its harbour found,
Measuring the gulf, it stoops, and dares the final bound.

O dreadful is the check—intense the agony—
When the ear begins to hear, and the eye begins to see;
When the pulse begins to throb—the brain to think again—
The soul to feel the flesh, and the flesh to feel the chain.

Yet I would lose no sting, would wish no torture less;
The more that anguish racks, the earlier it will bless;
And robed in fires of hell, or bright with heavenly shine,
If it but herald Death, the vision is divine.

EMILY BRONTË (1818–1848)

842 LAST LINES

No coward soul is mine,
No trembler in the world's storm-troubled sphere:
I see Heaven's glories shine,
And faith shines equal, arming me from fear.

O God within my breast,
Almighty, ever-present Deity!
Life—that in me has rest,
As I—undying Life—have power in Thee!

Vain are the thousand creeds
That move men's hearts: unutterably vain;
Worthless as wither'd weeds,
Or idlest froth amid the boundless main,

To waken doubt in one
Holding so fast by Thine infinity;
  So surely anchor'd on
The steadfast rock of immortality.

With wide-embracing love
Thy Spirit animates eternal years,
  Pervades and broods above,
Changes, sustains, dissolves, creates, and rears.

Though earth and man were gone,
And suns and universes cease to be,
  And Thou were left alone,
Every existence would exist in Thee.

There is not room for Death,
Nor atom that his might could render void:
  Thou—Thou art Being and Breath,
And what Thou art may never be destroyed.
Emily Brontë (1818–1848)

AIRLY BEACON   843

Airly Beacon, Airly Beacon;
  O the pleasant sight to see
Shires and towns from Airly Beacon,
  While my love climb'd up to me!

Airly Beacon, Airly Beacon;
  O the happy hours we lay
Deep in fern on Airly Beacon,
  Courting through the summer's day!

Airly Beacon, Airly Beacon;
  O the weary haunt for me,
All alone on Airly Beacon,
  With his baby on my knee!
Charles Kingsley (1819–1875)

THE SANDS OF DEE   844

"O Mary, go and call the cattle home,
    And call the cattle home,
    And call the cattle home,
    Across the sands of Dee."
The western wind was wild and dark with foam
    And all alone went she.

The western tide crept up along the sand,
    And o'er and o'er the sand,
    And round and round the sand,
    As far as eye could see.
The rolling mist came down and hid the land;
    And never home came she.

"O is it weed, or fish, or floating hair—
    A tress of golden hair,
    A drownèd maiden's hair,
    Above the nets at sea?"
Was never salmon yet that shone so fair
    Among the stakes on Dee.

They rowed her in across the rolling foam,
    The cruel crawling foam,
    The cruel hungry foam,
    To her grave beside the sea.
But still the boatmen hear her call the cattle home
    Across the sands of Dee.

CHARLES KINGSLEY (1819–1875)

845   SAY NOT THE STRUGGLE NAUGHT AVAILETH

Say not the struggle naught availeth,
    The labour and the wounds are vain,
The enemy faints not, nor faileth,
    And as things have been they remain.

If hopes were dupes, fears may be liars;
    It may be, in yon smoke conceal'd,
Your comrades chase e'en now the fliers,
    And, but for you, possess the field.

For while the tired waves, vainly breaking,
    Seem here no painful inch to gain,
Far back, through creeks and inlets making,
    Comes silent, flooding in, the main.

And not by eastern windows only,
    When daylight comes, comes in the light;
In front the sun climbs slow, how slowly!
    But westward, look, the land is bright!

ARTHUR HUGH CLOUGH (1819–1861)

846   THE IMPRISONED SOUL

At the last, tenderly,
From the walls of the powerful, fortress'd house,
From the clasp of the knitted locks—from the keep of the well-closed doors,
Let me be wafted.

Let me glide noiselessly forth;
With the key of softness unlock the locks—with a whisper
Set ope the doors, O soul!

Tenderly! be not impatient!
(Strong is your hold, O mortal flesh!
Strong is your hold, O love!)

WALT WHITMAN (1819–1892)

O Captain! My Captain!   847

O Captain! my Captain! our fearful trip is done,
The ship has weather'd every rack, the prize we sought is won,
The port is near, the bells I hear, the people all exulting,
While follow eyes the steady keel, the vessel grim and daring;
    But O heart! heart! heart!
      O the bleeding drops of red!
        Where on the deck my Captain lies,
          Fallen cold and dead.

O Captain! my Captain! rise up and hear the bells;
Rise up—for you the flag is flung—for you the bugle trills,
For you bouquets and ribbon'd wreaths—for you the shores crowding,
For you they call, the swaying mass, their eager faces turning;
    Here, Captain! dear father!
      This arm beneath your head!
        It is some dream that on the deck
          You've fallen cold and dead.

My Captain does not answer, his lips are pale and still,
My father does not feel my arm, he has no pulse nor will;
The ship is anchor'd safe and sound, its voyage closed and done,
From fearful trip the victor ship comes in with object won;
    Exult, O shores! and ring, O bells!
      But I, with mournful tread,
        Walk the deck my Captain lies,
          Fallen cold and dead.
                        WALT WHITMAN (1819–1892)

Trust Thou Thy Love   848

Trust thou thy Love: if she be proud, is she not sweet?
Trust thou thy Love: if she be mute, is she not pure?
Lay thou thy soul full in her hands, low at her feet;
Fail, Sun and Breath!—yet, for thy peace, She shall endure.
                        JOHN RUSKIN (1819–1900)

When the World is burning   849

    When the world is burning,
    Fired within, yet turning
      Round with face unscathed;
    Ere fierce flames, uprushing,
    O'er all lands leap, crushing,
      Till earth fall, fire-swathed;
    Up amidst the meadows,
    Gently through the shadows,
      Gentle flames will glide,
    Small, and blue, and golden.
    Though by bard beholden,
    When in calm dreams folden,—
      Calm his dreams will bide.

    Where the dance is sweeping,
    Through the greensward peeping,
      Shall the soft lights start;
    Laughing maids, unstaying,

　　　　　　Deeming it trick-playing,
　　　　　　High their robes upswaying,
　　　　　　　O'er the lights shall dart;
　　　　　　And the woodland haunter
　　　　　　Shall not cease to saunter
　　　　　　　When, far down some glade,
　　　　　　Of the great world's burning,
　　　　　　One soft flame upturning
　　　　　　Seems, to his discerning,
　　　　　　　Crocus in the shade.
　　　　　　　　　　EBENEZER JONES (1820–1860)

850　　　　　AT HER WINDOW
　　　　Beating Heart! we come again
　　　　　Where my Love reposes;
　　　　This is Mabel's window-pane;
　　　　　These are Mabel's roses.

　　　　Is she nested? Does she kneel
　　　　　In the twilight stilly,
　　　　Lily clad from throat to heel,
　　　　　She, my virgin Lily?

　　　　Soon the wan, the wistful stars,
　　　　　Fading, will forsake her;
　　　　Elves of light, on beamy bars,
　　　　　Whisper then, and wake her.

　　　　Let this friendly pebble plead
　　　　　At her flowery grating;
　　　　If she hear me will she heed?
　　　　　Mabel, I am waiting.

　　　　Mabel will be deck'd anon,
　　　　　Zoned in bride's apparel;
　　　　Happy zone! O hark to yon
　　　　　Passion-shaken carol!

　　　　Sing thy song, thou tranced thrush,
　　　　　Pipe thy best, thy clearest;—
　　　　Hush, her lattice moves, O hush—
　　　　　Dearest Mabel!—dearest...
　　　　　　　FREDERICK LOCKER-LAMPSON (1821–1895)

851　　　　THE FORSAKEN MERMAN
　　　Come, dear children, let us away;
　　　　Down and away below.
　　　Now my brothers call from the bay;
　　　Now the great winds shoreward blow;
　　　Now the salt tides seaward flow;
　　　Now the wild white horses play,
　　　Champ and chafe and toss in the spray.
　　　　Children dear, let us away.
　　　　This way, this way!

Call her once before you go.
    Call once yet.
In a voice that she will know:
 "Margaret! Margaret!"
Children's voices should be dear
(Call once more) to a mother's ear;
Children's voices, wild with pain.
Surely she will come again.
Call her once and come away.
    This way, this way!
"Mother dear, we cannot stay."
The wild white horses foam and fret.
    Margaret! Margaret!

Come, dear children, come away down.
    Call no more.
One last look at the white-wall'd town,
And the little grey church on the windy shore.
    Then come down.
She will not come though you call all day.
    Come away, come away.
Children dear, was it yesterday
We heard the sweet bells over the bay?
In the caverns where we lay,
Through the surf and through the swell,
The far-off sound of a silver bell?
Sand-strewn caverns, cool and deep,
Where the winds are all asleep;
Where the spent lights quiver and gleam;
Where the salt weed sways in the stream;
Where the sea-beasts, ranged all round,
Feed in the ooze of their pasture-ground;
Where the sea-snakes coil and twine,
Dry their mail, and bask in the brine;
Where great whales come sailing by,
Sail and sail, with unshut eye,
Round the world for ever and aye?
When did music come this way?
Children dear, was it yesterday?

Children dear, was it yesterday
(Call yet once) that she went away?
Once she sate with you and me,
On a red gold throne in the heart of the sea,
  And the youngest sate on her knee.
She comb'd its bright hair, and she tended it well,
When down swung the sound of the far-off bell.
She sigh'd, she look'd up through the clear green sea.
She said, "I must go, for my kinsfolk pray
In the little grey church on the shore to-day.
'Twill be Easter-time in the world—ah me!
And I lose my poor soul, Merman, here with thee."

I said, "Go up, dear heart, through the waves.
Say thy prayer, and come back to the kind sea-caves."
She smiled, she went up through the surf in the bay.
  Children dear, was it yesterday?

  Children dear, were we long alone?
"The sea grows stormy, the little ones moan.
Long prayers," I said, "in the world they say.
Come," I said, and we rose through the surf in the bay.
We went up the beach, by the sandy down
Where the sea-stocks bloom, to the white-wall'd town.
Through the narrow paved streets, where all was still,
To the little grey church on the windy hill.
From the church came a murmur of folk at their prayers,
But we stood without in the cold-blowing airs.
We climb'd on the graves, on the stones worn with rains,
And we gazed up the aisle through the small leaded panes.
  She sate by the pillar; we saw her dear:
  "Margaret, hist! come quick, we are here.
  Dear heart," I said, "we are long alone.
  The sea grows stormy, the little ones moan."
But, ah! she gave me never a look,
For her eyes were seal'd to the holy book.
Loud prays the priest; shut stands the door.
  Came away, children, call no more.
  Come away, come down, call no more.

    Down, down, down;
  Down to the depths of the sea.
She sits at her wheel in the humming town,
  Singing most joyfully.
Hark what she sings: "O joy, O joy,
For the humming street, and the child with its toy.
For the priest, and the bell, and the holy well.
  For the wheel where I spun,
  And the blessed light of the sun."
And so she sings her fill,
  Singing most joyfully,
Till the shuttle falls from her hand,
And the whizzing wheel stands still.
She steals to the window, and looks at the sand;
  And over the sand at the sea;
  And her eyes are set in a stare;
  And anon there breaks a sigh,
  And anon there drops a tear,
  From a sorrow-clouded eye,
  And a heart sorrow-laden,
    A long, long sigh
For the cold strange eyes of a little Mermaiden,
  And the gleam of her golden hair.

Come away, away, children.
Come children, come down.
The hoarse wind blows colder;
Lights shine in the town.
She will start from her slumber
When gusts shake the door;
She will hear the winds howling,
Will hear the waves roar.
We shall see, while above us
The waves roar and whirl,
A ceiling of amber,
A pavement of pearl.
Singing, "Here came a mortal,
But faithless was she:
And alone dwell for ever
The kings of the sea."

But, children, at midnight,
When soft the winds blow;
When clear falls the moonlight;
When spring-tides are low:
When sweet airs come seaward
From heaths starr'd with broom;
And high rocks throw mildly
On the blanch'd sands a gloom:
Up the still, glistening beaches,
Up the creeks we will hie;
Over banks of bright seaweed
The ebb-tide leaves dry.
We will gaze, from the sand-hills,
At the white, sleeping town;
At the church on the hill-side—
  And then come back down.
Singing, "There dwells a loved one,
  But cruel is she.
She left lonely for ever
  The kings of the sea."

MATTHEW ARNOLD (1822–1888)

THE SONG OF CALLICLES   852

Through the black, rushing smoke-bursts,
Thick breaks the red flame.
All Etna heaves fiercely
Her forest-clothed frame.

Not here, O Apollo!
Are haunts meet for thee.
But, where Helicon breaks down
In cliff to the sea.

Where the moon-silver'd inlets
Send far their light voice
Up the still vale of Thisbe,
O speed, and rejoice!

On the sward at the cliff-top,
Lie strewn the white flocks;
On the cliff-side, the pigeons
Roost deep in the rocks.

In the moonlight the shepherds,
Soft lull'd by the rills,
Lie wrapt in their blankets,
Asleep on the hills.

—What forms are these coming
So white through the gloom?
What garments out-glistening
The gold-flower'd broom?

What sweet-breathing Presence
Out-perfumes the thyme?
What voices enrapture
The night's balmy prime?—

'Tis Apollo comes leading
His choir, The Nine.
—The Leader is fairest,
But all are divine.

They are lost in the hollows.
They stream up again.
What seeks on this mountain
The glorified train?—

They bathe on this mountain,
In the spring by their road.
Then on to Olympus,
Their endless abode.

—Whose praise do they mention:
Of what is it told?—
What will be for ever.
What was from of old.

First hymn they the Father
Of all things: and then,
The rest of Immortals,
The action of men.

The Day in his hotness,
The strife with the palm;
The Night in her silence,
The Stars in their calm.

MATTHEW ARNOLD (1822–1888)

To Marguerite 853

Yes: in the sea of life enisled,
  With echoing straits between us thrown.
Dotting the shoreless watery wild,
  We mortal millions live *alone*.
The islands feel the enclasping flow,
And then their endless bounds they know.

But when the moon their hollows lights,
  And they are swept by balms of spring,
And in their glens, on starry nights,
  The nightingales divinely sing;
And lovely notes, from shore to shore,
Across the sounds and channels pour;

O then a longing like despair
  Is to their farthest caverns sent!
For surely once, they feel, we were
  Parts of a single continent.
Now round us spreads the watery plain—
O might our marges meet again!

Who order'd that their longing's fire
  Should be, as soon as kindled, cool'd?
Who renders vain their deep desire?—
  A God, a God their severance ruled;
And bade betwixt their shores to be
The unplumb'd, salt, estranging sea.

                MATTHEW ARNOLD (1822–1888)

Requiescat 854

Strew on her roses, roses,
  And never a spray of yew.
In quiet she reposes:
  Ah! would that I did too.

Her mirth the world required:
  She bathed it in smiles of glee.
But her heart was tired, tired,
  And now they let her be.

Her life was turning, turning,
  In mazes of heat and sound.
But for peace her soul was yearning,
  And now peace laps her round.

Her cabin'd, ample Spirit,
  It flutter'd and fail'd for breath.
To-night it doth inherit
  The vasty hall of Death.

                MATTHEW ARNOLD (1822–1888)

855   THE SCHOLAR-GIPSY

Go, for they call you, Shepherd, from the hill;
  Go, Shepherd, and untie the wattled cotes:
    No longer leave thy wistful flock unfed,
  Nor let thy bawling fellows rack their throats,
    Nor the cropp'd grasses shoot another head.
      But when the fields are still,
  And the tired men and dogs all gone to rest,
    And only the white sheep are sometimes seen
      Cross and recross the strips of moon-blanch'd green;
Come Shepherd, and again begin the quest.

Here, where the reaper was at work of late,
  In this high field's dark corner, where he leaves
    His coat, his basket, and his earthen cruise,
  And in the sun all morning binds the sheaves,
    Then here, at noon, comes back his stores to use;
      Here will I sit and wait,
  While to my ear from uplands far away
    The bleating of the folded flocks is borne,
      With distant cries of reapers in the corn—
All the live murmur of a summer's day.

Screen'd is this nook o'er the high, half-reap'd field,
  And here till sundown, Shepherd, will I be.
    Through the thick corn the scarlet poppies peep,
  And round green roots and yellowing stalks I see
    Pale blue convolvulus in tendrils creep:
      And air-swept lindens yield
  Their scent, and rustle down their perfumed showers
    Of bloom on the bent grass where I am laid,
      And bower me from the August sun with shade;
And the eye travels down to Oxford's towers:

And near me on the grass lies Glanvil's book—
  Come, let me read the oft-read tale again:
    The story of that Oxford scholar poor,
  Of pregnant parts and quick inventive brain,
    Who, tired of knocking at Preferment's door,
      One summer morn forsook
  His friends, and went to learn the Gipsy lore,
    And roam'd the world with that wild brotherhood,
      And came, as most men deem'd, to little good,
But came to Oxford and his friends no more.

But once, years after, in the country lanes,
  Two scholars, whom at college erst he knew,
    Met him, and of his way of life inquired.
  Whereat he answer'd that the Gipsy crew,

His mates, had arts to rule as they desired
  The workings of men's brains;
And they can bind them to what thoughts they will:
"And I," he said, "the secret of their art,
  When fully learn'd, will to the world impart:
But it needs Heaven-sent moments for this skill!"

This said, he left them, and return'd no more,
  But rumours hung about the country-side,
    That the lost Scholar long was seen to stray,
  Seen by rare glimpses, pensive and tongue-tied,
  In hat of antique shape, and cloak of grey,
    The same the Gipsies wore.
  Shepherds had met him on the Hurst in spring;
    At some lone alehouse in the Berkshire moors,
    On the warm ingle-bench, the smock-frock'd boors
  Had found him seated at their entering,

But 'mid their drink and clatter, he would fly:
  And I myself seem half to know thy looks,
    And put the shepherds, Wanderer, on thy trace;
  And boys who in lone wheatfields scare the rooks
  I ask if thou hast pass'd their quiet place;
    Or in my boat I lie
  Moor'd to the cool bank in the summer heats,
    'Mid wide grass meadows which the sunshine fills,
    And watch the warm green-muffled Cumnor hills,
  And wonder if thou haunt'st their shy retreats.

For most, I know, thou lov'st retired ground.
  Thee, at the ferry, Oxford riders blithe,
    Returning home on summer nights, have met
  Crossing the stripling Thames at Bablock-hithe,
    Trailing in the cool stream thy fingers wet,
      As the slow punt swings round:
  And leaning backwards in a pensive dream,
    And fostering in thy lap a heap of flowers
    Pluck'd in shy fields and distant Wychwood bowers,
  And thine eyes resting on the moonlit stream:

And then they land, and thou art seen no more.
  Maidens who from the distant hamlets come
    To dance around the Fyfield elm in May,
  Oft through the darkening fields have seen thee roam,
    Or cross a stile into the public way.
      Oft thou hast given them store
  Of flowers—the frail-leaf'd, white anemone—
    Dark bluebells drench'd with dews of summer eves,
    And purple orchises with spotted leaves—
  But none has words she can report of thee.

And, above Godstow Bridge, when hay-time's here
  In June, and many a scythe in sunshine flames,
    Men who through those wide fields of breezy grass
  Where black-wing'd swallows haunt the glittering Thames,
    To bathe in the abandon'd lasher pass,
      Have often pass'd thee near
  Sitting upon the river bank o'ergrown:
    Mark'd thine outlandish garb, thy figure spare,
    Thy dark vague eyes, and soft abstracted air;
  But, when they came from bathing, thou wert gone.

At some lone homestead in the Cumnor hills,
  Where at her open door the housewife darns,
    Thou hast been seen, or hanging on a gate
  To watch the threshers in the mossy barns.
    Children, who early range these slopes and late
      For cresses from the rills,
  Have known thee watching, all an April day,
    The springing pastures and the feeding kine;
    And mark'd thee, when the stars come out and shine,
  Through the long dewy grass move slow away.

In autumn, on the skirts of Bagley Wood,
  Where most the Gipsies by the turf-edged way
    Pitch their smoked tents, and every bush you see
  With scarlet patches tagg'd and shreds of gray,
    Above the forest-ground call'd Thessaly—
      The blackbird picking food
  Sees thee, nor stops his meal, nor fears at all;
    So often has he known thee past him stray
    Rapt, twirling in thy hand a wither'd spray,
  And waiting for the spark from Heaven to fall.

And once, in winter, on the causeway chill
  Where home through flooded fields foot-travellers go,
    Have I not pass'd thee on the wooden bridge
  Wrapt in thy cloak and battling with the snow,
    Thy face towards Hinksey and its wintry ridge?
      And thou hast climb'd the hill
  And gain'd the white brow of the Cumnor range;
    Turn'd once to watch, while thick the snowflakes fall,
    The line of festal light in Christ Church hall—
  Then sought thy straw in some sequester'd grange.

But what—I dream! Two hundred years are flown
  Since first thy story ran through Oxford halls,
    And the grave Glanvil did the tale inscribe
  That thou wert wander'd from the studious walls
    To learn strange arts, and join a Gipsy tribe:
      And thou from earth art gone
  Long since and in some quiet churchyard laid;
    Some country nook, where o'er thy unknown grave
    Tall grasses and white flowering nettles wave—
  Under a dark red-fruited yew-tree's shade.

—No, no, thou hast not felt the lapse of hours.
  For what wears out the life of mortal men?
    'Tis that from change to change their being rolls:
  'Tis that repeated shocks, again, again,
    Exhaust the energy of strongest souls,
      And numb the elastic powers.
  Till having used our nerves with bliss and teen,
    And tired upon a thousand schemes our wit,
    To the just-pausing Genius we remit
  Our worn-out life, and are—what we have been.

Thou hast not lived, why shouldst thou perish, so?
  Thou hadst *one* aim, *one* business, *one* desire:
    Else wert thou long since number'd with the dead—
  Else hadst thou spent, like other men, thy fire.
    The generations of thy peers are fled,
      And we ourselves shall go;
  But thou possessest an immortal lot,
    And we imagine thee exempt from age
    And living as thou liv'st on Glanvil's page,
  Because thou hadst—what we, alas, have not!

For early didst thou leave the world, with powers
  Fresh, undiverted to the world without,
    Firm to their mark, not spent on other things;
  Free from the sick fatigue, the languid doubt,
    Which much to have tried, in much been baffled, brings.
      O Life unlike to ours!
  Who fluctuate idly without term or scope,
    Of whom each strives, nor knows for what he strives,
    And each half lives a hundred different lives;
  Who wait like thee, but not, like thee, in hope.

Thou waitest for the spark from Heaven: and we,
  Vague half-believers of our casual creeds,
    Who never deeply felt, nor clearly will'd,
  Whose insight never has borne fruit in deeds,
    Whose weak resolves never have been fulfill'd;
      For whom each year we see
  Breeds new beginnings, disappointments new;
    Who hesitate and falter life away,
    And lose to-morrow the ground won to-day—
  Ah, do not we, Wanderer, await it too?

Yes, we await it, but it still delays,
  And then we suffer; and amongst us One,
    Who most has suffer'd, takes dejectedly
  His seat upon the intellectual throne;

And all his store of sad experience he
   Lays bare of wretched days;
Tells us his misery's birth and growth and signs,
   And how the dying spark of hope was fed,
   And how the breast was soothed, and how the head,
And all his hourly varied anodynes.

This for our wisest: and we others pine,
   And wish the long unhappy dream would end,
   And waive all claim to bliss, and try to bear,
With close-lipp'd Patience for our only friend,
   Sad Patience, too near neighbour to Despair:
     But none has hope like thine.
Thou through the fields and through the woods dost stray,
   Roaming the country-side, a truant boy,
   Nursing thy project in unclouded joy,
And every doubt long blown by time away.

O born in days when wits were fresh and clear,
   And life ran gaily as the sparkling Thames;
   Before this strange disease of modern life,
With its sick hurry, its divided aims,
   Its heads o'ertax'd, its palsied hearts, was rife—
     Fly hence, our contact fear!
Still fly, plunge deeper in the bowering wood!
   Averse, as Dido did with gesture stern
   From her false friend's approach in Hades turn,
Wave us away, and keep thy solitude.

Still nursing the unconquerable hope,
   Still clutching the inviolable shade,
   With a free onward impulse brushing through,
By night, the silver'd branches of the glade—
   Far on the forest-skirts, where none pursue,
     On some mild pastoral slope
Emerge, and resting on the moonlit pales,
   Freshen they flowers, as in former years,
   With dew, or listen with enchanted ears,
From the dark dingles, to the nightingales.

But fly our paths, our feverish contact fly!
   For strong the infection of our mental strife,
   Which, though it gives no bliss, yet spoils for rest;
And we should win thee from they own fair life,
   Like us distracted, and like us unblest.
     Soon, soon thy cheer would die,
Thy hopes grow timorous, and unfix'd they powers,
   And they clear aims be cross and shifting made:
   And then thy glad perennial youth would fade,
Fade, and grow old at last, and die like ours.

Then fly our greetings, fly our speech and smiles!
  —As some grave Tyrian trader, from the sea,
    Descried at sunrise an emerging prow
Lifting the cool-hair'd creepers stealthily,
    The fringes of a southward-facing brow
      Among the Ægean isles;
And saw the merry Grecian coaster come,
    Freighted with amber grapes, and Chian wine,
    Green bursting figs, and tunnies steep'd in brine;
And knew the intruders on his ancient home,

The young light-hearted Masters of the waves;
  And snatch'd his rudder, and shook out more sail,
    And day and night held on indignantly
O'er the blue Midland waters with the gale,
    Betwixt the Syrtes and soft Sicily,
      To where the Atlantic raves
Outside the Western Straits, and unbent sails
    There, where down cloudy cliffs, through sheets of foam,
    Shy traffickers, the dark Iberians come;
And on the beach undid his corded bales.

MATTHEW ARNOLD (1822–1888)

PHILOMELA   856

Hark! ah, the Nightingale!
The tawny-throated!
Hark! from that moonlit cedar what a burst!
What triumph! hark—what pain!

O Wanderer from a Grecian shore,
Still, after many years, in distant lands,
Still nourishing in thy bewilder'd brain
That wild, unquench'd, deep-sunken, old-world pain—
  Say, will it never heal?
And can this fragrant lawn
With its cool trees, and night,
And the sweet, tranquil Thames,
And moonshine, and the dew,
To thy rack'd heart and brain
  Afford no balm?

  Dost thou to-night behold
Here, through the moonlight on this English grass,
The unfriendly palace in the Thracian wild?
  Dost thou again peruse
With hot cheeks and sear'd eyes
The too clear web, and thy dumb Sister's shame?
  Dost thou once more assay
Thy flight, and feel come over thee,
Poor Fugitive, the feathery change
Once more, and once more seem to make resound
With love and hate, triumph and agony,
Lone Daulis, and the high Cephissian vale?

Listen, Eugenia—
How thick the bursts come crowding through the leaves!
Again—thou hearest!
Eternal Passion!
Eternal Pain!

MATTHEW ARNOLD (1822–1888)

857 SHAKESPEARE

Others abide our question. Thou art free.
We ask and ask: Thou smilest and art still,
Out-topping knowledge. For the loftiest hill
That to the stars uncrowns his majesty,
Planting his steadfast footsteps in the sea,
Making the heaven of heavens his dwelling-place,
Spares but the cloudy border of his base
To the foil'd searching of mortality;
And thou, who didst the stars and sunbeams know,
Self-school'd, self-scann'd, self-honour'd, self-secure,
Didst walk on earth unguess'd at. Better so!
All pains the immortal spirit must endure,
   All weakness that impairs, all griefs that bow,
Find their sole voice in that victorious brow.

MATTHEW ARNOLD (1822–1888)

858 FROM THE HYMN OF EMPEDOCLES

  Is it so small a thing
  To have enjoy'd the sun,
  To have lived light in the spring,
  To have loved, to have thought, to have done;
To have advanced true friends, and beat down baffling foes;

  That we must feign a bliss
  Of doubtful future date,
  And while we dream on this
  Lose all our present state,
And relegate to worlds yet distant our repose?

  Not much, I know, you prize
  What pleasures may be had,
  Who look on life with eyes
  Estranged, like mine, and sad:
And yet the village churl feels the truth more than you;

  Who's loth to leave this life
  Which to him little yields:
  His hard-task'd sunburnt wife,
  His often-labour'd fields;
The boors with whom he talk'd, the country spots he knew.

  But thou, because thou hear'st
  Men scoff at Heaven and Fate;
  Because the gods thou fear'st
  Fail to make blest thy state,
Tremblest, and wilt not dare to trust the joys there are.

I say, Fear not! life still
Leaves human effort scope.
But, since life teems with ill,
Nurse no extravagant hope.
Because thou must not dream, thou need'st not then despair.
        MATTHEW ARNOLD (1822–1888)

THE FLOWERS   859

When Love arose in heart and deed
 To wake the world to greater joy,
"What can she give me now?" said Greed,
 Who thought to win some costly toy.

He rose, he ran, he stoop'd, he clutch'd;
 And soon the Flowers, that Love let fall,
In Greed's hot grasp were fray'd and smutch'd,
 And Greed said, "Flowers! Can this be all?"

He flung them down and went his way,
 He cared no jot for thyme or rose;
But boys and girls came out to play,
 And some took these and some took those—

Red, blue, and white, and green and gold;
 And at their touch the dew return'd,
And all the bloom a thousandfold—
 So red, so ripe, the roses burn'd!
       WILLIAM BRIGHTY RANDS (1823–1880)

THE THOUGHT   860

Into the skies, one summer's day,
I sent a little Thought away;
Up to where, in the blue round,
The sun sat shining without sound.

Then my Thought came back to me.—
Little Thought, what did you see
In the regions whence you come?
And when I spoke, my Thought was dumb.

But she breathed of what was there,
In the pure bright upper air;
And, because my Thought so shone,
I knew she had been shone upon.

Next, by night a Thought I sent
Up into the firmament;
When the eager stars were out,
And the still moon shone about.

And my Thought went past the moon
In between the stars, but soon
Held her breath and durst not stir,
For the fear that covered her;
Then she thought, in this demur:

"Dare I look beneath the shade,
Into where the worlds are made;
Where the suns and stars are wrought?
Shall I meet another Thought?

"Will that other Thought have wings?
Shall I meet strange, heavenly things?
Thought of Thoughts, and Light of Lights,
Breath of Breaths, and Night of Nights?"

Then my Thought began to hark
In the illuminated dark,
Till the silence, over, under,
Made her heart beat more than thunder.

And my Thought, came trembling back,
But with something on her track,
And with something at her side;
Nor till she has lived and died,
Lived and died, and lived again,
Will that awful thing seem plain.
                        WILLIAM BRIGHTY RANDS (1823–1880)

MARITÆ SUÆ
I

Of all the flowers rising now,
  Thou only saw'st the head
Of that unopen'd drop of snow
  I placed beside thy bed.

In all the blooms that blow so fast,
  Thou hast no further part,
Save those the hour I saw thee last,
  I laid above thy heart.

Two snowdrops for our boy and girl,
  A primrose blown for me,
Wreathed with one often-play'd-with curl
  From each bright head for thee.

And so I graced thee for thy grave,
  And made these tokens fast
With that old silver heart I gave,
  My first gift—and my last.

II

I dream'd, her babe upon her breast,
Here she might lie and calmly rest
Her happy eyes on that far hill
That backs the landscape fresh and still.

I hoped her thoughts would thrid the boughs
Where careless birds on love carouse,
And gaze those apple-blossoms through
To revel in the boundless blue.

But now her faculty of sight
Is elder sister to the light,
And travels free and unconfined
Through dense and rare, through form and mind.

Or else her life to be complete
Hath found new channels full and meet—
Then, O, what eyes are leaning o'er,
If fairer than they were before!

WILLIAM PHILPOT (1823–1889)

MIMNERMUS IN CHURCH 862

You promise heavens free from strife,
   Pure truth, and perfect change of will;
But sweet, sweet is this human life,
   So sweet, I fain would breathe it still;
Your chilly stars I can forgo,
This warm kind world is all I know.

You say there is no substance here,
   One great reality above:
Back from that void I shrink in fear,
   And child-like hide myself in love:
Show me what angels feel. Till then
I cling, a mere weak man, to men.

You bid me lift my mean desires
   From faltering lips and fitful veins
To sexless souls, ideal quires,
   Unwearied voices, wordless strains:
My mind with fonder welcome owns
One dear dead friend's remember'd tones.

Forsooth the present we must give
   To that which cannot pass away;
All beauteous things for which we live
   By laws of time and space decay.
But O, the very reason why
I clasp them, is because they die.

WILLIAM (JOHNSON) CORY (1823–1892)

HERACLITUS 863

They told me, Heraclitus, they told me you were dead,
They brought me bitter news to hear and bitter tears to shed.
I wept as I remember'd how often you and I
Had tired the sun with talking and sent him down the sky.

And now that thou art lying, my dear old Carian guest,
A handful of grey ashes, long, long ago at rest,
Still are thy pleasant voices, thy nightingales, awake;
For Death, he taketh all away, but them he cannot take.

WILLIAM (JOHNSON) CORY (1823–1892)

864   THE MARRIED LOVER
Why, having won her, do I woo?
    Because her spirit's vestal grace
Provokes me always to pursue,
    But, spirit-like, eludes embrace;
Because her womanhood is such
    That, as on court-days subjects kiss
The Queen's hand, yet so near a touch
    Affirms no mean familiarness;
Nay, rather marks more fair the height
    Which can with safety so neglect
To dread, as lower ladies might,
    That grace could meet with disrespect;
Thus she with happy favour feeds
    Allegiance from a love so high
That thence no false conceit proceeds
    Of difference bridged, or state put by;
Because although in act and word
    As lowly as a wife can be,
Her manners, when they call me lord,
    Remind me 'tis by courtesy;
Not with her least consent of will,
    Which would my proud affection hurt,
But by the noble style that still
    Imputes an unattain'd desert;
Because her gay and lofty brows,
    When all is won which hope can ask,
Reflect a light of hopeless snows
    That bright in virgin ether bask;
Because, though free of the outer court
    I am, this Temple keeps its shrine
Sacred to Heaven; because, in short,
    She's not and never can be mine.
                COVENTRY PATMORE (1823–1896)

865   IF I WERE DEAD
"If I were dead, you'd sometimes say, Poor Child!"
The dear lips quiver'd as they spake,
And the tears brake
From eyes which, not to grieve me, brightly smiled.
Poor Child, poor Child!
I seem to hear your laugh, your talk, your song.
It is not true that Love will do no wrong.
Poor Child!
And did you think, when you so cried and smiled,
How I, in lonely nights, should lie awake,
And of those words your full avengers make?
Poor Child, poor Child!
And now, unless it be
That sweet amends thrice told are come to thee,
O God, have Thou no mercy upon me!
Poor Child!
                COVENTRY PATMORE (1823–1896)

Departure   866

It was not like your great and gracious ways!
Do you, that have naught other to lament,
Never, my Love, repent
Of how, that July afternoon,
You went,
With sudden, unintelligible phrase,
And frighten'd eye,
Upon your journey of so many days
Without a single kiss, or a good-bye?
I knew, indeed, that you were parting soon;
And so we sate, within the low sun's rays,
You whispering to me, for your voice was weak,
Your harrowing praise.
Well, it was well
To hear you such things speak,
And I could tell
What made your eyes a growing gloom of love,
As a warm South-wind sombres a March grove.
And it was like your great and gracious ways
To turn your talk on daily things, my Dear,
Lifting the luminous, pathetic lash
To let the laughter flash,
Whilst I drew near,
Because you spoke so low that I could scarcely hear.
But all at once to leave me at the last,
More at the wonder than the loss aghast,
With huddled, unintelligible phrase,
And frighten'd eye,
And go your journey of all days
With not one kiss, or a good-bye,
And the only loveless look the look with which you pass'd:
'Twas all unlike your great and gracious ways.

COVENTRY PATMORE (1823–1896)

The Toys   867

My little Son, who look'd from thoughtful eyes
And moved and spoke in quiet grown-up wise,
Having my law the seventh time disobey'd,
I struck him, and dismiss'd
With hard words and unkiss'd,
—His Mother, who was patient, being dead.
Then, fearing lest his grief should hinder sleep,
I visited his bed,
But found him slumbering deep,
With darken'd eyelids, and their lashes yet
From his late sobbing wet.
And I, with moan,
Kissing away his tears, left others of my own;
For, on a table drawn beside his head,
He had put, within his reach,
A box of counters and a red-vein'd stone,

A piece of glass abraded by the beach,
And six or seven shells,
A bottle with bluebells,
And two French copper coins, ranged there with careful art,
To comfort his sad heart.
So when that night I pray'd
To God, I wept, and said:
Ah, when at last we lie with trancèd breath,
Not vexing Thee in death,
And Thou rememberest of what toys
We made our joys,
How weakly understood
Thy great commanded good,
Then, fatherly not less
Than I whom Thou hast moulded from the clay,
Thou'lt leave Thy wrath, and say,
"I will be sorry for their childishness."
COVENTRY PATMORE (1823–1896)

868   A FAREWELL

With all my will, but much against my heart,
We two now part.
My Very Dear,
Our solace is, the sad road lies so clear.
It needs no art,
With faint, averted feet
And many a tear,
In our opposed paths to persevere.
Go thou to East, I West.
We will not say
There's any hope, it is so far away.
But, O, my Best,
When the one darling of our widowhead,
The nursling Grief,
Is dead,
And no dews blur our eyes
To see the peach-bloom come in evening skies,
Perchance we may,
Where now this night is day,
And even through faith of still averted feet,
Making full circle of our banishment,
Amazèd meet;
The bitter journey to the bourne so sweet
Seasoning the termless feast of our content
With tears of recognition never dry.
COVENTRY PATMORE (1823–1896)

869   THE BALLAD OF KEITH OF RAVELSTON

The murmur of the mourning ghost
  That keeps the shadowy kine,
"O Keith of Ravelston,
  The sorrows of thy line!"

Ravelston, Ravelston,
  The merry path that leads
Down the golden morning hill,
  And thro' the silver meads;

Ravelston, Ravelston,
  The stile beneath the tree,
The maid that kept her mother's kine,
  The song that sang she!

She sang her song, she kept her kine,
  She sat beneath the thorn,
When Andrew Keith of Ravelston
  Rode thro' the Monday morn.

His henchman sing, his hawk-bells ring,
  His belted jewels shine;
O Keith of Ravelston,
  The sorrows of thy line!

Year after year, where Andrew came,
  Comes evening down the glade,
And still there sits a moonshine ghost
  Where sat the sunshine maid.

Her misty hair is faint and fair,
  She keeps the shadowy kine;
O Keith of Ravelston,
  The sorrows of thy line!

I lay my hand upon the stile,
  The stile is lone and cold,
The burnie that goes babbling by
  Says naught that can be told.

Yet, stranger! here, from year to year,
  She keeps her shadowy kine;
O Keith of Ravelston,
  The sorrows of thy line!

Step out three steps, where Andrew stood—
  Why blanch thy cheeks for fear?
The ancient stile is not alone,
  'Tis not the burn I hear!

She makes her immemorial moan,
  She keeps her shadowy kine;
O Keith of Ravelston,
  The sorrows of thy line!

                SYDNEY DOBELL (1824–1874)

870   RETURN!

Return, return! all night my lamp is burning,
All night, like it, my wide eyes watch and burn;
Like it, I fade and pale, when day returning
Bears witness that the absent can return,
      Return, return.

Like it, I lessen with a lengthening sadness,
Like it, I burn to waste and waste to burn,
Like it, I spend the golden oil of gladness
To feed the sorrowy signal for return,
      Return, return.

Like it, like it, whene'er the east wind sings,
I bend and shake; like it, I quake and yearn,
When Hope's late butterflies, with whispering wings,
Fly in out of the dark, to fall and burn—
  Burn in the watchfire of return,
      Return, return.

Like it, the very flame whereby I pine
Consumes me to its nature. While I mourn
My soul becomes a better soul than mine,
And from its brightening beacon I discern
My starry love go forth from me, and shine
Across the seas a path for thy return,
      Return, return.

Return, return! all night I see it burn,
All night it prays like me, and lifts a twin
Of palmèd praying hands that meet and yearn—
Yearn to the impleaded skies for thy return.
Day, like a golden fetter, locks them in,
And wans the light that withers, tho' it burn
  As warmly still for thy return;
Still thro' the splendid load uplifts the thin
Pale, paler, palest patience that can learn
Naught but that votive sign for thy return—
That single suppliant sign for thy return,
      Return, return.

Return, return! lest haply, love, or e'er
Thou touch the lamp the light have ceased to burn,
And thou, who thro' the window didst discern
The wonted flame, shalt reach the topmost stair
  To find no wide eyes watching there,
No wither'd welcome waiting thy return!
A passing ghost, a smoke-wreath in the air,
The flameless ashes, and the soulless urn,

Warm with the famish'd fire that lived to burn—
Burn out its lingering life for thy return,
Its last of lingering life for thy return,
Its last of lingering life to light thy late return,
    Return, return.

SYDNEY DOBELL (1824–1874)

A CHANTED CALENDAR   871

First came the primrose,
On the bank high,
Like a maiden looking forth
From the window of a tower
When the battle rolls below,
So look'd she,
And saw the storms go by.

Then came the wind-flower
In the valley left behind,
As a wounded maiden, pale
With purple streaks of woe,
When the battle has roll'd by
Wanders to and fro,
So totter'd she,
Dishevell'd in the wind.

Then came the daisies,
On the first of May,
Like a banner'd show's advance
While the crowd runs by the way,
With ten thousand flowers about them
they came trooping through the fields.

As a happy people come,
So came they,
As a happy people come
When the war has roll'd away,
With dance and tabor, pipe and drum,
And all make holiday.

Then came the cowslip,
Like a dancer in the fair,
She spread her little mat of green,
And on it danced she.
With a fillet bound about her brow,
A fillet round her happy brow,
A golden fillet round her brow,
And rubies in her hair.

SYDNEY DOBELL (1824–1874)

LAUS DEO   872

In the hall the coffin waits, and the idle armourer stands.
At his belt the coffin nails, and the hammer in his hands.
The bed of state is hung with crape—the grand old bed where she was wed—

And like an upright corpse she sitteth gazing dumbly at the bed.
Hour by hour her serving-men enter by the curtain'd door,
And with steps of muffled woe pass breathless o'er the silent floor,
And marshal mutely round, and look from each to each with eyelids red;

"Touch him not," she shriek'd and cried, "he is but newly dead!"
"O my own dear mistress," the ancient Nurse did say,
"Seven long days and seven long nights you have watch'd him where he lay."
"Seven long days and seven long nights," the hoary Steward said;
"Seven long days and seven long nights," groan'd the Warrener gray;
"Seven," said the old Henchman, and bow'd his aged head;
"On your lives!" she shriek'd and cried, "he is but newly dead!"
    Then a father Priest they sought,
    The Priest that taught her all she knew,
    And they told him of her loss.
    "For she is mild and sweet of will,
    She loved him, and his words are peace,
    And he shall heal her ill."
    But her watch she did not cease.
    He bless'd her where she sat distraught,
    And show'd her holy cross,—
    The cross she kiss'd from year to year—
    But she neither saw nor heard;
    And said he in her deaf ear
    All he had been wont to teach,
    All she had been fond to hear,
    Missall'd prayer, and solemn speech,
    But she answer'd not a word.
Only when he turn'd to speak with those who wept about the bed,
"On your lives!" she shriek'd and cried, 'he is but newly dead!'
Then how sadly he turn'd from her, it were wonderful to tell,
And he stood beside the death-bed as by one who slumbers well,
And he lean'd o'er him who lay there, and in cautious whisper low,
"He is not dead, but sleepeth," said the Priest, and smooth'd his brow.
"Sleepeth?" said she, looking up, and the sun rose in her face!
"He must be better than I thought, for the sleep is very sound."
"He is better," said the Priest, and call'd her maidens round.
  With them came that ancient dame who nursed her when a child;
"O Nurse!" she sigh'd, "O Nurse!" she cried "O Nurse!" and then she smiled,
    And then she wept; with that they drew
    About her, as of old;
    Her dying eyes were sweet and blue,
    Her trembling touch was cold;
    But she said, "My maidens true,
    No more weeping and well-away;
    Let them kill the feast.
    I would be happy in my soul.
    'He is better,' saith the Priest;
    He did but sleep the weary day,
    And will waken whole.
    Carry me to his dear side,

    And let the halls be trim;
Whistly, whistly," said she,
"I am wan with watching and wail,
He must not wake to see me pale,
Let me sleep with him.
See you keep the tryst for me,
I would rest till he awake
And rise up like a bride.
But whistly, whistly!" said she.
"Yet rejoice your Lord doth live;
And for His dear sake
Say *Laus, Domine.*"
Silent they cast down their eyes,
And every breast a sob did rive,
She lifted her in wild surprise
And they dared not disobey.
"*Laus Deo,*" said the Steward, hoary when her days were new;
"*Laus Deo,*" said the Warrener, whiter than the warren snows;
"*Laus Deo,*" the bald Henchman, who had nursed her on his knee.
    The old Nurse moved her lips in vain,
And she stood among the train
Like a dead tree shaking dew.
Then the Priest he softly stept
Midway in the little band,
And he took the Lady's hand.
"*Laus Deo,*" he said aloud,
"*Laus Deo,*" they said again,
Yet again, and yet again,
Humbly cross'd and lowly bow'd,
Till in wont and fear it rose
To the Sabbath strain.
But she neither turn'd her head
Nor "Whistly, whistly," said she.
Her hands were folded as in grace,
We laid her with her ancient race
And all the village wept.

SYDNEY DOBELL (1824–1874)

THE FAIRIES 873

Up the airy mountain,
  Down the rushy glen,
We daren't go a-hunting
  For fear of little men;
Wee folk, good folk,
  Trooping all together;
Green jacket, red cap,
  And white owl's feather!

Down along the rocky shore
  Some make their home,
They live on crispy pancakes
  Of yellow tide-foam;

Some in the reeds
  Of the black mountain lake,
With frogs for their watch-dogs,
  All night awake.

High on the hill-top
  The old King sits;
He is now so old and gray
  He's nigh lost his wits.
With a bridge of white mist
  Columbkill he crosses,
On his stately journeys
  From Slieveleague to Rosses;
Or going up with music
  On cold starry nights
To sup with the Queen
  Of the gay Northern Lights.

They stole little Bridget
  For seven years long;
When she came down again
  Her friends were all gone.
They took her lightly back,
  Between the night and morrow,
They thought that she was fast asleep,
  But she was dead with sorrow.
They have kept her ever since
  Deep within the lake,
On a bed of flag-leaves,
  Watching till she wake.

By the craggy hill-side,
  Through the mosses bare,
They have planted thorn-trees
  For pleasure here and there.
If any man so daring
  As dig them up in spite,
He shall find their sharpest thorns
  In his bed at night.

Up the airy mountain,
  Down the rushy glen,
We daren't go a-hunting
  For fear of little men;
Wee folk, good folk,
  Trooping all together;
Green jacket, red cap,
  And white owl's feather!

WILLIAM ALLINGHAM (1824–1889)

That Holy Thing 874

They all were looking for a king
  To slay their foes and lift them high:
Thou cam'st, a little baby thing
  That made a woman cry.

O Son of Man, to right my lot
  Naught but Thy presence can avail;
Yet on the road Thy wheels are not,
  Nor on the sea Thy sail!

My how or when Thou wilt not heed,
  But come down Thine own secret stair,
That Thou mayst answer all my need—
  Yea, every bygone prayer.

GEORGE MACDONALD (1824–1905)

The Blessèd Damozel 875

The blessèd Damozel lean'd out
  From the gold bar of Heaven:
Her blue grave eyes were deeper much
  Than a deep water, even.
She had three lilies in her hand,
  And the stars in her hair were seven.

Her robe, ungirt from clasp to hem,
  No wrought flowers did adorn,
But a white rose of Mary's gift
  On the neck meetly worn;
And her hair, lying down her back,
  Was yellow like ripe corn.

Herseem'd she scarce had been a day
  One of God's choristers;
The wonder was not yet quite gone
  From that still look of hers;
Albeit, to them she left, her day
  Had counted as ten years.

(To one it is ten years of years:
  ...Yet now, here in this place,
Surely she lean'd o'er me,—her hair
  Fell all about my face....
Nothing: the Autumn-fall of leaves.
  The whole year sets apace.)

It was the terrace of God's house
  That she was standing on,—
By God built over the sheer depth
  In which Space is begun;
So high, that looking downward thence,
  She scarce could see the sun.

It lies from Heaven across the flood
    Of ether, as a bridge.
Beneath, the tides of day and night
    With flame and darkness ridge
The void, as low as where this earth
    Spins like a fretful midge.

But in those tracts, with her, it was
    The peace of utter light
And silence. For no breeze may stir
    Along the steady flight
Of seraphim; no echo there,
    Beyond all depth or height.

Heard hardly, some of her new friends,
    Playing at holy games,
Spake gentle-mouth'd, among themselves,
    Their virginal chaste names;
And the souls, mounting up to God,
    Went by her like thin flames.

And still she bow'd herself, and stoop'd
    Into the vast waste calm;
Till her bosom's pressure must have made
    The bar she lean'd on warm,
And the lilies lay as if asleep
    Along her bended arm.

From the fixt lull of Heaven, she saw
    Time, like a pulse, shake fierce
Through all the worlds. Her gaze still strove,
    In that steep gulf, to pierce
The swarm; and then she spoke, as when
    The stars sang in their spheres.

"I wish that he were come to me,
    For he will come," she said.
"Have I not pray'd in solemn Heaven?
    On earth, has he not pray'd?
Are not two prayers a perfect strength?
    And shall I feel afraid?

"When round his head the aureole clings,
    And he is clothed in white,
I'll take his hand, and go with him
    To the deep wells of light,
And we will step down as to a stream
    And bathe there in God's sight.

"We two will stand beside that shrine,
    Occult, withheld, untrod,
Whose lamps tremble continually
    With prayer sent up to God;
And where each need, reveal'd, expects
    Its patient period.

"We two will lie i' the shadow of
  That living mystic tree
Within whose secret growth the Dove
  Sometimes is felt to be,
While every leaf that His plumes touch
  Saith His name audibly.

"And I myself will teach to him,—
  I myself, lying so,—
The songs I sing here; which his mouth
  Shall pause in, hush'd and slow,
Finding some knowledge at each pause,
  And some new thing to know."

(Alas! to *her* wise simple mind
  These things were all but known
Before: they trembled on her sense,—
  Her voice had caught their tone.
Alas for lonely Heaven! Alas
  For life wrung out alone!

Alas, and though the end were reach'd?...
  Was *thy* part understood
Or borne in trust? And for her sake
  Shall this too be found good?—
May the close lips that knew not prayer
  Praise ever, though they would?)

"We two," she said, "will seek the groves
  Where the lady Mary is,
With her five handmaidens, whose names
  Are five sweet symphonies:—
Cecily, Gertrude, Magdalen,
  Margaret and Rosalys.

"Circle-wise sit they, with bound locks
  And bosoms covered;
Into the fine cloth, white like flame,
  Weaving the golden thread,
To fashion the birth-robes for them
  Who are just born, being dead.

"He shall fear, haply, and be dumb.
  Then I will lay my cheek
To his, and tell about our love,
  Not once abash'd or weak:
And the dear Mother will approve
  My pride, and let me speak.

"Herself shall bring us, hand in hand,
  To Him round whom all souls
Kneel—the unnumber'd solemn heads
  Bow'd with their aureoles:
And Angels, meeting us, shall sing
  To their citherns and citoles.

"There will I ask of Christ the Lord
  Thus much for him and me:—
To have more blessing than on earth
  In nowise; but to be
As then we were,—being as then
  At peace. Yea, verily.

"Yea, verily; when he is come
  We will do thus and thus:
Till this my vigil seem quite strange
  And almost fabulous;
We two will live at once, one life;
  And peace shall be with us."

She gazed, and listen'd, and then said,
  Less sad of speech than mild,—
"All this is when he comes." She ceased:
  The light thrill'd past her, fill'd
With Angels, in strong level lapse.
  Her eyes pray'd, and she smiled.

(I saw her smile.) But soon their flight
  Was vague 'mid the poised spheres.
And then she cast her arms along
  The golden barriers,
And laid her face between her hands,
  And wept. (I heard her tears.)
            DANTE GABRIEL ROSSETTI (1828–1882)

876   PHŒBUS WITH ADMETUS

When by Zeus relenting the mandate was revoked,
  Sentencing to exile the bright Sun-God,
Mindful were the ploughmen of who the steer had yoked,
  Who: and what a track show'd the upturn'd sod!
Mindful were the shepherds, as now the noon severe
  Bent a burning eyebrow to brown evetide,
How the rustic flute drew the silver to the sphere,
  Sister of his own, till her rays fell wide.
      God! of whom music
      And song and blood are pure,
      The day is never darken'd
      That had thee here obscure.

Chirping none, the scarlet cicalas crouch'd in ranks:
  Slack the thistle-head piled its down-silk gray:
Scarce the stony lizard suck'd hollows in his flanks:
  Thick on spots of umbrage our drowsed flocks lay.

Sudden bow'd the chestnuts beneath a wind unheard,
  Lengthen'd ran the grasses, the sky grew slate:
Then amid a swift flight of wing'd seed white as curd,
  Clear of limb a Youth smote the master's gate.
      God! of whom music
      And song and blood are pure,
      The day is never darken'd
      That had thee here obscure.

Water, first of singers, o'er rocky mount and mead,
  First of earthly singers, the sun-loved rill,
Sang of him, and flooded the ripples on the reed,
  Seeking whom to waken and what ear fill.
Water, sweetest soother to kiss a wound and cool,
  Sweetest and divinest, the sky-born brook,
Chuckled, with a whimper, and made a mirror-pool
  Round the guest we welcomed, the strange hand shook.
      God! of whom music
      And song and blood are pure,
      The day is never darken'd
      That had thee here obscure.

Many swarms of wild bees descended on our fields:
  Stately stood the wheatstalk with head bent high:
Big of heart we labour'd at storing mighty yields,
  Wool and corn, and clusters to make men cry!
Hand-like rush'd the vintage; we strung the bellied skins
  Plump, and at the sealing the Youth's voice rose:
Maidens clung in circle, on little fists their chins;
  Gentle beasties through push'd a cold long nose.
      God! of whom music
      And song and blood are pure,
      The day is never darken'd
      That had thee here obscure.

Foot to fire in snowtime we trimm'd the slender shaft:
  Often down the pit spied the lean wolf's teeth
Grin against his will, trapp'd by masterstrokes of craft;
  Helpless in his froth-wrath as green logs seethe!
Safe the tender lambs tugg'd the teats, and winter sped
  Whirl'd before the crocus, the year's new gold.
Hung the hooky beak up aloft, the arrowhead
  Redden'd through his feathers for our dear fold.
      God! of whom music
      And song and blood are pure,
      The day is never darken'd
      That had thee here obscure.

Tales we drank of giants at war with gods above:
  Rocks were they to look on, and earth climb'd air!
Tales of search for simples, and those who sought of love
  Ease because the creature was all too fair.

Pleasant ran our thinking that while our work was good.
  Sure as fruits for sweat would the praise come fast.
He that wrestled stoutest and tamed the billow-brood
  Danced in rings with girls, like a sail-flapp'd mast.
      God! of whom music
      And song and blood are pure,
      The day is never darken'd
      That had thee here obscure.

Lo, the herb of healing, when once the herb is known,
  Shines in shady woods bright as new-sprung flame.
Ere the string was tighten'd we heard the mellow tone,
  After he had taught how the sweet sounds came.
Stretch'd about his feet, labour done, 'twas as you see
  Red pomegranates tumble and burst hard rind.
So began contention to give delight and be
  Excellent in things aim'd to make life kind.
      God! of whom music
      And song and blood are pure,
      The day is never darken'd
      That had thee here obscure.

You with shelly horns, rams! and, promontory goats,
  You whose browsing beards dip in coldest dew!
Bulls, that walk the pastures in kingly-flashing coats!
  Laurel, ivy, vine, wreathed for feasts not few!
You that build the shade-roof, and you that court the rays,
  You that leap besprinkling the rock stream-rent:
He has been our fellow, the morning of our days;
  Us he chose for housemates, and this way went.
      God! of whom music
      And song and blood are pure,
      The day is never darken'd
      That had thee here obscure.
              GEORGE MEREDITH (1828–1909)

877   TARDY SPRING
  Now the North wind ceases,
  The warm South-west awakes;
  Swift fly the fleeces,
  Thick the blossom-flakes.

Now hill to hill has made the stride,
And distance waves the without-end:
Now in the breast a door flings wide;
Our farthest smiles, our next is friend.
And song of England's rush of flowers
Is this full breeze with mellow stops,
That spins the lark for shine, for showers;
He drinks his hurried flight, and drops.
The stir in memory seem these things,
Which out of moisten'd turf and clay,
Astrain for light push patient rings,
Or leap to find the waterway.

'Tis equal to a wonder done,
Whatever simple lives renew
Their tricks beneath the father sun,
As though they caught a broken clue:
So hard was earth an eyewink back;
But now the common life has come,
The blotting cloud a dappled pack,
The grasses one vast underhum.
A City clothed in snow and soot,
With lamps for day in ghostly rows,
Breaks to the scene of hosts afoot,
The river that reflective flows:
And there did fog down crypts of street
Play spectre upon eye and mouth:—
Their faces are a glass to greet
This magic of the whirl for South.
A burly joy each creature swells
With sound of its own hungry quest;
Earth has to fill her empty wells,
And speed the service of the nest;
The phantom of the snow-wreath melt,
That haunts the farmer's look abroad,
Who sees what tomb a white night built,
Where flocks now bleat and sprouts the clod.
For iron Winter held her firm;
Across her sky he laid his hand;
And bird he starved, he stiffen'd worm;
A sightless heaven, a shaven land.
Her shivering Spring feign'd fast asleep,
The bitten buds dared not unfold:
We raced on roads and ice to keep
Thought of the girl we love from cold.

    But now the North wind ceases,
    The warm South-west awakes,
    The heavens are out in fleeces,
    And earth's green banner shakes.

GEORGE MEREDITH (1828–1909)

LOVE'S GRAVE

Mark where the pressing wind shoots javelin-like,
Its skeleton shadow on the broad-back'd wave!
Here is a fitting spot to dig Love's grave;
Here where the ponderous breakers plunge and strike,
And dart their hissing tongues high up the sand:
In hearing of the ocean, and in sight
Of those ribb'd wind-streaks running into white.
If I the death of Love had deeply plann'd,
I never could have made it half so sure,
As by the unblest kisses which upbraid
The full-waked sense; or failing that, degrade!
'Tis morning: but no morning can restore

What we have forfeited. I see no sin:
The wrong is mix'd. In tragic life, God wot,
No villain need be! Passions spin the plot:
We are betray'd by what is false within.
                              GEORGE MEREDITH (1828–1909)

879   LUCIFER IN STARLIGHT
On a starr'd night Prince Lucifer uprose.
  Tired of his dark dominion swung the fiend
  Above the rolling ball in cloud part screen'd,
Where sinners hugg'd their spectre of repose.
Poor prey to his hot fit of pride were those.
  And now upon his western wing he lean'd,
  Now his huge bulk o'er Afric's sands careen'd,
Now the black planet shadow'd Arctic snows.
Soaring through wider zones that prick'd his scars
  With memory of the old revolt from Awe,
He reach'd a middle height, and at the stars,
Which are the brain of heaven, he look'd, and sank.
Around the ancient track march'd, rank on rank,
  The army of unalterable law.
                              GEORGE MEREDITH (1828–1909)

880   LOVE
The fierce exulting worlds, the motes in rays,
  The churlish thistles, scented briers,
The wind-swept bluebells on the sunny braes,
  Down to the central fires,

Exist alike in Love. Love is a sea
  Filling all the abysses dim
Of lornest space, in whose deeps regally
  Suns and their bright broods swim.

This mighty sea of Love, with wondrous tides,
  Is sternly just to sun and grain;
'Tis laving at this moment Saturn's sides,
  'Tis in my blood and brain.

All things have something more than barren use;
  There is a scent upon the brier,
A tremulous splendour in the autumn dews,
  Cold morns are fringed with fire.

The clodded earth goes up in sweet-breath'd flowers;
  In music dies poor human speech,
And into beauty blow those hearts of ours
  When Love is born in each.

Daisies are white upon the churchyard sod,
  Sweet tears the clouds lean down and give.
The world is very lovely. O my God,
  I thank Thee that I live!
                              ALEXANDER SMITH (1829–1867)

BARBARA 881

    On the Sabbath-day,
    Through the churchyard old and gray,
Over the crisp and yellow leaves I held my rustling way;
And amid the words of mercy, falling on my soul like balms,
'Mid the gorgeous storms of music—in the mellow organ-calms,
'Mid the upward-streaming prayers, and the rich and solemn psalms,
    I stood careless, Barbara.

    My heart was otherwhere,
    While the organ shook the air,
And the priest, with outspread hands, bless'd the people with a prayer;
But when rising to go homeward, with a mild and saintlike shine
Gleam'd a face of airy beauty with its heavenly eyes on mine—
Gleam'd and vanish'd in a moment—O that face was surely thine
    Out of heaven, Barbara!

    O pallid, pallid face!
    O earnest eyes of grace!
When last I saw thee, dearest, it was in another place.
You came running forth to meet me with my love-gift on your wrist:
The flutter of a long white dress, then all was lost in mist—
A purple stain of agony was on the mouth I kiss'd,
    That wild morning, Barbara.

    I search'd, in my despair,
    Sunny noon and midnight air;
I could not drive away the thought that you were lingering there.
O many and many a winter night I sat when you were gone,
My worn face buried in my hands, beside the fire alone—
Within the dripping churchyard, the rain plashing on your stone,
    You were sleeping, Barbara.

    'Mong angels, do you think
    Of the precious golden link
I clasp'd around your happy arm while sitting by yon brink?
Or when that night of gliding dance, of laughter and guitars,
Was emptied of its music, and we watch'd, through lattice-bars,
The silent midnight heaven creeping o'er us with its stars,
    Till the day broke, Barbara?

    In the years I've changed;
    Wild and far my heart has ranged,
And many sins and errors now have been on me avenged;
But to you I have been faithful whatsoever good I lack'd:
I loved you, and above my life still hangs that love intact—
Your love the trembling rainbow, I the reckless cataract.
    Still I love you. Barbara.

Yet, Love, I am unblest;
  With many doubts opprest,
I wander like the desert wind without a place of rest.
Could I but win you for an hour from off that starry shore,
The hunger of my soul were still'd; for Death hath told you more
Than the melancholy world doth know—things deeper than all lore
  You could teach me, Barbara.

  In vain, in vain, in vain!
  You will never come again.
There droops upon the dreary hills a mournful fringe of rain;
The gloaming closes slowly round, loud winds are in the tree,
Round selfish shores for ever moans the hurt and wounded sea;
There is no rest upon the earth, peace is with Death and thee—
  Barbara!

ALEXANDER SMITH (1829–1867)

882 BRIDE SONG
  Too late for love, too late for joy,
    Too late, too late!
  You loiter'd on the road too long,
    You trifled at the gate:
  The enchanted dove upon her branch
    Died without a mate;
  The enchanted princess in her tower
    Slept, died, behind the grate;
  Her heart was starving all this while
    You made it wait.

  Ten years ago, five years ago,
    One year ago,
  Even then you had arrived in time,
    Though somewhat slow;
  Then you had known her living face
    Which now you cannot know:
  The frozen fountain would have leap'd,
    The buds gone on to blow,
  The warm south wind would have awaked
    To melt the snow.

  Is she fair now as she lies?
    Once she was fair;
  Meet queen for any kingly king,
    With gold-dust on her hair.
  Now there are poppies in her locks,
    White poppies she must wear;
  Must wear a veil to shroud her face
    And the want graven there:
  Or is the hunger fed at length,
    Cast off the care?

We never saw her with a smile
  Or with a frown;
Her bed seem'd never soft to her,
  Though toss'd of down;
She little heeded what she wore,
  Kirtle, or wreath, or gown;
We think her white brows often ached
  Beneath her crown,
Till silvery hairs show'd in her locks
  That used to be so brown.

We never heard her speak in haste:
  Her tones were sweet,
And modulated just so much
  As it was meet:
Her heart sat silent through the noise
  And concourse of the street.
There was no hurry in her hands,
  No hurry in her feet;
There was no bliss drew nigh to her,
  That she might run to greet.

You should have wept her yesterday,
  Wasting upon her bed:
But wherefore should you weep to-day
  That she is dead?
Lo, we who love weep not to-day,
  But crown her royal head.
Let be these poppies that we strew,
  Your roses are too red:
Let be these poppies, not for you
  Cut down and spread.
                CHRISTINA GEORGINA ROSSETTI (1830–1894)
                         from "The Prince's Progress"

A BIRTHDAY   883
My heart is like a singing bird
  Whose nest is in a water'd shoot;
My heart is like an apple-tree
  Whose boughs are bent with thick-set fruit;
My heart is like a rainbow shell
  That paddles in a halcyon sea;
My heart is gladder than all these,
  Because my love is come to me.

Raise me a daïs of silk and down;
  Hang it with vair and purple dyes;
Carve it in doves and pomegranates,
  And peacocks with a hundred eyes;
Work it in gold and silver grapes,
  In leaves and silver fleurs-de-lys;
Because the birthday of my life
  Is come, my love is come to me.
                CHRISTINA GEORGINA ROSSETTI (1830–1894)

884 SONG

When I am dead, my dearest,
  Sing no sad songs for me;
Plant thou no roses at my head,
  Nor shady cypress tree:
Be the green grass above me
  With showers and dewdrops wet;
And if thou wilt, remember,
  And if thou wilt, forget.

I shall not see the shadows,
  I shall not feel the rain;
I shall not hear the nightingale
  Sing on, as if in pain;
And dreaming through the twilight
  That doth not rise nor set,
Haply I may remember,
  And haply may forget.
            CHRISTINA GEORGINA ROSSETTI (1830–1894)

885 TWICE

I took my heart in my hand
  (O my love, O my love),
I said: Let me fall or stand,
  Let me live or die,
But this once hear me speak
  (O my love, O my love)—
Yet a woman's words are weak;
  You should speak, not I.

You took my heart in your hand
  With a friendly smile,
With a critical eye you scann'd,
  Then set it down,
And said, "It is still unripe,
  Better wait awhile;
Wait while the skylarks pipe,
  Till the corn grows brown."
As you set it down it broke—
  Broke, but I did not wince;
I smiled at the speech you spoke,
  At your judgement I heard:
But I have not often smiled
  Since then, nor question'd since,
Nor cared for cornflowers wild,
  Nor sung with the singing bird.

I take my heart in my hand,
  O my God, O my God,
My broken heart in my hand:
  Thou hast seen, judge Thou.

My hope was written on sand,
  O my God, O my God:
Now let thy judgement stand—
  Yea, judge me now.

This contemn'd of a man,
  This marr'd one heedless day,
This heart take thou to scan
  Both within and without:
Refine with fire its gold,
  Purge Thou its dross away—
Yea, hold it in Thy hold,
  Whence none can pluck it out.

I take my heart in my hand—
  I shall not die, but live—
Before Thy face I stand;
  I, for Thou callest such:
All that I have I bring,
  All that I am I give,
Smile Thou and I shall sing,
  But shall not question much.
            CHRISTINA GEORGINA ROSSETTI (1830–1894)

UPHILL   886

Does the road wind uphill all the way?
  Yes, to the very end.
Will the day's journey take the whole long day?
  From morn to night, my friend.

But is there for the night a resting-place?
  A roof for when the slow, dark hours begin.
May not the darkness hide it from my face?
  You cannot miss that inn.

Shall I meet other wayfarers at night?
  Those who have gone before.
Then must I knock, or call when just in sight?
  They will not keep you waiting at that door.

Shall I find comfort, travel-sore and weak?
  Of labour you shall find the sum.
Will there be beds for me and all who seek?
  Yea, beds for all who come.
            CHRISTINA GEORGINA ROSSETTI (1830–1894)

PASSING AWAY   887

Passing away, saith the World, passing away:
Chances, beauty and youth sapp'd day by day:
Thy life never continueth in one stay.
Is the eye waxen dim, is the dark hair changing to gray
That hath won neither laurel nor bay?
I shall clothe myself in Spring and bud in May:
Thou, root-stricken, shalt not rebuild thy decay
On my bosom for aye.
Then I answer'd: Yea.

Passing away, saith my Soul, passing away:
With its burden of fear and hope, of labour and play,
Hearken what the past doth witness and say:
Rust in thy gold, a moth is in thine array,
A canker is in thy bud, thy leaf must decay.
At midnight, at cockcrow, at morning, one certain day,
Lo, the Bridegroom shall come and shall not delay:
Watch thou and pray.
Then I answer'd: Yea.

Passing away, saith my God, passing away:
Winter passeth after the long delay:
New grapes on the vine, new figs on the tender spray,
Turtle calleth turtle in Heaven's May.
Though I tarry, wait for me, trust me, watch and pray.
Arise, come away; night is past, and lo, it is day;
My love, my sister, my spouse, thou shalt hear me say—
Then I answer'd: Yea.
Christina Georgina Rossetti (1830–1894)

888   Marvel of Marvels

Marvel of marvels, if I myself shall behold
With mine own eyes my King in His city of gold;
Where the least of lambs is spotless white in the fold,
Where the least and last of saints in spotless white is stoled,
Where the dimmest head beyond a moon is aureoled.
O saints, my beloved, now mouldering to mould in the mould,
Shall I see you lift your heads, see your cerements unroll'd,
See with these very eyes? who now in darkness and cold
Tremble for the midnight cry, the rapture, the tale untold,—
The Bridegroom cometh, cometh, His Bride to enfold!

Cold it is, my belovèd, since your funeral bell was toll'd:
Cold it is, O my King, how cold alone on the wold!
Christina Georgina Rossetti (1830–1894)

889   Is it Well with the Child?

   Safe where I cannot die yet,
     Safe where I hope to lie too,
   Safe from the fume and the fret;
       You, and you,
     Whom I never forget.
   Safe from the frost and the snow,
     Safe from the storm and the sun,
   Safe where the seeds wait to grow
       One by one,
     And to come back in blow.
Christina Georgina Rossetti (1830–1894)

890   Remember

Remember me when I am gone away,
  Gone far away into the silent land;
  When you can no more hold me by the hand,
Nor I half turn to go, yet turning stay.

Remember me when no more day by day
   You tell me of our future that you plann'd:
   Only remember me; you understand
It will be late to counsel then or pray.
Yet if you should forget me for a while
   And afterwards remember, do not grieve:
   For if the darkness and corruption leave
   A vestige of the thoughts that once I had,
Better by far you should forget and smile
   Than that you should remember and be sad.
                   CHRISTINA GEORGINA ROSSETTI (1830–1894)

ALOOF   891

The irresponsive silence of the land,
   The irresponsive sounding of the sea,
   Speak both one message of one sense to me:—
Aloof, aloof, we stand aloof, so stand
Thou too aloof, bound with the flawless band
   Of inner solitude; we bind not thee;
   But who from thy self-chain shall set thee free?
What heart shall touch thy heart? What hand thy hand?
And I am sometimes proud and sometimes meek,
   And sometimes I remember days of old
When fellowship seem'd not so far to seek,
   And all the world and I seem'd much less cold,
   And at the rainbow's foot lay surely gold,
And hope felt strong, and life itself not weak.
                   CHRISTINA GEORGINA ROSSETTI (1830–1894)

REST   892

O Earth, lie heavily upon her eyes;
   Seal her sweet eyes weary of watching, Earth;
   Lie close around her; leave no room for mirth
With its harsh laughter, nor for sound of sighs.
She hath no questions, she hath no replies,
   Hush'd in and curtain'd with a blessèd dearth
   Of all that irk'd her from the hour of birth;
With stillness that is almost Paradise.
Darkness more clear than noonday holdeth her,
   Silence more musical than any song;
Even her very heart has ceased to stir:
Until the morning of Eternity
   Her rest shall not begin nor end, but be;
   And when she wakes she will not think it long.
                   CHRISTINA GEORGINA ROSSETTI (1830–1894)

DORA   893

She knelt upon her brother's grave,
   My little girl of six years old—
He used to be so good and brave,
   The sweetest lamb of all our fold;
He used to shout, he used to sing,
   Of all our tribe the little king—
And so unto the turf her ear she laid,
To hark if still in that dark place he play'd.

No sound! no sound!
Death's silence was profound;
And horror crept
Into her aching heart, and Dora wept.
If this is as it ought to be,
My God, I leave it unto Thee.
                    THOMAS EDWARD BROWN (1830–1897)

894   JESSIE

When Jessie comes with her soft breast,
  And yields the golden keys,
Then is it as if God caress'd
  Twin babes upon His knees—
Twin babes that, each to other press'd,
Just feel the Father's arms, wherewith they both are bless'd.

But when I think if we must part,
  And all this personal dream be fled—
O then my heart! O then my useless heart!
  Would God that thou wert dead—
A clod insensible to joys and ills—
A stone remote in some bleak gully of the hills!
                    THOMAS EDWARD BROWN (1830–1897)

895   SALVE!

To live within a cave—it is most good;
    But, if God make a day,
    And some one come, and say,
"Lo! I have gather'd faggots in the wood!"
    E'en let him stay,
And light a fire, and fan a temporal mood!

So sit till morning! when the light is grown
    That he the path can read,
    Then bid the man God-speed!
His morning is not thine: yet must thou own
They have a cheerful warmth—those ashes on the stone.
                    THOMAS EDWARD BROWN (1830–1897)

896   MY GARDEN

    A garden is a lovesome thing, God wot!
      Rose plot,
      Fringed pool,
    Fern'd grot—
      The veriest school
      Of peace; and yet the fool
    Contends that God is not—
Not God! in gardens! when the eve is cool?
      Nay, but I have a sign;
    'Tis very sure God walks in mine.
                    THOMAS EDWARD BROWN (1830–1897)

A NIGHT IN ITALY

Sweet are the rosy memories of the lips
   That first kiss'd ours, albeit they kiss no more:
Sweet is the sight of sunset-sailing ships,
   Altho' they leave us on a lonely shore:
Sweet are familiar songs, tho' Music dips
   Her hollow shell in Thought's forlornest wells:
   And sweet, tho' sad, the sound of midnight bells
When the oped casement with the night-rain drips.

There is a pleasure which is born of pain:
   The grave of all things hath its violet.
Else why, thro' days which never come again,
   Roams Hope with that strange longing, like Regret?
Why put the posy in the cold dead hand?
   Why plant the rose above the lonely grave?
   Why bring the corpse across the salt sea-wave?
Why deem the dead more near in native land?

Thy name hath been a silence in my life
   So long, it falters upon language now,
O more to me than sister or than wife
   Once ... and now—nothing! It is hard to know
That such things have been, and are not; and yet
   Life loiters, keeps a pulse at even measure,
   And goes upon its business and its pleasure,
And knows not all the depths of its regret....

Ah, could the memory cast her spots, as do
   The snake's brood theirs in spring! and be once more
Wholly renew'd, to dwell i' the time that's new,
   With no reiterance of those pangs of yore.
Peace, peace! My wild song will go wandering
   Too wantonly, down paths a private pain
   Hath trodden bare. What was it jarr'd the strain?
Some crush'd illusion, left with crumpled wing

Tangled in Music's web of twined strings—
   That started that false note, and crack'd the tune
In its beginning. Ah, forgotten things
   Stumble back strangely! and the ghost of June
Stands by December's fire, cold, cold! and puts
   The last spark out.—How could I sing aright
   With those old airs haunting me all the night
And those old steps that sound when daylight shuts?

For back she comes, and moves reproachfully,
   The mistress of my moods, and looks bereft
(Cruel to the last!) as tho' 'twere I, not she,
   That did the wrong, and broke the spell, and left
Memory comfortless.—Away! away!
   Phantoms, about whose brows the bindweed clings,
   Hopeless regret! In thinking of these things
Some men have lost their minds, and others may.

Yet, O for one deep draught in this dull hour!
  One deep, deep draught of the departed time!
O for one brief strong pulse of ancient power,
  To beat and breathe thro' all the valves of rhyme!
Thou, Memory, with thy downward eyes, that art
  The cup-bearer of gods, pour deep and long,
  Brim all the vacant chalices of song
With health! Droop down thine urn. I hold my heart

One draught of what I shall not taste again
  Save when my brain with thy dark wine is brimm'd,—
One draught! and then straight onward, spite of pain,
  And spite of all things changed, with gaze undimm'd,
Love's footsteps thro' the waning Past to explore
  Undaunted; and to carve in the wan light
  Of Hope's last outposts, on Song's utmost height,
The sad resemblance of an hour or more.

Midnight, and love, and youth, and Italy!
  Love in the land where love most lovely seems!
Land of my love, tho' I be far from thee,
  Lend, for love's sake, the light of thy moonbeams,
The spirit of thy cypress-groves and all
  Thy dark-eyed beauty for a little while
  To my desire. Yet once more let her smile
Fall o'er me: o'er me let her long hair fall....

Under the blessèd darkness unreproved
  We were alone, in that best hour of time
Which first reveal'd to us how much we loved,
  'Neath the thick starlight. The young night sublime
Hung trembling o'er us. At her feet I knelt,
  And gazed up from her feet into her eyes.
  Her face was bow'd: we breathed each other's sighs:
We did not speak: not move: we look'd: we felt.

The night said not a word. The breeze was dead.
  The leaf lay without whispering on the tree,
As I lay at her feet. Droop'd was her head:
  One hand in mine: and one still pensively
Went wandering through my hair. We were together.
  How? Where? What matter? Somewhere in a dream,
  Drifting, slow drifting down a wizard stream:
Whither? Together: then what matter whither?

It was enough for me to clasp her hand:
  To blend with her love-looks my own: no more.
Enough (with thoughts like ships that cannot land,
  Blown by faint winds about a magic shore)
To realize, in each mysterious feeling,
  The droop of the warm cheek so near my own:
  The cool white arm about my shoulder thrown:
Those exquisite fair feet where I was kneeling.

How little know they life's divinest bliss,
   That know not to possess and yet refrain!
Let the young Psyche roam, a fleeting kiss:
   Grasp it—a few poor grains of dust remain.
See how those floating flowers, the butterflies,
   Hover the garden thro', and take no root!
   Desire for ever hath a flying foot:
Free pleasure comes and goes beneath the skies.

Close not thy hand upon the innocent joy
   That trusts itself within thy reach. It may,
Or may not, linger. Thou canst but destroy
   The wingèd wanderer. Let it go or stay.
Love thou the rose, yet leave it on its stem.
   Think! Midas starved by turning all to gold.
   Blessèd are those that spare, and that withhold;
Because the whole world shall be trusted them.

The foolish Faun pursues the unwilling Nymph
   That culls her flowers beside the precipice
Or dips her shining ankles in the lymph:
   But, just when she must perish or be his,
Heaven puts an arm out. She is safe. The shore
   Gains some new fountain; or the lilied lawn
   A rarer sort of rose: but ah, poor Faun!
To thee she shall be changed for evermore.

Chase not too close the fading rapture. Leave
   To Love his long auroras, slowly seen.
Be ready to release as to receive.
   Deem those the nearest, soul to soul, between
Whose lips yet lingers reverence on a sigh.
   Judge what thy sense can reach not, most thine own,
   If once thy soul hath seized it. The unknown
Is life to love, religion, poetry.

The moon had set. There was not any light,
   Save of the lonely legion'd watch-stars pale
In outer air, and what by fits made bright
   Hot oleanders in a rosy vale
Search'd by the lamping fly, whose little spark
   Went in and out, like passion's bashful hope.
   Meanwhile the sleepy globe began to slope
A ponderous shoulder sunward thro' the dark.

And the night pass'd in beauty like a dream.
   Aloof in those dark heavens paused Destiny,
With her last star descending in the gleam
   Of the cold morrow, from the emptied sky.
The hour, the distance from her old self, all
   The novelty and loneness of the place
   Had left a lovely awe on that fair face,
And all the land grew strange and magical.

As droops some billowy cloud to the crouch'd hill,
   Heavy with all heaven's tears, for all earth's care,
She droop'd unto me, without force or will,
   And sank upon my bosom, murmuring there
A woman's inarticulate passionate words.
   O moment of all moments upon earth!
   O life's supreme! How worth, how wildly worth,
Whole worlds of flame, to know this world affords.

What even Eternity can not restore!
   When all the ends of life take hands and meet
Round centres of sweet fire. Ah, never more,
   Ah never, shall the bitter with the sweet
Be mingled so in the pale after-years!
   One hour of life immortal spirits possess.
   This drains the world, and leaves but weariness,
And parching passion, and perplexing tears.

Sad is it, that we cannot even keep
   That hour to sweeten life's last toil: but Youth
Grasps all, and leaves us: and when we would weep,
   We dare not let our tears fall, lest, in truth,
They fall upon our work which must be done.
   And so we bind up our torn hearts from breaking:
   Our eyes from weeping, and our brows from aching:
And follow the long pathway all alone.
      EDWARD ROBERT BULWER LYTTON, EARL OF LYTTON (1831–1892)

898   THE LAST WISH
   Since all that I can ever do for thee
   Is to do nothing, this my prayer must be:
   That thou mayst never guess nor ever see
   The all-endured this nothing-done costs me.
      EDWARD ROBERT BULWER LYTTON, EARL OF LYTTON (1831–1892)

899   IN THE TRAIN
   As we rush, as we rush in the Train,
      The trees and the houses go wheeling back,
   But the starry heavens above the plain
      Come flying on our track.

   All the beautiful stars of the sky,
      The silver doves of the forest of Night,
   Over the dull earth swarm and fly,
      Companions of our flight.

   We will rush ever on without fear;
      Let the goal be far, the flight be fleet!
   For we carry the Heavens with us, dear,
      While the Earth slips from our feet!
               JAMES THOMSON (1834–1882)

Sunday up the River 900

My love o'er the water bends dreaming;
  It glideth and glideth away:
She sees there her own beauty, gleaming
  Through shadow and ripple and spray.

O tell her, thou murmuring river,
  As past her your light wavelets roll,
How steadfast that image for ever
  Shines pure in pure depths of my soul.

                      JAMES THOMSON (1834–1882)

Gifts 901

Give a man a horse he can ride,
  Give a man a boat he can sail;
And his rank and wealth, his strength and health,
  On sea nor shore shall fail.

Give a man a pipe he can smoke,
  Give a man a book he can read:
And his home is bright with a calm delight,
  Though the room be poor indeed.

Give a man a girl he can love,
  As I, O my love, love thee;
And his heart is great with the pulse of Fate,
  At home, on land, on sea.

                      JAMES THOMSON (1834–1882)

The Vine 902

The wine of Love is music,
  And the feast of Love is song:
And when Love sits down to the banquet,
  Love sits long:

Sits long and arises drunken,
  But not with the feast and the wine;
He reeleth with his own heart,
  That great, rich Vine.

                      JAMES THOMSON (1834–1882)

Summer Dawn 903

Pray but one prayer for me 'twixt thy closed lips,
  Think but one thought of me up in the stars.
The summer night waneth, the morning light slips
  Faint and gray 'twixt the leaves of the aspen, betwixt the cloud-bars,
That are patiently waiting there for the dawn:
  Patient and colourless, though Heaven's gold
Waits to float through them along with the sun.
Far out in the meadows, above the young corn,
  The heavy elms wait, and restless and cold
The uneasy wind rises; the roses are dun;
Through the long twilight they pray for the dawn

Round the lone house in the midst of the corn.
    Speak but one word to me over the corn,
    Over the tender, bow'd locks of the corn.
                            WILLIAM MORRIS (1834–1896)

904   LOVE IS ENOUGH
Love is enough: though the World be a-waning,
And the woods have no voice but the voice of complaining,
   Though the sky be too dark for dim eyes to discover
The gold-cups and daisies fair blooming thereunder,
Though the hills be held shadows, and the sea a dark wonder,
   And this day draw a veil over all deeds pass'd over,
Yet their hands shall not tremble, their feet shall not falter;
The void shall not weary, the fear shall not alter
   These lips and these eyes of the loved and the lover.
                            WILLIAM MORRIS (1834–1896)

905   THE NYMPH'S SONG TO HYLAS
        I know a little garden-close
        Set thick with lily and red rose,
        Where I would wander if I might
        From dewy dawn to dewy night,
        And have one with me wandering.

        And though within it no birds sing,
        And though no pillar'd house is there,
        And though the apple boughs are bare
        Of fruit and blossom, would to God,
        Her feet upon the green grass trod,
        And I beheld them as before!

        There comes a murmur from the shore,
        And in the place two fair streams are,
        Drawn from the purple hills afar,
        Drawn down unto the restless sea;
        The hills whose flowers ne'er fed the bee,
        The shore no ship has ever seen,
        Still beaten by the billows green,
        Whose murmur comes unceasingly
        Unto the place for which I cry.

        For which I cry both day and night,
        For which I let slip all delight,
        That maketh me both deaf and blind,
        Careless to win, unskill'd to find,
        And quick to lose what all men seek.

        Yet tottering as I am, and weak,
        Still have I left a little breath
        To seek within the jaws of death
        An entrance to that happy place;
        To seek the unforgotten face
        Once seen, once kiss'd, once reft from me
        Anigh the murmuring of the sea.
                            WILLIAM MORRIS (1834–1896)

THE WATER-NYMPH AND THE BOY 906

I flung me round him,
I drew him under;
I clung, I drown'd him,
My own white wonder!...

Father and mother,
Weeping and wild,
Came to the forest,
Calling the child,
Came from the palace,
Down to the pool,
Calling my darling,
My beautiful!
Under the water,
Cold and so pale!
Could it be love made
Beauty to fail?

Ah me for mortals!
In a few moons,
If I had left him,
After some Junes
He would have faded,
Faded away,
He, the young monarch, whom
All would obey,
Fairer than day;
Alien to springtime,
Joyless and gray,
He would have faded,
Faded away,
Moving a mockery,
Scorn'd of the day!
Now I have taken him
All in his prime,
Saved from slow poisoning
Pitiless Time,
Fill'd with his happiness,
One with the prime,
Saved from the cruel
Dishonour of Time.
Laid him, my beautiful,
Laid him to rest,
Loving, adorable,
Softly to rest,
Here in my crystalline,
Here in my breast!

RODEN BERKELEY WRIOTHESLEY NOEL (1834–1894)

907   THE OLD
They are waiting on the shore
　　For the bark to take them home:
They will toil and grieve no more;
　　The hour for release hath come.

All their long life lies behind
　　Like a dimly blending dream:
There is nothing left to bind
　　To the realms that only seem.

They are waiting for the boat;
　　There is nothing left to do:
What was near them grows remote,
　　Happy silence falls like dew;
Now the shadowy bark is come,
And the weary may go home.

By still water they would rest
　　In the shadow of the tree:
After battle sleep is best,
　　After noise, tranquillity.
　　　　RODEN BERKELEY WRIOTHESLEY NOEL (1834–1894)

908   MEET WE NO ANGELS, PANSIE?
Came, on a Sabbath noon, my sweet,
　　In white, to find her lover;
The grass grew proud beneath her feet,
　　The green elm-leaves above her:—
　　　Meet we no angels, Pansie?

She said, "We meet no angels now";
　　And soft lights stream'd upon her;
And with white hand she touch'd a bough;
　　She did it that great honour:—
　　　What! meet no angels, Pansie?

O sweet brown hat, brown hair, brown eyes,
　　Down-dropp'd brown eyes, so tender!
Then what said I? Gallant replies
　　Seem flattery, and offend her:—
　　　But—meet no angels, Pansie?
　　　　　　　THOMAS ASHE (1836–1889)

909   TO TWO BEREAVED
You must be sad; for though it is to Heaven,
'Tis hard to yield a little girl of seven.
Alas, for me 'tis hard my grief to rule,
Who only met her as she went to school;

Who never heard the little lips so sweet
Say even "Good-morning," though our eyes would meet
As whose would fain be friends! How must you sigh,
Sick for your loss, when even so sad am I,
Who never clasp'd the small hands any day!
Fair flowers thrive round the little grave, I pray.
THOMAS ASHE (1836–1889)

910 WASSAIL CHORUS AT THE MERMAID TAVERN

    Christmas knows a merry, merry place,
      Where he goes with fondest face,
    Brightest eye, brightest hair:
      Tell the Mermaid where is that one place,
        Where?

Raleigh. 'Tis by Devon's glorious halls,
    Whence, dear Ben, I come again:
  Bright of golden roofs and walls—
    El Dorado's rare domain—
  Seem those halls when sunlight launches
    Shafts of gold thro' leafless branches,
  Where the winter's feathery mantle blanches
    Field and farm and lane.

CHORUS. Christmas knows a merry, merry place, &c.

Drayton. 'Tis where Avon's wood-sprites weave
    Through the boughs a lace of rime,
  While the bells of Christmas Eve
    Fling for Will the Stratford-chime
  O'er the river-flags emboss'd
    Rich with flowery runes of frost—
  O'er the meads where snowy tufts are toss'd—
    Strains of olden time.

CHORUS. Christmas knows a merry, merry place, &c.

Shakespeare's Friend.
    'Tis, methinks, on any ground
      Where our Shakespeare's feet are set.
    There smiles Christmas, holly-crown'd
      With his blithest coronet:
    Friendship's face he loveth well:
      'Tis a countenance whose spell
    Sheds a balm o'er every mead and dell
      Where we used to fret.

CHORUS. Christmas knows a merry, merry place, &c.

Heywood. More than all the pictures, Ben,
    Winter weaves by wood or stream,
  Christmas loves our London, when

                        Rise thy clouds of wassail-steam—
                    Clouds like these, that, curling, take
                        Forms of faces gone, and wake
                    Many a lay from lips we loved, and make
                        London like a dream.

CHORUS. Christmas knows a merry, merry place, &c.

*Ben Jonson*Love's old songs shall never die,
                    Yet the new shall suffer proof:
                Love's old drink of Yule brew I
                    Wassail for new love's behoof.
                        Drink the drink I brew, and sing
                        Till the berried branches swing,
                        Till our song make all the Mermaid ring—
                    Yea, from rush to roof.

                            FINALE.
                Christmas loves this merry, merry place;
                    Christmas saith with fondest face,
                    Brightest eye, brightest hair:
                "Ben, the drink tastes rare of sack and mace:
                    Rare!"
                                    THEODORE WATTS-DUNTON (1836–1914)

911   CHORUS FROM "ATALANTA"

When the hounds of spring are on winter's traces,
    The mother of months in meadow or plain
Fills the shadows and windy places
    With lisp of leaves and ripple of rain;
And the brown bright nightingale amorous
Is half assuaged for Itylus,
For the Thracian ships and the foreign faces.
    The tongueless vigil, and all the pain.

Come with bows bent and with emptying of quivers,
    Maiden most perfect, lady of light,
With a noise of winds and many rivers,
    With a clamour of waters, and with might;
Bind on thy sandals, O thou most fleet,
Over the splendour and speed of thy feet;
For the faint east quickens, the wan west shivers,
    Round the feet of the day and the feet of the night.

Where shall we find her, how shall we sing to her,
    Fold our hands round her knees, and cling?
O that man's heart were as fire and could spring to her,
    Fire, or the strength of the streams that spring!
For the stars and the winds are unto her
As raiment, as songs of the harp-player;
For the risen stars and the fallen cling to her,
    And the southwest-wind and the west-wind sing.

For winter's rains and ruins are over,
   And all the season of snows and sins;
The days dividing lover and lover,
   The light that loses, the night that wins;
And time remember'd is grief forgotten,
And frosts are slain and flowers begotten,
And in green underwood and cover
   Blossom by blossom the spring begins.

The full streams feed on flower of rushes,
   Ripe grasses trammel a travelling foot,
The faint fresh flame of the young year flushes
   From leaf to flower and flower to fruit;
And fruit and leaf are as gold and fire,
And the oat is heard above the lyre,
And the hoofèd heel of a satyr crushes
   The chestnut-husk at the chestnut-root.

And Pan by noon and Bacchus by night,
   Fleeter of foot than the fleet-foot kid,
Follows with dancing and fills with delight
   The Maenad and the Bassarid;
And soft as lips that laugh and hide
The laughing leaves of the trees divide,
And screen from seeing and leave in sight
   The god pursuing, the maiden hid.

The ivy falls with the Bacchanal's hair
   Over her eyebrows hiding her eyes;
The wild vine slipping down leaves bare
   Her bright breast shortening into sighs;
The wild vine slips with the weight of its leaves,
But the berried ivy catches and cleaves
To the limbs that glitter, the feet that scare
   The wolf that follows, the fawn that flies.
               ALGERNON CHARLES SWINBURNE (1837–1909)

HERTHA

I am that which began;
    Out of me the years roll;
    Out of me God and man;
    I am equal and whole;
God changes, and man, and the form of them bodily;
I am the soul.

    Before ever land was,
      Before ever the sea,
    Or soft hair of the grass,
      Or fair limbs of the tree,
Or the flesh-colour'd fruit of my branches,
I was, and thy soul was in me.

   First life on my sources
    First drifted and swam;
   Out of me are the forces
    That save it or damn;
Out of me man and woman, and wild-beast and bird:
before God was, I am.

   Beside or above me
    Naught is there to go;
   Love or unlove me,
    Unknow me or know,
I am that which unloves me and loves;
I am stricken, and I am the blow.

   I the mark that is miss'd
    And the arrows that miss,
   I the mouth that is kiss'd
    And the breath in the kiss,
The search, and the sought, and the seeker,
the soul and the body that is.

   I am that thing which blesses
    My spirit elate;
   That which caresses
    With hands uncreate
My limbs unbegotten that measure
the length of the measure of fate.

   But what thing dost thou now,
    Looking Godward, to cry,
   "I am I, thou art thou,
    I am low, thou art high"?
I am thou, whom thou seekest to find him;
find thou but thyself, thou art I.

   I the grain and the furrow,
    The plough-cloven clod
   And the ploughshare drawn thorough,
    The germ and the sod,
The deed and the doer, the seed and the sower,
the dust which is God.

   Hast thou known how I fashion'd thee,
    Child, underground?
   Fire that impassion'd thee,
    Iron that bound,
Dim changes of water, what thing of all these
hast thou known of or found?

   Canst thou say in thine heart
    Thou hast seen with thine eyes
   With what cunning of art
    Thou wast wrought in what wise,
By what force of what stuff thou wast shapen,
and shown on my breast to the skies?

Who hath given, who hath sold it thee,
    Knowledge of me?
Has the wilderness told it thee?
    Hast thou learnt of the sea?
Hast thou communed in spirit with night?
Have the winds taken counsel with thee?

Have I set such a star
    To show light on thy brow
That thou sawest from afar
    What I show to thee now?
Have ye spoken as brethren together,
the sun and the mountains and thou?

What is here, dost thou know it?
    What was, hast thou known?
Prophet nor poet
    Nor tripod nor throne
Nor spirit nor flesh can make answer,
but only thy mother alone.

Mother, not maker,
    Born, and not made;
Though her children forsake her,
    Allured or afraid,
Praying prayers to the God of their fashion,
she stirs not for all that have pray'd.

A creed is a rod,
    And a crown is of night;
But this thing is God,
    To be man with thy might,
To grow straight in the strength of thy spirit,
and live out thy life as the light.

I am in thee to save thee,
    As my soul in thee saith;
Give thou as I gave thee,
    Thy life-blood and breath,
Green leaves of thy labour, white flowers of thy thought,
and red fruit of thy death.

Be the ways of thy giving
    As mine were to thee;
The free life of thy living,
    Be the gift of it free;
Not as servant to lord, nor as master to slave,
shalt thou give thee to me.

   O children of banishment,
    Souls overcast,
   Were the lights ye see vanish meant
    Alway to last,
Ye would know not the sun overshining
the shadows and stars overpast.

   I that saw where ye trod
    The dim paths of the night
   Set the shadow call'd God
    In your skies to give light;
But the morning of manhood is risen,
and the shadowless soul is in sight.

   The tree many-rooted
    That swells to the sky
   With frondage red-fruited,
    The life-tree am I;
In the buds of your lives is the sap of my leaves:
ye shall live and not die.

   But the Gods of your fashion
    That take and that give,
   In their pity and passion
    That scourge and forgive,
They are worms that are bred in the bark that falls off;
they shall die and not live.

   My own blood is what stanches
    The wounds in my bark;
   Stars caught in my branches
    Make day of the dark,
And are worshipp'd as suns till the sunrise
shall tread out their fires as a spark.

   Where dead ages hide under
    The live roots of the tree,
   In my darkness the thunder
    Makes utterance of me;
In the clash of my boughs with each other ye hear
the waves sound of the sea.

   That noise is of Time,
    As his feathers are spread
   And his feet set to climb
    Through the boughs overhead,
And my foliage rings round him and rustles,
and branches are bent with his tread.

   The storm-winds of ages
    Blow through me and cease,
   The war-wind that rages,
    The spring-wind of peace,
Ere the breath of them roughen my tresses,
ere one of my blossoms increase.

All sounds of all changes,
    All shadows and lights
On the world's mountain-ranges
    And stream-riven heights,
Whose tongue is the wind's tongue and language
of storm-clouds on earth-shaking nights;

All forms of all faces,
    All works of all hands
In unsearchable places
    Of time-stricken lands,
All death and all life, and all reigns and all ruins,
drop through me as sands.

Though sore be my burden
    And more than ye know,
And my growth have no guerdon
    But only to grow,
Yet I fail not of growing for lightnings above me
or deathworms below.

These too have their part in me,
    As I too in these;
Such fire is at heart in me,
    Such sap is this tree's,
Which hath in it all sounds and all secrets
of infinite lands and of seas.

In the spring-colour'd hours
    When my mind was as May's
There brake forth of me flowers
    By centuries of days,
Strong blossoms with perfume of manhood,
shot out from my spirit as rays.

And the sound of them springing
    And smell of their shoots
Were as warmth and sweet singing
    And strength to my roots;
And the lives of my children made perfect
with freedom of soul were my fruits.

I bid you but be;
    I have need not of prayer;
I have need of you free
    As your mouths of mine air;
That my heart may be greater within me,
beholding the fruits of me fair.

>   More fair than strange fruit is
>   Of faiths ye espouse;
>   In me only the root is
>   That blooms in your boughs;
> Behold now your God that ye made you,
> to feed him with faith of your vows.
>
>   In the darkening and whitening
>   Abysses adored,
>   With dayspring and lightning
>   For lamp and for sword,
> God thunders in heaven, and his angels are red
> with the wrath of the Lord.
>
>   O my sons, O too dutiful
>   Toward Gods not of me,
>   Was not I enough beautiful?
>   Was it hard to be free?
> For behold, I am with you, am in you and of you;
> look forth now and see.
>
>   Lo, wing'd with world's wonders,
>   With miracles shod,
>   With the fires of his thunders
>   For raiment and rod,
> God trembles in heaven, and his angels are white
> with the terror of God.
>
>   For his twilight is come on him,
>   His anguish is here;
>   And his spirits gaze dumb on him,
>   Grown gray from his fear;
> And his hour taketh hold on him stricken,
> the last of his infinite year.
>
>   Thought made him and breaks him,
>   Truth slays and forgives;
>   But to you, as time takes him,
>   This new thing it gives,
> Even love, the belovèd Republic,
> that feeds upon freedom and lives.
>
>   For truth only is living,
>   Truth only is whole,
>   And the love of his giving
>   Man's polestar and pole;
> Man, pulse of my centre, and fruit of my body,
> and seed of my soul.

    One birth of my bosom;
      One beam of mine eye;
    One topmost blossom
      That scales the sky;
Man, equal and one with me,
  man that is made of me,
    man that is I.

          ALGERNON CHARLES SWINBURNE (1837–1909)

ITYLUS   913

Swallow, my sister, O sister swallow,
  How can thine heart be full of the spring?
    A thousand summers are over and dead.
What hast thou found in the spring to follow?
  What hast thou found in thine heart to sing?
    What wilt thou do when the summer is shed?

O swallow, sister, O fair swift swallow,
  Why wilt thou fly after spring to the south,
    The soft south whither thine heart is set?
Shall not the grief of the old time follow?
  Shall not the song thereof cleave to thy mouth?
    Hast thou forgotten ere I forget?

Sister, my sister, O fleet sweet swallow,
  Thy way is long to the sun and the south;
    But I, fulfill'd of my heart's desire,
Shedding my song upon height, upon hollow,
  From tawny body and sweet small mouth
    Feed the heart of the night with fire.

I the nightingale all spring through,
  O swallow, sister, O changing swallow,
    All spring through till the spring be done,
Clothed with the light of the night on the dew,
  Sing, while the hours and the wild birds follow,
    Take flight and follow and find the sun.

Sister, my sister, O soft light swallow,
  Though all things feast in the spring's guest-chamber,
    How hast thou heart to be glad thereof yet?
For where thou fliest I shall not follow,
  Till life forget and death remember,
    Till thou remember and I forget.

Swallow, my sister, O singing swallow,
  I know not how thou hast heart to sing.
    Hast thou the heart? is it all past over?
Thy lord the summer is good to follow,
  And fair the feet of thy lover the spring:
    But what wilt thou say to the spring thy lover?

O swallow, sister, O fleeting swallow,
  My heart in me is a molten ember
    And over my head the waves have met.
But thou wouldst tarry or I would follow
  Could I forget or thou remember,
    Couldst thou remember and I forget.

O sweet stray sister, O shifting swallow,
  The heart's division divideth us.
    Thy heart is light as a leaf of a tree;
But mine goes forth among sea-gulfs hollow
  To the place of the slaying of Itylus,
    The feast of Daulis, the Thracian sea.

O swallow, sister, O rapid swallow,
  I pray thee sing not a little space.
    Are not the roofs and the lintels wet?
The woven web that was plain to follow,
  The small slain body, the flower-like face,
    Can I remember if thou forget?

O sister, sister, thy first-begotten!
  The hands that cling and the feet that follow,
    The voice of the child's blood crying yet,
  Who hath remember'd me? who hath forgotten?
    Thou hast forgotten, O summer swallow,
      But the world shall end when I forget.

ALGERNON CHARLES SWINBURNE (1837–1909)

914   EARLIEST SPRING

Tossing his mane of snows in wildest eddies and tangles,
  Lion-like March cometh in, hoarse, with tempestuous breath,
Through all the moaning chimneys, and 'thwart all the hollows and angles
  Round the shuddering house, threating of winter and death.

But in my heart I feel the life of the wood and the meadow
  Thrilling the pulses that own kindred with fibres that lift
Bud and blade to the sunward, within the inscrutable shadow,
  Deep in the oak's chill core, under the gathering drift.

Nay, to earth's life in mine some prescience, or dream, or desire
  (How shall I name it aright?) comes for a moment and goes—
Rapture of life ineffable, perfect—as if in the brier,
  Leafless there by my door, trembled a sense of the rose.

WILLIAM DEAN HOWELLS (1837–1920)

915   WHAT THE BULLET SANG

O joy of creation,
    To be!
O rapture, to fly
    And be free!
Be the battle lost or won,
Though its smoke shall hide the sun,
I shall find my love—the one
    Born for me!

                    I shall know him where he stands
                            All alone,
                    With the power in his hands
                            Not o'erthrown;
                    I shall know him by his face,
                    By his godlike front and grace;
                    I shall hold him for a space
                            All my own!

                    It is he—O my love!
                            So bold!
                    It is I—all thy love
                            Foretold!
                    It is I—O love, what bliss!
                    Dost thou answer to my kiss?
                    O sweetheart! what is this
                            Lieth there so cold?
                                            BRET HARTE (1839–1902)

                            MAUREEN   916
O, you plant the pain in my heart with your wistful eyes,
        Girl of my choice, Maureen!
Will you drive me mad for the kisses your shy, sweet mouth denies,
        Maureen?

Like a walking ghost I am, and no words to woo,
        White rose of the West, Maureen:
For it's pale you are, and the fear that's on you is over me too,
        Maureen!

Sure it's one complaint that's on us, asthore, this day,
        Bride of my dreams, Maureen:
The smart of the bee that stung us his honey must cure, they say,
        Maureen!

I'll coax the light to your eyes, and the rose to your face,
        Mavourneen, my own Maureen!
When I feel the warmth of your breast, and your nest is my arm's
    embrace,
        Maureen!

O where was the King o' the World that day—only me?
        My one true love, Maureen!
And you the Queen with me there, and your throne in my heart, machree,
        Maureen!
                                        JOHN TODHUNTER (1839–1916)

                            AGHADOE   917
    There's a glade in Aghadoe, Aghadoe, Aghadoe,
        There's a green and silent glade in Aghadoe,
    Where we met, my love and I, Love's fair planet in the sky,
        O'er that sweet and silent glade in Aghadoe.

There's a glen in Aghadoe, Aghadoe, Aghadoe,
  There's a deep and secret glen in Aghadoe,
Where I hid from the eyes of the red-coats and their spies,
  That year the trouble came to Aghadoe.

O, my curse on one black heart in Aghadoe, Aghadoe,
  On Shaun Dhu, my mother's son in Aghadoe!
When your throat fries in hell's drouth, salt the flame be in your mouth,
  For the treachery you did in Aghadoe!

For they track'd me to that glen in Aghadoe, Aghadoe,
  When the price was on his head in Aghadoe:
O'er the mountain, through the wood, as I stole to him with food,
  Where in hiding lone he lay in Aghadoe.

But they never took him living in Aghadoe, Aghadoe;
  With the bullets in his heart in Aghadoe,
There he lay, the head, my breast keeps the warmth of where 'twould rest,
  Gone, to win the traitor's gold, from Aghadoe!

I walk'd to Mallow town from Aghadoe, Aghadoe,
  Brought his head from the gaol's gate to Aghadoe;
Then I cover'd him with fern, and I piled on him the cairn,
  Like an Irish King he sleeps in Aghadoe.

O, to creep into that cairn in Aghadoe, Aghadoe!
  There to rest upon his breast in Aghadoe!
Sure your dog for you could die with no truer heart than I,
  Your own love, cold on your cairn in Aghadoe.
JOHN TODHUNTER (1839–1916)

918   SONG
    O fly not, Pleasure, pleasant-hearted Pleasure;
      Fold me thy wings, I prithee, yet and stay:
          For my heart no measure
          Knows, nor other treasure
      To buy a garland for my love to-day.

    And thou, too, Sorrow, tender-hearted Sorrow,
      Thou gray-eyed mourner, fly not yet away:
          For I fain would borrow
          Thy sad weeds to-morrow,
      To make a mourning for love's yesterday.

    The voice of Pity, Time's divine dear Pity,
      Moved me to tears: I dared not say them nay,
          But passed forth from the city,
          Making thus my ditty
      Of fair love lost for ever and a day.
WILFRID SCAWEN BLUNT (1840–1922)

919   THE DESOLATE CITY
  Dark to me is the earth. Dark to me are the heavens.
    Where is she that I loved, the woman with eyes like stars?
  Desolate are the streets. Desolate is the city.
    A city taken by storm, where none are left but the slain.

Sadly I rose at dawn, undid the latch of my shutters,
  Thinking to let in light, but I only let in love.
Birds in the boughs were awake; I listen'd to their chaunting;
  Each one sang to his love; only I was alone.

This, I said in my heart, is the hour of life and of pleasure.
  Now each creature on earth has his joy, and lives in the sun,
Each in another's eyes finds light, the light of compassion,
  This is the moment of pity, this is the moment of love.

Speak, O desolate city! Speak, O silence in sadness!
  Where is she that I loved in my strength, that spoke to my soul?
Where are those passionate eyes that appeal'd to my eyes in passion?
  Where is the mouth that kiss'd me, the breast I laid to my own?

Speak, thou soul of my soul, for rage in my heart is kindled.
  Tell me, where didst thou flee in the day of destruction and fear?
See, my arms still enfold thee, enfolding thus all heaven,
  See, my desire is fulfill'd in thee, for it fills the earth.

Thus in my grief I lamented. Then turn'd I from the window,
  Turn'd to the stair, and the open door, and the empty street,
Crying aloud in my grief, for there was none to chide me,
  None to mock my weakness, none to behold my tears.

Groping I went, as blind. I sought her house, my beloved's.
  There I stopp'd at the silent door, and listen'd and tried the latch.
Love, I cried, dost thou slumber? This is no hour for slumber,
  This is the hour of love, and love I bring in my hand.

I knew the house, with its windows barr'd, and its leafless fig-tree,
  Climbing round by the doorstep, the only one in the street;
I knew where my hope had climb'd to its goal and there encircled
  All that those desolate walls once held, my beloved's heart.

There in my grief she consoled me. She loved me when I loved not.
  She put her hand in my hand, and set her lips to my lips.
She told me all her pain and show'd me all her trouble.
  I, like a fool, scarce heard, hardly return'd her kiss.

Love, thy eyes were like torches. They changed as I beheld them.
  Love, thy lips were like gems, the seal thou settest on my life.
Love, if I loved not then, behold this hour thy vengeance;
  This is the fruit of thy love and thee, the unwise grown wise.

Weeping strangled my voice. I call'd out, but none answer'd;
  Blindly the windows gazed back at me, dumbly the door;
See whom I love, who loved me, look'd not on my yearning,
  Gave me no more her hands to kiss, show'd me no more her soul.

Therefore the earth is dark to me, the sunlight blackness,
  Therefore I go in tears and alone, by night and day;
  Therefore I find no love in heaven, no light, no beauty,
  A heaven taken by storm, where none are left but the slain!
                                WILFRID SCAWEN BLUNT (1840–1922)

920   WITH ESTHER

He who has once been happy is for aye
  Out of destruction's reach. His fortune then
Holds nothing secret; and Eternity,
  Which is a mystery to other men,
Has like a woman given him its joy.
  Time is his conquest. Life, if it should fret.
Has paid him tribute. He can bear to die,
  He who has once been happy! When I set
The world before me and survey its range,
  Its mean ambitions, its scant fantasies,
The shreds of pleasure which for lack of change
  Men wrap around them and call happiness,
The poor delights which are the tale and sum
Of the world's courage in its martyrdom;

When I hear laughter from a tavern door,
  When I see crowds agape and in the rain
Watching on tiptoe and with stifled roar
  To see a rocket fired or a bull slain,
When misers handle gold, when orators
  Touch strong men's hearts with glory till they weep,
When cities deck their streets for barren wars
  Which have laid waste their youth, and when I keep
Calmly the count of my own life and see
  On what poor stuff my manhood's dreams were fed
Till I too learn'd what dole of vanity
  Will serve a human soul for daily bread,
—Then I remember that I once was young
And lived with Esther the world's gods among.
                                WILFRID SCAWEN BLUNT (1840–1922)

921   TO MANON, ON HIS FORTUNE IN LOVING HER

I did not choose thee, dearest. It was Love
That made the choice, not I. Mine eyes were blind
As a rude shepherd's who to some lone grove
His offering brings and cares not at what shrine
He bends his knee. The gifts alone were mine;
The rest was Love's. He took me by the hand,
And fired the sacrifice, and poured the wine,
And spoke the words I might not understand.
  I was unwise in all but the dear chance
Which was my fortune, and the blind desire
Which led my foolish steps to Love's abode,
And youth's sublime unreason'd prescience
Which raised an altar and inscribed in fire
Its dedication *To the Unknown God.*
                                WILFRID SCAWEN BLUNT (1840–1922)

St. Valentine's Day 922

To-day, all day, I rode upon the down,
With hounds and horsemen, a brave company
On this side in its glory lay the sea,
On that the Sussex weald, a sea of brown.
The wind was light, and brightly the sun shone,
And still we gallop'd on from gorse to gorse:
And once, when check'd, a thrush sang, and my horse
Prick'd his quick ears as to a sound unknown.
  I knew the Spring was come. I knew it even
Better than all by this, that through my chase
In bush and stone and hill and sea and heaven
I seem'd to see and follow still your face.
Your face my quarry was. For it I rode,
My horse a thing of wings, myself a god.
                    WILFRID SCAWEN BLUNT (1840–1922)

Gibraltar 923

Seven weeks of sea, and twice seven days of storm
Upon the huge Atlantic, and once more
We ride into still water and the calm
Of a sweet evening, screen'd by either shore
Of Spain and Barbary. Our toils are o'er,
Our exile is accomplish'd. Once again
We look on Europe, mistress as of yore
Of the fair earth and of the hearts of men.
  Ay, this is the famed rock which Hercules
And Goth and Moor bequeath'd us. At this door
England stands sentry. God! to hear the shrill
Sweet treble of her fifes upon the breeze,
And at the summons of the rock gun's roar
To see her red coats marching from the hill!
                    WILFRID SCAWEN BLUNT (1840–1922)

Written at Florence 924

O world, in very truth thou art too young;
When wilt thou learn to wear the garb of age?
World, with thy covering of yellow flowers,
Hast thou forgot what generations sprung
Out of thy loins and loved thee and are gone?
Hast thou no place in all their heritage
Where thou dost only weep, that I may come
Nor fear the mockery of thy yellow flowers?
  O world, in very truth thou art too young.
The heroic wealth of passionate emprize
Built thee fair cities for thy naked plains:
How hast thou set thy summer growth among
The broken stones which were their palaces!
Hast thou forgot the darkness where *he* lies
Who made thee beautiful, or have thy bees
Found out his grave to build their honeycombs?

O world, in very truth thou art too young:
They gave thee love who measured out thy skies,
And, when they found for thee another star,
Who made a festival and straightway hung
The jewel on thy neck. O merry world,
Hast thou forgot the glory of those eyes
Which first look'd love in thine? Thou hast not furl'd
One banner of thy bridal car for them.
  O world, in very truth thou art too young.
There was a voice which sang about thy spring,
Till winter froze the sweetness of his lips,
And lo, the worms had hardly left his tongue
Before thy nightingales were come again.
O world, what courage hast thou thus to sing?
Say, has thy merriment no secret pain,
No sudden weariness that thou art young?
              WILFRID SCAWEN BLUNT (1840–1922)

925   THE TWO HIGHWAYMEN
I long have had a quarrel set with Time
Because he robb'd me. Every day of life
Was wrested from me after bitter strife:
I never yet could see the sun go down
But I was angry in my heart, nor hear
The leaves fall in the wind without a tear
Over the dying summer. I have known
No truce with Time nor Time's accomplice, Death.
  The fair world is the witness of a crime
Repeated every hour. For life and breath
Are sweet to all who live; and bitterly
The voices of these robbers of the heath
Sound in each ear and chill the passer-by.
—What have we done to thee, thou monstrous Time?
What have we done to Death that we must die?
              WILFRID SCAWEN BLUNT (1840–1922)

926   A GARDEN SONG
      Here in this sequester'd close
      Bloom the hyacinth and rose,
      Here beside the modest stock
      Flaunts the flaring hollyhock;
      Here, without a pang, one sees
      Ranks, conditions, and degrees.

      All the seasons run their race
      In this quiet resting-place;
      Peach and apricot and fig
      Here will ripen and grow big;
      Here is store and overplus,—
      More had not Alcinoüs!

Here, in alleys cool and green,
Far ahead the thrush is seen;
Here along the southern wall
Keeps the bee his festival;
All is quiet else—afar
Sounds of toil and turmoil are.

Here be shadows large and long;
Here be spaces meet for song;
Grant, O garden-god, that I,
Now that none profane is nigh,—
Now that mood and moment please,—
Find the fair Pierides!

HENRY AUSTIN DOBSON (1840–1921)

URCEUS EXIT 927
TRIOLET

I intended an Ode,
  And it turn'd to a Sonnet
It began *à la mode*,
I intended an Ode;
But Rose cross'd the road
  In her latest new bonnet;
I intended an Ode;
  And it turn'd to a Sonnet.

HENRY AUSTIN DOBSON (1840–1921)

IN AFTER DAYS 928
RONDEAU

In after days when grasses high
O'er-top the stone where I shall lie,
  Though ill or well the world adjust
  My slender claim to honour'd dust,
I shall not question nor reply.

I shall not see the morning sky;
I shall not hear the night-wind sigh;
  I shall be mute, as all men must
    In after days!

But yet, now living, fain would I
That some one then should testify,
  Saying—"He held his pen in trust
  To Art, not serving shame or lust."
Will none?—Then let my memory die
    In after days!

HENRY AUSTIN DOBSON (1840–1921)

MOONI 929

He that is by Mooni now
Sees the water-sapphires gleaming
Where the River Spirit, dreaming,
Sleeps by fall and fountain streaming

Under lute of leaf and bough!—
Hears what stamp of Storm with stress is,
Psalms from unseen wildernesses
Deep amongst far hill-recesses—
   He that is by Mooni now.

Yea, for him by Mooni's marge
Sings the yellow-hair'd September,
With the face the gods remember,
When the ridge is burnt to ember,
   And the dumb sea chains the barge!
Where the mount like molten brass is,
Down beneath fern-feather'd passes
Noonday dew in cool green grasses
   Gleams on him by Mooni's marge.

Who that dwells by Mooni yet,
Feels in flowerful forest arches
Smiting wings and breath that parches
Where strong Summer's path of march is,
   And the suns in thunder set!
Housed beneath the gracious kirtle
Of the shadowy water-myrtle—
Winds may kiss with heat and hurtle,
   He is safe by Mooni yet!

Days there were when he who sings
(Dumb so long through passion's losses)
Stood where Mooni's water crosses
Shining tracks of green-hair'd mosses,
   Like a soul with radiant wings:
Then the psalm the wind rehearses—
Then the song the stream disperses—
Lent a beauty to his verses,
   Who to-night of Mooni sings.

Ah, the theme—the sad, gray theme!
Certain days are not above me,
Certain hearts have ceased to love me,
Certain fancies fail to move me,
   Like the effluent morning dream.
Head whereon the white is stealing,
Heart whose hurts are past all healing,
Where is now the first, pure feeling?
   Ah, the theme—the sad, gray theme!

— — —

Still to be by Mooni cool—
Where the water-blossoms glister,
And by gleaming vale and vista
Sits the English April's sister,
   Soft and sweet and wonderful!
Just to rest beneath the burning

Outer world—its sneers and spurning—
Ah, my heart—my heart is yearning
  Still to be by Mooni cool!
            HENRY CLARENCE KENDALL (1841–1882)

ODE 930

We are the music-makers,
  And we are the dreamers of dreams,
Wandering by lone sea-breakers,
  And sitting by desolate streams;
World-losers and world-forsakers,
  On whom the pale moon gleams:
Yet we are the movers and shakers
  Of the world for ever, it seems.

With wonderful deathless ditties
We build up the world's great cities,
  And out of a fabulous story
  We fashion an empire's glory:
One man with a dream, at pleasure,
  Shall go forth and conquer a crown;
And three with a new song's measure
  Can trample an empire down.

We, in the ages lying
  In the buried past of the earth,
Built Nineveh with our sighing,
  And Babel itself with our mirth;
And o'erthrew them with prophesying
  To the old of the new world's worth;
For each age is a dream that is dying,
  Or one that is coming to birth.
      ARTHUR WILLIAM EDGAR O'SHAUGHNESSY (1844–1881)

SONG 931

I made another garden, yea,
  For my new Love:
I left the dead rose where it lay
  And set the new above.
Why did my Summer not begin?
  Why did my heart not haste?
My old Love came and walk'd therein,
  And laid the garden waste.

She enter'd with her weary smile,
  Just as of old;
She look'd around a little while
  And shiver'd with the cold:
Her passing touch was death to all,
  Her passing look a blight;
She made the white rose-petals fall,
  And turn'd the red rose white.

Her pale robe clinging to the grass
  Seem'd like a snake
That bit the grass and ground, alas!
  And a sad trail did make.
She went up slowly to the gate,
  And then, just as of yore,
She turn'd back at the last to wait
  And say farewell once more.
        ARTHUR WILLIAM EDGAR O'SHAUGHNESSY (1844–1881)

932   THE FOUNTAIN OF TEARS
If you go over desert and mountain,
  Far into the country of Sorrow,
  To-day and to-night and to-morrow,
And maybe for months and for years;
  You shall come with a heart that is bursting
  For trouble and toiling and thirsting,
You shall certainly come to the fountain
At length,—to the Fountain of Tears.

Very peaceful the place is, and solely
  For piteous lamenting and sighing,
  And those who come living or dying
Alike from their hopes and their fears;
  Full of cypress-like shadows the place is,
  And statues that cover their faces:
But out of the gloom springs the holy
And beautiful Fountain of Tears.

And it flows and it flows with a motion
  So gentle and lovely and listless,
  And murmurs a tune so resistless
To him who hath suffer'd and hears—
  You shall surely—without a word spoken,
  Kneel down there and know your heart broken,
And yield to the long-curb'd emotion
That day by the Fountain of Tears.

For it grows and it grows, as though leaping
  Up higher the more one is thinking;
  And ever its tunes go on sinking
More poignantly into the ears:
  Yea, so blessèd and good seems that fountain,
  Reach'd after dry desert and mountain,
You shall fall down at length in your weeping
And bathe your sad face in the tears.

Then alas! while you lie there a season
  And sob between living and dying,
  And give up the land you were trying
To find 'mid your hopes and your fears;

—O the world shall come up and pass o'er you,
     Strong men shall not stay to care for you,
   Nor wonder indeed for what reason
   Your way should seem harder than theirs.

   But perhaps, while you lie, never lifting
     Your cheek from the wet leaves it presses,
     Nor caring to raise your wet tresses
   And look how the cold world appears—
     O perhaps the mere silences round you—
     All things in that place Grief hath found you—
   Yea, e'en to the clouds o'er you drifting,
   May soothe you somewhat through your tears.

   You may feel, when a falling leaf brushes
     Your face, as though some one had kiss'd you,
     Or think at least some one who miss'd you
   Had sent you a thought,—if that cheers;
     Or a bird's little song, faint and broken,
     May pass for a tender word spoken:
   —Enough, while around you there rushes
   That life-drowning torrent of tears.

   And the tears shall flow faster and faster,
     Brim over and baffle resistance,
     And roll down blear'd roads to each distance
   Of past desolation and years;
     Till they cover the place of each sorrow,
     And leave you no past and no morrow:
   For what man is able to master
   And stem the great Fountain of Tears?

   But the floods and the tears meet and gather;
     The sound of them all grows like thunder:
     —O into what bosom, I wonder,
   Is pour'd the whole sorrow of years?
     For Eternity only seems keeping
     Account of the great human weeping:
   May God, then, the Maker and Father—
   May He find a place for the tears!
             ARTHUR WILLIAM EDGAR O'SHAUGHNESSY (1844–1881)

              A WHITE ROSE   933
         The red rose whispers of passion,
           And the white rose breathes of love;
         O the red rose is a falcon,
           And the white rose is a dove.

         But I send you a cream-white rosebud
           With a flush on its petal tips;
         For the love that is purest and sweetest
           Has a kiss of desire on the lips.
                         JOHN BOYLE O'REILLY (1844–1890)

934　　　　　　MY DELIGHT AND THY DELIGHT
My delight and thy delight
Walking, like two angels white,
In the gardens of the night:

My desire and thy desire
Twining to a tongue of fire,
Leaping live, and laughing higher:

Thro' the everlasting strife
In the mystery of life.

Love, from whom the world begun,
Hath the secret of the sun.

Love can tell, and love alone,
Whence the million stars were strewn,
Why each atom knows its own,
How, in spite of woe and death,
Gay is life, and sweet is breath:

This he taught us, this we knew,
Happy in his science true,
Hand in hand as we stood
'Neath the shadows of the wood,
Heart to heart as we lay
In the dawning of the day.
　　　　　　　　　　ROBERT BRIDGES (1844–1930)

935　　　　　　　　SPIRITS
Angel spirits of sleep,
White-robed, with silver hair,
In your meadows fair,
Where the willows weep,
And the sad moonbeam
On the gliding stream
Writes her scatter'd dream:

Angel spirits of sleep,
Dancing to the weir
In the hollow roar
Of its waters deep;
Know ye how men say
That ye haunt no more
Isle and grassy shore
With your moonlit play;
That ye dance not here,
White-robed spirits of sleep,
All the summer night
Threading dances light?
　　　　　　　　　　ROBERT BRIDGES (1844–1930)

NIGHTINGALES 936

Beautiful must be the mountains whence ye come,
  And bright in the fruitful valleys the streams, wherefrom
      Ye learn your song:
Where are those starry woods? O might I wander there,
  Among the flowers, which in that heavenly air
      Bloom the year long!

Nay, barren are those mountains and spent the streams:
  Our song is the voice of desire, that haunts our dreams,
      A throe of the heart,
Whose pining visions dim, forbidden hopes profound,
  No dying cadence nor long sigh can sound,
      For all our art.

Alone, aloud in the raptured ear of men
  We pour our dark nocturnal secret; and then,
      As night is withdrawn
From these sweet-springing meads and bursting boughs of May,
  Dream, while the innumerable choir of day
      Welcome the dawn.

                           ROBERT BRIDGES (1844–1930)

A PASSER-BY 937

Whither, O splendid ship, thy white sails crowding,
  Leaning across the bosom of the urgent West,
That fearest nor sea rising, nor sky clouding,
  Whither away, fair rover, and what thy quest?
  Ah! soon, when Winter has all our vales opprest,
When skies are cold and misty, and hail is hurling,
  Wilt thoù glide on the blue Pacific, or rest
In a summer haven asleep, thy white sails furling.

I there before thee, in the country that well thou knowest,
  Already arrived am inhaling the odorous air:
I watch thee enter unerringly where thou goest,
  And anchor queen of the strange shipping there,
  Thy sails for awnings spread, thy masts bare:
Nor is aught from the foaming reef to the snow-capp'd grandest
  Peak, that is over the feathery palms, more fair
Than thou, so upright, so stately and still thou standest.

And yet, O splendid ship, unhail'd and nameless,
  I know not if, aiming a fancy, I rightly divine
That thou hast a purpose joyful, a courage blameless,
  Thy port assured in a happier land than mine.
  But for all I have given thee, beauty enough is thine,
As thou, aslant with trim tackle and shrouding,
  From the proud nostril curve of a prow's line
In the offing scatterest foam, thy white sails crowding.

                           ROBERT BRIDGES (1844–1930)

938 ## ABSENCE

When my love was away,
Full three days were not sped,
I caught my fancy astray
Thinking if she were dead,

And I alone, alone:
It seem'd in my misery
In all the world was none
Ever so lone as I.

I wept; but it did not shame
Nor comfort my heart: away
I rode as I might, and came
To my love at close of day.

The sight of her still'd my fears,
My fairest-hearted love:
And yet in her eyes were tears:
Which when I question'd of,

"O now thou art come," she cried,
"'Tis fled: but I thought to-day
I never could here abide,
If thou wert longer away."

      ROBERT BRIDGES (1844–1930)

939 ## ON A DEAD CHILD

Perfect little body, without fault or stain on thee,
 With promise of strength and manhood full and fair!
  Though cold and stark and bare,
The bloom and the charm of life doth awhile remain on thee.

Thy mother's treasure wert thou;—alas! no longer
 To visit her heart with wondrous joy; to be
  Thy father's pride:—ah, he
Must gather his faith together, and his strength make stronger.

To me, as I move thee now in the last duty,
 Dost thou with a turn or gesture anon respond;
  Startling my fancy fond
With a chance attitude of the head, a freak of beauty.

Thy hand clasps, as 'twas wont, my finger, and holds it:
 But the grasp is the clasp of Death, heartbreaking and stiff;
  Yet feels to my hand as if
'Twas still thy will, thy pleasure and trust that enfolds it.

So I lay thee there, thy sunken eyelids closing,—
 Go lie thou there in thy coffin, thy last little bed!—
  Propping thy wise, sad head,
Thy firm, pale hands across thy chest disposing.

So quiet! doth the change content thee?—Death, whither hath he taken
    thee?
  To a world, do I think, that rights the disaster of this?
        The vision of which I miss,
Who weep for the body, and wish but to warm thee and awaken thee?

Ah! little at best can all our hopes avail us
  To lift this sorrow, or cheer us, when in the dark,
        Unwilling, alone we embark,
And the things we have seen and have known and have heard of, fail us.
                            ROBERT BRIDGES (1844–1930)

PATER FILIO 940

Sense with keenest edge unusèd,
  Yet unsteel'd by scathing fire;
Lovely feet as yet unbruisèd
  On the ways of dark desire;
Sweetest hope that lookest smiling
O'er the wilderness defiling!

Why such beauty, to be blighted
  By the swarm of foul destruction?
Why such innocence delighted,
  When sin stalks to thy seduction?
All the litanies e'er chaunted
Shall not keep thy faith undaunted.

I have pray'd the sainted Morning
  To unclasp her hands to hold thee;
From resignful Eve's adorning
  Stol'n a robe of peace to enfold thee;
With all charms of man's contriving
Arm'd thee for thy lonely striving.

Me too once unthinking Nature,
  —Whence Love's timeless mockery took me,—
Fashion'd so divine a creature,
  Yea, and like a beast forsook me.
I forgave, but tell the measure
Of her crime in thee, my treasure.
                            ROBERT BRIDGES (1844–1930)

WINTER NIGHTFALL 941

The day begins to droop,—
  Its course is done:
But nothing tells the place
  Of the setting sun.

The hazy darkness deepens,
  And up the lane
You may hear, but cannot see,
  The homing wain.

        An engine pants and hums
           In the farm hard by:
        Its lowering smoke is lost
           In the lowering sky.

        The soaking branches drip,
           And all night through
        The dropping will not cease
           In the avenue.

        A tall man there in the house
           Must keep his chair:
        He knows he will never again
           Breathe the spring air:

        His heart is worn with work;
           He is giddy and sick
        If he rise to go as far
           As the nearest rick:

        He thinks of his morn of life,
           His hale, strong years;
        And braves as he may the night
           Of darkness and tears.
                      ROBERT BRIDGES (1844–1930)

942   WHEN DEATH TO EITHER SHALL COME

        When Death to either shall come,—
           I pray it be first to me,—
        Be happy as ever at home,
           If so, as I wish, it be.

        Possess thy heart, my own;
           And sing to the child on thy knee,
        Or read to thyself alone
           The songs that I made for thee.
                      ROBERT BRIDGES (1844–1930)

943   THE ODYSSEY

As one that for a weary space has lain
   Lull'd by the song of Circe and her wine
   In gardens near the pale of Proserpine,
Where that Ææan isle forgets the main,
And only the low lutes of love complain,
   And only shadows of wan lovers pine—
   As such an one were glad to know the brine
Salt on his lips, and the large air again—
So gladly from the songs of modern speech
   Men turn, and see the stars, and feel the free
     Shrill wind beyond the close of heavy flowers,
     And through the music of the languid hours
   They hear like Ocean on a western beach
     The surge and thunder of the Odyssey.
                      ANDREW LANG (1844–1912)

INVICTUS 944

Out of the night that covers me,
  Black as the pit from pole to pole,
I thank whatever gods may be
  For my unconquerable soul.

In the fell clutch of circumstance
  I have not winced nor cried aloud.
Under the bludgeonings of chance
  My head is bloody, but unbow'd.

Beyond this place of wrath and tears
  Looms but the Horror of the shade,
And yet the menace of the years
  Finds and shall find me unafraid.

It matters not how strait the gate,
  How charged with punishments the scroll,
I am the master of my fate:
I am the captain of my soul.

    WILLIAM ERNEST HENLEY (1849–1903)

MARGARITAE SORORI 945

A late lark twitters from the quiet skies:
And from the west,
Where the sun, his day's work ended,
Lingers as in content,
There falls on the old, gray city
An influence luminous and serene,
A shining peace.

The smoke ascends
In a rosy-and-golden haze. The spires
Shine and are changed. In the valley
Shadows rise. The lark sings on. The sun,
Closing his benediction,
Sinks, and the darkening air
Thrills with a sense of the triumphing night—
Night with her train of stars
And her great gift of sleep.

So be my passing!
My task accomplish'd and the long day done,
My wages taken, and in my heart
Some late lark singing,
Let me be gather'd to the quiet west,
The sundown splendid and serene,
Death.

    WILLIAM ERNEST HENLEY (1849–1903)

ENGLAND, MY ENGLAND 946

What have I done for you,
  England, my England?
What is there I would not do,
  England, my own?

With your glorious eyes austere,
As the Lord were walking near,
Whispering terrible things and dear
  As the Song on your bugles blown,
    England—
  Round the world on your bugles blown!

Where shall the watchful sun,
  England, my England,
Match the master-work you've done,
  England, my own?
When shall he rejoice agen
Such a breed of mighty men
As come forward, one to ten,
  To the Song on your bugles blown,
    England—
  Down the years on your bugles blown?

Ever the faith endures,
  England, my England:—
"Take and break us: we are yours,
  England, my own!
Life is good, and joy runs high
Between English earth and sky:
Death is death; but we shall die
  To the Song on your bugles blown,
    England—
  To the stars on your bugles blown!"

They call you proud and hard,
  England, my England:
You with worlds to watch and ward,
  England, my own!
You whose mail'd hand keeps the keys
Of such teeming destinies,
You could know nor dread nor ease
  Were the Song on your bugles blown,
    England,
  Round the Pit on your bugles blown!

Mother of Ships whose might,
  England, my England,
Is the fierce old Sea's delight,
  England, my own,
Chosen daughter of the Lord,
Spouse-in-Chief of the ancient Sword,
There's the menace of the Word
  In the Song on your bugles blown,
    England—
  Out of heaven on your bugles blown!
WILLIAM ERNEST HENLEY (1849–1903)

Revelation 947

Into the silver night
  She brought with her pale hand
The topaz lanthorn-light,
And darted splendour o'er the land;
  Around her in a band,
Ringstraked and pied, the great soft moths came flying,
  And flapping with their mad wings, fann'd
The flickering flame, ascending, falling, dying.

Behind the thorny pink
  Close wall of blossom'd may,
I gazed thro' one green chink
And saw no more than thousands may,—
  Saw sweetness, tender and gay,—
Saw full rose lips as rounded as the cherry,
  Saw braided locks more dark than bay,
And flashing eyes decorous, pure, and merry.

With food for furry friends
  She pass'd, her lamp and she,
Till eaves and gable-ends
Hid all that saffron sheen from me:
  Around my rosy tree
Once more the silver-starry night was shining,
  With depths of heaven, dewy and free,
And crystals of a carven moon declining.

Alas! for him who dwells
  In frigid air of thought,
When warmer light dispels
The frozen calm his spirit sought;
  By life too lately taught
He sees the ecstatic Human from him stealing;
  Reels from the joy experience brought,
And dares not clutch what Love was half revealing.

                    EDMUND GOSSE (1849–1928)

Dominus Illuminatio Mea 948

In the hour of death, after this life's whim,
When the heart beats low, and the eyes grow dim,
And pain has exhausted every limb—
  The lover of the Lord shall trust in Him.

When the will has forgotten the lifelong aim,
And the mind can only disgrace its fame,
And a man is uncertain of his own name—
  The power of the Lord shall fill this frame.

When the last sigh is heaved, and the last tear shed,
And the coffin is waiting beside the bed,
And the widow and child forsake the dead—
  The angel of the Lord shall lift this head.

For even the purest delight may pall,
And power must fail, and the pride must fall,
And the love of the dearest friends grow small—
But the glory of the Lord is all in all.

ANONYMOUS (c. 19th Cent.)

949   A BOOK

There is no frigate like a book
  To take us lands away,
Nor any coursers like a page
  Of prancing poetry.
This traverse may the poorest take
  Without oppress of toll;
How frugal is the chariot
  That bears a human soul!

EMILY DICKINSON (1830–1886)

950   ADVICE AGAINST TRAVEL

Traverse not the globe for lore! The sternest
But the surest teacher is the heart;
Studying that and that alone, thou learnest
Best and soonest whence and what thou art.

Moor, Chinese, Egyptian, Russian, Roman,
Tread one common down-hill path of doom;
Everywhere the names are man and woman,
Everywhere the old sad sins find room.

Evil angels tempt us in all places.
What but sands or snows hath earth to give?
Dream not, friend, of deserts and oases;
But look inwards, and begin to live!

JAMES CLARENCE MANGAN (1803–1849)

951   THE BLACK KNIGHT

A beaten and a baffled man,
My life drags lamely day by day,
Too young to die, too old to plan,
  In failure grey.

The knights ride east, the knights ride west,
For ladyes' tokens blithe of cheer,
Each bound upon some gallant quest;
  While I rust here.

JOHN TODHUNTER (1839–1916)

952   MICROCOSM

His home a speck in a vast Universe,
  He a mere atom on that tiny speck,
Victim of countless evils that coerce
  And force him onward on a pathless track:
And yet a being made to dominate
  O'er all things else by mind's controlling power:
Spoilt favourite at once and sport of fate,
  Football of fortune, time's consummate flower!

To him alone did Nature's self impart
  A spark of her divinest energy,
With power to create a world of Art,
  And intellect to solve all mystery:
So great and yet so little! blest and curst—
Nature's most noble offspring — yet her worst!
                    BERTRAM DOBELL (1842–1914)

THE BRIDGE 953

I stood on the bridge at midnight,
  As the clocks were striking the hour,
And the moon rose o'er the city,
  Behind the dark church-tower.

I saw her bright reflection
  In the waters under me,
Like a golden goblet falling
  And sinking into the sea.

And far in the hazy distance
  Of that lovely night in June,
The blaze of the flaming furnace
  Gleamed redder than the moon.

Among the long, black rafters
  The wavering shadows lay,
And the current that came from the ocean
  Seemed to lift and bear them away;

As, sweeping and eddying through them,
  Rose the belated tide,
And, streaming into the moonlight,
  The seaweed floated wide.

And like those waters rushing
  Among the wooden piers,
A flood of thoughts came o'er me
  That filled my eyes with tears.

How often, oh how often,
  In the days that had gone by,
I had stood on that bridge at midnight
  And gazed on that wave and sky!

How often, oh how often,
  I had wished that the ebbing tide
Would bear me away on its bosom
  O'er the ocean wild and wide!

For my heart was hot and restless,
  And my life was full of care,
And the burden laid upon me
  Seemed greater than I could bear.

But now it has fallen from me,
  It is buried in the sea;
And only the sorrow of others
  Throws its shadow over me,

Yet whenever I cross the river
  On its bridge with wooden piers,
Like the odor of brine from the ocean
  Comes the thought of other years.

And I think how many thousands
  Of care-encumbered men,
Each bearing his burden of sorrow,
  Have crossed the bridge since then.

I see the long procession
  Still passing to and fro,
The young heart hot and restless,
  And the old subdued and slow!

And forever and forever,
  As long as the river flows,
As long as the heart has passions,
  As long as life has woes;

The moon and its broken reflection
  And its shadows shall appear,
As the symbol of love in heaven,
  And its wavering image here.
                                HENRY WADSWORTH LONGFELLOW (1807–1882)

954   GOOD-BYE
Good-Bye, proud world! I'm going home:
Thou art not my friend, and I'm not thine.
Long through thy weary crowds I roam;
A river-ark on the ocean brine,
Long I've been tossed like the driven foam;
But now, proud world! I'm going home.

Good-bye to Flattery's fawning face;
To Grandeur with his wise grimace;
To upstart Wealth's averted eye;
To supple Office, low and high;
To crowded halls, to court and street;
To frozen hearts and hasting feet;
To those who go, and those who come;
Good-bye, proud world! I'm going home.

I am going to my own hearth-stone,
Bosomed in yon green hills alone,—
A secret nook in a pleasant land,
Whose groves the frolic fairies planned;

Where arches green, the livelong day,
Echo the blackbird's roundelay,
And vulgar feet have never trod
A spot that is sacred to thought and God.

O, when I am safe in my sylvan home,
I tread on the pride of Greece and Rome;
And when I am stretched beneath the pines,
Where the evening star so holy shines,
I laugh at the lore and the pride of man,
At the sophist schools and the learned clan;
For what are they all, in their high conceit,
When man in the bush with God may meet?
RALPH WALDO EMERSON (1803–1882)

THE CONQUEROR WORM   955

Lo! 'tis a gala night
   Within the lonesome latter years!
An angel throng, bewinged, bedight
   In veils, and drowned in tears,
Sit in a theatre, to see
   A play of hopes and fears,
While the orchestra breathes fitfully
   The music of the spheres.

Mimes, in the form of God on high,
   Mutter and mumble low,
And hither and thither fly—
   Mere puppets they, who come and go
At bidding of vast formless things
   That shift the scenery to and fro,
Flapping from out their Condor wings
   Invisible Woe!

That motley drama—oh, be sure
   It shall not be forgot!
With its Phantom chased for evermore,
   By a crowd that seize it not,
Through a circle that ever returneth in
   To the self-same spot,
And much of Madness, and more of Sin,
   And Horror the soul of the plot.

But see, amid the mimic rout
   A crawling shape intrude!
A blood-red thing that writhes from out
   The scenic solitude!
It writhes!—it writhes!—with mortal pangs
   The mimes become its food,
And seraphs sob at vermin fangs
   In human gore imbued.

Out—out are the lights—out all!
  And, over each quivering form,
The curtain, a funeral pall,
  Comes down with the rush of a storm,
While the angels, all pallid and wan,
  Uprising, unveiling, affirm
That the play is the tragedy, "Man,"
  And its hero the Conqueror Worm.
EDGAR ALLAN POE (1809–1849)

956   THE ARROW AND THE SONG

I shot an arrow into the air,
It fell to earth, I knew not where;
For, so swiftly it flew, the sight
Could not follow it in its flight.

I breathed a song into the air,
It fell to earth, I knew not where;
For who has sight so keen and strong
That it can follow the flight of song?

Long, long afterward, in an oak
I found the arrow, still unbroke;
And the song, from beginning to end,
I found again in the heart of a friend.
HENRY WADSWORTH LONGFELLOW (1807–1882)

957   TRUE ROYALTY

There was never a Queen like Balkis,
  From here to the wide world's end;
But Balkis talked to a butterfly
  As you would talk to a friend.

There was never a King like Solomon,
  Not since the world began;
But Solomon talked to a butterfly
  As a man would talk to a man.

She was Queen of Sabaea—
  And *he* was Asia's Lord—
But they both of 'em talked to butterflies
  When they took their walks abroad.
RUDYARD KIPLING (1865–1936)
from "The Just So Stories"

958   MY SHADOW

I have a little shadow that goes in and out with me,
And what can be the use of him is more than I can see.
He is very, very like me from the heels up to the head;
And I see him jump before me, when I jump into my bed.

The funniest thing about him is the way he likes to grow—
Not at all like proper children, which is always very slow;
For he sometimes shoots up taller like an india-rubber ball,
And he sometimes gets so little that there's none of him at all.

He hasn't got a notion of how children ought to play,
And can only make a fool of me in every sort of way.
He stays so close beside me, he's a coward, you can see;
I'd think shame to stick to nursie as that shadow sticks to me!

One morning, very early, before the sun was up,
I rose and found the shining dew on every buttercup;
But my lazy little shadow, like an arrant sleepy-head,
Had stayed at home behind me and was fast asleep in bed.
                    ROBERT LOUIS STEVENSON (1850–1894)

BED IN SUMMER 959

In Winter I get up at night
And dress by yellow candle light.
In Summer, quite the other way,
I have to go to bed by day.

I have to go to bed and see
The birds still hopping on the tree,
Or hear the grown-up people's feet
Still going past me in the street.

And does it not seem hard to you,
When all the sky is clear and blue,
And I should like so much to play,
To have to go to bed by day?
                    ROBERT LOUIS STEVENSON (1850–1894)

WYNKEN, BLYNKEN, AND NOD 960

Wynken, Blynken, and Nod one night
  Sailed off in a wooden shoe,—
Sailed on a river of crystal light
  Into a sea of dew.
"Where are you going, and what do you wish?"
  The old moon asked the three.
"We have come to fish for the herring-fish
  That live in this beautiful sea;
  Nets of silver and gold have we,"
        Said Wynken,
        Blynken,
        And Nod.

The old moon laughed and sang a song,
  As they rocked in the wooden shoe;
And the wind that sped them all night long
  Ruffled the waves of dew;
The little stars were the herring-fish
  That lived in the beautiful sea.
"Now cast your nets wherever you wish,—
  Never afeard are we!"
So cried the stars to the fishermen three,
        Wynken,
        Blynken,
        And Nod.

All night long their nets they threw
  To the stars in the twinkling foam,—
Then down from the skies came the wooden shoe,
  Bringing the fishermen home:
'Twas all so pretty a sail, it seemed
  As if it could not be;
And some folk thought 'twas a dream they'd dreamed
  Of sailing that beautiful sea;
  But I shall name you the fishermen three:
    Wynken,
      Blynken,
        And Nod.

Wynken and Blynken are two little eyes,
  And Nod is a little head,
And the wooden shoe that sailed the skies
  Is a wee one's trundle-bed;
So shut your eyes while Mother sings
  Of wonderful sights that be,
And you shall see the beautiful things
  As you rock on the misty sea
  Where the old shoe rocked the fishermen three,
    Wynken,
      Blynken,
        And Nod.

EUGENE FIELD (1850–1895)

961   THE DUEL

  The gingham dog and the calico cat
  Side by side on the table sat;
  'Twas half-past twelve, and (what do you think!)
  Nor one nor t'other had slept a wink!
  The old Dutch clock and the Chinese plate
  Appeared to know as sure as fate
  There was going to be a terrible spat.
  (I wasn't there; I simply state
  What was told to me by the Chinese plate!)

  The gingham dog went "bow-wow-wow!"
  And the calico cat replied "mee-ow!"
  The air was littered, an hour or so,
  With bits of gingham and calico,
  While the old Dutch clock in the chimney-place
  Up with its hands before its face,
  For it always dreaded a family row!
  (Now mind: I'm only telling you
  What the old Dutch clock declares is true!)

  The Chinese plate looked very blue,
  And wailed, "Oh, dear! what shall we do!"
  But the gingham dog and the calico cat
  Wallowed this way and tumbled that,

Employing every tooth and claw
In the awfullest way you ever saw—
And, oh! how the gingham and calico flew!
(*Don't fancy I exaggerate!
I got my views from the Chinese plate!*)

Next morning where the two had sat
They found no trace of the dog or cat;
And some folks think unto this day
That burglars stole the pair away!
But the truth about the cat and the pup
Is this: They ate each other up!
Now what do you really think of that!
(*The old Dutch clock it told me so,
And that is how I came to know.*)

EUGENE FIELD (1850–1895)

THE OVERLAND-MAIL 962

In the name of the Empress of India, make way,
O Lords of the Jungle wherever you roam,
The woods are astir at the close of the day—
We exiles are waiting for letters from Home—
Let the robber retreat; let the tiger turn tail,
In the name of the Empress the Overland-Mail!

With a jingle of bells as the dusk gathers in,
He turns to the foot-path that leads up the hill—
The bags on his back, and a cloth round his chin,
And, tucked in his belt, the Post-Office bill;—
"Despatched on this date, as received by the rail,
Per runner, two bags of the Overland-Mail."

Is the torrent in spate? He must ford it or swim.
Has the rain wrecked the road? He must climb by the cliff.
Does the tempest cry "Halt"? What are tempests to him?
The service admits not a "but" or an "if";
While the breath's in his mouth, he must bear without fail,
In the name of the Empress the Overland-Mail.

From aloe to rose-oak, from rose-oak to fir,
From level to upland, from upland to crest,
From rice-field to rock-ridge, from rock-ridge to spur,
Fly the soft-sandalled feet, strains the brawny brown chest.
From rail to ravine—to the peak from the vale—
Up, up through the night goes the Overland-Mail.

There's a speck on the hillside, a dot on the road—
A jingle of bells on the foot-path below—
There's a scuffle above in the monkeys' abode—
The world is awake, and the clouds are aglow—
For the great Sun himself must attend to the hail;—
In the name of the Empress the Overland-Mail.

RUDYARD KIPLING (1865–1936)

963   The Ballad Of The "Clampherdown"

It was our war-ship *Clampherdown*
 Would sweep the Channel clean,
Wherefore she kept her hatches close
When the merry Channel chops arose,
 To save the bleached marine.

She had one bow-gun of a hundred ton,
 And a great stern-gun beside;
They dipped their noses deep in the sea,
They racked their stays and stanchions free
 In the wash of the wind-whipped tide.

It was our war-ship *Clampherdown*,
 Fell in with a cruiser light
That carried the dainty Hotchkiss gun
And a pair o' heels wherewith to run,
 From the grip of a close-fought fight.

She opened fire at seven miles—
 As ye shoot at a bobbing cork—
And once she fired and twice she fired,
Till the bow-gun drooped like a lily tired
 That lolls upon the stalk.

"Captain, the bow-gun melts apace,
 The deck-beams break below,
'Twere well to rest for an hour or twain,
And botch the shattered plates again."
 And he answered, "Make it so."

She opened fire within the mile—
 As ye shoot at the flying duck—
And the great stern-gun shot fair and true,
With the heave of the ship, to the stainless blue,
 And the great stern-turret stuck.

"Captain, the turret fills with steam,
 The feed-pipes burst below—
You can hear the hiss of helpless ram,
You can hear the twisted runners jam."
 And he answered, "Turn and go!"

It was our war-ship *Clampherdown*,
 And grimly did she roll;
Swung round to take the cruiser's fire
As the White Whale faces the Thresher's ire,
 When they war by the frozen Pole.

"Captain, the shells are falling fast,
 And faster still fall we;
And it is not meet for English stock,
To bide in the heart of an eight-day clock,
 The death they cannot see."

"Lie down, lie down, my bold A.B.,
   We drift upon her beam;
We dare not ram, for she can run;
And dare ye fire another gun,
   And die in the peeling steam?"

It was our war-ship *Clampherdown*
   That carried an armour-belt;
But fifty feet at stern and bow,
Lay bare as the paunch of the purser's sow,
   To the hail of the Nordenfeldt.

"Captain, they lack us through and through;
   The chilled steel bolts are swift!
We have emptied the bunkers in open sea,
Their shrapnel bursts where our coal should be."
   And he answered, "Let her drift."

It was our war-ship *Clampherdown*,
   Swung round upon the tide.
Her two dumb guns glared south and north,
And the blood and the bubbling steam ran forth,
   And she ground the cruiser's side.

"Captain, they cry the fight is done,
   They bid you send your sword."
And he answered, "Grapple her stern and bow.
They have asked for the steel. They shall have it now;
   Out cutlasses and board!"

It was our war-ship *Clampherdown*,
   Spewed up four hundred men;
And the scalded stokers yelped delight,
As they rolled in the waist and heard the fight,
   Stamp o'er their steel-walled pen.

They cleared the cruiser end to end,
   From conning-tower to hold.
They fought as they fought in Nelson's fleet;
They were stripped to the waist, they were bare to the feet,
   As it was in the days of old.

It was the sinking *Clampherdown*
   Heaved up her battered side—
And carried a million pounds in steel,
To the cod and the corpse-fed conger-eel,
   And the scour of the Channel tide.

It was the crew of the *Clampherdown*
   Stood out to sweep the sea,
On a cruiser won from an ancient foe,
As it was in the days of long-ago,
   And as it still shall be.

                                          RUDYARD KIPLING (1865–1936)

964   MOLY

Traveller, pluck a stem of moly,
If thou touch at Circe's isle,—
Hermes' moly, growing solely
To undo enchanter's wile!
When she proffers thee her chalice,—
Wine and spices mixed with malice,—
When she smites thee with her staff
To transform thee, do thou laugh!
Safe thou art if thou but bear
The least leaf of moly rare.
Close it grows beside her portal,
Springing from a stock immortal,
Yes! and often has the Witch
Sought to tear it from its niche;
But to thwart her cruel will
The wise God renews it still.
Though it grows in soil perverse,
Heaven hath been its jealous nurse,
And a flower of snowy mark
Springs from root and sheathing dark;
Kingly safeguard, only herb
That can brutish passion curb!
Some do think its name should be
Shield-Heart, White Integrity.
Traveller, pluck a stem of moly,
If thou touch at Circe's isle,—
Hermes' moly, growing solely
To undo enchanter's wile!
                    EDITH M. THOMAS (1854–1925)

965   L'ENVOI

When Earth's last picture is painted, and the tubes are
        twisted and dried,
When the oldest colours have faded, and the youngest critic has died,
We shall rest, and, faith, we shall need it—lie down
        for an æon or two,
Till the Master of All Good Workmen shall set us to work anew!

And those who were good shall be happy: they shall sit
        in a golden chair;
They shall splash at a ten-league canvas with brushes of comet's hair;
They shall find real saints to draw from—Magdalene, Peter, and Paul;
They shall work for an age at a sitting and never be tired at all!

And only the Master shall praise us, and only the Master shall blame;
And no one shall work for money, and no one shall work for fame;
But each for the joy of the working, and each, in his separate star,
Shall draw the Thing as he sees It for the God of Things as They Are!
                    RUDYARD KIPLING (1865–1936)

The English Flag

[It is quite true that the English flag stands for freedom the world over. Wherever it floats almost any one is safe, whether English or not. – Ed.]

Winds of the World, give answer? They are whimpering to and fro—
And what should they know of England who only England know?—
The poor little street-bred people that vapour and fume and brag,
They are lifting their heads in the stillness to yelp at
      the English Flag!

Must we borrow a clout from the Boer—to plaster anew with dirt?
An Irish liar's bandage, or an English coward's shirt?
We may not speak of England; her Flag's to sell or share.
What is the Flag of England? Winds of the World, declare!

The North Wind blew:—"From Bergen my steel-shod van-guards go;
I chase your lazy whalers home from the Disko floe;
By the great North Lights above me I work the will of God,
That the liner splits on the ice-field or the Dogger fills with cod.

"I barred my gates with iron, I shuttered my doors with flame,
Because to force my ramparts your nutshell navies came;
I took the sun from their presence, I cut them down with my blast,
And they died, but the Flag of England blew free ere the spirit passed.

"The lean white bear hath seen it in the long, long Arctic night,
The musk-ox knows the standard that flouts the Northern Light:
What is the Flag of England? Ye have but my bergs to dare,
Ye have but my drifts to conquer. Go forth, for it is there!"

The South Wind sighed:—"From The Virgins my mid-sea course was ta'en
Over a thousand islands lost in an idle main,
Where the sea-egg flames on the coral and the long-backed
      breakers croon
Their endless ocean legends to the lazy, locked lagoon.

"Strayed amid lonely islets, mazed amid outer keys,
I waked the palms to laughter—I tossed the scud in the breeze—
Never was isle so little, never was sea so lone,
But over the scud and the palm-trees an English flag was flown.

"I have wrenched it free from the halliard to hang for a wisp
      on the Horn;
I have chased it north to the Lizard—ribboned and rolled and torn;
I have spread its fold o'er the dying, adrift in a hopeless sea;
I have hurled it swift on the slaver, and seen the slave set free.

"My basking sunfish know it, and wheeling albatross,
Where the lone wave fills with fire beneath the Southern Cross.
What is the Flag of England? Ye have but my reefs to dare,
Ye have but my seas to furrow. Go forth, for it is there!"

The East Wind roared:—"From the Kuriles, the Bitter Seas, I come,
And me men call the Home-Wind, for I bring the English home.
Look—look well to your shipping! By the breath of my mad typhoon
I swept your close-packed Praya and beached your best at Kowloon!

"The reeling junks behind me and the racing seas before,
I raped your richest roadstead—I plundered Singapore!
I set my hand on the Hoogli; as a hooded snake she rose,
And I flung your stoutest steamers to roost with the startled crows.

"Never the lotos closes, never the wild-fowl wake,
But a soul goes out on the East Wind that died for England's sake—
Man or woman or suckling, mother or bride or maid—
Because on the bones of the English the English Flag is stayed.

"The desert-dust hath dimmed it, the flying wild-ass knows.
The scared white leopard winds it across the taintless snows.
What is the Flag of England? Ye have but my sun to dare,
Ye have but my sands to travel. Go forth, for it is there!"

The West Wind called:—"In squadrons the thoughtless galleons fly
That bear the wheat and cattle lest street-bred people die.
They make my might their porter, they make my house their path,
Till I loose my neck from their rudder and whelm them all in my wrath.

"I draw the gliding fog-bank as a snake is drawn from the hole;
They bellow one to the other, the frightened ship-bells toll,
For day is a drifting terror till I raise the shroud with my breath,
And they see strange bows above them and the two go locked to death.

"But whether in calm or wrack-wreath, whether by dark or day,
I heave them whole to the conger or rip their plates away,
First of the scattered legions, under a shrieking sky,
Dipping between the rollers, the English Flag goes by.

"The dead dumb fog hath wrapped it—the frozen dews have kissed—
The naked stars have seen it, a fellow-star in the mist.
What is the Flag of England? Ye have but my breath to dare,
Ye have but my waves to conquer. Go forth, for it is there!"

RUDYARD KIPLING (1865–1936)

967   THE MAN WITH THE HOE

WRITTEN AFTER SEEING THE PAINTING BY MILLET.
*God made man in His own image,
in the image of God made He him.*
—GENESIS

Bowed by the weight of centuries he leans
Upon his hoe and gazes on the ground,
The emptiness of ages in his face,
And on his back the burden of the world.

Who made him dead to rapture and despair,
A thing that grieves not and that never hopes,
Stolid and stunned, a brother to the ox?
Who loosened and let down this brutal jaw?
Whose was the hand that slanted back this brow?
Whose breath blew out the light within this brain?

Is this the Thing the Lord God made and gave
To have dominion over sea and land;
To trace the stars and search the heavens for power;
To feel the passion of Eternity?
Is this the Dream He dreamed who shaped the suns
And marked their ways upon the ancient deep?
Down all the stretch of Hell to its last gulf
There is no shape more terrible than this—
More tongued with censure of the world's blind greed—
More filled with signs and portents for the soul—
More fraught with menace to the universe.

What gulfs between him and the seraphim!
Slave of the wheel of labour, what to him
Are Plato and the swing of Pleiades?
What the long reaches of the peaks of song,
The rift of dawn, the reddening of the rose?
Through this dread shape the suffering ages look;
Time's tragedy is in that aching stoop;
Through this dread shape humanity betrayed,
Plundered, profaned, and disinherited,
Cries protest to the Judges of the World,
A protest that is also prophecy.

O masters, lords, and rulers in all lands,
Is this the handiwork you give to God,
This monstrous thing distorted and soul-quenched?
How will you ever straighten up this shape;
Touch it again with immortality;
Give back the upward looking and the light;
Rebuild in it the music and the dream;
Make right the immemorial infamies,
Perfidious wrongs, immedicable woes?

O masters, lords, and rulers in all lands,
How will the future reckon with this Man?
How answer his brute question in that hour
When whirlwinds of rebellion shake the world?
How will it be with kingdoms and with kings—
With those who shaped him to the thing he is—
When this dumb Terror shall reply to God,
After the silence of the centuries?
EDWIN MARKHAM (1852–1940)

968 THE ROSEBUD

Queen of fragrance, lovely Rose,
The beauties of thy leaves disclose!
—But thou, fair Nymph, thyself survey
In this sweet offspring of a day.
That miracle of face must fail,
Thy charms are sweet, but charms are frail:
Swift as the short-lived flower they fly,
At morn they bloom, at evening die:
Though Sickness yet a while forbears,
Yet Time destroys what Sickness spares:
Now Helen lives alone in fame,
And Cleopatra's but a name:
Time must indent that heavenly brow,
And thou must be what they are now.

WILLIAM BROOME (1869?–1745)

969 BELINDA'S RECOVERY FROM SICKNESS

Thus when the silent grave becomes
Pregnant with life as fruitful wombs;
When the wide seas and spacious earth
  Resign us to our second birth;
Our moulder'd frame rebuilt assumes
New beauty, and for ever blooms,
And, crown'd with youth's immortal pride,
  We angels rise, who mortals died.

WILLIAM BROOME (1869?–1745)

970 ROMANCE

I will make you brooches and toys for your delight
Of bird-song at morning and star-shine at night.
I will make a palace fit for you and me,
Of green days in forests and blue days at sea.

I will make my kitchen, and you shall keep your room,
Where white flows the river and bright blows the broom,
And you shall wash your linen and keep your body white
In rainfall at morning and dewfall at night.

And this shall be for music when no one else is near,
The fine song for singing, the rare song to hear!
That only I remember, that only you admire,
Of the broad road that stretches and the roadside fire.

ROBERT LOUIS STEVENSON (1850–1894)

971 IN THE HIGHLANDS

In the highlands, in the country places,
Where the old plain men have rosy faces,
    And the young fair maidens
    Quiet eyes;
Where essential silence cheers and blesses,
And for ever in the hill-recesses
    Her more lovely music
    Broods and dies—

O to mount again where erst I haunted;
Where the old red hills are bird-enchanted,
    And the low green meadows
        Bright with sward;
And when even dies, the million-tinted,
And the night has come, and planets glinted,
    Lo, the valley hollow
        Lamp-bestarr'd!

O to dream, O to awake and wander
There, and with delight to take and render,
    Through the trance of silence,
        Quiet breath!
Lo! for there, among the flowers and grasses,
Only the mightier movement sounds and passes;
    Only winds and rivers,
        Life and death.
                ROBERT LOUIS STEVENSON (1850–1894)

REQUIEM   972
Under the wide and starry sky
    Dig the grave and let me lie:
Glad did I live and gladly die,
    And I laid me down with a will.

This be the verse you grave for me:
    Here he lies where he long'd to be;
Home is the sailor, home from sea,
    And the hunter home from the hill.
               ROBERT LOUIS STEVENSON (1850–1894)

THE DEAD AT CLONMACNOIS   973
FROM THE IRISH OF ANGUS O'GILLAN
In a quiet water'd land, a land of roses,
    Stands Saint Kieran's city fair;
And the warriors of Erin in their famous generations
    Slumber there.

There beneath the dewy hillside sleep the noblest
    Of the clan of Conn,
Each below his stone with name in branching Ogham
    And the sacred knot thereon.

There they laid to rest the seven Kings of Tara,
    There the sons of Cairbrè sleep—
Battle-banners of the Gael that in Kieran's plain of crosses
    Now their final hosting keep.

And in Clonmacnois they laid the men of Teffia,
    And right many a lord of Breagh;
Deep the sod above Clan Creidè and Clan Conaill,
    Kind in hall and fierce in fray.

Many and many a son of Conn the Hundred-Fighter
    In the red earth lies at rest;
Many a blue eye of Clan Colman the turf covers,
    Many a swan-white breast.

T. W. ROLLESON (1857–1920)

974   SONG

The boat is chafing at our long delay,
    And we must leave too soon
The spicy sea-pinks and the inborne spray,
    The tawny sands, the moon.

Keep us, O Thetis, in our western flight!
    Watch from thy pearly throne
Our vessel, plunging deeper into night
    To reach a land unknown.

JOHN DAVIDSON (1857–1909)

975   THE LAST ROSE

"O which is the last rose?"
A blossom of no name.
At midnight the snow came;
At daybreak a vast rose,
In darkness unfurl'd,
O'er-petall'd the world.

Its odourless pallor
Blossom'd forlorn,
Till radiant valour
Establish'd the morn—
Till the night
Was undone
In her fight
With the sun.

The brave orb in state rose,
And crimson he shone first;
While from the high vine
Of heaven the dawn burst,
Staining the great rose
From sky-line to sky-line.

The red rose of morn
A white rose at noon turn'd;
But at sunset reborn
All red again soon burn'd.
Then the pale rose of noonday
Rebloom'd in the night,
And spectrally white
  In the light
Of the moon lay.

But the vast rose
  Was scentless,
And this is the reason:
When the blast rose

　　　　Relentless,
　　And brought in due season
　　The snow rose, the last rose
　　Congeal'd in its breath,
　　Then came with it treason;
　　The traitor was Death.

　　In lee-valleys crowded,
　　The sheep and the birds
　　Were frozen and shrouded
　　In flights and in herds.
　　In highways
　　And byways
　　The young and the old
　　Were tortured and madden'd
　　And kill'd by the cold.
　　But many were gladden'd
　　By the beautiful last rose,
　　The blossom of no name
　　That came when the snow came,
　　In darkness unfurl'd—
　　The wonderful vast rose
　　That fill'd all the world.
　　　　　　　　　JOHN DAVIDSON (1857–1909)

SONG　　　　　　　　　　　　　　　976

　　April, April,
　　Laugh thy girlish laughter;
　　Then, the moment after,
　　Weep thy girlish tears!
　　April, that mine ears
　　Like a lover greetest,
　　If I tell thee, sweetest,
　　All my hopes and fears,
　　April, April,
　　Laugh thy golden laughter,
　　But, the moment after,
　　Weep thy golden tears!
　　　　　　　　　WILLIAM WATSON (1858–1935)

ODE IN MAY　　　　　　　　　　　977

Let me go forth, and share
　The overflowing Sun
　With one wise friend, or one
Better than wise, being fair,
Where the pewit wheels and dips
　On heights of bracken and ling,
And Earth, unto her leaflet tips,
　Tingles with the Spring.

What is so sweet and dear
　As a prosperous morn in May,
　The confident prime of the day,
And the dauntless youth of the year,

When nothing that asks for bliss,
  Asking aright, is denied,
And half of the world a bridegroom is,
  And half of the world a bride?

The Song of Mingling flows,
  Grave, ceremonial, pure,
  As once, from lips that endure,
The cosmic descant rose,
When the temporal lord of life,
  Going his golden way,
Had taken a wondrous maid to wife
  That long had said him nay.

For of old the Sun, our sire,
  Came wooing the mother of men,
  Earth, that was virginal then,
Vestal fire to his fire.
Silent her bosom and coy,
  But the strong god sued and press'd;
And born of their starry nuptial joy
  Are all that drink of her breast.

And the triumph of him that begot,
  And the travail of her that bore,
  Behold they are evermore
As warp and weft in our lot.
We are children of splendour and flame,
  Of shuddering, also, and tears.
Magnificent out of the dust we came,
  And abject from the Spheres.

O bright irresistible lord!
  We are fruit of Earth's womb, each one,
  And fruit of thy loins, O Sun,
Whence first was the seed outpour'd.
To thee as our Father we bow,
  Forbidden thy Father to see,
Who is older and greater than thou, as thou
  Art greater and older than we.

Thou art but as a word of his speech;
  Thou art but as a wave of his hand;
  Thou art brief as a glitter of sand
'Twixt tide and tide on his beach;
Thou art less than a spark of his fire,
  Or a moment's mood of his soul:
Thou art lost in the notes on the lips of his choir
  That chant the chant of the Whole.

WILLIAM WATSON (1858–1935)

THE GREAT MISGIVING 978

"Not ours," say some, "the thought of death to dread;
   Asking no heaven, we fear no fabled hell:
Life is a feast, and we have banqueted—
   Shall not the worms as well?

"The after-silence, when the feast is o'er,
   And void the places where the minstrels stood,
Differs in nought from what hath been before,
   And is nor ill nor good."

Ah, but the Apparition—the dumb sign—
   The beckoning finger bidding me forgo
The fellowship, the converse, and the wine,
   The songs, the festal glow!

And ah, to know not, while with friends I sit,
   And while the purple joy is pass'd about,
Whether 'tis ampler day divinelier lit
   Or homeless night without;

And whether, stepping forth, my soul shall see
   New prospects, or fall sheer—a blinded thing!
There is, O grave, thy hourly victory,
   And there, O death, thy sting.

WILLIAM WATSON (1858–1935)

PRAYERS 979

God who created me
   Nimble and light of limb,
In three elements free,
   To run, to ride, to swim:
Not when the sense is dim,
   But now from the heart of joy,
I would remember Him:
   Take the thanks of a boy.

Jesu, King and Lord,
   Whose are my foes to fight,
Gird me with Thy sword
   Swift and sharp and bright.
Thee would I serve if I might;
   And conquer if I can,
From day-dawn till night,
   Take the strength of a man.

Spirit of Love and Truth,
   Breathing in grosser clay,
The light and flame of youth,
   Delight of men in the fray,
Wisdom in strength's decay;
   From pain, strife, wrong to be free,
This best gift I pray,
   Take my spirit to Thee.

HENRY CHARLES BEECHING (1859–1919)

980   GOING DOWN HILL ON A BICYCLE
            A BOY'S SONG
    With lifted feet, hands still,
    I am poised, and down the hill
    Dart, with heedful mind;
    The air goes by in a wind.

    Swifter and yet more swift,
    Till the heart with a mighty lift
    Makes the lungs laugh, the throat cry:—
    "O bird, see; see, bird, I fly.

    "Is this, is this your joy?
    O bird, then I, though a boy
    For a golden moment share
    Your feathery life in air!"

    Say, heart, is there aught like this
    In a world that is full of bliss?
    'Tis more than skating, bound
    Steel-shod to the level ground.

    Speed slackens now, I float
    Awhile in my airy boat;
    Till, when the wheels scarce crawl,
    My feet to the treadles fall.

    Alas, that the longest hill
    Must end in a vale; but still,
    Who climbs with toil, wheresoe'er,
    Shall find wings waiting there.
                    HENRY CHARLES BEECHING (1859–1919)

981   WHY
    For a name unknown,
    Whose fame unblown
    Sleeps in the hills
        For ever and aye;

    For her who hears
    The stir of the years
    Go by on the wind
        By night and day;

    And heeds no thing
    Of the needs of spring,
    Of autumn's wonder
        Or winter's chill;

    For one who sees
    The great sun freeze,
    As he wanders a-cold
        From hill to hill;

And all her heart
Is a woven part
Of the flurry and drift
Of whirling snow;

For the sake of two
Sad eyes and true,
And the old, old love
So long ago.

BLISS CARMAN (1861–1929)

MY GRIEF ON THE SEA 982
FROM THE IRISH

My grief on the sea,
How the waves of it roll!
For they heave between me
And the love of my soul!

Abandon'd, forsaken,
To grief and to care,
Will the sea ever waken
Relief from despair?

My grief and my trouble!
Would he and I were,
In the province of Leinster,
Or County of Clare!

Were I and my darling—
O heart-bitter wound!—
On board of the ship
For America bound.

On a green bed of rushes
All last night I lay,
And I flung it abroad
With the heat of the day.

And my Love came behind me,
He came from the South;
His breast to my bosom,
His mouth to my mouth.

DOUGLAS HYDE (1861–1949)

THE PHŒNIX 983

By feathers green, across Casbeen
　The pilgrims track the Phœnix flown,
By gems he strew'd in waste and wood,
　And jewell'd plumes at random thrown.

Till wandering far, by moon and star,
　They stand beside the fruitful pyre,
Where breaking bright with sanguine light
　The impulsive bird forgets his sire.

>   Those ashes shine like ruby wine,
>   Like bag of Tyrian murex spilt,
>   The claw, the jowl of the flying fowl
>   Are with the glorious anguish gilt.
>
>   So rare the light, so rich the sight,
>   Those pilgrim men, on profit bent,
>   Drop hands and eyes and merchandise,
>   And are with gazing most content.
>
> ARTHUR CHRISTOPHER BENSON (1862–1925)

984   HE FELL AMONG THIEVES

"Ye have robb'd," said he, "ye have slaughter'd and made an end,
  Take your ill-got plunder, and bury the dead:
What will ye more of your guest and sometime friend?"
  "Blood for our blood," they said.

He laugh'd: "If one may settle the score for five,
  I am ready; but let the reckoning stand till day:
I have loved the sunlight as dearly as any alive."
  "You shall die at dawn," said they.

He flung his empty revolver down the slope,
  He climb'd alone to the Eastward edge of the trees;
All night long in a dream untroubled of hope
  He brooded, clasping his knees.

He did not hear the monotonous roar that fills
  The ravine where the Yassîn river sullenly flows;
He did not see the starlight on the Laspur hills,
  Or the far Afghan snows.

He saw the April noon on his books aglow,
  The wistaria trailing in at the window wide;
He heard his father's voice from the terrace below
  Calling him down to ride.

He saw the gray little church across the park,
  The mounds that hid the loved and honour'd dead;
The Norman arch, the chancel softly dark,
  The brasses black and red.

He saw the School Close, sunny and green,
  The runner beside him, the stand by the parapet wall,
The distant tape, and the crowd roaring between,
  His own name over all.

He saw the dark wainscot and timber'd roof,
  The long tables, and the faces merry and keen;
The College Eight and their trainer dining aloof,
  The Dons on the daïs serene.

He watch'd the liner's stem ploughing the foam,
  He felt her trembling speed and the thrash of her screw;
He heard the passengers' voices talking of home,
  He saw the flag she flew.

And now it was dawn. He rose strong on his feet,
  And strode to his ruin'd camp below the wood;
He drank the breath of the morning cool and sweet:
  His murderers round him stood.

Light on the Laspur hills was broadening fast,
  The blood-red snow-peaks chill'd to a dazzling white;
He turn'd, and saw the golden circle at last,
  Cut by the Eastern height.

"O glorious Life, Who dwellest in earth and sun,
  I have lived, I praise and adore Thee."
            A sword swept.
Over the pass the voices one by one
  Faded, and the hill slept.
                    HENRY NEWBOLT (1862–1938)

REUNITED   985

When you and I have play'd the little hour,
  Have seen the tall subaltern Life to Death
  Yield up his sword; and, smiling, draw the breath,
The first long breath of freedom; when the flower
Of Recompense hath flutter'd to our feet,
  As to an actor's; and, the curtain down,
  We turn to face each other all alone—
Alone, we two, who never yet did meet,
Alone, and absolute, and free: O then,
  O then, most dear, how shall be told the tale?
Clasp'd hands, press'd lips, and so clasp'd hands again;
  No words. But as the proud wind fills the sail,
    My love to yours shall reach, then one deep moan
    Of joy, and then our infinite Alone.
                    GILBERT PARKER (1862–1932)

WHERE MY BOOKS GO   986

All the words that I utter,
  And all the words that I write,
Must spread out their wings untiring,
  And never rest in their flight,
Till they come where your sad, sad heart is,
  And sing to you in the night,
Beyond where the waters are moving,
  Storm-darken'd or starry bright.
                    WILLIAM BUTLER YEATS (1865–1939)

THE SECOND COMING   987

Turning and turning in the widening gyre
The falcon cannot hear the falconer;
Things fall apart; the centre cannot hold;
Mere anarchy is loosed upon the world,
The blood-dimmed tide is loosed, and everywhere
The ceremony of innocence is drowned;
The best lack all conviction, while the worst
Are full of passionate intensity.

Surely some revelation is at hand;
Surely the Second Coming is at hand.
The Second Coming! Hardly are those words out
When a vast image out of Spiritus Mundi
Troubles my sight: somewhere in sands of the desert
A shape with lion body and the head of a man,
A gaze blank and pitiless as the sun,
Is moving its slow thighs, while all about it
Reel shadows of the indignant desert birds.
The darkness drops again; but now I know
That twenty centuries of stony sleep
Were vexed to nightmare by a rocking cradle,
And what rough beast, its hour come round at last,
Slouches towards Bethlehem to be born?
                              WILLIAM BUTLER YEATS (1865–1939)

988 WHEN YOU ARE OLD

When you are old and gray and full of sleep
  And nodding by the fire, take down this book,
  And slowly read, and dream of the soft look
Your eyes had once, and of their shadows deep;

How many loved your moments of glad grace,
  And loved your beauty with love false or true;
  But one man loved the pilgrim soul in you,
And loved the sorrows of your changing face.

And bending down beside the glowing bars,
  Murmur, a little sadly, how love fled
  And paced upon the mountains overhead,
And hid his face amid a crowd of stars.
                              WILLIAM BUTLER YEATS (1865–1939)

989 THE LAKE ISLE OF INNISFREE

I will arise and go now, and go to Innisfree,
And a small cabin build there, of clay and wattles made;
Nine bean rows will I have there, a hive for the honey bee,
  And live alone in the bee-loud glade.

And I shall have some peace there, for peace comes dropping slow,
Dropping from the veils of the morning to where the cricket sings;
There midnight's all a-glimmer, and noon a purple glow,
  And evening full of the linnet's wings.

I will arise and go now, for always night and day
I hear lake water lapping with low sounds by the shore;
While I stand on the roadway, or on the pavements gray,
  I hear it in the deep heart's core.
                              WILLIAM BUTLER YEATS (1865–1939)

990 A DEDICATION

My new-cut ashlar takes the light
  Where crimson-blank the windows flare;
By my own work, before the night,
  Great Overseer, I make my prayer.

If there be good in that I wrought,
  Thy hand compell'd it, Master, Thine;
Where I have fail'd to meet Thy thought
  I know, through Thee, the blame if mine.

One instant's toil to Thee denied
  Stands all Eternity's offence;
Of that I did with Thee to guide
  To Thee, through Thee, be excellence.

Who, lest all thought of Eden fade,
  Bring'st Eden to the craftsman's brain,
Godlike to muse o'er his own trade
  And manlike stand with God again.

The depth and dream of my desire,
  The bitter paths wherein I stray,
Thou knowest Who hast made the Fire,
  Thou knowest Who hast made the Clay.

One stone the more swings to her place
  In that dread Temple of Thy worth—
It is enough that through Thy grace
  I saw naught common on Thy earth.

Take not that vision from my ken;
  O, whatsoe'er may spoil or speed,
Help me to need no aid from men,
  That I may help such men as need!

                        RUDYARD KIPLING (1865–1936)

THE LONG TRAIL 991

There's a whisper down the field where the year has shot her yield
  And the ricks stand gray to the sun,
Singing:—"Over then, come over, for the bee has quit the clover
  And your English summer's done."
    You have heard the beat of the off-shore wind
    And the thresh of the deep-sea rain;
    You have heard the song—how long! how long!
    Pull out on the trail again!

Ha' done with the Tents of Shem, dear lass,
We've seen the seasons through,
And it's time to turn on the old trail, our own trail, the out trail,
Pull out, pull out, on the Long Trail—the trail that is always new.

It's North you may run to the rime-ring'd sun,
  Or South to the blind Horn's hate;
Or East all the way into Mississippi Bay,
  Or West to the Golden Gate;
Where the blindest bluffs hold good, dear lass,
And the wildest tales are true,
And the men bulk big on the old trail, our own trail, the out trail,
And life runs large on the Long Trail—the trail that is always new.

The days are sick and cold, and the skies are gray and old,
    And the twice-breathed airs blow damp;
And I'd sell my tired soul for the bucking beam-sea roll
    Of a black Bilbao tramp;
With her load-line over her hatch, dear lass,
And a drunken Dago crew,
And her nose held down on the old trail, our own trail, the out trail,
From Cadiz Bar on the Long Trail—the trail that is always new.

There be triple ways to take, of the eagle or the snake,
    Or the way of a man with a maid;
But the sweetest way to me is a ship's upon the sea
    In the heel of the North-East Trade.
Can you hear the crash on her bows, dear lass,
And the drum of the racing screw,
As she ships it green on the old trail, our own trail, the out trail,
As she lifts and 'scends on the Long Trail—the trail that is always new?

See the shaking funnels roar, with the Peter at the fore,
    And the fenders grind and heave,
And the derricks clack and grate, as the tackle hooks the crate,
    And the fall-rope whines through the sheave;
It's "Gang-plank up and in," dear lass,
It's "Hawsers warp her through!"
And it's "All clear aft" on the old trail, our own trail, the out trail,
We're backing down on the Long Trail—the trail that is always new.

O the mutter overside, when the port-fog holds us tied,
    And the sirens hoot their dread!
When foot by foot we creep o'er the hueless viewless deep
    To the sob of the questing lead!
It's down by the Lower Hope, dear lass,
With the Gunfleet Sands in view,
Till the Mouse swings green on the old trail, our own trail, the out trail,
And the Gull Light lifts on the Long Trail—the trail that is always new.

O the blazing tropic night, when the wake's a welt of light
    That holds the hot sky tame,
And the steady fore-foot snores through the planet-powder'd floors
    Where the scared whale flukes in flame!
Her plates are scarr'd by the sun, dear lass,
And her ropes are taut with the dew,
For we're booming down on the old trail, our own trail, the out trail,
We're sagging south on the Long Trail—the trail that is always new.

Then home, get her home, where the drunken rollers comb,
    And the shouting seas drive by,
And the engines stamp and ring, and the wet bows reel and swing,
    And the Southern Cross rides high!
Yes, the old lost stars wheel back, dear lass,
That blaze in the velvet blue.
They're all old friends on the old trail, our own trail, the outtrail,
They're God's own guides on the Long Trail—the trail that is always new.

Fly forward, O my heart, from the Foreland to the Start—
  We're steaming all too slow,
And it's twenty thousand mile to our little lazy isle
  Where the trumpet-orchids blow!
You have heard the call of the off-shore wind
And the voice of the deep-sea rain;
You have heard the song—how long! how long!
  Pull out on the trail again!

The Lord knows what we may find, dear lass,
And the deuce knows what we may do—
But we're back once more on the old trail, our own trail, the out trail,
We're down, hull down on the Long Trail—the trail that is always new.
                                        RUDYARD KIPLING (1865–1936)

THE GODS OF THE COPYBOOK HEADINGS   992

As I pass through my incarnations in every age and race,
I make my proper prostrations to the Gods of the Market Place.
Peering through reverent fingers I watch them flourish and fall,
And the Gods of the Copybook Headings, I notice, outlast them all.

We were living in trees when they met us. They showed us each in turn
That Water would certainly wet us, as Fire would certainly burn:
But we found them lacking in Uplift, Vision and Breadth of Mind,
So we left them to teach the Gorillas while we followed the March of Mankind.

We moved as the Spirit listed. They never altered their pace,
Being neither cloud nor wind-borne like the Gods of the Market Place,
But they always caught up with our progress, and presently word would come
That a tribe had been wiped off its icefield, or the lights had gone out in Rome.

With the Hopes that our World is built on they were utterly out of touch,
They denied that the Moon was Stilton; they denied she was even Dutch;
They denied that Wishes were Horses; they denied that a Pig had Wings;
So we worshipped the Gods of the Market Who promised these beautiful things.

When the Cambrian measures were forming, They promised perpetual peace.
They swore, if we gave them our weapons, that the wars of the tribes would cease.
But when we disarmed They sold us and delivered us bound to our foe,
And the Gods of the Copybook Headings said: *"Stick to the Devil you know."*

On the first Feminian Sandstones we were promised the Fuller Life
(Which started by loving our neighbour and ended by loving his wife)
Till our women had no more children and the men lost reason and faith,
And the Gods of the Copybook Headings said: *"The Wages of Sin is Death."*

In the Carboniferous Epoch we were promised abundance for all,
By robbing selected Peter to pay for collective Paul;
But, though we had plenty of money, there was nothing our money could buy,
And the Gods of the Copybook Headings said: *"If you don't work you die."*

Then the Gods of the Market tumbled, and their smooth-tongued wizards withdrew
And the hearts of the meanest were humbled and began to believe it was true
That All is not Gold that Glitters, and Two and Two make Four
And the Gods of the Copybook Headings limped up to explain it once more.

As it will be in the future, it was at the birth of Man
There are only four things certain since Social Progress began.
That the Dog returns to his Vomit and the Sow returns to her Mire,
And the burnt Fool's bandaged finger goes wabbling back to the Fire;

And that after this is accomplished, and the brave new world begins
When all men are paid for existing and no man must pay for his sins,
As surely as Water will wet us, as surely as Fire will burn,
The Gods of the Copybook Headings with terror and slaughter return!
Rudyard Kipling (1865–1936)

993   Recessional
June 22, 1897

    God of our fathers, known of old—
        Lord of our far-flung battle-line—
    Beneath whose awful Hand we hold
        Dominion over palm and pine—
    Lord God of Hosts, be with us yet,
    Lest we forget, lest we forget!

    The tumult and the shouting dies—
        The captains and the kings depart—
    Still stands Thine ancient sacrifice,
        An humble and a contrite heart.
    Lord God of Hosts, be with us yet,
    Lest we forget, lest we forget!

    Far-call'd our navies melt away—
        On dune and headland sinks the fire—
    Lo, all our pomp of yesterday
        Is one with Nineveh and Tyre!
    Judge of the Nations, spare us yet,
    Lest we forget, lest we forget!

    If, drunk with sight of power, we loose
        Wild tongues that have not Thee in awe—
    Such boasting as the Gentiles use
        Or lesser breeds without the Law—
    Lord God of Hosts, be with us yet,
    Lest we forget, lest we forget!

    For heathen heart that puts her trust
        In reeking tube and iron shard—
    All valiant dust that builds on dust,
        And guarding calls not Thee to guard—
    For frantic boast and foolish word,
    Thy Mercy on Thy People, Lord!
Rudyard Kipling (1865–1936)

Song 994

She's somewhere in the sunlight strong,
  Her tears are in the falling rain,
She calls me in the wind's soft song,
  And with the flowers she comes again.

Yon bird is but her messenger,
  The moon is but her silver car;
Yea! sun and moon are sent by her,
  And every wistful waiting star.

RICHARD LE GALLIENNE (1866–1947)

The Second Crucifixion 995

Loud mockers in the roaring street
  Say Christ is crucified again:
Twice pierced His gospel-bearing feet,
  Twice broken His great heart in vain.

I hear, and to myself I smile,
For Christ talks with me all the while.

No angel now to roll the stone
  From off His unawaking sleep,
In vain shall Mary watch alone,
  In vain the soldiers vigil keep.

Yet while they deem my Lord is dead
My eyes are on His shining head.

Ah! never more shall Mary hear
  That voice exceeding sweet and low
Within the garden calling clear:
  Her Lord is gone, and she must go.

Yet all the while my Lord I meet
In every London lane and street.

Poor Lazarus shall wait in vain,
  And Bartimaeus still go blind;
The healing hem shall ne'er again
  Be touch'd by suffering humankind.

Yet all the while I see them rest,
The poor and outcast, on His breast.

No more unto the stubborn heart
  With gentle knocking shall He plead,
No more the mystic pity start,
  For Christ twice dead is dead indeed.

So in the street I hear men say,
Yet Christ is with me all the day.

RICHARD LE GALLIENNE (1866–1947)

996   INVOCATION TO YOUTH

Come then, as ever, like the wind at morning!
Joyous, O Youth, in the agèd world renew
Freshness to feel the eternities around it,
   Rain, stars and clouds, light and the sacred dew.
      The strong sun shines above thee:
      That strength, that radiance bring!
      If Winter come to Winter,
      When shall men hope for Spring?
                      LAURENCE BINYON (1869–1943)

997   O WORLD, BE NOBLER

O World, be nobler, for her sake!
   If she but knew thee what thou art,
What wrongs are borne, what deeds are done
In thee, beneath thy daily sun,
   Know'st thou not that her tender heart
For pain and very shame would break?
O World, be nobler, for her sake!
                        LAURENCE BINYON (1869–1943)

998   BY THE MARGIN OF THE GREAT DEEP

When the breath of twilight blows to flame the misty skies,
All its vaporous sapphire, violet glow and silver gleam,
With their magic flood me through the gateway of the eyes;
   I am one with the twilight's dream.

When the trees and skies and fields are one in dusky mood,
Every heart of man is rapt within the mother's breast:
Full of peace and sleep and dreams in the vasty quietude,
   I am one with their hearts at rest.

From our immemorial joys of hearth and home and love
Stray'd away along the margin of the unknown tide,
All its reach of soundless calm can thrill me far above
   Word or touch from the lips beside.

Aye, and deep and deep and deeper let me drink and draw
From the olden fountain more than light or peace or dream,
Such primaeval being as o'erfills the heart with awe,
   Growing one with its silent stream.
                        GEORGE WILLIAM RUSSELL ('A. E.') (1853–1935)

999   THE GREAT BREATH

Its edges foam'd with amethyst and rose,
Withers once more the old blue flower of day:
There where the ether like a diamond glows,
   Its petals fade away.

A shadowy tumult stirs the dusky air;
Sparkle the delicate dews, the distant snows;
The great deep thrills—for through it everywhere
   The breath of Beauty blows.

I saw how all the trembling ages past,
Moulded to her by deep and deeper breath,
Near'd to the hour when Beauty breathes her last
    And knows herself in death.

GEORGE WILLIAM RUSSELL ('A. E.') (1853–1935)

A DUET 1000

"Flowers nodding gaily, scent in air,
Flowers posied, flowers for the hair,
Sleepy flowers, flowers bold to stare—"
    "O pick me some!"

"Shells with lip, or tooth, or bleeding gum,
Tell-tale shells, and shells that whisper Come,
Shells that stammer, blush, and yet are dumb—"
    "O let me hear."

"Eyes so black they draw one trembling near,
Brown eyes, caverns flooded with a tear,
Cloudless eyes, blue eyes so windy clear—"
    "O look at me!"

"Kisses sadly blown across the sea,
Darkling kisses, kisses fair and free,
Bob-a-cherry kisses 'neath a tree—"
    "O give me one!"

Thus said a king and queen in Babylon.

T. STURGE MOORE (1870–1944)

THE POPPY 1001

Summer set lip to earth's bosom bare,
And left the flush'd print in a poppy there;
Like a yawn of fire from the grass it came,
And the fanning wind puff'd it to flapping flame.

With burnt mouth red like a lion's it drank
The blood of the sun as he slaughter'd sank,
And dipp'd its cup in the purpurate shine
When the eastern conduits ran with wine.

Till it grew lethargied with fierce bliss,
And hot as a swinkèd gipsy is,
And drowsed in sleepy savageries,
With mouth wide a-pout for a sultry kiss.

A child and man paced side by side,
Treading the skirts of eventide;
But between the clasp of his hand and hers
Lay, felt not, twenty wither'd years.

She turn'd, with the rout of her dusk South hair,
And saw the sleeping gipsy there;
And snatch'd and snapp'd it in swift child's whim,
With—"Keep it, long as you live!"—to him.

And his smile, as nymphs from their laving meres,
Trembled up from a bath of tears;
And joy, like a mew sea-rock'd apart,
Toss'd on the wave of his troubled heart.

For *he* saw what she did not see,
That—as kindled by its own fervency—
The verge shrivell'd inward smoulderingly:

And suddenly 'twixt his hand and hers
He knew the twenty wither'd years—
No flower, but twenty shrivell'd years.

"Was never such thing until this hour,"
Low to his heart he said; "the flower
Of sleep brings wakening to me,
And of oblivion memory."

"Was never this thing to me," he said,
"Though with bruised poppies my feet are red!"
And again to his own heart very low:
"O child! I love, for I love and know;

"But you, who love nor know at all
The diverse chambers in Love's guest-hall,
Where some rise early, few sit long:
In how differing accents hear the throng
His great Pentecostal tongue;

"Who know not love from amity,
Nor my reported self from me;
A fair fit gift is this, meseems,
You give—this withering flower of dreams.

"O frankly fickle, and fickly true,
Do you know what the days will do to you?
To your Love and you what the days will do,
O frankly fickle, and fickly true?

"You have loved me, Fair, three lives—or days:
'Twill pass with the passing of my face.
But where *I* go, your face goes too,
To watch lest I play false to you.

"I am but, my sweet, your foster-lover,
Knowing well when certain years are over
You vanish from me to another;
Yet I know, and love, like the foster-mother.

"So frankly fickle, and fickly true!
For my brief life-while I take from you
This token, fair and fit, meseems,
For me—this withering flower of dreams."

The sleep-flower sways in the wheat its head,
Heavy with dreams, as that with bread:
The goodly grain and the sun-flush'd sleeper
The reaper reaps, and Time the reaper.

I hang 'mid men my needless head,
And my fruit is dreams, as theirs is bread:
The goodly men and the sun-hazed sleeper
Time shall reap, but after the reaper
The world shall glean of me, me the sleeper!

Love! love! your flower of wither'd dream
In leaved rhyme lies safe, I deem,
Shelter'd and shut in a nook of rhyme,
From the reaper man, and his reaper Time.

Love! *I* fall into the claws of Time:
But lasts within a leavèd rhyme
All that the world of me esteems—
My wither'd dreams, my wither'd dreams.
FRANCIS THOMPSON (1859–1907)

NON NOBIS 1002

Not unto us, O Lord,
Not unto us the rapture of the day,
The peace of night, or love's divine surprise,
High heart, high speech, high deeds 'mid honouring eyes;
For at Thy word
All these are taken away.

Not unto us, O Lord:
To us thou givest the scorn, the scourge, the scar,
The ache of life, the loneliness of death,
The insufferable sufficiency of breath;
And with Thy sword
Thou piercest very far.

Not unto us, O Lord:
Nay, Lord, but unto her be all things given—
My light and life and earth and sky be blasted—
But let not all that wealth of loss be wasted:
Let Hell afford
The pavement of her Heaven!
HENRY CUST (1861–1917)

SHEEP AND LAMBS 1003

All in the April morning,
  April airs were abroad;
The sheep with their little lambs
  Pass'd me by on the road.

The sheep with their little lambs
  Pass'd me by on the road;
All in an April evening
  I thought on the Lamb of God.

The lambs were weary, and crying
  With a weak human cry,
I thought on the Lamb of God
  Going meekly to die.

Up in the blue, blue mountains
  Dewy pastures are sweet:
Rest for the little bodies,
  Rest for the little feet.

Rest for the Lamb of God
  Up on the hill-top green,
Only a cross of shame
  Two stark crosses between.

All in the April evening,
  April airs were abroad;
I saw the sheep with their lambs,
  And thought on the Lamb of God.
                KATHARINE TYNAN HINKSON (1861–1931)

1004   AN UPPER CHAMBER
I came into the City and none knew me;
  None came forth, none shouted "He is here!"
Not a hand with laurel would bestrew me,
  All the way by which I drew anear—
  Night my banner, and my herald Fear.

But I knew where one so long had waited
  In the low room at the stairway's height,
Trembling lest my foot should be belated,
  Singing, sighing for the long hours' flight
  Towards the moment of our dear delight.

I came into the City when you hail'd me
  Saviour, and again your chosen Lord:—
Not one guessing what it was that fail'd me,
  While along the way as they adored
  Thousands, thousands, shouted in accord.

But through all the joy I knew—I only—
  How the hostel of my heart lay bare and cold,
Silent of its music, and how lonely!
  Never, though you crown me with your gold,
  Shall I find that little chamber as of old!
                    FRANCES BANNERMAN (1855–1940)

1005   RENOUNCEMENT
I must not think of thee; and, tired yet strong,
  I shun the love that lurks in all delight—
  The love of thee—and in the blue heaven's height,
And in the dearest passage of a song.

Oh, just beyond the sweetest thoughts that throng
  This breast, the thought of thee waits hidden yet bright;
  But it must never, never come in sight;
I must stop short of thee the whole day long.
But when sleep comes to close each difficult day,
  When night gives pause to the long watch I keep,
And all my bonds I needs must loose apart,
Must doff my will as raiment laid away,—
  With the first dream that comes with the first sleep
I run, I run, I am gather'd to thy heart.
ALICE MEYNELL (1850–1922)

THE LADY OF THE LAMBS   1006

She walks—the lady of my delight—
  A shepherdess of sheep.
Her flocks are thoughts. She keeps them white;
  She guards them from the steep.
She feeds them on the fragrant height,
  And folds them in for sleep.

She roams maternal hills and bright,
  Dark valleys safe and deep.
Her dreams are innocent at night;
  The chastest stars may peep.
She walks—the lady of my delight—
  A shepherdess of sheep.

She holds her little thoughts in sight,
  Though gay they run and leap.
She is so circumspect and right;
  She has her soul to keep.
She walks—the lady of my delight—
  A shepherdess of sheep.
ALICE MEYNELL (1850–1922)

IRELAND   1007

'Twas the dream of a God,
  And the mould of His hand,
That you shook 'neath His stroke,
That you trembled and broke
  To this beautiful land.

Here He loosed from His hold
  A brown tumult of wings,
Till the wind on the sea
Bore the strange melody
  Of an island that sings.

He made you all fair,
  You in purple and gold,
You in silver and green,
Till no eye that has seen
  Without love can behold.

I have left you behind
  In the path of the past,
With the white breath of flowers,
With the best of God's hours,
  I have left you at last.

DORA SIGERSON (1866–1918)

1008   GENIUS LOCI

Peace, Shepherd, peace! What boots it singing on?
  Since long ago grace-giving Phœbus died,
  And all the train that loved the stream-bright side
Of the poetic mount with him are gone
Beyond the shores of Styx and Acheron,
  In unexplorèd realms of night to hide.
  The clouds that strew their shadows far and wide
Are all of Heaven that visits Helicon.
Yet here, where never muse or god did haunt,
  Still may some nameless power of Nature stray,
Pleased with the reedy stream's continual chant
  And purple pomp of these broad fields in May.
The shepherds meet him where he herds the kine,
And careless pass him by whose is the gift divine.

MARGARET L. WOODS (1856–1945)

1009   A PARTING GUEST

What delightful hosts are they—
  Life and Love!
Lingeringly I turn away,
  This late hour, yet glad enough
They have not withheld from me
  Their high hospitality.
So, with face lit with delight
  And all gratitude, I stay
  Yet to press their hands and say,
"Thanks.— So fine a time! Good night."

JAMES WHITCOMB RILEY (1853–1916)

1010   A PENITENTIAL WEEK

The week had gloomily begun
For Willie Weeks, a poor man's
  SUN.

He was beset with bill and dun,
And he had very little
  MON.

"This cash," said he, "won't pay my dues,
I've nothing here but ones and
  TUES."

A bright thought struck him, and he said:
"The rich Miss Goldrocks I will
  WED."

But when he paid his court to her,
She lisped, but firmly said: "No,
  THUR."

"Alas," said he, "then I must die!
Although hereafter I may
  FRI."

They found his gloves, and coat, and hat;
The Coroner upon them
  SAT.

CAROLYN WELLS (1869–1942)

BALLAD FOR GLOOM   1011

For God, our God is a gallant foe
That playeth behind the veil.

I have loved my God as a child at heart
That seeketh deep bosoms for rest,
I have loved my God as a maid to man—
But lo, this thing is best:

To love your God as a gallant foe that plays behind the veil;
To meet your God as the night winds meet beyond Arcturus' pale.

I have played with God for a woman,
I have staked with my God for truth,
I have lost to my God as a man, clear-eyed—
 His dice be not of ruth.

For I am made as a naked blade,
 But hear ye this thing in sooth:

Who loseth to God as man to man
 Shall win at the turn of the game.
I have drawn my blade where the lightnings meet
 But the ending is the same:
Who loseth to God as the sword blades lose
 Shall win at the end of the game.

For God, our God is a gallant foe that playeth behind the veil.
Whom God deigns not to overthrow hath need of triple mail.

EZRA POUND (1885–1972)

THE BUILDER   1012

[This poem is noteworthy for its abrupt ending, birthing curious speculations that begin where Wattles' verse ends. – Ed.]

  Smoothing a cypress beam
   With a scarred hand,
  I saw a carpenter
  In a far land.

Down past the flat roofs
   Poured the white sun;
But still he bent his back,
   The patient one.

And I paused surprised
   In that queer place
To find an old man
   With a haunting face.

"Who art thou, carpenter,
   Of the bowed head;
And what buildest thou?"
   "Heaven," he said.
WILLARD WATTLES (1888–1950)

1013   DIOGENES

A hut, and a tree,
   And a hill for me,
And a piece of weedy meadow.
   I'll ask no thing,
   Of God or king,
But to clear away his shadow.
MAX EASTMAN (1883–1969)

1014   GRASS

Pile the bodies high at Austerlitz and Waterloo.
Shovel them under and let me work—
   I am the grass; I cover all.

And pile them high at Gettysburg
And pile them high at Ypres and Verdun.
Shovel them under and let me work.
Two years, ten years, and passengers ask the conductor:
   What place is this?
   Where are we now?

   I am the grass.
   Let me work.
CARL SANDBURG (1878–1867)

1015   I HAVE A RENDEZVOUS WITH DEATH

[Perhaps the greatest first line of any poem in this volume. Seeger kept his rendezvous, dying a hero's death on July 4, 1916 in the Battle of the Somme while serving in the French Foreign Legion. – Ed.]

I have a rendezvous with Death
At some disputed barricade,
When Spring comes back with rustling shade
And apple-blossoms fill the air—
I have a rendezvous with Death
When Spring brings back blue days and fair.

It may be he shall take my hand
And lead me into his dark land
And close my eyes and quench my breath—
It may be I shall pass him still.
I have a rendezvous with Death
On some scarred slope of battered hill,
When Spring comes round again this year
And the first meadow-flowers appear.

God knows 'twere better to be deep
Pillowed in silk and scented down,
Where love throbs out in blissful sleep,
Pulse nigh to pulse, and breath to breath,
Where hushed awakenings are dear...
But I've a rendezvous with Death
At midnight in some flaming town,
When Spring trips north again this year,
And I to my pledged word am true,
I shall not fail that rendezvous.

ALAN SEEGER (1888–1916)

MENDING WALL

1016

Something there is that doesn't love a wall,
That sends the frozen-ground-swell under it,
And spills the upper boulders in the sun;
And makes gaps even two can pass abreast.
The work of hunters is another thing:
I have come after them and made repair
Where they have left not one stone on stone,
But they would have the rabbit out of hiding,
To please the yelping dogs. The gaps I mean,
No one has seen them made or heard them made,
But at spring mending-time we find them there.
I let my neighbor know beyond the hill;
And on a day we meet to walk the line
And set the wall between us once again.
We keep the wall between us as we go.
To each the boulders that have fallen to each.
And some are loaves and some so nearly balls
We have to use a spell to make them balance:
"Stay where you are until our backs are turned!"
We wear our fingers rough with handling them.
Oh, just another kind of outdoor game,
One on a side. It comes to little more:
He is all pine and I am apple-orchard.
My apple trees will never get across
And eat the cones under his pines, I tell him.
He only says, "Good fences make good neighbors."
Spring is the mischief in me, and I wonder
If I could put a notion in his head:

"*Why* do they make good neighbors? Isn't it
Where there are cows? But here there are no cows.
Before I built a wall I'd ask to know
What I was walling in or walling out,
And to whom I was like to give offence.
Something there is that doesn't love a wall,
That wants it down!" I could say "Elves" to him,
But it's not elves exactly, and I'd rather
He said it for himself. I see him there,
Bringing a stone grasped firmly by the top
In each hand, like an old-stone savage armed.
He moves in darkness as it seems to me,
Not of woods only and the shade of trees.
He will not go behind his father's saying,
And he likes having thought of it so well
He says again, "Good fences make good neighbors."
                    ROBERT FROST (1874–1963)

1017   MORNING SONG FROM "SENLIN"
It is morning, Senlin says, and in the morning
When the light drips through the shutters like the dew,
I arise, I face the sunrise,
And do the things my fathers learned to do.
Stars in the purple dusk above the rooftops
Pale in a saffron mist and seem to die,
And I myself on swiftly tilting planet
Stand before a glass and tie my tie.

Vine-leaves tap my window,
Dew-drops sing to the garden stones,
The robin chirps in the chinaberry tree
Repeating three clear tones.

It is morning. I stand by the mirror
And tie my tie once more.
While waves far off in a pale rose twilight
Crash on a white sand shore.
I stand by a mirror and comb my hair:
How small and white my face!—
The green earth tilts through a sphere of air
And bathes in a flame of space.
There are houses hanging above the stars
And stars hung under a sea...
And a sun far off in a shell of silence
Dapples my walls for me....

It is morning, Senlin says, and in the morning
Should I not pause in the light to remember God?
Upright and firm I stand on a star unstable,
He is immense and lonely as a cloud.
I will dedicate this moment before my mirror
To him alone, for him I will comb my hair.
Accept these humble offerings, clouds of silence!
I will think of you as I descend the stair.

Vine-leaves tap my window,
The snail-track shines on the stones;
Dew-drops flash from the chinaberry tree
Repeating two clear tones.

It is morning, I awake from a bed of silence,
Shining I rise from the starless waters of sleep.
The walls are about me still as in the evening,
I am the same, and the same name still I keep.
The earth revolves with me, yet makes no motion,
The stars pale silently in a coral sky.
In a whistling void I stand before my mirror,
Unconcerned, and tie my tie.

There are horses neighing on far-off hills
Tossing their long white manes,
And mountains flash in the rose-white dusk,
Their shoulders black with rains....
It is morning, I stand by the mirror
And surprise my soul once more;
The blue air rushes above my ceiling,
There are suns beneath my floor....

...It is morning, Senlin says, I ascend from darkness
And depart on the winds of space for I know not where;
My watch is wound, a key is in my pocket,
And the sky is darkened as I descend the stair.
There are shadows across the windows, clouds in heaven,
And a god among the stars; and I will go
Thinking of him as I might think of daybreak
And humming a tune I know....

Vine-leaves tap at the window,
Dew-drops sing to the garden stones,
The robin chirps in the chinaberry tree
Repeating three dear tones.

CONRAD AIKEN (1889–1973)

OLD MANUSCRIPT

The sky
is that beautiful old parchment
in which the sun
and the moon
keep their diary.
To read it all,
one must be a linguist
more learned than Father Wisdom;
and a visionary
more clairvoyant than Mother Dream.
But to feel it,
one must be an apostle:

one who is more than intimate
In having been, always,
the only confidant—
like the earth
or the sea.

ALFRED KREYMBORG (1883–1966)

1019   RICHARD COREY

Whenever Richard Cory went down town,
  We people on the pavement looked at him:
He was a gentleman from sole to crown,
  Clean favored, and imperially slim.

And he was always quietly arrayed,
  And he was always human when he talked;
But still he fluttered pulses when he said,
  "Good-morning," and he glittered when he walked.

And he was rich — yes, richer than a king,
  And admirably schooled in every grace:
In fine, we thought that he was everything
  To make us wish that we were in his place.

So on we worked, and waited for the light,
  And went without the meat, and cursed the bread;
And Richard Cory, one calm summer night,
  Went home and put a bullet through his head.

EDWIN ARLINGTON ROBINSON (1869–1935)

1020   THE RICH MAN

The rich man has his motor-car,
  His country and his town estate.
He smokes a fifty-cent cigar
  And jeers at Fate.

He frivols through the livelong day,
  He knows not Poverty, her pinch.
His lot seems light, his heart seems gay;
  He has a cinch.

Yet though my lamp burns low and dim,
  Though I must slave for livelihood—
Think you that I would change with him?
  You bet I would!

FRANKLIN P. ADAMS (1881–1960)

1021   SILENCE

I have known the silence of the stars and of the sea,
And the silence of the city when it pauses,
And the silence of a man and a maid,
And the silence for which music alone finds the word,
And the silence of the woods before the winds of spring begin,
And the silence of the sick
When their eyes roam about the room.
And I ask: For the depths

Of what use is language?
A beast of the field moans a few times
When death takes its young.
And we are voiceless in the presence of realities—
We cannot speak.

A curious boy asks an old soldier
Sitting in front of the grocery store,
"How did you lose your leg?"
And the old soldier is struck with silence,
Or his mind flies away
Because he cannot concentrate it on Gettysburg.
It comes back jocosely
And he says, "A bear bit it off."
And the boy wonders, while the old soldier
Dumbly, feebly lives over
The flashes of guns, the thunder of cannon,
The shrieks of the slain,
And himself lying on the ground,
And the hospital surgeons, the knives,
And the long days in bed.
But if he could describe it all
He would be an artist.
But if he were an artist there would he deeper wounds
Which he could not describe.

There is the silence of a great hatred,
And the silence of a great love,
And the silence of a deep peace of mind,
And the silence of an embittered friendship,
There is the silence of a spiritual crisis,
Through which your soul, exquisitely tortured,
Comes with visions not to be uttered
Into a realm of higher life.
And the silence of the gods who understand each other without speech,
There is the silence of defeat.
There is the silence of those unjustly punished;
And the silence of the dying whose hand
Suddenly grips yours.
There is the silence between father and son,
When the father cannot explain his life,
Even though he be misunderstood for it.

There is the silence that comes between husband and wife.
There is the silence of those who have failed;
And the vast silence that covers
Broken nations and vanquished leaders.
There is the silence of Lincoln,
Thinking of the poverty of his youth.
And the silence of Napoleon
After Waterloo.

And the silence of Jeanne d'Arc
Saying amid the flames, "Blessèd Jesus"—
Revealing in two words all sorrow, all hope.
And there is the silence of age,
Too full of wisdom for the tongue to utter it
In words intelligible to those who have not lived
The great range of life.

And there is the silence of the dead.
If we who are in life cannot speak
Of profound experiences,
Why do you marvel that the dead
Do not tell you of death?
Their silence shall be interpreted
As we approach them.

EDGAR LEE MASTERS (1868–1950)

1022   TREES

    I think that I shall never see
    A poem lovely as a tree.

    A tree whose hungry mouth is prest
    Against the sweet earth's flowing breast;

    A tree that looks at God all day,
    And lifts her leafy arms to pray;

    A tree that may in summer wear
    A nest of robins in her hair;

    Upon whose bosom snow has lain;
    Who intimately lives with rain.

    Poems are made by fools like me,
    But only God can make a tree.

JOYCE KILMER (1886–1918)

1023   IF—

If you can keep your head when all about you
    Are losing theirs and blaming it on you,
If you can trust yourself when all men doubt you,
    But make allowance for their doubting too;
If you can wait and not be tired by waiting,
    Or being lied about, don't deal in lies,
Or being hated, don't give way to hating,
    And yet don't look too good, nor talk too wise:

If you can dream—and not make dreams your master;
    If you can think—and not make thoughts your aim;
If you can meet with Triumph and Disaster
    And treat those two impostors just the same;
If you can bear to hear the truth you've spoken
    Twisted by knaves to make a trap for fools,
Or watch the things you gave your life to, broken,
    And stoop and build 'em up with worn-out tools:

If you can make one heap of all your winnings
    And risk it on one turn of pitch-and-toss,
And lose, and start again at your beginnings
    And never breathe a word about your loss;
If you can force your heart and nerve and sinew
    To serve your turn long after they are gone,
And so hold on when there is nothing in you
    Except the Will which says to them: "Hold on!"

If you can talk with crowds and keep your virtue,
    Or walk with Kings—nor lose the common touch,
If neither foes nor loving friends can hurt you,
    If all men count with you, but none too much;
If you can fill the unforgiving minute
    With sixty seconds' worth of distance run,
Yours is the Earth and everything that's in it,
    And—which is more—you'll be a Man, my son!
RUDYARD KIPLING (1865–1936)

THE TOUCH OF THE MASTER'S HAND   1024

'Twas battered and scarred, and the auctioneer
    Thought it scarcely worth his while
To waste much time on the old violin,
    But held it up with a smile.
"What am I bidden, good folks," he cried,
    "Who'll start the bidding for me?"
"A dollar, a dollar. Then two! Only two?
    Two dollars, and who'll make it three?"

"Three dollars, once; three dollars, twice;
    Going for three..." But no,
From the room, far back, a grey-haired man
    Came forward and picked up the bow;
Then wiping the dust from the old violin,
    And tightening the loosened strings,
He played a melody pure and sweet,
    As a caroling angel sings.

The music ceased, and the auctioneer,
    With a voice that was quiet and low,
Said: "What am I bid for the old violin?"
    And he held it up with the bow.
"A thousand dollars, and who'll make it two?
    Two thousand! And who'll make it three?
Three thousand, once; three thousand, twice,
    And going and gone," said he.

The people cheered, but some of them cried,
    "We do not quite understand.
What changed its worth?" Swift came the reply:
    "The touch of the Master's hand."
And many a man with life out of tune,
    And battered and scarred with sin,
Is auctioned cheap to the thoughtless crowd
    Much like the old violin.

A "mess of pottage," a glass of wine,
    A game — and he travels on.
He is "going" once, and "going" twice,
    He's "going" and almost "gone."
But the Master comes, and the foolish crowd
    Never can quite understand
The worth of a soul and the change that is wrought
    By the touch of the Master's hand.
MYRA BROOKS WELCH (1877–1959)

1025 THE NIGHT HAS A THOUSAND EYES

The night has a thousand eyes,
    And the day but one;
Yet the light of the bright world dies
    With the dying sun.

The mind has a thousand eyes,
    And the heart but one;
Yet the light of a whole life dies
    When love is done.
FRANCIS WILLIAM BOURDILLON (1852–1921)

1026 MAN'S DAYS

A sudden wakin', a sudden weepin',
A li'l suckin', a li'l sleepin';
A cheel's full joys an' a cheel's short sorrows,
Wi' a power o' faith in gert to-morrows.

Young blood red-hot an' the love of a maid,
One glorious day as'll never fade;
Some shadows, some sunshine, some triumphs, some tears,
And a gatherin' weight o' the flyin' years.

Then old man's talk o' the days behind 'e,
Your darter's youngest darter to mind 'e;
A li'l dreamin', a li'l dyin':
A li'l lew corner o' airth to lie in.
EDEN PHILLPOTTS (1862–1960)

Author Index

Franklin P. Adams	The Rich Man	1020
Joseph Addison	Hymn	417
Conrad Aiken	Morning Song From "Senlin"	1017
Hew Ainslie	Willie and Helen	653
Mark Akenside	Amoret	451
	The Complaint	452
	The Nightingale	453
William Alexander, Earl of Stirling	Aurora	179
	To Aurora	251
Henry Alford	The Bride	819
William Allingham	The Fairies	873
Anonymous	This World's Joy	2
	Of a rose, a lovely rose	7
	May in the Green-Wood	11
	Carol	12
	Quia Amore Langueo	13
	The Nut-Brown Maid	14
	As ye came from the Holy Land	22
	The Lover in Winter Plaineth for the Spring	23
	Balow	24
	The Old Cloak	25
	When Flora had O'erfret the Firth	42
	Lusty May	43
	My Heart is High Above	44
	The Lovliness of Love	394
	Dominus Illuminatio Mea	948
Ballads and Songs By Unknown Authors	Sir Patrick Spens	348
	The Dowie Houms of Yarrow	349
	Clerk Saunders	350
	Edward, Edward	351
	The Queen's Marie	352
	Binnorie	353
	The Wife of Usher's Well	354
	The Three Ravens	355
	The Twa Corbies	356
	A Lyke-Wake Dirge	357
	The Seven Virgins.	358
	Two Rivers	359
	Cradle Song	360
	The Call	361
	The Bonny Earl of Murray	362
	Helen of Kirconnell	363
	Waly, Waly	364
	Barbara Allen's Cruelty	365
	Pipe and Can	366
	Love will find out the Way	367
	Phillada Flouts Me	368

Miscellanies & Songs by Unnamed or Uncertain Authors	Hey Nonny No!	45
	Preparations	46
	To Her Sea-faring Lover	53
	The Faithless Shepherdess	54
	Crabbed Age and Youth	55
	A Pedlar	263
	The Now Jerusalem	264
	Icarus	265
	Madrigal	266
	How Can The Heart Forget her?	267
	Tears	268
	My Lady's Tears	269
	Sister, Awake!	270
	Devotion	271
	Since First I Saw Your Face	272
	There is a Lady Sweet and Kind	273
	Love Not Me For Comely Grace	274
	The Wakening	275
Matthew Arnold	The Forsaken Merman	851
	The Song of Callicles	852
	To Marguerite	853
	Requiescat	854
	The Scholar-Gipsy	855
	Philomela	856
	Shakespeare	857
	From the Hymn of Empedocles	858
Thomas Ashe	Meet We no Angels, Pansie?	908
	To Two Bereaved	909
Alfred Austin	To America	763
Sir Robert Ayton	To His Forsaken Mistress	143
	To an Inconstant One	144
Francis Bacon	Life	255
Joanna Baillie	The Outlaw's Song	548
Lady Grisel Baillie	Werena my Heart's licht I wad dee	414
Frances Bannerman	An Upper Chamber	1004
Anna Lætitia Barbauld	Life	463
John Barbour	Freedom	3
Richard Barnefield	Philomel	164
William Barnes	Mater Dolorosa	767
	The Wife a-lost	768
James Beattie	An Epitaph	461
Francis Beaumont	On the Tombs in Westminster Abbey	192
Sir John Beaumont	Of his Dear Son, Gervase	181
Thomas Lovell Beddoes	Wolfram's Dirge	774
	Dream-Pedlary	775
	Song	776
Henry Charles Beeching	Prayers	979
	Going Down Hill on a Bicycle	980
Aphra Behn	Song	384

	The Libertine	385
Arthur Christopher Benson	The Phœnix	983
Laurence Binyon	Invocation to Youth	996
	O World, be Nobler	997
William Blake	A Dream	490
	To the Muses	521
	To Spring	522
	Song	523
	Reeds of Innocence	524
	The Little Black Boy	525
	Hear the Voice	526
	The Tiger	527
	Cradle Song	528
	Night	529
	Love's Secret	530
Wilfrid Scawen Blunt ...	Song	918
	The Desolate City	919
	With Esther	920
	To Manon, on his Fortune in Loving Her	921
	St. Valentine's Day	922
	Gibraltar	923
	Written at Florence	924
	The Two Highwaymen	925
Francis William Bourdillon	The Night Has a Thousand Eyes ...	1025
William Lisle Bowles	The Butterfly And The Bee	480
	Time and Grief	547
Mark Alexander Boyd ...	Sonet	91
Mary Emily Bradley	A Chrysalis	742
Nicholas Breton	Phillida and Coridon	47
	A Cradle Song	48
Ebenezer Cobham Brewer	Little Things	711
Robert Bridges	My Delight and Thy Delight	934
	Spirits	935
	Nightingales	936
	A Passer-by	937
	Absence	938
	On a Dead Child	939
	Pater Filio	940
	Winter Nightfall	941
	When Death to Either shall come ..	942
Alexander Brome	The Resolve	335
Richard Brome	Humility	433
Emily Brontë	My Lady's Grave	839
	Remembrance	840
	The Prisoner	841
	Last Lines	842
William Broome	The Rosebud	968
	Belinda's Recovery from Sickness ..	969

Thomas Edward Brown	Dora	893
	Jessie	894
	Salve!	895
	My Garden	896
William Browne, of Tavistock	A Welcome	196
	The Sirens' Song	197
	The Rose	198
	Song	199
	Memory	200
	An Epitaph	201
	On the Countess Dowager of Pembroke	202
Elizabeth Barrett Browning	Rosalind's Scroll	786
	The Deserted Garden	787
	Consolation	788
	Grief	789
	Sonnets from the Portuguese, No. 1	790
	Sonnets from the Portuguese, No. 3	791
	Sonnets from the Portuguese, No. 6	792
	Sonnets from the Portuguese, No. 14	793
	Sonnets from the Portuguese, No. 22	794
	A Musical Instrument	795
Robert Browning	An Incident Of The French Camp	724
	How They Brought The Good News From Ghent To Aix	745
	Rabbi Ben Ezra	759
	Prospice	760
	Hervé Riel	761
	Song from "Paracelsus"	821
	The Wanderers	822
	Thus the Mayne Glideth	823
	Pippa's Song	824
	You'll Love Me Yet	825
	Porphyria's Lover	826
	Song	827
	Earl Mertoun's Song	828
	In a Gondola	829
	Meeting at Night	830
	Parting at Morning	831
	The Lost Mistress	832
	The Last Ride together	833
	Misconceptions	834
	Home-thoughts, from Abroad	835
	Home-thoughts, from the Sea	836

Robert Mannyng of Brunne	Praise of Women	1
John Bunyan	The Shepherd Boy Sings in the Valley of Humiliation	347
Robert Burns	John Barleycorn	484
	To A Mouse, ...	486
	To A Mountain Daisy, ...	487
	Bannockburn	496
	Mary Morison	531
	Jean	532
	Auld Lang Syne	533
	My Bonnie Mary	534
	John Anderson, my Jo	535
	The Banks O' Doon	536
	Ae Fond Kiss	537
	Bonnie Lesley	538
	Highland Mary	539
	O were my Love yon Lilac fair	540
	A Red, Red Rose	541
	Lament for Culloden	542
	The Farewell	543
	Hark! the Mavis	544
John Burroughs	My Own Shall Come To Me	755
George Gordon Byron, Lord Byron	The Destruction Of Sennacherib ...	497
	The Eve Of Waterloo	501
	When We Two Parted	631
	For Music	632
	We'll Go No More A-Roving	633
	She walks in Beauty	634
	The Isles of Greece	635
	All For Love	689
	Elegy	690
	On the Castle of Chillon	699
	Youth and Age	701
Jeremiah Joseph Callanan	The Outlaw of Loch Lene	670
Thomas Campbell	Lord Ullin's Daughter	489
	Hohenlinden	495
	Ye Mariners of England	614
	The Battle of the Baltic	615
	Freedom and Love	692
	The Solider's Dream	705
	The River of Life	707
Thomas Campion	Cherry-Ripe	130
	Laura	131
	Devotion	132
	Follow Your Saint	133
	Vobiscum est Iope	134
	A Hymn in Praise of Neptune	135
	Winter Nights	136
	Integer Vitae	137

	O come quickly!	138
Thomas Carew	Song	243
	Persuasions to Joy: a Song	244
	To His Inconstant Mistress	245
	The Unfading Beauty	246
	Ingrateful Beauty Threatened	247
	On the Lady Mary Villiers	248
	An Epitaph	249
Henry Carey	Sally in our Alley	428
	A Drinking-Song	429
Bliss Carman	Why	981
Lewis Carroll	Father William	720
	Jabberwocky	721
	The Walrus and the Carpenter	722
William Cartwright	To Chloe	312
	Falsehood	313
	On the Queen's Return from the Low Countries	314
	On a Virtuous Young Gentlewoman That Died Suddenly	315
Margaret Cavendish, Duchess of Newcastle	The Pastime of the Queen of Fairies	398
George Chapman	Bridal Song	84
Thomas Chatterton	Song from Aella	517
Geoffrey Chaucer	The Love Unfeigned	4
	Balade	5
	Merciles Beaute	6
Colley Cibber	The Blind Boy	468
John Clare	Written in Northampton County Asylum	655
Arthur Hugh Clough	Say not the Struggle Naught Availeth	845
Hartley Coleridge	The Solitary-Hearted	675
	Song	676
	Early Death	677
	Friendship	678
Samuel Taylor Coleridge	The Rime of the Ancient Mariner	584
	Kubla Khan	585
	Love	586
	Youth and Age	587
	Time, Real and Imaginary	588
	Work without Hope	589
	Glycine's Song	590
Sara Coleridge	O sleep, my Babe	770
	The Child	771
William Collins	Ode to Simplicity	447
	How sleep the Brave	448
	Ode to Evening	449
	Fidele	450
	To Morrow	474
William Congreve	False though She be	415
	A Hue and Cry after Fair Amoret	416

Henry Constable	On the Death of Sir Philip Sidney ..	87
	Diaphenia	250
Susan Coolidge	How The Leaves Came Down	713
William (Johnson) Cory	Mimnermus in Church	862
	Heraclitus	863
Charles Cotton	To Cœlia	371
Abraham Cowley	Drinking	331
	The Epicure	332
	The Swallow	333
	The Wish	334
	A Supplication	395
William Cowper	The Nightingale And The Glow-worm	434
	The Solitude Of Alexander Selkirk .	435
	To Mary Unwin	459
	My Mary	460
	The Poplar Field	470
	To A Young Lady	471
George Crabbe	Meeting	518
	Late Wisdom	519
	A Marriage Ring	520
Richard Crashaw	Wishes to His Supposed Mistress ..	318
	The Weeper	319
	A Hymn to the Name and Honour of The Admirable Saint Teresa	320
	Upon the Book and Picture of The Seraphical Saint Teresa	321
	Verses from the Shepherds' Hymn .	322
	Christ Crucified	323
	An Epitaph upon Husband and Wife Who Died and were Buried Together	324
Allan Cunningham	The Sun rises bright in France	623
	Hame, Hame, Hame	624
	The Spring of the Year	625
	The Sea	698
Robert Cunninghame-Graham of Gartmore	If Doughty Deeds	458
Henry Cust	Non Nobis	1002
John Cutts, Lord Cutts .	Song	405
Thomas D'Urfey	Chloe Divine	401
Samuel Daniel	Love is a Sickness	88
	Ulysses and the Siren	89
	Beauty, Time, and Love	90
	Care-charmer Sleep	252
George Darley	Song	672
	To Helene	673
	The Fallen Star	674
Sir William Davenant ...	Aubade	283
	To a Mistress Dying	284
	Praise and Prayer	285

John Davidson	Song	974
	The Last Rose	975
Sir John Davies	Man	142
Aubrey Thomas De Vere	Serenade	837
	Sorrow	838
Sir Aubrey De Vere	The Children Band	636
Thomas Dekker	Sweet Content	165
Emily Dickinson	A Book	949
Bertram Dobell	Microcosm	952
Sydney Dobell	The Ballad of Keith of Ravelston ...	869
	Return!	870
	A Chanted Calendar	871
	Laus Deo	872
Henry Austin Dobson ..	A Garden Song	926
	Urceus Exit	927
	In After Days	928
George Bubb Dodington, Lord Melcombe	Shorten Sail	427
John Donne	Daybreak	156
	Song	157
	Time and Absence	158
	The Ecstasy	159
	The Dream	160
	The Funeral	161
	A Hymn to God the Father	162
	Death	163
Michael Drayton	To His Coy Love	93
	The Parting	94
	Sirena	95
	Agincourt	96
	To the Virginian Voyage	97
William Drummond, of Hawthornden	Invocation	182
	Madrigal	183
	Spring Bereaved 1	184
	Spring Bereaved 2	185
	Spring Bereaved 3	186
	Her Passing	187
	Inexorable	188
	Change Should Breed Change	189
	Saint John Baptist	190
	This Life Which Seems So fair	254
	The Lessons of Nature	256
	Doth Then The World Go Thus? ...	257
John Dryden	A Song for St. Cecilia's Day, 1687 .	373
	Ah, how sweet it is to love!	374
	Hidden Flame	375
	Song to a Fair Young Lady, Going Out of the Town in the Spring	376
William Dunbar	To a Lady	15
	In Honour of the City of London ...	16
	On the Nativity of Christ	17

	Lament for the Makers	18
Edward Dyer	Contentment	21
Max Eastman	Diogenes	1013
Richard Edwardes	Amantium Irae	39
George Eliot	The Choir Invisible	758
Jane Elliot	A Lament for Flodden	455
Ebenezer Elliott	Battle Song	621
	Plaint	622
Ralph Waldo Emerson	The Problem	762
	Give All to Love	777
	Uriel	778
	Bacchus	779
	Brahma	780
	Good-Bye	954
Sir George Etherege	Song	377
	How Long he Would Love	378
Sir Richard Fanshawe	A Rose	311
Sir Samuel Ferguson	Cean Dubh Deelish	820
Eugene Field	Wynken, Blynken, And Nod	960
	The Duel	961
James T. Fields	The Captain's Daughter	717
Edward Fitzgerald	Old Song	805
	From Omar Khayyám	806
Thomas Flatman	The Sad Day	380
Giles Fletcher	Wooing Song	191
John Fletcher	Sleep	168
	Bridal Song	169
	Aspatia's Song	170
	Hymn to Pan	171
	Away, Delights	172
	Love's Emblems	173
	Hear, ye Ladies	174
	God Lyaeus	175
	Beauty Clear and Fair	176
	Melancholy	177
	Weep No More	178
Phineas Fletcher	A Litany	180
John Ford	Dawn	193
Robert Frost	Mending Wall	1016
Richard Le Gallienne	Song	994
	The Second Crucifixion	995
George Gascoigne	A Lover's Lullaby	40
John Gay	Song	423
	Black-Eyed Susan	431
Oliver Goldsmith	Woman	456
	Memory	457
Edmund Gosse	Revelation	947
Hannah Flagg Gould	A Name In The Sand	508
James Graham, Marquis of Montrose	I'll never love Thee more	316
Thomas Gray	Elegy Written In A Country Churchyard	438

	The Curse upon Edward	444
	The Progress of Poesy	445
	On a Favourite Cat, Drowned in a Tub of Gold Fishes	446
	Ode on the Pleasure Arising From Vicissitude	467
	Hymn to Adversity	472
Robert Greene	Samela	81
	Fawnia	82
	Sephestia's Lullaby	83
	Content	260
Fanny Greville	Prayer for Indifference	464
Fulke Greville, Lord Brooke	Myra	74
Nicholas Grimald	A True Love	36
William Habington	To Roses in the Bosom of Castara	280
	Nox Nocti Indicat Scientiam	281
Fitz-Greene Halleck	Marco Bozzaris	494
Bret Harte	What the Bullet sang	915
Stephen Hawes	The True Knight	26
	An Epitaph	27
Robert Stephen Hawker	King Arthur's Waes-hael	782
	Are they not all Ministering Spirits?	783
Robert Heath	What is Love?	432
Felicia Dorothea Hemans	The Landing Of The Pilgrims	436
	The Voice Of Spring	437
	Casabianca	476
	Dirge	656
William Ernest Henley	Invictus	944
	Margaritae Sorori	945
	England, My England	946
George Herbert	Virtue	235
	Easter	236
	Discipline	237
	A Dialogue	238
	The Pulley	239
	Love	240
Robert Herrick	To the Virgins, to make much of Time	203
	To the Western Wind	204
	To Electra	205
	To Violets	206
	To Daffodils	207
	To Blossoms	208
	The Primrose	209
	The Funeral Rites of the Rose	210
	Cherry-Ripe	211
	A Meditation for his Mistress	212
	Delight in Disorder	213
	Upon Julia's Clothes	214

	The Bracelet: To Julia	215
	To Daisies, not to Shut So Soon	216
	The Night-piece: To Julia	217
	To Music, to Becalm his Fever	218
	To Dianeme	219
	To Œnone	220
	To Anthea, Who May Command Him Anything	221
	To the Willow-tree	222
	The Mad Maid's Song	223
	Comfort to a Youth that had Lost his Love	224
	To Meadows	225
	A Child's Grace	226
	An Epitaph upon a Child that Died	227
	His Winding-sheet	228
	Litany to the Holy Spirit	229
Thomas Heywood	Matin Song	166
	The Message	167
Katharine Tynan Hinkson	Sheep and Lambs	1003
Thomas Hoccleve	Lament for Chaucer	8
James Hogg	A Boy's Song	551
Thomas Jefferson Hogg	The Skylark	513
J.G. Holland	Heaven Is Not Reached At A Single Bound	736
Oliver Wendell Holmes	The Chambered Nautilus	737
Thomas Hood	I Remember, I Remember	498
	Autumn	679
	Silence	680
	Death	681
	Fair Ines	682
	Time of Roses	683
	Ruth	684
	The Death-bed	685
	The Bridge of Sighs	686
Richard Henry Horne	The Plough	781
Henry Howard, Earl of Surrey	Description of Spring	33
	Complaint of the Absence of Her Lover being upon the Sea	34
	The Means to Attain Happy Life	35
William Dean Howells	Earliest Spring	914
Mary Howitt	The Spider and the Fly	481
James Henry Leigh Hunt	Abou Ben Adhem	485
	The Glove And The Lions	502
	Cupid Drowned	506
	Jenny kiss'd Me	626
Douglas Hyde	My Grief on the Sea	982
Jean Ingelow	The Brides Of Enderby	756
Richard Jago	Absence	443

King James I of Scotland	Spring Song of the Birds	10
Samuel Johnson	One-and-Twenty	441
	On the Death of Mr. Robert Levet, A Practiser in Physic	442
Ebenezer Jones	When the World is burning	849
Sir William Jones	Epigram	466
Ben Jonson	Hymn to Diana	145
	To Celia	146
	Simplex Munditiis	147
	The Shadow	148
	The Triumph	149
	An Elegy	150
	A Farewell to the World	151
	The Noble Balm	152
	On Elizabeth L. H.	153
	On Salathiel Pavy, a child of Queen Elizabeth's Chapel	154
	A Part of an Ode	155
Thomas Jordan	Coronemus Nos Rosis Antequam Marcescant	317
John Keats	Ode to a Nightingale	657
	Ode on a Grecian Urn	658
	To Autumn	659
	Ode on Melancholy	660
	Fragment of an Ode to Maia	661
	Bards of Passion and of Mirth	662
	Fancy	663
	Stanzas	664
	Las Belle Dame sans Merci	665
	On First Looking into Chapman's Homer	666
	When I have Fears that I may Cease to Be	667
	To Sleep	668
	Last Sonnet	669
	The Human Seasons	708
John Keble	Burial of the Dead	654
Henry Clarence Kendall	Mooni	929
Francis Scott Key	The Star-Spangled Banner	479
Joyce Kilmer	Trees	1022
Henry King, Bishop of Chichester	A Contemplation upon Flowers	232
	A Renunciation	233
	Exequy on his Wife	234
Charles Kingsley	A Farewell	716
	Airly Beacon	843
	The Sands of Dee	844
Rudyard Kipling	True Royalty	957
	The Overland-mail	962
	The Ballad Of The "Clampherdown"	963
	L'Envoi	965

Seven Centuries of English Verse

	The English Flag	966
	A Dedication	990
	The Long Trail	991
	The Gods of the Copybook Headings	992
	Recessional	993
	If—	1023
William Knox	Mortality	515
Alfred Kreymborg	Old Manuscript	1018
Charles Lamb	The Old Familiar Faces	611
	Hester	612
	On an Infant dying as soon as born	613
Mary Lamb	A Child	549
Walter Savage Landor	The Maid's Lament	592
	Rose Aylmer	593
	Ianthe	594
	Twenty Years Hence	595
	Verse	596
	Proud Word You Never Spoke	597
	Resignation	598
	Mother, I cannot mind my Wheel	599
	Autumn	600
	Remain!	601
	Absence	602
	Of Clementina	603
	Ianthe's Question	604
	On Catullus	605
	Dirce	606
	Years	607
	Separation	608
	Late Leaves	609
	Finis	610
	Her Name	709
	On His Own Death	710
Andrew Lang	The Odyssey	943
Sidney Lanier	The Tournament	733
	Barnacles	749
Edward Lear	The Owl And The Pussy-cat	715
Catherine C. Liddell	Jesus The Carpenter	735
Lady Anne Lindsay	Auld Robin Gray	516
Frederick Locker-Lampson	At Her Window	850
Thomas Lodge	Rosalind's Madrigal	75
	Phillis 1	76
	Phillis 2	77
	Rosaline	78
John Logan	To the Cuckoo	465
Henry Wadsworth Longfellow	The Village Blacksmith	718
	Hiawatha's Childhood	729
	The Wreck Of The *Hesperus*	740
	A Psalm Of Life	748

	The Skeleton In Armour	752
	My Lost Youth	797
	The Bridge	953
	The Arrow and the Song	956
Richard Lovelace	To Lucasta, going to the Wars	325
	To Lucasta, going beyond the Seas	326
	Gratiana Dancing	327
	To Amarantha, that she Would Dishevel her Hair	328
	The Grasshopper	329
	To Althea, from Prison	330
James Russell Lowell	The Finding Of The Lyre	741
	The Shepherd Of King Admetus	744
	June	747
John Lydgate	Vox Ultima Crucis	9
John Lyly	Cards and Kisses	63
	Spring's Welcome	64
Henry Francis Lyte	Abide With Me	504
George Lyttelton, Lord Lyttelton	Tell me, my Heart, if this be Love	440
Edward Robert Bulwer Lytton, Earl of Lytton	A Night in Italy	897
	The Last Wish	898
George MacDonald	Little White Lily	712
	The Wind And The Moon	734
	That Holy Thing	874
Thomas Babington Macaulay, Lord Macaulay	Horatius At The Bridge	746
	A Jacobite's Epitaph	766
Charles Mackay	Song Of Life	725
Francis Mahony	The Bells of Shandon	785
James Clarence Mangan	Dark Rosaleen	772
	The Nameless One	773
	Advice Against Travel	950
Edwin Markham	The Man With The Hoe	967
Christopher Marlowe	The Passionate Shepherd to His Love	98
Andrew Marvell	On Paradise Lost	262
	An Horatian Ode	336
	A Garden	337
	To His Coy Mistress	338
	The Picture of Little T. C. In a Prospect of Flowers	339
	Thoughts in a Garden	340
	Songs of the Emigrants in Bermuda	341
	An Epitaph	342
	The Fair Singer	396
Edgar Lee Masters	Silence	1021
Jasper Mayne	Time	279

Isaac Mcclellan	The Death Of Napoleon	739
George Meredith	Phœbus with Admetus	876
	Tardy Spring	877
	Love's Grave	878
	Lucifer in Starlight	879
Alice Meynell	Renouncement	1005
	The Lady of the Lambs	1006
William Miller	Wee Willie Winkie	714
Richard Monckton Milnes, Lord Houghton .	Shadows	818
John Milton	Hymn on the Morning of Christ's Nativity	289
	On Time	290
	At a Solemn Musick	291
	L'Allegro	292
	Il Penseroso	293
	From "Arcades"	294
	The Star that Bids the Shepherd Fold	295
	Sweet Echo	296
	Sabrina Fair	297
	To the Ocean now I Fly	298
	Lycidas	299
	On His Blindness	300
	To Mr. Lawrence	301
	To Cyriack Skinner	302
	On His Deceased Wife	303
	Light	304
	Invincible Might	305
	His Uncontroulable Intent	306
	On the Late Massacre in Piemont ..	392
	When the Assault was Intended to the City	393
James Montgomery	Arnold Von Winkleried	512
Clement Clarke Moore ..	A Visit From St. Nicholas	478
T. Sturge Moore	A Duet	1000
Thomas Moore	The Last Rose Of Summer	505
	Cupid Stung	507
	The Harp That Once Through Tara's Halls	510
	The Young May Moon	616
	The Irish Peasant to His Mistress ..	617
	The Light of Other Days	618
	At the Mid Hour of Night	619
	How Sweet the Answer Echo Makes	694
	The Journey Onwards	695
	Pro Patria Mori	700
George Pope Morris	Woodman, Spare That Tree!	750
William Morris	Summer Dawn	903
	Love is Enough	904
	The Nymph's Song to Hylas	905
Anthony Munday	Beauty Bathing	65

Carolina Nairne, Lady Nairne	The Land o' the Leal	550
Thomas Nashe	Spring	128
	In Time of Pestilence	129
Henry Newbolt	He fell Among Thieves	984
John Henry Newman	Lead, Kindly Light	751
Roden Berkeley Wriothesley Noel	The Water-Nymph and the Boy	906
	The Old	907
Caroline Elizabeth Sarah Norton	I do not love Thee	800
John Boyle O'Reilly	A White Rose	933
Arthur William Edgar O'Shaughnessy	Ode	930
	Song	931
	The Fountain of Tears	932
John Oldham	A Quiet Soul	404
William Oldys	On a Fly drinking out of his Cup	422
Selleck Osborne	A Modest Wit	499
Thomas Otway	The Enchantment	403
Isobel Pagan	Ca' the Yowes to the Knowes	462
Gilbert Parker	Reunited	985
Thomas Parnell	Song	420
Coventry Patmore	The Married Lover	864
	If I Were Dead	865
	Departure	866
	The Toys	867
	A Farewell	868
John Howard Payne	Home, Sweet Home!	503
Thomas Love Peacock	Love and Age	627
	The Grave of Love	628
	Three Men of Gotham	629
George Peele	Fair and Fair	79
	A Farewell to Arms	80
Ambrose Philips	To Miss Charlotte Pulteney	430
Katherine Philips ("Orinda")	To One Persuading a Lady to Marriage	372
Eden Phillpotts	Man's Days	1026
William Philpot	Maritæ Suæ	861
John Pierpont	Warren's Address To The American Soldiers	482
Edgar Allan Poe	The Raven	757
	To Helen	802
	Annabel Lee	803
	For Annie	804
	The Conqueror Worm	955
Alexander Pope	Solitude	400
	On a certain Lady at Court	424
	Elegy to the Memory of an Unfortunate Lady	425
	The Dying Christian to his Soul	426
Walter Porter	Love in Thy Youth	259

Ezra Pound	Ballad for Gloom	1011
Winthrop Mackworth Praed	Fairy Song	769
Matthew Prior	The Question to Lisetta	406
	To a Child of Quality	407
	Song	408
	On My Birthday, July 21	409
	The Lady Who Offers Her Looking-Glass to Venus	410
	To Lady Margaret Cavendish Holles-Harley, When a Child	411
	For my own Monument	412
Francis Quarles	A Divine Rapture	230
	Respice Finem	231
Sir Walter Raleigh	The Lye	49
	The Silent Lover	56
	His Pilgrimage	57
	The Conclusion	58
	Her Reply	99
Allan Ramsay	Peggy	421
Thomas Randolph	A Devout Lover	282
William Brighty Rands .	The Flowers	859
	The Thought	860
Thomas Buchanan Read	Sheridan's Ride	726
James Whitcomb Riley .	A Parting Guest	1009
Edwin Arlington Robinson	Richard Corey	1019
Samuel Rogers	A Wish	509
	The Sleeping Beauty	688
T. W. Rolleson	The Dead at Clonmacnois	973
Christina Georgina Rossetti	Bride Song	882
	A Birthday	883
	Song	884
	Twice	885
	Uphill	886
	Passing Away	887
	Marvel of Marvels	888
	Is it Well with the Child?	889
	Remember	890
	Aloof	891
	Rest	892
Dante Gabriel Rossetti .	The Blessèd Damozel	875
Henry Rowe	Sun	545
	Moon	546
Richard Rowlands	Lullaby	127
John Ruskin	Trust Thou Thy Love	848
George William Russell ('A. E.')	By the Margin of the Great Deep ...	998
	The Great Breath	999

Charles Sackville, Earl of Dorset	Song	381
Carl Sandburg	Grass	1014
Epes Sargent	A Life On The Ocean Wave	730
Alexander Scott	A Bequest of His Heart	37
	A Rondel of Love	38
Sir Walter Scott	Lochinvar	488
	Gathering Song Of Donald Dhu	493
	Proud Maisie	578
	Brignall Banks	579
	Lucy Ashton's Song	580
	Answer	581
	The Rover's Adieu	582
	Breathes There The Man	583
	To A Lock of Hair	687
	Eleu loro	696
	The Maid of Neidpath	697
Sir Charles Sedley	To Chloris	382
	To Celia	383
Alan Seeger	I Have a Rendezvous with Death	1015
Helen Selina, Lady Dufferin	Lament of the Irish Emigrant	799
George Sewel	The Dying Man in his Garden	473
William Shakespeare	Polonius' Advice	50
	A Fragment From Mark Antony's Speech	51
	Silvia	100
	The Blossom	101
	When Daisies Pied and Violets Blue	102
	When Icicles Hang by the Wall	103
	Over Hill, Over Dale	104
	Spotted Snakes with Double Tongue	105
	Where the Bee Sucks	106
	Tell me Where is Fancy Bred	107
	Dirge	108
	It was a Lover and his Lass	109
	Aubade	110
	Bridal Song	111
	Dirge of the Three Queens	112
	Orpheus	113
	Sonnet, No. 18	114
	Sonnet, No. 30	115
	Sonnet, No. 31	116
	Sonnet, No. 53	117
	Sonnet, No. 57	118
	Sonnet, No. 94	119
	Sonnet, No. 97	120
	Sonnet, No. 102	121
	Sonnet, No. 104	122
	Sonnet, No. 106	123
	Sonnet, No. 116	124

	Sonnet, No. 129	125
	Sonnet, No. 146	126
John Sheffield, Duke of Buckinghamshire	The Reconcilement	390
	On One who Died Discovering her Kindness	391
Percy Bysshe Shelley	Ozymandias Of Egypt	514
	Hymn of Pan	639
	The Invitation	640
	Hellas	641
	To a Skylark	642
	The Moon	643
	Ode to the West Wind	644
	The Indian Serenade	645
	Night	646
	From the Arabic	647
	Lines	648
	To —	649
	The Question	650
	Remorse	651
	Music, when Soft Voices die	652
	Thy Kisses	691
	Love's Philosophy	693
	The Poet's Dream	706
James Shirley	A Hymn	241
	Death the Leveller	242
	The Last Conquerer	258
Sir Philip Sidney	The Bargain	66
	Song	67
	Voices at the Window	68
	Philomela	69
	The Highway	70
	This Lady's Cruelty	71
	Sleep	72
	Splendidis Longum Valedico Nugis	73
Dora Sigerson	Ireland	1007
John Skelton	To Mistress Margery Wentworth	19
	To Mistress Margaret Hussey	20
Alexander Smith	Love	880
	Barbara	881
Tobias George Smollett	To Leven Water	454
Caroline Southey	To Death	630
Robert Southey	The Battle Of Blenheim	491
	The Legend Of Bishop Hatto	500
	His Books	591
Robert Southwell	Times go by Turns	85
	The Burning Babe	86
Edmund Spenser	Whilst it is Prime	59
	A Ditty In praise of Eliza, Queen of the Shepherds	60
	From "Daphnaida"	61
	Easter	62

	One Day I Wrote Her Name Upon the Strand	261
Thomas Stanley	The Relapse	370
Robert Louis Stevenson	My Shadow	958
	Bed in Summer	959
	Romance	970
	In the Highlands	971
	Requiem	972
William Stevenson	Jolly Good Ale and Old	41
William Strode	Chloris in the Snow	369
Sir John Suckling	A Doubt of Martyrdom	307
	The Constant Lover	308
	Why so Pale and Wan?	309
	When, Dearest, I but think of Thee	310
Algernon Charles Swinburne	Chorus from "Atalanta"	911
	Hertha	912
	Itylus	913
Joshua Sylvester	Ubique	92
Jane Taylor	Twinkle, Twinkle, Little Star	475
	The Violet	477
Sir Henry Taylor	Elena's Song	765
Alfred Tennyson, Lord Tennyson	Sweet And Low	719
	Lady Clare	727
	The Lord Of Burleigh	728
	The Charge Of The Light Brigade	732
	Crossing The Bar	738
	The Brook	743
	The Revenge	753
	Sir Galahad	754
	Mariana	807
	The Lady of Shalott	808
	The Miller's Daughter	809
	Song of the Lotos-Eaters	810
	St. Agnes' Eve	811
	Blow, Bugle, blow	812
	Summer Night	813
	Come down, O Maid	814
	From "In Memoriam"	815
	Maud	816
	O that 'twere possible	817
Frederick Tennyson	The Holy Tide	796
William Makepeace Thackeray	Little Billee	723
Edith M. Thomas	Moly	964
Francis Thompson	The Poppy	1001
James Thomson	On the Death of a particular Friend	439
	Rule Britannia	469
	In the Train	899
	Sunday up the River	900

	Gifts	901
	The Vine	902
Edward Thurlow, Lord Thurlow	May	620
John Todhunter	Maureen	916
	Aghadoe	917
	The Black Knight	951
Thomas Traherne	News	379
Charles Tennyson Turner	Letty's Globe	801
Henry Vaughan	The Retreat	343
	Peace	344
	The Timber	345
	Friends Departed	346
Edward Vere, Earl of Oxford	A Renunciation	253
Thomas Wade	The Half-asleep	784
William Sidney Walker	Too Solemn for Day, Too Sweet for Night	671
Edmund Waller	On a Girdle	286
	Go, lovely Rose	287
	Old Age	288
William Walsh	Rivals	413
William Watson	Song	976
	Ode in May	977
	The Great Misgiving	978
Willard Wattles	The Builder	1012
Theodore Watts-Dunton	Wassail Chorus at the Mermaid Tavern	910
Isaac Watts	Let Dogs Delight To Bark And Bite	399
	The Day of Judgement	418
	A Cradle Hymn	419
Charles Webbe	Against Indifference	402
John Webster	A Dirge	276
	The Shrouding of The Duchess of Malfi	277
	Vanitas Vanitatum	278
Myra Brooks Welch	The Touch of the Master's Hand	1024
Carolyn Wells	A Penitential Week	1010
Robert Wever	In Youth is Pleasure	52
Walt Whitman	Song Of Myself	764
	The Imprisoned Soul	846
	O Captain! My Captain!	847
John Greenleaf Whittier	Barbara Frietchie	731
	Vesta	798
John Wilmot, Earl of Rochester	Return	386
	Love and Life	387
	Constancy	388
	To His Mistress	389
John Wilson	When on Mine Eyes Her Eyes First Shone	397

Author	Title	Page
George Wither	The Lover's Resolution	194
	A Widow's Hymn	195
Charles Wolfe	The Burial of Sir John Moore after Corunna	637
	To Mary	638
Margaret L. Woods	Genius Loci	1008
Samuel Woodworth	The Old Oaken Bucket	511
William Wordsworth	I Wandered Lonely As A Cloud	483
	Fidelity	492
	Strange Fits of Passion Have I Known	552
	She Dwelt Among the Untrodden Ways	553
	I Travell'd Among Unknown Men	554
	Three Years She Grew in Sun and Shower	555
	A Slumber Did My Spirit Seal	556
	Upon Westminster Bridge	557
	Evening on Calais Beach	558
	On the Extinction of The Venetian Republic, 1802	559
	O Friend! I Know Not Which Way I Must Look	560
	Milton! Thou Shouldst be Living at this Hour	561
	Great Men Have Been Among Us	562
	British Freedom	563
	When Men Change Swords for Ledgers	564
	The Solitary Reaper	565
	Perfect Woman	566
	Ode to Duty	567
	The Rainbow	568
	The Sonnet	569
	Scorn not the Sonnet	570
	The World	571
	Ode	572
	Desideria	573
	Valedictory Sonnet to the River Duddon	574
	Mutability	575
	The Trosachs	576
	Speak!	577
	Admonition to a Traveller	702
	To Sleep	703
	A Lesson	704
Sir Henry Wotton	Elizabeth of Bohemia	139
	The Character of a Happy Life	140
	Upon the Death of Sir Albert Morton's Wife	141
Sir Thomas Wyatt	Forget not yet	28
	The Appeal	29

	A Revocation	30
	Vixi Puellis Nuper Idoneus...	31
	To His Lute	32
William Butler Yeats	Where My Books Go	986
	The Second Coming	987
	When You are Old	988
	The Lake Isle of Innisfree	989

First Line Index

A Book of Verses underneath the Bough	806
A! Fredome is a noble thing!	3
A barking sound the Shepherd hears	492
A beaten and a baffled man	951
Abide with me! fast falls the eventide	504
Abou Ben Adhem (may his tribe increase!	485
Above yon sombre swell of land	781
Absence, hear thou my protestation	158
Absent from thee, I languish still	386
Accept, thou shrine of my dead saint	234
A chieftain, to the Highlands bound	489
A child's a plaything for an hour	549
Adieu, farewell earth's bliss!	129
Ae fond kiss, and then we sever	537
A flock of sheep that leisurely pass by	703
A garden is a lovesome thing, God wot!	896
Ah, Chloris! that I now could sit	382
Ah, how sweet it is to love!	374
A hut, and a tree	1013
Ah! were she pitiful as she is fair	82
Ah, what avails the sceptred race!	593
Airly Beacon, Airly Beacon	843
A late lark twitters from the quiet skies	945
Alexis, here she stay'd; among these pines	186
A life on the ocean wave	730
All Nature seems at work. Slugs leave their lair	589
All are not taken; there are left behind	788
Allas! my worthi maister honorable	8
All holy influences dwell within	636
All in the April morning	1003
All in the Downs the fleet was moor'd	431
All is best, though we oft doubt	306
All my past life is mine no more	387
All's over, then: does truth sound bitter	832
All the flowers of the spring	278
All the words that I utter	986
All thoughts, all passions, all delights	586
All under the leaves and the leaves of life	358
Alone I walked the ocean strand	508
Amarantha sweet and fair	328
And, like a dying lady lean and pale	643
And wilt thou leave me thus?	29
Angel, king of streaming morn	545
Angel spirits of sleep	935
A nightingale, that all day long	434
April, April	976
A rose, as fair as ever saw the North	198
Art thou poor, yet hast thou golden slumbers?	165
As I in hoary winter's night	86
As I pass through my incarnations in every age and race	992
As I was walking all alane	356
As doctors give physic by way of prevention	412

As it fell upon a day	164
Ask me no more where Jove bestows	243
Ask me why I send you here	209
Ask not the cause why sullen Spring	376
A slumber did my spirit seal	556
As one that for a weary space has lain	943
As slow our ship her foamy track	695
A star is gone! a star is gone!	674
As those we love decay, we die in part	439
A sudden wakin', a sudden weepin	1026
A sunny shaft did I behold	590
A supercilious nabob of the East	499
A sweet disorder in the dress	213
As we rush, as we rush in the Train	899
As ye came from the holy land	22
At Flores in the Azores Sir Richard Grenville lay	753
At her fair hands how have I grace entreated	267
A thousand martyrs I have made	385
At midnight, in his guarded tent	494
A traveller on a dusty road	725
At the last, tenderly	846
At the mid hour of night, when stars are weeping, I fly	619
Avenge, O Lord! Thy slaughter'd Saints, whose bones	392
Awake, Æolian lyre, awake	445
Awake, awake, my Lyre!	395
Away! away!	452
Away, delights! go seek some other dwelling	172
Away! the moor is dark beneath the moon	651
A weary lot is thine, fair maid	582
A wet sheet and a flowing sea	698
Bacchus must now his power resign	429
Balow my babe, lie still and sleep!	24
Bards of Passion and of Mirth	662
Beating Heart! we come again	850
Beautiful must be the mountains whence ye come	936
Beauty clear and fair	176
Beauty sat bathing by a spring	65
Behold her, single in the field	565
Being your slave, what should I do but tend	118
Be it right or wrong, these men among	14
Best and brightest, come away!	640
Bid me to live, and I will live	221
Bird of the wilderness	513
Blest pair of Sirens, pledges of Heav'ns joy	291
Blown in the morning, thou shalt fade ere noon	311
Bowed by the weight of centuries he leans	967
Brave flowers—that I could gallant it like you	232
Breathes there the man with soul so dead	583
Bright Star, would I were steadfast as thou art	669
Bright shone the lists, blue bent the skies	733
Bring me wine, but wine which never grew	779
Busy, curious, thirsty fly!	422

By feathers green, across Casbeen	983
By the shores of Gitche Gumee	729
Call for the robin-redbreast and the wren	276
Calm on the bosom of thy God	656
Came, on a Sabbath noon, my sweet	908
Captain, or Colonel, or Knight in arms	393
Care-charmer Sleep, son of the sable Night	252
Ca' the yowes to the knowes,	544
Ca' the yowes to the knowes	462
Charm me asleep, and melt me so	218
Cherry-Ripe, ripe, ripe, I cry	211
Chloe's a Nymph in flowery groves	401
Christmas knows a merry, merry place	910
Clerk Saunders and may Margaret	350
Cold in the earth—and the deep snow piled above thee	840
Come, Sleep; O Sleep! the certain knot of peace	72
Come, Sleep, and with thy sweet deceiving	168
Come away, come away, death	108
Come, dear children, let us away	851
Come down, O maid, from yonder mountain height	814
Come into the garden, Maud	816
Come, let us now resolve at last	390
Come little babe, come silly soul	48
Come live with me and be my Love	98
Come not in terrors clad, to claim	630
Come then, as ever, like the wind at morning!	996
Come thou, who are the wine and wit	228
Come, worthy Greek! Ulysses, come	89
Condemn'd to Hope's delusive mine	442
Count each affliction, whether light or grave	838
Crabbèd Age and Youth	55
Cupid and my Campaspe play'd	63
Cupid once upon a bed	507
Cynthia, to thy power and thee	169
Cyriack, whose Grandsire on the Royal Bench	302
Dark, deep, and cold the current flows	622
Dark to me is the earth. Dark to me are the heavens	919
Daughter of Jove, relentless power	472
Day, like our souls, is fiercely dark	621
Dear Lord, receive my son, whose winning love	181
Dear love, for nothing less than thee	160
Death, be not proud, though some have called thee	163
Death stands above me, whispering low	710
Deep on the convent-roof the snows	811
Diaphenia like the daffadowndilly	250
Does the road wind uphill all the way?	886
Doth then the world go thus, doth all thus move?	257
Down in a green and shady bed	477
"Do you remember me? or are you proud?"	604
Drink to me only with thine eyes	146
Drop, drop, slow tears	180
Earth has not anything to show more fair	557

E'en like two little bank-dividing brooks	230
Enough; and leave the rest to Fame!	342
Eternal Spirit of the chainless Mind!	699
Even such is Time, that takes in trust	58
Ever let the Fancy roam	663
Fain would I change that note	271
Fair Amoret is gone astray	416
Fair and fair, and twice so fair	79
Fair daffodils, we weep to see	207
Fair is my Love and cruel as she's fair	90
Fair pledges of a fruitful tree	208
Fair ship, that from the Italian shore	815
Fair stood the wind for France	96
False though she be to me and love	415
False world, good night! since thou hast brought	151
Fear death?—to feel the fog in my throat	760
Fine knacks for ladies! cheap, choice, brave, and new	263
First came the primrose	871
"Flowers nodding gaily, scent in air	1000
Fly envious Time, till thou run out thy race	290
Fly hence, shadows, that do keep	193
Follow a shadow, it still flies you	148
Follow thy fair sun, unhappy shadow!	132
Follow your saint, follow with accents sweet!	133
Foolish prater, what dost thou	333
For God, our God is a gallant foe	1011
For a name unknown	981
Forbear, bold youth; all's heaven here	372
Forget not yet the tried intent	28
For her gait, if she be walking	199
For knighthood is not in the feats of warre	26
Four Seasons fill the measure of the year	708
Fra bank to bank, fra wood to wood I rin	91
Fresh Spring, the herald of loves mighty king	59
From harmony, from heavenly harmony	373
From low to high doth dissolution climb	575
From the forests and highlands	639
From you, Ianthe, little troubles pass	594
Gather ye rosebuds while ye may	203
Give all to love	777
Give a man a horse he can ride	901
Give me my scallop-shell of quiet	57
Give pardon, blessèd soul, to my bold cries	87
Go and catch a falling star	157
God Lyaeus, ever young	175
God of our fathers, known of old	993
God who created me	979
Goe, soule, the bodie's guest	49
Go fetch to me a pint o' wine	534
Go, for they call you, Shepherd, from the hill	855
Go from me. Yet I feel that I shall stand	792
Go, lovely Rose	287

Gone were but the winter cold	625
Good-Bye, proud world! I'm going home	954
Good-morrow to the day so fair	223
Great men have been among us; hands that penn'd	562
Grow old along with me!	759
Had we but world enough, and time	338
Hail, beauteous stranger of the grove!	465
Hail holy light, ofspring of Heav'n first-born	304
Hail, sister springs	319
Hail to thee, blithe spirit!	642
Half a league, half a league	732
Hallow the threshold, crown the posts anew!	314
Hame, hame, hame, O hame fain wad I be	624
Happy the man, whose wish and care	400
Happy those early days, when I	343
Hark! Now everything is still	277
Hark! ah, the Nightingale!	856
Hark! hark! the lark at heaven's gate sings	110
Heap cassia, sandal-buds and stripes	821
Hear the voice of the Bard	526
Hear, ye ladies that despise	174
Heaven is not reached at a single bound	736
He first deceased; she for a little tried	141
He has conn'd the lesson now	769
Helen, thy beauty is to me	802
Hence, all you vain delights	177
Hence, heart, with her that must depart	37
Hence loathèd Melancholy	292
Hence vain deluding joyes	293
Here a little child I stand	226
Here, ever since you went abroad	602
Here in this sequester'd close	926
Here she lies, a pretty bud	227
Her eyes the glow-worm lend thee	217
He that is by Mooni now	929
He that is down needs fear no fall	347
He that loves a rosy cheek	246
He who has once been happy is for aye	920
Hey nonny no!	45
Hierusalem, my happy home	264
High-spirited friend	152
Highway, since you my chief Parnassus be	70
His golden locks Time hath to silver turn'd	80
His home a speck in a vast Universe	952
How dear to this heart are the scenes of my childhood	511
How delicious is the winning	692
How happy is he born and taught	140
How like a Winter hath my absence been	120
How many times do I love thee, dear?	776
How near me came the hand of Death	195
How sleep the brave, who sink to rest	448
How sweet the answer Echo makes	694

How vainly men themselves amaze	340
Hush! my dear, lie still and slumber	419
Hyd, Absolon, thy gilte tresses clere	5
I Said—Then, dearest, since 'tis so	833
I am monarch of all I survey	435
I am that which began	912
I am! yet what I am who cares, or knows?	655
I arise from dreams of thee	645
I ask no kind return of love	464
I came into the City and none knew me	1004
I cannot change as others do	388
I cannot eat but little meat	41
I celebrate myself, and sing myself	764
I chatter, chatter, as I flow	743
I come, I come! ye have called me long	437
I'd a dream to-night	767
I dare not ask a kiss	205
I did but look and love awhile	403
I did not choose thee, dearest. It was Love	921
I do confess thou'rt smooth and fair	143
I do not love thee!—no! I do not love thee!	800
I dream'd that, as I wander'd by the way	650
I dug, beneath the cypress shade	628
If I had thought thou couldst have died	638
"If I were dead, you'd sometimes say, Poor Child!"	865
If all the world and love were young	99
If aught of oaten stop, or pastoral song	449
If doughty deeds my lady please	458
I fear thy kisses, gentle maiden	691
I feed a flame within, which so torments me	375
I flung me round him	906
If rightly tuneful bards decide	451
If the quick spirits in your eye	244
If the red slayer think he slays	780
If there were dreams to sell	775
If thou must love me, let it be for naught	793
If thou wilt ease thine heart	774
If to be absent were to be	326
If women could be fair, and yet not fond	253
If you can keep your head when all about you	1023
If you go over desert and mountain	932
I got me flowers to straw Thy way	236
I have a little shadow that goes in and out with me	958
I have a mistress, for perfections rare	282
I have a rendezvous with Death	1015
I have had playmates, I have had companions	611
I have known the silence of the stars and of the sea	1021
I intended an Ode	927
I know a little garden-close	905
I know a thing that's most uncommon	424
I know my soul hath power to know all things	142
I left thee last, a child at heart	786

I like a church; I like a cowl	762
"I'll tell you how the leaves came down,"	713
I long have had a quarrel set with Time	925
I loved him not; and yet now he is gone	592
I loved thee once; I'll love no more	144
I made another garden, yea	931
I met a traveller from an antique land	514
I mind me in the days departed	787
I'm sittin' on the stile, Mary	799
I must not think of thee; and, tired yet strong	1005
I'm wearin' awa', John	550
I, my dear, was born to-day	409
In Clementina's artless mien	603
In Scarlet town, where I was born	365
In Winter I get up at night	959
In Xanadu did Kubla Khan	585
In a drear-nighted December	664
In after days when grasses high	928
In a harbour grene aslepe whereas I lay	52
In a quiet water'd land, a land of roses	973
In a valley of this restles mind	13
In going to my naked bed as one that would have slept	39
In her ear he whispers gaily	728
In somer when the shawes be sheyne	11
In the downhill of life, when I find I'm declining	474
In the hall the coffin waits, and the idle armourer stands	872
In the highlands, in the country places	971
In the hour of death, after this life's whim	948
In the hour of my distress	229
In the merry month of May	47
In the name of the Empress of India, make way	962
Into the silver night	947
Into the skies, one summer's day	860
I play'd with you 'mid cowslips blowing	627
I pray thee, leave, love me no more	93
I remember, I remember	498
I saw fair Chloris walk alone	369
I saw my Lady weep	269
I saw old Autumn in the misty morn	679
I saw where in the shroud did lurk	613
I sent a ring—a little band	673
I shot an arrow into the air	956
I sing of a maiden	12
Is it so small a thing	858
"Isn't this Joseph's son?"—ay, it is He	735
I sprang to the stirrup, and Joris, and he	745
I stood on the bridge at midnight	953
I strove with none, for none was worth my strife	610
I tell you, hopeless grief is passionless	789
It fell in the ancient periods	778
I that in heill was and gladnèss	18
I think that I shall never see	1022

I thought of Thee, my partner and my guide	574
I thought once how Theocritus had sung	790
I thought to meet no more, so dreary seem'd	654
It is a beauteous evening, calm and free	558
It is an ancient Mariner	584
It is morning, Senlin says, and in the morning	1017
It is not Beauty I demand	394
It is not, Celia, in our power	378
It is not death, that sometime in a sigh	681
It is not growing like a tree	155
It is not to be thought of that the flood	563
It is the miller's daughter	809
I took my heart in my hand	885
I travell'd among unknown men	554
Its edges foam'd with amethyst and rose	999
It was a' for our rightfu' King	543
It was a lover and his lass	109
It was a summer's evening	491
It was many and many a year ago	803
It was not in the Winter	683
It was not like your great and gracious ways!	866
It was our war-ship *Clampherdown*	963
It was the Winter wilde	289
It was the schooner *Hesperus*	740
It was the time when lilies blow	727
I've heard them lilting at our ewe-milking	455
I wandered lonely as a cloud	483
I will arise and go now, and go to Innisfree	989
I will make you brooches and toys for your delight	970
I wish I were where Helen lies	363
I, with whose colours Myra dress'd her head	74
Jenny kiss'd me when we met	626
John Anderson, my jo, John	535
King Francis was a hearty king, and loved a royal sport	502
Know, Celia, since thou art so proud	247
Ladies, though to your conquering eyes	377
Lars Porsena of Clusium	746
Late at een, drinkin' the wine	349
Lawrence of vertuous Father vertuous Son	301
Lay a garland on my herse	170
Lead, kindly Light, amid th' encircling gloom	751
Leave me, O Love, which reachest but to dust	73
Lestenyt, lordynges, both elde and yinge	7
Let dogs delight to bark and bite	399
Let me go forth, and share	977
Let me not to the marriage of true minds	124
Let us drink and be merry, dance, joke, and rejoice	317
Life! I know not what thou art	463
Like the Idalian queen	183
Like thee I once have stemm'd the sea of life	461
Like to Diana in her summer weed	81
Like to the clear in highest sphere	78

Little White Lily	712
Little drops of water	711
London, thou art of townes *A per se.*	16
Long-expected one-and-twenty	441
Look not thou on beauty's charming	580
Lo, quhat it is to love	38
Lords, knights, and squires, the numerous band	407
Lo! 'tis a gala night	955
Loud mockers in the roaring street	995
Love bade me welcome; yet my soul drew back	240
Love guards the roses of thy lips	77
Love in fantastic triumph sate	384
Love in my bosom like a bee	75
Love in thy youth, fair maid; be wise	259
Love is a sickness full of woes	88
Love is enough: though the World be a-waning	904
Love is the blossom where there blows	191
Love not me for comely grace	274
Love, thou are absolute, sole Lord	320
Love thy country, wish it well	427
Love wing'd my Hopes and taught me how to fly	265
"Make way for liberty!" he cried	512
Marie Hamilton's to the kirk gane	352
Mark where the pressing wind shoots javelin-like	878
Martial, the things that do attain	35
Marvel of marvels, if I myself shall behold	888
Mary! I want a lyre with other strings	459
May! Be thou never graced with birds that sing	201
May! queen of blossoms	620
Merry Margaret	20
Methought I heard a butterfly	480
Methought I saw my late espoused Saint	303
'Mid pleasures and palaces though we may roam	503
Mild is the parting year, and sweet	600
Milton! thou shouldst be living at this hour	561
Mine be a cot beside the hill	509
More love or more disdain I crave	402
Mortality, behold and fear!	192
Most glorious Lord of Lyfe! that, on this day	62
Mother, I cannot mind my wheel	599
Mother of Hermes! and still youthful Maia!	661
Much have I travell'd in the realms of gold	666
Music, when soft voices die	652
My Damon was the first to wake	518
My Love in her attire doth show her wit	266
My Peggy is a young thing	421
My Phillis hath the morning sun	76
My blood so red	361
My days among the Dead are past	591
My dear and only Love, I pray	316
My delight and thy delight	934
My faint spirit was sitting in the light	647

My fairest child, I have no song to give you	716
My good blade carves the casques of men	754
My grief on the sea	982
My heart aches, and a drowsy numbness pains	657
My heart is high above, my body is full of bliss	44
My heart is like a singing bird	883
My heart leaps up when I behold	568
My little Mädchen found one day	742
My little Son, who look'd from thoughtful eyes	867
My love is strengthen'd, though more weak in seeming	121
My love o'er the water bends dreaming	900
My lute, awake! perform the last	32
My mind to me a kingdom is	21
My mother bore me in the southern wild	525
My new-cut ashlar takes the light	990
My noble, lovely, little Peggy	411
My silks and fine array	523
My soul is sailing through the sea	749
My soul, sit thou a patient looker-on	231
My soul, there is a country	344
My thoughts hold mortal strife	188
My true love hath my heart, and I have his	66
Nay but you, who do not love her	827
Near to the silver *Trent*	95
Never seek to tell thy love	530
Never weather-beaten sail more willing bent to shore	138
New doth the sun appear	189
News from a foreign country came	379
Nobly, nobly Cape Saint Vincent to the North-west died away	836
No coward soul is mine	842
No, no! go not to Lethe, neither twist	660
Nor Love nor Fate dare I accuse	433
Not, Celia, that I juster am	383
Not a drum was heard, not a funeral note	637
No thyng ys to man so dere	1
"Not ours," say some, "the thought of death to dread	978
Not unto us, O Lord	1002
Now sleeps the crimson petal, now the white	813
Now the North wind ceases	877
Now the golden Morn aloft	467
Now the lusty spring is seen	173
Now winter nights enlarge	136
Nuns fret not at their convent's narrow room	569
O, Brignall banks are wild and fair	579
O Captain! my Captain! our fearful trip is done	847
O Christ of God! whose life and death	798
O Earth, lie heavily upon her eyes	892
O Friend! I know not which way I must look	560
O Mary, at thy window be	531
"O Mary, go and call the cattle home	844
O Memory, thou fond deceiver	457
O Sing unto my roundelay	517

O Time! who know'st a lenient hand to lay	547
O Waly, waly, up the bank	364
O Western wind, when wilt thou blow	23
O World, be nobler, for her sake!	997
O come, soft rest of cares! come, Night!	84
Of Nelson and the North	615
Of Neptune's empire let us sing	135
Of all the flowers rising now	861
Of all the girls that are so smart	428
Of all the torments, all the cares	413
Of a' the airts the wind can blaw	532
O fly, my Soul! What hangs upon	241
O fly not, Pleasure, pleasant-hearted Pleasure	918
O for some honest lover's ghost	307
O for the mighty wakening that aroused	784
Often I think of the beautiful town	797
Of this fair volume which we World do name	256
Oft, in the stilly night	618
O happy Tithon! if thou know'st thy hap	179
O happy dames! that may embrace	34
Oh how comely it is and how reviving	305
Oh, young Lochinvar is come out of the west	488
O if thou knew'st how thou thyself does harm	251
O joy of creation	915
O lovers' eyes are sharp to see	697
O lusty May, with Flora queen!	43
O many a day have I made good ale in the glen	670
O, may I join the choir invisible	758
O mortal folk, you may behold and see	27
O my Dark Rosaleen	772
O my Luve's like a red, red rose	541
O my deir hert, young Jesus sweit	360
On Linden, when the sun was low	495
On a Poet's lips I slept	706
On a day—alack the day!	101
On a starr'd night Prince Lucifer uprose	879
On a time the amorous Silvy	275
Once a dream did wave a shade	490
Once did she hold the gorgeous East in fee	559
Once upon a midnight dreary, while I pondered, weak and weary	757
One day I wrote her name upon the strand	261
On either side the river lie	808
One more Unfortunate	686
One word is too often profaned	649
Only tell her that I love	405
On parent knees, a naked new-born child	466
On the Sabbath-day	881
On the sea and at the Hogue, sixteen hundred ninety-two	761
On the wide level of a mountain's head	588
O're the smooth enameld green	294
Orpheus with his lute made trees	113
O ruddier than the cherry!	423

O saw ye bonnie Lesley	538
O saw ye not fair Ines?	682
O! say, can you see, by the dawn's early light	479
O say what is that thing call'd Light	468
O sleep, my babe, hear not the rippling wave	770
O snatch'd away in beauty's bloom!	690
O soft embalmer of the still midnight!	668
O talk not to me of a name great in story	689
O that 'twere possible	817
Others abide our question. Thou art free	857
O the sad day!	380
O thou, by Nature taught	447
O thou that swing'st upon the waving hair	329
O thou undaunted daughter of desires!	321
O thou with dewy locks, who lookest down	522
O, to be in England	835
O turn away those cruel eyes	370
Our bugles sang truce, for the night-cloud had lower'd	705
Out of the night that covers me	944
Out upon it, I have loved	308
Over hill, over dale	104
Over the mountains	367
Over the sea our galleys went	822
O were my Love yon lilac fair	540
O what a plague is love!	368
"O what can ail thee, knight-at-arms	665
"O which is the last rose?"	975
O why should the spirit of mortal be proud?	515
O wild West Wind, thou breath of Autumn's being	644
O world, in very truth thou art too young	924
O yonge fresshe folkes, he or she	4
O, you plant the pain in my heart with your wistful eyes	916
Pack, clouds, away! and welcome, day!	166
Passing away, saith the World, passing away	887
Passions are liken'd best to floods and streams	56
Past ruin'd Ilion Helen lives	596
Peace, Shepherd, peace! What boots it singing on?	1008
Perfect little body, without fault or stain on thee	939
Phœbus, arise!	182
Pibroch of Donuil Dhu	493
Pile the bodies high at Austerlitz and Waterloo	1014
Piping down the valleys wild	524
Poor soul, the centre of my sinful earth	126
Praise is devotion fit for mighty minds	285
Pray but one prayer for me 'twixt thy closed lips	903
Proud Maisie is in the wood	578
Proud word you never spoke, but you will speak	597
Pure stream, in whose transparent wave	454
Put your head, darling, darling, darling	820
Queen Mab and all her Fairy fry	398
Queen and huntress, chaste and fair	145
Queen of fragrance, lovely Rose	968

Quhen Flora had o'erfret the firth	42
Quoth tongue of neither maid nor wife	765
Remain, ah not in youth alone!	601
Remember me when I am gone away	890
Return, return! all night my lamp is burning	870
"Rise," said the Master, "come unto the feast."	819
Roll forth, my song, like the rushing river	773
Rorate coeli desuper!	17
Rose-cheek'd *Laura*, come	131
Roses, their sharp spines being gone	111
Round the cape of a sudden came the sea	831
Safe where I cannot die yet	889
Said the Wind to the Moon, "I will blow you out	734
Say not the struggle naught availeth	845
Says Tweed to Till	359
Scorn not the Sonnet; Critic, you have frown'd	570
Scots, wha hae wi' Wallace bled	496
Seamen three! What men be ye?	629
Season of mists and mellow fruitfulness!	659
See how the flowers, as at parade	337
See the Chariot at hand here of Love	149
See thou character. Give thy thoughts no tongue	50
See where she sits upon the grassie greene	60
See with what simplicity	339
See yon blithe child that dances in our sight!	771
Sense with keenest edge unusèd	940
Serene I fold my hands and wait	755
Seven weeks of sea, and twice seven days of storm	923
Shall I compare thee to a Summer's day?	114
Shall I thus ever long, and be no whit the neare?	53
Shall I, wasting in despair	194
She beat the happy pavèment	327
She dwelt among the untrodden ways	553
She fell away in her first ages spring	61
She is not fair to outward view	676
She knelt upon her brother's grave	893
She pass'd away like morning dew	677
She's somewhere in the sunlight strong	994
She stood breast-high amid the corn	684
She walks in beauty, like the night	634
She walks—the lady of my delight	1006
She was a phantom of delight	566
She was a queen of noble Nature's crowning	675
She who to Heaven more Heaven doth annex	315
Should auld acquaintance be forgot	533
Shut not so soon; the dull-eyed night	216
Since I noo mwore do zee your feäce	768
Since all that I can ever do for thee	898
Since first I saw your face I resolved to honour and renown ye	272
Since there's no help, come let us kiss and part	94
Sing his praises that doth keep	171
Sing lullaby, as women do	40

Sister, awake! close not your eyes!	270
Sleep on, and dream of Heaven awhile	688
Sleep, sleep, beauty bright	528
Smoothing a cypress beam	1012
Softly, O midnight Hours!	837
Something there is that doesn't love a wall	1016
Some vex their souls with jealous pain	391
So shuts the marigold her leaves	200
Sound, sound the clarion, fill the fife!	581
So, we'll go no more a-roving	633
"Speak! speak! thou fearful guest!	752
Spring, the sweet Spring, is the year's pleasant king	128
Stand close around, ye Stygian set	606
Stand! the ground's your own, my braves!	482
Stay, O sweet and do not rise!	156
Steer, hither steer your winged pines	197
Stern Daughter of the Voice of God!	567
Still do the stars impart their light	313
Still let my tyrants know, I am not doom'd to wear	841
Still to be neat, still to be drest	147
Strange fits of passion have I known	552
Strew on her roses, roses	854
Summer set lip to earth's bosom bare	1001
Sunset and evening star	738
Sure thou didst flourish once! and many springs	345
Surprised by joy—impatient as the Wind	573
Swallow, my sister, O sister swallow	913
Sweet Echo, sweetest Nymph that liv'st unseen	296
Sweet Spring, thou turn'st with all thy goodly train	185
Sweet and low, sweet and low	719
Sweet are the rosy memories of the lips	897
Sweet are the thoughts that savor of content	260
Sweet, be not proud of those two eyes	219
Sweet day, so cool, so calm, so bright!	235
Sweetest Saviour, if my soul	238
Sweet in her green dell the flower of beauty slumbers	672
Sweet rois of vertew and of gentilness	15
Sweet stream, that winds through yonder glade	471
Sweet western wind, whose luck it is	204
Swiftly walk o'er the western wave	646
Tarye no lenger; toward thyn heritage	9
Tell me not, Sweet, I am unkind	325
Tell me not, in mournful numbers	748
Tell me not of a face that's fair	335
Tell me not what too well I know	605
Tell me where is Fancy bred	107
Thank Heaven! the crisis	804
That which her slender waist confined	286
That zephyr every year	184
The Assyrian came down like a wolf on the fold	497
The Indian weed witherèd quite	366
The Lady Mary Villiers lies	248

The Nightingale, as soon as April bringeth	69
The Owl and the Pussy-Cat went to sea	715
The Rose was sick and smiling died	210
The Spirit epiloguizes:	298
The Spirit sings:	297
The Star that bids the Shepherd fold	295
The World's a bubble, and the Life of Man	255
The beauty and the life	187
The blessèd Damozel lean'd out	875
The boat is chafing at our long delay	974
The boy stood on the burning deck	476
The breaking waves dashed high	436
The chough and crow to roost are gone	548
The curfew tolls the knell of parting day	438
The day begins to droop	941
The days are sad, it is the Holy tide	796
Thee too, modest tressed maid	546
The fierce exulting worlds, the motes in rays	880
The forward youth that would appear	336
The fountains mingle with the river	693
The gingham dog and the calico cat	961
The glories of our blood and state	242
The gray sea and the long black land	830
The harp that once through Tara's halls	510
The irresponsive silence of the land	891
The isles of Greece! the isles of Greece	635
The king sits in Dunfermline town	348
The lark now leaves his wat'ry nest	283
The last and greatest Herald of Heaven's King	190
The leaves are falling; so am I	609
The linnet in the rocky dells	839
The loppèd tree in time may grow again	85
The lovely lass o' Inverness	542
The man of life upright	137
The merchant, to secure his treasure	408
The more we live, more brief appear	707
The moth's kiss, first!	829
The murmur of the mourning ghost	869
The night has a thousand eyes	1025
The old mayor climb'd the belfry tower	756
The poplars are fell'd, farewell to the shade	470
The rain set early in to-night	826
There ance was a may, and she lo'ed na men	414
There are two births; the one when light	312
There be none of Beauty's daughters	632
There came a youth upon the earth	744
The red rose whispers of passion	933
There is a Lady sweet and kind	273
There is a flower, the Lesser Celandine	704
There is a garden in her face	130
There is a mountain and a wood between us	608
There is a silence where hath been no sound	680

There is no frigate like a book	949
There is sweet music here that softer falls	810
There lay upon the ocean's shore	741
There lived a wife at Usher's well	354
There's a glade in Aghadoe, Aghadoe, Aghadoe	917
There's a whisper down the field where the year has shot her yield	991
There's a woman like a dewdrop, she's so purer than the purest	828
There's not a joy the world can give like that it takes away	701
There's not a nook within this solemn Pass	576
There was a sound of revelry by night	501
There was a time when meadow, grove, and stream	572
There was never a Queen like Balkis	957
There were three kings into the East	484
There were three ravens sat on a tree	355
There were three sailors of Bristol city	723
There were twa sisters sat in a bour	353
The rich man has his motor-car	1020
The ring, so worn as you behold	520
The seas are quiet when the winds give o'er	288
The sky	1018
The soote season, that bud and bloom forth brings	33
The spacious firmament on high	417
The splendour falls on castle walls	812
The summer and autumn had been so wet	500
The sun descending in the west	529
The sun rises bright in France	623
The sun was shining on the sea	722
The thirsty earth soaks up the rain	331
The twentieth year is wellnigh past	460
The week had gloomily begun	1010
The wine of Love is music	902
The world is too much with us; late and soon	571
The world's great age begins anew	641
Th' expense of Spirit in a waste of shame	125
They all were looking for a king	874
They are all gone into the world of light!	346
They are waiting on the shore	907
The year's at the spring	824
They flee from me that sometime did me seek	31
The young May moon is beaming, love	616
They seem'd, to those who saw them meet	818
They that have power to hurt and will do none	119
They told me, Heraclitus, they told me you were dead	863
This Life, which seems so fair	254
This ae nighte, this ae nighte	357
This is a spray the Bird clung to	834
This is the ship of pearl, which, poets feign	737
This little vault, this narrow room	249
This was the noblest Roman of them all	51
This winter's weather it waxeth cold	25
Thou art to all lost love the best	222
Though beauty be the mark of praise	150

Thou still unravish'd bride of quietness	658
Three years she grew in sun and shower	555
Through grief and through danger thy smile hath cheer'd my way	617
Through the black, rushing smoke-bursts	852
Throw away Thy rod	237
Thus the Mayne glideth	823
Thus when the silent grave becomes	969
Thy bosom is endeared with all hearts	116
Thy hue, dear pledge, is pure and bright	687
Thy restless feet now cannot go	323
Thy soul within such silent pomp did keep	404
Tiger, tiger, burning bright	527
Time is the feather'd thing	279
Timely blossom, Infant fair	430
'Tis a child of phansies getting	432
Tis a dull sight	805
'Tis the last rose of summer	505
To all you ladies now at land	381
To-day, all day, I rode upon the down	922
To fair Fidele's grassy tomb	450
To live within a cave—it is most good	895
To make a final conquest of all me	396
To me, fair friend, you never can be old	122
To my true king I offer'd free from stain	766
To-night retired, the queen of heaven	453
Too late for love, too late for joy	882
Too solemn for day, too sweet for night	671
Tossing his mane of snows in wildest eddies and tangles	914
T'other day as I was twining	506
To these whom death again did wed	324
Traveller, pluck a stem of moly	964
Traverse not the globe for lore! The sternest	950
Trust thou thy Love: if she be proud, is she not sweet?	848
Turning and turning in the widening gyre	987
'Twas battered and scarred, and the auctioneer	1024
'Twas brillig, and the slithy toves	721
Twas on a lofty vase's side	446
'Twas the dream of a God	1007
'Twas the night before Christmas, when all through the house	478
Twenty years hence my eyes may grow	595
Twinkle, twinkle, little star!	475
Under a spreading chestnut-tree	718
Underneath this myrtle shade	332
Underneath this sable herse	202
Under the wide and starry sky	972
Unlike are we, unlike, O princely Heart!	791
Up from the South at break of day	726
Up from the meadows rich with corn	731
Upon my lap my sovereign sits	127
Up the airy mountain	873
Urns and odours bring away!	112
Venus, take my votive glass	410

Verse, a breeze 'mid blossoms straying	587
Victorious men of earth, no more	258
Vital spark of heav'nly flame!	426
Waes-hael for knight and dame!	782
We are the music-makers	930
Weave the warp, and weave the woof	444
Wee Willie Winkie rins through the town	714
Wee, modest, crimson-tipped flower	487
Weep no more, nor sigh, nor groan	178
Weep not, my wanton, smile upon my knee	83
Weep with me, all you that read	154
Weep you no more, sad fountains	268
Wee, sleekit, cow'rin', tim'rous beastie	486
Welcome, maids of honour!	206
Welcome, welcome! do I sing,	196
Well I remember how you smiled	709
Well then! I now do plainly see	334
Were I as base as is the lowly plain	92
We saw Thee in Thy balmy nest	322
We see them not—we cannot hear	783
We, that did nothing study but the way	233
We've trod the maze of error round	519
We watch'd her breathing thro' the night	685
We were crowded in the cabin	717
"Wharefore sou'd ye talk o' love	653
What beck'ning ghost, along the moonlight shade	425
What bird so sings, yet so does wail?	64
What conscience, say, is it in thee	220
What delightful hosts are they	1009
What have I done for you	946
What is so rare as a day in June?	747
What is the voice I hear	763
What is your substance, whereof are you made	117
What needs complaints	224
What nymph should I admire or trust	406
What should I say?	30
What sweet relief the showers to thirsty plants we see	36
What was he doing, the great god Pan	795
When Britain first at Heaven's command	469
When, Cœlia, must my old day set	371
When Death to either shall come	942
When Delia on the plain appears	440
When Earth's last picture is painted, and the tubes are	965
When God at first made Man	239
When I am dead, my dearest	884
When I beheld the poet blind, yet bold	262
When I consider how my light is spent	300
When I have borne in memory what has tamed	564
When I have fears that I may cease to be	667
When I survey the bright	281
When Jessie comes with her soft breast	894
When Letty had scarce pass'd her third glad year	801

When Love arose in heart and deed	859
When Love with unconfinèd wings	330
Whenas in silks my Julia goes	214
When by Zeus relenting the mandate was revoked	876
When daisies pied and violets blue	102
When, dearest, I but think of thee	310
Whenever Richard Cory went down town	1019
When he who adores thee has left but the name	700
When icicles hang by the wall	103
When in the chronicle of wasted time	123
When lovely woman stoops to folly	456
When maidens such as Hester die	612
When my love was away	938
When on mine eyes her eyes first shone	397
When our two souls stand up erect and strong	794
When the breath of twilight blows to flame the misty skies	998
When the fierce North-wind with his airy forces	418
When the hounds of spring are on winter's traces	911
When the lamp is shatter'd	648
When the sheep are in the fauld, and the kye at hame	516
When the world is burning	849
When thou must home to shades of underground	134
When thou, poor Excommunicate	245
When thy beauty appears	420
When to the Sessions of sweet silent thought	115
When we two parted	631
When we were idlers with the loitering rills	678
When you and I have play'd the little hour	985
When you are old and gray and full of sleep	988
Where, like a pillow on a bed	159
Where shall the lover rest	696
Where the bee sucks, there suck I	106
Where the pools are bright and deep	551
Where the remote Bermudas ride	341
Whether on Ida's shady brow	521
While that the sun with his beams hot	54
Whither, O splendid ship, thy white sails crowding	937
Whoe'er she be	318
Whoever comes to shroud me, do not harm	161
Who hath his fancy pleased	67
Who is Silvia? What is she?	100
Who is it that, this dark night,	68
Why, Damon, with the forward day	473
Why I tie about thy wrist	215
Why art thou silent! Is thy love a plant	577
"Why does your brand sae drop wi' blude	351
Why dost thou shade thy lovely face? O why	389
Why, having won her, do I woo?	864
Why so pale and wan, fond lover?	309
Why, why repine, my pensive friend	598
Wild was the night, yet a wilder night	739
"Will you walk into my parlour?" said the Spider to the Fly	481

Wilt Thou forgive that sin where I begun	162
Winds of the World, give answer? They are whimpering to and fro	966
With all my will, but much against my heart	868
With blackest moss the flower-plots	807
With deep affection	785
With how sad steps, O moon, thou climb'st the skies!	71
With leaden foot Time creeps along	443
With lifted feet, hands still	980
With margerain gentle	19
Woodman, spare that tree!	750
Worschippe ye that loveris bene this May	10
Wouldst thou hear what Man can say	153
Wynken, Blynken, and Nod one night	960
Wynter wakeneth al my care	2
Ye Highlands and ye Lawlands	362
Ye Mariners of England	614
Years, many parti-colour'd years	607
Ye banks and braes and streams around	539
Ye blushing virgins happy are	280
Ye flowery banks o' bonnie Doon	536
Ye have been fresh and green	225
"Ye have robb'd," said he, "ye have slaughter'd and made an end	984
Ye little birds that sit and sing	167
Yes: in the sea of life enisled	853
Yes, there is holy pleasure in thine eye!	702
Yet if His Majesty, our sovereign lord	46
Yet once more, O ye Laurels, and once more	299
You are a tulip seen to-day	212
"You are old, Father William," the young man said	720
You brave heroic minds	97
You know, we French storm'd Ratisbon	724
You'll love me yet!—and I can tarry	825
You meaner beauties of the night	139
You must be sad; for though it is to Heaven	909
You promise heavens free from strife	862
Your beauty, ripe and calm and fresh	284
Your eyen two wol slee me sodenly	6
You spotted snakes with double tongue	105

www.ingramcontent.com/pod-product-compliance
Lightning Source LLC
Chambersburg PA
CBHW070711160426
43192CB00009B/1153